SPORTS, GAMES, AND PLAY
Social and Psychological Viewpoints

SPORTS, GAMES, AND PLAY
Social and Psychological Viewpoints

EDITED BY

Jeffrey H. Goldstein
Temple University

LAWRENCE ERLBAUM ASSOCIATES, PUBLISHERS
1979   Hillsdale, New Jersey

DISTRIBUTED BY THE HALSTED PRESS DIVISION OF
JOHN WILEY & SONS
New York   Toronto   London   Sydney

Lawrence Erlbaum Associates, Inc., Publishers
62 Maria Drive
Hillsdale, New Jersey 07642

Distributed solely by Halsted Press Division
John Wiley & Sons, Inc., New York

Library of Congress Cataloging in Publication Data
Main entry under title:
Sports, games, and play.

   Includes indexes.
   1. Sports—Social aspects—Addresses, essays,
lectures. 2. Sports—Psychological aspects—Addresses,
essays, lectures. 3. Games—Social aspects—Addresses,
essays, lectures. 4. Games—Psychological aspects—Addresses, essays, lectures. I. Goldstein, Jeffrey H.
GV706.5.S74   796'.01   78-21261
ISBN 0-470-26602-3

Printed in the United States of America

Contents

PART II: SPORTS OBSERVED: ANALYSES OF SPECTATORS

List of Contributors

Numbers in parentheses indicate the pages on which the authors' contributions begin.

JENNINGS BRYANT (297), Department of Communication Studies, University of Massachusetts, Amherst, Mass.

PETER S. K. CHI (115), Department of Sociology, Cornell University, Ithaca, N.Y.

GARRY E. CHICK (65), Department of Anthropology, University of Pittsburgh, Pittsburgh, Pa.

JOHN EDWARDS (409), Department of Psychology, Loyola University of Chicago, Chicago, Ill.

GEORGE GASKELL (263), Department of Psychology, London School of Economics and Political Science, London, England.

JEFFREY H. GOLDSTEIN (401), Department of Psychology, Temple University, Philadelphia, Pa.

ELIOT HEARST (29), Department of Psychology, Indiana University, Bloomington, Ind.

JAMES M. JONES (157), American Psychological Association, Washington, D.C.

JOHN P. KING (115), Department of Sociology, Mary Baldwin College, Staunton, Va., and Cornell University, Ithaca, N.Y.

LEON MANN (337), Department of Psychology, Flinders University of South Australia, Bedford Park, Australia.

FREDERICK MOSTELLER (371), Department of Statistics, Harvard University, Cambridge, Mass.

BRUCE C. OGILVIE (149), Department of Psychology, San Jose State University, San Jose, Calif.

ROBERT PEARTON (263), Department of Sociology, St. Mary's College, University of London, London, England.

JOHN M. ROBERTS (65), Department of Anthropology, University of Pittsburgh, Pittsburgh, Pa.

BARRY S. SAPOLSKY (297), Department of Mass Communication, Florida State University, Tallahassee, Fla.

LONNIE SHERROD (1), Department of Psychology, Yale University, New Haven, Conn.

JEROME L. SINGER (1), Department of Psychology, Yale University, New Haven, Conn.

LLOYD REYNOLDS SLOAN (219), Department of Psychology, Howard University, Washington, D.C.

THOMAS A. TUTKO (101), Department of Psychology, San Jose State University, San Jose, Calif.

STEPHEN A. WILLIAMSON (157), Department of Social Relations, Harvard University, Cambridge, Mass.

MICHAEL WIERZBICKI (29), Department of Psychology, Indiana University, Bloomington, Ind.

FRANK WINER (189), Private practice, Norwalk, Conn.

DOLF ZILLMANN (297), Department of Communications, Indiana University, Bloomington, Ind.

Preface

Recreation and leisure activities are often regarded as frivolous behaviors, particularly by social scientists. Yet they have both a noteworthy past in social science history and, I believe, an even more promising future. As for history, sports, games, and play have figured prominently in cultural anthropology, sociology, and psychology. In anthropology, Anthony R. Radcliffe-Brown's notion of "joking relationships" and the field work of Benedict, Mead, and other early cultural anthropologists have contributed greatly to the development of the field. The current interest in popular culture and folklore has its roots in this anthropological work. In sociology, George Herbert Mead, for one, used play both as a metaphor for social development and as an inherent part of his scheme of the social self. In psychology, where there has been less explicit concern with recreation and leisure, there have been no less important theoretical developments—such as Berlyne's work on exploratory behavior and White's concept of competence—in which games and play figure in important ways.

Despite these notable references to sports, games, and play in the theory and research of early 20th-century social science, such behaviors are generally regarded as mere curiosities or as incidental to the more conventional interests of the field. That is unfortunate, because not only do recreational activities occupy an increasing portion of the behavior of Western peoples, but they offer rich opportunities for the construction and testing of theory and for the development of methodology. It was with an eye toward their inherent interest and the great potential of sports, games, and play as vehicles for the furthering of scientific theory that I invited the contributors to this volume to summarize their recent work.

The purpose of this book is to bring together in a single volume work that reflects the wide range of interests that social and behavioral scientists have in recreational activities. There is no attempt made to present any single theoretical or methodological point of view. On the contrary, the purpose is to reflect the great diversity of approaches, both methodological and conceptual, that sociologists, anthropologists, and psychologists have brought to bear on the pervasive activities that sports, games, and play comprise. Implicit in this task is the notion that not only can the social and behavioral sciences teach us something about these seemingly frivolous behaviors but that recreational activities may help us to refine and extend our concepts and methodological techniques.

There is hardly a topic in modern social science that cannot be found among the complex behaviors that constitute sports, games, and play. Among the topics included in this volume are: organizational and social structure; attitudes and values; national, sex, and race differences; motivation and achievement; social learning; social influence; concept formation and problem solving; aggression; collective behavior; personality; aesthetics; mass media effects; and methodological approaches ranging from multi-dimensional scaling to quasi-experiments and naturalistic observation. Sports, games, and play have much to offer the social scientist, and, as the chapters in this volume attest, social science has much to contribute to our understanding of the nature and functions of recreation.

The chapters of this book are divided somewhat arbitrarily into three major sections: papers that are concerned with the effects of, or processes related to, participation in various sports and games; papers concerned with the spectators of sport; and papers that deal with factors influencing the outcome of sports. Other organizations of these diverse papers are, of course, possible, and more than one paper speaks to several of these broad topics.

As editor, I have chosen not to comment extensively on the papers that appear in *Sports, Games, and Play*. The book as a whole is not as much an attempt to solve a problem as it is an attempt to raise possibilities— possibilities for new and exciting areas of research. As such, the contributors to this volume represent a broad spectrum of social science orientations— from anthropologists to sociologists; to clinical, developmental, experimental, and social psychologists; and to those whose area of specialization is statistics and communications. Sports, games, and play clearly represent subject matter of cross-disciplinary boundaries. It can only be wished that interdisciplinary cooperation will arise in the study of these frivolous behaviors as it has not in the study of more pressing social problems.

JEFFREY H. GOLDSTEIN

SPORTS GAMES AND PLAY
Social and Psychological Viewpoints

SOCIAL AND PSYCHOLOGICAL STUDIES OF PARTICIPANTS IN SPORTS, GAMES, AND PLAY

1 The Development of Make-Believe Play

Lonnie Sherrod
Jerome L. Singer
Yale University

Matthew... comes into the kitchen holding a child-sized badminton racket... Mother: "Did you get it? Where did it go? Down there?" Matthew: "I got it!" and runs out of the kitchen after an imaginary shuttle-cock... Matthew swings the racket hitting the imaginary shuttlecock. Mother pretends to toss the shuttlecock back to Matthew. They continue, Matthew and mother taking turns hitting the shuttlecock. The game continues, becoming more sophisticated. Matthew seems to be timing his imaginary shots to follow mother's and looks up at the imaginary "birdie" each time it approaches. Matthew inadvertently drops the racket. Mother: "You lost your racket." Matthew: "Oh, I missed." Matthew pretends to serve and mother to return the serve. Matthew retrieves the imaginary shuttlecock from the hallway. They continue. Matthew calls: "Enough, enough." Matthew: "I want a drink of water." Mother gets a glassful: "Are you thirsty?"; as she holds the imaginary glass for Matthew to drink.
—Cited by Carew, Chan, & Halfer (Note 1, pp. 85–86)

LONNIE SHERROD received his Ph.D. in Developmental Psychology from Yale University and his M.S. from the University of Rochester. Mr. Sherrod's studies of sports and play reflect his interest in the development of adult recreation and imaginative expression and in the interrelations of social and cognitive development.

JEROME L. SINGER is Professor of Psychology and Director of the Clinical Psychology Training Program at Yale University. He received his Ph.D. in Clinical Psychology from the University of Pennsylvania in 1950. He has carried out an extensive series of studies on the psychology of imagination and daydreaming and their manifestations in children's play. He has also examined theoretical relationships between adolescent and preadolescent fantasies of sports, heroics, and adult development.

1

The foregoing description of a mother playing a purely imaginative badminton game with her 26-month-old son, Matthew, highlights the relevance of a chapter on make-believe play to a book on sports and games. Piaget (1962) characterizes three types of play: mastery, symbolic, and games with rules, Mastery play involves attempts of the child to gain motor control over the environment; building with blocks or learning to ride a tricycle are examples. Symbolic or pretend play involves the translation of the external world into structures reconcilable with the child's schemas of the world. Pretend drinking from an empty cup by a 2-year-old is one early example (Fein, 1975), but quite complex story sequences are often enacted by older children. Games with rules involve structured organized activities; hop-scotch, checkers and board games, and baseball are examples.

Piaget proposes that forms of play emerge naturally in the cognitive development of the child. The sensory-motor infant engages in mastery play; symbolic play emerges with the appearance of the ludic symbol, and games with rules make their appearance as the child begins to engage in social interaction, to become less egocentric, and to comprehend the notion of rule structures.

MAKE-BELIEVE PLAY AND ADULT IMAGERY

The connection between adult forms of recreation and amusement (sports such as football and tennis, games such as chess and charades, and fantasy activity such as daydreaming) and the earlier forms of child play are not necessarily trivial. It is not unreasonable to expect that we might learn something about adult recreation, sport, and fantasy activity from investigations of children's play. In this chapter we focus on make-believe or symbolic play (play involving the child's imagination). We do not directly assess the relevance of our material to all forms of adult play activity.

Consider, however, some of the following instances of adult fantasy play and imagery bearing on sports. Many early adolescents carry their interest in sports like baseball and football indoors in the form of board games. Such games, although played according to formal rules, also evoke much fantasy and imagery. From 10 to 14 years of age, a group of friends of one of the authors (Singer) improvised board games for baseball and football in which one called a play, spun a spinner or cast dice, and looked up the play under a heading such as Off-Tackle Run, where a 5 might yield "Gains 4 yards." They were not satisfied to simply call plays. Instead they created an entire make-believe atmosphere with players, each with his or her own style or career; they simulated radio announcers describing the game and generated in themselves and in the others the excitement of actually witnessing a game. It even seemed to them that their "stars" did better despite the presumably chance nature of the spinning or die-casting!

Board games of baseball based upon computerized analyses of batting patterns are currently extremely popular with adults and are creating a minor craze. David Eisenhower (who retreated into almost obsessive playing of this game during the "final days" of the Nixon administration), according to *Newsweek* ("Dice Baseball Fever," 1976), attributes its appeal to "part make-believe, part genius of the game. The sights, sounds, and smells of the ballpark come alive [p. 60]."

The imagery transformations of make-believe may have even more clearly adaptive implications for sports and athletic activities. In Australia, Richardson (1969) demonstrated that gymnasts who engaged in *mental* practice actually performed better than did athletes who occupied their minds with other activities. Suinn (1972, 1976) extends this approach to the systematic training of skiers to engage in mental "skiing of an entire course" as well as certain motor exercises. The great Jean-Claude Killy reports that engaging in mental practice of an entire downhill course as he was recovering from an injury led to one of his greatest performances. In controlled studies, Suinn was able to show decided advantages for the experimental group in their practice sessions, and for other individual skiers in actual international competitions. The make-believe play of childhood thus can be seen as a form of stretching and developing of skills that could be of great advantage to adults were they prepared to resort more frequently to the inner world of imagery.

DEFINITION AND DEVELOPMENT OF PLAY

The Definition of Play

The definitions of play are usually heavily embedded in the particular theory in which they are offered. Play generally is defined in terms of function (or the lack thereof) in relation to immediate biological need reduction (that is, play is not consummative behavior) or in terms of motivation (or the lack thereof): Play is not appetitive behavior; there is no play drive. Being neither consummative nor appetitive, play is quite a special behavior. Piaget (1962) offers a formalistic (or descriptive) definition of play rather than a causal, motivational (immediate efficient cause) or functional (goal) explanation. He defines pay as pure assimilation of the world to the ego. Play is behavior in which the external world is completely transformed to coincide with the internal world of the child and involves no accommodation of the child to the external world. Play is the opposite of imitation, which is pure accommodation of the child to the external world. Notice that Piaget's definition does not conflict with the other definitions of play but rather expands and elaborates those definitions.

Components of Pretend and Fantasy Activity

The special case of fantasy activity and pretend play actually represents a cluster of interrelated abilities or processes. It is useful to partition imaginative abilities into the following five components:

1. the ability to form images (irrespective of specific sensory modality);
2. skill in storing and retrieving the images already formed;
3. a store of images (quantity and quality);
4. skill in recombining, integrating, etc.—generally employing these images as a source of internal stimulation—and divorcing them from reality; and
5. reinforcement for skillful processing as described in (4).

Components (1) and (2) are primarily cognitive abilities studied under the rubrics of imagery and memory and are not unique to fantasy activity. The potential store of images is, of course, dependent on the information available in the individual's environment. Only components (4) and (5) are specific to imaginative play and other fantasy activity.

All five components operate together to determine the person's imaginative capacitites. Failure in one process influences the effectiveness of others. For example, having poor skill in storing and retrieving images decreases the supply of images and the overall adaptive value and reinforcement of using images. Success or skill in all five processes is necessary for a strong orientation toward imaginative activities. The more control and skill one develops in regard to these processes, the more reinforcement and positive affect that is generated by their use. Development of these processes without overlying control can lead to mental disorders—when people, for example, cannot determine whether they are attending to internal or external stimulation or when children are at the mercy of fears (of the dark, for example) generated by their imagination. The failure to develop adequate resources for fantasy play is even more likely to be associated with emotional or behavioral difficulty (Singer, 1973).

A consideration of make-believe play and imagination in childhood carries us far beyond the offered definition of play and illustrates the point that to study child play is to study one of the primary means by which chldren deal with their environments.

Description and Development of Pretend Play

The first appearance of pretend play occurs around 12 months of age and consists of the functional use of a schema outside its normal context. Drinking from an empty cup and pretending to go to sleep are examples. In

other words, the origins of make-believe play lie in the early sensory-motor activity of the child (Piaget, 1962).

By 18 months of age, pretend play includes activities directed to others, and it becomes independent of the features of immediate stimulation. And by 3 to 4 years of age, make-believe play seems to be deliberately used by children as a means of transcending immediate space and time. One author (Sherrod) was playing "Tarzan" with a 3½-year-old boy. The boy was Tarzan; the adult was a tiger. The boy was to run out of an adjoining room in order to save a train that the "tiger" was attacking. After being out of the room an unusually long time, the child came rushing back into the room, shouting "Wait a minute, wait a minute!" Then in a quite serious manner, he cautioned, "Remember, we're just pretending."

Fein (1975) extensively analyzes the development of make-believe activities. She describes the move from the nonpretend use of objects (drinking from a full cup) to the make-believe use (drinking from an empty cup) to finally using a pretend cup to give a doll a drink. She characterizes this move in terms of a shift from analog to digital processes. Early pretending is dependent on anchor supports; the child pretends to drink from an empty cup but does not yet use another object as a cup or pretend to feed a pretend character. Older children (2 years plus) can break representations into components and select relevant properties for use in pretend play; they are less dependent on anchor supports, or on reality-based objects in their play. Fein and Robertson (Note 2) and Pulaski (1973) demonstrate that older children prefer less-structured and less-defined objects in their play.

Golomb (Note 3) shows that training 4-year-olds in producing the transformations of pretend games can actually help them grasp the Piagetian principles of conservation at an age well before this is usually the case. By having 4-year-olds play at make-believe and by testing the limits of their credibility, she was able to show that they could later make better judgments about the fact that liquids of initially same amounts that were placed in differently shaped beakers were still equal.

Once the child has reached the digital-process stage of pretend development, make-believe play becomes increasingly less object-centered and more and more involves the enactment of scenarios (playing house, school, cowboys and Indians, and so on). Thus, with age, make-believe play becomes increasingly rich and elaborate and less directly dependent on immediate external stimulation. The frequency of pretend activity also increases with age. In a study of 3- and 4-year-old children, Singer and Singer (1973) observed that make-believe play constituted only about 10% of the child's total activity, but by 5 years of age, pretend activity was much more frequent (Freyberg, 1973; Pulaski, 1973).

Play also becomes with age increasingly social and cooperative. Garvey (1974) argues that three abilities underlie this blossoming of social play (both imaginative and nonimaginative play):

1. the ability to distinguish play and nonplay states;
2. the ability to abstract the organizing rule of the play; and
3. the ability to identify a theme of the play and contribute to its development.

By 3½ years of age, children show evidence of the ability to recognize and effectively to signal play and nonplay states; and by 5 years of age, children are capable of abstracting and contributing to the development of play themes and of organizing rules.

By adolescence, play has become totally social and predominantly involves games with rules. The pretend and imaginative aspects of human experience have become internalized and are expressed privately in the form of daydreams and fantasies and/or publicly through creative expression in the arts (painting, writing, and so on).

Continuity in Play Development

The pioneering work of Jean Piaget, which demonstrates that child development is characterized by continual qualitative reorganization of cognitive structures, has made evident the importance of the continuity issue. Kagan (1971) characterizes three types of continuity:

1. Homotypic continuity is defined as stability in the behavioral manifestations of an underlying process; the process itself may, however, change with age.
2. Heterotypic continuity is defined as change in the behavioral manifestations of a stable underlying process.
3. Complete continuity is defined as occurring when there is stability in both underlying process and behavioral manifestations of the process.

Kagan's characterization of the continuity issue stresses the distinction that must be made between overt behavior and underlying process in discussing the continuity issue. In regard to the development of play, one might ask whether adult recreation and children's play are manifestations of a stable underlying process. Clearly, the question can not be addressed in such a simplistic form, because one must first address the question of whether the different forms of child's play that coexist can indeed be included under the rubric of play. Perhaps if we limit the question to one type of child's play (e.g., pretend play) and one form of adult play (e.g., fantasy and daydreams), it will be less risky to tackle the question.

Though there have been few longitudinal studies of the development of play, several theorists have argued for continuity between adult fantasy activity and childhood symbolic play. The precise conceptions or definitions

of play and fantasy activity vary with the particular theory, but all the theories imply a heterotypic continuity between adult and child fantasy activity.

1. Piaget (1962) denotes the existence of two invariant functions in cognitive development, the conservative function of assimilation by which reality is adapted to the individual's cognitive structures and the adaptive function, or accommodation, by which the individuals adapt their cognitive structures to the environment. In fact, every confrontation between organisms and environment involves both assimilation and accommodation. One process may, however, predominate. Play is behavior in which assimilation predominates over accommodation. Thus, according to Piaget (1962), child's play is assimilation of reality to the ego. Assimilation of reality to the ego is an underlying process that is reflected by different behavioral manifestations of the child's development level. The sensory-motor child may go through the motions of drinking from an empty cup; the 4- to 5-year old child may elaborate a complex sociodramatic scene in which many roles are assumed. During adolescence, this assimilative activity becomes covert (as the child's overt behavior becomes more reality adapted) to constitute fantasy and daydreams. The development is characterized by heterotypic (process but not behavior) continuity.

2. The Freudian (1933) position is that play and fantasy (and dreams) are manifestations of primary process. Fantasy and play enable expression and temporary gratification of repressed drives. The tendency to express and temporarily to gratify repressed desires is an underlying process that gradually gains motor expression through play and fantasy. This position also espouses a heterotypically continuous development of play and fantasy; this theory differs from Piagetian theory in that play, rather than being an internalization of outside events to produce fantasy, constitutes an externalization of symbolic function (Rosenbaum, 1972). The earlier forms of the psychoanalytic theory implied, however, that both adult and chldhood fantasy were responses to conflict and deficiency and were regressive defenses.

3. Klinger (1969, 1971) advocates that play and fantasy are initially inseparable and that they become differentiated with age. Some covert process (such as a sequence of subvocal motor elements) finds motor expression in play. Gradually the connection between covert process and motor expression weakens and disappears. Only covert manifestations (fantasy) of the process are then evident. Fantasy is according to Klinger (1971), "mentation whose ideational products are not evaluated by the subject in terms of their usefulness in advancing some immediate goal extrinsic to the mentation itself [p. 10]," just as play is behavioral activity with no immediate goal other than the pleasure derived from executing the activities themselves. Again, heterotypic continuity is suggested.

4. Rosenbaum (1972) explains the development of play and fantasy as being due to the reification of cognitive residues. Cognitive residues are intact cognitive structure that have been displaced or absorbed by other cognitive structures. Reification is the tendency to seek fulfillment of expectation in as wide a range of experience as possible. To reify a cognitive structure is to predict and influence its reflection in the environment, and a structure can be considered reified once its expected reflection in the environment has occurred. Cognitive residues may accomplish reification through play and fantasy. This theory is also characterized by heterotypic continuity. The reification of cognitive structures is accomplished at different ages by either play or fantasy.

5. Bruner (1964) elaborates three modes of mental representation: sensory-motor, iconic, and symbolic The very young child utilizes motor expressions as representations of experience, the older child employs perceptual representations, and the adolescent can manipulate symbols. The play and fantasy activity of the child can be considered as reflections of these modes of representation. The sensory-motor child plays with objects, the older child pretends, and the adolescent can fantasize. Because Bruner does not argue that the three modes of representation are discontinuous, heterotypic continuity is again implied; change occurs in the overt behavior reflections of the underlying mode of representation.

Several different theories agree that child play is heterotypically continuous with adult fantasy. The only empirical finding relating to the continuity issue is that creative adults (e.g., artists) report higher levels of childhood imaginative play than do less creatively oriented adults (Singer, 1973). When choosing as limited a range as one type of child's play and one type of adult recreation, we find a paucity of experimental verification but a great deal of theoretical speculation on the continuity issue. Researchers and theoreticians in the field are therefore acknowledging the importance of the question of continuity; however, we are in need of longitudinal studies of the development of child and adult play (recreational *and* fantasy activities).

THE BENEFITS OF MAKE-BELIEVE PLAY

The need to consider the continuity issue becomes even more obvious when we examine the importance of make-believe play in the life of the child.

Singer and Singer (1976b), in an extensive review of the literature on children's make-believe play, conclude that skill in imaginative play is positively related to imagery capacity, verbal fluency, divergent thought, ability to tolerate redundant or monotonous stimulation, ability to control affect (to reduce aggression and to generate positive affect), ability to separate

reality and illusion, and lack of psychopathology. Saltz and Johnson (1977) argue further than fantasy play is intimately related to cognitive development —in the realm of representations and concept formation—and that make-believe play helps children to gain feelings of control over their environments.

The relation between make-believe play and cognitive abilities and processes such as imagery, representation, and concept formation is not to be minimized, but because these abilities are necessarily a part of fantasy activity, as we have argued in earlier sections, the development must be a two-way transactional system. It is almost impossible to argue other than that make-believe play and cognition facilitate each other. The two must develop in parallel; they form bidirectional, not two separate unidirectional, systems. Thus, studies (such as Saltz, Dixon & Johnson, Note 4) that train children or give them experience in imagery play should not be used to argue for the influence of imaginative play on cognitive development, because training in fantasy activity necessarily involves training also in cognitive skills such as representation and imagery.

The relation between fantasy play and verbal fluency and divergent thought can be explained, at least partially, by the relation between fantasy and cognition. Increases in fantasy ability necessarily involve an increase in imagery and representational skills, and these are, or at least can be, necessary for increases in verbal fluency and divergent thought. The more adaptive functions (e.g., control of affect) less obviously result from make-believe play; so we consider their relation in more detail.

Coping With Redundant Stimulation and the Control of Emotion

Singer and Singer (1976b) argue that imaginative play is a form of exploration, a controlled examination of novelty and gradual assimilation of that novelty that is much accompanied by the alternating affects of interest, surprise, and joy. The exploration is not one of the physical environment but of 'a stimulus field created by the child's own as yet insufficiently assimilated experiences and fantasies or memories of adult interactions or communications [pp. 33–34].'' Singer and Singer's argument is based on the affect that can be observed in children's imaginative play and on Tomkins' (1962, 1963) and Izard's (1971) theories of emotion. These theories propose that affect rather than drive plays the central role in human motivation and is related to the rate and persistence of new cognitive inputs with which the organism deals. Imaginative activities are especially likely to generate positive affects; because the child is dealing with an internal store of stimulation, he or she alone controls the rate and persistence of inputs.

There is very little empirical investigation of the relation between affect and imaginative activity. There are quite a number of studies demonstrating that imaginative abilities can be used to prevent or reduce unpleasant environmental circumstances and thereby indirectly control affect.

One major advantage of imaginative activity is that it provides a novel stimulus field and can be used as an escape from an unpleasant environment (Singer, 1961, 1966). The child is more likely to be able to tolerate waiting situations, polite adult gatherings, etc., and thereby is less likely to provoke the wrath of parents and other adults (Singer & Singer, 1976b; Saltz, Dixon, & Johnson, Note 4).

Adolescents showing evidence of high imaginative behavior are less likely to become involved in disciplinary problems (Spivack & Levine, Note 5). Kindergarten-age children showing many human movement responses on the Barron Inkblot tests (taken as a sign of creativity) are more likely to be capable of remaining quiet during an extended waiting period (Riess, Note 6). Singer (1961) reports that 6- to 9-year-old children who reported more imaginative play as part of their normal activity and reported imaginary companions were more likely to tolerate a long wait. The highly imaginative children sustained themselves during the waiting period by introducing play elements, as indicated by mouthing sound effects and by hand and body gestures. Imaginative play behavior has also been shown to be associated with greater abilities in concentration, and this is usually accompanied by positive affect (Singer, 1973).

Singer and Singer (1976b) and Rosenhan, Underwood, and Moore (1974) report that children who engage in imaginative activity that is associated with positive affect are less likely to be aggressive. Biblow (1973) directly assessed the influence of imaginative tendency on the expression of agression in 10-year-old children. All children were angered by having their work interfered with by an older child. The subjects were then exposed to either an aggressive, neutral, or pleasant television film. Compared to behavior immediately before the films (and after arousal), high-fantasy children showed a reduction in aggression during free play behavior following the aggressive film. Singer and Singer (1976a) suggest that these results imply that imaginative play distracts from the experience of frustration and is associated with positive affect, which changes the overall affective state of a frustrated subject.

One cannot, however, carry an escape hypothesis too far. We have argued that fantasy and pretend occur in situations involving highly redundant external stimulation—when the subject is bored—and serve as a mental escape valve when no physical one is possible. From personal experience, one might argue that make-believe play also occurs when the person has lots of mundane cares (if bombarded with work and problems); the aggression studies fit into this hypothesis as well. Perhaps daydreaming and fantasizing are lowest during some optimal level of external stimulation and increase if

stimulation goes above or below that level; that is, these skills serve as coping devices in the same way that infants use gaze aversion to avoid a stimulus that is either too novel or to which they have habituated. Persons with demands on their time and energy to meet survival requirements (poverty-ridden families, low-technology cultures, etc.) might resort to vicarious fantasy in the form of television, movies, rituals, and symbolic activities (more passive activities) but not necessarily in the form of private fantasy. Fein (Note 7) argues that one must differentiate between proximal and distal fantasies—"proximity being an index of the likelihood of the fantasy becoming connected to a realizable program of action." Thus, a cleaning woman can dream of becoming a private maid (proximal) or a glamorous movie star (distal). Fein also distinguishes free-flowing and problem-directed arousal and suggests that problem-directed arousal will facilitate proximal fantasies and that free-flowing arousal will facilitate more distal fantasies. Thus, according to the fantasy as coping-mechanism argument presented in the preceding paragraphs, proximal fantasies may increase as the pressure of survival requirements mounts, whereas distal fantasies may increase with boredom and redundant external stimulation. Such a proposal can be easily tested by asking individuals to report their fantasies in artifically constructed situations of varying redundancy, pressure, etc., and then measuring the "proximity" of their fantasy content.

Another way to examine these speculations is to examine adult fantasies and childhood pretend play in societies in different levels of technological advancement. Sutton-Smith and Roberts (1972) provide cross-cultural studies of play, but they concentrate mainly on games. These authors provide clear documentation for the connection between the structure of the society and the structure of games. Games fulfill needed functions within the society, almost mimicking the society at large. Thus, in societies undergoing rapid rates of change, technological advancement and so on, games of order and disorder predominate. These games provide a mechanism for experimenting with new roles and life styles in the changing society (Sutton-Smith, 1974). No one has, to date, provided such an examination of pretend play, but if we assume continuity between pretend play and games with rules, we might expect pretend play to serve similar functions earlier in the child's life.

Make-Believe Play as Reality-Testing

According to Singer and Singer (1976b), imaginative play may actually help children to discriminate fantasy and reality:

> The reasoning in part was based on the notion that the child's ability to produce transformations also offers the child experience in recognizing the sequences which are produced by itself and those which are demanded by others or by the

characteristics of the physical environment. A consequence of active play and replay of make-believe sequences may also be an enhancement of differentiated memory schemas [pp. 20–21].

Tucker (Note 8) tested the notion that differentiated schema were associated with playing out fantasy sequences over a period of time. The subjects were 9- to 11-year-old children. There were no differences in recall of adventure stories as a function of whether or not the stories were presented as truth or fiction However, children who were highly imaginative were more accurate in recall of the stories and were less prone to introduce gross distortion in the stories than were children who were less imaginative. High imaginative orientation, therefore, seems to be associated with increased ability to separate fantasy and reality rather than with the risk of confusing fantasy and reality. Saltz, Dixon, and Johnson (Note 4) found that preschoolers trained in thematic-fantasy play were later better at detecting absurdities and unrealities in pictures than were control children.

Carrying the foregoing point even further, Gould (1972) collected nursery school teachers' observations of preschoolers' ongoing make-believe play; analysis from a psychoanalytic viewpoint indicated that failure of development of imaginative play was a serious sign of pathology. Children past 3 years of age who have not developed a capacity for make-believe play are likely to show serious difficulties in self-delineation and in positive interaction with other people. Gould argues that imaginative symbolism enriches realistic thought and allows the child to work out, through make-believe play, methods for coping with conflicts, anxieties, and problems in real life.

INDIVIDUAL VARIATION IN
THE DEVELOPMENT OF MAKE-BELIEVE PLAY

Definition, Description, and Measurement

We have already alluded to the existence of individual differences between children in make-believe play. In light of the argument presented in the preceding section that make-believe play is a normal characteristic of child development that carries importance and satisfies functions crucial to normal development, it is appropriate now to consider the existence of individual variation and the possible promoting and maintaining factors of such individual differences.

Individual children vary along both quantitative and qualitative dimensions of imaginativeness. Some children simply engage in make-believe play and daydreaming less frequently than others. Other children also exhibit make-believe play that is more reality-based, less rich, and less elaborate; these children are unable to execute long or complex story sequences or to

decenter from the realities of the concrete world before them. The latter form of pretend play seems to be less advanced developmentally than the more elaborate, rich play.

Singer (1973) develops a method for measuring fantasy (imaginative play) predisposition in children. The method consists of an imaginative-play interview, which measures the child's report of the extent of his or her pretend activities, the child's responses on the Barron Inkblot test (or the Rorschach test for older children), and teacher ratings of the child's imaginative tendencies. Ratings of fantasy predisposition from these three measurements correlate highly with observed frequency of pretend play in 3- and 4-year-old children (Singer & Singer, 1973). Reliability of the measurements is quite high—95.5% , in fact (Dennis, Note 9).

We now consider possible factors involved in promoting and maintaining individual variation in imaginative activities.

Early Pretending: Differences in Infant Temperament and in Mother–Infant Interaction

By 12 months of age (at the very beginnings of pretend play), individual differences in quality and quantity are already in evidence (Fein, 1975). Thus, some factors before the appearance of make-believe play must be at least partially responsible for the emergence of individual differences in pretend. That is, the origins of individual differences in early symbolic behavior may lie in the nonsymbolic, sensorimotor activity of the individual. Piaget (1962) is very explicit, of course, in theorizing that the origins of symbolic functioning, in general, lie in the sensorimotor activity of the child. It is not unreasonable to expect the origins of individual differences in symbolic activity also to be found in nonsymbolic activity or related variables.

One likely target variable is differences in individual temperament or constitution. Thomas, Chess, and Birch (1968) and Escalona (1968) amply demonstrate the existence of individual diferences in temperament (activity level, rhythmicity, etc.) present at birth. Kagan (1971) likewise characterizes slow- and fast-tempo infants. Slow-tempo infants seem to visually fixate objects longer, to smile more, to habituate more slowly, to have longer attention spans in play, and to generally be less active than fast-tempo infants. Singer (1973) argues that the more passive, slow-tempo children are probably more prone to examine and assimilate environmental information available to them; the active child would be more externally oriented, continually jumping from one external stimulus to another, with less internal processing. Thus, there may exist constitutional, genetically programmed differences in the ability to attend to external stimulation sufficiently long to allow formation of mental representations of the stimulus and in the tendency to attend to such representations once they are formed and stored.

There is little information on the stability of such individual differences in infant temperament and style. Fenson, Snapper, and Minner (1974) found that, in slow- and fast-tempo infants, fixation time was stable in individuals over a 3-week period, but habituation rate was not. Whether such individual differences in infants are related to the dimension of impulsivity–reflectivity in older children is an open question.

If stability of such individual differences in constitution does exist, it must be at least partially dependent on environmental factors capable of maintaining the differences. The early caregiver–infant system undoubtedly exerts considerable influence on the development of individual differences. The caregiver–infant relationship is a two–way, transactional system (Sameroff & Chandler, 1975; Thomas, Chess, & Birch, 1968). The infant's interaction with the caregiver can exert considerable influence on the individual style that the infant brings to subsequent interaction; but likewise, the infant's individual style exerts considerable influence on the caregiver (Lewis & Rosenblum, 1974). Many cases exist in which parents' behavior has been shown to be significantly modified by the infant's temperament. Thus, parents who would otherwise be considered "good" caregivers by typical standards can become neglectful or even abusive when confronted for the first time with an infant who is chronically ill with colic or who has a difficult temperament.

Bell (1974) proposes that there are two social exchange systems between mother and infant: the caregiving one, designed to avoid undesirable, immediate, and long-range occurrences; and the social play exchange system, involving mutual, reciprocal, and social interaction. The former is aimed at avoiding negative affect; the latter at generating positive affect. By being sensitive to the cycling of infant behavior, by tracking infant behavior, by decreasing activity when the infant looks away, and by following periods of responding with periods of not responding, the caregiver gives the infant a chance to respond, to interact, and, by so doing, gives the infant experience in pacing attention to the environment (Brazelton, Koslowski, & Main, 1974; Richards, 1974). The caregiver may thus be instrumental in fostering the infant's tendency to attend to the environment. Interaction with a caregiver may also facilitate the discrimination of external and internal stimulus sources. Close contact with and separation from a caregiving figure may lead to the realization that the caregiver is outside and that the mental representation of caregiver is inside (Blatt & Wile, 1976). Such interaction usually occurs during the social play exchange system, thereby generating a great deal of positive affect, and may cause the formation, storage, retrieval, etc., of mental representations, which also occur in the context of social play, to become pleasurable. Colicky and other infants with difficult temperaments may maximize caregiving interaction and   minimize social play exchange,

thereby creating a situation conducive to the development of possibly already existing individual differences in temperament.

Both the constitution with which the infant is born and the type of social exchange system experienced during the first year may affect the infant's tendency to attend to the environment, to form representations, and to derive pleasure from these activities. Infant temperament and early caregiver–infant interaction thus influence both the store or representations that the 1-year-old child has available for pretending and the child's tendency to rely on such internal representations as a source of stimulation to be used in play.

Middle Childhood and Individual Variation in Pretend Play

The existence of individual differences become increasingly evident with age. By age 4 or 5, individual differences in fantasy activity are well developed (Franklin, Note 10)—so well-developed, in fact, that the individual differences in fantasy predisposition account for more of the variance than do sex differences or situational differences such as those involving specific toys or settings (Pulaski, 1973).

Earlier we discussed the shift from analog to digital processes in the development of pretend activity; the developmental shift from analog to digital processes in pretend activity may occur to different extents in different children. Thus, the pretend activity of the low-fantasy child may still rest heavily on analog processes, whereas the pretend activity of the high-fantasy child of the same age may be dependent on digital processes. That is low-fantasy children may for one reason or another become fixated in the first or second phase of the three-phase developmental sequence that Fein (1975) has described. Investigators who have observed individual differences in the quality and quantity of children's imaginative play generally report that low-fantasy children have less elaborate and less complex pretend play, which is more dependent on immediate reality, than do high-fantasy children (Eifermann, 1971; Murphy, 1972; Rubin, Maioni, & Hornung, 1976; Saltz & Johnson 1974, 1977; Smilansky, 1968; Stork, Note 11). None of these investigators, however, attempted to break down the fantasy activity of these children into components and determine in which components the low-fantasy children are deficient. Do these children have difficulty forming and retrieving images, or do they simply have an inadequate supply of images due to a stimulus-impoverish environment? Perhaps they are simply not reinforced for engaging in fantasy activity. It would be fairly straightforward to test low-fantasy and high-fantasy children on the abilities represented by the components of fantasy activity in order to determine on which components the children differ.

IMPROVING THE IMAGINATIVE PLAY OF CHILDREN

A number of studies have attempted to intervene in the lives of low-fantasy children and to provide them with training or experience in imaginative play. One major environmental variable that correlates with level and quality of children's imaginative activity is socioeconomic class; many of the intervention programs have, therefore, focused on children from disadvantaged backgrounds.

Smilansky (1968) observed that lower socioeconomic-class children engage in elaborate sociodramatic play much less frequently than do middle-class children, and Smilansky saw little change in the dramatic play of either lower-class or middle-class children after 3 years of age. Thus, she argues against a retardation explanation of the class differences in pretend play. Smilansky undertook an intervention program aimed at furthering either general cognitive ability, specific play ability, or both. The group given training only in cognitive skills evidenced no improvement in sociodramatic play; the group trained only in play and the group trained both in play and cognitive skill improved significantly, but the latter group showed the greatest benefit from the intervention. Improvement occurred in imitative role play, make-believe play in regard to objects, actions, and situations, persistence at tasks, social interaction, and verbal communication. Smilansky concludes that provision for cognitive ability alone will not improve the frequency and quality of children's play, but training in play skills themselves is also necessary—a finding that agrees with our analysis of fantasy activity in terms of component processes.

Eifermann (1971) argues that lower socioeconomic-class children do play sociodramatically but at older ages than middle-class children; the development of such play is simply retarded, she argues. Both Smilansky and Eifermann studied Israeli children. Stork (Note 11) observed children in a New Haven, Connecticut, nursery school and found that though the younger, lower-SES children initially evidenced less and simpler pretend activity than the middle-class children; by age 6, the lower-SES children had caught up with the middle-class ones—presumably as a result of the nursery school experience. The evidence is not strong, and Stork does not discuss the specific aspects of the experience that may have been crucial—except for mentioning that interaction with older and more skillful peers was probably important. Griffing (1974) studied the imaginative play of middle- and lower-SES blacks and found that the middle-class group showed far more make-believe play, although such play was in evidence in both SES groups.

Feitelson and Ross (1973) examined the influence of tutoring with play materials on the sociodramatic play of 5- to 6-year-old lower middle-class children. The children were divided into four groups: (1) tutoring with play materials; (2) availability of play materials without adult intervention; (3)

tutoring (music lessons) involving no play materials; and (4) control (neither play materials nor tutoring). Ten 30-minute sessions, one-half week apart, were offered. The authors report that, though there was a high variance in level of play at the beginning of the study, most play themes were stereotypic and influenced by the play props available. In group one (tutoring with play materials), mechanical and nonplay activity decreased; sequential, combinatorial, and innovative play increased. The reverse trend occurred in the other three groups. Feitelson and Ross, therefore, argue that thematic play does not develop spontaneously but that both a model and play materials must be available for such play to fluorish.

Saltz, Dixon, and Johnson (Note 4) have undertaken the largest and most comprehensive training study. Data from 4 years of the study have been reported. Lower-class children, aged 3 to 4 years, were given experience in thematic fantasy play (TFP), defined as *verbal role entacment in a group*. The teacher read traditional folk tales to the children; each child was assigned a part in the tale, and the teacher then helped the children to enact the tale. The same tale would be repeatedly enacted with the children playing different roles. Children were discouraged from improvising or being creative in their enactment of the fantasy. Three 15-minute sessions were carried out each week for 4- to 6-month periods. Training in TFP increased the frequency of spontaneous play, increased the children's ability to cognitively represent another's affective experience, increased the children's ability to tell and remember stories (to connect and integrate events over time in a story), and increased performance on IQ tests, tests of empathy, and ability to delay gratification. Thematic play was more effective than nonthematic play experience, and enactment of fantasy was necessary for the effects.

Neither Feitelson and Ross nor Saltz, Dixon, and Johnson report individual differences in ability to respond to the play training. It is unclear whether there were no such individual differences or whether these authors simply failed to report them.

Dansky and Silverman (1975) report that children in spontaneous play situations develop more uses for objects than children given imitative or intellectual training in object possibilities. The authors argue that playful activity, once flourishing, "can provide children with an opportunity to organize their experiences and to exercise their cognitive abilities in a manner that is likely to facilitate imaginative adaptation to future situations [p. 104]." Dansky and Silverman also do not report individual differences in ability to respond to imitative versus spontaneous play situations.

Freyberg (1973) found that as little as eight 20-minute training sessions over a 1-month period resulted in improvement in imaginative play and verbal communication and increased the positive affect and concentration of 5-year-olds. Training occurred in small groups and centered around an adult who introduced themes around various objects and toys available to the

children, encouraging the children to adopt roles in a story plot, etc. These children, however, did not, even after training, attain the levels of imaginative play observed in middle-class children (Pulaski, 1973). The children with high-fantasy predisposition benefited most from the program. This result, coupled with the small amount of training necessary to accomplish improvement, suggests that: (1) all children have at least a minimal capacity for imaginative play; and (2) the capacity, derived from previous experience, that the children bring to a particular program determines the extent to which they can benefit from the program.

Nahme-Huang, Singer, Singer, and Wheaton (1977) report increases in the frequency of imaginative play of emotionally disturbed children following intervention efforts centered around imaginative activities. Unfortunately, these emotionally disturbed children were not able, during the short duration of the intervention program, to consolidate the play pattern sufficiently well that the results of the intervention were lasting. This study, therefore, again demonstrates the existence of individual variation (disturbed versus nondisturbed, in this case) in the ability to respond to and benefit from training.

Marshall and Doshi (1965) trained preschoolers in doll-play fantasy. The frequency of dramatic play with peers increased if an adult had engaged in fantasy play with the child, enacting topics commonly used in children's dramatic play with peers. Training was the critical factor, not warmth and attention.

Singer and Singer (1976a) examined the influence of television versus a live adult model on children's imaginative play. Preschoolers either watched TV simply in large groups of children (one-half hour daily for 2 weeks); watched TV with an adult present who interpreted material, encouraged imitation of the material, etc.; or interacted with an adult (no TV) who generated a number of make-believe games and encouraged participation. Significant increases in imaginative play and positive affect resulted from the treatments. TV viewing was least effective, but adult alone was most effective. Thus, at this age, live social interaction with adults seems crucial to children's development of imaginative play.

In a more recent study, Singer, Singer, Tower, and Biggs (Note 12) exposed 3- and 4-year-olds to 2 weeks of daily showings of *Mister Roger's Neighborhood, Sesame Street,* or nature and animal films. Adults were seated with each of the three groups during their viewings. Subsequently, children exposed to the *Mister Roger's* show demonstrated a greater increase imaginatively than those watching *Sesame Street* and the control films. This effect was strongest for the initially less imaginative children.

Several other training programs have employed play and fantasy as training devices even though the programs were not directly aimed at facilitating the development of play itself. Lovinger (Note 13) reports that 25

weeks of training in make-believe play increased children's language usage skills. Friedrich and Stein (1975) demonstrate that kindergarten children learn the prosocial content of TV programs and generalize that learning to other situations. Their groups watched neutral or prosocial television programs and were offered either irrelevant, verbal-label, or role-playing training. Role-playing training increased nonverbal helping behavior, especially for boys. Verbal-label training facilitated verbal performance on learning tasks. The authors do not, however, report measures of play behavior. In the study by Singer et al., just cited, children viewing *Mister Roger's* showed an increase in positive affect and less dependence on adults in the nursery school.

Meichenbaum (1977) has generated a series of methods using self-instructional plans, "coping imagery," and fantasy play aimed at facilitating the development of self-control. For example, impulsive children gradually learned to slow down their own movements through a combination of imagery and self-instruction. None of Meichenbaum's methods have been employed specifically to increase the elaborateness of fantasy play, though it seems reasonable to expect such an increase to result from some of the methods.

It is difficult to argue that the factors that training provides are also necessarily those that are normally present in development. The interaction with adults and other aspects of training could be substitutes for the normal facilitators of imaginative play. This argument, however, appears untenable in the light of experiential and family correlates of high-fantasy predisposition, discussed in the following section.

In addition, one might explain the differences in fantasy predisposition (especially in regard to SES differences) in terms of performance rather than competence. The training studies may, therefore, simply facilitate performance rather than increasing competence—by making the children less ill at ease and more comfortable in the situations. The performance explanation, however, seems unlikely. First of all, the argument seems most applicable to social class differences in play, but both individual variation and the effects of training also exist within, in addition to between, socioeconomic classes (Griffing, 1974). Secondly, the differences are often observed in spontaneous free play in the children's natural setting and should not, therefore, be extremely susceptible to "strange" context influences. Finally, if the training influences were simply putting the children more at ease, we would expect differential experiences (cognitive only versus fantasy play only versus both) to be equally effective when, in fact, they are not.

We would, therefore, conclude that the individual differences in fantasy activity are at least not entirely performance differences due to adaptability to novel situations and that the training experiences influence competence as well as performance. Thus, we would argue that even very limited interaction

with an adult who provides material to be used in imaginative play and encourages such play, thereby initiating practice in the behaviors necessary to imaginative play, is effective in increasing the quantity and quality of children's imaginative play. Generally, the training studies indicate that all the components of fantasy activity are being influenced by training. For example, the ability of children to form representations of their environments, to store and retrieve the representations, to recombine, resynthesize already stored images, to increase the quality and quantity of the store of images, and to gain pleasure from such activity, are all facilitated by supervised experience in fantasy activity. Fantasy training, of course, facilitates those cognitive processes involved in fantasy activity as well as the processes specific to fantasy. Once flourishing, spontaneous play can provide the mechanism for its own continued development; each component feeds the other in a spiraling type of interaction leading to the further development of ability in and tendency to fantasize. The capacity for pretend play that the children bring to the training situation, however, determines the extent to which they can benefit from such experience. Few of the training studies, however, examine the possible reasons for these initial individual differences in fantasy activity.

PERSONALITY AND EXPERIENTIAL CORRELATES OF PRETEND PLAY

Fantasy predispositions (as measured by the Singer method) correlate with a number of personality factors and aspects of the child's functioning. Fantasy predisposition correlates positively with ability to wait (Singer, 1973; Saltz, Dixon & Johnson, Note 4), positive affect displayed in pretend play (Marshall & Doshi, 1965; Singer & Singer, 1973; Singer & Singer, 1976b), complexity of verbal communication (Smilansky, 1968; Stork, Note 11), ability to concentrate (Singer, 1973), ability to benefit from training in imaginative-play techniques (Freyberg, 1973; Singer & Singer, 1973; Smilansky, 1968), amounts of peer-play interaction and frequency of friendly peer interaction (Marshall & Doshi, 1965), and amount of mother–infant imaginative play interaction and amount of maternal schooling (Dennis, Note 9). Fantasy predisposition correlates negatively with aggressive play and motoric play (Biblow, 1973; Singer, 1973), tendency to model observed aggression (Biblow, 1973), and maternal restrictiveness (Dennis, Note 9). In addition, make-believe play correlates with child (as opposed to adult) orientation of the individual, with the characteristics of being loving, sociable, and withdrawn, and with the tendency to engage in complementary behavior. Boys engage in more fantasy activity than do girls (Emmerich, 1971) at least under some circumstance. Fantasy predisposition is unrelated to achievement motivation (Freyberg, 1973). Freyberg (1973) reports that

fantasy predisposition is unrelated to IQ; Dennis (Note 9) reports that IQ predicts fantasy predisposition.

Marshall (1961) observed that the frequency of dramatic play language and of hostility with peers increased with peer acceptance of such behaviors, with home experience with dramatic play topics, increased for boys and decreased for girls as fathers agreed with PARI scales emphasizing punitive control, and decreased as fathers agreed with PARI scales of overpossessiveness and with time spent simply talking with adults.

Certain family experiential factors correlate with the fantasy-predisposition measure. Children with high-fantasy predispositions tend to be only or oldest children (to have fewer siblings), to have more living space at home, and to have more educated parents who are more tolerant and encouraging of make-believe and fantasy, and they tend to be closer to one parent (usually the mother) (Freyberg, 1973). Singer (1973) interprets these results to imply that the factors essential for the development of high-fantasy predispositions are: (1) the close identification and frequent interaction with one parent who provides a model of behaviors to be used in play; and (2) some opportunities for privacy in order to permit the child to reprocess and integrate the experiences occurring in interaction with the parent.

Dennis (Note 9) set out to test Singer's hypothesis and to examine the family background factors that encourage or discourage imaginative play. She found no relation between the child's level of fantasy orientation and: (1) the fantasy orientation of the parents or the siblings; (2) the abstractness of the parents' conceptual system; (3) the father's restrictiveness of the play environment in the home; and (4) the amount of privacy in the home. High-fantasy children, however, when compared to low-fantasy children tended to have mothers who were less restrictive of the home play environment and who engaged in imaginative-play interaction with the child and to have fathers who did not in any way discourage imaginative activity. Dennis cautions, however, that due to the two-way transactional nature of mother–child interaction, it is impossible to establish the direction of causality. High-fantasy children may promote imaginative-play interaction between their mothers and themselves, and imaginative play may not necessitate the restrictions of frequent and active motoric play.

Gershowitz (Note 14) has investigated the effects of adult–child interaction on the expression of fantasy predisposition. He reports that adults with experience or training in child work are much more effective at encouraging make-believe play than are other adults. Emotional involvement of the adult and the lack of restrictions or amount of leeway allowed in the play are crucial to the encouragement of imaginative activity. Cross-lag correlation techniques demonstrate that adult involvement in the initial stages of play interaction followed by a loosening of adult intervention is most likely to facilitate play development.

Another area in which family correlates of imaginative predisposition have been investigated is the special case of imaginary companions. The child invents a friend who he or she plays with, talks to, and generally interacts with—usually in the absence of other persons. Frequency estimates of imaginary companions usually vary from 12% to 33%, and imaginary companions are most likely to be present in the 3- to 5-year-old group (Manosevitz, Prentice, Wilson, 1973). Imaginary companions themselves can be quite diverse and interesting; Dennis (Note 9) reports a case of an imaginary companion named the "abdominal snow man." Imaginary companions can also be quite realistic in nature; a case in point is an imaginary companion named Jethro who makes the child get up every night for a glass of water (Dennis, Note 9). Manosevitz and colleagues have investigated the various personal and demographic correlates of imaginary companions. More firstborns and only children tend to have imaginary companions, and females are more likely to have imaginary companions than are males. Nuclear-family disruption is not a factor nor is the number of friends, siblings, pets, and so on. Parental attitudes, characterized by lack of disapproval, do seem to be important (Manosevitz et al., 1973). Unlike other forms of pretend play, the presence of imaginary companions does not correlate with intelligence, creativity, or waiting ability (Manosevitz & Fling, Note 15). Retrospectively, however, creative adults report that they were more likely to have had make-believe playmates in childhood (Schaefer, 1969; Schaefer & Anastasi, 1968).

Modeling Influences

Thus, both the training studies and the family correlates of a high-fantasy predisposition indicate that lack of overt disapproval of imaginative play and some experience with a parent or other adult in imaginative activity are necessary if such play is to flourish. That is, the availability of some sort of model of behaviors to be used in play, of some encouragement to engage in such play, and even some direct instruction in "how to" play imaginatively are important to the expressions of imaginative play in children. These functions need not necessarily be served by a parent, but it seems that the person most likely to be in a position to perform these functions is a parent. Thus, parents who have one rather than several children, who are themselves rather imaginative, who frequently fantasize, and who have enough home space, time, and energy to interact with the child, are the parents most likely to naturally and spontaneously teach and encourage imaginative activity by the child. On the other hand, parents who must work two jobs in order to support a large family, who live under crowded, unpleasant conditions, etc., are probably much less likely to have the time and energy to engage in fantasy activity themselves, much less to encourage such in their children. Such a

suggestion might be especially pertinent to an explanation of socioeconomic class differences in children's fantasy activities. Meichenbaum and Turk (1972), in fact, cite evidence that the life circumstances of disadvantaged families tend to mitigate against elaborate, playful, or attentive interchange between adults and children. Pavenstedt (1967) reports, from a longitudinal study of multiproblem families, witnessing actual discouragement of and interference with children's play by the adults. She cites one particularly sad example of a boy playing with a wooden airplane he himself had made. The boy's father mocked the child's play and called the plane a piece of junk; other family members then destroyed the plane.

At any rate, modeling influences seem to be especially crucial to the development of individual differences in fantasy predisposition. Gottlieb (1973) studied modeling in 10- to 14-year-olds. Exposure to imaginative models enhanced imaginative behavior; exposure to realistic or ambiguous model behavior resulted in observer factualism and realistic behavior. Modeling superseded the imaginative predisposition of the young children. The older children structured the task in their own terms; high-fantasy children produced divergent behavior, and low-fantasy subjects were bound to detail and literalness. Likewise, Biblow (1973) observed that only low-fantasy children tended to have aggression enhanced by observed violent behavior; high-fantasy children could reduce aggression through fantasy. Fantasy predisposition, therefore, once developed, can affect the influence of a modeling situation on the child just as it influenced the child's capacity to benefit from direct training in and encouragement of imaginative play.

There are several ways modeling behavior could influence fantasy predisposition. One influence, as in Gottlieb's study, is that children could directly model the imaginative behavior of their parents (or any other attractive model). Because most of adults' imaginative behavior, except that directed specifically to children, is covert, it is doubtful if this aspect of modeling of adults is very important in accounting for intrasocietal variation—though it may be relevant to the influence of older children. Rather, we would expect the influence of parents to operate mainly through direct training and encouragement. The second possible influence of modeling processes is that the model can serve as a source of information on content for play behaviors. Thus, children model parental roles and activities. Such modeling is, indeed, widespread; children in a variety of cultures carry out the dominant roles of their parents in their pretend play. For example, Rajput children play at cooking and farming, the major activities of their parents; children of Okinawa often imitate their mothers visiting each other ceremoniously, imitating their voices, and so on (Whiting, 1963). Just as the earliest form of pretend play reflects the functional use of an acquired activity (Piaget, 1962; Fein, Note 16), so the first role-playing by children may reflect the functional use (or trying out) of the role behaviors acquired through observational learning.

Franklin (Note 10) has carried out a study on the influence of modeling on block play in 4- to 5-year-old children. She reports that children are much more likely to model an adult who engages in fantasy than in concrete play. Even more interesting is that during spontaneous play the children adapt the model's behavior to their own style; mimicry, therefore, was a minor feature of the effect of the model. Thus, children model both the type of play and the content; but the individual differences, preferences, and so on that the children bring to the situation (as in the training studies) determine the behaviors the children select to model and determine the reproduction of the behaviors by the children.

The number and diversity of models the child has available may be one source of imaginative predisposition in children. Such a suggestion at first seems at variance with Singer's (1973) argument that high-fantasy predisposition correlates positively with small family size, closeness with one parent, etc. The latter factors may function at earlier ages when pretend play is first emerging. Number and diversity of models may function later when the child is actively engaged in role-playing. In addition, Singer (1966) has proposed a two-part system to modeling—selection of a model and adherence to its values and behaviors in order to enhance positive affect. Further, the extent of modeling depends on the model's reactions to the modeling attempt (Bandura, 1971). Thus, the low-fantasy predisposition children even though from a large family, may have fewer persons whose behaviors they see reinforced and who reinforce the modeling of their behavior than the high-fantasy children, who, perhaps having fewer individuals available, have a larger number of suitable models.

We have been considering failures on the part of the model to facilitate modeling; on the contrary, there may be individual differences in tendency to model. Bruner (1972) has argued for the development of differential "tutor proneness" or tendency to model the parent's behavior. Bandura (1971) suggests that modeling phenomena are governed by four processes; attention, retention (both verbal and imaginal), motoric reproduction, and reinforcement and motivation. Low-fantasy predisposition may, therefore, develop due to a failure to model—as a result of misfunction in one of these four processes. Though there is evidence that children already high in fantasy predisposition are more innovative and not as imitative in their modeling behavior as low-fantasy predisposition children (Gottlieb, 1973; Franklin, Note 10), no one has looked to see if children high in fantasy predisposition at time $x + 1$ were more effective modelers at time x.

There has been little consideration of the developmental sequence of modeling behavior; because it is a phenomenon conceived and nourished by social-learning theories, little attention has been devoted to possible qualitative differences in modeling behavior according to developmental level. Bandura (1971) characterized four possible aspects of modeling:

1. observational learning—the observer can witness responses not yet made and later reproduce them in identical form;
2. inhibiting effects, decrements in modeled behaviors, or reduction of responses as a result of seeing a model punished;
3. disinhibitory effects—increase in performance of formerly inhibited behaviors after seeing a model do them without getting punished; and
4. response facilitation effect—facilitation of performance of existing responses in the same general class.

Thus, different aspects may be especially prominent at different developmental levels, or children of different age may be more susceptible to modeling influences. Gottlieb's work (1973), in fact, demonstrated the differential influence of models on children of different ages and of different fantasy predispositions.

ACKNOWLEDGMENTS

The authors wish to thank Greta Fein, Michael Lamb, Victoria Seitz, and Deborah Stipek for critical readings of the manuscript and for much useful exchange.

REFERENCE NOTES

1. Carew, J., Chan, I., & Halfer, C. *Observing intelligence in young children: Eight case studies.* Englewood Cliffs, N.J.: Prentice-Hall, 1976.
2. Fein, G., & Robertson, A. *Cognitive and social dimensions of pretending in two-year olds.* Mimeographed report, Yale University, 1974.
3. Golomb, C. Pretense play: A cognitive perspective. *Wheelock College Symposium on Symbolization and the Young Child,* 1976.
4. Saltz, E., Dixon, D., & Johnson, I. *Training disadvantaged preschoolers on various fantasy activities: Effects on cognitive functioning and impulse control.* (Tech. Rep. #8, Studies in Intellectual Development). Detroit: Wayne State University, 1976.
5. Spivack, G., & Levine, M. *Self-regulation and acting-out in normal adolescents* (Prog. Rep for National Institute of Mental Health Grant M-4531). Devon, Pa.: Devereaux Foundation, 1964.
6. Reiss, A. A. *Study of some genetic behavioral correlates of human movement responses in children's Rorschach protocols.* Unpublished doctoral dissertation, New York University, 1957.
7. Fein, G. Personal Communication, August, 1975.
8. Tucker, J. *The role of fantasy in cognitive-affective functioning: Does reality make a difference in remembering?* Unpublished doctoral dissertation, Teachers College, Columbia University, 1975.
9. Dennis, L. B. *Individual and familial correlates of children's fantasy play.* Unpublished doctoral dissertation, University of Florida, 1976.
10. Franklin, D. *Block play modeling and its relationship to imaginativeness, impulsivity-reflection and internal-external control.* Unpublished predissertation research, Yale University, 1975.

11. Stork, L. *Observations on make-believe play in lower- and middle-class children from three to six years of age.* Unpublished manuscript, Yale University, 1974.
12. Singer, J. L., Singer, D. G., Tower, R., & Biggs, A. *Preschoolers watch* Mister Rogers *and* Sesame Street: *Some effects on recall and imagination.* In preparation, Yale University, 1976.
13. Lovinger, S. L. *Sociodramatic play and language development in preschool disadvantaged children.* Unpublished manuscript, Central Michigan University, 1973.
14. Gershowitz, M. *Fantasy behaviors of clinic-referred children in play encounters with college undergraduates.* Unpublished doctoral dissertation, Michigan State University, 1974.
15. Manosevitz, M., & Fling, S. *The relation of imaginary companions in young children to intelligence, creativity, and waiting ability.* Paper presented at the Meetings of the Society for Research in Child Development, Denver, April 1975.
16. Fein, G. *Structure and continuity: The anatomy of play during the second year of life.* Unpublished manuscript, Yale University, 1974.

REFERENCES

Bandura, A. *Psychological modeling: Conflicting theories.* Chicago: Aldine-Atherton, 1971.
Bell, R. Q. Contributions of human infants to caregiving and social interaction. In M. Lewis & L. A. Rosenblum (Eds.), *The effect of the infant on its caregiver.* New York: Wiley, 1974.
Biblow, E. Imaginative play and the control of aggressive behavior. In J. L. Singer (Ed.), *The child's world of make-believe.* New York: Academic press, 1973.
Blatt, S. J., & Wild, C. M. *Schizophrenia: A development analysis.* New York: Academic Pres, 1976.
Brazelton, T. B., Koslowski, B., & Main, M. The origins of reciprocity: The early mother–infant interaction. In M. Lewis & L. A. Rosenblum (Eds.), *The effect of the infant on its caregiver.* New York: Wiley, 1974.
Bruner, J. S. The course of cognitive growth. *American Psychologist,* 1964, *19,* 1–15.
Bruner, J. S. The nature and uses of immaturity. *American Psychologist,* 1972, *27,* 687–709.
Dansky, J. L., & Silverman, I. W. Play: A general facilitator of associative fluency. *Developmental Psychology,* 1975, *11,* 104.
Dice baseball fever. *Newsweek,* August 23, 1976, pp. 60–61.
Eifermann, R. R. Social play in childhood. In R. Herron & B. Sutton-Smith (Eds.), *Child's play.* New York: Wiley, 1971.
Emmerich, W. Structure and development of personal-social behaviors in preschool settings. Princeton, Educational Testing Service, 1971.
Escalona, S. K. *The roots of individuality.* New York: Basic Books, 1968.
Fein, G. A transformational analysis of pretending. *Developmental Psychology,* 1975, *11,* 291–296.
Feitelson, D., & Ross, G. S. The neglected factor: Play. *Human Development,* 1973, *16,* 202–223.
Fenson, C., Sapper, V., & Minner, D. G. Attention and manipulative play in the one year old child. *Child Development,* 1974, *45,* 757–764.
Freud, S. *New introductory lectures on psychoanalysis.* New York: W. W. Norton and Co., 1933.
Freyberg, J. T. Increasing the imaginative play of urban disadvantaged kindergarten children through systematic training. In J. L. Singer (Ed.), *The child's world of make-believe.* New York: Academic Press, 1973.
Friedrich, L. K., & Stein, A. H. Prosocial television and young children: The effects of verbal labeling and role playing on learning and behavior. *Child Development,* 1975, *46,* 27–38.

Garvey, C. Some properties of social play. *Merrill Palmer Quarterly,* 1974, *20*(3), 163–180.

Gottlieb, S. Modeling effects upon fantasy. In J. L. Singer (Ed.), *The child's world of make-believe.* New York: Academic Press, 1973.

Gould, R. *Child studies through fantasy.* New York: Quadrangle Books, 1972.

Griffing, P. Sociodramatic play among young black children. *Theory into Research,* 1974, *13,* 257–264.

Izard, C. *The face of emotion.* NewYork: Appleton-Century-Crofts, 1971.

Kagan, J. *Change and continuity in infancy.* New York: Wiley, 1971.

Klinger, E. Development of imaginative behavior: Implications of play for a theory of fantasy. *Psychological Bulletin,* 1969, *72,* 277–298.

Klinger, E. *Structure and functions of fantasy.* New York: Wiley-Interscience, 1971.

Lewis, M., & Rosenblum, L. A. *The effect of the infant on its caregiver.* NewYork: Wiley, 1974.

Manosevitz, M., Prentice, N. M., & Wilson, F. Individual and family correlates of imaginary companions in preschool children. *Developmental Psychology,* 1973, *8,* 72–79.

Marshall, H. R. Relations between home experiences and children's use of language in play interactions with peers. *Psychological Monographs,* 1961, *75*(5, Whole No. 509).

Marshall, H. R., & Doshi, R. Aspects of experience revealed through doll play of preschool children. *Journal of Psychology,* 1965, *61,* 47–57.

Meichenbaum, D. *Cognitive behavior modification,* New York: Plenum, 1977.

Meichenbaum, D. & Turk, L. Implications of research on disadvantaged children and cognitive training programs for educational television: Ways of improving Sesame Street. *Journal of Social Education,* 1972, *6,* 27–41.

Murphy, L. B. Infants' play and cognitive development. In M. W. Piers (Ed.), *Play and development.* New York: W. W. Norton and Co., 1972.

Nahme-Huang, L., Singer, D. G., Singer, J. L., & Wheaton, A. Imaginative play and perceptual-motor intervention methods with emotionally-disturbed, hospitalized children: An evaluation study. *American Journal of Orthopsychiatry,* 1977, *47,* 238–247.

Pavenstedt, E. (Ed.) *The drifters.* Boston, Mass.: Little, Brown, & Co., 1967.

Piaget, J. *Play, dreams and imitation in childhood.* New York: W. W. Norton and Co., 1962.

Pulaski, M. A. Toys and imaginative play. In J. L. Singer (Ed.), *The child's world of make-believe.* New York: Academic Press, 1973.

Richards, M. P. M. First steps in becoming social. In M. P. Richards (Ed.), *The integration of a child into a social world.* Cambridge, England: Cambridge University Press, 1974.

Richardson, A. *Mental imagery.* New York: Springer, 1969.

Rosenbaum, D. A. The theory of cognitive residues: A new view of fantasy. *Psychological Review,* 1972, *79,* 471–486.

Rosenhan, D., Underwood, B., & Moore, B. Affect moderates, self-gratification and altruism. *Journal of personality and social psychology,* 1974, *30,* 546–552.

Rubin, K. H., Maioni, T. L., & Hornung, M. Free play behaviors in middle and lower class preschoolers: Parten and Piaget revisited. *Child Development,* 1976, *47*(2), 414–419.

Saltz, E., & Johnson, I. Training of thematic-fantasy play in culturally-disadvantaged children: Preliminary results. *Journal of Educational Psychology,* 1974, *66,* 623–630.

Saltz, E., & Johnson, J. Fantasy and cognitive representation in culturally-disadvantaged children. In M. Spenakis & H. Kasten (Eds.), *Comparative studies of a child's social development.* Donauworth: Auer, 1977. (English Trans.)

Sameroff, A., & Chandler, M. Reproduction risk and the continuum of caretaking casualty. In F. D. Horowitz (Ed.), *Review of child development research* (Vol. 4). Chicago: University of Chicago Press, 1975.

Schaefer, C. E. Imaginary companions and creative adolescents. *Developmental Psychology,* 1969, *1,* 747–749.

Schaefer, C. E., & Anastasi, A. A biographical inventory for identifying creativity in adolescent boys. *Journal of Applied Psychology,* 1968, *52,* 42–48.

Singer, J. L. Imagination and waiting ability in young children. *Journal of Personality,* 1961, *29,* 396–413.

Singer, J. L. *Daydreaming.* New York: Random House, 1966.

Singer, J. L. *The child's world of make-believe.* New York: Academic Press, 1973.

Singer, J. L., & Singer, D. Some characteristics of make-believe play in nursery school children: An observational study. In J. L. Singer (Ed.), *The child's world of make-believe.* New York: Academic Press, 1973.

Singer, J. L., & Singer, D. Can TV stimulate imaginative play?*Journal of Communications,* 1976, *26,* 74–80. (a)

Singer J. L., & Singer, D. Imaginative play and pretending in early childhood: Some experimental approaches. In A. Davids (Ed.), *Child personality and psychopathology* (Vol. 3). New York: Wiley, 1976. (b)

Smilansky, S. *Effects of sociodramatic play on disadvantaged preschool children.* New York: Wiley, 1968.

Suinn, R. M. Behavior rehearsal training for ski racers. *Behavior Theory,* 1972 ,*3*(No. 509).

Suinn, R. M. Body thinking: Psychology for Olympic champs. *Psychology Today,* July 1976, *10,* 38–43.

Sutton-Smith, B. Toward an anthropology of play. *Newsletter of the Association for Anthropological Study,* 1974, *1,* 8–15.

Sutton-Smith, B., & Roberts, J. M. The cross-cultural and psychological study of games. In B. Sutton-Smith (Ed.), *The folkgames of children.* Austin, Texas: University of Texas Press, 1972.

Thomas, A., Chess, S., & Birch, H. *Temperament and behavior disorders in children.* New York: University Press, 1968.

Tomkins, S. S. *Affect, imagery, consciousness* (Vols. 1 and 2). New York: Springer, 1962, 1963.

Whiting, B. *Six cultures: Studies of child rearing.* New York: Wiley, 1963.

2 Battle Royal: Psychology and the Chessplayer

Eliot Hearst
Michael Wierzbicki
Indiana University

> *Life is a kind of chess, in which we have often points to gain, and competitors or adversaries to contend with .... Several very valuable qualities of the mind, useful in the course of human life, are to be acquired or strengthened by [chess play] so as to become habits, ready on all occasions.*
>
> —Benjamin Franklin (1786)

> *Chess is the royal game for many reasons. It crystallizes within its elaborate structure the family romance, is replete with symbolism, and has rich potentialities for granting satisfactions and for sublimations of drives. Not without reason it is the one game that, since its invention around A.D. 600, has been played in most of the world, has captivated the imagination and interest of millions, and has been the source of great sorrows and great pleasures.*
>
> —Norman Reider (1959)

> *Chess is a foolish expedient for making idle people believe they are doing something very clever when they are only wasting their time.*
>
> —George Bernard Shaw (1905)

ELIOT HEARST is an experimental psychologist, and MICHAEL WIERZBICKI is a clinical psychologist. Both are experienced chessplayers. Hearst is a U.S. Senior Master and Life Master and has been captain of the U.S. Olympic Chess Team (1962), a vice-president of the U.S. Chess Federation (1956–1959), and a regular columnist on international and national chess affairs for *Chess Life* (1960–1964). Wierzbicki has won the U.S. Junior Open Championship (1973) and is currently rated an Expert by the U.S. Chess Federation.

INTRODUCTION

In 1972, a world championship match between an urbane and articulate Russian grandmaster and a crude and uncommunicative American chess genius captured newspaper and television headlines around the world. In the United States, the movements of 32 pieces over 64 squares—and the between-game antics, opinions, and tactics of the players and their advisors—were followed with the kind of attention usually reserved for events like the World Series or the Super Bowl. Millions of Americans wondered whether Bobby Fischer had simply "psyched-out" Boris Spassky or whether Fischer was really the greatest chessplayer in the history of the game, as he had been insisting for a long time. Membership in the U.S. Chess Federation (USCF) soon surpassed 60,000 players, a tripling of its numbers, and department stores exhausted their supply of chess sets and chess books almost as rapidly as these items appeared on display. After the match, Bobby Fischer's views on life, women, and psychology were as much in demand on television talk shows as were the comments of Mark Spitz, Jimmy Connors, or Wilt Chamberlain. Chess as a sport had apparently come of age in the Western hemisphere.

Now, after 5 years featured by Fischer's complete withdrawal from chess competition and by the coronation of Russia's phlegmatic and unaggressive Anatoly Karpov as world champion, the Royal Game has clearly been unable to maintain the level of popular excitement it achieved during that summer in Iceland. This slackening of interest is of course no surprise, because a really outstanding matchup like the Fischer–Spassky struggle is rare in any individual sport, and continued public attention generally depends on frequent appearances by some brilliant and colorful individuals. Where would boxing be without Muhammad Ali? However, even though news broadcasts in the United States no longer carry the latest chess results, the game remains a very popular sports activity.

Regardless of the international popularity of chess at any given time, experimental and clinical psychologists have been interested in the game ever since psychology became a separate discipline in the 19th century. The great psychometrician Alfred Binet was curious about the qualities and techniques involved in the ability of blindfolded chessplayers to play several games simultaneously. Beginning 50 years ago, psychoanalysts came to view the game as a symbolic reenactment of the Oedipal conflict, with the un-conscious goal of father murder (manifested as trapping the king, which is close to the literal meaning of the word *checkmate*). Child prodigies, like José Capablanca, Samuel Reshevsky, and Bobby Fischer, who attained master strength before they were teenagers, caused researchers to wonder what chess might have in common with mathematics and music, the other two major areas in which prodigies occur.

Several psychologists have asked what unique qualities, if any, distinguish master players from weaker players or nonplayers. Experimentalists who study learning, memory, and imagery have found chess a good tool for analyzing human thought processes because of the complex cognitive nature of the game and its well-defined rules; these workers have performed experiments in which players of various strengths must select a move while analyzing aloud or must recall positions that they have been permitted to study for only a few seconds. This research has often been undertaken in conjunction with the development of specific computer programs or models of human cognition and problem solving. Furthermore, in 1968, several experts in the field of artificial intelligence made a famous bet (one they will almost surely lose!) that they would produce a program capable of defeating International Master David Levy of Scotland by the year 1978. The best computer programs "practice" each year in the national computer chess championship, which takes place during the meetings of the Association for Computing Machinery (ACM) and is considered by many computer scientists to be one of the highlights of the convention. Along with their interests in the mind and personality of the chessplayer, psychologists and experts in other fields have investigated: (1) whether increasing age affects chess skill as it does achievement in other sports and in the sciences; and (2) whether the definite differences that exist between the skills and accomplishments of male and female chessplayers reflect mere differences in their upbringing or are traceable to actual biological differences between the sexes with respect to hemispheric specialization in the brain.

In our opinion, the psychological ramifications of chess are at least as numerous as for any other sport or game. Its attractions may be hard for an outsider to understand. For some players the game becomes a complete obsession or addiction; a remorseful minister in 1680 wrote that chess "hath not done with me when I have done with it [cited in Reider, 1959, p. 2]." Stefan Zweig (1944) and Vladimir Nabokov (1964) wrote novels about individuals who were totally devoted to chess. H. G. Wells (1898) called chess "an unaccountable passion" that "slaps the theory of natural selection in the face. . . it annihilates a man [cited in Reider, 1959, p. 2]."

Other players seem more dispassionate about the game; they are attracted by the challenge of its seemingly limitless complexities—its basic insolubility —and they may regard chess as a mental or intellectual exercise that fosters the development of good habits related to self-reliance, self-criticism, patience, and long-range planning. Such devotees, like Benjamin Franklin, often praise chess as a contest in which luck plays little or no role; they fall into the second of Collins' (1880) categories: "There are two classes of men, those who are content to yield to circumstances, and who play whist; and those who aim to control circumstances, who play chess [cited in Reider, 1959, p. 3]." In

a similar vein, the behaviorist B. F. Skinner (1948) describes the promotion of only two games in his utopian society, *Walden Two*. Frazier, the fictional founder of that society, explains that "we don't encourage competitive games with the exception of tennis or chess, where the exercise of skill is as important as the outcome of the game [p. 169]."

Many chessplayers are undoubtedly drawn to the game because of its competitive–aggressive aspects. In their view, a chess victory that "crushes someone's ego," as Bobby Fischer would phrase it, is even more satisfying than is a victory in team sports or in individual games based on luck or physical prowess. Conversely, defeats in chess seem particularly hard for many persons to accept, perhaps because they greatly value intellectual abilities and regard a loss as somehow reflecting mental inferiority to their opponent.

There are other chess devotees, for example the great artist Marcel Duchamp, who consider the game primarily a creative esthetic endeavor, an amalgam of beauty and reason (see Margulies, 1977). Duchamp stated that all chessplayers are really artists. Because actual competitive play, with its strict time limits, is so likely to be marred by errors, persons who strive for beauty and perfection in the game often turn to the slower pace of chess by mail or to the composition and solution of chess problems; however, prizes for the most "brilliant" game are still awarded in some tournaments. Other chessplayers are thrill-seekers; they find chess competition tremendously exciting, particularly when they are under extreme time pressure and have to make five or 10 moves in less than a minute. For spectators and players, a time-pressure scramble can be as hair-raising as a last-minute touchdown drive in football. Finally, to conclude our brief categorization of several of the motives for playing chess, there are those who treat the game as a recreation or hobby that momentarily takes the mind off the problems of life.

In this chapter we summarize and assess some of the tentative conclusions that psychologists have reached concerning the thought processes and personality attributes of chessplayers, in the context of the topics mentioned earlier. Our statements and evaluations represent a mixture of fact and speculation, the latter based on our own experiences as psychologists and chess experts. Before delving into the psychology of chess, we describe the general nature of competitive chess and mention some of its features that resemble or differ from features of other sports or games.

VARIETIES AND CHARACTERISTICS OF CHESS

Tournament Chess

Except for the series of individual elimination matches that produce the world champion's new challenger every 3 years, almost all important competitive chess involves tournaments composed of 14 or more players. The most

prestigious of these events are usually restricted to fewer than 20 invited participants, and all players meet every other competitor once (a round-robin tournament). In contrast, open tournaments (with unrestricted entries, sometimes reaching 400 or 500 players) are planned to last from six to 12 rounds; opponents for each round are selected according to the Swiss System, whereby players with the same or very similar cumulative scores are paired with each other. In both round-robin and Swiss events, a player will normally have the white pieces against a randomly assigned half of his opponents and the black pieces against the other half. Because white moves first and has a small advantage [statistics show that white wins about 53% of the decisive (nondrawn) games in high-level tournament chess (e.g., in Rubin, 1973)], players are eager to receive white against the strongest players and invariably grumble if they do not.

In all these competitions, the players are forced to adhere to a strict time limit. In the middle of the 19th century, chess clocks were not used and games frequently lasted for more than 10 consecutive hours. To speed up play, some tournament directors tried the idea of imposing a fine for every 15 minutes taken above a regulation limit of 10 moves per hour. However, this system evoked justifiable criticism, because it discriminated in favor of the wealthier players and did not stop stalling even among the less wealthy.

Nowadays, the two players share the use of a device that comprises two independently operating clocks. Upon making a move, one player pushes a button that stops his own clock and starts the clock of his opponent. In an important competition, each player must make 40 moves in 2½ hours—an average of fewer than 4 minutes a move—or lose the game on a time forfeit. Thus most sessions last approximately 4 or 5 hours, and unfinished games are then adjourned and continued later under a new time control. A player can distribute his time allotment in any way he desires, so that it is not uncommon for someone to consume 2 hours and 29 minutes for his first 30 moves and then be forced to make 10 moves in the final minute. Nonchessplayers may have a difficult time imagining the stress and pressure that many competitors feel when faced with 5, 10, or 20 moves to complete in a minute or so. The player cannot call a timeout to collect his thoughts or plan ahead; he cannot afford to walk around while his opponent is thinking. And if the opponent plays a move that is both surprising and powerful, its effect sometimes resembles that of a boxer's solid punch to the jaw: The recipient's whole body sags and his eyes turn glassy.

For outstanding success in tournaments, a fairly aggressive style is necessary. A large number of draws, for which each player receives ½ point, generally dooms an individual to the middle of the scoretable. Chess games can be drawn in a variety of ways, but draws most commonly occur by agreement between the two players [e.g., 83% of all draws in Rubin's (1973) sample.] This outcome may take place at any point in the game and for several different reasons: The players may be afraid of each other; they may be

satisfied with their current position in the tournament and not want to jeopardize it by taking any risks; one player may be winning but is either tired or very short of time and settles for a draw; or the position is completely equal, and there is virtually no chance for anyone to win. Some players are well known as "drawing masters" and are content to draw almost every game. Bobby Fischer and Boris Spassky, along with Viktor Korchnoi, Mikhail Tal, and Bent Larsen, have been very successful tournament players because they play to win in almost every game. They may occasionally overextend themselves and lose a game or two in an important tournament, but their relatively greater number of victories (for which one point is awarded) generally places them at or near the top.

Match Play

Matches involve one-on-one competition between two players. From 1951 to 1972, all matches in the world-championship cycle had a maximum length (e.g., 24 games), so that once a player captured the lead it was to his advantage to take no risks and attempt to draw all the rest of the games. With support from most masters and chess fans, Bobby Fischer argued vociferously and unyieldingly that the fairest method for match play was one in which draws did not count and the first player to win a certain number of games (e.g., 8 or 10) would be the winner. This method forces both players to be more aggressive and should prevent a dull, conservative player from winning the world title, as Tigran Petrosian of the USSR had done in 1963. Petrosian rarely won major tournaments but was extremely difficult to defeat in matches. He took advantage of the occasional mistakes made by his match opponents, committed very few himself, and was content to play solidly and draw a large proportion of the other games.

Fischer's suggestions were for the most part accepted and implemented by the international chess federation (FIDE), but because one or two of his relatively minor requests were disallowed, he resigned the world title in 1975. By doing so, he turned his back on the $5 million stakes offered by the Phillipine organizers for the scheduled match between him and Karpov. Had the match been held, the total prize money would have been second only to that of the Foreman–Ali fight in the history of individual sport.

Masters prepare for matches and tournaments by examining the past games of their prospective opponents, which are recorded in chess notation during actual play and later published in bulletins of each major tourney or match. Such preparation entails a search for the opponents' strengths and weaknesses, in much the same fashion as a basketball coaching staff would carefully examine past game films of upcoming foes. Like other sports, too, the grandmaster might play practice games against players whose styles or nervous mannerisms resemble those of forthcoming opponents. Masters also

study the latest theoretical articles, mainly in Russian or Yugoslavian publications, which collate and evaluate novel moves or ideas that have recently been adopted or suggested.

As further preparation for serious competition, many players adhere to a strict physical regimen. Ex-world champion Mikhail Botvinnik customarily jogged several miles a day and engaged in other strenuous physical exercises like skiing and canoeing. Fischer swims and plays tennis regularly; he says, "I gotta stay in shape or its's all over." Spassky skis and plays soccer. As in other competitive sports, fitness and stamina are important ingredients of success, in addition to positive attitudes and specific skills, techniques, and knowledge.

Exhibitions and Diversions

Masters often play speed chess for "relaxation." Five-minute chess is the most common version and involves the use of regular chess clocks. The player who first exceeds 5 minutes for all his moves is the loser; most games are over before then, however, because of checkmate or the opponent's resignation. Ten-seconds-a-move chess is popular in some clubs; a bell rings every 10 seconds, and the player whose turn it is to move must do so immediately or forfeit the game. Blitz chess, or move-on-move chess, is frequent among masters; each player must move as fast as possible (i.e., within a second after the opponent's last move), and games usually end in 2 or 3 minutes. Skilled chessplayers can play "masterful" games at this speed, which, as we discuss later, indicates that they do not need to calculate ahead to play excellent chess.

There are a variety of exhibitions that chess professionals occasionally give when they are not competing in tournaments or matches. The most common of these is a "simultaneous," in which a master takes on all comers at the same time. The boards are normally arranged in a rectangle and the exhibitor walks in a regular sequence from one game to the next, answering his opponents' moves within seconds. The world's record for simultaneous play is 250 games played in 1950 by Argentine master Miguel Najdorf, who took 11 hours to score 226 wins, 14 draws, and 10 losses. Because the quality of the opposition is generally not high in such events (masters have nothing to gain and consider it bad form or beneath their dignity to play in a simultaneous that another master is giving), the principal problem the exhibitor faces is one of physical endurance. Timeouts or rest periods are usually not given to the exhibitor during the course of play, unless the event is expected to last more than 5 or 6 hours.

A blindfold demonstration is particularly impressive, even for the more jaded chess fan. In such an exhibition, the master is not literally "blindfolded" but sits with his back to all his opponents and announces his moves aloud in

the chess notation system. His opponents have regular sets and boards in front of them and make their moves as in a standard simultaneous exhibition, but the master must rely completely on his memory of the different games and positions. The play shifts successively from one board to the next, and a referee tells the exhibitor only the number of the board and the opponent's latest move.

In 1783, Philidor played two games blindfolded while also contesting a third game with sight of the board; one writer described his feat as a "phenomenon in the history of man." In 1858–1859, Paul Morphy played eight blindfold simultaneous games on three different occasions in Europe. The world's simultaneous blindfold record has climbed by leaps and bounds since then and is currently 52 games, held by Janos Flesch of Hungary. Later in this chapter we return to a discussion of the techniques and abilities that seem crucial for playing good blindfold chess.

COGNITIVE ASPECTS OF CHESS

Some Fallacies About Chess Abilities

Outsiders usually regard the chessmaster as a person who possesses an incredible memory capacity, must calculate many moves ahead with lightning rapidity, is able to present very definite reasons for all his decisions, and has an astronomical IQ. All of these beliefs are false.

Memory. Several studies (for reviews and comments, see Charness, 1976, 1977, and Simon & Chase, 1973), have shown that masters and Class A players perform no better than much weaker players when they are given material to memorize that is nonchessical in nature (e.g., verbal items like consonant trigrams) or that involves pieces arranged randomly on the chessboard. Furthermore, the notion is erroneous that master play is critically dependent on an encyclopedic move-by-move knowledge of opening variations, endgame techniques, and prior games played by the master himself and other champions. Unfortunately, this view has been fostered by numerous chess writers, usually not grandmasters, who imply that young players should exhaustively study reams of opening analysis and retain as much specific information as possible. Although for practical reasons (e.g., avoidance of time pressure) a master must certainly be familiar with a reasonable amount of opening and endgame detail, the form or organization of this knowledge and the way in which it is acquired (by rote or through understanding of general principles) seem to be the factors that are important in his ability to apply the knowledge effectively in actual game situations. The Russian master, Znosko-Borovsky, said that chess is a game of understand-

ing, not memory. Danish Grandmaster Bent Larsen cautions against "learning variations, not chess." Masters often speak contemptuously of "book players" who know *Modern Chess Openings* almost by heart but who typically go astray as soon as well-charted positions are left behind.

Men played master chess long before the end of the 19th century, when extensive published analysis first became available. Emanuel Lasker, who was world champion for 27 years (1894–1921), remarked that "I have stored little in my memory, but I can apply that little." His successor as world champion, José Capablanca, often boasted that he had hardly ever opened a chess book. In any event, there are very few games between high-level players that cannot be saved even when one side does obtain a definite advantage early in the contest. An alert player ordinarily has several "second chances" to rescue a game later on, because even grandmasters rarely conduct a full game impeccably. Fischer and Karpov have often won or drawn objectively lost positions against grandmasters of the highest strength, which indicates that there is much more to top-level chess than mnemonic skill and encyclopedic knowledge.

While studying the psychological capacities of great chessplayers in the 19th century, Binet (1893/1966) was surprised to discover that they do not have "photographic minds"—exact visualization of chess positions while recalling old games or playing chess blindfolded; their images were abstract, in the sense that specific details were often omitted. When asked to describe games played months or years previously, expert players were most likely to forget isolated moves that were not well integrated with the rest of the game. They remembered ideas, patterns, plans, and the type of tactical finale rather than individual moves. Their memory was organized so that they retained some general scheme, from which they could reconstruct many specific details.

There seems nothing special about chessmasters in this connection. The memory processes of all normal human beings seem to operate mainly in terms of general principles and economical organization of related material. Otherwise, we would have to waste time searching through a mass of irrelevant or unimportant details in solving new problems or recalling solutions to old ones.

Calculation.   Edgar Allen Poe dismissed chess as a process of calculation, that is, seeing many moves ahead and examining numerous side variations. However, the fact that masters can play excellent chess at the rate of 1 or 2 seconds per move, or when in extreme time pressure, seems to demonstrate that they need not calculate far ahead in order to play well. U.S. Grandmaster Robert Byrne (in Collins, 1974), after remarking that memory is not a major ingredient of the great chess mind, added that calculation is not so important, either. Likewise, Grandmaster William Lombardy (in Collins, 1974) insisted

that the accurate setting of goals ("combined with appropriate smoke screens") and the accumulation of small advantages—not exact calculations —are the keys to master chess: "Calculation most often comes after the goal is achieved, the moment when a winning position converts into a mathematically forced win [p. 143]."

Most masters, whether because of laziness, fear of time pressure, the risk of making a calculational error, or mere economy of thinking, actually avoid elaborate calculations during competitive play. It is rarely worth the time to delve deeply into a particular variation unless certain ill-defined features suggest to the master that an unexpected trap or pretty combination might be hidden there. de Groot's (1965) comparisons of masters, experts, and weaker players, who were asked to analyze aloud while selecting a move in positions that they had not seen before, revealed no differences between the different groups in breadth and depth of their calculations (see also Charness, 1977). Concrete calculations are obviously necessary in chess, but they are less important than outsiders believe. Instead of examining many more moves than weaker players, masters simply consider better ones.

Verbalizability of Decisions.   Another widespread belief about master play is the notion that masters can verbalize very specific criteria for their choice of a given move. This misconception has led some computer scientists to think that all one has to do to create an expert chess program is to ask masters why they played particular moves and then somehow to incorporate these criteria as strict rules or algorithms within the program. However, unless some specific tactical points are involved, masters often explain their moves with such vague comments as, "It looked good," or "That had to be the correct move." They are frequently unable or reluctant to elaborate their reasons in detail. Very few rules are independent of the given position of all the pieces, and masters apparently consider many global and specific factors simultaneously. After masters lose a game, they often do not know where they committed their decisive mistakes. Karpov asked Petrosian after a defeat in 1973, "Please, where did I make my mistake?" It might have taken both of them hours, days or months before the crucial error was finally isolated.

In psychological research (see Hammond, 1971) with human subjects who must learn to make complex decisions based on a variety of cues—none of which is invariably correct—the subjects who produce superior judgments are frequently unable to provide a clear explanation of exactly how they do it. In real-life situations, interviewers have discovered that the more experienced stockbrokers are less able to describe their judgments than are the less experienced. Our current knowledge of basic principles of human learning, thinking, and problem solving is not sufficient to explain how these intuitive, poorly articulated judgments are made.

A similar phenomenon seems also to occur in athletic competition. William James (1890) praises an article by A. T. Dudley about the mental qualities of athletes, in which Dudley states that the distinguishing feature of a good player involves his ability to trust entirely to "impulse" and not to think out every move. "The poor player, unable to trust his impulsive actions, is compelled to think carefully all the time [p. 539]" and thus loses opportunities through his slowness. On the other hand, the good player does not know how he performed a certain act and often says that he did it by instinct.

General Intelligence. Contrary to Goethe's contention that "chess is the test-block of the mind," psychological studies and personal observations of players do not substantiate the belief that chessmasters have exceptionally high general intelligence. In one of the first extensive discussions of chess by a psychologist, Cleveland (1907) expressed his view that chess skill is not a valid index of high mental endowment. de Groot, a successful chessmaster and psychologist, believes that masters would score well above the average on spatial-imagination tests of nonverbal abilities (e.g., tests involving mental rotation of block designs), but he, too, does not believe that extraordinary verbal intelligence is an indispensable requirement. Likewise, Simon and Chase (1973) state that "there is no evidence that masters demonstrate more than above-average competence on basic intellectual factors; their talents are chess-specific [p. 403]." On the other hand, a blockhead like Mirko Czentovic, a major character in Zweig's novella, *The Royal Game* (1944), probably could not have become world champion, as he was in the story.

Our own subjective judgments agree with those aforementioned: Chessmasters would probably score no higher on tests of general intelligence (i.e., verbal and quantitative aptitude) than other persons with similar family backgrounds and education. However, masters do have the ability, at least in chess, to acquire new ideas rapidly, to create and handle novel positions, to recognize and quickly evaluate similarities and differences between various complex situations, and to isolate the core of a difficult problem without much hesitation—ingredients of what some people might be willing to label high intelligence. These characteristics probably come closer to describing a master's distinctive skills and, for that matter, the talents of a good problem solver in any field than do exceptional memory capacity, calculational ability, and fluency of verbalization. It would be worthwhile to determine whether chessmasters also display excellent problem-solving abilities in complex tasks unrelated to chess.

An interesting and relevant question concerns the extent to which chess ability is limited by genetic factors. Binet (1893/1966) expressed the opinion that "one may *attain* average standing, whereas one is *born* a chessmaster [p. 137]." Obviously one is not literally born a chessmaster, because knowledge

and practice are crucial for the manifestation of chess skills, but the experience of the present authors certainly suggests that you cannot select just any person and expect to convert him into a master, even if you are given total control over his life. Despite the tremendous dedication, good nerves, and extensive practice that many ambitious players bring to the chessboard, they never achieve master status. Some kind of special talent seems necessary, but we cannot support this strong impression of ours with any concrete data.

Characteristics of Chess Thinking and Learning

In the context of a recent analysis of systematic differences between the methods employed by computers and human beings in selecting a chess move, one of the present authors (Hearst, 1977; see also Hearst, 1967) suggested the following features as characteristic of the thinking and learning of the strong human chessplayer.

Focused or Restricted Search.   A chessplayer ordinarily considers only two or three first moves in any position, analyzes a few sample variations, and then decides on a move. In 1907, Cleveland remarked on the selectivity of chess thinking and the grasp of essentials and "position sense" that strong players possess. Unlike an unfortunate computer, the human being does not have to examine thousands of irrelevant moves or variations, many of which are refuted by the same basic reply. High on the human's list of heuristics is "ignore *x, y, z*, etc."; the human conforms to William James' (1890) dictum that "the art of being wise is the art of knowing what to overlook."

Progressive Deepening.   In his pioneering work on thought and choice in chess, de Groot (1965) asked chessplayers to think aloud while choosing their moves. Expert and master players displayed a continuous reevaluation of ideas and specific moves in a given position. Such *progressive deepening,* as he called this process, was rare in weak players. When a human being analyzes in this manner, he often reinvestigates the same moves again and again. A move that was rejected or put aside a few moments before because it did not fulfill the specific goals or plans considered by the player at that time, is reanalyzed—but now with a different goal in mind.
    This process of progressive deepening probably characterizes superior problem solving in many situations besides chess. Reasonable-looking ideas are not permanently discarded after their first (superficial) examination fails to bear fruit. Persistent reconsideration and reevaluation of the possibilities usually produce keener understanding of their relevance and applicability.

Control by Plans and Patterns.   If chess skill is not simply a matter of the calculation or memory of specific moves or move-sequences, as we have

maintained, then what positive criteria guide the strong player's choices of moves? Apparently he selects his moves mainly on the basis of a plan or typical technique for handling that kind of position, as determined by its relatively permanent aspects. Pawn formations, for example, are very important in guiding a master's choice of moves. If the pawns on the queenside are arranged in a certain way after his opponent has declined the Queen's Gambit, a master will probably pursue the "minority attack" on the queenside and hardly consider any moves that do not contribute to this well-known strategy. The master's general goals in such a position may not shift for many moves unless the opponent's replies force a radical revision of strategy or suggest to the master that another plan would now be even more effective, perhaps in conjunction with pursuit of the minority attack.

Strong chessplayers rely so much on plans and general principles rather than specific move analysis that they sometimes overlook a simple way of winning because it does not fit into their general strategy. Therefore an over-reliance on rules or principles can lead to a stereotyped play and prove disadvantageous. An appropriate balance between concrete move analysis (i.e., focused calculation) and adherence to general principles or plans seems to be the hallmark of master play.

Psychological research (see Charness, 1976, 1977; Frey & Adesman, 1976; Simon & Chase, 1973) indicates that expert chess and Go players apparently store old positions and games in their memory, and analyze new positions, in terms of larger "chunks" or perceptual units, than do weak players. Similarly, Morse Code experts can decode a message faster and remember it better than amateurs because they presumably process the material in terms of larger units (words, phrases, sentences) than their inexperienced counterparts, who must plod along letter by letter.

Along the same lines, studies of human learning and memory, performed with verbal or pictorial material by experimental psychologists, have revealed that subjects categorize or organize small bits of specific information into larger meaningful units (unless no organizing principle is present, in which case rote learning may be the only recourse). Anyone who wants to "develop an exceptional memory"—to remember, for example, phone numbers or the names of many new acquaintances—usually benefits greatly from training in mnemonic techniques that have been used by orators and actors for many centuries. The recent nationwide popularity of Lorayne and Lucas' *The Memory Book* (1975) is a tribute to the utility of these methods for coding and organizing verbal and numerical material. Incidentally, Jerry Lucas, one of the authors of the book and an All-American in basketball at Ohio State, gives examples of how these techniques can be used to memorize fairly complex plays in basketball or football. Lucas reports that players were always running over to ask him for the details of a play they could not remember.

Thus patterns, relationships, and organized configurations seem to control the play of the chessmaster (and probably the thought and planning of experts in any sport, game, or problem-solving activity) rather than disconnected elements of the situation—in chess, the moves of the various pieces. Accordingly, if a chessplayer wants to improve, he probably ought not to concentrate on memorizing opening variations but rather to play many games with stronger players and to study books that stress general ideas, plans, and patterns that are appropriate in different kinds of positions. As a youth 30 years ago, one of the present authors (Hearst) learned the openings mainly in this fashion, by means of Reuben Fine's *The Ideas Behind the Chess Openings* (1943); he has not suffered very much from a relative lack of detailed knowledge about specific variations in each opening.

Acute Sensitivity to Positive and Negative Consequences. Simon and Chase (1973; see also Chase & Simon, 1973) answer the question, "How does one become a master in the first place?", with the simple word: *practice.* For them, this is "the overriding factor in chess skill," as with any skilled task including football and music. These writers interpret practice in chess to involve the buildup in long-term memory of a vast repertoire of patterns and associated plausible moves, which are eventually used almost automatically.

Practice and experience, as used by these writers, are rather empty concepts. How does practice lead directly or indirectly to improvement, and what kinds of experiences are better than others? Such analyses of the development of chess skill, although certainly of value as far as they go, reflect the focus of many contemporary cognitive psychologists on perception and memory rather than on learning and behavior and thus seem incomplete to us. It is obvious that merely showing a person thousands of chess diagrams or patterns will not improve his chess play very much, if at all. Some kind of contingent feedback, or shaping of appropriate behaviors, seems indispensable to understanding how "practice" has its effects. A human being gains proficiency at chess not just by watching others play, or simply by learning general principles and specific maneuvers from books or instructors, but mainly by receiving feedback about the strength or weakness of particular moves or plans that he adopts in actual games.

The machinery of living organisms is arranged so that they can profit directly from the consequences of their actions. Good chess ideas frequently lead to quick victory, bad blunders to rapid defeat. Because the chessplayer's choices of moves are constantly being shaped by immediate or delayed consequences, he eventually learns which types of positional features, patterns, and tactical devices are likely to be significant or relevant in certain types of positions and which are likely to be ineffective or disastrous. Chessplayers somehow refine their concepts of what a good or bad outcome is, perhaps without being aware of it. They play thousands of actual games

and analyze in privacy numerous annotated games of masters and their own past encounters. They continuously ask: What was the move or plan that led to victory or defeat? As a result, the experienced player's ability to vary his plans depending on specific arrangements of the chess pieces often becomes extremely keen—he can isolate the "core" of the problem quickly—even though he may not be able to verbalize very well the exact reasons for his decisions, as we mentioned earlier. Analogously, people can speak and write English beautifully without being able to verbalize the specific grammatical rules they follow.

Champions in any sport must be expert perceivers and learners. They must be attentive to small changes in the external situation as well as to global features. They must be self-critical and able to modify their behavior when there is evidence that their actions are not optimal. Particularly acute sensitivity to positive and negative consequences, coupled with high motivation and a capacity for hard work, plays a large role in the development of a champion.

Chessmaster Versus Chess Computer

In the 18th and 19th centuries, exhibitions of Kempelen's and Maelzel's chess machines (for a summary see Carroll, 1975) were huge commercial successes and stimulated many authors, technologists, and philosophers to speculate about the relationships between man and machine. Of course, a human being who played expert chess was cleverly concealed inside each of these early automata. Today no such tricks are played on gullible audiences. Actual computer programs have been developed that play a reasonable, but certainly not master, level of chess. We cannot pursue the question of the successes and failures of computer chess in any depth here, but a few comments seem worthy of mention. Interested readers may consult Frey (1977) and Newborn (1975) for extensive discussion of the issues.

Many outsiders do not realize the complexity of chess. It is important to point out that even though it may be theoretically possible for a computer to play a perfect game by analyzing every variation to completion, such a task is far beyond the computer's practical powers. A computer that analyzed all first moves to their legal ending in a win, loss, or draw and was capable of examining a thousand billion billion variations a second would still take more than 10^{91} years to calculate its first move, which is appreciably longer than the age of the universe. Therefore, no machine can be expected to play perfect chess. The work of the machine in calculating variations must be cut down through the use of certain rules or criteria, by means of which moves can be evaluated.

Two standards can be applied for deciding whether a chess program is successful. The first is based on its *achievement:* Can it play as well as a human

expert? The second is based on the *process* it uses to select its moves: Does it think like an expert?

By the first criterion—and despite what numerous newspaper and television commentators and many workers in the field of artificial intelligence have claimed—the overall results have not been tremendously impressive. Work on construction of chess programs began about 20 years ago, and in 1967 MacHack Six was the first program to compete in several tourneys against human opponents. It achieved a USCF rating of 1400–1450 in its last two appearances. These results placed it in USCF category Class C (Class B players range from 1600 to 1799, Class A players from 1800 to 1999, Experts from 2000 to 2199, Masters from 2200 to 2399, and Senior Masters above 2400).

Today, 10 years later, most chess programs still play at Class C level or worse, which means that these programs are weaker than 25,000 North American chessplayers and hundreds of thousands of players in the Soviet Union. However, Northwestern University's program, developed by David Slate and Larry Atkin (Slate & Atkin, 1977) into the winner of six of the first seven U.S. Computer Championships, won a California Class B tournament in 1976 and the Minnesota Open Championship in early 1977 against human competition, although it later did poorly in the Minnesota Closed Championship (in which no masters played). It is distinctly better than the other available programs, including the U.S.S.R.'s KAISSA, but still falls consistently short of master strength. As of the summer of 1977, the program had never defeated a top expert or master in serious tournament competition. In 1975, Earl Hunt concluded that "today's [chess] programs are trivial opponents for master players [p. 442]," and his statement would still be true in 1978 even in light of definite recent improvements in their achievement made possible mainly by the phenomenal speed of new computers.

In terms of our second criterion for evaluating the success of a chess program, it is clear that computer chessplayers do not "think" like real experts. However, in certain important respects, a program actually possesses advantages over human players! If no technical problems arise during a game, the best-constructed programs will never commit simple blunders, such as leaving a queen or bishop to be taken for nothing or overlooking a checkmate in one or two moves, and they will immediately take advantage of such mistakes by an opponent. The computer will never fall victim to fatigue or inattention, and it will store and retrieve thousands of specific opening variations better than a human. Therefore, Northwestern's program can perform very well in speed chess against masters, since the master's big strategic advantages are somewhat balanced by the likelihood of his committing some kind of blunder in very fast chess.

Most of the other differences between human and computer players strongly favor the human. Once the human knows the computer's

weaknesses, he can take advantage of them (for suggestions see Hearst, 1977). Programs engage in bulldozer-like evaluation of tens or hundreds of thousands of positions resulting from analysis that extends four or five half-moves deep (i.e., two or three by the machine, two by the opponent). Humans restrict their analysis to feasible possibilities, whereas the computer uncomplainingly analyzes a large number of irrelevant moves or variations before reaching its decision; it is as if a person had to scan his entire vocabulary before he could utter an appropriate English word or sentence. Programs may notice attacks and defenses but have no mechanism for storing and remembering this information; they start from scratch on the next move and therefore exhibit little in the way of long-range planning. Humans are rather flexible with regard to how deeply they analyze certain variations, whereas most computer programs are designed to look ahead no more than four or five half-moves. Computer programs do not display progressive deepening; a computer usually dismisses a move from further consideration once it fails to meet certain predetermined criteria or is judged much weaker than some other alternatives. Furthermore, computer programs are rarely designed to analyze patterns or configurations of pieces (for a program that does attempt such analysis, see Zobrist & Carlson, 1973), in obvious contrast to the perceptual skills of strong chessplayers, as already discussed. Finally, although the possibility may prove technically feasible in the future, there are today no chess computer programs that "learn from experience"; they can only follow the explicit instructions of a human being who works out the important factors to be taken into account and then corrects the program on the basis of its general performance.

In summary, the value of chess as an object for computer simulation of human thought processes is yet to be clearly demonstrated. Work on computerized chess has not progressed very much if we measure its progress in terms of the capacity of the programs to imitate human chess thought.

One other aspect of computer chess merits brief mention. Many Class A and B players performed far below their usual strength when opposing the Northwestern program. They reported being "unnerved" in such competition. David Levy (1977) suggests that human reactions to intellectual encounters with computers may provide an unexplored and worthwhile topic for psychologists to study.

Blindfold Chess

Almost any master can play three or four games of blindfold chess simultaneously, but few are willing to endure the strain necessary to contest 10 or more. As a matter of fact, there is a strong rule against blindfold exhibitions in the Soviet Union. Besides viewing such exhibitions as a bourgeois stunt, the Russians believe that the strain of blindfold chess is

hazardous to one's health and may lead to mental breakdown. They maintain that three of the greatest blindfold players in history (Morphy, Pillsbury, and Zukertort) died while suffering from a psychosis—a diagnosis that is, in fact, almost surely wrong for at least one of the cases.

There should be nothing particularly strange about a master's ability to play chess blindfolded, because even a standard game requires much analysis in one's head.[1] Grandmaster Siegbert Tarrasch said that the actual sight of the chessmen often disturbed his analysis in a regular tournament game. Incidentally, some experts at blindfold play (for example, George Koltanowski) like to have an empty board in front of them as an aid to visualization, whereas others (for example, Reuben Fine) find it more of a hindrance than a help.

Alfred Binet (1893/1966) was the first psychologist to attempt an analysis of the apparently incredible memory feats of blindfold players. Binet concluded, not too surprisingly, that physical endurance, excellent concentration, vast knowledge of the game, a good memory, and ability at visual imagery (but, as we discuss later, not perfectly detailed visualization) were essential requirements for skill at blindfold chess. However, blindfold play has developed substantially since Binet's time, and the more recent discussions by Alekhine (1931/1971), de Groot (1965), and Fine (1965) are also of considerable interest, especially because these writers were all master chessplayers, unlike Binet. Fine has defeated players of master strength during blindfold exhibitions in which he played only one player at a time but at the very fast rate of 10 seconds per move. (Normally there is no time limit on the blindfold player's moves, and sometimes simultaneous exhibitions of more than 20 boards last longer than 15 hours.)

Descriptions of visual imagery during blindfold play are not completely consistent from player to player. Fine remarked that he visualized each position as it came up. Although he (Fine, 1965) stated that blindfold chess "depends upon the capacity to visualize the board with full clarity [p. 366]," he did not describe in detail the character or concreteness of his own visual images. On the other hand, there are players who claim that they can play blindfold chess without visualizing the board at all. Pillsbury once declared that he did not see actual images of the chess board in his mental vision; there were "no definite patterns of the game" in his mind, and it was, as far as he could say, "a memorization of the moves" as he went along in the games. The games would come up before him in an indistinct way, and his moves would be made from a "sort of formless vision of the positions."

---

[1]There have been four or five master chessplayers who were actually blind, including Albert Sandrin of Chicago. Perhaps the strongest of these was T. H. Tylor of England, who was blind for his entire chess career, unlike Sandrin. Tylor defeated Tartakower and Flohr and drew with Alekhine and Vidmar in regular tournament games. Tarshis (1964) has written an interesting article on how the blind play chess.

Most reports about visualization in blindfold chess seem to fall somewhere in between Fine's and Pillsbury's descriptions. One of Binet's correspondents wrote: "I only know that it is a knight or a pawn without bothering about anything else." Squares on the board generally have no distinct color for most blindfolded players, only vaguely defined boundaries. Players state that they never visualize all 64 squares at once. Alekhine reported that he visualized the pieces functionally as "lines of force." The bishop is not a piece with a clergyman's miter on it but is a diagonal force; the rook does not look like the tower of a castle but is a horizontal–vertical cross. In the same vein, Tarrasch said that "the shapes of the pieces are indistinct; I consider principally their capacity for action."

Alekhine (1931/1971) summarized his techniques in the following way: "The player does not try to recreate before his eyes the whole board with its white and black squares, its white and black pieces—the way, incidentally, the majority of the uninitiated visualize it—but he recollects only some characteristic move, the configuration of a part of the board.... This is how, to the best of my knowledge, all masters of blindfold chess play [p. 523]."

Another commentator on blindfold chess, Henri Bergson (1902, cited in de Groot, 1965, pp. 5–6) similarly concluded that detailed, picture-like visualization was not crucially involved in concentrated mental efforts of this kind but rather sme abstract or geometrical general scheme (the "character" of the position) that indicates the rules or operations one must follow to reconstruct the position. The master might mentally note: "The game on Board 5 is a Sicilian Defense, Dragon Variation, in which I am attacking black's castled king on the open King's Rook's file." Memory of the opening, the columns (files) that have no pawns on them, and the position of the opponent's king should enable him to *reconstruct* most of the details of the position. When an opponent's move is announced in a blindfold exhibition, the whole position in that game does not immediately leap to the master's mind; he recalls it progressively via sequences of connected ideas and themes.

Fine (1965) and Alekhine (1931/1971) reported some of the specific methods that they applied to prevent confusion among all the games being played simultaneously. They agreed that the greatest demands in this respect occur in the opening stages of the exhibition, when the positions in many games remain quite similar. In order to create distinctiveness among the different games, Fine opened with a different first move (P-QB4, P-Q4, P-K4, and P-KB4) in each one of a group of four adjacent games (say, Boards 1–4) and repeated the same sequence of different opening moves in each additional set of four games (Boards 5–8, Boards 9–12). The types of game that develop from each of these four opening moves are usually quite different. Alekhine also planned his openings systematically before a blindfold exhibition; in one 26-board exhibition in New York, he played a Queen's Pawn Opening on Boards 1–6, a King's Pawn on Boards 7–12, a

Queen's Pawn on Boards 13–18, a King's Pawn on Boards 19–24, and an English Opening on Boards 25 and 26.

A few moments of thought by the reader should reveal that the blindfold player is sure to be delighted when an opponent tries to confuse him by choosing an unusual first move or by making some bizarre, totally unwarranted move shortly afterward. As Fine (1965) said, "This immediately gives the game an individual cast and solves the blindfold player's problem [p. 357]" of keeping one board distinct from the other. However, unsophisticated opponents often try this scheme, because they think that the blindfold player is attempting to repeat previously memorized, fixed move sequences; therefore, they suppose that a novel move will spoil the master's train of thought (this error derives from the common misconception, mentioned earlier, that masters possess an exceptional memory and select moves primarily on the basis of some detailed move-by-move knowledge of chess). Fine commented that he did not feel completely comfortable until the standardized opening moves in a blindfold exhibition were over and distinctive patterns of play were unfolding on each board. Real difficulties arose when two or more games had reached almost identical positions.

Fine's (1965) further analysis of blindfold chess focused on the importance of past associative learning in facilitating his recall of the specific features of a certain position. For example, white's king usually ends up on King's-Knight-One (KN1) due to castling early in the game, and therefore the position of the king need not be reviewed constantly after castling. Different squares have a host of different associations; a pawn on the first row is impossible, and therefore pawns are never "seen" there; bishops end up on QB4 or KN2 much more often than on KN8. Different pieces normally reach different squares; knights, queens, or rooks rarely stand on KN2, but a bishop there is very common. Relatively permanent features like pawn structures (the pattern of pawns that generally separate the more powerful pieces of one army from the other) are extremely important in organizing a particular position. These pawn configurations signify where the major pieces are likely to be stationed and toward what points attacks are likely to be directed.

Thus the experienced player, with or without a blindfold, does not conceive a chess position as a conglomeration of scattered squares and pieces but rather as an organized pattern (like the "Gestalt," or integrated configuration, emphasized by the Gestalt psychologists). As Tarrasch once said: "A good game of chess can be told as a series of interrelated facts." No position changes completely with a single move. Binet noted that if a master player can remember a total of 500 moves played in 5 or 10 simultaneous games, and a novice is totally unable to do so, it is because the master understands the reasons that produced the moves and because he has a clear notion of the psychological development of the game.

One final note on blindfold play, which may help to explain the inattention of certain chessplaying college students while their professors are lecturing: It is of course possible for both players to play blindfolded. In his college days, chessmaster Neumann used to write his moves on scraps of paper and pass them back and forth to neighboring students. Sometimes five or six different games were going on during a particularly boring lecture.

FACTORS RELATED TO CHESS SKILL[2]

Age

There are two especially interesting general aspects of the relationship between age and chess skill. The first of these involves the relatively high incidence of child prodigies in the field of chess. The second concerns the age at which peak performance occurs among master players and the rate of subsequent decline in their achievements. Does increasing age affect chess skill as it does performance in other sports or productivity in scientific fields? A third related question involves the longevity of master chessplayers; do they generally die younger or older than nonchessplayers or weaker players?

Chess Prodigies.   As in music or mathematics, chess talent may show itself very early in life. Capablanca learned chess at the age of 4 while watching his father play against a fellow soldier on duty at Morro Castle in Havana. Capablanca pointed out an illegal knight move and then won his very first game with the elder Capablanca. By the time he was 12, he was the best player in Cuba. Paul Morphy learned the game before he was 8 and defeated Johann Lowenthal, one of the best players in the world, a month prior to his 13th birthday. Samuel Reshevsky gave successful simultaneous exhibitions throughout Europe between the ages of 5 and 8. Bobby Fischer and Boris Spassky were of master strength by the time they were 12 or 13. Fischer actually won his first U. S. Championship in 1957 at the age of 14, and a year later he became the youngest grandmaster in chess history.

It is extremely rare for anyone to learn the game after 20 and become a leading master; in fact, we know of no one who has accomplished this feat. Most of the world's top players were all of master strength before they were legally old enough to marry or vote. Of course, there are strong social factors

---

[2]In addition to age and sex, discussed later, some writers have suggested that such factors as educational background and specialty, race, and occupation are correlated with chess aptitude or achievement. The evidence for their conclusions is admittedly weak, and therefore we do not pursue these topics in the present chapter.

that may make age an irrelevant consideration here. Once a person is old enough to have completed his education, found a job and started to raise a family, he probably will not have the free time necessary for learning and mastering chess. Teen-age boys most easily succumb to chess fever and, as we see later, the psychoanalysts draw significant inferences from this fact.

What do music, mathematics, and chess share that spawns prodigies in these fields? We could speculate that they involve relatively limited and isolated subject-matter areas that do not require a great deal of knowledge or experience in other fields; no prodigies appear in sociology or biochemistry. The three areas involve tasks that are basically nonverbal, contain a rather small number of relatively specific rules, and have a simple and logical fundamental structure that, however, can be permuted so as to yield exceptionally complex combinations and relationships. The three areas do not demand physical maturity, as would be the case for outstanding performance in such sports as professional football or basketball. It is of additional interest that very few great contributions have been made to the three areas by women—a topic to which we return shortly when discussing sex differences in chess ability.

Peak Performance and Decline.   Several researchers (Buttenwieser, 1936; Draper, 1963; Elo, 1965; Rubin, 1960) have examined the performance of masters as a function of age. Most grandmasters have scored their greatest victories between the ages of 25 and 40. Buttenwieser (1936) performed a statistical analysis of 100 chessplayers and concluded that there was an improvement in skill from approximately 20 to 40 years of age, after which a plateau was reached extending through the forties. From 50 to 70 years of age there was a steady but not very large drop in performance. Another researcher, Rubin (1960), concluded that after 40 the quality of tournament chess play decreases appreciably. A Russian study by Strumilin (cited in Krogius, 1976) reported that peak performance occurs around 32 or 33 years of age, with a "catastrophic fall" after 60.

However, the best-controlled and most analytical study of age and chess performance was carried out by Professor Arpad Elo, who has been mainly responsible for developing the details of the American (USCF) and International (FIDE) rating systems. This system is completely objective, is based on sound statistical principles, and can be used to calculate ratings for masters who died long before the system was developed.

Drawing from a pool of 51 masters whose careers spanned at least 30 years during the period 1855 to 1963, Elo found that peak performance occurred at about age 36 with a relatively gradual decline thereafter. Average performance at age 63 was about the same as that at age 21. A recent analysis of tournament results by Krogius (1976) revealed findings that were not very

different: A great chessplayer attains his best performances at about age 35, and a particularly noticeable decline starts at the age of 47.

These findings can be compared with those in other sports. Lehman (1953) has done the most extensive work concerning the relationship between age and athletic performance. He found that participants in aggressive physical activities like professional football and ice hockey reach a peak earlier (around age 25) and do not last as long as those in less violent sports. When Lehman examined performance in sports that involve coordination and precision but no physical contact—such as rifle-shooting, billiards, golf, and bowling—peak performance was found to occur during the early or mid-thirties, a result very similar to his findings with respect to the productivity of scientists. Lehman concluded that peak performance in tasks that entail self-pacing, fine motor activities, or creative thinking occur at roughly similar ages. Elo's data for chessmasters are generally consistent with Lehman's conclusions.

As would be expected, Lehman also found that proficiency in precision sports declined more rapidly with increasing age than did scientific productivity. His age-decline curves for scientific performance resemble those that Elo obtained for chessmasters, although the measures are different and not easily compared. Lehman also discovered that proficiency in sports like golf, archery, and bowling, which are self-initiated and self-paced, can be maintained at reasonably high levels for many years. However, when older individuals have to perceive quickly and respond accordingly, or when they have to perform tasks requiring large amounts of strength, endurance, speed, and flexibility, they are at a disadvantage.

Chess under a time limit contains some of the elements that should produce a definite deterioration in performance with increasing age. Former world champion Mikhail Botvinnik has remarked that one's ability to calculate quickly and accurately declines with age, although one's strategic or positional sense may stay the same or even improve. Excellent physical endurance, as pointed out earlier, is very important for top-notch chess performance. A 4- or 5-hour game is terribly hard on competitors who are not in good physical condition. As he grows older, a chess veteran is more and more likely to accept his opponent's offer of a draw (Draper, 1963; Rubin, 1960), even when the oldster is quite aware that he has the better position. Thus he settles for a half point, instead of the full point that follows a win. Very often he is afraid to take the risks necessary to score the victory because he is worried about the possibility of a error in calculation due to his increasing susceptibility to fatigue.

However, lest senior citizens become discouraged about their chances for success in chess tourneys, it is worth pointing out that Emanuel Lasker finished third in an international tournament of grandmasters when he was 67

years old, and Samuel Reshevsky is still competing with success in American championships at the age of 66.

Longevity. Barry (1969) has studied the longevity of 32 outstanding chessplayers. He found that the 13 players (including four world champions) who also pursued professions apart from chess lived significantly longer (an average of 66.1 years) than the 19 players (including five world champions) whose only profession was chess (an average of 56.0 years). The average longevity of 26 composers of chess problems was 69.0 years, and of 23 minor masters, 68.1 years. Barry concluded that outstanding chess achievement alone is not a good predictor of longevity but that social–intellectual superiority (as reflected in success outside chess) is correlated with long life span; the intense efforts, unending competition, continuous travel, and exaggerated ambitions of chess professionals may play a role in decreasing their life span. The latter individuals may not be as able to cope well with the inevitable decline in their powers after age 40 or 50 as the masters who have other interests and rewards to sustain them.

Sex

Chess devotees often tease their wives or girlfriends by pointing out how much better men are at chess than women. No woman has ever reached grandmaster status, even though in countries like the Soviet Union and Yugoslavia there are top-notch coaches available and tremendous rewards for a successful woman player in terms of recognition, salaries, and travel opportunities. The present authors know of no American woman who has ever played master-level chess, even though we are acquainted with many females who study industriously and participate in numerous tournaments. In 1893, Binet (see Binet, 1893/1966) remarked that "the best female player in Paris is no better than any mediocre amateur [p. 132]." Bobby Fischer has put it more crudely: "They're all weak, all women. They're stupid compared to men. They shouldn't play chess, you know."

Actually, two or three women have been able to provide reasonably powerful and consistent opposition for male masters, if not for grandmasters. One of these was Vera Menchik, who was killed in England during a World War II air raid; she had defeated such players as Max Euwe and Samuel Reshevsky in tournament competition. Nona Gaprindashvili, women's world champion since 1962, has achieved several excellent results in mixed competition within and outside the USSR, as has Alla Kushnir, formerly of Russia but a recent emigrant to Israel.

In this day and age, it requires a certain amount of fortitude to embark on a discussion of potential reasons for this definite sex difference in chess achievements (and for the relatively few important contributions by women in the other two major fields that spawn prodigies: music and mathematics).

Both males and females often display emotional behavior when the topic arises. However, we press on regardless (see also Reider, 1964).

Gray (1973) attributes sex differences in mathematics, music, and chess to sociocultural factors. As far as chess is concerned, she reiterates the point that other writers (e.g., Sen, 1972) have made, namely that women are generally brought up to avoid aggressiveness and competition, especially with men. Furthermore, the attention of women is continuously divided; they are typically expected to participate in and worry about family life and social matters and thus cannot pursue chess with the single-minded dedication and aggressive self-centeredness necessary for outstanding success. Other women who actually achieve some success may stop at a point where a man continues to seek improvement, simply because they measure themselves against other women; according to Gray (1973), the "absolute goal of greatness remains ungained. . . and unsought [p. 31]." There are no female grandmasters to serve as role models for the ambitious women player. Gray recommends that if girls were conditioned to be more independent and to avoid the compassion and consideration that distracts them from serious work, we would then expect and obtain real creativity from women in music, mathematics, and chess.

Psychoanalysts have stressed a different reason for the absence of chess success by women. They trace it to the female's lack of unconscious desires to murder her father. The chief object of her hostility is presumably not the father but the mother. Thus chess does not offer women any outlet for their matricidal impulses. We further discuss the psychoanalytic approach to chess in the next section of this chapter. However, our opinion is that this type of explanation is farfetched, unsupported by any objective data, and at best a gross oversimplification. Furthermore, we have never noticed that women players have any particular tendency to attack their opponent's queen.

Developmental psychologists interested in hemispheric specialization in the brain have recently begun to discuss chess within the context of sex differences in spatial ability. Harris (1978) speculates that the male superiority in chess may reflect a basic cognitive process that is less common or less well developed in women than in men. Among other sources of evidence that chess involves spatial skills, Harris cites Chase and Simon's (1973) and de Groot's (1965) conclusions that chess necessitates a great deal of visual–perceptual processing—a theme reiterated earlier in this chapter. Crucial to Harris' argument is the fact that probably the most persistent and reliable of all the known individual differences in cognitive skills is a sex difference in spatial ability: Males do consistently better than females on embedded-figures tasks, mental rotation problems, solid geometry tests, maze learning, map reading, etc. The difference is generally stronger and more consistent in older children and adults, although significant differences have appeared at least as early as 4 years of age.

Harris presents experimental and clinical evidence in support of the hypothesis that sex differences in spatial ability are traceable to the extent of

lateralization of language and spatial–perceptual skills in the left and right brain hemispheres, respectively, with greater lateralization in the male brain than in the female brain. Thus, in females more than in males, language functions are bilaterally represented, with a negative effect on spatial ability. In accordance with this general hypothesis, Witelson (1976) found that boys performed a spatial-processing task in a manner consistent with right-hemisphere specialization as early as the age of 6, whereas girls continued to show evidence of bilateral representation until the age of 13.

Clearly, no final answer is possible concerning the relative roles of sociocultural versus inborn-biological factors in an account of the males' chess superiority. We think that cultural factors of the kind discussed by Gray must certainly be involved. However, in view of the consistent correlations between brain function, sex, and spatial ability—and the appearance of these correlations very early in life—it seems unlikely to us that the male superiority can be totally attributed to the different ways boys and girls are brought up.

MOTIVATION, EMOTION, AND PERSONALITY IN CHESS

In the introduction to this chapter, we listed some of the motives, needs, and functions that the game of chess presumably serves for different individuals. It may be an outlet for aggression or a substitute for war; a thrill-seeking activity; a "moral" exercise that aids in developing the qualities of self-reliance, self-criticism, patience, and long-range planning; a challenging, insoluble intellectual puzzle devoid of luck; an artistic creation; a recreation or diversion that restores energy for more demanding aspects of life; or a source of power, status, or financial rewards. In this section of the chapter, we first describe some features of the psychoanalytic interpretation of chess; this approach has provoked many positive and negative reactions and constitutes a substantial portion of the psychological literature on the game (for reviews, see Cockburn, 1974, and Reider, 1959). Then we comment briefly on possible personality differences between those who play chess and those who engage in competitive athletics, and we touch upon the question of whether an individual chess style—aggressive or defensive, tactical or strategical—somehow reflects a person's overall personality characteristics. Finally, the personalities and behavior of some famous players in chess history are discussed.

Psychoanalyzing Chessplayers

Freud himself was the first psychoanalyst to mention chess when in 1913 he compared the learning of psychoanalytic techniques with the steps required to master the elements of the game. It was not until 1925, however, that

Alexander Herbstman, a well-known Russian chess problem composer as well as a physician, spelled out the general theme that has since pervaded psychoanalytic opinion about chess: The king and queen symbolize the father and mother. Consequently, a game of chess serves as a symbolic restaging of the Oedipal conflict, with father murder as its unconscious goal. Herbstman's paper was apparently not accessible to analysts in Western Europe, and it remained for Ernest Jones, Freud's major biographer, to propose essentially the same thesis and develop it extensively in his paper on Paul Morphy (Jones, 1931). In his opinion, the chessplayer experiences a kind of mystical union with kings and queens, which adds immeasurably to the attractions of the game.

Reider (1959) beautifully summarized the history and legends that are relevant to the psychoanalytic point of view. He adduced as evidence for the theme of patricide a variety of myths surrounding the origin of chess. One, for example, attributes the invention of the game to an Eastern philosopher named Xerses, who tried to cure King Evil-Merodach of his madness. Evil-Merodach (who incidentally, is mentioned very kindly in the Bible) had apparently turned insane after chopping the body of his father, Nebuchadnezzar, into 300 pieces and throwing them to 300 vultures.

With the development of the rules of chess over many centuries, the mobility of the queen increased markedly to the point where she is now the most powerful piece on the board. All chessplayers know that the goal of the game is to trap the king; despite its importance and irreplaceability, however, the king is weak in terms of mobility and requires constant protection. Ernest Jones (1931) remarked that it will not surprise the psychoanalyst to learn that in attacking the father the most potent assistance is afforded by the mother (= queen).

According to the psychoanalysts, it is not only the king and queen that serve as specific symbols in chess combat. Checkmate itself may imply castration and exposure of weakness. Reuben Fine (1967), in his role as a clinical psychologist, stated that rooks, bishops, knights, and pawns frequently symbolize the penis; the bishop may literally refer to some person who molds our conscience; the knight may symbolize a horse; and pawns may symbolize little boys. In general, Fine views chess as involving sublimation of homosexual and hostile impulses.

Psychoanalysts are entitled to their opinions about the real meaning of chess. Readers who find psychoanalytic approaches fruitful in formulating hypotheses about personality conflicts and disorders, and in understanding behavior, can probably accept the chess interpretation without much difficulty. However, as research-oriented psychologists, the present authors would like to see more than dogmatic opinion, myth, legend, and anecdote presented as the major bases for such an interpretation. We know of no objective tests of the theory, nor can we conceive of any clear way of validating or disproving it.

The Personalities of Chessplayers and Athletes

Alderman (1974) summarized the literature with respect to the personality traits that seem characteristic of successful athletes. They tend to be outgoing and socially at ease, self-assertive and tough, self-confident and cheerful, conventional and conservative. However, the data are not clear concerning the hypothesis that various sports can be distinguished on the basis of different personalities (i.e., do athletes with certain personality traits tend to be attracted to specific kinds of sports, or to individual versus team sports?).

It would be valuable to carefully collect some objective personality data from successful chessplayers and to compare them to the general profile for athletes. However, to our knowledge, no worthwhile studies have been conducted along these lines. The absence of data encourages us to speculate on the topic. We think that chessplayers would yield a somewhat different profile from athletes. The most obvious difference would probably lie along the conventionality–conservativeness dimension. The typical chessmaster of our acquaintance cares little about the "proper" ways of doing things, is politically rather left-wing, usually expresses atheistic or agnostic views, and has a "show me" attitude about most issues. We agree with de Groot (1965, p. 347) that skepticism is a valuable quality over the chessboard, and, like him, we think it is reflected in the general behavior of many chessmasters.

Furthermore, our guess is that chessplayers would generally prove to be more introverted and socially ill at ease than is apparently the case for successful athletes. Of course, successful athletes may gain more experience handling fans, interviewers, and community gatherings than do chessmasters, at least in the United States, and they may therefore have more opportunity to develop certain social skills. And, despite extensive training programs and organizations in some countries, chessplayers usually develop their abilities in an individualistic way—relying greatly on their own study and play and relatively little on coaches, teachers, or trainers—whereas most athletes, even in individual sports, must continuously interact with others in developing and polishing their skills. Chess can be "studied" anytime and anywhere, with or without a chessboard, in bed or in the office; but a golfer, runner, or tennis champion requires certain physical settings to effectively practice skills.

Chessmasters are generally very amusing companions, especially if you enjoy verbal wit of an insulting or self-deprecatory nature. They are more likely to engage in puns or quips than in pranks, horseplay, or any form of slapstick. It would be interesting to determine whether participants in different types of sports prefer different kinds of humor.

Chess Style and Individual Personality

Top-flight chess in the 1970s is as much psychological battle as it is a manifestation of technical knowledge and ability. Most successful competi-

tors play the "man" as well as the "board.". This approach necessitates a pregame analysis of the opponent's likes and dislikes and of his particular psychological strengths and weaknesses—a willingness to take tactical risks, a preference for defensive or cramped positions, overconfidence in certain types of situations, avoidance of unclear variations, impatience after obtaining the advantage, and rigidity in choice of openings. Even in Binet's time, his correspondents spoke of the ardor and fierceness of La Bourdonnais' play, the blind impetuosity of Cochrane, the finesse of von der Lasa. Some players are boxers and others sluggers; Petrósian prefers to "shift wood" patiently, waiting for a mistake, whereas Tal is happiest when the game is incredibly complicated and risky. There are players who are easily discouraged when they "lose the initiative" (a phrase comparable to the word "momentum" in other sports, which has become a football or basketball commentator's cliche), whereas other masters play superbly when their backs are to the wall.

The question of whether a master's chess personality corresponds to his personality away from the board in an unexplored one. Fine (1967) remarked that the connection between individual personality and chess style cannot be reduced to any formula. We think he is right, although our impression is that "drawing masters," who generally play unaggressive, solid chess, are rarely likely to have bubbling, vivacious personalities away from the chess board (unlike the supreme tactician Tal, who is a very funny, outgoing person).

Analysis of Famous Masters

Paul Morphy was a chess prodigy from New Orleans, the acknowledged world champion in 1858, a true gentleman (unlike many players of his and other eras), one of the first experts at blindfold chess, and an apparent victim of schizophrenia when he died at 47. In his classic psychoanalytic contribution, Jones (1931) attributed Morphy's love of chess to an unconscious desire to overcome his father. Insofar as Morphy's final illness was concerned, Jones attached great significance to the refusal of Howard Staunton of England to play him a match. Staunton was one of the strongest players in the world, but he was obviously afraid of losing to Morphy. While viciously attacking the American and his abilities in a chess column in the 1858 *Illustrated London News,* Staunton manufactured all kinds of excuses to avoid meeting him across the chessboard.

Jones theorized that because Morphy could not meet and defeat this father figure, his unconscious desires were thwarted, precipitating his later psychosis. Besides being farfetched (e.g., Morphy's illness did not begin until years afterward), Jones' entire argument is somewhat fallacious, because the acknowledged world champion at the time was Adolph Anderssen of Germany, whom Morphy did play and beat decisively. Why then, asks Fine (1967), should Morphy have been so disturbed by Staunton's refusal to face

him? Besides reiterating this vexing question, Lawson (1976), in his definitive biography of Morphy, proceeds to point out some glaring inaccuracies that Jones and Fine made in their descriptions of Morphy's life, personality, and illness.

Reuben Fine's monograph (1967) figuratively placed many of the world's greatest masters on his psychoanalytic couch. Like other analysts, he believes that the grim motive of father-murder is pervasive in chess. All the world champions came under Fine's scrutiny, and he classified them into two categories, heroes and nonheroes, depending on whether they seriously pursued interests apart from chess. According to Fine, the heroes (Morphy, Steinitz, Capablanca, and Alekhine) used chess to satisfy fantasies of omnipotence and showed considerable emotional disturbance. The non-heroes were more emotionally stable and treated chess as one of many intellectual endeavors; they displayed accomplishment in other areas as well (mathematics, philosophy, engineering).

An example of Fine's specific analysis is his description of Capablanca as the Don Juan of the chessworld. Women flocked around the handsome Cuban wherever he went, and some of his most effective strategies at important tourneys did not involve chess at all. At the peak of his career, Capa often remarked that he could not possibly lose a single game of chess (in fact, during one span of 8 years, he never did get beaten and he lost only 35 games of the 700 he played during his career). Said Fine (1967): "The dreamland where one can never be beaten is a familiar one; it is the return to the mother. In him the oral fixation was strong. It does not surprise us to learn that Capablanca was exceptionally fond of cooking and that he had several favorite restaurants where he went to prepare his own meals [pp. 50–51]." Fine's opinion is worth considering, but there are certainly many chessmasters of our acquaintance who lack great self-confidence and yet are also exceptionally fond of good cooking. And some of the most self-confident chessmasters are hardly gourmets.

There have been numerous books written about the lives, chess feats, and eccentricities of the great chessmasters. We refer our readers to the best of these volumes, Schonberg's *Grandmasters of Chess* (1973). Brad Darrach's book, *Bobby Fischer vs. the Rest of the World* (1974), is sensationalistic and often inaccurate, but on the basis of our own experience, we think it is not tremendously off the mark in its characterization of America's moody ex-world champion.

TRICKS AND GAMESMANSHIP
IN CHESS COMPETITION

Up to now we have tried to present a relatively serious summary of the psychological factors involved in the game of chess. We have avoided mention of ruses and stratagems that skirt the edge of legality, respectability,

and consideration for one's opponent. Crass examples of these tricks can be observed daily in any chess club. Players will twiddle, quiver, sing, shake, tap, whistle, and cluck while their opponents are trying to think, and then insist these forms of behavior are unconscious and unintentional if their opponent complains. Some persons believe that the more loudly they bang down a chess piece, the stronger its effect on the opponent. This tactic calls to mind T. E. Lawrence's report that Arabs were inordinately afraid of cannons: "They thought weapons destructive in proportion to their noise." At any rate, chess clubs are not the austere, noiseless places that outsiders imagine them to be or club directors usually would like them to be.

Gamesmanship occurs even in high-level chess competition, although the techniques that prevail there are typically more subtle and refined than among weaker players (see Krogius, 1976). Mikhail Tal is well known for his extracurricular strategy. He often gazes so intensely at his opponents that he has been accused of hypnotizing them into surrender. Imagine having to face an evil eye, in addition to a grandmaster's standard arsenal of weapons over the chessboard. Pal Benko, the Hungarian–American grandmaster, wore dark sunglasses when he had to play Tal, in an attempt to minimize the effect of his fierce stare. In 1974, both Karpov and Viktor Korchnoi accused each other of using the evil-eye tactic in their world championship challengers' match.

According to some reports, Korchnoi had to be physically restrained from attacking Petrosian during one of their important matches. He complained that Petrosian was tapping his feet up and down while Korchnoi was trying to think, although Petrosian claimed that he was doing nothing of the sort. Incidentally, Petrosian has a definite psychological advantage over his opponents because he is somewhat deaf and normally wears a hearing aid. Whenever the audience's chatter or street noises rise above a certain level, he merely turns off the device. Robert Hubner of West Germany resigned a close and very important match to Petrosian in 1971 rather than continue play amidst noisy conditions, which hardly affected the tuned-out Petrosian.

Some masters have developed the habit (of course not illegal) of thinking for 15 or 20 minutes on a move they had planned long before; they want to deceive their opponent as to the surprise value of his last move and perhaps lull him into a false sense of security. Returning to finish an adjourned game that everyone believed an easy win for his opponent, world champion Mikhail Botvinnik did not bring along his usual thermos of coffee. During home analysis, he had discovered some promising but still futile resources, and he wanted his opponent to think that he expected the game to last only a few more moves. His opponent played carelessly and Botvinnik held the game.

Different players adopt different measures when they suddenly realize that they have just committed a bad blunder, or when their opponent, as he is preparing to reply, writes down on his scoresheet the most-feared move. Some players immediately get up and walk around happily, whereas others sit

still and smile serenely in these emotionally charged situations. During one of the first games between Tal and Fischer, Tal looked so calm after Fischer wrote down a winning move that Bobby eventually crossed out the move and played one that was far inferior. Tal won the game.

When it is not a player's turn to move, he is free to leave the board. Although several masters have been caught between moves analyzing the game on their pocket chess set in a toilet stall, most players would not be so unethical. They do, however, circle the table, stand behind their opponent, or lean over the board to "get a better look" at the clock. It is difficult to prove malicious intent in most such cases, and referees are somewhat powerless to stop the behavior unless it is particularly blatant and the offender has been given several previous warnings.

When one or both players are in time pressure, a great variety of picturesque behaviors may often be observed. Staccato coughing, rhythmic swaying, and hand-hovering are commonplace. Clocks are frequently knocked off the table and onto the floor in the player's haste to move and push the button that starts the opponent's clock. Some players say "j'adoube" as often as possible, adjusting several of their pieces so that they are centered exactly on their respective squares (a player is permitted to touch a piece without moving it as long as he first announces "j'adoube," French for "I adjust"). Their poor opponent, ready to reply immediately to a move of some touched piece, is understandably rattled by such tactics but often will not protest to the tournament director because there is so little time left. In one famous time scramble, Grandmaster Milan Matulovic of Yugoslavia, who has a well-earned reputation for unethical play, once shouted "j'adoube!" *after* making a losing move and then replaced the blunder with a better move. To this day no one knows exactly how he was able to get away with taking back a move in grandmaster competition, but ever since that time, he has had to suffer from the nickname "J'adoubovic." Apparently he has not suffered too much, however, because he successfully managed to take back another move against the same opponent in a subsequent tournament.

Straightforward verbal ploys are often more effective in upsetting a self-assured opponent than those described so far. Like saying at the start of play: "I see you weren't invited to that big tournament in Moscow." Or perhaps later in the evening: "How come your wife hasn't been in the tournament room for the last hour?" At the peak of excitement just before the Fischer–Spassky match, most newspaper and television commentators suggested that Bobby was trying to "psych-out" Spassky with his verbal demands and unyielding behavior. This seems very unlikely to us. Fischer is an extremely ethical player, who simply will not budge until the tournament conditions meet his personal standards of perfection.

Despite warnings by tournament organizers and referees, it is very hard to prevent the fixing of a game by two players. The most common version of

such a contract is for good friends, or competitors from the same country, to agree to a draw in private before the game, and then to stay in the playing room only long enough to make 20 or 30 innocuous or rehearsed moves. Then they shake hands, signifying a draw by mutual agreement. In 1975, Samuel Reshevsky had the audacity to complain to the tournament director that Pal Benko had not kept a pregame agreement about a fixed draw and had actually played to win a final-round game between them in the U.S. Championship. As we have noted, it is virtually impossible to prevent private agreements of this kind, but when a tournament official possesses definite evidence about such arrangements, he has the power to impose severe penalties and probably should do so.

Tournament competitors have to be careful about spectators, too. One player and his confederate were asked to resign from one of New York's leading chess clubs because the confederate, a chessmaster, was transmitting moves to the player by means of a prearranged code based on finger movements. Watching for a signal may be legal in baseball, but not in chess. Bobby Fischer has often claimed, on the basis of minimal evidence, that members of the Russian group accompanying their players to various tourneys in the early 1960s were passing valuable information to his Soviet opponents during their games with him. He forced the tournament directors to prohibit any conversations during actual play. Later he wrote inflammatory articles listing the ways in which the Russians had cheated him out of the world title. Some of his preconditions for the Spassky match and for the ill-fated Karpov match were intended to prevent what he considered any form of hanky-panky on the part of the Russians.

Gamesmanship is a factor in virtually every type of sports competition. Well-chosen taunts, misleading smiles and frowns, complicated bluffs, and similar tactics occur in boxing, tennis, and football. It may surprise some nonchessplayers to learn that, in this respect, the Royal Game—that serious, intellectual, legalistic struggle—takes second place to no other sport. And psychologists interested in sports, games, and play will find chess an even more intricate form of human competition and interaction than they might have suspected initially.

REFERENCES

Alderman, R. B. *Psychological behavior in sport.* Philadelphia: W. B. Saunders, 1974.

Alekhine, A. [The blindfold game] (A. Buschke, trans.). *Chess Life and Review*, 1971, *26*, 522–523. (Originally published, 1931.)

Barry, H. Longevity of outstanding chess players. *Journal of Genetic Psychology*, 1969, *115*, 143–148.

Binet, A. [Mnemonic virtuosity: A study of chessplayers] (M. L. Simmel & S. B. Barron, trans.). *Genetic Psychology Monographs*, 1966, *74*, 127–162. (Originally published, 1893.)

Buttenwieser, P. *The relation of age to skill of expert chess players.* Unpublished doctoral dissertation, Stanford University, 1936.

Carroll, C. M. *The great chess automaton.* New York: Dover, 1975.

Charness, N. Memory for chess positions: Resistence to interference. *Journal of Experimental Psychology: Human Learning and Memory,* 1976, *2,* 641–653.

Charness, N. Human chess skill. In P. Frey (Ed.), *Chess skill in man and machine.* New York: Springer, 1977.

Chase, W. G., & Simon, H. A. The mind's eye in chess. In W. G. Chase (Ed.), *Visual information processing.* New York: Academic Press, 1973.

Cleveland, A. A. The psychology of chess and of learning to play it. *American Journal of Psychology,* 1907, *18,* 269–308.

Cockburn, A. *Idle passion: Chess and the dance of death.* New York: Simon & Schuster, 1974.

Collins, J. W. *My seven chess prodigies.* New York: Simon & Schuster, 1974.

Collins, M. "Frances." In F. Karslake (Ed.), *Attic salt.* London: Karslake & Co., 1909. (Originally published, 1880.)

Darrach, B. *Bobby Fischer vs. the rest of the world.* New York: Stein and Day, 1974.

de Groot, A. D. *Thought and choice in chess.* The Hague: Mouton, 1965.

Draper, N. Does age affect master chess? *Journal of the Royal Statistical Society,* 1963, *126,* 120–127.

Elo, A. Age changes in master chess performance. *Journal of Gerontology,* 1965, *20,* 289–299.

Fine, R. *The ideas behind the chess openings.* New York: David McKay, 1943.

Fine, R. The psychology of blindfold chess: An introspective account. *Acta Psychologica,* 1965, *24,* 352–370.

Fine, R. *The psychology of the chess player.* New York: Dover, 1967.

Franklin, B. The morals of chess. *Columbian Magazine,* December 1786.

Frey, P. (Ed.). *Chess skill in man and machine.* New York: Springer, 1977.

Frey, P., & Adesman, P. Recall memory for visually presented chess positions. *Memory and Cognition,* 1976, *4,* 541–547.

Gray, M. Pawn to Queen-3. *The Sciences,* June 1973, p. 31.

Hammond, K. R. Computer graphics as an aid to learning. *Science,* 1971, *172,* 903–908.

Harris, L. J. Sex differences in spatial ability: Possible environmental, genetic, and neurological factors. In M. Kinsbourne (Ed.), *Asymmetrical function of the brain.* Cambridge, England: Cambridge University Press, 1978.

Hearst, E. Psychology across the chessboard. *Psychology Today,* June 1967, pp. 28–37.

Hearst, E. Man and machine: Chess achievements and chess thinking. In P. Frey (Ed.), *Chess skill in man and machine.* New York: Springer, 1977.

Hunt, E. *Artificial intelligence.* New York: Academic Press, 1975.

James, W. *The principles of psychology* (Vol. 2). New York: Henry Holt, 1890.

Jones, E. The problem of Paul Morphy. *International Journal of Psychoanalysis,* 1931, *12,* 1–23.

Krogius, N. *Psychology in chess.* New York: RHM Press, 1976.

Lawson, D. *Paul Morphy: The pride and sorrow of chess.* New York: David McKay, 1976.

Lehman, H. C. *Age and achievement.* Princeton, N.J.: Princeton University Press, 1953.

Levy, D. Invasion from Cyberland. *Chess Life and Review,* 1977, *32,* 312–313.

Lorayne, H., & Lucas, J. *The memory book.* New York: Ballantine Books, 1975.

Margulies, S. Principles of beauty. *Psychological Reports,* 1977, *41,* 3–11.

Nabokov, V. *The defense.* New York: G. P. Putnam, 1964.

Newborn, M. *Computer chess.* New York: Academic Press, 1975.

Reider, N. Chess, Oedipus, and the mater dolorosa. *International Journal of Psychoanalysis,* 1959, *40,* 1–14.

Reider, N. The natural inferiority of women chessplayers. *Chessworld,* May–June 1964, pp. 12–19.

Rubin, E. The age factor in master chess. *The American Statistician*, 1960, *14*, 19–21.

Rubin, E. How games end in master chess tournaments. *The American Statistician*, 1973, *27*, 119–122.

Schonberg, H. C. *Grandmasters of chess*. Philadelphia: J. B. Lippincott, 1973.

Sen, C. T. Women and chess. *Ms*, December 1972, pp. 88–91; 107.

Shaw, G. B. *The irrational knot*. New York: Brentano, 1905.

Simon, H. A., & Chase, W. G. Skill in chess. *American Scientist*, 1973, *61*, 394–403.

Skinner, B. F. *Walden two*. New York: Macmillan, 1948.

Slate, D., & Atkin, L. Chess 4.5: The Northwestern University chess program. In P. Frey (Ed.), *Chess skill in man and machine*. New York: Springer, 1977.

Tarshis, J. How the blind play chess. *Chessworld*, January–February 1964, pp. 20–25.

Wells, H. G. *Certain personal matters*. London: Lawrence & Bullen, 1898.

Witelson, S. Sex and the single hemisphere: Specialization of the right hemisphere for spatial processing. *Science*, 1976, *193*, 425–427.

Zobrist, A., & Carlson, F. R. An advice-taking chess computer. *Scientific American*, 1973, *228*, 92–105.

Zweig, S. *The royal game*. New York: Viking Press, 1944.

3 Butler County Eight Ball: A Behavioral Space Analysis

John M. Roberts
Garry E. Chick
University of Pittsburgh

INTRODUCTION

The Monday Nite pool League of western Pennsylvania is primarily in southern Butler County and secondarily in northern Allegheny County. The League, one of several like organizations in Butler County, furthers the play of eight ball, a two-person game of physical skill with strategy that belongs to the pocket billiards or pool group of games. This study presents some ethnographic information on the League and on the play of eight ball by its members (approximately 150 men) that may be a contribution to our knowledge of American popular culture. The chief concern of this chapter, however, is the presentation of the descriptive approach to eight ball which has been termed "behavioral space analysis."

This descriptive approach may illustrate a newer type of ethnography for it combines the use of psycholinguistic and quantitative techniques with the use of such older anthropological techniques as participant observation and the employment of informed judges as observers and informants to construct a different view of a familiar game. This chapter also deals with the difference between the attitudes of the expert players in the League and those of the

JOHN M. ROBERTS is Andrew Mellon Professor of Anthropology at the University of Pittsburgh. He received his Ph.D. in anthropology at Yale University and has taught at the University of Minnesota, Harvard University, the University of Nebraska and Cornell University. He has served as President of the American Ethnological Society and the Society for Cross-Cultural Research.

GARRY E. CHICK is a doctoral candidate in the Department of Anthropology at the University of Pittsburgh.

more ordinary players and the implications of these differences for an understanding of the game.

This investigation of the game of eight ball has its place in a series of studies dealing with games from a behavioral scientific point of view. Since preceding publications have appeared in varied and even obscure outlets, it is useful to cite them in chronological order here: Roberts, Arth, and Bush (1959); Roberts and Sutton-Smith (1962); Sutton-Smith, Roberts, and Kozelka (1963); Roberts, Sutton-Smith, and Kendon (1963); Sutton-Smith and Roberts (1964); Roberts, Hoffmann, and Sutton-Smith (1965); Roberts and Sutton-Smith (1966); Sutton-Smith and Roberts (1967); Roberts and Koening (1968); Roberts, Koenig, and Stark (1969); Sutton-Smith and Roberts (1970); Roberts and Forman (1971); Roberts, Meeker, and Aller (1972); Barry and Roberts (1972); Roberts and Barry (1976); and Roberts and Kundrat (1978). The publications cited deal with cross-cultural associations found with games of various types, the play of a game of strategy (tick, tack, toe), team compositions, and with game involvements, but the present report is the first in the series to deal with a specific game of physical skill with strategy.

Although this report constitutes the first anthropological use of behavioral space analysis in the description of a game, many of the elements used in the analysis are familiar to anthroplogists. The mapping of high-concordance linguistic codes within perceptual and conceptual domains, for example, is now an old technique in anthropology, cf. the mapping of Zuni and English color terms in Lennenberg and Roberts (1956) and the mapping of preferences for shirts and shoes in Roberts, Strand, and Burmeister (1971). Multidimensional scaling and clustering techniques have also been used (cf. Romney, Shephard, and Nerlove, 1972; and D'Andrade, 1978). It is only the combination of these familiar elements into behavioral space analysis that is new.

The first study in this genre was an analysis of behaviors displayed by obstetrical nurses within obstetrical wards. Here, linguistic expressions were obtained for a sample of behaviors, good and bad, interesting and uninteresting, important and unimportant, which an informed judge thought could serve as a model of the full behavioral array. These expressions were then mapped into a four-dimensional space through the use of the multidimensional scaling of a similarity matrix based on the judgments of similarity made by a sample of nurses. The resultant conceptual model of an actual behavioral space has both ethnographic interest and salience for decision makers (Roberts, Skoner, and Hogner, Note 1).

In this investigation of eight ball, an informed judge listed 60, eight ball behaviors, good and bad, important and unimportant, interesting and uninteresting, which he felt represented the full behavior array found in eight ball. Obviously this is only ethnographic judgment, but the judge was a long-

term player who was completely familiar with the League. For better or worse, these 60 behaviors constitute a "model" of the eight ball behavioral space.

Next, the common English expressions for these behaviors (i.e., elements in a high-concordance code) were entered on cards. Forty-five experienced members of the League were given the cards individually and each individual sorted them into piles based on the similarities that he felt the various behaviors had for each other. Then the aggregate similarity matrix based on the sorting was clustered. Each of the main clusters was then treated as a domain and the behaviors within the domain were subjected to multidimensional scaling. It is argued that both the clusters and the dimensions produced by these procedures have ethnographic import. They must be understood if people are to understand the play of the game as it actually occurs.

Finally an attitudinal study of a small sample of experts and a small sample of more ordinary players was conducted. All of the players scaled all of the behaviors associated with actual play in terms of the fun experienced when they performed them. Again players scaled their estimates of the amounts of concentration that a set of behaviors required and the amount of concentration experienced when they performed these behaviors. For another set of behaviors, the players considered the degree which their concentration was broken when they practiced these behaviors.

The total analysis, then, deals with a sample of actual behaviors occurring in the space on and around the pool table in the course of the play of eight ball and with the conceptual space into which the players map this play. Then, to a degree, attitudes toward concentration and fun are also mapped within this space. The total description leads to a better understanding of the game.

BUTLER COUNTY EIGHT BALL

It is impossible to interpret the quantitative data presented in this chapter if the reader does not have some understanding of eight ball and of the context in which it is played. An informal sampling of academic readers showed that many did not know the game at all. Although eight ball must be played by millions, those millions may fall in socioeconomic categories differing from those of most of the professional writers on games. It is for this reason that we describe eight ball in some detail.

The Monday Nite Pool League (which is devoted to eight ball) was organized in 1966 when the owners of six small town and rural taverns (the rural Pike Restaurant, Rugh's Tavern in Saxonburg, the rural Sarver VFW, the rural Frank's Tavern, the White Star Club in Freeport, and Alexander's Inn in Knox Chapel, familiarly known as Sadie and Violet's) decided that the play of the League would foster business on Monday evenings which were

usually slow. Each tavern had at least one coin-operated pool table, 7 feet in length and 3½ feet in width (two feet shorter and a half foot narrower than the standard table), which released the balls needed for a game when a quarter was placed in the slot, a selection of cue sticks, and other accessories needed for the play of the game. Furthermore, there were enough regular customers interested in eight ball at each tavern to staff a team. Incidentally, the League proved to be good business venture for the owners and now whenever a participating tavern is sold, other taverns in the region display interest in getting a place in the League.

The 20-article constitution of the Monday Nite Pool League establishes the structure and governance of the League. The League has also promulgated 18 special rules for the play of eight ball in the League context. A special meeting is held each summer when the League's officers, a president, a vice-president, a secretary, and a treasurer are elected. During the season of play, each of the six teams sends two elected representatives to meet with the officers of the League each month and such meetings are held on a few occasions during the off-season. Membership in the League is restricted to "Any male person of good moral character who has attained 21 years of age or over." Each member pays a $5.00 membership fee each year and must also purchase at least one $10.00 raffle ticket each year (nonmembers may also buy raffle tickets). The membership fees and proceeds from the sale of raffle tickets are used only to finance the operations of the League and no profits accrue to any of the League officers, members or tavern owners. Two of the owners of the taverns are also members of the League, but they have no political power in the organization.

Each team has a captain who is usually chosen through informal consensus and who is marked by a willingness to take the job. Although a total of 15 members of each team play in any given match, team membership can range from approximately 22 to 36 members (the average is about 25 to 28 members). The members of these teams rarely, if ever, hold formal meetings.

Members range in age from 21 to 70 years, but the average is 35 to 40 years. The members are varied in occupation: truck drivers, machinists, school teachers, bartenders, mushroom farm workers, steel workers, garage mechanics, supermarket managers, restaurant managers, draftsmen and other occupations are represented in the League.

The 24 League matches are played every year from early October through March on Monday evenings between 8:00 p.m. and about 10:30 p.m. The "season" is divided into halves of 12 matches each. On any given Monday night, games are played at three "home" taverns. The allocation of visiting and home games, however, is evenly distributed among the six taverns. At the end of the season, the winning teams from each half have a play-off for the championship while the remaining teams play for third place. The top player

from each team is also pitted in a round-robin tournament to determine the League's best individual player.

The first raffle drawing is held in January, and drawings continue for several weeks with the prizes increasing each week from $15 to $25 to $50 and , finally, to $100. The annual banquet at the end of the season at the White Star Club is financed in part by membership dues and in part by the sale of the raffle tickets. Trophies for the winning teams and individuals are awarded at the banquet.

Each match consists of 15 games of eight ball played by 15 different players from each of the two competing teams. Team players are chosen by lot from the team members present in the tavern before the match begins (usually 18 to 20 team members appear for each match). Members who are unsuccessful in the lottery one week are guaranteed the opportunity to play the following week. If a team has less than 15 players present in the tavern, it must forfeit those games for which no player is available. Because team standings are based on the total number of games (rather than matches) won during the series, each team tries to win each match by the widest margin possible. Thus every game played has equal value.

Although the games seem to have little attraction for casual spectators, most of the players watch the games in each match with interest. Few players leave a match early, even if they have already played, and many, after their own match is finished, go to one of the other bars in the League to see how the other teams have fared that evening. Occasionally wives and girlfriends are present and on any average evening one or two women watch the play. Indeed, a few women attend matches quite consistnetly.

Players tend to arrive 30 to 45 minutes early in order to play one or two practice games and to have drink or two before the action begins. At 8:00 p.m., each team captain counts the number of players available for the team. The home-team's captain then places 15 numbered plastic "pills" in a small plastic bottle along with as many blank "pills" as are necessary to equal the total number of players available on the visiting team. These "pills" are then randomly distributed to the visiting team members. Players' names are then listed according to the number of the game that they have drawn. Should any players be present who received blank "pills" on the previous Monday, they draw before the blank "pills" are added to the bottle. Then the same process is repeated by the visiting team's captain for the home team. This random drawing for playing positions prevents teams from matching their better players against the poorer players of the opposing team.

Most players prefer to play in the fourth and fifth games of the evening because the first three games are particularly nerve-wracking. Initial interest is always high and there are 30 to 40 other players who are watching the play. In addition, although the spectators may not offer advice on the play of

particular shots, heckling is at a peak during the early games. Players are under such pressure to perform well that they often relieve their nervousness with drinks, a custom that works to the disadvantage of the early game players who have had too few drinks to be effective while players of the late games may have had too many.

Players who have already played or who are waiting to play often converse or encourage a team member to play well. They may heckle an opposing player, but such heckling is almost always goodnatured, for good sportsmanship is highly encouraged. Team members who are present, but who did not draw a numbered "pill" often drink through the evening. A few play Liar's Poker, a gambling game based on forming poker hands from the serial numbers of dollar bills.

In the play of eight ball the League uses the smaller, coin-operated tables found in taverns (incidentally, the tavern owners provide the 15 quarters needed for the play of the League matches in their taverns). Each table has a felt playing surface and six pockets, one at each corner and one in the center of each long side of the table. The 15 numbered composition balls cannot be retrieved once they have gone into the pockets for they can only be released by the deposit of another quarter in the slot. The unnumbered, white cue ball is slightly larger and heavier than the other balls so that it can be retrieved after it falls through the pocket. The fact that the numbered balls cannot be retrieved dictates differences in rules from the regulation game of eight ball that deal, mainly, with "spotting," or replacing balls on the table, when an infraction of some other rule has occured.

Each tavern has one or more racks of approximately 20 wooden cues that vary in weight from 14 to 21 ounces, but roughly one-third of the players bring their own two-piece cues. Chalk for the cues and talcum powder for the hands of the players are also provided. The chalk is applied to the leather or composition cue tip, so a shot will not be spoiled by a slip. Talcum powder helps the cue stick slide easily through the fingers. A wooden or plastic triangular frame or rack is used for grouping the balls and a bridge (sometimes called a rake because of its physical resemblance to a garden rake) is available to support the cue stick when the cue ball is so far from the edge of the table that the player cannot easily use the hand to support the tip end of the stick.

The 15 numbered balls are racked and spotted at one end of the table with the eight ball in the center. The other balls in the triangular group are roughly alternated in terms of their being either low numbered or high numbered. Thus, the ball at the apex of the triangular group may be a low ball, numbered one through seven, with the next ball being high, numbered 10 through 15, and so on. The balls are alternated so that there will not be a strong chance that several balls of either the high or low group will go into pockets to the exclusion of other balls.

The first player shoots the cue ball at the triangular rack of balls from the other end of the table as hard as possible so that as many balls as possible will be driven into pockets and about two-thirds of the time at least one ball is made. Except for the eight ball there is no need, as in other pool games, to call or indicate the pocket into which one intends to shoot a ball. If a player makes one or more of either the low numbered balls or the high numbered balls on the break, he must then sink the remaining balls in that group before he can attempt to make the eight ball. If a player makes at least one high and one low ball on the break, he may then choose to shoot either the remaining low numbered or the remaining high numbered balls. The choice, of course, is based on the positions of the balls on the table. If the first player fails to sink one or more balls on the break, his opponent may then choose to play either the low numbered or the high numbered balls. A player who makes the eight ball on the break wins the game (the only instance in which the pocket into which the eight ball is to be shot need not be called in advance), but this rarely happens because the eight ball is in the exact center of the rack where it is surrounded by the other balls. Each player continues to shoot until he misses a shot.

A player may not hit one of his opponent's designated balls (a "bad hit") with the cue ball before it strikes one of his own balls. If he does, he loses his turn. Similarly, a player also looses his turn if he "scratches" by either shooting the cue ball into one of the pockets or off the table (a "table scratch"). The game continues as each player attempts, in turn, to put the seven designated balls, either high or low in number, into the pockets. After a player has sunk all seven balls, he then attempts to shoot the eight ball into a pocket that he "calls" in advance. Should he either make the eight ball in any pocket other than the designated one, or scratch in the process of shooting, regardless of whether or not the eight ball is made, the game is lost. If the eight ball is missed, the game continues until one of the players succeeds in making it.

Some of the techniques used in shooting pool figure in the behavioral space to be considered later. A player selects a cue on the basis of his preference for weight and shaft thickness. He then "chalks" the tip of the stick with a 1-inch cube of chalk to prevent the tip's skidding or slipping (a miscue) on the cue ball when a shot is made. Then the player positions himself at the table for the shot. He may lean over the table, but one of his feet must remain on the floor at all times. If the player is right handed, the left hand is positioned on the table approximately 6 to 8 inches from the cue ball (this distance varies with the nature of the shot and with the configuration of the balls on the table) and forms a "bridge" with the hand on which to cradle the cue stick, leaving enough of the stick protruding beyond the hand so that the ball may be struck with the tip of the stick. The player grips the cue stick with the right hand, usually about a foot from the end, and with the forearm in essentially a

vertical position and swinging like a pendulum, he "strokes" or, in effect, aims the cue stick at the cue ball. This stroking resembles, in kind, the practice swings a batter takes in baseball before the pitch is actually thrown. After the player is satisfied with his position, he follows through with the cue stick and strikes the cue ball which, in turn, knocks the object ball into the pocket.

Obviously, some shots, such as those where neither the cue ball nor the object ball must travel a long distance to the pocket, are easier to execute than others. Therefore, it is strategic to cause the cue ball to come to rest after each shot in a position that offers another relatively simple shot. There are three primary methods of "shooting for position." First, the player must choose a sequence of shots, by observing the distribution of object balls on the table, which will facilitate the cue ball's coming to rest in a good position for the next shot after each shot. Second, the force with which the cue ball is struck by the cue stick is a determining factor in the cue ball's travel after it strikes the object ball. Finally, the player may apply "English" or spin to the cue ball which will affect the actions of both the cue ball and object balls.

The concept of "English" requires some elaboration. The cue ball may be struck with center "English," imparting no spin to the ball, so that it skids across the table until an object ball is struck. If the shot is a long one, or if the cue ball is hit softly, the ball will pick up some top spin from the friction produced by the felt surface of the table. If a cue ball that lacks spin strikes an object ball flush in the center, it will impart all of its forward motion to the object ball and stop instantly. If the player wants the cue ball to "follow" or to continue rolling in the same direction as the object ball, he may apply high "English" to the cue ball by striking the cue ball slightly above center (no more than the width of the tip of the cue stick) with the cue. Here the cue tip must be well chalked to prevent miscueing, but an attempt to impart too much "English" either by striking the cue ball too hard or by hitting it too far from its center may result in a miscue. Low "English" or backspin is achieved by striking the cue ball below center and this will cause the cue ball to back up toward the shooter (i.e., "drawing" the cue ball). Right or left "English" is achieved by striking the cue ball slightly to the right or left of center and this will cause the cue ball to be kicked slightly in one direction and the object ball in the other. For example, on a straight-in shot where the cue ball and the object ball are directly in line with a pocket, right "English," which gives the cue ball a counter clockwise rotation when viewed from above, will kick the object ball slightly to the left and the cue ball slightly to the right. Combined effects are also possible: low left "English," high right "English," and so on. In addition, because many, if not most, shots are not straight-in shots, the player must have knowledge of the ways in which "English" affects the movements of both the cue and object balls when the paths between the cue ball, the object

ball, and the pocket form an angle (a "cut" shot). Finally "English" may be used to affect the angle with which a ball bounces off the rail of the table.

The majority of the expressions used for the behaviors listed later are either self explanatory or have already been explained, but some are either very colloquial or obscure. These expressions merit some explanation.

When the balls are racked prior to the start of the game, the player who is to shoot first, that is, to break the rack, may place the cue ball anywhere in an area at the end of the table opposite the end where the balls are racked. This area is circumscribed by the sides (rails) of the table and an imaginary line across the table between dots or diamonds, on the two side rails and it constitutes approximately one-fourth of the playing surface. Similarly, after the opposing player has committed a scratch, a player may place the cue ball anywhere within the same area in preparation for the next shot but may not, however, shoot at an object ball that lies within that area.

A "bank shot" is simply a shot in which either the cue ball or the object ball is banked off one or more of the rails in the attempt to make the shot. A "reverse bank" is a type of bank shot wherein the player is attempting to cause the object ball to be banked back approximately into the area from which the cue ball is shot. This contrasts with the standard bank shot in which the included angle between the directions of the paths of the cue ball and the object ball, after it is banked, is usually somewhere between about 30° and 120°. "Banking off the diamonds" is a bank shot in which the player utilizes small diamonds that are inlaid on the rails at intervals as an aid in the calculation of angles on bankshots.

In a "combination shot," the player attempts to make a ball by hitting another object ball into it. Thus, there may be two-ball, three-ball, or several-ball combinations that involve two, three or more object balls, plus the cue ball. Obviously, if multiple object balls are involved in a combination shot, greater skill is necessary and the chances for success are poorer. Few players will attempt a three-ball or more combination except in desperation or in a situation where they are presented with a dead combination. A "dead combination" is one in which the object ball need only be hit in the correct general direction and because of its relationship, usually contact, with other balls on the table, it will go in the desired pocket. The "kiss shot" is a type of combination shot that is similar to a bank shot except that either the cue ball, or more commonly, the object ball is banked, or "kissed," off another ball instead of the rail. Related to the combination and kiss shots are the "slop shot" and "double kiss." The "slop shot" is simply where the player makes a shot quite by accident. It may not even be the ball originally intended to be made, or the chosen pocket, but it must be one of his own balls. Sometimes, in desperate situations, a player may attempt to make a slop shot by "blasting,"

or hitting the cue ball very hard into a cluster of object balls, in the hope that something will go in. The slop shot is legal on all shots except the eight ball since that ball must be shot into a predesignated pocket. A "double kiss" is where, usually after a miss, the cue ball strikes the object ball a second time, occasionally knocking it into the pocket.

Blasting for a slop shot is both unreliable and risky. The success rate is poor and the player may actually sink one or more of the opponent's balls. Even worse, the player may accidentally make the eight ball and lose the game. Therefore, most players will shoot "safe," ostensibly trying to make a shot but really being more concerned with leaving the cue ball in a position where the opponent has few or no good shots available. Playing "defense" is similar, except that the player is really attempting to make shots but is careful that, should he miss, his opponent will be in a poor position. Overly blatant "safe" or "defensive" play is frowned upon and considered unsportsmanlike. Thus, a player who is faced with little chance of making a shot must make some token effort to make a shot, when his real intent is to shoot safe.

The "massé" shot is one in which the cue stick is held high, almost perpendicular to the table surface, in the attempt to impart so much spin, or "English," to the cue ball that it will curve, usually around another ball, and strike the object ball. It is an extremely difficult shot and is rarely used. Finally, the "table foul" is moving a ball on the table accidentally with the hand or arm, perhaps when attempting a shot. The "table foul" also requires loss of turn.

The differences in skill found among the members of the League must also be considered. Most of the players in the League began playing pool in high school or earlier. Since few, if any, of the young players in this area come from homes with pool tables, the game is learned in regular pool halls and in teenage hangouts with coin-operated tables. By the time players join a pool league team they are already experienced.

The superior players have already spent much time in pool halls where, for example, they have played straight pool, a game in which all shots must be called [i.e., each ball must be shot into a pocket designated by the player before each shot, and any ball that falls into a wrong pocket must be replaced (spotted) on the table]. Since straight pool does not allow for accidental shots (slop shots) and the winner is determined by the total number of balls made (the first player to reach a predetermined number of balls, usually 125, is the winner), the level of both physical skill and strategy are higher in the play of straight pool than it is for the play of eight ball in the League.

Although no one in the League is a poor player, few members belong to the tournament player class. Some of the very best players, however, were once better players, but for one reason or another they must now play less frequently than they formerly did. They have joined the League to keep their

hand in the game as well as to have a night out. They still suffer, though, from a lack of practice.

Other superior players in the area find it frustrating to play a single game in an evening and they derive less pleasure from the social aspects of the League. These players play in other bars or pool halls where they can both play more games and bet on the outcomes. The League does not permit betting on games although in several bars, players sometimes bet a dollar or two a game after the League games are over.

High stake games in western Pennsylvania are played only by skillful players who rarely, if ever, play eight ball. Nine ball is the game used for gambling. Here balls numbered one through nine are racked in a diamond shape. The object of the game is to make the five ball (which is placed in the center of the rack of balls) and the nine ball (which is placed at the apex of the diamond farthest from the player breaking the rack). Twice as much money is bet on the nine ball, as much as $50, as on the five ball. The players must shoot in rotation, that is, they must shoot the balls in numerical sequence, lowest to highest. A player, though, may shoot combination shots, striking the proper numbered ball first, but then knocking either it or the cue ball into the nine ball or the five ball. Normally, the game is won through these combination shots. Nine ball demands higher skill than eight ball because of the need to shoot in rotation and the need for the ability to shoot combination shots. The fact that money has been bet also increases the pressure on the players.

Those players who play several nights a week or who wager fairly large sums of money on their game do not find the League congenial, but players of this type often join the League after they have ceased to play highly competitive pool. Since the League encourages sportsmanship, the intense competitiveness of the high stakes money players is not welcomed. The players who belong to the League are better than beginning players, but poorer, with two or three exceptions, than tournament players or the high-stake gamblers. Within these limits, though, there are substantial differences in skill among the members of the League.

THE EIGHT-BALL BEHAVIORAL SPACE

In 1975 a well-qualified informed judge selected 60 of the numerous behaviors, important and unimportant, good and bad, interesting and uninteresting, that regularly occur in the course of League play and which can be identified by a relatively short English expression or tags. Hereafter, these 60 behaviors will be treated as representative of the whole. The names or labels for these behaviors are also elements in a high concordance linguistic code for they were easily recognized by each and every player (cf. Roberts, Strand, & Burmeister, 1971).

The 60 behaviors are listed in Fig. 3.1, which also gives the hierarchical clustering solution used here. The similarity matrices for the clustering were obtained by typing on a card the expression for each behavior and by giving the shuffled deck of typed cards to informants who then sorted them into piles on the basis of the similarities that these behaviors had for each other in their view. The informants were told that they must have more than one and less than 60 piles. The minimum and maximum number of piles obtained was three and 23. This sorting was done by 45 regularly playing League members (i.e., nearly one-third of the total membership). The 45 similarity matrices were then summed to produce the aggregate matrix that was entered into the clustering program. This matrix was clustered through the use of the U-statistic clustering technique, a nonparametric method of hierarchical clustering that groups clusters on the basis of the best mean rank of proximity scores connecting potential clusters. This technique has been found to be more accurate in recovering the structure of error-perturbed data than either the single-link or complete-link method (D'Andrade, 1978).

A small number of players from the League examined the clustering solution presented in Fig. 3.1 and stated that it fitted their experience with the game. Certainly the three largest clusters made particular ethnographic sense. The uppermost large cluster in Fig. 3.1 groups 10 preparatory and facilitating behaviors into an "instrumental" cluster. The large central cluster of 35 behaviors pertains to proper play and this, to use an archaic term, is the "seemly" cluster. The third and bottom cluster of 15 behaviors groups incorrect and nonskillful play into an "unseemly" cluster.

The seemly cluster is further subdivided into four obvious clusters. The uppermost group of 11 behaviors includes the types of shots that are standard in play. The next lower cluster of 10 behaviors groups behaviors related to cue ball control. The next lower cluster of seven behaviors is strategic in character. Finally, the bottom cluster of seven behaviors is obviously a game-winning cluster.

Since the three principle clusters defined an overall pattern that is acceptable to eight ball players, it was thought that each of these major clusters might be mapped into a structured domain. The similarity matrices for the three clusters, therefore, were subjected to multidimensional scaling (the KYST program; Kruskal, Young, & Seery, Note 2). The three solutions will be discussed later.

Because the instrumental cluster is essentially irrelevant as far as the play of the game is concerned, it will only receive brief attention. The final configuration of 10 points in two dimensions had a stress of .075, and it is presented in Table 3.1 and Fig. 3.2. The key for the letters appearing in Fig. 3.2 is given in Table 3.1. A similar usage holds for Figs. 3.3 and 3.4, where the keys appear in Tables 3.2 and 3.3.

Although the two dimensions found in the solution were uninterpretable, the plot (Fig. 3.2) of the solution showed that six behaviors (racking the balls,

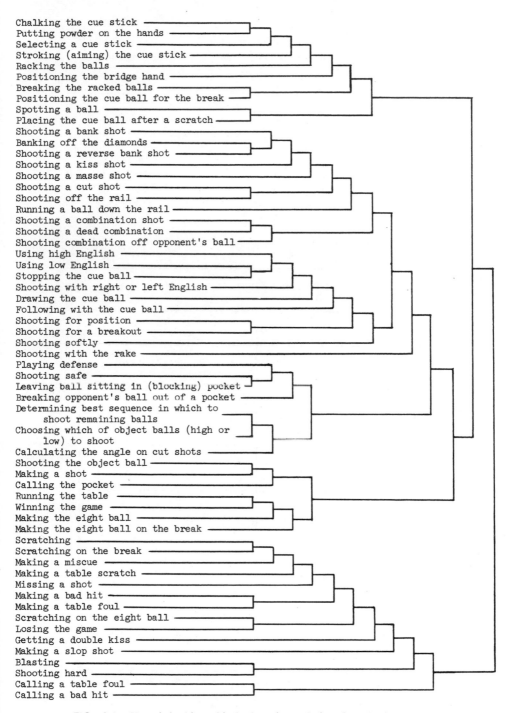

FIG. 3.1. U-statistic hierarchical clustering solution for 60 eight-ball behaviors.

TABLE 3.1

TABLE 3.1
Multidimensional Scaling Solution for the Instrumental Cluster

Behaviors		Dimensions	
		I	II
A.	Placing the cue ball after a scratch	1.337	−.453
B.	Selecting a cue stick	.988	.761
C.	Spotting a ball	.808	−1.242
D.	Breaking the racked balls	.645	1.126
E.	Racking the balls	−.536	.250
F.	Positioning the bridge hand	−.579	−.315
G.	Putting powder on the hands	−.623	−.034
H.	Chalking the cue stick	−.647	−.051
I.	Positioning the cue ball for the break	−.693	.032
J.	Stroking the cue stick	−.700	.073

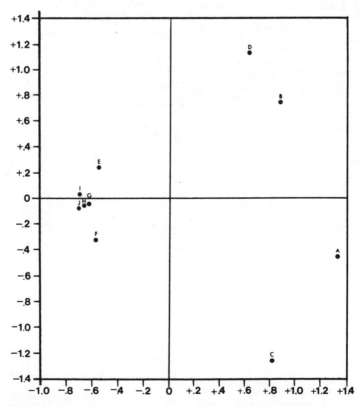

FIG. 3.2. Two-dimensional representation of interpoint distances among 10 instrumental eight-ball behaviors.

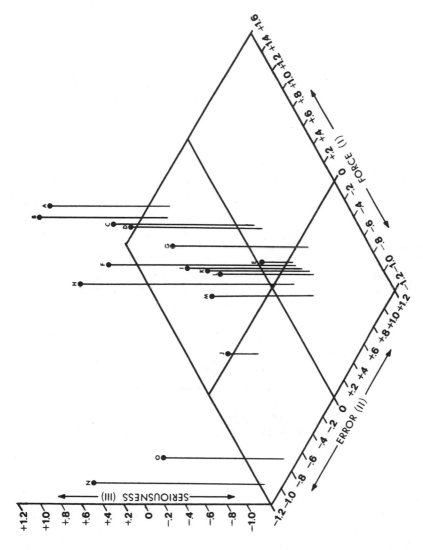

FIG. 3.3.   Three-dimensional representation of interpoint distances among 15 unseemly eight-ball behaviors.

TABLE 3.2
Multidimensional Scaling Solution for the Unseemly Cluster

		Dimensions		
		I	II	III
Behaviors		Force	Error	Seriousness
A.	Calling a bad hit	1.477	−.515	−.050
B.	Calling a table foul	1.427	−.585	.012
C.	Making a table foul	.549	.183	.187
D.	Making a bad hit	.436	.301	.084
E.	Getting a double kiss	−.052	.394	−.873
F.	Scratching on the eight ball	−.114	.341	.665
G.	Missing a shot	−.134	.594	.140
H.	Losing the game	−.182	.219	.895
I.	Making a miscue	−.189	.398	−.063
J.	Making a slop shot	−.265	−.424	−.957
K.	Scratching on the break	−.305	.461	−.194
L.	Scratching	−.350	.472	.002
M.	Making a table scratch	−.477	.352	−.192
N.	Shooting hard	−.860	−1.269	.429
O.	Blasting	−.961	−.922	−.086

positioning the cue ball for the break, stroking the cue stick, chalking the cue stick, putting powder on the hands, and positioning the bridge hand—a near outlier) seem to constitute a pre-shot preparation group of some ethnographic interest. The remaining four behaviors appear to have unique characteristics that, while still instrumental in nature, are not closely related to the other behaviors in this cluster.

The unseemly cluster had a final configuration of 15 points in three dimensions with a stress of .051. This solution is presented in Table 3.2 and Fig. 3.3.

The three dimensions in the unseemly cluster are both interpretable and ethnographically interesting. Dimension I, a "force" dimension, ranges from violent physical activity, such as blasting and shooting hard, to low physical force, e.g., making a table foul, to nonphysical force, e.g., calling a bad hit and calling a table foul. Indeed, these last two activities are not even controlled by the shooter, for they are initiated by his opponent. Dimension II seems to be an error-class dimension that ranges from overt to potential errors or from errors where the consequences are known, to errors where the consequences are problematic. Finally, dimension III seems to be a seriousness dimension that ranges from the most serious, which included bad luck, to the least serious, which includes good luck. Good luck, by the way, is still unseemly— ideally a player wins through skill.

The clusters found in this solution are also interpretable. One cluster groups the common mistakes, such as missing a shot, scratching, scratching

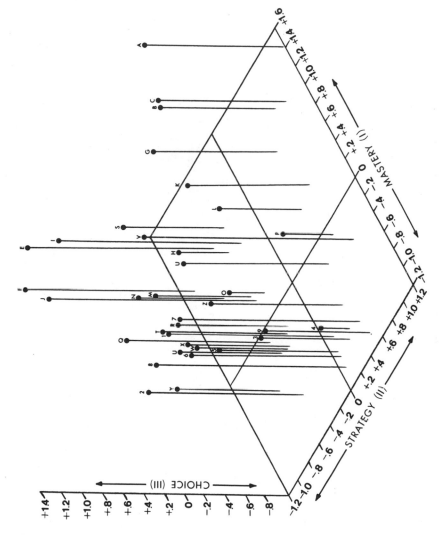

FIG. 3.4. Three-dimensional representation of interpoint distances among 35 seemly eight-ball behaviors.

TABLE 3.3
Multidimensional Scaling Solution for the Seemly cluster

		Dimensions		
Behaviors		I *Mastery*	II *Strategic*	III *Choice*
A.	Making the eight ball on the break	1.427	1.186	.193
B.	Making the eight ball	1.163	.773	−.073
C.	Winning the game	1.090	.919	.056
D.	Determining the best sequence in which to shoot remaining balls	.978	−.404	−.263
E.	Leaving a ball sitting in (blocking) pocket	.968	−.627	.603
F.	Breaking opponent's ball out of a pocket	.888	−1.051	.439
G.	Running the table	.863	.512	.030
H.	Choosing which of the balls (high or low) to shoot	.813	−.475	−.710
I.	Shooting safe	.702	−.498	.566
J.	Playing defense	.588	−.750	.503
K.	Making a shot	.403	.682	−.027
L.	Calling the pocket	.331	.483	−.390
M.	Shooting for position	.299	−.489	−.247
N.	Shooting for a breakout	.236	−.460	−.054
O.	Calculating the angle on cut shots	.212	−.344	−.856
P.	Shooting the object ball	−.094	.626	−.720
Q.	Shooting softly	−.131	−.563	.189
R.	Drawing the cue ball	−.199	−.294	−.224
S.	Running a ball down the rail	−.215	.442	.235
T.	Shooting with right or left English	−.242	−.352	−.026
U.	Stopping the cue ball	−.297	−.448	−.216
V.	Shooting a dead combination	−.344	.828	.828
W.	Using high English	−.344	−.428	−.315
X.	Using low English	−.349	−.418	−.225
Y.	Following with the cue ball	−.493	−.707	−.185
Z.	Shooting a kiss shot	−.604	.366	.062
1.	Banking off the diamonds	−.713	.122	.412
2.	Shooting a massé shot	−.754	−.350	.336
3.	Shooting a cut shot	−.773	.251	−.315
4.	Shooting with the rake	−.807	.304	−.932
5.	Shooting a reverse bank shot	−.838	.071	.085
6.	Shooting a bank shot	−.849	.089	.212
7.	shooting a combination shot	−.881	.450	.571
8.	Shooting a combination off opponent's ball	−1.011	.068	.667
9.	Shooting off the rail	−1.024	.486	−.209

on the break, making a miscue, making a table scratch, and missing a shot. One two-element cluster, making a table foul and making a bad hit, and another two-element cluster, calling a table foul and calling a bad hit, are related in that both refer to the same errors, but different players figure as the actor in the situation. Scratching on the eight ball and losing the game are also closely related for they pertain to ultimate failure. Shooting hard and blasting constitute a cluster of shots which are physically alike, but which differ strategically. These last shots are not really errors in and of themselves, but they are risky shots with a high probability of unfortunate outcomes. Finally, making a slop shot is not closely related to any other shot except getting a double kiss on the seriousness dimension. Getting a double kiss is an outlier as well, although it is related to the common mistake cluster along dimensions I and II and to making a slop shot on dimension III. The problematic nature of this shot accounts for its distinct position. A double kiss is never, with the possible exception of a type of trick shot, a desirable way in which to execute a shot even though the result is sometimes successful. Yet a double kiss is not such a bad behavior for the shot might be made and if it isn't, the player only misses a shot that was poorly played and which, in all probability, would have been missed in any case.

The unseemly dimensions merit further comment. The force dimension I reflects the players' concern for the movement of the balls on the table. Although good players occasionally see the need for blasting or shooting hard, they also know that the possibility of error increases with an increase in the use of physical force, a relationship which has been effectively discussed by Fels (1977). Several players in the League do shoot harder than most of the better players with some success, but they are often criticized by other players who feel that they would do even better if they shot in a softer, more controlled and deliberate manner. Shooting hard, of course, is clearly poor strategy in shooting for position.

The behaviors of low physical force and no physical force at the other end of dimension I are of less consequence in the overall strategy of play. Making a table foul, for instance, is always accidental and it is usually tolerated by an opposing player without requiring a forfeit of the turn. The offending player simply moves the bumped ball back to its original position (often this action is accompanied by jeers of "move them wherever you want them" from spectators). Making a bad hit and calling a bad hit are more serious, for these behaviors are likely to result in loss of turn for the offender. Making a bad hit is often accidental, consisting of a player's lightly ticking one of the opponent's object balls before striking one's own. Thus, the error may result in a miniscule movement of the ball, but it is a foul, nonetheless.

The error class dimension (II) orders behaviors that, on the one hand, are overt errors whose effects are self evident, and on the other, are plays that

cannot really be described as errors (e.g., shooting hard or calling a table foul) because they may be correct under some circumstance. Calling bad hits or table fouls, however, are unpleasant acts for most players since the League's emphasis on sportsmanship dictates that a player should immediately acknowledge a foul without the need of the opponent's calling it, with the result that when a foul is called, the opponent's poor sportsmanship is underscored. Similarly, a situation may warrant shooting hard, or blasting, and making a slop shot aids in winning the game. Yet none of these behaviors are considered to be skill shots and unlike the behaviors at the other end of the dimension, their effect on the game is more probabilistic and uncertain. They lack style.

The seriousness dimension (III), ranges from relatively less bad actions, such as making a slop shot, to clearly bad actions, such as losing the game or scratching on the eight ball. Parenthetically, it can be noted that luck can be important in eight ball. Clearly, making a slopshot is a lucky break for it results from the missing of a shot and losing the game can be the result of a lucky shot by the opponent or an unlucky shot by oneself. Actually the players may even overestimate the importance of this component of luck in eight ball.

The most important cluster for the play of the game is the 35 behavior seemly cluster. The final configuration in three dimensions has a stress of .099 (cf. Table 3.3 and Fig. 3.4). Dimension I is a mastery dimension, which ranges from concrete behaviors to abstract or strategic behaviors. Dimension II pertains to strategy for it ranges from offense to defense through the control of the object ball on to the control of the cue ball. Dimension III is a choice dimension which ranges from plays in which there are options, to those where the action is forced or dictated by the situation.

The mastery dimension (I) seems to contrast the mastery of fine-grained, specific shots and cue ball manipulations with the general mastery of the play and the outcome of the game. Thus, such concrete behaviors as shooting a massé shot, shooting with the rake, shooting off the rail, and shooting a bank shot appear at the fine-grained end of the dimension, in contrast with such behaviors as winning the game, making a shot, playing defense, and determining the best sequence in which to shoot remaining balls which appear at the general mastery or abstract end.

Strategy in pool or other games has several aspects or levels: the desired outcome, the plan or strategy to achieve that outcome, and the methods by which the plan is carried out. The strategic dimension (II) compares the tactics used in eight ball (such as shooting for a breakout) and the specific manipulations of the cue ball, (using high "English," stopping the cue ball, etc.) which are used to carry out a strategic behavior with the types of shots in which the strategy and cue ball control are used (e.g., shooting a cut shot, shooting a bank shot, or shooting a combination shot) and the outcomes, if

the tactics are applied successfully, (i.e., making a shot, winning the game, or making the eight ball.)

The choice dimension (III) deals with the decisions players make in regard to shots. There is often more than one shot available to a player although only one of these may be the best choice in the situation. Sometimes, however, there are free options in shot choice, but other behaviors are forced as in shooting the object ball or calculating the angle on cut shots (which must be done for every shot in order to determine whether the shot is, in fact, a cut shot) and still others are situationally specific as in choosing which of the balls (high or low) to shoot and shooting with the rake where the behavior is forced. This dimension, then, describes the range of options available to the player. It seems to be the case that those behaviors offering little or no option are less interesting than those where flexibility of choice is involved. Interesting optional shots include shooting a dead combination, shooting a combination off an opponent's ball, and leaving a ball sitting in (blocking) a pocket.

The clusters in the three dimensional solution (cf. Fig. 3.4) can be characterized. One cluster (making the eight ball on the break, winning the game, making the eight ball, running the table, making a shot, and calling the pocket) is a "win" or success cluster. A second cluster (shooting off the rail, shooting with the rake, and shooting a cut shot) can be contrasted with a third (shooting a kiss shot, banking off the diamonds, shooting a bank shot, shooting a reverse bank shot, shooting a combination shot, and shooting a combination off opponent's ball) in the sense that the former includes relatively unspectacular, standard shots while the latter groups more spectacular and difficult shots. Another cluster (using high "English," using low "English," using right or left "English," drawing the cue ball, shooting softly, stopping the cue ball, following with the cue ball, and shooting a massé shot) deals with the control of the cue ball, especially through the application of "English" to the cue ball. There is a small, offensive strategy cluster (shooting for position and shooting for a breakout) and a defensive strategy cluster [playing defense, leaving a ball sitting in (blocking) pocket, and shooting safe]. Finally, there is a combined strategy cluster [choosing which of the balls (high or low) to shoot and determining the best sequence in which to shoot remaining balls], wherein the player determines how best to attack the game given the positions of the balls on the table.

As with the unseemly cluster, there are a few outliers. Shooting the object ball, calculating the angle on cut shots, and making the eight ball on the break are outliers with their own distinctive characteristics.

The data presented thus far represent a general cultural approximation. It is now possible to go beyond this to consider differences between the expert and the more ordinary players in the League.

Observation of the play of eight ball showed that the players often discussed concentration. In their view bad play was often the result of poor

concentration and bad play further destroyed concentration. On the other hand, good play was sustained by concentration. It was thought that expert players had a greater ability to maintain concentration than did ordinary players. It was decided, therefore, to scale the 35 behaviors in the seemly cluster on the concentration experienced by the players when they performed those behaviors and on the estimate by the players of the amount of concentration required if the behavior were to be performed properly.

All of the players considered the play of eight ball to be fun, but it was thought that there would be differences in fun between the seemly and unseemly clusters and differences in fun within the major clusters. Thus, the behaviors in the two clusters were scaled on the amount of fun experienced by the players.

Unfortunately, substantial samples of expert and ordinary players could not be obtained, but nine experts and 11 ordinary players agreed to participate in the scaling exercise. The expert players were distinguished from the ordinary players on the basis of their play in the League over a period of years. Indeed, there was consensus among League members that the nine experts were truly expert by the League standards. The 11 ordinary players represented a range of ordinary play within the League.

In 1976, the 20 players scaled the behaviors in each group by laying out cards with the behaviors written on them along a meter stick.[1] Then the scale value of each behavior was entered in centimeters. Each player scaled fun for both groups, concentration broken for the unseemly cluster, and concentration experienced and concentration required for the seemly cluster, five scaling operations in all.

Table 3.4 presents the average scale values for fun for the expert and the ordinary players. The two sets of players seem to have similar views, for the two sets of fun values have a correlation of .957 (significance = .001). Both kinds of players, for example, regard making a slop shot, shooting hard, and blasting as unseemly behaviors which are still fun. The experts, on the other hand, get significantly less fun from shooting hard and blasting than do the ordinary players whereas the ordinary players get more fun from calling a table foul (an action that is usually a basis for joking and frivolity). the experts also get more fun out of making a bad hit.

Table 3.5 gives the average scale values for the breaking of concentration for the unseemly cluster. The sets of values for the experts and the ordinary players have a correlation of .805 (significance level = .001). On the whole,

---

[1]The authors were influenced in selecting this scaling technique by Roy G. D'Andrade who, in turn, owed much to Norman Anderson for stimulation. The authors are so indebted to Roy G. D'Andrade that the conventional acknowledgment seems inadequate. Not only did D'Andrade introduce the authors to "U-Statistic Hierarchical Clustering," but he actually did the clustering given in this chapter. He also aided in the interpretation of the clusters and dimensions. As a matter of fact, the entire chapter owes much to his stimualtion and creativity. The authors appreciate his help.

TABLE 3.4
Average Scale Values for Expert and Ordinary Players for the "Fun" Variable with Behaviors from the Unseemly Cluster

	Expert Class		Ordinary Class	
Rank	Behaviors	Ave. Scale Value	Behaviors	Ave. Scale Value
1.	Making a slop shot	80.0	Making a slop shot	88.4
2.	Shooting hard	57.4[a]	Blasting	84.5[a]
3.	Blasting	55.2[a]	Shooting hard	79.0[a]
4.	Getting a double kiss	36.7	Getting a double kiss	45.3
5.	Making a table scratch	24.8	Calling a table foul	24.5[a]
6.	Missing a shot	24.1	Making a table scratch	24.3
7.	Scratching on the break	22.8	Missing a shot	21.8
8.	Making a table foul	21.4	Scratching on the break	21.4
9.	Scratching	20.6	Making a table foul	20.1
10.	Making a bad hit	18.3[a]	Scratching	19.2
11.	Calling a table foul	10.3[a]	Calling a bad hit	17.0
12.	Making a miscue	9.3	Making a miscue	13.1
13.	Calling a bad hit	8.3	Making a bad hit	10.8[a]
14.	Losing the game	4.0	Losing the game	4.9
15.	Scratching on the eight ball	2.9	Scratching on the eight ball	1.3

[a]Significance leve for "*t* test" of less than .05.

TABLE 3.5
Average Scale Values for Expert and Ordinary Players for the "Concentration Broken" Variable with Behaviors from the Unseemly Cluster

	Expert Class		Ordinary Class	
Rank	Behaviors	Ave. Scale Value	Behaviors	Ave. Scale Value
1.	Scratching on the eight ball	80.9[a]	Scratching on the eight ball	94.8[a]
2.	Making a miscue	72.7	Scratching	76.0[a]
3.	Making a bad hit	69.1	Losing the game	75.3
4.	Scratching	62.2[a]	Making a miscue	71.5
5.	Making a table scratch	57.7	Making a bad hit	66.8
6.	Missing a shot	46.4	Making a table scratch	65.5
7.	Making a table foul	39.6	Calling a bad hit	51.9[a]
8.	Losing the game	36.3	Making a table foul	56.4
9.	Getting a double kiss	35.7	Missing a shot	49.5
10.	Scratching on the break	33.4	Scratching on the break	41.3
11.	Blasting	30.9[b]	Getting a double kiss	38.8
12.	Shooting hard	29.3	Calling a table foul	34.6[b]
13.	Calling a bad hit	21.3	Shooting hard	20.7
14.	Making a slop shot	11.7	Blasting	17.9[b]
15.	Calling a table foul	7.7[a]	Making a slop shot	8.5

[a]Significance levels for the "*t* test" of less than .05.
[b]Significance levels for the "*t* test" of less than .10.

there is agreement among the expert and the ordinary players, but the experts are less disturbed than the ordinary players by scratching on the eight ball, scratching, calling a bad hit, and calling a table foul. On the other hand, at a directional level, the expert is more bothered by blasting than is the ordinary player.

Table 3.6 below gives the average scale values for the behaviors in the seemly cluster for fun. The correlation between the values of the experts and the ordinary players is .905 (significance = .001). Once again the two sets of players have similar attitudes toward fun, but the ordinary players found more fun than the experts in making the eight ball on the break, using low "English," banking off the diamonds, stopping the cue ball, directionally making the eight ball, and directionally shooting softly whereas the experts were higher than the ordinary players in shooting for position, shooting the object ball, determining the best sequence in which to shoot remaining balls, and directionally shooting with the rake. The ordinary players found fun in successful outcomes and in clever plays whereas the expert players were more concerned with the play of the game.

The average scale values for concentration experienced for the behaviors in the seemly cluster is given in Table 3.7. The correlation between the values of the experts and the ordinary players is .859 (significance = .001). Although there is agreement between the two sets of players, there is a significant difference between the overall averages for concentration experienced (experts = 68.492, s.d. 18.780, and ordinary players = 58.683, s.d. 19.015; t = 2.171, $p < .02$). Not only did the experts experience more concentration, but they reported experiencing significantly more concentration than did the ordinary players for shooting for position, shooting for a breakout, shooting a combination shot, determining the best sequence in which to shoot remaining balls, breaking the opponent's ball out of a pocket, shooting a dead combination, choosing which of the object balls (high or low) to shoot, calling the pocket, directionally shooting a kiss shot, directionally calculating the angle on cut shots, and directionally following with the cue ball. The ordinary players, however, reported experiencing significantly greater concentration when playing defense than did the experts.

Unlike the other scales, the concentration-required scale is based on estimates and not reports of experience. The average concentration-required estimates are given in Table 3.8. The values for the experts and the ordinary players have a correlation of .858 (significance = .001). The concentration-experienced scale and the concentration-required scale for the experts had a correlation of .867 (significance = .01) and the same two scales had a correlation of .919 (significance = .001) for the ordinary players. There was a significant difference between the overall average of the average concentration estimates for the experts (71.867) and ordinary players (64.586) (t = 1.825, $p < .05$). The expert players also estimated that more concentration was required for shooting for position, shooting for a breakout, shooting a

TABLE 3.6
Average Scale Values for Expert and Ordinary Players for the "Fun" Variable with Behaviors from the Seemly Cluster

	Expert Class		Ordinary Class	
Rank	Behaviors	Ave. Scale Value	Behaviors	Ave. Scale Value
1.	Running the table	99.1	Making the eight ball on the break	98.0[a]
2.	Making the eight ball on the break	95.7[a]	Running the table	97.9
3.	Winning the game	95.7	Winning the game	96.3
4.	Making the eight ball	91.4[b]	Making the eight ball	95.2[b]
5.	Shooting for position	86.1[a]	Making a shot	83.2
6.	Making a shot	83.8	Shooting a massé shot	78.9
7.	Shooting a bank shot	81.7	Shooting a reverse bank shot	78.5
8.	Shooting a massé shot	81.7	Shooting a bank shot	77.6
9.	Shooting a kiss shot	80.6	Breaking opponent's ball out of a pocket	76.7
10.	Shooting a combination shot	79.9	Shooting a combination shot	75.3
11.	Shooting for a breakout	75.4	Shooting a kiss shot	74.5
12.	Breaking opponent's ball out of a pocket	73.1	Drawing the cue ball	72.5
13.	Leaving a ball sitting in (blocking) pocket	72.7	Shooting for a breakout	71.8
14.	Shooting a reverse bank shot	72.6	Shooting a cut shot	70.9
15.	Shooting a dead combination	69.0	Banking off the diamonds	70.8[a]
16.	Drawing the cue ball	66.6	Shooting for position	70.2[a]
17.	Shooting with right or left English	66.2	Shooting a dead combination	68.7
18.	Shooting a cut shot	63.8	Using low English	67.8[a]
19.	Shooting the object ball	62.4[a]	Leaving a ball sitting in (blocking) pocket	64.8
20.	Calling the pocket	60.4	Shooting with right or left English	64.3
21.	Following with the cue ball	56.9	Stopping the cue ball	61.9[a]
22.	Shooting combination off opponent's ball	56.1	Using high English	58.9
23.	Playing defense	55.7	Shooting combination off opponent's ball	51.7
24.	Using high English	55.1	Following with the cue ball	50.3
25.	Using low English	53.7[a]	Shooting softly	49.9[b]
26.	Banking off the diamonds	53.6[a]	Shooting off the rail	49.8
27.	Determining the best sequence in which to shoot remaining balls	52.6[a]	Running a ball down the rail	48.7
28.	Stopping the cue ball	51.9[a]	Playing defense	46.9
29.	Running a ball down the rail	50.9	Calling the pocket	46.4
30.	Shooting off the rail	49.2	Shooting the object ball	42.5[a]
31.	Calculating the angle on cut shots	45.0	Calculating the angle on cut shots	39.3
32.	Shooting softly	39.4[b]	Determining the best sequence in which to shoot remaining balls	30.3[a]
33.	Shooting safe	36.6	Shooting safe	24.9
34.	Choosing which of object balls (high or low) to shoot	34.3	Choosing which of object balls (high or low) to shoot	27.4
35.	Shooting with the rake	28.9[b]	Shooting with the rake	17.5[b]

[a]Significance level for the "t test" of less than .05.
[b]Significance level for the "t test" of less than .01.

TABLE 3.7
Average Scale Values for Expert and Ordinary Players for the "Concentration Experienced" Variable with Behaviors from the Seemly Cluster

	Expert Class		Ordinary Class	
Rank	Behaviors	Ave. Scale Value	Behaviors	Ave. Scale Value
1.	Making the eight ball	98.1	Running the table	90.6
2.	Running the table	97.7	Making the eight ball	90.3
3.	Shooting for position	94.8[a]	Winning the game	86.4
4.	Winning the game	91.8	Making a shot	83.2
5.	Shooting for a breakout	86.1[a]	Shooting a bank shot	78.6
6.	Shooting a combination shot	85.3[a]	Shooting a cut shot	75.7
7.	Making a shot	82.1	Shooting a combination shot	75.5[a]
8.	Shooting a bank shot	81.6	Running a ball down the rail	74.5
9.	Running a ball down the rail	80.3	Shooting for position	72.7[a]
10.	Shooting a cut shot	80.1	Shooting a reverse bank shot	70.1
11.	Shooting a kiss shot	79.4[b]	Shooting the object ball	68.8
12.	Shooting off the rail	79.3	Shooting a kiss shot	64.5[b]
13.	Shooting the object ball	77.6	Shooting with right or left English	64.5
14.	Shooting a reverse bank shot	76.9	Shooting for a breakout	64.2[a]
15.	Calculating the angle on cut shots	75.7[b]	Calculating the angle on cut shots	63.9[b]
16.	Determining the best sequence in which to shoot remaining balls	74.8[a]	Using low English	62.5
17.	Breaking the opponent's ball out of a pocket	74.6[a]	Shooting softly	61.6
18.	Shooting with right or left English	72.7	Drawing the cue ball	61.4
19.	Shooting softly	71.0	Playing defense	57.5[b]
20.	Drawing the cue ball	69.8	Using high English	57.0
21.	Shooting a dead combination	66.9[a]	Shooting off the rail	56.0
22.	Choosing which of the object balls (high or low) to shoot	63.9[a]	Determining the best sequence in which to shoot remaining balls	54.7[a]
23.	Following with the cue ball	63.6[b]	Shooting a massé shot	54.0
24.	Shooting a massé shot	60.9	Stopping the cue ball	54.0
25.	Using high English	60.3	Banking off the diamonds	53.7
26.	Using low English	59.3	Following with the cue ball	52.6[b]
27.	Shooting a combination off opponent's ball	58.2	Shooting a combination off opponent's ball	51.3
28.	Stopping the cue ball	56.7	Breaking the opponent's ball out of a pocket	48.9[a]
29.	Shooting with the rake	53.4	Shooting safe	41.7
30.	Playing defense	45.9[b]	Shooting with the rake	40.2
31.	Shooting safe	44.8	Shooting a dead combination	34.8[a]
32.	Banking off the diamonds	44.7	Choosing which of the object balls (high or low) to shoot	34.8[a]
33.	Calling the pocket	40.6[a]	Leaving ball sitting in (blocking) pocket	25.3
34.	Leaving ball sitting in (blocking) pocket	34.3	Calling the pocket	15.9[a]
35.	Making the eight ball on the break	14.2	Making the eight ball on the break	12.8

[a]Significance level for the "*t* test" of less than .05.
[b]Significance level for the "*t* test" of less than .10.

TABLE 3.8
Average Scale Values for Expert and Ordinary Players for the "Concentration Required"
Variable with Behaviors from the Seemly Cluster

	Expert Class		Ordinary Class	
Rank	Behaviors	Ave. Scale Value	Behaviors	Ave. Scale Value
1.	Running the table	96.9	Running the table	92.7
2.	Shooting for position	93.1[a]	Winning the game	90.8
3.	Winning the game	92.6	Making the eight ball	87.3
4.	Shooting for a breakout	91.8[a]	Shooting for position	82.7[a]
5.	Making the eight ball	89.8	Banking off the diamonds	79.8[b]
6.	Shooting a combination shot	88.1[a]	Shooting a combination shot	78.4[a]
7.	Shooting a massé shot	86.3[a]	Shooting a bank shot	76.3
8.	Shooting a kiss shot	85.4[a]	Running a ball down the rail	75.8
9.	Shooting a bank shot	82.6	Shooting a cut shot	75.3
10.	Determining best sequence in which to shoot remaining balls	80.0[a]	Shooting a kiss shot	74.9[a]
11.	Breaking opponent's ball out of a pocket	79.2[a]	Shooting for a breakout	71.5[a]
12.	Shooting a reverse bank shot	78.3	Making a shot	70.7
13.	Running a ball down the rail	78.2	Shooting with right or left English	69.7
14.	Shooting with the rake	77.0[a]	Shooting a reverse bank shot	69.8
15.	Making a shot	76.3	Shooting the object ball	69.1
16.	Calculating the angle on cut shots	76.0[b]	Shooting a massé	69.0[a]
17.	shooting with right or left English	75.9	Calculating the angle on cut shots	64.8[b]
18.	Drawing the cue ball	75.4[a]	Breaking opponent's ball out of a pocket	64.4[a]
19.	Shooting combination off opponent's ball	75.2[a]	Using high English	63.9
20.	Shooting a cut shot	73.0	Playing defense	63.9
21.	Shooting the object ball	72.8	Drawing the cue ball	62.8[a]
22.	Shooting off the rail	71.6[a]	Stopping the cue ball	62.3
23.	Banking off the diamonds	66.3[b]	Using low English	62.1
24.	Using low English	65.9	Shooting softly	62.0
25.	Following with the cue ball	65.6	Shooting combination off opponent's ball	60.9[a]
26.	Choosing which of the object balls (high or low) to shoot	65.6[a]	Shooting with the rake	60.3[a]
27.	Shooting softly	64.8	Shooting safe	59.9
28.	Playing defense	64.3	Following with the cue ball	58.4
29.	Using high English	62.0	Shooting off the rail	58.0[a]
30.	Stopping the cue ball	61.6	Determining best sequence in which to shoot remaining balls	54.8[a]
31.	Shooting safe	61.4	Shooting a dead combination	43.8[a]
32.	Shooting a dead combination	61.2[a]	Leaving ball sitting in (blocking) pocket	39.8
33.	Leaving ball sitting in (blocking) pocket	37.4	Choosing which of the object balls (high or low) to shoot	35.8[a]
34.	Calling the pocket	25.0	Making the eight ball on the break	26.9
35.	Making the eight ball on the break	18.7	Calling the pocket	22.2

[a]Significance level for the "*t* test" of less than .05. [b]Significance level for the "*t* test" of less than .10.

combination shot, shooting a massé shot, shooting a kiss shot, determining best sequence in which to shoot remaining balls, breaking opponent's ball out of a pocket, shooting with the rake, drawing the cue ball, shooting combination off opponent's ball, shooting off the rail, choosing which of the object balls (high or low) to shoot, and shooting a dead combination than did the ordinary players, and, directionally, calculating the angle on cut shots, but the ordinary players thought that, directionally, banking off the diamonds required more concentration. The general import of these findings is to show that the experts considered concentration more salient in their game playing than did the ordinary players.

The differences between the experts and the ordinary players can be considered in yet another way. The 35 behaviors in the seemly cluster differed in the degree to which they emphasized strategy and physical skill: 11 were judged high in strategy and low in physical skill [playing defense, leaving ball sitting in (blocking) pocket, determining best sequence in which to shoot remaining balls, choosing which of the object balls (high or low) to shoot, calculating the angle on cut shots, calling the pocket, shooting a dead combination, shooting for position, shooting for a breakout, shooting softly, and shooting safe]; 13 were judged medium in strategy and medium in physical skill (shooting combination off opponent's ball, shooting with right or left "English," drawing the cue ball, breaking the opponent's ball out of a pocket, shooting a combination shot, using low "English," running the table, winning the game, making the eight ball on the break, banking off the diamonds, shooting a kiss shot, stopping the cue ball, and following with the cue ball); and 11 were judged to be low in strategy and high in physical skill (making the eight ball, making a shot, using high "English," running a ball down the rail, shooting a cut shot, shooting the object ball, shooting with the rake, and shooting off the rail).

Table 3.9 gives the averages of the behaviors for the experts and the ordinary players for fun in the three categories. Table 3.10 gives the two-way analysis of variance. Note that there is no significant difference between the two sets of players when it comes to fun, but that the category of behaviors judged as medium in strategy and medium in physical skill was the highest in fun and the category of behaviors judged high in strategy and low in physical skill was the lowest.

With the concentration-experienced variable, however, there was a significant difference between the experts and the ordinary players and there were significant differences among the groups of behaviors (cf. Tables 3.11 and 3.12). The behaviors that were low in strategy and high in physical skill provided the most concentration and those that were high in strategy and low in physical skill provided the least. The estimate of concentration required presented a picture similar to that provided by the concentration experienced variable. There was a directional difference between the experts and the ordinary players and the same sort of relationship among the groups of behaviors.

TABLE 3.9

Average Fun for Behaviors Ordered on the Basis of Relative
Amounts of Physical Skill and Strategy Present

Behaviors	Expert	Ordinary	Total
Low strategy, high physical skill	65.6	63.8	64.6
Medium strategy medium physical skill	71.5	73.7	72.7
High strategy, high physical skill	57.0	49.2	52.7
Total	64.7	62.2	

TABLE 3.10

Two-Way Analysis of Variance of Fun for the Relative Amounts
of Strategy and Physical Skill Present in Behaviors
(High, Medium, and Low) by Player Expertise

Source of Variance	SS	df	ms	F	p
A (Degree of strategy)	4540.332	2	2270.166	6.814	.005
B (Expert and ordinary)	106.789	1	106.789	0.321	n.s.
A × B	304.579	2	152.289	0.457	n.s.
Residual (error)	21323.208	64	333.175		

TABLE 3.11

Average Concentration Experienced for Behaviors
Ordered on the Basis of Relative Amounts of
Physical Skill and Strategy Present

Behaviors	Expert	Ordinary	Total
Low strategy, high physical skill	75.5	68.0	71.4
Medium strategy, medium physical skill	66.8	59.9	63.0
High strategy, low physical skill	63.5	47.9	54.9
Total	68.6	58.6	

TABLE 3.12

Two-Way Analysis of Variance of Concentration Experienced for the
Relative Amounts of Strategy and Physical Skill Present in Behaviors
(High, Medium, and Low) by Player Expertise

Source of Variance	SS	df	ms	F	p
A (Degree of strategy)	2837.490	2	1418.745	4.288	.025
B (Expert and ordinary)	1734.624	1	1734.624	5.242	.05
A × B	270.028	2	135.014	0.408	n.s.
Residual (error)	21177.646	64	330.901		

The seemly cluster presented in Fig. 3.1 is further subdivided into four
clusters—standard shots, cue ball control, strategic moves, and game winning
behaviors. Similar clusters are represented in the two-dimensional plot of the
space defined by dimension I and dimension II (see Fig. 3.3). The standard
shot group is found in the area defined by the negative scores for both the
mastery dimension (I) and the strategic dimension (II). The cue ball control
group is found in the quadrant defined by the negative scores on the mastery
dimension and on the strategic dimension. The strategic moves group is found
in the quadrant defined by the positive scores on the mastery dimension and
by negative scores on the strategic dimension. Finally, the game winning
group is found in the quadrant defined by positive scores on both the mastery
and the strategic dimensions.

These four groups were considered in terms of the fun, concentration-
experienced, and concentration-required variables. Tables 3.13 and 3.14
show that there is no significant difference between the experts and the
ordinary players for the fun variable as far as the two-way analysis of variance
is concerned, but that there are significant differences for the groups of
behaviors. the game winning behaviors were the most fun and the strategic
moves were the least. The standard shots and the cue ball control behaviors
were intermediate.

TABLE 3.13

Average Fun Experienced for Behaviors Found
in Four Subclusters

Subcluster	Experts	Ordinary	Total
Win	87.7	86.2	86.8
Shot	62.4	60.5	61.4
Cue ball control	58.9	63.1	61.2
Strategy	59.0	50.3	54.2
Total	67.0	65.0	

TABLE 3.14
Two-Way Analysis of Variance of Fun for Four Subclusters
(Shot Cluster, Cue Ball Control Cluster,
Strategy Cluster, and Win Cluster) by Player Expertise

Source of Variance	SS	df	ms	F	p
A (Subclusters)	8176.250	3	2725.417	9.582	.001
B (Expert and ordinary)	66.284	1	66.284	0.233	n.s.
A × B	357.448	3	119.149	0.419	n.s.
Residual (error)	17634.420	62	284.426		

The two-way analysis of variance for the concentration-experienced variable failed to show differences among the groups, but there was a directional difference between the experts and the ordinary players with the experts displaying more concentration for each group. The two-way analysis of variable yielded no significant results for the concentration-required variable.

The foregoing treatment has dealt with the eight ball behavioral space. This space has been described in terms of hierarchical clusters, multidimensional scaling solutions, and attitudes toward fun and concentration displayed by expert and ordinary players.

DISCUSSION

The investigation reported here must be regarded as small scale, exploratory research. This is unfortunate for the complexities of Butler County eight ball merit a monograph rather than a single chapter. Perhaps more can be done in the future.

The exploratory nature of this research was dictated by the total absence of research funds and by the fact that much of the inquiry led into uncharted territory. It is at precisely this stage in anthropological research when the best use can be made of informed judges, certainly heavy reliance was placed on such judges in the selection of the 60 behaviors to be considered in detail, in the choice of the attitudinal variables of fun, concentration broken, and concentration experienced, in the identification of the nine expert players and of the 11 ordinary players, in the coding of the 35 behaviors from the seemly cluster on the basis of relative amounts of physical skill and strategy, and in the interpretation of some of the results. It is doubtful if any interpretation could have been made of dimensions and clusters if an informed judge had not been available. The use of quantitative techniques developed the need for more ethnographic information of a traditional sort rather than less. In this research, informed judges were indispensable.

It is true, of course, that the ethnography of the Monday Night Pool League has interest for students of American popular culture. Space did not permit a full ethnographic statement on the League. Perhaps this will be possible at a later date because relatively little is known of the rural or small town beer tavern and its place in the expressive life of its patrons.

Turning now to eight ball itself, the basic clustering solution is the foundation for the description offered here. If the instrumental cluster is ignored as not pertaining to the direct play of the game two main clusters remain, the unseemly and seemly clusters. Here, at least, there seems to be fundamental opposition between things to go right and things that go wrong, an opposition that probably exists not only in other games, but in other cultural patterns yielding outcomes that can be judged as being good or bad. This opposition may represent an important structural principle.

The dimensions of the unseemly and seemly clusters are also descriptively important. The force, error class, and seriousness dimensions of the unseemly cluster seem to have generality, for most gamesters can see that unseemly behaviors can range from the physical to the mental (force), from the certain to the possible or probable (error), and from the inconsequential to the consequential (seriousness). These dimensions seem solidly grounded in ethnographic experience and an on-going study of women's tennis has yielded a similar error space. Perhaps, other studies of women's field hockey and men's soccer will do the same. In some respects, these dimensions may be quite specific to Butler County eight ball, but this can only be determined through comparative research.

The dimensions for the seemly cluster may be less general. The mastery, strategy, and choice dimensions seem appropriate for game research, but they were not recognized by informed judges as being "right" to the same degree as were the clusters or the dimensions of the unseemly group. Actually, the use of a five dimensional solution was considered, for it had a lower stress value and the two additional dimensions, auxilliary command of the table and location, were interpretable, but this solution was finally rejected because informed judges considered it to be more uncertain than the three-dimensional solution. Once again, it will be interesting to see whether or not a mastery dimension (fine-grained to general), a strategic dimension (offense to defense), and a choice dimension (forced choice to optional choice) appear in the studies of tennis, volleyball, and field hockey that are currently in progress.

Five attitudinal variables were used with the behaviors in the seemly and unseemly clusters. For the unseemly cluster, it was evident that the behaviors varied in the degree to which they contributed to broken concentration for the experts and the ordinary players. The ordinary players found a number of behaviors to be more disturbing than did the experts.

Some of the unseemly behaviors, such as making a slop shot, shooting hard, and blasting, appeared to be genuine fun for both the experts and the ordinary players, but even the other behaviors could be ranked in terms of the degree to which they are fun. This fun with error may be an important dynamic in the learning of the game, since it is somewhat contradictory to have unseemly play rewarded by fun. In other games, too, some errors are fun.

For the seemly cluster the estimate of the concentration needed or required for a behavior produced results that were largely congruent with the report on the concentration experienced for each behavior. The experts and ordinary players differed most with this variable not only in terms of the report of concentration experienced for particular behaviors, but also in the overall amount of concentration experienced. It would appear that the experts were more likely to experience concentration and that they were less likely to have their concentration broken.

There was, however, less difference between the experts and the ordinary players when it came to the experience of fun. Physical skill behaviors that included some strategy seemed to be the most fun and physical skill behaviors seemed to require the most concentration. Although the experts were more aware of the strategic aspects of the game than were the ordinary players, they still found the strategic behaviors to be less fun and less demanding of concentration. The emphasis in eight ball is on physical skill.

Finally, one question can be raised about the ways in which ordinary players become experts. If we assume that the ordinary players represent one stage of development and the experts another, it can be seen that although the pattern of fun changes somewhat for the experts, the dramatic change occurs in the area of concentration. The experts must develop more concentration and more of an ability to sustain concentration. Or, alternatively, as they progress in the game, only those ordinary players who have these concentrational abilities become experts. Of course, some players must fall in between. Do the experts become expert through learning or are they self-selected on the basis of their abilities or both? This problem must be faced in future research.

The fact that experts appear to have different cognitive maps of the game than ordinary players has general anthropological implications. Such differences raise the problems of sampling for some cultural patterns since only experts can give the most advanced, technical, or developed view of the pattern. The view of the ordinary participant, of course, is important too, particulary if there is mass involvement in the pattern.

The analysis presented here adds descriptive depth to our knowledge of eight ball, but it is still incomplete and static. More must be done with actual play and studies of other games now in progress may improve on this approach.

ACKNOWLEDGMENTS

The research reported in this chapter was unfunded, so the provision of computer time by the University of Pittsburgh is greatly appreciated by the authors. The authors are also grateful to Roy G. D'Andrade, Allen L. Tan, Richard Scaglion, Randall J. Kendis, Alan T. Cypher, Leslie H. Passarelli, the members of the Monday Night Pool League and the tavern owners who cooperated in the study.

REFERENCE NOTES

1. Roberts, J. M., Skoner, M., & Hogner, R. H. Working behaviors for obstetrical nurses. Unpublished manuscript.
2. Kruskal, J. B., Young, F. W., & Seery, J. B. How to use KYST, a very flexible program to do multidimensional scaling and unfolding. Unpublished manuscript. Bell Telephone Laboratories, 1973.

REFERENCES

Barry, H., III, & Roberts, J. M. Infant socialization and games of chance. *Ethnology*, 1972, *11*, 296 308.

D'Andrade, R. G. U-statistic hierarchical clustering. *Psychometrika*, 1978, *43*, 59–67.

Fels, G. *Mastering pool.* Chicago: Contemporary Books, Inc., 1977.

Lenneberg, E. H., & Roberts, J. M. The language of experience: A study in methodology. Memoir 13, *International Journal of American Linguistics*. Bloomington: Indiana University Publications in Anthropology and Linguistics, 1956.

Roberts, J. M., Arth, M. J., & Bush, R. R. Games in culture. *American Anthropologist*, 1959, *61*, 597–605.

Roberts, J. M., & Barry, H., III. Inculcated traits and game-type combinations: A cross-cultural view. T. T. Craig (Ed.), *The humanistic and mental health aspects of sports, exercise and recreation.* Chicago: Amer. Medical Assoc., 1976.

Roberts, J. M., & Forman, M. L. Riddles: Expressive models of interrogation. *Ethnology*, 1971, *10*, 509–533.

Roberts, J. M., Hoffman, H., & Sutton-Smith, B. Pattern and competence: A consideration of tick, tack, toe. *El Palacio*, 1965, *72*, 17–30.

Roberts, J. M., & Koenig, F. Focused and distributed status affinity. *Sociological Quarterly*, 1968, *9*, 150–157.

Roberts, J. M., Koenig, F., & Stark, R. B. Judged display: A consideration of a craft show. *Journal of Leisure Research*, 1969, *1*, 163–179.

Roberts, J. M., & Kundrat, D. F. Variation in expressive balances and competence for sports car rally teams. *Urban Life*, 1978, *7*, 231–251; 275–280.

Roberts, J. M., Meeker, Q. S., & Aller, J. Action styles and management game performance: An exploratory consideration. *Naval War College Review*, 1972, *24* (10), 65–81.

Roberts, J. M., Strand, R. F., & Burmeister, E. Preferential pattern analysis. In P. Kay (Ed.), *Explorations in mathematical anthropology.* Cambridge: M.I.T. Press, 1971.

Roberts, J. M., & Sutton-Smith, B. Child training and game involvement. *Ethnology*, 1962, *1*, 166–185.

Roberts, J. M., & Sutton-Smith, B. Cross-cultural correlates of games of chance. *Behavior Science Notes*, 1966, *1*, 131–144.

Roberts, J. M., Sutton-Smith, B., & Kendon, A. Strategy in games and folk tales. *Journal of Social Psychology*, 1963, *61*, 185–199.

Romney, A. K., Shepard, N., & Nerlove, S. B. (Eds.). *Multidimensional scaling: Theory and applications in the behavioral sciences.* N.Y.: Seminar Press 1972.

Sutton-Smith, B., & Roberts, J. M. Rubrics of competitive behavior. *Journal of Genetic Psychology*, 1964, *105*, 13–37.

Sutton-Smith, B., & Roberts, J. M. Studies of an elementary game of strategy. *Genetic Psychology Monographs*, 1967, *75*, 3–42.

Sutton-Smith, B., & Roberts, J. M. The cross-cultural and psychological study of games. In G. Luschen (Ed.), *The cross-cultural analysis of sport and games.* Champaign, Ill.: Stipes, 1970.

Sutton-Smith, B., Roberts, J. M., & Kozelka, R. M. Game involvement in adults. *Journal of Social Psychology*, 1963, *60*, 15–30.

4 Personality Change in the American Sport Scene

Thomas A. Tutko
San Jose State University

INTRODUCTION

The growing significance of athletics in this country has reached staggering proportions. Attendance figures at athletic contests reach new highs, leagues are expanding with franchises in every corner of the country, new leagues are formed and although some fail, surviving teams from bankrupt leagues join the old and established groups. Sports previously thought to be foreign, such as soccer, are slowly but surely becoming part of the American scene.

These are not the only signs of the growing prominence of athletics. Within each major sport, the seasons have grown longer and there are more "exhibition" games than ever before. In professional football, for example, training camp begins in July and the final game, the Super Bowl, is in January, a period of 7 months. Professional basketball begins in September and the final play-off games continue as long as June, a remarkable period of 10 months. There are periods during the year when professional baseball, football, basketball and hockey are being played simultaneously. This is not to mention golf, tennis and several other sports also being played at the same time.

THOMAS A. TUTKO is Professor of Psychology in the Department of Psychology at San Jose State University. He has been a consultant to numerous professional and amateur sports teams and is author of a number of books on psychology and sports, among them *SportsPsyching, The Psychology of Coaching,* and, with Bruce Ogilvie, *Problem Athletes and How to Handle Them.*

A true sports fan can spend every hour of the waking day keeping track of the various teams and the thousands of athletes involved. At the same time this craze is taking place in professional athletics, it is being matched, if not superseded, by the fanaticism on the college level. The collegiate system is so close to the professionals that the average person can barely determine the difference between the two.

As a further testimony to sports popularity and importance, one need only refer to the proliferation of books, magazines, length of sports pages and sports news to get a feel for the emotional impact of the jock world. Political figures, including presidents, senators, congresspersons, etc., are frequent visitors to the athletic scene and the political expediency of being a fan can never be underestimated. In his book, *Fans: How We Go Crazy Over Sports,* Michael Roberts (1976) points out that political favors as well as decisions are made as a result of athletic influence

Television time has grown steadily to the point that weekends, during playoffs and championships, and weekdays have become dominated by a smorgasbord of jock activity. As if current contests aren't enough, we have replays, reviews, and reliving of old events—the great moments in sports. The Super Bowl attracts over 90 million people annually and has become an American holiday. What is ironic is that it takes 2 weeks' preparation for approximately 5 minutes of action. Monday night football has become our new religion. If as many people attended church on Sunday as watched football on Monday evening, the clergy would believe that a miracle had occurred and that we all might be "saved." If the parishoners at Sunday services demonstrated the same enthusiasm, dedication, loyalty and hope as Monday night football, the clergy would be right.

Many see athletic events and sports contests as the backbone of America and that what we see displayed on the playing field stands for, and represents all of the virtuous characteristics that make this country great. In a philosophical sense the sporting scene does represent a slice of this country's culture. If it didn't, it could not survive, let alone thrive, in this nation. But there can be another view of athletics. Some contend that it is a growing monster, leaving in its path physical, economic and psychological destruction and that the values being displayed and practiced have little redeeming features.

Looking at these two views we might say that investigating the sports scene is like evaluating a manure pile. You can either see it as a waste—something to be discarded because it is messy and basically just stinks. Or you can view it as a fertilizer, a source from which great things may grow. The purpose of this chapter is to present a position that explores both sides from a social as well as clinical psychological viewpoint. Perhaps both sides have something important to say.

WHAT WE BELIEVE ABOUT ATHLETICS—
THE HALO AND HEAVEN

There is a long-standing belief in this country that sports builds character. A comparison has often been made between the athletic field and the battlefield. Because as a nation we have never "lost" a war, the assumption is made that our successes on the battlefield have grown out of our successes on the playing field. We further assume that the athletic field is directly responsible and that all things attained from athletics are good for growth and development. Sports are supposed to bring out the "best" in us.

There can be little doubt that the athletic area has become a center for taking care of our emotional needs. We participate in and are spectators of the emotional charge. If athletics did not provide the excitement it would be gone in a short period. We look forward to indulging in the "joys" of victory but all too often steep in the "agony" of defeat. Without that occasional emotional charge, life would be a little bit duller—a little bit less "alive" and perhaps even have less meaning.

To this emotional charge we respond in various ways. The behavior we see during the excitement becomes tied to all types of "courageous" as well as "cowardly" behavior. During the emotional high of a contest, athletes may perform far beyond their usual expectations while others suddenly fall below their usual game. The emotion tied to the game produces not only unexpected circumstances but unexpected behaviors. For this reason sports carry an immense appeal. No two contests can ever be repeated exactly and we are constantly expecting the unexpected (as contradictory as that may sound).

It is usually the winner that gets the attention and becomes the center of focus. Whatever he or she does or says becomes our model and these descriptions are frequently on a personal psychological level. Although we may admire and respect talent, our personal opinion of the winner becomes, in our mind, the reason the winners are able to manifest their talent.

Another assumption that we make is that to be a winner you have to be a "good" guy. In all of our folklore it is always the "clean cut," wholesome American kid who finally comes through in the end. We cannot conceive of a "bad" guy, a S. O. B., being a winner. Somehow that picture, that image, destroys our illusions. In order to keep the picture complete and in line with mythology, the winners can only be good. By the same token, losers must be "bad." They must be tainted in some way or have some flaw that keeps them from attaining the Holy Grail (otherwise known as the Stanley Cup or the Super Bowl Trophy). We cannot think that a team or player can be corrupt or dirty and God knows we cannot even entertain the thought that accepted behavior within some sports may be corrupt or destructive.

And so we devise terms to describe our heroes and heroines and place them on pedestals so they may act as models. We develop a whole new jock vocabulary that incorporates all of the cultural values. We then point out how these values are crystallized in sports. Our winning athletes are courageous, loyal, competitive, dedicated, fierce, determined, aggressive, team persons, tough-minded, psyched-up, motivated, etc. Not only that, they give 110%, they never say die, play with pain, or give till it hurts. Winning athletes are a cross between Superman, the Bionic Man and the Boy Scout Oath. These simple one-word descriptions are fortified with locker rooms filled with slogans that further describe the winner. We all know that "winners never quit and quitters never win," and Leo Durocher's expression that went something like, "You show me a good loser and I'll show you a real loser." Perhaps the two most famous of the expressions came from leaders of this country. Richard Nixon had on his desk the old favorite, "When the going gets tough, the tough get going," and, of course, there is always Vince Lombardi's dictum, "Winning isn't everything—it's the only thing."

As if this were not enough of a reminder, we develop nicknames for teams and players to remind us of the psychological dimensions. We have Minnesota's "Purple People Eaters," the Los Angeles Rams' "Fearsome Foursome" and the Cincinnati's "Big Red Machine." We have "Mean Joe" Green, "Hustlin' Pete Rose" and in addition we have hundreds of pro, college, and high school teams with animal and mythical names that indicate strength, fierceness, quickness, etc.

Descriptions of contests in newspapers and magazines remind us of the emotional and personal element in the game. "Reds blast Padres," "Colts manhandle Seahawks," "Bullets outhussle Hawks," etc., are all sports headlines that reawaken us for a brief moment to the feeling tone and the emotional characteristics of the game.

Perhaps the greatest belief that sports build character comes from two other sources. One is our personal encounters with athletics and the second is the observation of contests where we have been able to witness exceptional performances.

Anyone who has had the opportunity to participate in an athletic contest, and most of us have, knows the joy of participation. There is the emotional response of being able to cope with it or finding yourself being overcome by it. Many aspects of our personal identity have been involved. Moreover, most of us have had the experience of success if only to a slight degree. The tie shot that went well, scoring a basket or getting a base hit, all of these experiences provide us with a temporary sense of identity and of well being. At times it gives us temporary fulfillment. In many instances we find ourselves responding in ways that may even shock us. We may jump up and down with joy at a hit, argue with the umpire over a "bad" call, disagree with an opponent on the legality or illegality of a play. The game awakens in us some

dormant aspect of our personality that the dullness of normal everyday life tends to gloss over or make little use of.

The surprising part about athletics is that it excites our dominant personality features. Our personality traits become more apparent to ourselves and others. At times we may be embarrassed, at other times we are shocked and maybe even proud of the ways we handled ourselves. When we see an athletic contest we are able to see in the performer certain characteristics that are a reminder of trials, tribulations and pressures that we have. Because of our experiences we are able to empathize with this position. The athlete (or team) and ourselves become one. To see a performance where the athlete does well is tied to the "good" feeling inside of us—that feeling of trying and doing well. We assume that the good feeling is tied to all of the positive characteristics that make up character.

We have read about, heard about, or seen heroic performances that serve as an inspiration. Examples are endless like athletes playing in extreme pain, the "washed out" athlete who makes a comeback, an underdog who overcomes the extreme odds and produces an upset. These incidents, however remote, rare, and statistically improbable as they may be, are displayed as reminders of the Horatio Alger effect that sports can produce. As the old saying goes, "The game isn't over until the last man is out."

These spectacular performances are tied to ambition, hard work, dedication, assertiveness, handling pressure, etc. How then can anything be bad about sports and athletics? They can only hold the highest values.

WHAT WE SEE IN ATHLETICS— THE HARASSMENT AND HELL

Despite the fact that we continuously toss around platitudes and praise the godly merits of athletics, the average person, even the avid sports enthusiast, cannot help but feel all is not well in athletics. Something seems wrong. Players jump from team to team becoming instant millionaires. From one year to another it becomes difficult to have a predictable lineup on the field. Managers and coaches are fired almost in routine fashion and at times without apparent logic; some, in fact, after having winning, and, in some cases, championship seasons. Players are battling owners and managers, let alone opponents. In one case a player "punched out" his manager.

The description does not seem to stop there. There are countless cases of all sorts including violence in hockey, breaking of contracts, suits involving accusations that there is a criminal element in sports, etc. Fans are rioting in Cleveland and in New York, players are being hit by cups of beer in Boston and officials are being hit by whiskey bottles in Bloomington, Minnesota. Owners are thought to be crazy for paying ludicrous sums of money for free agents and commissioners are being condemned for not being strong enough

to keep order in this "zoo." One wonders whether sports are building character or developing "characters." One cannot help but wonder what has happened in athletics. How can an area generally considered one that produces character as well as serves as a source of entertainment and recreation become a battlefield?

In their book entitled *Winning Is Everything and Other American Myths,* Tutko and Bruns (1976) point out that there has been a change in philosophy from, "It is not whether you win or lose but how you play the game," to the present mania of, "Winning is the only thing." Although the latter philosophy may ostensibly encompass all of the American values, it has some inherent drawbacks. For one thing, this approach tends to proliferate losers. In a league of four, there are three losers, one winner; in a league of eight, seven to one, and in the NFL—28 teams, 27 losers, and one winner.

When you put together 28 highly talented competitive teams and eventually boil it down to one winner symptoms are bound to emerge. There is an old theory in psychology called the frustration–aggression hypothesis. Although the theory has had some questionable validity, it does, nonetheless, have application here. The 27 losers in the NFL (and it must be remembered this group is being used as an example), have to have some form of recognition, some form of identity, some way of either making it to the top or being a winner in some way. The disruptive behaviors we see on the sports pages each day are really symptoms–reactions to frustration that highly competitive people feel. Tutko and Bruns point out the major symptoms that emerge in such an environment. For the purposes of this chapter, we briefly describe the destructive behavior in athletics—those characteristics that do not build character.

The first of these is the aggressiveness and violence we witness. Although one can accept the assertiveness required in a game—whether it is hard tackling or body checking or screening—it becomes a different dimension when the goal is to intentionally hurt or intimidate someone. The amount of violence in athletics has become so common that in some areas, such as hockey, it has become part of the coaching philosophy. One intentionally tries to put the other guy out of commission.

The natural result of over aggressiveness and violence is an increase in injuries. In their book, Tutko and Bruns dedicate one full chapter to injuries in various sports. As an example, over one-half of all high school football players in the state of North Carolina were injured enough to be out of at least two games in a season; 100,000 boys develop chronic elbow strain in a single year in Little League baseball and in a study done in Southern California all Little League pitchers who have pitched for 2 or more years regularly had elbow damage. There are unique and frequent injuries in Youth Football, ice hockey, swimming, gymnastics and baseball.

Drugs have become one of the more subtle symptoms of the sports scene. They can be used to hype up, put on bulk, calm down, face an over-zealous opponent, or just get away from it all. In his book, *North Dallas Forty,* Pete Gent (1973) gives one an insight into not only the frequent usage but also the massive reliance on the elixirs used to cope with the stress of athletics.

Neurotic behavior has become an everyday acceptable part of athletic viewing. Athletes literally work all year round to the point of working themselves into poor condition. Playing with pain has become more than something one discusses, it has become an expectation. Rarely do professional athletes become fully healed before going back into full competition. In a sense it is absurd to ignore nature's way of telling when something is wrong. The fear of losing, the fear of being demoted, the fear of being left out, are all incentives to play with pain and ignore nature's signs that one may be harming oneself.

As the emphasis on winning has become intensified, our view on what it takes to be a winner has changed. The heavy emphasis on recruiting, particularly on a college level, has led to massive lying and cheating not only to prospective athletes but to colleagues, other colleges, and anyone else who might question. Honest recruiting is not only ineffective, it is seen as naive. Lying and cheating become models for young athletes along with egocentrism, greed, disloyalty and inability to handle defeat. Immature behavior is the standard and all of those virtuous characteristics previously thought to be emerging from athletes seem in fact to be quite the reverse—at least in the present competitive format.

Here, then, are the two positions on athletics—one espousing the merits of athletic competition and eventual long range benefits and the other pointing out the destruction of values and the moral decay emerging.

It is apparent that each one sees athletics through one's own bias. If two people viewing the same behavior have different reference points, they tend to see the behavior in line with their own belief system. Thus a smashing tackle in football can be seen as a competitive assertive move, behavior related to a trait that will serve as a benefit to the athlete later in life. It also fits into the rugged individualism of the American idea—"the basis on which this country was founded." On the other hand, it can be seen as brutal and destructive, undermining the possibility of a cooperative effort by being bullish and destructive.

We end up with different names for the behaviors. Unfortunately, because the sports scene has become more intense and winning has become our prime target, many behaviors that are socially unacceptable are given socially acceptable titles to justify their existence. The same tackle mentioned previously should injure or at least intimidate the opponent because it puts us in the winner's circle.

We can devise socially acceptable titles for behaviors that can be destructive, almost pathological in nature. Let us consider some commonly accepted values and how they may be distorted in order to produce winning. As long as one is successful we can make all kinds of excuses for one's behavior. Let us consider first the more commonly accepted characteristics related to winning—the characteristics that supposedly lead to success, not just as in athletics but later in life as well:

Ambition—the desire to be on top, to be number one, to be the very best; the setting of successful goals and attaining them; to be the best in your field; to reach for maximum potential; to reach perfection.

Determination—the willingness to work hard to fulfull one's goals; to put in the time and effort necessary to reach these goals rather than give up or quit without reaching one's best.

Dedication—to become committed to some goal; to find an aim or purpose where one may manifest one's talent; to become committed to a purpose.

Assertiveness—ability to defend oneself, to stick up for oneself; to make things happen rather than wait for them to happen; to expand the personal domain.

Leadership—to assume responsibility for others and work with them to develop their talents as well as one's own; to help the team reach its maximum potential.

Respect for authority—trainable—the willingness to learn from others more knowledgeable; to try new and different ideas; to attempt new systems and expand one's knowledge; to work with authorities in an harmonious relationship.

Handling pressure—to be calm and think clearly as well as plan effectively in the face of threat, frustration, conflict and danger; to turn an anxious situation into a productive situation.

Mental toughness—to handle setbacks; to learn to face defeat—learn from it and ultimately turn it to advantage; to learn from failure in order to become more successful.

Cooperation—to work with others toward a larger goal—something bigger than individual personal needs; to learn sacrifice and appreciate contribution to a larger group.

Confidence—to develop faith and belief in oneself and one's abilities; to test one's limits and learn to play continually near one's maximum potential.

One can hardly disagree with these characteristics. Although there may seem to be an overlap, for the most part, they describe the ideal from a competitive standpoint. Although they may read like a page from the *"Goodie-Goodie Two Shoes Handbook,"* they do represent a positive approach toward fulfilling one's life. If these were being demonstrated and practiced in athletics, one could hardly doubt their positive influence.

The paradox of the situation is that it is commonly felt that if we win we are ambitious, determined, dedicated, assertive, etc., and this in turn will assure us of success in other aspects of life. Once again we use anecdotal data and personal testimonies of a small few as justification for the many. What is really happening in many instances is that a different set of behaviors is being practiced, some opposite to the socially acceptable ones but we need to see these characteristics in socially acceptable ways. Let us use the same label as was previously mentioned but now describe the common behaviors that accompany these. Perhaps we may be able to see the distortion.

Ambition—to be continually dissatisfied unless you are on top, the best— unbeatable. When you reach the top, not to be satisfied until you've built a dynasty and set higher standards so you are beating people by higher scores. In essence, never feel happy and content where you are but be obsessed with where you should be—perfect. As one coach put it, "It's not just that I have to win but I have to see the other guy lose."

Determination—work continually as long, as hard, and as miserably as possible otherwise you should feel that it is of no value. Never take any breaks otherwise you should feel you are "goofing" off. Pain should be an incentive to drive yourself harder. Pain, torture, and agony should be constant companions. Never feel you are putting in enough time unless you are completely miserable. No matter how hard you have worked, if you don't win you haven't worked hard enough.

Dedication—you should have a single, narrow-minded aim in your life and that is, being number one. To try to be a rounded individual, one with numerous interests, is detracting from your main purpose in your life—your sport. Your life has one purpose and all your efforts should go in that direction. You will sacrifice anything and anyone in order to reach the top and use any moral code to get there.

Assertiveness—you must learn to be assertive to the point of being destructive, even violent if necessary. If people accuse you of being mean, point out to them that you hate to lose. View everything in athletics as a dog- eat-dog world. If you don't get him first and put him away, he'll do it to you. Learn to intimidate—there is an advantage in having the opponent fear you, especially if he has more talent. If it involves hurting the other guy, that's the name of the game. He'd do it to you.

Leadership—power over others is important. If they don't listen to you— out they go. Take charge, tell others what to do, eliminate the rebels and have others completely subservient. The only way things work is when people do what they are told and shut up. A democratic approach is a sign of disrespect to the coach's authority. Besides, it is not expedient. Anyone who can't get others to follow this way is weak.

Respect for authority—trainable—winning is the only criterion for respect. If authorities can't help you win you don't have to pay attention because they

probably don't know what they're talking about anyway. If the authorities aren't winners you're better off by yourself or rebelling. If the authorities are winners, imitate them completely. Don't try to do your own thinking but be completely dedicated to the winning authority. Try to copy all that the winning authority says and does, because that is obviously the way to do it. Never respect officials since they are not really authorities. Treat them as if they are wrong and against you.

Handling pressure—if you don't win you can't handle pressure—regardless of the type. You're a flake because you blow the big ones or fold in the clutch or shy away from the tough ones. Only winners are able to win the big ones—the rest are flakes. It is okay to throw temper tantrums, destroy equipment, demean others as long as it helps you reduce your own tension and eventually win. You can manifest immature behavior as long as you are successful.

Mental toughness—nothing is of value in a loss. "Losing is worse than dying because you have to live with losing." Anyone who loses obviously has not put it all together and is too sensitive. You've got to be thick skinned and not let anything bother you. You should never take pride in a loss, regardless of the circumstances. You should be self punishing and feel badly when losing. Do not forgive yourself until you win. When you get a chance to return the loss make it more than you lost by. Never admit a loss—find some excuse or scapegoat.

Cooperation—you come first. You cooperate only when it is to your benefit. You owe no allegiance to anyone. Once you're out there you're on your own. You're number one and you play for yourself otherwise how are the scouts going to see you to give you a scholarship? If you don't consider yourself, how else are you going to sign a gigantic contract? You're only number one when you get the most—this way everyone knows.

Confidence—no matter how good you are or how good your ability is, if you aren't winning you aren't confident enough. What's more if you aren't winning, you have no right to feel confident, in fact, if you are losing you should be losing your confidence as well. If you win you should not only be confident but cocky as well. You should always believe you are going to win no matter how much larger or bigger or more talented your opponent may be. If you're confident you don't need anyone.

The descriptions have been exaggerated to make a point, however, many responses in this latter list have not only been tolerated and justified but exemplified as "the way" a competitor acts. We can rationalize and justify almost any behavior in the guise of winning. It is unfortunate that many of the behaviors described in the latter traits have been viewed by most of us as traits or characteristics of a winner. By giving them socially acceptable titles we dupe ourselves into believing they are positive characteristics, ones that will leave a personal, fulfilling effect. They are, in fact, personally destructive,

whatever the label. Not only are they detrimental as a model for the present but may have long range effects hindering, rather than helping, individuals from reaching their goals.

What may be more upsetting about the overall picture is that the characteristics described lastly probably are related to success in athletics. As a result, rather than sports being a medium through which positive characteristics may be developed that may carry one through difficult times later in life, it becomes an area where one learns characteristics that may be instrumental in causing problems later in life. For the short term and short sighted goal of winning, we may be sacrificing the long-range goal of coping with life's problems.

THE REASON FOR CHANGE IN
THE AMERICAN SPORTS SCENE

We may rightfully ask ourselves, "How has athletics gotten out of hand? How can the American public become so enthusiastic over an area that may only lead to greater pain and destructiveness? How can we distort our perceptions to the point of seeing potentially destructive psychological behavior as the model to emulate?"

To answer these questions we must begin by realizing that our society is immensely competitive. Each day the average citizen is innundated with examples of competition, whether it is in work, social relationships, or even recreation, each person is in a continual set of challenges.

The vast majority of us get little recognition from work sources and yet we are constantly being reminded of those who are making it "big." Although the athletic arena is not a vital part of our lives, it crystallizes all of the many values as well as fantasies that we have been trained to believe as children. Each decade seems to bring about an era of life that captures it all. We are now going through the sports era.

What are these values—what does the sports world bring together in terms of values? To begin with it is now the glamor world. Sports figures have become our modern day heroes. The rags-to-riches stories impress all of us as rags-to-riches stories have in the past. A boy who is broke and family starving can go from back farmland to the big time to be a millionnaire. A relatively unknown shy small-town boy can go from coal pit to the nation's sex symbol. A black boy can be the hope of his ghetto community. In addition to all the riches, there is also the fame—TV, radio, magazines, etc. We can live out our dreams in their accomplishments. In essence, sports can give us an identity. We can wear caps, buttons, symbols, and garments that make us Raiders, Pirates, Buccaneers or Packers. What's more sports can provide us heroes. We all need models, heroes whom we can look up to, people who can give us

hope, personalities we can live and die with (or at least pass, catch or score touchdowns with); someone with whom we can empathize, feel for and become part of, if only in fantasy. In our heads we can make them as exciting as we wish.

When our teams win, we become winners and our identity is assured. We are all one. It is not uncommon for a fan to say something like, "Whom do we play tonight?" as if he or she is on the team. His or her identity is complete. The magic of being a fan is that you are in a no-lose situation because if your team doesn't win you can be an instant expert. It is hard to mention a sports fan who does not have the solution to his team's problem. "We need more pitching," "If we had another good receiver, we would have no trouble," "One more rebounder and we're in." Name the problem; the fan has the answer. Fans go undefeated, it is only their teams that lose.

The sports enthusiasts have other advantages as well. The cathartic effect of sports should not be overlooked. The frustrations of work, the freeway, the wife and kids, and the world situation can always be worked off at the game. To let loose and yell or express an opinion or disagree with the authorities, either coach or officials, can have a draining effect for the bottled-up anger.

There's always the entertainment and the sociability aspect. A bunch of people crowded together in a common cause where they can laugh, cry, kibbitz, exchange and get the emotional high during the tense moments of the game or the "on the edge of your seat" tension and we can see how athletics provide a unique charge. Even if you lose, there are enough high points to get you prepared for next week or next month or next year. Mentally you can always be building.

The value of a sporting contest is that in a short period of time there is a clear cut winner and loser, things are black or white, good or bad, there is little ambiguity. As if that weren't enough, this same bit of obsessive compulsion can be repeated again tomorrow or next week or in a short period of time. Added to that, the same pattern and process can be done in a number of different sports.

In the long run, then, we become intricately tied to athletics. We cannot help but become part of the process. It is hard for us to see anything wrong or corrupt or bad in it since it is as if we are admitting our own faults—our own weaknesses. It is hard to accept the disruptive feature for it would have to change ourselves. It is more than a game being played out there—our very personalities are on the line.

CHANGES

Because these characteristics exist does not mean that they are doomed—that they cannot change. Many of the characteristics mentioned as positive traits can be learned through athletics but it will take a revamping of the present

sports scene. One major change that will be necessary is to alter the model being viewed by children. Their heroes on television continually exhibit many of the behaviors labeled as destructive. Children cannot help but think it is the "proper" way of doing things. A child who sees his super star start a fight on the hockey rink accepts that as a role model and an acceptable way of resolving problems. Unless properly taught he cannot learn otherwise.

A second way to change this trend is to train individuals who are responsible for athletes, particularly young athletes, the proper methods of bringing about behavioral change. Many of our coaches, managers and physical educators are not trained in the child rearing or psychological areas including communication, motivation, personality, etc. Rarely is it made part of a required program. Proper education as well as proper training can bring about dramatic effects since most people, particularly young people, are eager to learn and are quite responsive.

Many of the behavior modification techniques lend themselves quite readily to bringing about change. Rushall and Siedentop (1972) have written a complete text dealing with fundamentals of this approach and have applied it quite successfully in their work.

What may be more important, however, than all of the foregoing is that the world of athletics should take a good look at its value structure. If athletics are a slice of the American culture and many of the behaviors described do represent destructiveness based on a win-at-all-costs philosophy, perhaps we may be able to see why nationally we have the same symptoms, only in greater proportion. It may be that we are so enmeshed in it that we cannot see the conflict between what we say and what we do. No wonder other nations may see us far more differently than we see ourselves. Our sports conflicts are only mirroring our societal conflicts, and until we can come to grips with the conflict, little can be expected to be done. That would be tragic since the athletic world represents one of the few ways whereby we can instill positive values, productive work habits and personal growth while at the same time developing socially and physically. There is no area with greater potential for overall development than that of physical activity through sports and athletics. With proper planning we can bring about that change.

REFERENCES

Gent, P. *North Dallas Forty.* New York: Morrow Book Co., 1973

Roberts, M. *Fans: How we go crazy over sports.* Washington, D.C.: New Republic Book Co., 1976.

Rushall, B. S., & Siedentop, D. *The development and control of behavior in sport and physical education.* Philadelphia, Pa.: Lea & Febiger, 1972.

Tutko, T. A., & Bruns, W. *Winning is everything and other American myths.* New York: Macmillan, 1976.

5

Social Structure, Sex-Roles, and Personality: Comparisons of Male/Female Athletes/Nonathletes

John P. King
*Virginia Polytechnic Institute
and State University*

Peter S. K. Chi
Cornell University

INTRODUCTION

The idea that there exists an "athletic personality" is one that has enjoyed wide, popular appeal for many years and one that has increasingly attracted the attention of researchers. Athletes are seen by many as special kinds of people who are different not only in terms of their skills and physical abilities, but also in their personalities and general social behavior. Researchers have directed their efforts towards the determination of just how athletes may differ from nonathletes and, indeed, a great deal of the literature indicates that athletes and nonathletes do have different personality characteristics (Alderman, 1974; Berlin, 1974; Cooper, 1969; Kane, 1970, 1972; Ogilvie, 1967, 1970; Schandel, 1965; Werner & Gottheil, 1976). Researchers have also

JOHN P. KING did his graduate work for the Ph.D. at Cornell University in the Department of Sociology. His dissertation, entitled "Social Structure, Sex Roles, and Personality: A Study of the Relationships of Family Background, College Environment, and School Activities to Personality with Special Attention to Athletic Participation," represents, in part, a further continuation and refinement of the research interests discussed in this chapter. He was the recipient of an NIGMS training grant for study in the interdepartmental program in social psychology and personality at Cornell. He previously taught at Mary Baldwin College. His research interests include the study of social structure and personality, sex roles (male and female), social inequality, social control, and the sociological and social psychological analyses of social institutions (family, neighborhoods, and sports).

PETER S. K. CHI received his Ph.D. from the Department of Sociology at Brown University. He is an Assistant Professor in the Department of Consumer Economics and Housing at Cornell University. His research interests include sociological analyses of social institutions (family, housing, and sports), migration and residential mobility, and consumer health status.

115

explored the question of whether or not athletes differ among themselves according to their level of skill or competition and the type of sport in which they participate. Again, the evidence seems to indicate that such differences do exist (Berlin, 1974; Flanagan, 1951; Kane, 1972; Kroll & Peterson, 1965; Malumphy, 1968; Ogilvie, 1970; Peterson, Weber, & Trousdale, 1967; Singer, 1969; Straub & Davis, 1971).

In spite of research findings that support the concept of an "athletic" or "sports personality," many scholars have remained unconvinced that such assertions are indeed valid. Their doubts seem to arise from two sources: (1) inconsistencies in results from one study to another; and (2) the deficiencies in the designs of the studies. Although some studies have found personality differences either between athletes and nonathletes or among athletes at different skill or competition levels or in different kinds of sports, other studies have not found such differences (Rushall, 1976; Sage, 1976). Even in those studies where differences were found, the situation is confused: One set of personality traits may significantly differentiate the various groups in one study but not in the other. Furthermore, significant differences may show up in two studies on the same personality trait, but the differences may be in opposite directions. Sometimes when different samples are combined, the significant differences that were found in the original samples disappear (Lakie, 1962; and cf. Fisher, 1976a; Martens, 1976; Ryan, 1976). An examination of the literature shows clearly that athletes vary markedly in their personality profiles whether they are viewed as a whole, in terms of skill or competition level, or in relation to kinds of sports participated in (cf. Hardman, 1973).

Although the problem of inconsistent results poses serious questions about this line of research, calls to abandon such research seem premature (cf. Fisher, 1976a; Martens, 1976; Ryan, 1976). Rather, an attempt should be made to determine the factors that are operating to produce the inconsistent results. Are there really no differences between the various subgroups? Or, are there differences that are being mediated by other variables that have not received adequate attention? Criticisms of the research designs (or nature of the studies) point up two major areas of deficiency in the research. One is the lack of attention given to cultural, social structural, and demographic factors and the other the lack of attention given to personality theory.

Whether comparing athletes with nonathletes or athletes with other athletes, most of the researchers have merely administered personality inventories and described the categories of personality that appear to differentiate the groups from one another. Often, athletes are simply described as scoring above or below average on the personality traits measured. On the basis of these limited analyses, researchers have tended to make a direct linkage between certain kinds of personality configurations and the likelihood of athletic participation. To be successful, however, any

attempt to link personality variables with athletic participation must explain: (1) what personality is; and (2) how and why certain personality characteristics are more likely than others to be related to athletic participation. Failure to address these questions explicitly has led to serious problems within this field of research and to difficulties in interpreting the various findings meaningfully (Fisher, 1976a; Kroll, 1976; Martens, 1976; Ryan, 1976).

Most research in the area of personality and athletic participation seems to assume implicitly that personality is a uniquely psychological construct and that personality and behavior are directly related (cf. Fisher, 1976a; Martens, 1976) without regard to the influence of situational or environmental variables. This line of research also fails to recognize athletics as a functioning social system with its own unique subsystems (cf. Loy, 1969; King & Chi, 1974). We discuss these points only briefly as they receive more detailed attention later in the chapter.

The importance of environmental factors in explaining behavior is well documented in the literature (see, e.g., Mischel, 1968; Yinger, 1965). In view of the findings in this area, any study that attempts to explain athletic participation on the basis of personality alone is, at best, incomplete (cf. Fisher, 1976a; Martens, 1976). An interactionist approach, which emphasizes the importance of both individual and environmental variables, is as necessary in the study of behavior in athletics as it is in the study of any behavior. An interactionist approach likewise stresses the importance of psychological, social, and cultural factors in personality development. The validity of this approach has been amply demonstrated in both the theoretical and empirical literature (Levine, 1974; Lewin, 1935; Mead, 1934; Smelser & Smelser, 1963; Yinger, 1965).

The application of an interactionist approach to the study of personality and participation in specific subsystems of a larger society and culture has proved to be especially useful and is of particular interest (see Argyris, 1954; Greenstein, 1969; Merton, 1940; Spiegel, 1971; Yinger, 1965, 1970). Using this approach, the system properties of the particular institution, organization, or social group that frame the individual's behavior are identified, then an attempt is made to relate those system properties to individual personality. Since athletics may be viewed as a subsystem of a larger society and culture, it would seem logical to approach the study of personality and athletic participation in the same way.

In an earlier study (King & Chi, 1974), we examined athletics as a social system and demonstrated that this system is composed of its own unique subsystems. The system properties of athletics can be expected to vary according to the particular subsystem being examined. For example, our earlier study pointed to differences between individual-oriented and group-oriented sports. Differences between athletes and nonathletes, and among

athletes themselves, can be examined most fruitfully by focusing attention upon the system properties of specific athletic subsystems. Once the differentiating system properties are identified, it is then possible to examine athletic participation in relation to personality. Furthermore, differences in the athletic social system may also arise because of a particular location in the larger social system and because of demographic and background differences among athletic participants. Attention will also have to be directed toward the distinguishing characteristics of the individuals who participate in each athletic social system, such as age, sex, and social class background. For instance, until recently, very little attention was given to the study of women's participation in sports. Most discussions of athletes and athletic participation have been limited to male athletes. To make generalizations across all athletes on this basis is clearly misleading. In addition, it is also of great importance to identify exactly where the athletic social system stands in relation to the larger social system. For example, when dealing with college athletes, we must recognize that the athletic social system is a part of the college social system. Colleges vary in their regional and cultural milieu, and they may provide their students with different athletic environments. Therefore, athletes even in the same sports and at the same skill and competition level may differ in personality simply because they are in different colleges.

The Background of the Present Study

The present study is a continuation and extension of our previous study in which an interactionist approach was used. In the previous study (King & Chi, 1974), the authors found that differences in personality profiles between athletes and nonathletes and between athletes from different sports could be explained in terms of "athletic social system theory." The theory states that participation in a particular social system or subsystem (such as an athletic social system) necessarily embeds the individual within certain spheres of interaction that place explicit demands and expectations upon the individual. Not only are demands made in regard to behavior but there are also demands that the individual view the world in a certain way, be a certain "type" of person, and display certain characteristics. To successfully participate and commit oneself to such a system, the individual must reach an accommodation with the demands and expectations of the spheres of interaction. At the same time, if the individual's participation is needed or valued, then others in the social system, as well as the system itself, must also accommodate themselves to the individual. There is, then, a continual give and take between the individual and the social system. As a result of this process, both the individual and the social system develop their own unique characters. In the case of the individual we may say that there has been a process of personality

development or adjustment.[1] As we described it in the earlier study, there is a meshing of the individual and the social system.

An individual, of course, participates simultaneously in several social systems, each of which has its own demands. It is our contention, however, that any individual's participation in, and commitment to, the different social systems or spheres of interaction are not of equal intensity or duration. Some will have a greater impact than others upon the individual; only in those systems may we expect to see the connection between the properties of the social system and the individual's total personality configuration. Participation in the athletic social system of intercollegiate competition and its subsystems represents the type of involvement and commitment that might be expected to influence the individual's total personality configuration.

An individual's actual behavior in the athletic social system is assumed to rest upon both personality structure and the system properties of athletics. The system properties of athletics may, in turn, influence the individual's basic personality structure. As the individual continues to participate in the athletic social system and is committed to such participation, we may expect that those characteristics demanded of the individual by the system will be reflected in the individual's total personality structure. By identifying the system properties of athletics and the demands it makes upon its participants, we may be able to see how and why personality is related to athletic participation.

In the previous study, personality differences (looked at in terms of the total personality configuration and in terms of individual personality traits) were found between athletes and nonathletes and between athletes in individual-oriented, less team-structured sports and those in group-oriented, more team-structured sports. All the differences pointed to the influence of the unique system properties of the athletic social system in general and of its subsystems (individual-oriented and group-oriented sports) in particular. An additional finding was that athletes who had participated in the college athletic social system for differing periods of time were also characterized by different personality profiles.

THE PRESENT STUDY

At the conclusion of our previous study it was noted that in the future it would be desirable to study athletic participation and personality within the context of a larger social system, particularly the college social system. The present

---

[1]See the various definitions of personality presented in Yinger (1965).

study attempts to do this explicitly. In addition, the interplay between sex role, college social system, athletic social system, and individual personality is systematically examined.

Theoretical Perspective

It is our contention that inconsistent findings on the relationship between personality and athletic participation are due to the fact that most studies have examined only a particular athletic social system and ignored the larger social system of which the athletic social system is a part. The fact that a large number of studies have used college samples increases the possibility that this may indeed be the case (see Lakie, 1962; Singer, 1975). Colleges differ greatly on a number of factors: size, location, sexual composition, academic and extracurricular programs offered, among others. It is expected that different types of people are attracted to different types of colleges and that these colleges, in turn, affect the personality development of their students in different ways. In the present study we have drawn samples from three different colleges. These colleges have been matched in terms of location, size, and academic programs but they vary in terms of the sexual composition of their student bodies.

The introduction of sex as a variable into our study allows us to examine not only the impact of college sexual composition but also the influence of sex roles on athletic personality development. Traditionally, as we are all well aware, differential expectations and demands have been placed upon males and females, and different patterns of behavior for each sex have been "encouraged" through social sanctions (see Chafetz, 1974; Farrell, 1975; Hartley, 1974; Maccoby & Jacklin, 1974; Pleck & Sawyer, 1974; Weitz, 1977). Athletics and masculinity have traditionally been linked in the public mind. Men are expected to be both athletic and competitive in general, and formal athletic participation is one way for a male to prove his masculinity (Beisser, 1972; Farrell, 1975). Societal sanctions, sometimes quite harsh, are used to back up these expectations. The male who cannot or will not compete in athletics may be labeled a "sissy" (cf. Candell, 1974; Gagnon, 1974; Lester, 1974; *Out in Right Field*, 1974). Women, on the other hand, are expected to be neither athletic nor competitive. While athletics and masculinity are assumed to go together, athletics and femininity are assumed to be diametrically opposed. The female who does participate in athletics often has her womanhood or femininity questioned (Berlin, 1974; Felshin, 1974; Gerber, 1974; Harris, 1973; Hart, 1972a; Metheny, 1972).

Why is athletic participation differentially associated with masculinity and femininity? An athlete is popularly considered to be physically and emotionally strong, tough, brave, adventuresome, assertive, aggressive, competitive, and achievement-oriented. Athletic participation places one in

the public arena where one must prove oneself before all. And to prove oneself publicly in athletics, as in other fields of endeavor, is to attest to one's importance as a force in both the social and physical world (Metheny, 1972; Felshin, 1974). These are all factors that are associated with the traditional male sex role.

The traditional (and often misinformed) conception of the female sex role, on the other hand, has stressed just the opposite characteristics. The image of the woman has been that of a weak, dependent, passive, sensitive, cooperative, and emotional individual who remains outside the public arena and proves herself not by her accomplishments or achievements, but by her ability to find a man and to express herself through her family. To be a woman in a "man's world" is to be unimportant as a force in the social and physical world. The female, at least in modern western society, has also been valued for her soft and delicate body and good looks. All of these characteristics have been assumed to be incompatible with the physical vigor, strength, and force supposedly required for athletic competition.

Given the popular images of athletics, masculinity and femininity, it is not surprising to find that males are channeled into athletics while females are not.[2] As a matter of fact, athletics have been described as a masculine rite of passage (Beisser, 1972). Furthermore, the general social environment not only makes it easier for males to participate in athletics but also makes it harder for females to do so. The limited range of facilities and programs provided for females in schools and colleges, compared with those available to men, is just one example.

In spite of the considerations discussed above, girls and women have participated in athletics to a fairly considerable degree. However, as historical and cross-cultural studies (Gerber, 1974; Spears, 1974; Sutton-Smith & Morgan, 1963; Sutton-Smith, Roberts, & Kozelka, 1969; Swanson, 1974) indicate, this participation has been limited until recently in terms of the types of activities judged acceptable and suitable for females, and the degree of commitment expected and accepted for female athletic participants. Given this background, several crucial questions may be raised: How do we explain female athletic participation? Are so-called feminine qualities really incompatible with athletic participation? Must a female become more masculine or less feminine in order to be a successful athletic participant? The existing literature may provide partial answers to these questions.

First of all, studies of female physiology have largely discounted the idea that women are unfit for athletic participation. Women athletes are neither

---

[2]At first, it may appear that the "tomboy" proves this assertion wrong. However, there usually comes a time when the "tomboy" is encouraged or forced to turn away from athletics to more feminine endeavors. In addition, when girls and women do participate in athletics, it is usually limited to a few sports out of the total range of sports open to boys and men.

physically damaged nor is their physical appearance adversely affected (Boslooper & Hayes, 1973; Harris, 1973; Shaffer, 1972). In regard to the claim that women are not or cannot be assertive, aggressive, competitive, bold, etc., the evidence indicates first, that these characteristics are socially conditioned and, second, that they are present in women but may be displayed in ways that differ from their display in males (see Maccoby & Jacklin, 1974; Sherif, 1972; Smith, 1972; Weitz, 1977). In the realm of athletics women have, indeed, demonstrated these very characteristics. This is not to say that they have performed "like men" but rather that they have performed in ways that are clearly goal oriented. Most importantly, as Sandra Bem (1974) has demonstrated, the characteristics that have been traditionally associated with masculinity and femininity are not mutually exclusive. An individual can have both so-called masculine and feminine traits without the presence of one necessarily entailing the absence or diminution of the other. Bem further asserts that the truly healthy and fully functioning individual is the one who can incorporate both traditionally ascribed masculine and feminine characteristics into his/her behavioral repertoire and therefore face all situations flexibly and competently. The same thing might be said about individuals engaged in athletic competition. For example, two of the most important traditional female traits would seem to be of direct relevance to some forms of athletics. These are the ability to get along with and cooperate with others and the ability to be sensitive to the needs and feelings of others. These characteristics are especially important in developing the cohesiveness and team spirit needed in group-oriented and team structured sports. Such characteristics, along with some of the more traditional masculine character-istics, would be valuable assets for all athletes.

Because athletics has been considered a predominantly male domain, the woman athlete, at least in the past, has had to cope with a certain degree of dissonance and anxiety about her athletic participation. This ambivalence has direct implications in regard to one's own self concept and one's concern with self-presentations to others (Berlin, 1974; Boslooper, 1973; Felshin, 1974; Harris, 1973; Gerber, 1974; Maccoby, 1963; Metheny, 1972; Tyler, 1973). Various ways of coping with this situation have been noted in the literature. The strategy of role segregation [or the "chameleon syndrome" as Harris (1973) calls it] was one way of dealing with this ambivalence. The female athlete could attempt to separate her athletic participation from the rest of her social life, displaying characteristics associated with athletics only at the times of active participation [see Allen's (1972) discussion of the "athlete self" and the "feminine self"]. In this way the female athlete could prove she was feminine (as demonstrated in her other activities and behaviors) in spite of her athletic participation.

As mentioned earlier, female athletes were (and still are to a certain extent) limited in the range of activities open to them. Those activities that were

acceptable for females, then, could be justified as either not detracting from one's femininity or as even contributing to one's femininity. Athletics stressing gracefulness or other aesthetic features are clear examples of this (see Metheny, 1972). It should be made clear that the ambivalence experienced by female athletes was not necessarily the result of individual self doubts. Rather, social pressures and sanctions may have forced female athletes to adopt the strategies mentioned earlier. Given the fact that the roles of males and females in society have been clearly differentiated from one another, the participation of females in a traditionally male domain could call into question the very underpinnings of this sex-role differentiation. However, as we have seen, female athletic participation has been accommodated in a way that this has, until recently, been avoided. The strategies employed by female athletes, then, can partially be understood as responses to the demands of societal conventions.

Of course, the situation is changing dramatically today. As Felshin (1974) points out, women are feeling much less anxiety and dissonance about their participation in athletics, and the larger society is slowly coming to accept the equality of women in this domain as in others. Girls and women, today as in the past, are choosing to participate in sports for reasons that largely have to do with the personal satisfaction that can be obtained from such participation. The fact that females are not as pressured as males to be athletic may mean that their choice to be athletic participants is based upon goal-oriented reasons clearly related to the pursuit of athletics in and of itself. This would be in contrast to those males who participate in athletics because of pressures to "prove" their masculinity.

In the present study our concern is with the question of how different types of college environments—male, female, and coed colleges—influence the relationship between sex roles, athletic participation, and personality. Given the different types of college environments, or social systems, it may be expected that the traditional sex-role demands and male/female patterns of athletic participation will vary from college to college. The examination of athlete/nonathlete differences, differences between athletes in different types of sports and between athletes receiving varsity letters for different numbers of years, is made in relation to sex roles and college environment. It is our contention that the particular design of this study clarifies some of the inconsistencies and confusion in the research on personality and intercollegiate athletic participation.

The Research Design

The present study has drawn four samples of athletes and nonathletes from three different private colleges: two samples of female athletes and nonathletes, and two samples of male athletes and nonathletes. One female

sample was drawn from a small women's liberal arts college; the other, from a small coeducational liberal arts college. The male samples were drawn from a small men's liberal arts college and from the same small coed liberal arts college as the second female sample. As in our previous study, the athlete samples were drawn from individuals who had received a varsity letter in intercollegiate athletics. The nonathlete samples were drawn from students who had not lettered. Each athlete sample was divided into those who participated in individually-oriented, less team-structured sports, and those who participated in group-oriented, more team-structured sports.[3] (Distribution of sample sizes is presented in the appendix.) In addition, the athletes were identified according to the number of years they had participated in varsity athletics.

The three colleges sampled are all located within a radius of approximately 30 miles in the Shenandoah Valley of Virginia. Each college has a liberal arts orientation and each could be considered relatively small. There is, however, some variation in these two factors. The men's college is somewhat larger than the other two colleges and has somewhat more of a "career preparation" orientation. All these colleges, being in the same area, draw their students from the same general region, predominantly the southeast and middle-atlantic states. Each is located within a small-town community that is relatively isolated from large population concentrations. The male college is an independent institution; the female and coed colleges are church related. The racial and ethnic composition of each college is quite homogeneous with very few minority group students in any of them. A greater proportion of students at the men's and women's colleges seem to come from families with higher socioeconomic status than students at the coed college. Although there is some variation among the three colleges, they are similar in most aspects. The only major difference among the three colleges is the factor of sexual composition.

---

[3]The women's college had the following individual sports: tennis, riding, golf, and fencing; and the following group sport: basketball. The coed female program had the following individual sport: tennis; and the following group sports: basketball, field hockey, lacrosse, volleyball, and tennis. The coed male program was composed of the following individual sports: track, cross-country, tennis, golf; and the following group sports: football, basketball, and baseball. The men's college had the following individual sports: swimming, wrestling, track, cross country, golf. The samples for each college were drawn from the whole range of sports offered at the college and divided according to participation in individual or group sports. For those few athletes who participated in both types of sports, a determination was made as to the type of sport of greatest significance to that individual and she/he was so classified. The differences that do exist in the sports programs are clearly indicative of the historical (and present) roles of men and women in athletics. For example, the types of sports offered for women (particularly at the women's college) are clearly in line with those sports which have traditionally been acceptable for women. For historical treatments of women in athletics, see Gerber, 1974; Spears, 1974; and Swanson, 1974. In addition, Sutton-Smith and Morgan, 1963, and Sutton-Smith et al., 1969 provide cross-cultural analyses of the avenues of game and sport involvement open to women and girls.

In general, all three colleges have relatively modest athletic budgets; the men's college has the largest and the women's college the smallest. All three colleges have fairly diverse intercollegiate athletic programs, but the men's college has substantially greater diversity. The intercollegiate athletics offered at the women's college are concentrated in the individual-oriented, less team-structured sports, whereas those for women at the coed college are concentrated in the group-oriented, more team-structured sports. The male college and male sports program at the coed college have the same number of individual and group sports; both emphasize the group-oriented, more structured sports more than the individual sports.[4]

The levels of competition at the three colleges are in the moderate range, although there is some variability in each college in regard to particular sports. The women's college has a particularly strong tennis program, the coed college has a strong program for males in baseball, and the male college has a particularly strong program in lacrosse.

This unique research design allows us to investigate the independent and interactive effects of sex factors, types and duration of athletic participation, and the college social system upon personality traits.

Measurement

The major measurement instruments used in this study are the Cattell 16 PF personality inventory (Cattell, 1972; Cattell, Eber, & Tatsuoka, 1970) and the Bem sex-role identity scale (Bem, 1974).

The 16 PF seeks to measure 16 primary source traits of personality: (A) reserved/outgoing; (B) intelligence; (C) emotionality; (E) assertiveness; (F) surgency (sober/happy-go-lucky); (G) conscientiousness; (H) venturesome-ness; (I) sensitivity (tough-minded/sensitive); (L) trusting/suspicious; (M) practical/imaginative; (N) forthright/shrewd; (O) apprehensiveness (self-assured/apprehensive); (Q1) conservative/experimenting; (Q2) group depen-dent/self-sufficient; (Q3) self control; (Q4) tension (relaxed/tense). From these primary personality factors various second-order personality factors may be derived. Those of greatest interest to us are: (SI) introversion/extra-version; (SII) anxiety; (SIII) emotional poise; (SIV) group-dependent/inde-pendent.[5] The source traits measured by the 16 PF are considered to be the underlying sources of the individual's actual behavior. Those behaviors that appear together as the individual navigates through the social world are what Cattell calls surface traits. Cattell points out that there is an interaction

---

[4]See footnote 3.

[5]When one trait is mentioned for the personality factor, the measurement is for the degree of that trait, a higher score representing a higher degree. When two traits are mentioned, the measurement is for a continuum, a lower score representing the first trait mentioned and a higher score the second one.

between the two sets of traits: Source traits influence surface traits and are in turn influenced by surface traits. This interactionist conception of personality fits well with our basic theoretical assumptions (see the background discussion).

The Bem sex-role identity scales are composed of a masculinity scale, a femininity scale, and a social desirability scale. As mentioned before, masculinity and femininity do not represent the end points of a single continuum but are treated as independent factors. An individual's score on one scale does not necessarily diminish his/her score on the other. A measure of androgyny is computed by subtracting the femininity score from the masculinity score and represents the degree of deviation from an equal combination of masculine and feminine traits. The closer the score is to zero, the more balanced or androgynous is the individual (the social desirability scale is not used in the present analysis).

Methods of Analysis

First, within each of the four samples (the women's college, men's college, and male and female coed college samples), individual and group sports athletes are each independently compared with nonathletes on the basis of each group's personality configurations, using both the profile of the 16 primary factors and the profile of the four second-order factors. The pattern similarity coefficient, r_p, is used to make the within-sample comparisons between the individual-sports athletes and nonathletes and the group-sports athletes and nonathletes. The r_p measures the degree of similarity between two groups based on any number of factors and has roughly the same meaning as the correlation coeficient.[6]

The second step in the analysis is to make selected cross-college comparisons. The female college athletes are compared with their female counterparts at the coed college, and a similar comparison is made across the two male samples. The third set of comparisons is cross-sex in nature—the contrast between male and female athletes at the coed college. These cross-college and cross-sex comparisons allow us to examine the effects of the different college social systems and the effects of sex roles on the relationship between personality and athletic participation. T-tests are computed for the comparisons on the personality and sex-role identity measures.

Following these analyses, all four samples are combined and used in a set of analyses of variance. First, the combined sample of athletes and nonathletes is used in a three-way ANOVA, testing the effects of sex, college membership,

---

[6]The r_p's calculated will actually underestimate the differences between the groups. This follows from our inability to assign integer weights to the 16 PF traits. The assignment of such weights is specific to the groups being compared and takes into consideration the "importance" of those traits for the criterion group (see Cattell et al., 1970).

and athletic participation on the personality and sex-role identity measures. Second, the combined athlete samples are used in a four-way ANOVA, testing the effects of sex, college membership, type of sport participation, and number of years lettered on the personality and sex-role identity measures. Given the fact that sex and college membership are interrelated, multiple classification analysis (MCA) is consulted to insure that sex and college membership do indeed contribute independently to variations in the personality and sex-role identity measures.

ANALYSES AND FINDINGS

Within-Sample Comparisons on Athletes and Nonathletes

Due to the different characteristics of the three college social systems and the types of demands that one may expect to be placed upon the males and females in each system, it is expected that the rank order of pattern similarity coefficients calculated between individual sports athletes and nonathletes and between group sports athletes and nonathletes varies according to the sex of the athletes and the college being examined.

The Female College Sample. Given the unique environment of the women's college, it is hypothesized that the individual sport/nonathlete r_p score is relatively larger than the group sport/nonathlete r_p; that is, personality differences between group sport athletes and nonathletes are expected to be greater than those between individual-sport athletes and nonathletes.

Two factors are of particular relevance. First, participation in group-oriented sports places the individual in a situation where there is increased interaction with other athletes; this situation, coupled with the more structured team organization, should firmly embed the individual in the athletic social system. Given this greater embeddedness, one would expect that those personality characteristics that differentiate athletes from nonathletes may be more firmly reinforced in the group-sport members than in the individual-sport members. Second, although athletic participation is traditionally not a highly valued form of female behavior, the female environment of a women's college may force women to take on the "campus roles" that are usually played by men. This type of institutional setting may not only provide a greater tolerance for intercollegiate athletic activities but also support and encourage such behavior. Therefore, in this particular setting we would expect a relatively low level of effect from any countervailing forces that might pull women away from their embeddedness in the athletic social system. Hence, those athletes more embedded in the athletic social

system, the group athletes, are expected to show a relatively smaller degree of similarity (as measured by the r_p) to the nonathletes than the individual-sports athletes.

The pattern similarity coefficients for the womens college comparisons are shown in panel A of Table 5.1. For both the 16 primary and four second-order personality profiles, the nonathlete/group sports r_p comparison is relatively smaller than the nonathlete/individual sports r_p. This finding supports our hypothesis.

The Female Coed College Sample.   It is hypothesized that the r_p rank order for the individual-sport athlete/nonathlete and group-sport athlete/ nonathlete comparisons for this sample may follow a reverse pattern of what was found for the women's college sample. The rationale of this hypothesis lies in the consideration of the larger college social system: The coed college represents a social environment where the potential for structured sex-role differentiation may exist. Traditional sex-role expectations and behaviors are

TABLE 5.1
Pattern Similarity Coefficients (r_p)[a]

	Nonathletes	Athletes	
		Individual Sports	Group Sports
Panel A			
Women's College			
Nonathletes	—	.83	.59
Individual sports	.76	—	.51
Group sports	.62	.18	—
Panel B			
Coed College Females			
Nonathletes	—	.81	.89
Individual sports	.71	—	.84
Group sports	.95	.88	—
Panel C			
Men's College			
Nonathletes	—	.87	.92
Individual sports	.88	—	.80
Group sports	.98	.83	—
Panel D			
Coed College Males			
Nonathletes	—	.81	.76
Individual sports	.87	—	.89
Group sports	.79	.88	—

[a]Computed for the personality profile based on the 16 primary personality scores (upper diagonal) and the profile based on the four second-order scores (lower diagonal).

likely to be present if only because of social inertia. Although athletic participation for females is encouraged at the coed college, women in this college could still face pressure from the general college social system, particularly from the male students, that could draw them away from full commitment to athletics. Unlike the situation in the women's college, males are present and may be expected to lay claim to those "campus roles" that have traditionally been theirs. Such a situation could work to push women's athletics into a position subordinate to that of men's athletics and, therefore, lead to a situation in which other, more traditional female roles are stressed. As discussed earlier, the female athlete would then be faced with some degree of anxiety or dissonance about her athletic participation. The group-sport situation would certainly help the individual in dealing with this ambivalence. Traditionally, this ambivalence was handled in a way that led the female athlete to emphasize her "feminine self" over her "athletic self." Given the fact that traditional sex-role stereotypes have not yet been fully overcome, we may expect that this same type of coping strategy is still used to some extent among the female athletes at the coed college being examined. The increased interaction and group support of the group sports for women could, therefore, actually work in a way to check the individual's commitment to athletics. Indeed, female athletes in the group-sport situation at the coed school could be encouraged to express a greater commitment to their "female social selves" than to their "athletic social selves." The female group athlete is in a situation of intense interaction with other athletes who may caution her if she deviates too far from the "feminine ideal," and thus may prevent the greater effects of athletic participation on personality.

Although the female individual-sport athlete at the coed college would likely face the same ambivalence as the group-sport athlete and attempt to deal with it in a similar way, her efforts would probably be more clearly segregated from her actual athletic participation. Consequently, the individual-sport athlete could actually be more embedded in the athletic social system than the group-sport athlete. The effect of athletic participation upon the personality profiles of individual-sport athletes would therefore be greater and would show up more strongly in their comparisons with nonathletes.

Panel B of Table 5.1 indicates that the individual-sport athlete/nonathlete r_ps for both personality profiles are relatively smaller than the group-sport athlete/nonathlete r_ps. Our hypothesis is therefore supported.

The Coed Male and the Men's College Samples.   In contrast to the female samples, it is expected that the types of processes at work in regard to athletic participation may be similar for both male samples. Therefore, the coed male and men's college samples are expected to display the same type of pattern in the individual-sport athlete and group-sport athlete comparisons with nonathletes. Although many of the characteristics encouraged for athletic

participants are the same as those encouraged for all males, it is anticipated that participation in the athletic social system still works to differentiate athletes from nonathletes. This is expected simply because participation in athletics is likely to give these characteristics greater salience for the individuals so involved. Given the greater intensity of interaction and embeddedness found within group sports, athletes in these sports are expected to differ from nonathletes more than the individual-sport athletes do.

Findings in panel D of Table 5.1 support our predictions for the male coed sample: Athletes in individual sports have a relatively greater degree of similarity to the nonathletes than do the group-sport athletes. However, the results from the male college sample in panel C contradict the expectations; on both profiles, group-sport athletes show a relatively greater level of similarity to nonathletes than do the individual-sport athletes.[7]

Cross-Sample Comparisons

In order to examine the importance of the larger college social system and the variable of sex, we report the results from three cross-sample comparisons:[8] women's college vs. coed college females, men's college vs. coed college males, males vs. females at the coed college.

Cross-College Comparisons of the Female Athlete Samples. As discussed before, the female athletes at the coed college are assumed to face greater cross-pressures from the general college social system than their counterparts at the women's college. Contradictory messages stressing the importance of athletics, on the one hand, and of being feminine, on the other

---

[7]This finding, indeed, appears puzzling. However, we will attempt to offer a purely speculative explanation for it that runs much along the same lines as that used for the similar pattern found in the female coed sample. Given the all-male environment, it may be expected that competitive social comparison processes are quite pronounced (see Farrell, 1975; Pleck & Sawyer, 1974). As discussed earlier, the traits associated with the athlete are much the same as those associated with men in general. Perhaps the general college population and the group sports athletes are being told the same things. The individual sports athletes are not in the same type of group structured situation as the group sports athletes and, therefore, may be freer of pressures to conform to the predominant campus stereotype. They have already proved themselves as men through their athletic participation and, without the group pressures found in team sports, may be freer to explore just how they will be men. Scott (1971) has especially called attention to the stereotyped patterns of behavior and characteristics expected of all athletes and Farrell (1975) has pointed out that these are similar to those found for most men's groups in general. In this situation, it would be only the males who have already proved their masculinity and who are outside intense group interaction situations who could escape the demands and pressures that they be a certain type of man.

[8]All further analyses were conducted using computer programs from the *Statistical Package for Social Sciences* (Nie, Hull, Jenkins, Steinbrenner, & Bent, 1975).

hand, are likely to cause greater ambivalence in the coed college female athletes. The women's college athletes are likely to receive greater support for their athletic participation simply because they are the college's only athletes and do not have to compete with males for the support and encouragement of the wider college community. Therefore, the system properties of the athletic social system are expected to have a greater effect on the personality profiles of the athletes at the women's college than on those of the female athletes at the coed college; that is, the women's college athletes would be more likely to exhibit personality characteristics associated with athletic participation such as assertiveness, conscientiousness, venturesomeness, toughmindedness, and forthrightness (see Ogilvie, 1967, 1970). They are likely to be more experimenting and independent as well. On personality factors such as anxiety, poise, tension, self control, self assurance, and emotionality, it is expected that the female athletes at the coed college score in directions that would be indicative of greater stress. This hypothesis is based on the assumption that these female athletes experience greater cross-pressures and ambivalence than the women's college athletes. On the sex-role identity measures, it is hypothesized that the two groups score equally on the femininity scale, but that the women's college sample scores higher on the masculinity scale. On the androgyny factor, therefore, we expect that the female college sample deviates more in the masculine direction than the female coed sample.

The findings lend support to our expectations (see panel A of Table 5.2). The women's college sample is significantly more assertive, more conscientious, more venturesome, more toughminded, more experimenting, more extroverted, and more independent than the coed female sample. There seems to be a tendency for the females from the women's college to be more outgoing and emotionally poised as well, but tests on both measures are not statistically significant. There were no other differences on the personality factors that might indicate the consequences of stress or ambivalence. As predicted, the two samples score equally on the femininity scale, and there is a trend toward greater masculinity for the women's college sample. On the androgyny score, the coed sample tends to score slightly closer to zero; the female college sample deviates in the masculine direction while the coed sample deviates in the feminine direction.

Cross-College Comparisons of the Male Athlete Samples. In line with our basic theoretical position, it is expected that differences between the male athletes on the personality and sex-role identity measures arise because of the two distinct types of college environments they come from. In contrast to our expectations for the female samples, it is expected that the athletes at the men's college exhibit characteristics more in line with traditional sex-role ascriptions than the athletes at the coed college. Analyses of male to male interactions (see Farrell, 1975, and Pleck & Sawyer, 1974) have indicated that

TABLE 5.2

Significance Levels for t-tests of Cross-Sample Differences with Respect to Personality and Sex-Role Identity Measures[a] (Athletes Only)

Measure	A. Women's College vs Coed College Females			B. Men's College vs Coed College Males			C. Coed College Males vs Coed College Females		
	t	df	p	t	df	p	t	df	p
A: Reserved/Outgoing	1.49	64	.07 (W)	—	—	—	—	—	—
B: Intelligence	—	—	—	—	—	—	—	—	—
C: Emotionality	—	—	—	—	—	—	—	—	—
E: Assertiveness	2.68	64	.01 (W)	2.66	87	.01 (M)	-2.31	71	.01 (Ma)
F: Surgency	—	—	—	—	—	—	1.38	71	.09 (Fe)
G: Conscientiousness	1.96	64	.03 (W)	—	—	—	—	—	—
H: Venturesomeness	1.71	64	.05 (W)	—	—	—	—	—	—
I: Tough-Minded/Sensitive	-1.86	64	.04 (C)	1.69	91[b]	.05 (M)	3.95	71	.01 (Fe)
L: Trusting/Suspicious	—	—	—	—	—	—	—	—	—
M: Practical/Imaginative	—	—	—	3.10	87	.01 (M)	—	—	—
N: Forthright/Shrewd	—	—	—	—	—	—	1.85	71	.04 (Fe)
O: Self-Assured/Apprehensive	—	—	—	—	—	—	—	—	—
Q1: Conservative/Experimenting	2.66	64	.01 (W)	2.36	87	.01 (M)	—	—	—
Q2: Group-dependent/Self-sufficient	—	—	—	—	—	—	-1.26	71	.10 (Ma)
Q3: Self-Control	—	—	—	—	—	—	1.54	71	.07 (Fe)
Q4: Relaxed/Tense	—	—	—	—	—	—	—	—	—
SI: Introversion/Extroversion	1.69	64	.05 (W)	—	—	—	—	—	—
SII: Anxiety	—	—	—	—	—	—	—	—	—
SIII: Emotional poise	1.43	64	.08 (W)	—	—	—	-2.65	71	.01 (Ma)
SIV: Group-dependent/Independent	2.71	64	.01 (W)	3.26	87	.01 (M)	-2.10	71	.02 (Ma)
Masculinity	1.65	64	.06 (W)	—	—	—	-3.54	71	.01 (Ma)
Femininity	—	—	—	-1.62	62[b]	.06 (C)	1.61	71	.06 (Fe)
Androgyny	1.45	64	.08 (C)	1.47	87	.08 (C)	-4.15	71	.01 (Fe)

[a]The letters in parentheses indicate the group that scored highest on that factor; W = Women's College, C = Coed College, M = Men's College, Ma = Male, Fe = Female.

[b]Degree of freedom (df) differs because the F-test of homogeneity of variance indicated that separate variance estimates should be used and this sometimes changes the df.

interactions in all male group situations are likely to evoke processes that push the participants in the direction of displaying quite forcefully those characteristics traditionally ascribed to males. For this reason, it is expected that the men's college athletes differ from the coed college male athletes on the personality measures in the direction of traditionally ascribed male characteristics. It is also expected that the men's college athletes, on the average, have higher masculinity and lower femininity scores than their counterparts at the coed college. Concomitantly, the androgyny score of the coed college male athletes would be closer to zero.

Panel B of Table 5.2 presents the results of the cross-college male comparisons. The men's college atheletes are more assertive, imaginative, experimenting, and independent than the coed college male athletes. All of these traits are part of the traditional male sex-role stereotype. The finding that the men's college athletes are more-sensitive/less-tough-minded than the male athletes at the coed college does not, however, fit into the traditional masculine stereotype.

On the sex-role identity scores, no differences were found between the two groups on the masculinity score. As predicted, however, the coed college sample does show a trend toward greater femininity than the men's college sample and scored slightly closer to zero on the androgyny factor.

Comparisons of the Male and Female Coed College Samples.   These comparisons give us an opportunity to test directly whether or not the influence of athletic participation on personality transcends the influence of sex roles. The hypothesis tested is that differences between the male and female athletes on the personality and sex-role identity measures are in line with traditional sex-role expectations.

The results shown in panel C of Table 5.2, support the prediction. Each of the five significant differences between the male and female coed college samples follows traditional sex-role expectations: The male athletes are more assertive, tough-minded, forthright, poised, and self-sufficient than the female athletes. Also in line with traditional sex-role expectations are the trends toward greater independence among the male athletes and toward greater self-control among the female athletes. Although statistically insignificant, one deviation from the expected pattern appears: There is a trend toward greater surgency on the part of the females.

Findings on the sex-role identity measures are as expected: The males are more masculine and the females more feminine. The females scored closer to zero on the androgyny score, indicating a greater balance of masculinity and femininity. The males deviated from zero in the masculine direction.

Summary.   The three cross-sample comparisons clearly indicate that the relationship between personality and athletic participation cannot be fully understood unless other mediating variables such as sex-roles and college

social system are taken into account. The fact that differences between the athletes were found in these cross-sample comparisons clearly shows that it is meaningless to talk about athletes as if they were a universally homogeneous group of people. In order to determine more precisely the relative importance of sex, college social system, and athletic participation in regard to personality, analyses of variance are performed on the combined athlete and nonathlete samples and on the combined athlete samples only.

Multivariate Analyses

Three-Way Analysis of Variance on the Combined Athlete and Nonathlete Samples. The first analysis of variance (ANOVA) includes the total combined samples classified by the control variables of sex, college, and participation or nonparticipation in athletics. Each of the personality trait and sex-role identity measures is tested against these controls separately. Given the preliminary findings from the cross-sample comparisons, it is hypothesized that sex and college membership have strongest independent main effects on the dependent variables while the effects of athletic status are principally in interaction with these two variables. Multiple classification analysis (MCA) is used to test the independent effects of sex and college membership on the personality and sex-role identity measures, but the data are not presented. The significant findings from the ANOVA are presented in Table 5.3.[9]

Significant main and intractive effects were found for 19 out of the total 23 measures. Sex and/or college have significant main effects on 16 of the measures and athletic participation has main effects on six. Significant interaction effects are found on six of the measures. Interpretations of these findings are presented.

On factor A, outgoing/reserved, sex and college are the significant main effects. The females are more outgoing than the males, and those individuals who attend the single-sex institutions are more outgoing than those who attend the coed college. Of the two single-sex institutions, when the effect of sex is controlled in MCA, the men's college students are the most outgoing. An interaction effect between sex and athletic participation was also found on factor A. Among the females, the nonathletes are more outgoing than the athletes, while among the males it is the athletes who are more outgoing than the nonathletes. The females, whether athletes or nonathletes, are more outgoing than either of the male groups.

On factors E (assertiveness) and F (surgency), sex and college were found to have significant main effects. The males are more assertive than the

---

[9]Space limitations preclude inclusion of all means and standard deviations in the tables. The discussions of the findings indicate how the groups compare with one another on the scores.

females, and the females are more happy-go-lucky (or surgent) than the males. The two groups of single-sex college students are more assertive than the coed college students, with the men's college students ranking first on this factor. When sex is controlled in the MCA, the men's college students come out as being the most surgent, followed by the women's college students.

On factor G (conscientiousness), athletic participation is the only significant main effect. Athletes, both male and female, and irrespective of college, are significantly more conscientious than nonathletes.

On factor H (shy/venturesome), the significant main effect on sex reveals that the females are more venturesome than the males. There is also a significant two-way interaction (athletic participation by sex). As was found in the analysis of factor A, the athlete/nonathlete differences were in opposite directions for the males and females. Female nonathletes are more venturesome than female athletes, while male athletes are more venturesome

TABLE 5.3
Three-Way Analysis of Variance on Combined Samples of Athletes and Nonathletes
(Significant F-Values Only)

Measure	Source of Variation	F	df	P
A: Outgoing/reserved	Sex	13.51	1	.001
	College	18.86	2	.005
	Sex by athletic participation	8.65	1	.003
E: Assertiveness	Sex	4.02	1	.043
	College	9.52	2	.001
F: Surgency	Sex	15.28	1	.001
	College	2.99	2	.050
G: Conscientiousness	Athletic participation	4.07	1	.042
H: Venturesomeness	Sex	3.86	1	.048
	Sex by athletic participation	3.65	1	.05
I: Tough-minded/sensitive	Sex	31.67	1	.001
	Athletic participation	3.84	1	.048
L: Trusting/suspicious	College	4.17	2	.016
M: Practical/imaginative	Athletic participation	4.83	1	.027
	Sex by athletic participation	7.06	1	.008
	College by athletic participation	5.43	2	.005
N: Forthright/shrewd	Athletic participation	7.03	1	.008
O: Self-assured/apprehensive	Sex	5.48	1	.019

(continued)

TABLE 5.3 *(continued)*

Measure	Source of Variation	F	df	P
Q1: Conservative/experimenting	Sex	12.31	1	.001
	College	2.88	2	.050
Q2: Group-dependent/self-sufficient	Sex	3.65	1	.050
Q3: Self-control	College	3.89	2	.021
SI: Introversion/extroversion	Sex	6.78	1	.009
	College	4.81	2	.009
	Sex by athletic participation	7.54	1	.006
	College by athletic participation	4.24	2	.015
SIII: Emotional poise	Sex	10.60	1	.001
	Athletic participation	3.86	1	.047
SIV: Group-dependent/independent	Sex	10.89	1	.001
	College	10.23	2	.001
Masculinity	Sex	6.15	1	.013
	College	5.59	2	.004
	Athletic participation	13.52	1	.001
	College by athletic participation	3.52	2	.030
Feminity	Sex	25.93	1	.001
	Sex by athletic participation	4.46	1	.033
Androgyny	Sex	29.47	1	.001
	College	4.86	2	.008
	Athletic participation	16.45	1	.001

than male nonathletes. The females, whether athletes or nonathletes, are more venturesome than either of the male groups. This latter finding clearly contradicts the traditional sex-role stereotypes of the timid female and bold male. Another surprising finding is that the nonathlete females are more venturesome than the athlete females. Given the fact that female athletes are venturing into a traditionally male domain would lead one to expect the opposite.

On factor I (tough-minded/sensitive), sex and athletic participation were found to have significant main effects. In line with traditional expectations, the females are more sensitive than the males, and the athletes are more tough-minded than the nonathletes.

On factor L (trusting/suspicious), college shows as the only significant main effect. The coed students are the most suspicious and the men's college students are the most trusting.

Analysis of factor M (practical/imaginative), reveals that athletic participation has the only main effect, the athletes being more practical than the nonathletes. Inspection of the sex by athletic participation interaction effect, however, reveals that all females, whether they are athletes or nonathletes, are more practical/less imaginative than either of the two male groups. Within sex, the relationship between practicality and athletic participation does hold up, but across sex lines it does not.

There is also a second interaction effect on factor M, college by athletic participation. Inspection of this interaction effect reveals that the other observed relationships on this factor are further mediated by the influence of the college social system. Both groups from the men's college were more imaginative/less practical than all other groups, but the men's college athletes were more imaginative than their nonathlete counterparts. Within the women's college a similar pattern was found, the athletes being more imaginative than the nonathletes. Only within the coed college were the athletes more practical/less imaginative than the nonathletes. The coed college nonathletes, in addition, were more imaginative than either of the two women's college groups. The most practical of all groups were the coed college athletes.

The main effect of athletic participation on factor N (forthrightness), indicates that athletes regardless of sex or college are more forthright than nonathletes. Sex is the only main effect found for factor O (self-assured/apprehensive): The females are significantly more apprehensive than the males.

Sex and college are shown as significant main effects on the conservative/experimenting factor (Q1). Males, whether or not athletes, are significantly more experimenting than females. In the MCA, with sex controlled, the men's college students are most experimenting and coed college students the most conservative. On factor Q2 (group-dependent/self-sufficient), the only significant effect is by sex—the males are significantly more self-sufficient than the females. On the self-control factor (Q3), college has the only significant main effect. When controlled for sex in the MCA, the coed college students are the most self-controlled and the women's college students the least self-controlled.

On the second-order factor of introversion/extroversion (SI), there are two significant main effects, sex and college, and two significant interaction effects, sex by athletic participation and college by athletic participation. The females are more extroverted than the males and (when controlled for sex in the MCA), the men's college students are the most extroverted and the coed college students the most introverted. The sex by athletic participation interaction reveals that the relationship between athletic participation and introversion/extroversion differs for the two sexes. While female nonathletes are more extroverted than female athletes, it is the male athletes who are more

extroverted than the male nonathletes. Examination of the second interaction (college by athletic participation) reveals that the women's college athletes and nonathletes, in that order, are the most extroverted and the coed college nonathletes and athletes are the most introverted; the men's college nonathletes and athletes, in that order, follow the women's college groups.

Factor SIII (emotional poise) shows two significant main effects, sex and athletic participation. The males are significantly more emotionally poised than the females, and the athletic participants are more emotionally poised than the nonparticipants. The group-dependent/self-sufficient second-order factor (SIV) is characterized by two significant main effects, sex and college. Males in general are more independent than the females but when sex is controlled in the MCA, the men's college students are more group-dependent than the students from the other two colleges.

Sex, college, and athletic participation all show significant main effects on the masculinity scale. The males are more masculine than the females and athletes, regardless of sex, more masculine than nonathletes; the men's college students are the most masculine and the coed college students, the least. In addition, there is a significant college by athletic participation interaction. The men's college athletes and nonathletes are the most masculine, followed by the women's college and coed college athletes, and the women's college, and coed college nonathletes, in that order.

On the femininity scale, sex has the only significant and entirely predictable main effect: The females are more feminine than the males. There is also a significant sex by athletic participation interaction; female nonathletes are the most feminine followed by female athletes, male athletes, and male nonathletes. The finding that male athletes are more feminine than the male nonathletes is particularly significant in light of the earlier contention that traditional female characteristics could prove to be valuable in athletics.

Sex, college, and athletic participation all have significant main effects on the androgyny score. Females are closer to zero than males and nonathletes closer than athletes, and athletes deviate more toward masculinity. The coed college students are closest to zero, and the men's college students are farthest from zero.

Summary. The overall pattern of the results clearly indicates the importance of taking into consideration additional variables when attempting to investigate the relationship between athletic participation and personality. The interaction effects are particularly revealing in this respect. On factors A (outgoing/reserved), H (shy/venturesome), M (practical/ imaginative), and SI (introversion/extroversion) the sex by athletic participation interactions revealed that the relationships between personality and athletic participation were in the exact opposite directions for males and females. The college by athletic participation interactions on factors M

(practical/imaginative) and SI (introversion/extroversion) indicated that relationships between athletic participation and personality vary according to the college social system.

Athletic participation, however, does have independent main effects on several of the personality and sex-role identity variables that hold across sex and college lines: conscientiousness (G), toughmindedness (I), forthrightness (N), emotional poise (SII), masculinity and androgyny. Athletes, regardless of sex and college, are more conscientious, toughminded, forthright, emotionally poised, and masculine than nonathletes. These findings are consistent with earlier findings. These findings, however, should not blind us to the fact that other variables must also be investigated before direct relationships between personality and athletic participation are posited. The significant interaction effects and main effects of sex and college clearly attest to this type of position.

Four-Way Analysis of Variance on the Combined Athlete Samples.   The previous analyses of the within-sample comparisons of individual-sport athletes and group-sport athletes with nonathletes indicated that the two types of athletic participation may have differential effects upon personality. Early studies have also documented personality differences between athletes in different types of sports and between athletes lettering different numbers of years (e.g., King & Chi, 1974). The previous analyses also revealed that the relationship between personality and type of sport differs according to the sex of the athlete and the college social system the athlete is in. In order to investigate the relative importance of type of sport and number of years lettered when sex and college social system are controlled for, the combined samples of athletes is used in four-way ANOVA. This analysis examines how well the variables of type of sport (individual versus group sports), number of years lettered, sex, and college can explain the variations in the personality and sex-role identity scores found among the athletes from the combined samples. It is hypothesized that sex and college have the most important main effects, with the effects of variables pertaining to athletic participation evident basically in interaction with these two variables. The results of the analysis of variance are presented in Table 5.4.[10] As expected, sex and college are the most important main effects in explaining variations in athletic personality. For none of the personality and sex-role identity measures was type of athletic participation or number of years lettered a main effect. The effects of individual versus group sport participation and intensity of participation as measured by number of years lettered are only seen to be significant in interaction with college or sex.

---

[10]Space limitations preclude inclusion of all means and standard deviations in the tables. The discussion of the findings indicate how the groups compare with one another on the scores.

On factor E (assertiveness), there are two significant main effects, sex and college. Male athletes are more assertive than their female counterparts; the men's college athletes are the most assertive and the coed college athletes, the least. The effect of college remains when sex is controlled in MCA. There is also a significant interaction effect (college by type of sports by number of

TABLE 5.4
Four-Way Analysis of Variance for Combined Samples of Athletes
(Significant *F*-values Only)

Measure	Source of Variation	F	df	p
E: Assertiveness	Sex	4.09	1	.043
	College	6.78	2	.002
	College by type of sport by years	2.34	5	.045
F: Surgency	College by type of sport	3.91	2	.022
G: conscientiousness	College by years	3.06	6	.008
	Sex by type of sport by years	3.40	5	.020
I: Tough-minded/sensitive	Sex	14.38	1	.001
N: Forthright/shrewd	Sex by type of sport by years	3.06	3	.030
Q1: Conservative/experimenting	College	6.46	2	.002
Q3: Self-control	Sex	4.57	1	.033
	College by type of sport	2.34	2	.035
	Type of sport by years	2.60	3	.050
	Sex by type of sport by years	2.85	8	.005
	College by type of sport by years	2.34	5	.045
SI: Introversion/extroversion	College by type of sport	3.46	2	.034
SIII: Anxiety	Sex	7.14	1	.008
	Sex by years	3.55	3	.016
SIV: Group-dependent/independent	Sex	3.71	1	.050
	College	12.29	2	.001
Masculinity	Sex	8.28	1	.005
Feminity	Sex	3.83	1	.05
	College by type of sport	7.85	2	.001
	Sex by type of sport by years	3.80	3	.012
Androgyny	Sex	14.56	1	.01
	College by type of sport	5.03	2	.008
	Sex by type of sport by years	3.31	3	.022

years lettered). The interaction effect indicates that within each college the individual-sport athletes who have lettered a lesser number of years are the most assertive and the group-sport athletes lettering a greater number of years the least. But comparison of these groups across college lines does not necessarily reveal the same type of relationship. The group that is least assertive within one college may still be more assertive than the most assertive group in another college.

The significant interaction effect of college by type of sport for factor F (surgency) reveals a situation similar to that found for factor E. Within each college the group-sport athletes are more surgent than the individual-sport athletes, but comparisons across the men's and coed colleges reveal that the men's college individual athletes are more surgent than the coed college group athletes. Comparisons across the men's and women's colleges and the women's and coed colleges, however, are in line with the basic relationship of surgency and type of sport.

Examination of factor G (conscientiousness) reveals two significant interactions, college by number of years lettered and sex by type of sports by number of years lettered. Although it is found that within each college those lettering a lesser number of years are more conscientious, we cannot say that they are more conscientious than those lettering a greater number of years in another college; both lettering groups in the women's college are more conscientious than all the groups in the men's and coed colleges. Comparisons across the men's and coed colleges, however, indicate that the relationship of conscientiousness to lesser number of years lettered does hold up across these colleges.

From the second interaction, we see that within each sex group, athletes who have lettered the least number of years are the most conscientious, followed by individual athletes lettering a lesser number of years. The group athletes who have lettered a greater number of years are the least conscientious. However, each female group that has lettered a lesser number of years is more conscientious than either of the male groups that have lettered a lesser number of years. Again, female athletes lettering a larger number of years are more conscientious than their male counterparts.

On factor I (tough-minded/sensitive), there is one significant main effect: The females are more sensitive than the males. Factor N (forthrightness) reveals one significant interaction effect, sex by type of sport by number of years lettered. For each sex, group athletes who had lettered a lesser number of years are most forthright, followed by group athletes who had lettered a greater number of years. Individual athletes lettering a greater number of years are the least forthright group. This pattern, however, does not show up in comparisons across sex. All of the female groups, in general, are more forthright than any of the male groups.

On the conservative/experimenting factor (Q1), college is the only significant main effect. The athletes at the men's college are the most

experimenting and the coed college athletes are the most conservative. On factor Q3 (self-control), one significant main effect (sex) is found. Females are significantly more self-controlled than males. In addition, several interaction effects are apparent. The college by type of sports interaction reveals that within each college, group-sports athletes are more self-controlled than individual-sports athletes. Comparisons across the women's and coed colleges repeats this pattern. However, both the group- and individual-sports athletes at the male college score substantially lower on self-control than those of either the women's or the coed colleges. Another interaction term, college by type of sport by number of years lettered, repeats the pattern of the two-way interaction with an additional finding that, within each college, those who had lettered a greater number of years are more self-controlled. The third interaction (sex by type of sport by number of years lettered) shows that within each sex the same pattern as that for within each college is present. However, across sex lines all female groups are more self-controlled than even the male individual-sports athletes who had lettered a greater number of years.

Analysis of the second-order factor SIII (emotional poise) reveals two significant findings. There is a significant main effect for sex—the males being more emotionally poised than the females—and a significant interaction, sex by number of years lettered. Within each sex, those who had lettered fewer years are more emotionally poised than those who had lettered more years. However, even the male athletes who had lettered more years were more emotionally poised than the female athletes who had lettered fewer years.

On the group-dependent/self-sufficient second-order factor (SIV), two significant effects can be seen. First, males are more independent than females and second, the athletes from the men's college are the most selfsufficient while the athletes from the coed college are the most group dependent.

On the masculinity and femininity scales, sex has the only significant main effect, and the effect is in the expected direction. Analyses of the femininity scale also reveal two significant interactions: college by type of sport and sex by type of sport by number of years lettered. The two-way interaction reveals that within each college, group athletes score higher on femininity than individual athletes. All the women's college athletes score higher than all other groups, and all athletes in the coed college score higher than those in the men's college. Examination of the main effects in the MCA reveals that this same pattern would hold even when controlling for sex. The three-way interaction (sex by type of sports by number of years lettered) indicates that, within each sex, as within college and across sex, female athletes in both individual and group sports score higher on femininity than even the male group-sport athletes. The interaction also shows that those who either participate very little or a great deal score higher on femininity, whereas those who participate to a more moderate extent score lower. Again all females, regardless of number of years lettered, scored higher than any of the males.

The finding that both male and female group-sport athletes score higher on femininity than their individual-sport counterparts confirms our earlier speculation that traditionally feminine characteristics would seem to be quite important for all group-sport athletes. This finding, coupled with the finding that male athletes are more feminine than male nonathletes, certainly adds credence to Bem's (1974) contention that both masculine and feminine characteristics are needed by an individual if he/she is to be successful in his/her pursuits.

Examination of the androgyny factor reveals a significant main effect for sex: Females are more adrogynous than males. A significant college by type of sport interaction indicates that both sports types at the women's college are most androgynous, whereas both sports types at the men's college are least adrogynous, whereas both sports types at the men's college are least androgynous. Within each college, the group-sport athletes are slightly more androgynous than the individual-sport athletes.

Summary. The results from the second set of analyses of variance are clearly in line with the basic hypotheses tested and, when combined with the findings from the first set of ANOVA's, lend increased support to the contention that the relationship between personality and athletic participation is understandable or meaningful only when additional variables such as sex and college social structure are taken into account. It was hypothesized that the variations in the personality and sex-role identity measures within the combined samples of athletes would be explained more substantially by the sex and college social system variables than by such variables as type of sports and number of years lettered. Indeed, sex and college proved to have the only significant independent main effects. Looking at the entire group of athletes, type of sport and number of years lettered failed to explain significant variations. Examinations of the interaction effects, however, revealed that these variables did explain the variation in some of the personality and sex-role identity measures within sex and college categories. The particular relationships between personality or sex-role identity and type of sports or number of years lettered did not, however, remain constant across sex and college lines. Within one college or sex group one relationship may be found, while in another college or sex group the other type of relationship exists.

SUMMARY AND IMPLICATIONS

The study of the relationship between athletic participation and personality variation is still in the exploratory stage. Although the quantity of research in this area is increasing, little progress has been made in detemining how and why athletic participation might be related to personality. Researchers often conduct studies using personality inventories and then report whatever

differences show up as giving support to their hypotheses of the prior existence of personality differences. The inadequacies and shortcomings of this type of research have been discussed.

The present study, as a continuation of an earlier study, attempts to develop a general theoretical framework for studying athletic personality. In the earlier study (King & Chi, 1974), we suggested that athletic participation could best be understood when athletes are viewed as a functioning social system composed of various other athletic subsystems. Linking this consideration with an interactionist model of personality allowed us to posit the types of relationships we expected to find between athletic participation and personality. The present research was an attempt to add further evidence to support this approach and to build upon and extend it. We attempted to show that the athletic social system and its subsystems are parts of a larger social system, in this case a college social system, and that the larger system produces variations within the athletic social system. The effect of participation in the athletic social system and its subsystems upon personality was posited to be mediated by the larger social system (the college). The findings seem to support this prediction. In addition, a consideration of sex roles was integrated into the present study to show how additional individual, social, and cultural factors mediate between the relationship of personality and athletic participation.

Our earlier study concluded that the system properties of athletic participation are linked to personality variations between athletes and nonathletes and between athletes in different types of sports. The between-sample comparisons and the two ANOVAs reported in the present study revealed that athletic participation and type of athletic participation are still important variables in understanding personality variations, but that the influence of these variables depends upon the sex of the athletes and the college social system of which the athletic system is a part. It was demonstrated that sex and college membership often submerge the effects of athletic participation. Indeed, the effects of sex and college social system appear to be the major sources of personality variation, at least in terms of main effects.

Although our research has greatly clarified and expanded the study of personality and athletic participation, it does not represent the greatest level of complexity to be reached; for example, we used only college sexual composition as a variable and held constant such variables as location and academic nature of the college. Needless to say, these and other similar variables should be investigated independently. Future research should also focus on the primary socialization and continuing socialization of individuals who become athletic competitors. Consideration of such factors as parental encouragement, social class background, availability of facilities, the types of communities lived in, the particular past and present interests and activities of

APPENDIX TABLE
Distribution of Sample Size by Sex, College, Athletic Status, and Types of Sports

| | Men's College | Women's College | Coed College | | Total |
			Male	Female	
Athletic Status					
Nonathletes	53	63	47	47	210
Athletes	56	31	36	36	159
Total	109	94	83	83	369
Types of Sports					
Individual sports	17	21	17	7	62
Group sports	36	9	19	28	92
Total	53	30	36	35	154[a]

[a]Missing data for five athletes led to their exclusion from the individual/group sports classification, thereby giving us the figure of 154 rather than 159.

individuals, and similar variables, would have great theoretical relevance. Such a line of research would increase our understanding of athletic participation and personality and at the same time broaden our knowledge of social and personality systems in general.

ACKNOWLEDGMENTS

This research was supported in part by grants to the senior author from NIGMS Training Grant #GMO1941 (administered by the Department of Sociology, Cornell University), and from the Mary Baldwin College Faculty Development Fund. Additional assistance was given by the Department of Sociology, and the Department of Consumer Economics and Housing, Cornell University.

REFERENCES

Alderman, R. B. *Psychological behavior in sport.* Philadelphia, Pa.: W. B. Saunders, 1974.
Allen, D. Self concept and the female participant. In D. V. Harris (Ed.), *Women and sport: A national research conference. Proceedings.* University Park: Pennsylvania State University, College of Health, Physical Education and Recreation (Penn State HPER Series No. 2), 1972.
Argyris, C. *Organization of a bank.* New Haven, Conn.: Labor and Management Center, Yale University, 1954.

Beisser, A. R. The American seasonal masculinity rites. In M. M. Hart (Ed.), *Sport in the socio-cultural process*. Dubuque, Iowa: William C. Brown Co., 1972.

Bem, S. L. The measurement of psychological androgyny. *Journal of Consulting and Clinical Psychology*, 1974, *42*, 155–162.

Berlin, P. The woman athlete. In E. W. Gerber, J. Felshin, P. Berlin & W. Wyrick (Eds.), *The American woman in sport*. Reading, Mass.: Addison-Wesley, 1974.

Boslooper, T., & Hayes, M. *The feminity game*. New York: Stein & Day, 1973.

Candell, P. When I was about fourteen. In J. H. Pleck & J. Sawyer (Eds.), *Men and masculinity*. Englewood Cliffs, N.J.: Prentice-Hall, 1974.

Cattell, R. B. r_p and other coefficients of personality. *Psychometrika*, 1949, *14*, 279–298.

Cattell, R. B. *Manual for the 16 PF*. Champaign, Ill.: Institute for Personality and Ability Testing. 1972.

Cattell, R. B., Eber, H. W., & Tatsuoka, M. M. *Handbook for the sixteen personality factor questionnaire* (16 PF). Champaign, Ill.: Institute for Personality and Ability Testing, 1970.

Chafetz, J. S. *Masculine/feminine or human? An overview of the sociology of sex roles*. Itasca, Ill.: F. E. Peacock, 1974.

Cooper, L. Athletics, activity, and personality. *Research Quarterly*, 1969, *40*, 17–22.

Farrell, W. *The liberated man: Beyond masculinity: Freeing men and their relationships with women*. New York: Bantam Books, Inc., 1975.

Felshin, J. The social view. In E. W. Gerber, J. Felshin, P. Berlin, & W. Wyrick (Eds.), *The American woman in sport*. Reading, Mass.: Addison-Wesley, 1974.

Fisher, A. C. In search of the albatross. In A. C. Fisher (Ed.), *Psychology of sport: Issues and insights*. Palo Alto, Calif.: Mayfield Publ. Co., 1976. (a)

Fisher, A. C. (Ed.). *Psychology of sport: Issue and insights*. Palo Alto, Calif.: Mayfield Publ. Co., 1976. (b)

Flanagan, L. A study of some personality traits of different physical activity groups. *Research Quarterly*, 1951, *22*, 312–323.

Gagnon, J. H. Physical strength, once of significance. In J. H. Pleck & J. Sawyer (Eds.), *Men and masculinity*. Englewood Cliffs, N. J.: Prentice-Hall, 1974.

Gerber, E.W. Chronicle of participation. In E. W. Gerber, J. Felshin, P. Berlin, & W. Wyrick (Eds.), *The American woman in sport*. Reading, Mass.: Addison-Wesley, 1974.

Greenstein, F. *Personality and politics*. Chicago: Markham, 1969.

Hardman, K. A dual approach to the study of personality and performance in sport. In H. T. A. Whiting, K. Hardman, L. B. Hendry, & M. G. Jones (Eds.), *Personality and performance in physical education and sport*. Lafayette, Ind.: Balt Publ., 1973.

Harris, D. V. (Ed.). *Women and sport: A national research conference. Proceedings*. University Park: Pennsylvania State University, College of Health, Physical Education and Recreation (Penn State HPER Series No. 2), 1972.

Harris, D. V. *Involvement in sport: A somatopsychic rationale for physical activity*. Philadelphia, Pa.: Lea V. Febiger, 1973.

Hart, M. M. On being female in sport. In M. M. Hart (Ed.), *Sport in the socio-cultural process*. Dubuque, Iowa: William C. Brown Co., 1972. (a)

Hart, M. M. (Ed.). *Sport in the socio-cultural process*. Dubuque, Iowa: William C. Brown Co., 1972. (b)

Hartley, R. E. Sex-role pressure and the socialization of the male child. In J. H. Pleck & J. Sawyer (Eds.), *Men and masculinity*. Englewood Cliffs, N.J.: Prentice-Hall, 1974.

Kane, J. E. Personality and physical activity. In G. S. Kenyon (Ed.), *Contemporary psychology of sport*. Chicago: Athletic Institute, 1970.

Kane, J. E. Psychological aspects of sport with special reference to the female. In D. V. Harris (Ed.), *Women and sport: A national research conference. Proceedings*. University Park:

Pennsylvania State University,. College of Health, Physical Education and Recreation (Penn State HPER Series No. 2), 1972.

King, J. P., & Chi, P. S. K. Personality and the athletic social structure: A case study. *Human Relations,* 1974, *27,* 179–193.

Kroll, W. Current strategies and problems in personality assessment of athletes. In A. Fisher (Ed.), *Psychology of sport: Issues and insights.* Palo Alto, Calif.: Mayfield Publ. Co., 1976.

Kroll, W., & Peterson, K. Personality factor profiles of college football teams. *Research Quarterly,* 1965, *36,* 443–447.

Lakie, W. L. Personality characteristics of certain groups of intercollegiate athletes. *Reseach Quarterly,* 1962, *33,* 566–573.

Lester, J. Being a boy. In J. H. Pleck & J. Sawyer (Eds.), *Men and masculinity.* Englewood Cliffs, N.J.: Prentice-Hall, 1974.

Levine, R. A. *Culture, behavior, and personality.* Chicago: Aldine Publ. Co., 1973.

Lewin, K. *A dyanamic theory of personality: Selected papers.* New York: McGraw-Hill, 1935.

Loy, J. W., Jr. The nature of sport. In J. W. Loy, Jr. & G. S. Kenyon (Eds.), *Sport, culture, and society: A reader on the sociology of sport.* New York: Macmillan, 1969. (a)

Loy, J. W., Jr., & Kenyon, G. S. (Eds.), Sport and small groups: Overview: The sport group as a micro-social system. In J. W. Loy, Jr. & G. S. Kenyon (Eds.), *Sport, culture, and society: A reader on the sociology of sport.* New York: Macmillan, 1969. (b)

Loy, J. W., Jr., & Kenyon, G. S. (Eds.). *Sport, culture and society: A reader on the sociology of sport.* New York: Macmillan, 1969. (c)

Maccoby, E. E. Woman's Intellect. In S. Farber & R. Wilson (Eds.), *The Potential of Woman.* New York: New York: McGraw Hill, 1963.

Maccoby, E. E., & Jacklin, C. N. *The psychology of sex differences.* Stanford, University Press, 1974.

Malumphy, T. Personality of women athletes in intercollegiate competition. *Research Quarterly,* 1968, *39,* 610.

Martens, R. The paradigmatic crises in American sport personology. In A. Fisher (Ed.), *Psychology of sport: Issues and insights.* Palo Alto, Calif.: Mayfield Publ. Co., 1976.

Mead, G. H. *Mind, self and society.* Chicago: University of Chicago Press, 1934.

Merton, R. Bureaucratic structures and personality. *Social Forces,* 1940, *18,* 560–568.

Metheny, E. Symbolic forms of movement: The feminine image in sports. In H. M. Hart (Ed.), *Sport in the socio-cultural process.* Dubuque, Iowa: William C. Brown Co., 1972.

Mischel, W. *Personality and assessment.* New York: Wiley, 1968.

Morgan, W. P. (Ed.). *Contemporary reading in sport psychology.* Springfield, Ill.: Charles C. Thomas, 1970.

Nie, N., Hull, C. H. Jenkins, J. G., Steinbrenner, K., & Bent, D. H. *Statistical package for the social sciences.* New York: McGraw-Hill, 1975.

Ogilvie, B. C. Psychological consistencies within the personality of high-level competitors. In W. P. Morgan (Ed.), *Contemporary reading in sport psychology.* Springfield, Ill.: Charles C. Thomas, 1970.

Out in right field. In J. H. Pleck & J. Sawyer (Eds.), *Men and masculinity.* Englewood Cliffs, N. J.: Prentice-Hall, 1974.

Peterson, S., Weber, J., & Trousdale, W. Personality traits of women in team sports vs. women in individual sports. *Research Quarterly,* 1967, *38,* 686–690.

Pleck, J. H., & Sawyer, J. (Eds.). *Men and masculinity.* Englewood Cliffs, N. J.: Prentice-Hall, 1974.

Rushall, B. S. Three studies relating personality variables to football performance. In A. Fisher (Ed.), *Psychology of sport: Issues and insights.* Palo Alto, Calif.: Mayfield Publ. Co., 1976.

Ryan, E. D. The questions we ask and the decisions we make. In A. Fisher (Ed.), *Psychology of sport: Issues and insights.* Palo Alto, Calif.: Mayfield Publ. Co., 1976.

Sage, G. H. An assessment of personality profiles between and within intercollegiate athletics from eight different sports. In A. Fisher (Ed.), *Psychology of sport: Issues and insights.* Palo Alto, Calif.: Mayfield Publ. Co., 1976.

Schandel, J. Psychological differences between athletes and nonparticipants in athletics at three educational levels. *Research Quarterly,* 1965, *36,* 52-67.

Scott, J. *The athletic revolution.* New York: The Free Press, 1971.

Shaffer, T. E. Physiological considerations of the female participant. In D. V. Harris (Ed.), *Women and sport: A national research conference. Proceedings.* University Park: Pennsylvania State University, College of Health, Physical Education and Recreation (Penn State HPER Series No. 2), 1972.

Sherif, C. Females in the competitive process. In D. V. Harris (Ed.), *Women and sport: A national research conference. Proceedings.* University Park: Pennsylvania State University, College of Health, Physical Education and Recreation (Penn State HPER Series No. 2), 1972.

Singer, R. N. Personality differences between and within baseball and tennis players. *Research Quarterly,* 1969, *40,* 582-588.

Singer, R. N. *Myths and truths in sports psychology.* New York: Harper & Row, 1975.

Smelser, N. J., & Smelser, W. T. (Eds.). *Personality and social systems.* New York: Wiley, 1963.

Smith, M. Aggression and the female athlete. In D. V. Harris (Ed.), *Women and sport: A national research conference. Proceedings.* University Park: Pennsylvania State University, College of Health, Physical Education and Recreation (Penn State HPER Series No. 2), 1972.

Spears, B. The emergence of women in sport. In B. J. Hoepner (Ed.), *Women's athletics: Coping with controversy.* DWGS Report. Washington, D.C.: American Association for Health, Physical Education & Recreation, Aapher Publications, 1974.

Spiegel, J. *Transactions: The interplay between individual, family, and society.* New York: Science House, 1971.

Straub, W., & Davis, S. Personality traits of college football players who participated at different levels of competition. *Medicine and Science in Sports,* 1971, *3,* 39-43.

Sutton-Smith, B., Roberts, J. M., & Kozelka, R. M. Game involvement in adults. In J. W. Loy, Jr. & G. S. Kenyon (Eds.), *Sport, culture, and society: A reader on the sociology of sport.* New York: Macmillan, 1969.

Swanson, R. A. From glide to stride: Significant events in a century of American women's sport. In B. J. Hoepner (Ed.), *Women's athletics: Coping with controversy.* DGWS Report. Washington, D.C.: American Association for Health, Physical Education & Recreation, Aapher Publications, 1974.

Tyler, S. Adolescent crisis: Sport participation for the female. In D. V. Harris (Ed.), *Women and sport: A national research conference. Proceedings.* University Park: Pennsylvania State University, College of Health, Physical Education and Recreation (Penn State HPER Series No. 2), 1972.

Weitz, S. *Sex Roles: Biological, psychological, and social foundations.* New York: Oxford University Press, 1977.

Werner, A. C., & Gottheil, E. Personality development and participation in college athletics. In A Fisher (Ed.), *Psychology of sport: Issues and insights.* Palo Alto, Calif.: Mayfield Publ. Co., 1976.

Yinger, J. M. *Toward a field theory of behavior.* New York: McGraw-Hill, 1965.

Yinger, J. M. *The scientific study of religion.* New York: McGraw-Hill, 1970.

6 The Personality of Those Women Who Have Dared To Succeed in Sport

Bruce C. Ogilvie
San Jose State University

This is a significant moment in our history to examine some of the central problems faced by the women who seek to excel in our society. It is incidental to our discussion whether our female achiever is found in the world of science, the arts, politics, sports, or any other area of accomplishment. There are those few exceptions where the achiever has been trained from infancy to resist being defined by the prevailing stereotypes in our culture. Excluding this small sample, the great majority of women are trapped by a form of ambivalence that leads to an inhibition of the fullest expression of their potential talent. The extreme manifestion of this ambivalence may take the form of a true "success phobic" reaction.

The waste of feminine potential for those who are burdened with this unconscious fear with respect to the expression of their skill, aptitude or talent cannot accurately be estimated. Though it is evident that an increasing number of women are standing on the threshold of creative freedom, far too many are experiencing the negation of their potential by the unconscious social fears that block their freedom of action.

The fundamental cause of this inhibition has borne many labels. Among those to be used as points of reference in this discussion are "social role expectancies," "early role definition," "sex identification," and "cultural

BRUCE OGILVIE received his Ph.D. at the University of London, Institute of Psychiatry. He is currently Professor of Counseling and Psychology at San Jose State University, coordinator of the Institute for the Study of Athletic Motivation and a Consultant for Sports Science Associates, Inc., Denver. He has been a consultant to U.S. Olympic teams since 1964, 12 teams in the National Football League, 13 national baseball teams, and four teams in the National Basketball Association.

female modeling." Each shares the common causal chain of circumstances and therefore contributes to preconceptions as to how a women must define herself in order to avoid identity conflicts. Independent of the capriciousness or the arbitrariness of these role definitions and societal pressures, the ascribed model takes on the structure of an absolute. The assumption is made that once she integrates within her personality these gender absolutes, she becomes conflict-free because she is acting consistent with her psychological, social, and physical nature. Both consciously and unconsciously she absorbs those attitudes and integrates those values that are rewarded, and extinguishes those for which she is punished. Early career identification is an excellent example of the imposition of cultural bias upon human ability.

It has been only most recently in our history that quotas set for women seeking to enter the professions have been branded as illegal. The 1972 investigation in the state of California of the relationship of gender to the probability of completing university training offers substantial evidence with respect to bias and the consequent role conflict for women. It was found that females scored significantly higher than males with regard to academic preparation when entering as freshmen. In spite of academic superiority the proportion of females completing their degree was only 30% as compared to 70% of the males. The same study completed in 1976 gives strong evidence that the conflict may be diminishing because the percentage of females who graduated had reached 40%. Examples of "role ambivalence" of this magnitude can be documented throughout our entire social structure. The data from every investigation illustrates the intrusion of unconscious negative feelings or conflictive attitudes that form the basis for her role ambivalence. Should she succumb to these cultural pressures and become imbued with the myth as to what constitutes acceptable feminine behavior, she becomes the prisoner of an absurdity. Aptitude, talent, ability, and intelligence know no gender, each defines a human quality and has only a most limited relationship to one's biology.

Our abysmal ignorance about successful women gives evidence once again of our social priorities in terms of interest. It is possible to read the entire literature about them during a single weekend. The growing curiosity about these women makes it essential that we begin to use the meager information that is available to us. At the present time it will offer us the most objective means for expanding our understanding of how the female achiever has warded off cultural conformity and maintained a strong personal identity. When we begin to comprehend the personality structure of even a select sample of successful women, we should be able to discern the attributes that have enabled them to counter cultural stereotyping.

In terms of role expectancies, how do these women ward off manipulation of this kind and still function efficiently? What motivation attributes do they ascribe to themselves that produces the energy as well as the freedom to set

their own priorities? The data presented are based on interpretations of psychometric studies and depth interviews with female athletes. The samples include 16 women selected by the U.S. Parachute Association as the most outstanding national competitors; 14 established licensed drivers who were actively competing, identified by Sports Car Clubs of America as outstanding women competitors; 26 women fencers from the 1968 National Championships; the 1968 U.S. basketball team; the California State intercollegiate swimming champions; 40 Olympic women swimmers, including those who received either gold, silver, or bronze medals; Olympic women's track and field athletes. Other inferences are drawn from women competitors in tennis, golf, skiing, water skiing and aerobatics. The husbands' comments were collected whenever the opportunity presented itself, usually at the competition site.

During an interview with a woman who was among the best professionals in her field and was distinguished by her international reptuation, she described herself as a "cultural mutant." She stated that she was the only female in her family to ever gain independence. What does it take in terms of personality to be able to stand in the face of enormous prejudice and make the "leap of freedom?"

Women who have been able to penetrate the myth can provide us with the psychological insight that can enable us to better prepare other striving women. Based upon extensive interviews plus responses to a number of personality inventories, a highly consistent motivational picture emerges. The woman who appears best prepared in terms of personality to avoid career ambivalence or success-phobia describes herself as if she had experienced a culture that is quite different from that of women in general. They proved to be candid, open, nondefensive subjects of study. The interview was perceived as just another interesting challenge where they could match their response tendencies against others.

Now let her tell her own story, how she sees herself, and how she tends to respond in a wide variety of situations:

I am deeply imbued with the drive for success which means I set high goals for myself and for those with whom I become involved. In my fantasies I often see myself as receiving recognition and acclaim for expressing my talent. I have a very positive mental set and feel I can accomplish anything to which I put my hand. It is extremely easy for me to express contrary thoughts or ideas. Subordinating myself to the will of others comes very hard for me even when they hold positions of power over me. Following the advice, counsel or leadership of others would take a very special effort on my part.

I respond poorly to the dependency needs of others. Passive-dependency tends to turn me off because I become impatient and resentful when I'm leaned on. Self-direction and independence of action are amongst the highest developed traits in my personality. It is easy for me to become aggressive,

particularly when standing up for something in which I have a deep investment. Condescension to others simply because they have titles or the mantel of authority would be most rare indeed.

I actively seek the leadership role and enjoy making the final decisions. Others seek me out as leader and select me as the one to settle disputes. Supervising, directing or influencing the actions of others seems to come natural for me.

I am socially bold and uninhibited in my life style. There is a strong tendency within me toward nonconformity. Traditional values, cultural definitions as to what constitutes right or correct behavior influence me only slightly. I see the role of woman much as I would view a cafeteria table where I am free to select those forms of human behavior that are consistent with my personal view of my own nature.

I have a hard nosed view of reality which inclines me toward seeing things precisely as they are in the world. It is easy for me to turn off my emotions when there is a danger that they might diminish my capacity for sound judgement. I seem to have good control over inner emotional urgencies which could color my perception of the hard facts. Although I know guilt, it would rarely become the basis for motivating my actions. Mistakes, errors and failures are quickly brushed out of consciousness. It is a great waste of time to engage in self-punishing thoughts or actions. I avoid intropunitivenss because it tends to disturb my capacity for making sound decisions. Societal pressures as to the correctness of human behavior might distress me but don't significantly change the choice I make. I feel guilt is basically a destructive emotional force and therefore should be shunned.

My enthusiasm causes me to take on more projects than I can usually handle. Perseverence is not one of my long suits as it is extremely difficult for me to stay with things without getting distracted. My mind seems to race ahead to new or different concerns. Boredom comes very quickly particularly when locked into the requirement of the routine application of my talent. Part of my success has been my willingness to admit this fault and then compensate by training someone else to handle details. If I had four lifetimes, I could never complete all the projects I have in mind right at this moment.

Confrontation, which requires the expressing of my natural aggression, does not cause me to feel uneasy or guilty. Contrary views or interpretations that differ from my own tend to pull me out of myself in the form of doing battle. I can take a strong stand and actively argue for my point of view. Though I support the women's rights, I have never participated actively in the movement. I know this is because I have had more space in which to be a person than the average women in this society.

I feel most fortunate to be gifted with excellent physical health. Rarely have I ever used physical symptoms as an excuse to escape from emotional pressure. My mood tends to be quite stable. Should I get depressed it passes rapidly and I'm on my way up again. I experience my body as highly charged with vital energy. I seem to thrive on mental and physical activities. I possess a healthy libido and have a most permissive view with regard to sex.

Experimentation with new and different types of experiences is most natural for me. I like to travel and enjoy the variety of experience found in change. I am

much inclined toward risk taking and find tremendous excitement when I am living on the fine edge of my existence. I tend to seek out social, emotional or physical risks which turn others off. I enjoy sound mental health and feel that I function on a high level of ego integration. When facing exaggerated threats of any kind rather than retreating behind some neurotic defense I tend to attack the source.

Let me sum myself up as best I can from looking objectively at myself. I am different from most women in my aggression, ambition, self-direction, exhibitionism, dominance, surgency, assertiveness, tough-mindedness, self-assurance, impulsiveness, health both physical and mental, need for action, risk-taking and low tendency to feel guilt. I am inner motivated and therefore I have a low need to seek social approval. I choose my own values and life-styles.

The foregoing summation of her self-picture forces the conclusion that in her close personal relationships she is a most formidable lady. Therefore, experiencing her through the eyes of the significant other in her life will greatly enrich our insight:

She studiously avoids people who want to lay out their life story of toil and tears or expose their personal problems. If I should complain or try to manipulate her in order to get emotional support, she becomes cool and analytic. Even my minor illnesses will cause her to retreat and become less giving. She often can make me feel that in her eyes I am not moving ahead fast enough. She frequently is critical of those whom she views as just standing still or treading water. One of her most characteristic responses would be, "Why don't they get off their dead butt and get going?" She consistently sees those who continually fail as individuals who are unwilling to pay the price she has paid for success.

Her restlessness and high energy level at times are hard for me to take, particularly when I'm in need of a tranquil period. At times she seems only to exist as a positive creature when she is confronting another challenge. Even our recreational life must be expressed in some form of physical action. When she gets tense or anxious you can bet that she will turn quickly to some form of physical outlet. Rumination over past blunders or mistakes is certainly not her style. The arguments we had last week are a dead issue, it's what we are going to do about the here and now that counts with her. Her impulsiveness probably causes me the most distress in our relationship. I find myself continually running around trying to tie up loose ends because of her lack of concern for planning ahead.

She is quite modest in terms of making emotional demands upon me. I feel that I enjoy much more freedom in my relationship than activities we share. She will beat me in checkers, poker, tennis or first in the shower; it makes no difference. I can stand the heat she generates because she is a most exciting lady even though at times I feel I am hanging on the tail of a tornado. I know that the last thing I can do is to ever take her for granted. Should I ever be so inclined I must be prepared for a long drop.

It is reasonable to assume that as our society produces ever increasing numbers of counter-culture females like these women, the threat imposed upon tradition-bound males magnifies proportionately. Sex stereotypes die slowly, if they ever die. It is apparent that the greater the cultural reinforcement of a concept of women as passive, dependent, willingly submissive, servants to men and whose basic motive for existence is her nesting instinct, the more difficult will be her quest for freedom. The repression and denial she is forced to master in order to meet these role expectancies produces a prisonlike effect that can seal away her potential forever.

Should we decide that for the improvement of our society, or simply on the basis of human justice, we must produce increasing numbers of women with the character structure defined here, what are the implications with respect to male adjustment? Should she make a total commitment to her talent, the one most obvious implication has to be the ego threat for the average male. It has been the exceptional male who has been able to avoid getting into some unhealthy form of competition with the investment the achievement-oriented woman must make in order to excel. Many respond to her interest in a career as if it were another lover vieing for her affection. The consequences of this form of insecurity contribute to an attempt to undermine or devalue her career commitment. Any attempt to produce feelings of guilt create self-doubt with respect to her appropriate role and can become the basis for producing severe conflicts in the relationship. The greater the masculine insecurity the more intense will be the need to reestablish himself as the number one priority in her life. Compound this form of insecurity with a myopic view of the nature of women and you have the picture of the male who is least likely to live in a complimentary partnership with her.

In social evolutionary terms we have been listening to and hearing about women who may be considered in terms of the present standard as true cultural mutants. Social, psychological, and physical rebellion have been essential characteristics that have enabled her to ward off external definitions as to the true nature of woman. She refused to be manipulated by traditional stereotypes and has the intestinal fortitude to seek a deeply personal concept of "womenness." She learns quickly that rebellion is not true freedom because it is too bound up with negative or angry emotions that deplete her valuable energy. She does experience it as a necessary first step that equips her to stand above the culture and make freer personal choices. It has not been too many years since every form of female self determination was defined negatively such as overcompensation, masculine protest and even penis envy. The personality attributes that these women have ascribed to themselves appear essential if they are to free themselves from the intrusion of bias, prejudice and most importantly, ignorance about human nature. When it is possible to arrange the personality traits of successful women in hierarchical order, we may have produced the ideal model for the woman of the future.

It also becomes imperative that we educate the women with high levels of aspiration that there is a negative side to the quest for success. She must be alerted to the danger of losing the tender and giving side of her nature in the ruthless competitive marketplace that is so much of her reality.

It appears quite possible that our cultural mutant may have little insight into the type of threat that she imposes upon others. Her natural vitality and positive investment in life cause her to appear exciting and socially desirable. The constantly changing moods and her tendency to become bored easily may place excessive demands upon others.

The degree to which this personality organization has affected her capacity to adjust in other areas of her life needs to be investigated. Successful professional women in their autobiographies describe the strong convictions that are essential for them to establish personal priorities. Such examples as delaying marriage in order to complete their education, choosing to establish themselves in their professions before fulfilling childbearing needs, and making the adjustment to their children's needs only until she feels the children will not be negatively affected by substitute parental care. She also chooses to restrict the number of children she will bear.

Janet Cuca reporting in the *APA Monitor,* January, 1976, offers some strong evidence with respect to the relationship of the institution of marriage and professional achievement for women in the field of psychology. She reports the marked differences between men and women psychologists and between women with masters degree level training and those with Ph.D. In the combined women professionals, 22% never married, whereas only 8% of the males never married. Of the males, 5% are separated or divorced, and 13% of the women are separated or divorced. Educational levels of the professional women proved to discriminate even more dramatically the adjustment factors associated with high levels of attainment. Although only 18% of women with masters never married, over 28% of women with Ph.D. never married. The fact that only 53% of females with Ph.D. marry, whereas between 90 and 95% of males with the same level of professional training marry, clearly substantiates that the women were subjected to pressures that forced them to alter their priorities.

The National Science Foundation report showed clearly that this finding was not unique to women psychologists because women sociologists, anthropologists, and other social scientists are avoiding or dissolving marriages at an even greater rate. The social and emotional cost for the female achiever should be a serious area of study. During personal interviews and within the privacy of the privileged communication the near-universal concern expressed by these women was the maintenance of close personal or intimate relationships. It would be premature to suggest that this is more evident in her life than that of her less competitive sisters.

In closing, it should be stated that it is impossible to estimate the loss of creative energy or potential talent caused by the unconscious fear of success

that is conditioned in the female. This is equally true in terms of those young women who purchase uncritically the myth as to the nature of women. The central conflict ultimately boils down to that of the free expression of her talent rather than to continually look back over her shoulder for some sign of social approval. She must be able to leave behind any of the remnants of doubt or guilt because she has refused ever again to be defined by others. She knows that she must be constantly on guard against those culturally repressive features that would drive her off her chosen course. As stated previously, she must brand upon her brain the following truth: talent, success, achievement and creativity know no gender; each describes a human potential. When she fully accepts that truth, she can truly make the leap for freedom.

7

Athletic Profile Inventory (API): Assessment of Athletes' Attitudes and Values

James M. Jones
American Psychological Association

Stephen A. Williamson
Harvard University

INTRODUCTION

America is an achieving society. As such, the merits of an individual's life are based upon successful acquisition or accomplishment. Nearly every means of judging success follows from attempts to quantify the sum of a person's activities over some specified period of time (e.g., how many years of school, how much income, homes owned, cars, TVs, books written, articles written, movies produced, share of viewing audience and so on). Employing the

JAMES M. JONES is currently Director of the Minority Fellowship Program of the American Psychological Association in Washington, D.C. The research reported in this chapter was conducted while he was an associate professor of social psychology at Harvard University. Dr. Jones received his B.A. from Oberlin College, M.A. from Temple University and his Ph.D. from Yale in 1970. His research interests include sports personality and social-dynamics. He has written a book about 5'5" ex-NFL running back Mack Herron that is now in search of a publisher. Dr. Jones also does research in humor, having spent a year in Trinidad as a Guggenheim Fellow in 1973–1974 studying Calypso. He is currently working on a revision of his *Prejudice and Racism* (Addison-Wesley, 1972) and a critique of cultural biases in American Social Science research under a Ford Foundation grant.

STEPHEN A. WILLIAMSON recently completed his Ph.D. in social psychology at Harvard University where he worked with Dr. Jones on the research reported in this chapter. Dr. Williamson completed his A.B. at Brown University in 1971, and has worked for several years as a consultant to a variety of organizations involved in major change programs. He currently has a private consulting practice, is an associate of McBer, Inc. (a Boston consulting firm), and is conducting research on small group behavior, organizational development, performance evaluation and the relationship of playing and working. With R. F. Bales and S. P. Cohen, he is about to publish a book on a new method of systematic observation, and is presently working on a book developing a theory of play in work settings.

157

standard assessment tool of almost anything (call it the Richter Scale Measure of Success), "On a scale of one to ten," we evaluate conduct, performance, and progress.

"Winning isn't everything, it's the only thing." This statement was attributed to the late and legendary Vince Lombardi. In no other area of human performance are the canons of achievement orientation more conspicuously applied than in organized athletics. In no other domain is winning more definite and public. Competition is the driving force behind much of the achievement aspirations of many people in our society. Competition follows from the situation where a desirable goal can only be reached by fewer than the number of people who desire it. In many everyday circumstances, failure to achieve a specific goal is muted by the well known Freudian gambits of substitution, sublimation and rationalization. But, in organized athletics, winning is the only thing.

We began our research into the attitudes and philosophy of athletes several years ago because it seemed to be such a rich forum for scrutinizing many of the empirical and theoretical questions of social scientific interest in an achieving society. This field is rich for social psychology in particular for a number of reasons:

1. The essence of team sports is the effective integration of the individual with the team in pursuit of a common goal.
2. Behaviors are easily quantified and can be systematically compared to attitude domains.
3. Social organization is clear, and authority structures are easily described.
4. Interracial contact is extensive and subject to the attendant conflicts and occasional successes.
5. Women have always been peripheral participants, but promise to move increasingly into the mainstream of organized athletic activity, raising the issue of sex roles in this domain.

Although we had this very broad-based view of the merits of sports research, the specific impetus for undertaking a research program was an empirical observation concerning basketball players. Worthy and Markle (1970) and Jones and Hochner (1973) have shown that white basketball players are more accurate free-throw shooters, while black players are either more accurate or not significantly different in field goal accuracy than white players. Whereas Worthy and Markle chose to embed this observation in an imperative scheme emphasizing the descriptive characteristics of the two performance activities (*self-paced* to describe free throws, and *reactive* to describe field goals), and further to implicate physiological racial differences in the explanation (Worthy, Note 1), Jones and Hochner offered a sociocultural rationale, based on the principles of "technique" and "style".

Sports Personality.   We described a three-factor personality orientation with each factor consisting of a bipolar attitude domain.

1. ACHIEVEMENT

success..style

2. POWER

competition.....................................play

3. AFFILIATION

team ....individual

This model assumes that the overall issues represented by each motivational factor are applicable to everyone, but that relatively different psychological emphases distinguish one pole from the other. For example, in achievement, everyone wishes to play well, but the basis for judgment of good performance varies. A "success" player (this was a poor choice of terms, "technique" would have been better) learns by the book, is highly coachable, and tends to do things in the prescribed manner. For example, Rick Barry as a free-throw shooter epitomizes this orientation. He has mastered the mechanics of free-throw shooting to a fluid underhand motion that can be repeated with great accuracy time and again.

By contrast, the "style" player often brings a unique set of skills to the performance of the same activities. To highlight this distinction, let us describe the Slam Dunk competition sponsored by CBS for players in the National Basketball Association. Two players compete in a match consisting of five attempts at slam dunking the ball through the basket. Each made dunk counts two points. In addition, a panel of three judges evaluates the overall 'style' of the five dunks on a scale of 1–10. The maximum score is 40 (three judges give 10 each, all dunks are made). There are several interesting observations to be made about this competition. First, it is the first time that style has been explicitly recognized in major American sports. The only other sports where points are actually awarded on style are in swimming, gymnastics and figure skating.[1] The second thing to be noted is the interplay between style and technique. The most successful performer must not only make all of the dunks but do it with style. Superstars in any sport are noted because they not only have an element of unique style, but they necessarily possess extraordinary technical skills. The third point is simply that, in general, style is much more difficult to measure and hence, in the arena of numbers and quantifications, more difficult to serve as a basis for evaluation.

---

[1]It is also interesting to note that, in all three of these, women participate in fairly large numbers. Style in basketball is clearly the outgrowth of the influx of black players. This suggests that style per se is a counter establishment orientation.

The *Power* factor is critical and probably serves to weed people out as they progress up the sports competition ladder. It is unlikely that many athletes would ever reach the professional level without intense competitive drive. Two cases stand out to highlight this dimension. Both Bill Walton (Portland center) and Dave Cowens (Boston center) have had problems stabilizing in their professional careers. Both are extraordinary and gifted athletes. It appears that Cowens' problem may be that he is too competitive. In Boston, there are legendary stories and photos of Cowens flying through the air parallel to the floor in quest of a loose ball. Walton, on the other hand, appears to be a more passive, easy-going person for whom raising competitive instincts to such a high pitch causes some pain. In general, then, power factor refers to individualized competitive concerns (cf. McClelland, Davis, Kalin, & Wanner, 1972). Our notion corresponds to the concept of *p*-Power in their scheme.

The *Affiliation* factor was more of an overall orientation toward social-psychological relationships. A team-oriented person would gain more from the association with other players. That is, being part of the team with all that issued from that affiliation would be a strong motivational force for this athlete. The individual-oriented athlete might participate for more personal reasons. This factor might relate to outside sports activities or actual on-the-field activities. Of the three, it is probably the least important in terms of evaluating athletic performance.

Attitudes Toward Achievement. The classic approach toward achievement motivation is given in the work of McClelland, Atkinson, and Clark (1953), who summarize the general notion as:

> Achievement is the latent disposition to compete with a standard of excellence that involves both a persistent desire for such competition and an emotional concern with it. The assumed motive is expressed by the individual as affective concern about or preoccupation with doing well in relation to achievement goals. Unique accomplishments, instrumental acts toward attainment, obstacles to overcome and prospects of success and failure operationally define the concerns indicative of need achievement [p. 32].

The development of achievement motivation theory has progressed with attempts to specify the psychological parameters and behavioral consequences of the motive. For example, Atkinson, (1974) and Atkinson and Feather, (1966) have taken a conflicting approach that views achievement motivation as the resultant positive approach (goal directed) tendency and a negative avoidance (fear of failure) tendency. In the athletic context, which of these tendencies dominates could have very significant implications for

performance style and coachability. A player motivated more by fear of failure will likely take more conservative approaches to performance and play well enough to avoid criticism from coaches. A player motivated more strongly by desire for success will likely be more aggressive in performance and respond more to praise from coaches. In fact, a player so motivated might well find excessive concern for eliminating mistakes to have an inhibiting effect on performance.

Another approach to achievement is given by Weiner, Frieze, Kukla, Reed, Rest, and Rosenbaum (1971); Kukla (1970); and Weiner (1973). Weiner hypothesizes that individuals utilize four elements of ascription in their attempt to make interpretations and predictions about achievement-related events. These four elements are ability (A), effort (E), task difficulty (T), and luck (L), which represent the cells of a 2×2 matrix of causal determinants of achievement outcomes. The variables considered in this ascription model of achievement outcomes are locus of control (internal, external) and stability of outcome (stable, unstable). An internal locus and stable outcome suggests ability-caused achievment. An internal locus and unstable outcome suggests variable effort is responsible for the outcome. External locus ascriptions suggest either task properties (stable) or luck (unstable) is responsible for the outcome.

Employing this conception of achievement-related behavioral attribution, Weiner and Kukla (1970) found that, in general, effort is a more salient determinant of the distribution of rewards and punishments than is ability. College subjects role-played grade school teachers and distributed rewards and punishments for exam performance. In each ability level, high effort was rewarded more than low effort. However, for each level of effort, low ability was rewarded more than high ability.

Another finding suggests that individuals with relatively high achievement needs tend to ascribe the causes of the performance (both success and failure) to internal attributes (ability and/or effort) (Weiner & Kukla, 1970; Weiner & Potepan, 1970). In addition, high achievers typically see their failure as due to lack of effort, while low achievers more frequently see failure as an indication of lack of ability. Weiner et al. (1971) interpret this as evidence that high achievers see failure as alterable and hence a basis for increased motivation and effort. Low achievers, on the other hand, see this as evidence for a basic incapacity and hence reason to stop trying.

The implications of this analysis for achievement-related athletic perform-ance are considerable. Consider some of the slogans that are commonly found on locker room walls. "Anybody can be ordinary, but it takes guts to excel." "Dedication and devotion are keys to success." "Good training makes a good athlete." A summary of athletic sloganeering suggests quite clearly that hard work and sacrifice (effort), as much or more than natural ability are the

important attributes of a successful athlete. The willingness to work hard and sacrifice is summarized by coaches under the term "good attitude."[2]

Let us consider an athlete who has substantial ability, and participates in a sport as an expression of that ability. The athlete is out to develop further and express that which he or she does well, not to overcome ability deficiency with ever-increasing levels of effort expenditure. To the extent that a coach elects to focus on specific components of performance and to evaluate players in part on their willingness to demonstrate great effort toward improving their performances, a player with relatively more ability is very likely to be discredited by a coach who measures achievement in terms of effort. As with the student in the classroom, possessing ability can, for an athlete, be a basis for being denied rather than receiving rewards.

An important issue for an athlete who is judged under the scrutiny of traditional achievement norms is the extent to which he or she accepts those same norms as the motivational dynamic in his or her own performance. If the intrinsic reward contingency makes effort salient as a motive to perform, the athlete will behave in ways that are rewarded by the coach. If effort per se is not intrinsically rewarding, the athlete is likely to rate a "poor" attitude by the coach, and his or her performance opportunities are likely to be adversely affected.

This distinction suggests that there may well be differences in achievement-oriented behavior that emanate from different attitudes toward achievement. For example, in track, it has been long accepted (although African runners are forcing a refinement of the notion) that black runners were good at short distances, but not over 400 meters. White runners critize blacks for not having the stamina and guts to work hard to develop a distance capacity. Black runners, conversely, wonder why runners get pleasure in the agony of anaerobic exhaustion.

Without judging the relative capacity for distance training, or leg to torso length, or spur heel characteristic of black athletes, (cf. Kane, 1971, for an evaluation of racial differences among athletes), we suggest that a substantial part of the explanation can be found in the attitudes toward achievement and the implication of those attitudes for athletic preference and performance. Black athletes tend to define achievement in terms of the realization of specific abilities that they possess. Because each athlete has a unique configuration of abilities, the standard of achievement tends to be individualistic. One indication of this tendency is the greater variability in performance styles among black athletes.

---

[2]Tutko and Ogilvie (1967, 1971) have developed the Athletic Motivation Inventory (AMI) to assess "good attitude." It consists of 190 multiple-choice items which are scored in 11 subscales. Three of the subscales, determination (willing to practice long and hard), drive (desire to win or be successful), and coachability (respects coaches, cooperates with authority), are manifestations of what is considered "Good Attitude."

When achievement is defined in terms of hard work or effort, as it normatively is, then the details of the skill are spelled out and athletes are able to work at developing them. With skill so defined, performance standards vary with effort. This standard is congruent with the orientation of the traditional high achiever where success or failure lies only with the level of effort expended.

Athletic Profile Inventory (API). In an attempt to assess attitudinal variations that could distinguish among these orientations for athletes, Jones and Williamson (1976) developed an Athletic Profile Inventory (API). The API consisted of four sections generally designed to obtain sociodemographic background information, attitudes toward traditional sloganeering in athletics, Rotter's locus of control perceptions, and finally, role-playing estimates of psychological reactions to hypothetical athletic situations. Two hundred and five athletes representing nine sports, at college and high school levels, filled out the API.

A factor analysis of the sports slogans revealed a dominant factor reflecting traditional attitudes toward achievement. These items comprised 13 of the 24 total (loadings greater than .49) and accounted for 32% of the common variance. They all emphasized hard work, sacrifice and effort ("The will to win is the will to work," had the highest loading). Using factor scores as a measure of an athlete's endorsement of traditional achievement attitude, we found a variety of differences on other aspects of the API.

The most powerful and interesting finding concerned reactions to the hypothetical performance situations. When personal success was pitted against team failure and vice versa, those athletes with traditional achievement attitudes based their own reaction on *team* outcomes, while those who did not endorse traditional achievement based their reactions on personal performance. In addition, those with traditional achievement attitudes were more frequently starting performers, and had been involved with athletics for a longer time. Here we report the results of additional studies with a revised API, a larger and more varied sample of athletes and the addition of projective measures of achievement.

METHOD

Procedure

The final sample of subjects for this study was obtained in two ways. First, a random sample of college and high school athletic directors were selected from the NCAA national directory and from high school athletic director registers for Massachusetts, New York, New Jersey, Washington, D.C., Florida, Ohio, Oklahoma, Nebraska, South Dakota, North Dakota, and

California. Letters were then sent to the 59 college athletic directors and 40 high school athletic directors, asking for their participation in the survey by serving as coordinators for the distribution of the questionnaire to a range of athletes at their respective schools. Twenty-five replies (41%) were received from the college athletic directors, and 11 (28%) from high school athletic directors. Questionnaires were sent to this group, with a final return from 12 colleges and six high schools of 199 fully completed questionnaires. The colleges represented in this sample are located in New York, Michigan, Ohio, Georgia, Illinois, Minnesota, North Carolina, Florida, Louisiana, and Connecticut. The high schools represented are located in Ohio, Florida, North Dakota, Oklahoma, California, and New York.

Second, three undergraduate theses conducted under our guidance generated three other samples of respondents from three high schools and three colleges in the Boston area. In each of these samples the athletic director or coach of a specific sport was contacted by the researcher and asked for permission to have athletes fill out the questionnaire. Athletes were then contacted directly by the researcher, asked to fill out the questionnaire and return it to the researcher. This procedure resulted in a nearly perfect response rate, adding 245 respondents to the sample.

Athletes.   Table 7.1 gives the percentage distribution of our final sample of 444 respondents across relevant demographic variables. The general two-state sampling plan did not yield a random probability sample of high school and college athletes. There are three reasons for this. First, responses to the initial inquiry were underrepresentative of colleges with large athletic programs. Colleges such as Alabama, Oklahoma, and Notre Dame did not respond. Second, when an athletic director did elect to participate in the study, there was no control over which athletes were recruited to fill out the API. Third, we do not assume that the particular athletes we have in our sample are necessarily *typical* of those who participate in the same sport. The range of athletes, however, is quite broad and we feel as a group they constitute a reasonable sample of "athletes."

The general character of our sample, evident from Table 7.1, is white males playing major sports and living on the eastern half of the United States. They are generally middle class, and live in and around large cities.

Athletic Profile Inventory (API).   The Athletic Profile Inventory (API) was the basic instrument employed in the research. However, two of the thesis subsamples utilized slightly modified versions (in which questions on particular topics such as family influence on sports participation, or sources of rewards in athletic performance, were added). The present version of the API was divided into five sections:

Section 1, entitled *General Sports Background Information,* contained general demographic questions concerning the respondents' background,

TABLE 7.1
Characteristics of the Sample ($N = 444$)

Sport[a]		Sex		Race		City Size		SES		Region		Education	
Football	33.8%	Male	77.5%	Latin	1.6%	Large urban	12.9%	Upper	15.1%	Northeast	19.8%	High school	25.0%
Baseball	11.5	Female	22.5	Black	6.6					Eastern seaboard	36.0	College	75.0
Basketball	19.8			White	87.6	Medium urban	20.2	Lower-middle	18.2	Midwest	20.9		
Track	15.1			Other	4.2	Suburban	39.7	Lower	2.5	South	4.7		
Tennis	1.8					Small town	22.0			Southeast	10.6		
Squash	1.3									Northwest	5.9		
Golf	1.3					Rural	5.2			No response	2.1		
Swimming	6.7												
Wrestling	9.4												
Soccer	4.0												
Lacrosse	1.8												
Hockey	1.3												
Boxing	.2												
Crew	14.4												

[a]These percentages sum to greater than 100%, because respondents were permitted to record more than one sport played.

165

early socialization influences into sports, and a general assessment of their experiences in organized athletics. It was felt that responses to these questions would be useful in determining possible antecedents at various stages of athletic development of their present attitudes toward achievement. Included in this section were questions about practice behavior, positive and negative, social, psychological, and academic effects.

Section 2, entitled *General Opinion Survey,* consisted of 25 generalized value statements selected from Bales' (1970) three-dimensional model of interpersonal behavior in small groups. The statements represent typical values expressed in interpersonal relationships, arrayed along the dimensions of power, affectivity, and conservatism (e.g., "cooperation is far more enjoyable than competition"). Several items were selected to represent both ends of each dimension, and responses were made by checking agree, disagree, or undecided. These items were expected to provide important data on the relationship of athletic attitudes and experiences on more generalized values held in this society.

Section 3, entitled *Sports Attitude Survey,* consisted of 24 common locker room slogans (see Snyder, 1971). Respondents were asked to indicate the extent of their agreement with each of the slogans on 9-point Likert scales from strongly agree (9) to strongly disagree (1). The slogans were used to represent the traditional range of attitudes, values and norms that permeate organized athletics, (e.g., "winning isn't everything, it's the only thing"). The items emphasize winning, hard work, sacrifice and team loyalty. Endorsement of the items suggests a general endorsement of the normative structure of organized sports in America today,[3] and a more specific endorsement of the value of achievement.

Section 4, entitled *Perception of Situations,* was presented as a role-play situation in which respondents were asked to imagine themselves actually in the performance situation described. After reading the hypothetical situations, respondents were asked to rate their feelings on 9-point Likert scales from very happy (1) to very unhappy (9). Two situations were described—one for basketball and one for baseball:

> *Basketball* Your basketball team has had a far better season than anyone expected. If you can win one more game you will have a chance to go to the national tournament. Your team's opponents are strong, tall and fast. You are not given much chance to win. However, you personally have an outstanding game. The score is tied coming down to the final 15 seconds of the game and you have scored 38 points. After a time out, you are set up to take the final shot. As you are maneuvering for your shot, the man guarding you steals the ball and dribbles down to make a final basket for your defeat.

---

[3]Because the slogans were taken from a basketball locker room, there is a likely bias toward team sport attitudes.

After reading this description respondents answered the following two questions: (1) "How do you feel now?"; and (2) "How would you feel if you had scored but 2 points, but your team had won the game?"

> *Baseball* You have had a bad day at the plate, going 0 for 4 and striking out three times. However, in the final game of the conference championship series, your team is ahead 3 to 1 in the last inning. The first two batters for the opposition go out routinely. The next batter hits the ball to you but instead of making what would be the final out of the game, you bobble the ball for an error. The next batter hits a home run to tie the game. However, in the twelfth inning your right fielder hits a home run and your team goes on to win the conference championship.

After reading this description, respondents answered the following two questions: (1) "How do you feel now?"; and (2) "How would you feel if you had gone 4 for 4 and made several good fielding plays but your team had lost the game?"

It was felt that, in the absence of more direct data on reactions to real athletic situations, these role-play situations would provide some insight into the important link of athletic attitudes of behavior. The situations also directly assess reactions to personal vs. team performance and winning vs. losing.

The second part of this section presented subjects with a similar task— writing TAT stories to one-sentence verbal cues. Three such cues were presented: (1) "David is looking into his microscope;" (2) "John is walking along a busy street in New York City;" and (3) "As the leader of the group of men and women, Bill has the final say on all decisions of the group." In accord with typical TAT instructions, respondents were asked to create a story, keeping in mind the following questions: (1) "What is happening? Who are the people?"; (2) "What has led up to the situation? That is, what has happened in the past?"; (3) "What is being thought and felt? What is wanted? By whom?"; and (4) "What will happen? What will be done?" It was felt that inclusion of the TAT stories would provide data on the interplay of attitudes toward achievement and power, individual values, and motivational dynamics as typically assessed in the personality literature. The first cue typically "pulls for" power motivation. The second cue was included as a "filler."

RESULTS

Sports Attitude Profile

Following the procedures employed in previous work (Jones, Note 2; Jones & Williamson, 1976), the locker room slogans from Section III of the API were factor analyzed via the DATATEXT (Armour, 1971) program for

orthogonal varimax rotation. A three-factor solution was suggested that accounted for 35.4% of the common variance. The fourth factor accounted for less than 3% and was not amenable to a useful interpretation. Table 7.2 gives the item loadings for the three factors. Interpretations of the factors were made for all items loading above .40 or below –.40.

Traditional Achievement.   In previous work, the emphasis on hard work and training were considered to represent the achievement-oriented view of

TABLE 7.2
Sports-Attitude Profile—Item Loadings

Sports Items	Traditional Achievement	Power	Anti-Establishment
Dedication and devotion are the keys to success	(.66)	.01	–.22
There is no substitute for hard work.	(.61)	.04	–.26
A team succeeds when no one cares who gets the credit.	(.58)	.14	(–.35)
It's not the size of the man in the fight, but the size of the fight in the man.	(.58)	.08	–.12
Good players help others to be good players.	(.56)	–.08	–.01
Champions come in all sizes.	(.53)	–.19	–.01
The will to win is the will to work.	(.53)	.11	(–.40)
An athlete is a gentleman who represents his school.	(.48)	.17	–.21
Hustle and desire make a winning team.	(.46)	.04	(–.52)
An ounce of loyalty to the team is worth a pound of cleverness.	(.43)	.19	–.12
Anyone can be ordinary, but it takes guts to excel.	(.43)	.29	(–.35)
Good training makes a good athlete.	(.40)	.04	(–.54)
Show me a 'good' loser and I'll show you a loser.	.07	(.68)	–.04
Winning isn't everything, it's the only thing.	.28	(.67)	–.04
The winner gets the glory, the loser gets the shame.	–.13	(.61)	.05
The high point of any contest is the demoralization of your opponent.	.01	(.59)	–.15
Nice guys don't win.	.01	(.59)	–.15
They ask not how you played the game, but whether you won or lost.	.05	(.52)	.16
It is important to win by as large a margin as possible.	–.12	(.44)	–.25
Anger is a sign of weakness	.01	.03	(–.64)
Winners are made, not born.	.25	.04	(–.44)
Percent of variance	15.4%	12.1%	7.9%

effort expanded in pursuit of a goal. The first factor includes all of the hard work items but, in addition, includes items that emphasize teamwork and group goals. We have labeled this factor "traditional achievement," because it combines the effort of individual goal-oriented aspiration as well as the cooperative interaction of individuals in pursuit of group-goals.

Power.   The second factor is similarly clear and consists of those items that emphsize winning. Whereas traditional achievement stresses the means by which the goal is achieved, the power dimension is concerned only with the goal itself. It reflects competition in its purest form as a zero-sum contest with one winner and one loser. Individuals who endorse this factor want to win, period.

Anti-Establishment.   The third factor is different from any obtained in previous studies in that it appears to be a general one spanning all of the items and characterized by omnibus negativity. Only two items in the entire list achieved positive loadings and these were not significantly different from zero. If we can describe the implication of most of the items as suggesting that success comes from submitting to the established order, regime of training, hard work, sacrifice, and selflessness, then this factor appears to be a rejection of all of that. It would not be surprising to find that an athlete who loaded heavily on this factor would have difficulty getting along in many of the highly regimented athletic programs around the country.

Value Attitude Profile

The value items from the Bales (1970) list in Section II of the API were also factor analyzed with an orthogonal varimax rotation. The item loadings above and below .40 and –.40 respectively were again used for interpretation. (See Table 7.3.)

Puritanism.   The first factor accounted for 10.7% of the variance and has been labeled *puritanism.* The items loading positively on this factor reflect the religious elements of the Protestant ethic as reflected in the writings of John Calvin and given expression in America by the Puritans of New England. As with the *Achievement* factor in the previous section, these items emphasize conformity, hard work and group cohesion, self-sacrifice and selflessness. One would expect that this factor would be highly correlated with the *Traditional Achievement* factor.

Individualism.   The second factor implicates the individual as the measure of success. Rugged individualism of the pioneer days, coupled with the material view of a society in which money is the only meaningful measure—hence the object of all endeavor. One might suspect that a rugged

TABLE 7.3
Value-Attitude Profile—Item Loadings

Value Items	Puritanism	Individualism	Humanism
The chief of man is nothing other than eternal salvation.	(.70)	.17	.14
Every person should have complete faith in some supernatural power whose decisions should be obeyed without question.	(.63)	.25	−.03
Life would hardly be worth living without the promise of immortality and life after death.	(.62)	.14	.13
One should hold high ideals, purify himself, restrain his desires for pleasure.	(.43)	.00	.04
An individual finds himself in merging with with a social group, joining with others in resolute and determined activity.	(.35)	−.01	.33
The individualist is the person who is most likely to discover the best road to a new future.	−.05	(.57)	.05
In life an individual for the most part should 'go it alone,' assuring himself of privacy and attempting to control his own life.	−.18	(.56)	.10
It is the man who stands alone who excites our admiration.	−.05	(.50)	.18
People really have very little in common with each other.	−.07	(.50)	−.33
Money is the measuring stick of scientific, artistic, moral and all other values in a society.	.20	(.46)	−.06
In any group, it is more important to keep a friendly atmosphere than to be efficient.	.02	.08	(.56)
A group of equals will work a lot better than a group with a rigid hierarchy.	.13	.01	(.49)
People are basically and innately good.	.08	−.07	(.48)
Cooperation is far more enjoyable and desirable than competition.	−.10	.01	(.44)
We are all born to love—it is the principle of existence and it's only true end.	.27	.01	(.43)
Divorce should be subject to fewer old-fashioned restrictions and become more a matter of mutual consent.	(−.40)	.15	.14
Christianity and all other religions are at best only partly true.	(−.68)	.18	.05
Percent of variance	10.7%	8.0%	7.8%

individualist and power-oriented person, as indicated by the power scale, would have a lot in common.

Humanism. The third factor was almost as strong as the second, accounting for 7.8% of the variance. The interpretation of humanism may seem a little strong but is made on the basis of a general prosocial orientation. That is, the positive aspects of individual attributes (people are innately good) and positive interaction goals (cooperation, equality, friendliness, and love) combine to give a strong argument for the humanism interpretation.

Scale Construction and Intercorrelations

While the three-factor solutions were arrived at independently for each of the Sports and Value Profiles, it is apparent from the interpretations that some degree of overlap exists. To assess the interrelatedness of the two scales, a varimax rotation was performed and individual subject factor scores were computed. Factor scores are computed independently for each factor and have the useful property of having both a mean and sum across all respondents equal to zero. Each subject's factor scores for all six factors were computed and keypunched on IBM cards along with all other relevant data for that subject.

Table 7.4 shows the intercorrelations among the factor scores for the Sports Attitude and General Value profiles. The largest association is between the Puritanism and Traditional Achievement Scales. This is to be expected if we consider the Puritanism scale to tap the ideology of the Protestant Ethic. It is this philosophy that underlies the traditional conceptions of achievement motivation (McClelland, 1961). It is also not surprising to find that the Anti-Establishment scale is negatively related to

TABLE 7.4
Intercorrelations Among Sports- and Value-Attitude Profiles

Sports Attitude Profile	Value-Attitude Profile		
	Puritanism	Individualism	Humanism
Traditional Achievement	.28^c	.07	.10
Power	.07	.20^c	-.10
Anti-establishment	-.23^c	-.11^a	-.14^b

Note: N for each correlation is 444; *df* = 442.
[a]*p* = .05.
[b]*p* = .01.
[c]*p* = .001.

Puritanism (r = .23). It is largely the regimentation, denial and sacrifice characteristic of puritan philosophy that the Anti-Establishment scale rejects.

It is also noteworthy that the winning philosophy of the Power scale is reflected in a significant correlation with the Individualism scale (r = .20; p = .001). As described earlier, Power as here measured reflects a competitive zero-sum orientation that could be characterized as a kind of rugged individualism.

We should note that while the Puritanism scale is positively related to Traditional Achievement, and the Individualism scale is positively related to the Power scale, the Humanism scale bears no positive relationship to any of the Sports scales. Similarly, the Anti-Establishment scale bears no positive relationship to *any other* scale. To summarize these relationships, it seems that one factor reflects Traditional Achievement as expressed in the Protestant ethic, a second factor expressed Individual Accomplishment and Victory as expressed in personalized power and rugged individualism; a third factor represents a rejection of the established order of regimented self-denial, obedience and conformity; and a fourth represents an overall prosocial orientation toward human interaction and individual worth.

Sports-Attitude Group Profile

In previous research (Jones & Williamson, 1976), it was found that the Sports slogan factors accounted for a significantly greater degree of the variation in athletic behavior and attitude than did other attitude dimensions. Furthermore, among those sports attitude profile factors, Achievement accounted for the major proportion of observed effects. In an attempt to combine all of the sports factors in a composite profile, the following analysis was performed. First, subjects were divided in three groups, low, medium, and high for each of the three factors. This was accomplished by selecting those subjects whose factor scores fell within $\frac{1}{2}S_D$ above and below the mean of zero (i.e., −.50 score + .50), for the medium range, and subjects whose scores were greater than +.50 for high and less than −.50 for low. This procedure resulted in a 3 × 3 matrix of 27 cells such that each subject could be located in one and only one cell.

Because positive loadings on the first two factors strongly suggest that the kind of attitude a coach would look for in the ball players and because a positive loading on the third factor implied a high probabiity of trouble between coach and athlete, a gradient from "coach's dream" to "athletic dropout" was constructed. This profile of coach's dream corresponds to the profile suggested in Tutko and Ogilvie (1971). Specifically, the following four subscales of the athletic motivation inventory describe the same profile:

Drive: desire to win or to be successful
Determination: willing to practice long and hard

Coachability: respects coaches; cooperates with authority
Conscientiousness: likes to do things exactly right; goal of team above self

Table 7.5 shows how these groups were ordered and the frequencies and percentages of athletes falling into each. Because a high loading on Traditional Achievement and Power were considered to be positive attributes in the existing coaching philosophy, scoring high on both and moderate or low on the third factor was considered to produce a coach's dream (13.51% of the sample). The next best combination was scoring high on Traditional Achievement and moderate or low on Power and Anti-Establishment (19.59%), followed by high on power and moderate or low on the other two factors (10.81%). Taken together, 195, or 43.91% of the entire sample could be described as having a strong positive orientation to the prevailing coaching and performance standards of organized sports.

On the other hand, any athlete who scored high on the Anti-Establishment scale and moderate or low on Traditional Achievement and Power was considered to have a short life in established big time sports programs, or at

TABLE 7.5
Frequencies and Percentages of Athletes in Sports-Attitude Groupings

Group Type[a]						
Traditional Achievement	*Power*	*Anti-Establish-ment*	*Group Level*	*N*		*% Total Sample*
Low	Low	High	Dropouts	93		20.95%
Moderate	Moderate	High				
Moderate	Low	High				
Low	Moderate	High				
Low	Low	Low	Low power	56		12.61%
Moderate	Low	Moderate				
Moderate	Low	Low				
Low	Low	Moderate				
Low	Moderate	Moderate	Low achievement	30		6.76%
Low	Moderate	Low			179	
Moderate	Moderate	Low				40.32% Dropouts
High	Moderate	High				
High	Low	High				
Low	High	High				
Moderate	High	High				
High	High	High				
Moderate	Moderate	Moderate			70	15.77% Moderates

(continued)

TABLE 7.5 *(continued)*

Traditional Achievement	Power	Anti-Establish-ment	Group Level	N		% Total Sample	
High	Moderate	Moderate	High achievement	87		19.59%	
High	Low	Moderate					
High	Low	Low					
High	Moderate	Low					
Low	High	Low	High power	48		10.81%	
Moderate	High	Moderate					
Low	High	Moderate					
Moderate	High	Low					
High	High	Low	Coach's Dreams	60		13.51%	
High	High	Moderate			195	43.91%	Coach's dreams

Group Type[a]

[a]Assignment to Groupings are based on individual subject factor scores where:

Low = $< -.50$

Moderate = $> -.50$ and $< +.50$

High = $> +.50$.

best a career characterized by conflict. Ninety-three athletes (20.95%) fell into this category, which we summarize with the label "dropouts." In addition, we judged that any athlete who failed to score high on either Traditional Achievement (6.76%) or Power (12.61%) was also likely to be in a marginal position. Thus these three groupings represent the opposite end from the coach's dreams (we might call them coach's nightmares), and constitute 179 subjects or 40.32% of the sample.

The middle group was uneven and couldn't be conveniently labeled. They are simply characterized by being positively loaded on the Anti-Establishment factor, and positive on either Traditional Achievement, Power or both. We also included subjects who were moderate on all three factors, because they seemed to be legitimately middle-of-the-roaders. This entire group only accounted for 15.77% of the total sample.

In the analyses that follow, we have simplified the 27 possible cells to three to reflect the groupings discussed above. They are coach's dreams, moderates, and dropouts. It is assumed that these groups reflect an implicit attitude-continuum from Pro-Establishment to Anti-Establishment. We should emphasize that this attitude continuum is not necessarily correlated with actual athletic ability. As indicated earlier, great emphasis is placed on "Attitude" in athletics and this is what our groupings represent.

General Characteristics of Sports-Attitude Groups

Table 7.6 summarizes the frequencies in select demographic characteristics by sports-attitude groups. First we can see that females fall disproportionately high in the dropout group (55%), and correspondingly low in the coach's dream group (29%). Males are more evenly distributed across these groups, although slightly more represented in the coach's dream group (48% compared to 43.9% for the total sample). These differences for sex require a cautious interpretation, however. It is quite evident that, in general, the API is worded to reflect a male orientation. Although only two of the sports items ("nice guys don't win" and "an athlete is a gentleman who represents his school") make any reference to male gender, the Value items are heavily biased toward a male gender identification. Because the Value items preceded the sports items, it is entirely possible that a general reaction to this bias could have produced more general negativity in female responses on the sports items. This reaction would have had the effect of making female respondents more anti-establishment, hence a relatively higher percentage among them would fall in the dropout category. Yet to some extent this sexist bias is inherent in the substance and implication of many of the slogans so we would not want to conclude that the phenomenon is entirely artifactual.

We can also see that black respondents fall more frequently in the dropout (57%) than the coach's dream group (21%). This observation is consistent with data and arguments advanced in previous work (Jones & Hochner, 1973; Jones, Note 2). That is, black athletes are characterized in performance as representing style—a personalized means orientation toward a goal. This is contrasted with the rule-governed formalized approach of traditional agreed-upon means to the same goals. For example, outfielders are 'taught' to field ground balls to the outfield between their legs, going down on one knee to keep the ball from getting past them. Willie Mays 'instructs' would-be outfielders in the art of racing alongside the ball, sweeping it up with the glove and in one motion transferring and throwing it to the appropriate base (see Schrag, 1971, for a tribute to Mays' style; and Axthelm, 1970, for description of style in street basketball).

While we can describe style as a personalized approach to achievement, it is clear that an individual expression may not be congruent with a coach's expectations or desires. Over the years there have been many *incidents* between coaches and black players (see, e.g., Olsen, 1969). The present data offer an interpretation of these strained relationships based in part on differences in attitudes about the critical dimensions of achievement.

Although we interpret this negative loading as reflective of "style" for black athletes, it should be noted that our conception of style is a positive expression. However, the characteristics of style do not lend themselves to sloganeering because they are so individualized. A better test of the attitude

TABLE 7.6

Characteristics of Sport-Attitude Group as a Function of Sex, Race, Education Level, and Sports Involvement

Sports-Attitude Group	Sex		Race		Education Level		Number of Sports Played	
	Male %	Female %	Black %	White %	High School %	College %	One %	More than 1 %
Dropouts	124(37.1)	55(56.1)	16(57)	146(39)	37(34)	140(43)	55(51)	46(27)
Moderates	44(13.2)	114(14.3)	6(21)	57(15)	13(12)	55(17)	14(13)	28(16)
Coach's dreams	166(49.7)	29(29.6)	6(22)	171(46)	58(54)	129(40)	39(36)	99(57)
	334	198	28	374	108	324	108	173
Probability[a]	$p = .005$		$p = .02$		$p = .01$		$p = .009$	

[a]Probability levels are based on chi-square analysis.

differences suggested would be to include examples of both a style and traditional achievement approach in the same instrument.

The observation from Table 7.6 that high-school respondents were very highly represented in the coach's dream group (54%) but college respondents in this category fell to 40% has implications for the socialization of sports attitudes. It appears that high-school-age athletes are relatively accepting of the tenets of the sports establishment. If these attitudes are what gets taught, then perhaps it is a matter of maturation and experience with counter-examples that causes a diminution in adherence to the established attitude system characterized by college athletes. Indeed, the more complex an athlete's life becomes, the more difficult it is for him/her to adhere to the strictest interpretation of the pro-establishment attitude (e.g., "An athlete is a gentleman who represents his school," or "You live the way you play").

Finally, we note that athletes who play multiple sports are more likely to accept pro-establishment attitudes (57%) than those who concentrate on one sport. Perhaps this result indicates that to perform successfully in different sports settings with varying characteristics of abilities, temperament, physical and emotional requirements, coaching techniques and philosophies and so on, an athlete must have a positive attitude that enables him/her to maintain a constant and forward focus. In part, this focus is what is provided by adherence to the attitudes reflected in the coach's dream category.

Sociobehavioral Correlates of Sports-Attitude Groups

On the assumption that the accepted or established sports system consists of a way of life, a coherent set of attitudes or philosophies, and behavioral styles that are recognizable and fairly uniform among adherents to the philosophy, we asked a number of questions that had bearing on these issues. Table 7.7 gives a summary of those relationships that attained statistical significance in a one-way analysis of variance for the sports-attitude groups.

Size.   First we can note that as we go from dropouts to coach's dreams the athletes get taller and heavier. We have already noted that about one-third of the sample of dropouts were females, hence this result is neither surprising nor of great significance.

Practice Behavior.   Respondents were asked to indicate the age at which they began their organized sports careers, the number of hours they spent practicing alone between the ages of 10 and 15, and the number of hours they spend practicing alone now. In general, the results for all of these items suggest that the involvement of dropouts is less and covers a shorter period of time. That is, the average age at which respondents in the dropout group began sports was 9.94, compared to 9.24 for coach's dreams. They also

TABLE 7.7
Socio-Behavioral Relationships Among Sports-Attitude Types

Sociobehavioral Indices	Sports-Attitude Group			
	Dropouts	Middle	Dreams	Probability[a]
Height	69.50 in.	70.94	70.58	$p = .05$
Weight	156.33 lb	167.00	170.00	.02
Age (org. sports)	9.94	9.45	9.24	.004
Time practice (10–15)	1.27	1.62	1.68	.001
Practice now	1.24	1.21	1.55	.02
Status enhanced	1.27	1.46	1.60	.009
Effect on life	2.52	2.63	2.83	.001
Family attend	2.87	3.21	3.52	.002
Sport talk at meals	2.91	3.18	3.52	.046
Effect on family	2.98	3.41	3.92	.001
Percent athletic friends	51.4%	56.2%	67.2%	.055
Outside interests	3.51	2.86	2.82	.053

[a]Probabilities are based on one-way analysis of variance.

practiced significantly less when younger (1.27 vs. 1.68 hours per day), and continue to practice less (1.24 vs. 1.55.)

Again there is a possible sex effect confounding these results. It is well documented that there are fewer organized sports activities for young girls (at least for the present sample. Events like Title IX, and a general increase in support for female involvement in sports is changing this pattern.) With no organized opportunity to play, and no recognized incentive to practice, a young girl could be expected to report fewer practice hours.

Social Relationships.   The athlete-hero is a popular figure from high school (cf. Coleman, 1961) to the Olympics (Bruce Jenner's *Time* cover appearance) with immodest sorties into college and professional sports. A number of questions were asked about the general effect of sports in the lives of our respondents. Respondents were asked if their social status in school was enhanced as a result of their participation in sports; if sports had made their lives better, worse, or had mixed or no effect; if their families attended their performances, if they talked about sports at meals, and if their family had been positively influenced by their sports participation. Finally, respondents were asked to indicate what percentage of their friends were also athletes.

The results of these questions, summarized in Table 7.7, maintain the profile that is emerging. Coach's dreams indicate a significantly more positive experience as well as greater family involvement. In addition, these respondents show a deeper involvement with sports itself (as given by the

practice hours shown above) and others who play sports (67.2% athlete friends compared to 51.4% for dropouts). Also coach's dreams indicated fewer outside interests (2.82%) than dropouts (3.51%). To the extent that sports is a closed system with very extensive and demanding regimentation and order, it would seem to follow that an individual who prefers a more open and varied life style would have problems. It further seems that the deep commitment and involvement required for participation may simply overwhelm an individual even if he/she has a pro-establishment attitude (i.e., coach's dream) and is a highly successful performer. Immediately one thinks of Dave Meggyssey (1970), Bill Walton, and Dave Cowens, among many others who have shown evidence of the strain high-powered sports involvement can cause.

Performance Variations. One of the assumptions of this attitude-structure approach is that important aspects of an individual athlete's performance can be predicted from their attitudes. Social psychology has a long history of trying to show the extent to which this association can be demonstrated (see Wicker, 1969, for a recent review of the current status of this work). Because coaches often implicate "attitude" in their assessment of a given athlete, and the presumed implication is that certain critical behaviors will be affected in a positive (good attitude) or negative (bad attitude) way, then it is important to assess possible differences in attitude and their implications for behavior.

Ideally, we would have developed a behavioral inventory that could then be administered in the context of a series of athletic encounters. The results of this behavioral inventory could then be cross checked with the attitude profile and a determination of the link between the attitudes and behaviors could be made. We have, so far, focussed on the attitude portion and only alluded to the behavioral dimension by using a role-play procedure.

The two hypothetical situations described in the method section were given as behavioral correlates. In each example, the target person's performance was qualitatively at variance with the team outcome. It is evident from the slogans that winning is very important and team success is held above all. Therefore, one would expect that pro-establishment athletes would evaluate their own performance and the consequences of their performance on self-satisfaction in accordance with team outcomes. Conversely, dropouts, who reject much of this sloganeering, would be more inclined to evaluate their performances directly.

To test the extent to which the above reasoning could be demonstrated, two measures were computed. First, a personal score was created by adding the obtained scores for a good performance by the target (scored 38 points in the basketball situation and went 4 for 4 in baseball). Second, a team score was created by adding the scores for those situations in which the team won but

the target performed poorly. The resultant numbers are higher to the extent that respondents were happy with their performance (personal) or the team's victory (team). These numbers were then analyzed in a 2 × 3 (performance satisfaction × sports-attitude group) repeated measures analysis of variance. Table 7.8 gives these mean figures for personal and team evaluations of target performance as a function of attitude groups.

First, we should note that a strong main effect for performance satisfaction criteria shows that team outcome was significantly more important than personal outcome in general satisfaction. This suggests that our sample did adhere to the basic notion that winning is the most important thing. The main effect for sports group did not reach statistical significance. The significant interaction prediction was obtained, however. That is, dropouts were more inclined to be satisfied when they had performed well, whereas coach's dreams were relatively more inclined to indicate high satisfaction when the team had won.

The result obtained is a good reflection of the distribution of attitudes about performance and winning among athletes. The obtained interaction shows that athletes differ in the extent to which they embrace the philosophy of total selflessness. Certainly it is not unreasonable to be happy with an outstanding performance even in defeat. Articulating personal satisfaction in the context of team defeat is counter to established norms, and athletes who do so are generally viewed with suspicion (i.e., their loyalty to the team may come under question.)

The main effect for team outcome, however, is very strong. The variation described by the interaction occurs within an overall adherence to the popular norm of victory as the primary goal. Among most of the conspicuously successful professional basketball players (Wilt Chamberlain, Bill Russell, Oscar Robertson), the measure of success has often been the number of world championships won. Chamberlain 'outperformed' Russell statistically, but 11

TABLE 7.8
Personal and Team Outcome Criteria as a Function of
Sports-Attitude Group

Performance Satisfaction Criteria	Sports-Attitude Group			
	Dropouts	Moderate	Coach's Dream	
Personal outcome	2.72	2.53	2.31	2.50
Team outcome	6.78	7.02	7.35	7.10
Total	4.75	4.77	4.88	4.80

$F_{PSC} = df = 1,439; \quad p < .01.$
$F_{SAG \times PSC} = df = 2,439; \quad p < .05.$

world championships for Russell's Boston Celtics to 1 for Chamberlain's Philadelphia team told the final tale. Robertson was one of the very best ever but his career was not complete until in his final years he teamed with Abdul-Jabbar to win a world title in Milwaukee.

The trade-off between individual performance and team success is the essence of social psychological inquiry. The society of sports and the behavior of individual athletes within it provides a major real world laboratory for the study of key social psychological variables. Although the present role-play study is but a small step in this direction, it does conform to empirical observations and is encouraging for further research efforts in this area.

Achievement Imagery

Although a major element of the present conceptualization of the relationship between sports attitudes and athletic performance concerns achievement behavior, we have no direct measures of it. Another methodological effort to obtain additional measures of achievement was to include a sentence-cued TAT protocol. It has been shown that one can obtain reliable thematic imagery material with simple sentence cues instead of the traditional pictures (Horner, 1971). One of the cues that has been shown to elicit achievement imagery was "David (Alice) is looking into his (her) microscope." Respondents were asked to tell a story suggested by this sentence, and to include in that story "What is happening? Who are the people? What has led up to the situation? That is, what has happened in the past? What is being thought and felt? What is wanted? By whom? What will happen? What will be done?"

A complete analysis of the protocols generated by these cues has yet to be conducted. We received stories from a little over one third of our sample. The stories were sorted into categories based on the sports-attitude group into which the story's author fell. For illustrative purposes, we have selected 15 stories from the most extreme groups (eight from coach's dreams HH* and seven from dropouts **H). Table 7.9 gives the text for the stories given by dropouts, and Table 7.10 the stories for coach's dreams.

A formal analysis has not been performed on these stories. However, it is possible to form some impressions from a comparison of the stories given by dropouts and coach's dreams. For dropouts, several of the stories are unconventional. For example, two of them end in death (#s 4, 6); two are allegorical (#s 2, 7); two express a desire for peace, harmony (#s 1, 5), and the remaining story, although more conventional than the others, still manages to have a girl scream and a slide knocked to the floor.

The iconoclastic, alienated tone of these stories fits with the overall characterization of the dropouts as Anti-Establishment. Table 7.4 showed that these same people were negatively disposed toward each of the Value Attitude Profiles, and significantly so. It is as if the modern world in its

TABLE 7.9
TAT Stories for Achievement Imagery Among the Dropout Sports-Attitude Group

1

He is a student (4th grade) in a science class. It is the first time he has ever viewed through the microscope. The other children are busy running around the room during this lab time, but David is so intent upon examining his drop of pond water that he hears no one. He is totally fascinated and feels a kind of inner peace and harmony in this small world. He doesn't understand all that is happening but is intrigued. Probably nothing important will result.

2

Once upon a time, there was a young man named David. Early one Monday morning David got ready to go to his eight o'clock lab. He had been up late the night before and he was a little tired. When he got to class, the lab was to examine various one-celled animals. On one particular slide, David discovered that there was a rare one-celled animal that didn't look anything at all like the others. As he looked closer, David found more of these different animals. He found that these small animals were actually intelligent beings. They appeared to be communicating with each other and each animal followed a definite pathway. Naturally, David couldn't believe his eyes. He thought that he might be seeing things because he didn't have enough sleep. David just changed the slide and didn't say anything to anybody. To this day no one else has seen nor heard anything about intelligent one-celled animals.

3

David is looking at protozoan in his microscope. His biology classmates are also looking through the microscope at the protozoan. David must look at these one-celled creatures because the teacher has assigned this project to him. David feels satisfied that he has so successfully isolated the protozoan. All of a sudden, a girl screams, as she drops the slide and microscope. Now David is slightly upset, but since most of his classmates had seen the slide, David proceeds in cleaning up the slide.

4

As David was looking through the microscope, he started dreaming of the day he would be out of school. When he could go home to his wife and child. He now only has one more year to go. He hasn't seen them in years. All of a sudden a shot rang out. David fell dead.

5

The world is peaceful. There is no war going on and everyone is living in harmony. Still many domestic problems: poverty, unemployment. The three big powers of the world have decided to try and live together. Money is no longer the most precious thing in the world. People only want to have enough to live comfortably; no greed. Eventually some will start another war and this peaceful attitude about the world will disappear again for another couple of decades.

6

David is one of those individuals who is trying to discover himself. The question is "how?" One day while in Chemistry he sets down to the microscope and begins his study on the crawling things under the glass plate. His mind is wondering and he finds himself in a deep doze, thinking about nothing, yet thinking about everything. It's been so long since he decided to find himself, the real David. Many times he had asked God to speak to him, to show him some sign that He would help.
But nothing ever happened.

(continued)

TABLE 7.9 *(continued)*

In school David was one of those common goodie-two-shoe guys. Always doing something for someone else, he felt like he should be patted on the head, to reward himself.

The bell rang which ended the class. He gathered up his books and headed to his car for lunch. He didn't even make it to the car. He was hit and killed by a car as he crossed the street to his car. Maybe this was God's way of having David meet him. Maybe God planned for David to find himself through God. How will each of us meet God and find ourselves?

7

David is looking at a group of ameba. They are moving around content with their work. Another single-celled animal enters the picture. This one doesn't want anything; just wants to be left alone and do its own business. Finally, the group of ameba get together and force the other animal out of the picture because it is different from them. Dave then switches slides but is sad that life is that way.

TABLE 7.10
TAT Stories for Achievement Imagery Among the Coach's Dream Sports-Attitude Group

8

In school one day, David and his friends were discussing the looks of different kinds of hair. Although some of his friends thought there was no difference, David asserted that there was. To prove his point, David looked into a microscope at the hairs of three of his friends. When David looked, his point was proven, the hairs had different structures. He then asked his friends, after they looked at the hairs, if they got the hairs they looked at last week from different people with different kinds of hair (curly, straight, fuzzy, etc.). When his friends said no, he explained to them the importance and bearing it had.

9

Dave is the new student at Bluffington High. Dave has made his mind up to become the envy of all his new classmates. Dave's previous High School, Jamestown South, had left him with a bad impression. Dave now feels that he has to be looked up to. When his new classmates wanted someone to do their experiment for them, this was Dave's chance. Dave tried so hard to succeed at his first real chance that he failed. He had made himself look ridiculous. For some unknown reason, after all the students had left the room laughing, one nice-looking girl stayed. This was Dave's true hope. The chance to have a close friend.

10

David is in Biology class (lab). Most of the people in the class are good friends of David. David was just chosen by the teacher to pick out and identify specific objects in a universal microscope slide of a common plant cell. David is somewhat embarrassed for he was talking to his lab partner while the teacher was lecturing. His thoughts toward the teacher are not very pleasant. However David identifies all the objects asked for by the teacher. So he now feels he has fooled the teacher.

11

He sees cells and small microscopic animals.
The people around him are students.

(continued)

TABLE 7.10 *(continued)*

He is a biological student studying blood types.
He is really amazed at how the cells move and float about and wonders how the process happens.
He wants to know how this takes place.
He will find out from his professor.
He will later become one of the best biologists in the United States.

12

David is sitting in his Biology class in High School and Mr. Bezdek, the teacher has just instructed David on the proper use of the microscope. Mr. Bezdek has given David the task of looking at an amoeba. David was bored earlier in the semester by the dry lecturing, but being able to see the amoeba has helped to make the boring lectures a little more meaningful.

David did feel as though he was wasting his time in class, but now he realizes what was done during the lectures was necessary to make this experience with the microscope more worthwhile. David feels bad because Mr. Bezdek did help him learn about small animals that he had never seen before. He will study harder.

13

David is a biology major who has an ambition to be a doctor. David is in his biology lab studying a chicken embryo. He is in the lab since there is a test tomorrow. David knows that if he can do well on this test then he has a chance to get a B in the course. He also realizes that if this extra work pays off then the self-satisfaction he gains will be quite beneficial toward his final exams.

14

David is looking into his microscope as he is trying to make up a slide containing a rock section. He is noticing the minute sections into which it is broken. As he sees the different sections he identifies them and writes them down. After he has written all that he can identify he turns it in for comparison by the instructor. After the comparison is made if he has the majority correct he goes on to another slide. If he has missed several he goes over that same slide once more.

15

Davis is not doing as well as he should in Biology. Therefore he is spending more time now looking into his microscope to improve himself in the course, as this is his weakness in the course and he realizes it now.

---

material, spiritual and social aspects does not provide support for the needs or hopes of these people.

By contrast, the stories told by the coach's dreams are highly conventional and serve almost as models for the achievement image. The two dominant themes are success or accomplishment (#s 8, 9, 10, 11, 13) and hard work and improved perforamnce (#s 12, 13, 15). Story number 14 does not directly implicate either of these two themes, but is characterized by attention to procedure and instruction.

It is compelling to see products of free response to the simple sentence cue fall so neatly into the categories derived from the factor analytic procedures. The story patterns reinforce the interpretations of the factors and the subsequent respondent groupings.

DISCUSSION

We began our research program in an attempt to show that behind the performance differences noted by Worthy and Markle (1970) and Jones and Hochner (1973) lay basic attitudinal differences that derived from a broader pattern of sociocultural relationships with specific implications for achievement behavior. The results obtained in our work with the API outline a range of relationships consistent with this viewpoint.

Combining the Sports and Value Profiles, we have identified four attitudinal clusters:

1. *Traditional Achievement and Puritanism*—characterized by belief in hard work, dedication, sacrifice, selflessness, triumph of effort over and above ability, denial, and obedience to authority.
2. *Power and Individualism*—characterized by consuming desire to win, to dominate and demoralize an opponent, to promote self, to stand aloof from others.
3. *Anti-Establishment*—characterized by general rejection of all platitudes and principles of achievement, authority, sacrifice and idealism.
4. *Humanism*—characterized by a desire to promote prosocial relationships, belief in the basic goodness of people, preference for understanding and friendliness over achievement and progress.

We are here suggesting that the four attitude clusters described above characterize the dominant positions among the people involved in athletics. We further suggest that clusters 1 and 2 are basically normative within the subculture of sports, and as such serve as a mirror of society (Boyle, 1962). The Protestant (Puritan) ethic giving rise to achievement motivation and the rugged individualism of frontier days giving rise to motives toward power and domination of men and environment are the cultural underpinnings of sports as well.

If we view Clusters 1 and 2 as normative within the sports complex, then Cluster 3 and 4 must be considered nonnormative and athletes who express these sentiments as deviant. We are here speaking of attitudes and values, not performance. The assumption, however, is that variations in performance can, in part, be accounted for in terms of these attitudinal orientations.

We began our study by noting the racial performance differences in free-throw and field goal shooting accuracy. Whereas Worthy and Markle (1970) attempted to account for these differences in terms of the self-paced (free throws) or reactive (field goals) nature of the performance, we offer the following view. The performance principles (and indeed the practice) of free-throw shooting rest largely in the domain of Traditional Achievement. To perfect the skill is to compete with a standard of excellence (100% accuracy),

and to undertake a commitment to perfecting the technique with repeated practice.

Field goal shooting, by nature, is less amenable to such a performance standard, because of the variable context of competition with an opponent. We argue that superior skill at field goal shooting comes, in part, from a stronger motivation toward Power and Individualism. Whereas a white player may have spent hours shooting free throws at a basket on the garage, a black player is more likely to have spent hours playing one-on-one basketball in the school playground. Is this then simply a socioeconomic rather than a sociocultural difference?

In our earlier attempt to account for these racial differences in performance (Jones & Hochner, 1973), we postulated that "style" is an important ingredient in the performance of many black athletes. We represent style here as an initial element of individualism, and hence closer to the attitude orientation of Cluster 2 than 1. Thus, a person with a strong orientation on 2 would possibly have a unique, individualistic way of performing and attempt to dominate another player with that style. Pete Maravich, Julius Erving, Paul Westphal and Earl Monroe are considered style players, while Jo Jo White, Oscar Robertson, Jerry West and John Havlicek are not.

What produces the racial variations we observe is more a matter of how the four clusters are represented in a given athlete or group of athletes than in specific attributes of race. We reject the notion of high versus low achievement motivation as a focus on Traditional Achievement alone would force us to, but propose that there are several different achievement systems. Each system has its own reward structure and is capable of rewarding different behaviors (in the elemental sense of increasing the probability of their occurrence). Racial differences in sports performance can, in part, be attributed to different reinforcement contingencies.

We believe the attitude clusters represented in the API are central to the motivational systems of athletes. The view of sports as a social system organized around these motivational principles could serve as an orientation toward the systematic research of important issues in social psychology such as the relationship between attitudes and behavior; behavioral consequences of personality profiles; obedience and authority; social facilitation; competition and aggression; individual versus group performance; normative behavior and deviance and many other issues.

Although we have offered far reaching discussions of the implications of the results obtained with the API, it should be noted that there are limits to simple paper-and-pencil techniques. The utility of the API in addressing the issues posed requires not only considerably more refinement and validity and reliability studies, but the careful blending with other measures and observations from many other contexts for successful application. We do feel

that the API has proven to offer interesting insights into the attitudinal domains of athletes and that further research and development would likely be productive.

REFERENCE NOTES

1. Worthy, M. *Eye darkness, race, and self-paced athletic performance.* Paper presented at Southeastern Psychological Association Meeting, Miami, Fla., April 1971.
2. Jones, J. M.. *Psychological contours of black athletic performance and expression.* Paper presented to the Physical Education Symposium on Race and Sport, Slippery Rock State College, Pennsylvania, June 19–23, 1972.

REFERENCES

Armour, D. *DATATEXT*, Harvard University, 1971.

Atkinson, J. W. *Motivation and achievement.* New York: Halsted Press, 1974.

Atkinson, J. W., & Feather, N. T. (Eds.). *A theory of achievement motivation.* New York: Wiley, 1966.

Axthelm, P. *The city game.* New York: Anchor Press, 1970.

Bales, R. F. *Personality and interpersonal behavior.* New York: Holt, Rinehart & Winston, 1970.

Boyle, A. *Sport as a mirror of society.*

Coleman, J. C. *The adolescent society,* New York: The Free Press, 1961.

Frieze, I., & Weiner, B. Cue utilization and attributional judgments for success and failure. *Journal of Personality,* 1971, *39,* 591–606.

Horner, M. *The motive to avoid success.* Unpublished doctoral dissertation, University of Michigan, 1966.

Jones, J. M., & Hochner, A. Racial differences in sports activities: A look at the self-paced versus reactive hypothesis. *Journal of Personality and Social Psychology,* 1973, *27,* 86–95.

Jones, J. M., & Williamson, S. A model of athlete's attitudes toward sports performance. *International Journal of Sport Psychology,* 1976, *7,* 82–106.

Kane, M. An assessment of "Black is best." *Sports Illustrated,* 1971, *34,* 72–83.

Kukla, A. *Cognitive determinants of achieving behavior.* Unpublished doctoral dissertation, University of California, Los Angeles, 1970.

McClelland, D. C. *The achieving society.* Princeton: Von Nostrand, 1961.

McClelland, D. C., Atkinson, J. W.,& Clark,. *The achievment motive.* New York: Appleton-Century, 1953.

McClelland, D. C., Davis, W. N., Kalin, R., & Wanner, E. *The drinking man.* New York: Free Press, 1972.

Meggyesy, D. *Out of their league.* Berkeley: Ramparts Press, 1970.

Olsen, J. *The black athlete: A shameful story.* New York: Time-Life Books, 1969.

Schrag, P. The age of Willie Mays. *Saturday Review,* 1971, *54,* 15–17, 42–43.

Snyder, E. Athletic dressing room slogans as folklore: A means of socialization. *International Review of Sport Sociology,* 1972, *7,* 89–102.

Tutko, T., & Ogilvie, B. Sports: If you want to build character, try something else. *Psychology Today,* 1971, *5*, 61–63.

Weiner, B. *Theories of motivation.* Chicago: Markham Publ. Co., 1972.

Weiner, B., & Kukla, A. An attributional analysis of achievement motivation. *Journal of Personality and Social Psychology,* 1970, *15,* 1–20.

Weiner, B., Frieze, I., Kukla, A., Reed, L., Rest, S., & Rosenbaum, R. M. *Perceiving the causes of success and failure.* New York: General Learning Press, 1971.

Weiner, B., & Potepan, P. A. Personality correlates and affective reations toward exams of succeeding and failing college students. *Journal of Educational Psychology,* 1970, *65*, 144–151.

Wicker, A. Attitudes versus actions: The relationship of verbal and overt behavioral responses to attitude objects. *Journal of Social Issues,* 1969, *25*, 41–78.

Worthy, M., & Markle, A. Racial differences in reactive versus self-paced sports activities. *Journal of Personality and Social Psychology,* 1970, *16*, 439–443.

8

The Elderly Jock and How He Got That Way

Frank Winer

I am an elderly jock. I'm 60 years old and I play tennis and volleyball regularly and avidly. Occasionally, I play paddleball, and when I do, it is with similar enthusiasm. I look forward eagerly to Sunday mornings and Tuesday evenings, which are my regular playing times for tennis and volleyball. As a matter of fact, Tuesdays are generally made pleasant by the anticipation of the evening, and I'm so eager that I usually have prepared my gym bag well in advance of leaving home for the gym. I feel like a kid sometimes; I will play whenever I have the chance. If for some reason I am unable to play when scheduled, I am quite disappointed. I do not take missing my scheduled athletic times lightly, and even when I am away on a pleasant vacation with my wife, I experience occasional twinges at missing my regular games. My tennis racquet accompanies me on vacations so that I can play if I am fortunate enough to encounter the possibility.

For the past several years a heart condition has required that I play less strenuously. Of several adjustments that I have had to make following my illness, the requirement to ease up is the most difficult. In play, I am often in conflict. I have a very hard time holding myself in check, and I am frequently unsuccessful. Sometimes after an effort that I should not have made, I feel scared, and, for short periods, withdrawn and self preoccupied. Some day, I

FRANK WINER received his Ph.D. from N.Y.U. and certification from the Postgraduate Center for Mental Health (N.Y.). Over the past 30 years Dr. Winer has engaged in the practice and teaching of psychotherapy and family counseling. He has been on the faculties of the University of Minnesota, Fairfield University, and the Westchester Center for the Study of Psychoanalysis and Psychotherapy. Frank Winer died suddenly of a heart attack on February 17, 1977, while playing volleyball.

will have to quit volleyball and tennis, probably in that order. When that happens, I will feel some relief from conflict, but I know also that I will feel miserable. I am prepared to allow myself to be miserable; I am even going to insist on it and permit myself to mourn the ending of my competitive athletic participation, because such an event merits mourning. But, I hope that soon after I retire as an active participant, I will be healthy enough to coach a teenage volleyball team, and if I can't find one to coach, I will try to organize one.

A number of my friends and acquaintances are elderly jocks, including one brother of 65 who still plays handball and paddleball. These men play regularly and spiritedly. Some argue over plays and points as if murder were impending, but they get along with each other nonetheless. For various reasons, including having more free time, some play more frequently than when they were younger. They adhere rigidly to their sports schedules, which constitute a significant portion of their recreational time. Their wives, like my wife I suspect, have mostly come to terms with their husbands' obsessional pursuits, whether in resigned surrender or in more cheerful acceptance.

As a young man I had played varsity college football and had enjoyed very much the recognition that accompanied being on the football team. I had rather assumed that, like myself, most of my fellow jocks had been members of school teams in either high school or college, and that all of us, to some varying or substantial degree, were reliving our days of athletic prestige. Without having thought much about it, it had also seemed to me that elderly jocks must all have once been young jocks. But when I asked them I learned, to my surprise, that by and large my jock comrades had neither been outstanding athletes nor had most of them participated on school teams. Nor had all been fervent jocks as young adults, some not having been involved actively from their adolescence to their late thirties or forties, when family obligations had abated. All, however, had in common a past love for physical activity, sports, and games originating in childhood. When they refer to their childhood participation in sports, I notice that my jock comrades speak wistfully and nostalgically. Most, I gather, had, as kids, been fairly sturdy, or wiry and agile, and maybe able to run a little bit faster or jump a little farther than others. My jock friends were, as kids, avid in their athletic interests, but by no means distinguished.

So, I was struck with the observation that old jocks were in their youth neither outstanding athletes nor necessarily once young jocks. And then I had a corollary realization that many ex–athletes do not continue their interest in jock pursuits into middle age and beyond, but drop out long before. It also occurred to me that among the young jocks with whom I currently play, certain ones would probably quit sports before becoming old jocks for psychological reasons that I discuss later.

Restriction of my definition of the jocks to males is not intended as an ideological or discriminatory statement against women. It is, instead, a reflection of two things: my ignorance of the subject of women as sports enthusiasts, and respect for the presumed etymology of the word "jock."

At any rate, the realization of discontinuity between young and old jocks, and the discovery that old jocks were not all exathletes, led me to think more about my own history and motives, as well as to make further speculations about my elderly colleagues. But first I would like to define what I mean by an elderly jock, and to elaborate and justify my definition.

An elderly jock is a man who continues to play regularly and wholeheartedly into his fifties and sixties and beyond, such competitive and physically demanding games as tennis, paddleball, racquet ball, platform tennis, squash, badminton, handball and volleyball. The elderly jock, to earn the name, needs take the game seriously, play hard, and struggle and scratch for points. As a result of an evolutionary selective attrition process, a concept that I will explain presently, elderly jocks, as a group, are well able to bear losing, but aim to win, or at least to give a good accounting of themselves. The jock is so competition-oriented that he tends to be, in my experience, impatient with warmups and practice, although nonetheless he tries to discipline himself to be diligent in pursuit of technique, and obsessive about strategies, as if he were a kid with a long career in sports ahead of him.

There are doubtlessly many elderly participants in sports who don't care much about struggling to win which, from the point of view of my definition, disqualifies them as jocks. There are those who play tennis, golf or bowl, either on a regular or occasional basis, but mostly for fun, diversion, exercise, relaxation, or to maintain body tone, or in the search for better health and longevity. Others may delight also in the motor pleasure of physical activity, or enjoy the explosive freedom of whacking a ball, or just in being outdoors. Games may be enjoyed furthermore, precisely for their meaninglessness, triviality or silliness. Some may play for the opportunity to enjoy whimsical impulse, as in the exuberance of tossing a soaring frisbee.

But jocks are different. Not that jocks can't or don't enjoy such experiences. Certainly jocks, no less than others, want good body tone, trimness and the like. And without doubt the pleasures of running, reaching, stretching and hitting are no less meaningful to jocks than to others. And, of course, whim, impulse, laughter, silliness, "horse play" are not lost on most jocks. The fact is, however, that the jock's essential relation to his game is a serious matter to him. The game serves purposes for the jock that are, for him, meaningful and significant, contrary to those of nonjocks.

Watch an elderly jock at play: It is abundantly clear, for example, that he is not playing for his health. Jocks are more prone in their play to threaten their health than to maintain it. They tend to extend themselves physically beyond

what is prudent for their years. They play too long in hot sun or inclement weather, when good sense would caution otherwise, and they often aggravate inflamed joints by a need to play even when medical advice calls for inactivity and rest.

Nor is the motive of relaxation or tension–reduction visible in the ordinary play of elderly jocks. If the motives for play can be divided between those who seek equilibrium, tension–reduction and relaxation, and those who seek tension–maintenance, disequilibrium, struggle, there can be little question as to the camp in which the elderly jock belongs.

Many people take up sports to lose weight. But the elderly jock's purpose is the other way around. He likes to lose weight so he can play better, or over more years. Most elderly jocks want to continue to play for just as long as they can, and for them slimness and trimness are instrumental to that end—a bonus also, if you will, but not the end itself.

I have become painfully aware of the differential motives of jocks and nonjocks in our gym on volleyball nights, each group resenting the other because of lack of reconciliation of motives. The nonjocks who show up sometimes find the jocks grim and fanatical in their insistence on all–out effort; while jocks feel, with validity, that the nonjocks "spoil" the game because they don't try very hard to win.

But seriousness of purpose and effort is not the only criterion for my definition of jock. Joggers (as joggers) are not jocks, however serious, committed or disciplined they may be. The serious jogger's pleasure is focused on his own self-development, on acquiring endurance, speed and toughness of mind and body. He has no opponent. He runs for himself and against himself, his own pleasure in running, and his improvement is sufficient motivation for his effort. For the jock, on the other hand, self-improvement is less an end in itself, serving largely an instrumental function, the jock requiring for his fullest satisfaction an opponent with whom to do battle.

By the same token, even serious golfers and bowlers are not jocks. Although, to be sure, the presence of an adversary usually enlivens and enhances these games, competition with another is not the essence of the game. On the other hand, jock games are truly adversary proceedings, the competition being direct, immediate and continually operative during play. Each player acts and reacts in opposition to the other, moving and countermoving with the actions of the other. The very purpose of the game is thwarted unless each player tries to best the other.

On the other hand, the game of golf does not require an adversary since its essential object is the completion of a course in as few strokes as possible. Competition with an opponent in golf is neither direct nor immediate, but of a remote nature. In golf it is quite possible to compete with someone removed in time and space, or even to play alone. Also, competition in golf is not continuous throughout a match but directed generally at a final score. The

activity of opponents in golf is parallel rather than interactive; each player has his own ball, takes his turn, plays his own game, alongside but independent of the other. Aside from the various courtesies of golf designed to avoid interferences between players, each plays essentially by, for and against himself. The golfer is unencumbered by, and even tries to be nonresponsive to, the play of those with whom he plays; in this sense, the game of golf is a more egocentric activity, with no pejorative intent implied by such characterization.

While games are objectively defined by their purposes and structures, the nature of games is also influenced by their particular players. By virtue of their wishes, motives and personalities, the players may distort and confuse or clarify the abstract differences among the various games and sports. Without doubt there are highly competitive people playing golf who bring out whatever competitive potential resides in the game. And most of us know serious golfers who can enjoy a round of golf alone, without an opponent. But these individual differences between golfers are essentially irrelevant to my reasoning in excluding even serious golfers as jocks. The point is that with reference to the purpose and structure of the game of golf itself, the conflict with an opponent is no more than peripheral. The insignificance of competition in the game of golf is perhaps affirmed among many golfers who, in their desire to make the game more competitive than it naturally is, regularly bet on its outcome. In other words, if golf were competitive in its nature, I would think there would be little need to elaborate it with the common practice of betting.

And of course, self-development as a primary motive may be found among serious participants of jock sports. In tennis, for example, it is possible for players of a particular match to reconcile their competitive purpose with their efforts to improve their skill. However, there are decided limits to such reconciliation of aims. Certainly, at some point, if one's focus in a game is too heavily placed on self-development, the motive to win is subverted, and the game is apt to lose interest for one's more competitive-minded opponent.

Now of course, in the final analysis, players can make anything of a game they wish and enjoy it, as long as they agree. The distinctions I have drawn between the social and competitive jock games, and the asocial and self-developmental games, apply only with reference to those who subscribe to the schema and potential of the game. But, for example, not all golfers care about their scores or their form; nor do all tennis players seek competition. There are seekers of fun and relaxation who can find it as well on a tennis court as on a golf course. Some enjoy hitting a ball—tennis, golf or other; stretching legs and arms in release from cramped workaday existence. There are those capable of resisting both any impulse to physical self-improvement, or to struggle with an opponent. As it relates to them, my distinctions are irrelevant, because for their purposes either kind of activity will do as well.

Distinctions between the cooperative–competitive jock games and the nonjock self-development games may be further elaborated as they apply to the rules of the game. In a completely individual activity, such as jogging, there are no rules. In golf and bowling, rules may be meaningful but remain simple. However, in the highly competitive jock games, rules are explicit, standardized, detailed, and significant.

The basic function of the rules of games is to place opponents on an equal footing. Where there are no opponents, rules are not needed. Whether it is tossing a frisbee back and forth or hitting a tennis ball to and fro, if the participants do not mutually define themselves as opponents, rules are mostly irrelevant. In such a case it makes no difference to anyone whether you hit a tennis ball on one bounce or two, foot fault, and so forth.

In a particular match the stringency with which rules are observed will depend on how competitive the situation is regarded. In an impromptu beach volleyball game, for example, where people care little about winning and losing, the rules provide a structure for the procedure, but little more. Lines may be drawn in the sand, and certain primary rules of the game observed in rough fashion. But the rules may be applied carelessly and selectively, more stringently against stronger players, loosely against weaker players.

In such instances, where the rules of the game are unimportant to the participants, or where the rules are applied haphazardly and easily disregarded for convenience's sake, then it may be said that the game is played truly in the service of the individual players. The game, then, is merely instrumental, unimportant in itself, and each individual participant's whim, impulse or wish is paramount. However, when the players' joint purpose is to struggle competitively with each other on an equal footing, significance must be accorded to the rules and to the game itself. The rules must then take on a compelling importance, overriding, to a considerable degree, the individual whims, impulses and wishes of the separate players. The players then assign to the game—its object and rules—an obligatory reality to which they then must conform. It may then be said that the rules, procedures and object of the game govern the players, and not the other way around. That is the case with jocks. The jock adjusts and surrenders himself to the game, but willingly and even, more or less, fervently. The procedure of a willing surrender to forces outside ourselves is often identified with the concept of "love." On this basis, the jock is to be regarded as "loving" his sport.

Elderly jocks, then, are "loving" players of adversary games, games in which opponents are pitted in direct, interactive struggle, where the purpose of the game is to try to win over an opponent, with whom one struggles on equal footing. The jock assigns obligatory powers to the game's competitive purpose, as well as to its procedures and rules. For the jock, the game is the thing!

The jock's ideal goal, I believe, is to deliver himself to the game. He seeks absorption in the game and tries to eliminate obstacles to his concentration.

He would like to give the game his very best so that he can successfully adapt to its demands, as imposed on him through his opponent as these tasks shift and vary, moment by moment, with the ball's movement. Jocks are characterized by the relative wholeheartedness of their play, by their determination and zealousness. Jocks like to pit their full resources against the full resources of an opponent; halfhearted play by either is generally enjoyed by neither.

The jock seeks to tap his inner resources, resources not easily called forth except by difficulties. He calls this "playing over his head". He wants to concentrate hard, to integrate his energies so as to drag from himself the best of his skills. As in life generally, there are those who in adversity or crisis successfully achieve higher levels of integration and tap inner resources not ordinarily accessible. So, in just that sense, in play jocks create crises against which they organize their resources.

In this context, what does it mean to create crises? It means that the adversaries agree that the object, rules and procedures of the game itself are to be regarded as having importance and value, and will be treated as compelling realities to be complied with and not to be violated simply for the sake of ease and convenience. It means that the adversaries agree to try their best, within the schema of the game, to make matters difficult for each other; each will make wholehearted efforts to win. It means, furthermore, that one selects as adversaries players of at least equal caliber, who are capable of summoning one's best efforts. Many jocks even prefer playing against others who are a bit better than themselves, because of the spur to effort evoked by superior competition, while spurning inferior opposition since no crisis of effort is entailed.

Elderly jocks are searching via their struggles, challenges, difficulties, and demands of the game, a feeling of momentary wholeness. Gordon Allport (1960, p. 68) defined happiness as the glow that attends the integration of the person while pursuing or contemplating the attainment of goals. A thrill resides, for the elderly jock, in what in athletic parlance is called "putting it all together," an integration of form, energy, power and concentration, making for intended performance. He would like to be able, in a given instance of play, to do precisely what he chooses to do. His ideal is to achieve a mastery of himself in playing by reaching into himself as deeply as is potentially possible for him: The strength of his will power, the extent of his stamina and speed, the best of his technique, all the tactical wisdom and judgment he has acquired, and whatever self-confidence he can muster to add polish and decisiveness to his movements and strokes.

Jocks generally have some ideal vision of their possibilities and potentialities which urge and inspire them helpfully in play. But in the case of the elderly jock in particular, he must carry, along with such a vision, both a realistic acceptance of his own limitations and considerable respect for the ability of his opponent to thwart him. The jock may, for inspiration, give full

rein to the range of his glorious imagination, but he must not confuse his fantasy with reality. He must accept that the ecstatic moments of putting it all together are few and far between. This he can best do if he has found satisfaction and value in the act of striving itself. He must accept that, strictly speaking, his vision of integrating at one moment all his capacities is in fact attainable only rarely, but that more constant excitement and thrill may be found in the effort itself.

If one requires for one's well being the actual success of "putting it all together," being an elderly jock is hardly rewarding. Nor does the future bode well; athletic activity does not improve with age. The elderly jock's pleasure needs more substantial, constant and reliable sources than the precious few moments of integrating his various physical and psychological attributes. One such source derives from the wholeheartedness and sincerity of his efforts.

To play sincerely or wholeheartedly means to lose oneself, relatively speaking, in the game. It means to win over self-consciousness, intimidation and vanity; it means the summoning of courage to expose one's self to defeat despite one's full efforts; it means the mastery of various anxieties and apprehensions that divert and dilute one's efforts; it means the self-imposition of discipline and concentration; it means stubbornness and persistence even when tired. The jock's phrase for this wholeheartedness and sincerity is "hanging in there."

Winning has, I imagine, the same meaning for elderly jocks as reaching the top of the mountain has for the mountain climber. Whatever the thrill upon arrival on a mountain peak, it would be without much meaning if the climber had been transported there effortlessly by helicopter. The mountain top is a symbol, and attaining it is confirmation of obstacles overcome. Its meaning resides for the climber in the struggle he has made and the difficulties mastered en route. The motives of mountain climbers and jocks have in common a wish to confront physical obstacles and to surmount them. The message their achievements impart is not only about their physical abilities, but of qualities of character as well.

I see another similarity between the two. In one sense, winning and getting to the top of the mountain are the motives of the jock and mountain climber respectively, but in another sense they are not. The mountain peak maps the climber's upward destination. It tells us where he is headed, but not his reasons for making the trip. And so it is with the jock. Winning describes the direction (or goal) of his efforts, but not why he is making the effort. But somehow, if we are to understand the jock, we need to see beyond his desire to win and focus attention instead on the significance of struggle for him. A jock who seeks easy victories is a seduced jock. For the most part elderly jocks, at least, repudiate the temptation to seek cheap victories. So dear to him are striving and struggling that the elderly jock lays himself open to snobbishness

and intolerance, because he may avoid playing with inferior players. His pride is invested with taking on tough and difficult challenges, so that he must extend himself, both physically and psychologically, to his limits and beyond.

So wrapped up are elderly jocks in struggle and challenge that they tend to be impatient, as I know I am, in warming up before matches. I am sometimes amused at our impatience. We older fellows, with our creaky joints and inelastic muscles, know fully well that we should have long, easy warm–ups. But each of us impatiently waits for his comrades to indicate their readiness and we generally rush to start before we should.

What about losing? Can the competitive elderly jock be a good sport about losing? My answer is "yes." I have witnessed some younger jocks who, over the years, in response to the threat of losing, cheat and become quarrelsome or abusive, and who upon actually losing become depressed and terribly sullen. My hunch is that young jocks who have such problems with losing retire before becoming old jocks, perhaps becoming golfers and coaches instead. Old jocks, on the other hand, at least in my limited experience, while scrappy and testy and not above crabbing over whether a ball was in or out, make a point of trying hard to be scrupulous and are usually, if not always, painstakingly fair. The elderly jocks that I know maintain, and I've seen no real evidence to the contrary, that they suffer no depression or loss of self-esteem whatever the outcome of play, indeed coming back to play, time after time, with regularity. Younger jocks, the men in their thirties and forties who have enjoyed and played sports in their twenties, sometimes have problems accepting losing. I've noticed this among certain of our volleyball players. It seems to me that they are still undergoing difficulty in coming to terms with physical changes associated with aging.

Elderly jocks are, after all, the distillation of a selective, evolutionary process dating back over a number of years. The elderly jock, whatever his earlier competence, can no longer confidently regard himself as a good player, but must accept himself as "good for my age," and then as time goes on, take consolation in still playing hard, and then finally find solace in managing to play at all. Period. If he cannot accept, respect and feel pride even as his abilities diminish, he will drop out, becoming an ex–jock, instead of being an elderly one.

I have never met an elderly jock who was abashed by his relish and pleasure winning, or who made more than perfunctory noises to minimize his competitive nature. But the strong wish to win should not be automatically equated with the compulsion to win. They are not the same. The compulsion to win is narrow and rigid, allowing no room for the dignity of the loser. It is based on anxiety that stems from the belief that losing is a humiliating and ridiculing experience, and that losers are inferiors. The compulsion to win has desperation and fear behind it, the aim being to avoid a demeaned, shameful

position by achieving through victory a superior and arrogant one. The compulsive need to win allows no room for the loser's self-esteem and dignity. Because the consequences of losing are so demeaning and humiliating in compulsive competition, defeat must be avoided at all costs. Therefore, the threat of losing, for compulsive winners, leads easily in sports to hostility, cheating, disparaging, blaming others, complaining, and rationalizing in urgent efforts to ward off feelings of self-contempt, or the projected contempt and hostility of others.

A young man who played volleyball years ago in a group of which I was a part offers a good illustration of the compulsion to win. Even though we played informally and with "pick up" sides, our games were hard fought and vigorous. As a group we struggled with each other but enjoyed our play and each other. The young man in question played as hard and easily as well as anyone else but never with pleasure. If his team fell behind, a process ensued, so regularly as to be considered automatic: He would start out by criticizing unmercifully members of his own team; then he would accuse his opponents of cheating; this would be accompanied by his own cheating, first subtly, then outrageously; and if we were using a referee, he would find fault with the referee and on several occasions so hostile and accusing was he that fist fights were only narrowly averted.

I don't know for sure whether he has remained a jock, as he has since moved out of the area. But I would think, in view of his problem with losing, that he probably dropped out long ago.

But my experience with this young man is indeed different from my experience with elderly jocks generally. There are many crabby, cantankerous elderly jocks, but their crabbiness is usually associated not with fears of losing, but with their being sticklers for compliance with the rules. Most elderly jocks are strict about observance of the rules of the game, and take great pride in their being fair-minded. The relationship among the older men I play with tends to be warm and friendly, characterized by comaraderie and mutual identification, rather than hostility and disparagement. Whatever competitive barbs ensue, and there are some, are pretty much restricted to teasing and humorous banter. These jocks allow ample space for the dignity of the loser of a match, while they permit the winner his share of expressed pride and pleasure. To be sure, elderly jocks are compulsive, but a distinction needs to be made between the compulsion to win, and the compulsion to engage in struggle. It is the latter that characterizes the elderly jocks, not the former.

The competition of jocks is, paradoxically and as previously indicated, a cooperative venture. Each tries his best to win, and receives, through evocation, the best efforts of the other. Each contributes to the excellence of the other's play, thus giving precise and accurate meaning to "giving and getting." Furthermore, each has the good will of the other, and it is

characteristic of our groups of jocks to offer encouragement and guidance to each other. Especially when a game is hard fought, and the exchange between adversaries is roughly equal, do the players tend even more deeply to regard each other with mutual respect and appreciation. Play between jocks, furthermore, often results in a "we" feeling, a sense of belonging.

Thus, having an opponent whom one can meet on an equal footing is a basic requirement for the elderly jock. He enjoys competition and struggle. But, inevitably, times arise when one does play an opponent with abilities so superior to one's own that the contest is clearly unequal. In such instances, the cooperative competition described previously is impossible to achieve, and both players are generally better if both recognize that fact. Whether at such times the competitive–cooperative schema is abandoned in favor of some more relaxed noncompetitive basis for play will depend on individual cases. However, if the players do continue to compete, it is my experience that elderly jocks continue usually to try their very best, even when hopelessly outclassed. They feel they owe that to their opponents, even if it means being trounced.

Conversely, despite the narcissistic reassurance in winning, most elderly jocks I know would as soon be trounced as trounce an opponent. Many of us are embarrassed by the discomfiture of a badly beaten opponent. I recall on one occasion our volleyball group, which was fairly experienced, was matched with a group from another city who were still learning the game. Our opponents became increasingly intimidated, frustrated and demoralized, while after a brief cockiness at winning we became more and more embarrassed and uncomfortable with their demoralization. We didn't know how to respond in order to help matters. We were fearful that if we relaxed in our play too much, they would feel more, rather than less, humiliated. It took several frustrating games, during which incipient quarrels developed among them, before they accepted the reality of the large differential in abilities, and ceased feeling humiliated. Then, as if all of us suddenly developed good sense, we relaxed and made a playful, noncompetitive evening of it.

Various circumstances contribute to a man's propensity to remain or abandon being a jock into his older years, first among them, without doubt, being the state of his health and physical condition. But among the various circumstances and conditions related to the outcome, the jock's relationship to his wife is highly influential. Given normal circumstances, and a preceding adequate relationship, I believe that there is a strong tendency for husbands and wives to be drawn closer together and to become more mutually dependent as they age. A number of social–psychological factors contribute to this phenomenon, not least of which is the fact that with children grown up and gone from the home, husband and wife are now more exclusively in each other's company. If, as I said before, they have enjoyed each other over the years together, the couple tend to become now even more companionable,

doing more and more things together, including hobbies, recreational activities, marketing and the like.

Many of my friends have moved gracefully into this pattern, naturally and without struggle; some even eagerly. In such instances, and I believe it common, these men over a period of time terminate their regularly scheduled athletic competitive activities with all-male companions, and adopt new modes of activity, including those of an athletic nature, that now involve their wives' participation. Tennis players may find the change easier than my volleyball or paddleball friends, since mixed doubles offer a convenient transitional alternative, not available to the others.

But other older men, including myself, cling harder to their jock activities, even while feeling the increasing desire and need to spend more time with their wives. Some wives, and I include my own, appreciate the great importance of jock activities to their husbands and altruistically encourage them to continue. Also, some wives have independent activities of their own to pursue, which are important to them; others, I am sure, feel resentful about being left alone evenings and weekends.

The issue is a real one for elderly jocks and their wives, and the ambivalence elderly jocks feel in pursuit of their activities is probably both common and substantial. It is a tribute to the strength of the drive to remain a jock that, despite the very strong natural pull toward spending more time with their wives as both grow older, there are so many elderly jocks around. My own resolve to remain one continues, with great strength.

I associated my jock activities, their competitiveness and aggressiveness, their physicality and roughness, their all-male companionability, with my masculinity. At the same time, I associate growing older and the gradual loss of my physical powers with a demasculinizing process, a process the inevitability of which I accept and understand. But, I don't welcome it and would like to retard it by playing my games just as long as I can. Perhaps, but I am vague about what I feel, I regard the pulls toward my wife, with our increased need for each other and consequent desire for closeness that accompanies our getting older, as also demasculinizing in effect. At any rate, even though we enjoy each other, I remain determined that it not keep me from remaining a jock.

So much for my exposition of the elderly jock. How did he get that way? It is a safe assumption that various elderly jocks used various routes to get to their station. Furthermore, no single explanation can encompass how even one elderly jock got there. But I have a historical concept of how I became an elderly jock, perhaps aspects of which are relevant to the development of other jocks.

I think that one source for a later strong interest in competitive sports is situated in the struggle of children who, in forming peer relationships, are almost inevitably faced with reconciling their natural reaching out for

friendly relations with their equally natural apprehensions about being accepted on equal terms. I think that jocks are people who try through sports to combine both their desire for a friendly relationship and to establish to an adversary, proof of one's substantiality. Stated another way, competitive sports encourage an aggressive expression of one's ability, yet in a setting of play.

Quite early in childhood, certainly by the time we have attended school for a year or so, most of us are well involved in efforts at achieving friendly relationships with other children. We learn the rudiments of sharing and exchange. We learn how to comply to others, and to obey the rules. To guide us further in our interactions, we develop a knowledge and a sense of fair play and justice. And if our efforts at establishing friendly relationships are more or less successful, we acquire increased self-confidence, a sense of group affiliation from which we gain inner security and, in time, a network of mutual loyalties that provide roots and orientation.

But these efforts at making friends and getting along with other children are not without fears, nor without friction, nor without struggle and pain, and not without their failures. Establishing and maintaining friendly relations with others are seldom problem-free. All of us experience rejection, sometimes real, sometimes imagined, and sometimes just anticipated. None of us is without immunity, in group situations, from being attacked, intimidated, humiliated, exploited, shamed, ridiculed or otherwise subjected to negative treatment.

Establishing and maintaining peer relationships, thus, have their harrassing and frightening aspects, to which each individual need address himself to find his own solutions. To be sure, the process of establishing friendly relations involves the overcoming of our egocentric biases and the learning of sharing, giving, complying and sacrificing, but it certainly evokes also the need for individual strengthening and toughening, the development of one's inner resources to withstand adverse interpersonal experiences, and the development of certain abilities to defend one's self from the abuse and animosity of others.

We need to learn to defend, assert and stand up for ourselves. We need to learn to make demands, too. We need to develop the ability to resist and, at times, to defy. We need to learn how to fight; how to disagree, and how to take independent and unpopular action in the face of others' disapproval, and even despite our own fears. We must also learn to tolerate our own aggressiveness and anger, and to channel them for effectiveness. We need to develop the strength to take risks and to tolerate our own aggressiveness and anger, and to channel them for effectiveness. We need to develop the strength to take risks and to tolerate our failures and mistakes, so that we may learn from them. We need to develop adequate belief in our individual worth and the confidence in our ability to defend it against those who would demean us. And we need to

acquire some adequate measures of courage, fortitude, resolve, toughness, persistence and coolness in the face of threat, abuse and rejection. In short, we need to learn to develop our nerve, overcome fears and to confront the inevitable challenges that arise in working out peer relationships. We need to surmount at least some of these challenges, and in so doing learn and strengthen ourselves in the direction of autonomy and self-confidence.

These tasks of self-development, with all their emphasis on strength and autonomy, are not antithetical to the development of friendly relations with others. Instead, the achievement of these developmental tasks is contributory, if not a requirement, for comfortable and reciprocal peer relations. Satisfactory peer relations require, it seems to me, a feeling of equal worth with others, and such feelings depend on the ability to stand up for one's self. The failure to achieve relative autonomy and strength may condemn one to relationships infused with fears and tentativeness. In such instances, children are apt to try to make their relationships palatable by various artificial strategies, with constant loss of spontaneous and natural expression. Such strategies are designed to make one safe, as for example, in self-effacing, dependent behavior. Others may seek their safety in isolation, responding to their fears of encounters with peers by introversion and withdrawal.

I recall that among my larger worries as a child was the possibility of being bullied by another child, my concern being whether I would, in a given instance, stand up to intimidation. I think that probably my greatest dread, as a child, was of feeling or being helpless in the face of threat. Whatever early notions I had about the ideal of masculinity, I am sure that central to my concept was the courage, as much as the ability, to stand up to bullying behavior, submission being in some way related to effeminancy and homosexuality.

Be that as it may, however, I believe that most of us learn fairly early in life that if you don't want to be pushed around by others, it is a good idea to stand up for your rights. Furthermore, if we tolerate unequal treatment without resistance, we are apt, we discover, to feel inferior. To be sure, those children who feel less substantial than others in the first place are most vulnerable to bullying, because of their difficulty in mustering the courage to assert or defend themselves. But, at the same time, the reverse is also true. Our self-esteem as children is dependent on how insistent we are in being treated by others as no less significant, substantial or worthy than they.

As a youngster, I took it for granted that fist fights, although fearsome, were a required price that one had to pay, from time to time, to maintain both practical and psychological equality with others. My friends, and my brothers as well, also regarded the necessity to fight as a commonplace and unremarkable reality. Nor do I have any question but that my parents, like most other parents in our neighborhood, would expect that their children fight, under ordinary circumstances, rather than tolerate abuse. I don't mean

that we kids fought constantly. We didn't. It was only that given the provocation, fighting was accepted as normal, and we had to be willing to fight.

Our neighborhood was actually a tough one in a factory city and consisted largely of poor laboring new immigrant Italians and second generation Irish. While hostile toward each other, they had in common hostility to the sprinkling of immigrant Jewish families who also lived there. Not that the Jewish families were without hostility of their own to the others, but being a tiny minority they just couldn't afford to exercise it as freely and openly. Some of the ethnic hostility of the parents was visited upon the children, but not all of it. For to a fair degree we played together after school. In school, too, we kids get along reasonably well.

Outside of school, status among us as young boys was mostly a matter of physical toughness and the willingness and ability to fight. Children seemed to find, in some rough fashion but not a static one, a rank order for themselves and others that identified one's standing as a fighter. A lowly position on this totem pole could spell trouble for a youngster who tolerated it too easily, because he would be vulnerable as a scapegoat for bullying behavior from others.

We all need, for our well-being, to be able to evaluate ourselves with some consistency as adequate and competent. In our neighborhood, with its emphasis on aggression, it would be very difficult for a child, even one as young as 7 or 8, who was too fearful to fight, to have an adequate image of himself. By that age we already placed much value on the ability and courage to fight, with disdain and contempt for cowardice. Like others, I assessed myself with these values in mind and perceived others according to the same standards. Somewhere around the age of 8 or 9, I learned that I was quite strong for my age, a very comforting realization, which I clearly recall having achieved dramatically and suddenly as a result of a fight. Yet, I remember also from that age period being ashamed of my being fat, because it seemed to me to indicate softness, weakness, and girlishness.

We Jewish kids in the immediate neighborhood hung together, although we had friends and playmates among both the Italians and Irish children. Especially as we got older and our games became organized sport, encompassing, by necessity, larger numbers of children, our after-school play included the melange of ethnic backgrounds. We formed teams, shared most of the same childhood cultural values, shared the same play areas and vacant lots, had the same neighborhood school loyalties, but nonetheless our religious and cultural differences were lost on none of us.

There was no doubt but that in certain respects the Jewish children felt like outsiders in their own neighborhood, and were subject to the resentment and disparagement of other children, albeit less so when the personal contact with a particular child was daily and immediate. Especially in our encounters with

certain cliques or gangs of Italian boys would we be subjected to threat, intimidation, challenges or derision.

Experiencing the hostility of the others, the Jewish boys often felt apprehensive and defensive. We had our own clique, but we were of insufficient number to gain great confidence from that, but nonetheless we were sturdy enough to be of mutual support to each other, with assistance from older brothers. The older we got, the more aware we became of our difference, but at the same time more confident of defending ourselves. In the face of derision and intimidation, it would have been easy for use to react with demoralization and to accept opprobrium, but on the whole and especially with increasing maturity, we felt a determination that whatever our ethnic differences from other boys, it not be confused by anyone, them or us, with inferiority.

Certainly, with sufficient discretion and the practical sense to avoid confrontations in certain instances and with certain kids, generally we did not shrink from encounters, from competitive games, nor from the playgrounds and vacant lots of our neighborhood. Nor did we run from fights. For the most part, we were prideful enough to defend and give a good accounting of ourselves.

My parents had led hard lives; they were also both political radicals and militant labor-union people, and their beliefs and experiences were well reflected in their individual characters. They were used to adversity, and they were tough and realistic. They encouraged and expected of their four sons and one daughter the development of personal courage and self-assertion. They were both social idealists, but they also believed in the realities and necessity of fighting to protect one's rights and dignity, life having always involved such struggle for them. Their beliefs made good sense in our neighborhood.

My brother Sol, 5 years older than I, was obsessed with the "manly arts of self-defense" and infected me with his bug, although I don't think I ever quite reached his degree of preoccupation. As I recall it, when he was about 12 or 13 years old, he was constantly clipping out magazine ads and sending away through the mails for Jiu-Jitsu lessons, wrestling holds, and the like. He usually contented himself with receiving the "free introductory offers," which abounded in the pulp magazines of those days. Sol had the patience to be forever practicing these newly acquired techniques.

I was his pupil, protegé, assistant, victim, "patsy," depending on his mood and on my degree of willingness to participate on a particular day. At any rate, he practiced his tricks and holds on me, a process which though painful at times, was edifying for both of us. I'm not sure with what degrees of love or revenge, but I in turn played the same role with my younger brother, Joe. Interestingly, some of these techniques that we acquired through the magazine ads actually worked, and to this day I remember them.

Sol was a strong, tough boy and, unlike me, slim and tall for his age. He was on the track team in high school, and he high jumped, ran the quarter mile, broad jumped, and threw the discus. Through him, some of us kids on the block learned something of the techniques of these activities. I recall my father's making high jump standards for us, which we used for a number of years. We were forever running races "around the block" and beginning new training regimens, inspired by my brother.

But Sol also had a reputation as a fighter. He was not only protective, but an ideal to emulate, as well. Boxers were heroes in the 1920's among us kids, and I think most poor neighborhoods had at least several boys of 15 to 16 and up who boxed in what were called "the amateurs," a euphemism for exploitation, these boys fighting for paying audiences for several dollars a fight. Amateur boxers were respected and feared in our neighborhood.

Jack Dempsey was world heavyweight champion when I was eight or nine. The barbershop featured photos of boxers, standing knock-kneed and bare-torsoed, somehow vulnerable looking in their partial nakedness. But not Jack Dempsey! His photos showed him crouching formidably—no knock knees for him; tough, scowling face in need of a shave; bristling short hairs on his head. He was a fearless brawler, with a fierce left hook, eager to absorb punishment so as to be in position to deliver it. To me, he was an awesome man and probably so for my brothers and our friends as well.

But Gene Tunney, who replaced him, was much more my hero, commanding my loyalty because he encompassed within himself not only toughness and fighting ability, but he presumably possessed, as well, social virtues, intelligence and respect for education. Tunney was a "white hat" hero; he boxed standing straight and tall, cool and courageous, feinting, parrying, jabbing.

To me, Dempsey and Tunney were symbols, who blended easily with the romantic, medieval tripe we were learning about in school at the time: the knights of King Arthur lore. Dempsey was a "black knight," alienated, unlovable and unloved, antisocial and brutal, but fearsome and awesome in his prowess and meanness. Tunney was his antithesis, cultivated, honorable and unwilling to take unfair or even accidental advantage.

Fighting among us young children in our neighborhood, as is probably true among children elsewhere, was regulated by certain rules and procedures that approximated those of boxing matches. You were not supposed to punch a "man" on the ground or hit "below the belt," nor continue to fight after the other had conceded. Biting, scratching, kicking, hairpulling were not only regarded as unfair, but unbecoming and unmanly as well, implying hysteria and loss of self-control. The rules, while not always observed well, and at times even dispensed with, nonetheless represented an ethical ideal, and as such were accorded importance and were influential in determining fighting

behavior. Breaking of the rules invited the risk of social disapproval, with loss of status. Furthermore, the rules were subject to enforcement by any or all onlookers with sufficient bravery or inclination to do so.

While the concept of fairness is sensible, our notion of fair play was influenced by the romantic distortions of the "Western" movies, which we gobbled up weekly for a nickel apiece. Villains fought unfairly, whether with guns or otherwise, while the price one paid for the role of hero involved a willingness to fight, usually at considerable disadvantage. But nonetheless, we also knew that no matter the disadvantage or cost, it was the villain and not the hero who paid the ultimate price.

For us younger children, the rules of fighting were reassuring. The rules tended to protect, by limiting wanton aggressive behavior, and a sensible youngster in a tough neighborhood welcomes and values rules.

A fight was a serious enough event for us children to be entered into ordinarily with apprehension. But there were many times also when fighting had a play-acting, charade-like quality, a going-through-the-motions, in which bluff or one-upmanship substituted to a great degree for a serious effort to hurt one another. In such instances fighting resembled a game or quasi-sport, inasmuch as the victory being sought was a symbolic one. This was the case when a fight evolved from a competitive jockeying for feelings of superiority or higher status, satisfaction being obtained after a brief ritualistic fight, with one accepting the intimidation of the other. Such fights ended before too much injury could be inflicted. In such instances, the rules of fighting tend to be given exaggerated importance, not simply to keep the encounter on a fair and equal basis, but to protect the combatants from injuring each other too severely.

But this sort of ritualistic fighting, this play-acting, this quasisport, this fighting by the rules, could no longer serve us as we grew into teenagers. Fighting for teenagers is a more grim and serious matter, more fierce and dangerous, and sometimes even vicious and maiming. Teenagers fought less frequently than younger children, but their ability and propensity to inflict pain and injury on each other did not lend itself to, or even permit, the perpetuation of the amorphous, ritualistic game-like fighting of younger children. In short, the distinctions between fighting and games become more urgent as children grow older.

When I was about 12 or 13, I had a fist fight with a boy that seems, in retrospect, very significant in my growing up. It was not only the bloodiest fight that I had ever had with anyone until then, but the most serious and wholehearted fight, as well. I think the same was true for him. We knew and disliked each other, and this was a grudge match. We were more or less of equal strength and we fought on equal terms. Unlike most of my prior fights, this one went on and on, neither of us willing to concede to the other. There was a large crowd present at the ball park where the fight was held, but no one

interfered. The fight ended only after my opponent's father, who ran a shoe repair shop several blocks away, got wind of the fight and came running with a large leather strap, which he flailed about. I just know that that fight was my signal of changing from a child to a man.

There are times in a child's life when there may be no adequate alternative to a fight. It may be an occasion of fury or vindictiveness, possibly in response to an outrage, or a time when self-protection requires it, or an effort to rid oneself of a bully. But who really likes a fight? There are some hostile, bellicose people who, with confidence in their ability to fight, enjoy it. But for most of us, the prospect of a fight is grim, and it makes us apprehensive.

At any rate, that is how I felt as a child. I was neither hostile nor bellicose. I didn't want to beat up others or to make myself vulnerable to that possibility. Nor did I want to bully others. When I had a fight, it was either to defend myself and my self-respect, or out of anger at some other offense. And when I asserted myself verbally, I was far from arrogant or assaultive. Like many children, I was unsure of myself and, if anything, somewhat shy.

So, as a child I placed a great deal of value on strength, courage, self-assertion, as well as on the ability to fight; I didn't want fights. I wanted, instead, to be able to exercise these qualities by means other than fighting. Also, I wanted for others to recognize these attributes in me. I wanted to combine my being friendly with others and to maintain self-respect and respect of others. I wanted to feel, and to feel from others, that I was as significant, substantial, and capable as they were. As a child, I was certainly not always sure of my equality, and I desired ways to establish it for myself and others.

Who has the rare good fortune to grow up in such a loving atmosphere that he feels always easy and secure in his self-esteem and equality to others? Whatever the variations among individuals, practically all of us, to a substantial degree, must engage in struggle to gain and maintain confidence in our equality to others. And each child, in growing up, has to struggle in his own way and discover his own solutions. For me, competitive sports offered one solution, being both conducive to friendship and yet expressive of attributes I valued. I learned that in sports I could be tough, assertive, aggressive, daring, courageous, exhibit physical prowess, and still be friendly. Unlike fighting, competitive sports did not necessarily imply hostility, anger, threats to self-respect.

To be sure, a more hostile youngster might well utilize competitive sports as a vehicle for his hostility, and as a substitute (rather than alternative) for fighting. And many do. Yet, the rules of games and sports, and the spirit of sportsmanship, to the degree to which its is present in the life of a particular child, tempers and limits hostile and angry expression.

Competitive sports had other advantages, too. While some competitiveness can be hurtful, and therefore frightening, they are less so on both counts than

is fighting. A desirable aspect of sports is that it makes a game out of combat. With all the aggressiveness of competitive sports, the struggle among adversaries is merely symbolic, with winning and losing having no substantive meaning. Fighting, on the other hand, is starkly real, with more disturbing possible implications for winner and loser. Furthermore competitive sports, at least ideally, provide ample room for the dignity, confidence and self-respect of the loser, especially one whose efforts have been all-out, while in fighting the dignity and respect accorded a loser are a matter of happenstance, and the threat to self-esteem of far greater significance.

At any rate, the competitive sport which, at first, seemed to me to exemplify best all these very precious attributes was the sport that most closely resembled fighting. That sport is boxing, and I wanted very much to be a good boxer. Boxing is the most prototypical and primitive of sports and is often confused with fighting. But boxing as a fighting technique and boxing as a sport are, at least abstractly, two different entities. Both were popular in my neighborhood when I was a child. As already indicated, boxers were folk heroes for us children, and in accordance with the vogue in the 1920s, we kids extolled not only Dempsey and Tunney, but fighters of the day, such as Benny Leonard, Jack Sharkey and Mickey Walker, who were as important to us as Babe Ruth, Ty Cobb and Lou Gehrig. Also, our neighborhood had a hall where boxing matches were held regularly. Boxing was so popular in those days that even amidst the poverty of the neighborhood, in which sports equipment was, to say the least, very meager, sets of scuffed boxing gloves would always appear at the proper moment. Boxing matches, complete with gloves, impromptu referees and boxing rings formed by onlookers, were a common aspect of our informal recreational activities.

In those days, also, the city playgrounds sponsored boxing among their charges, and boxing was one of our gym activities in junior high school. Also, boxing gloves were brought out by adults, when children argued, as a presumably civilized way to settle disputes. But while boxing as a sport has an identity of its own, it is, nevertheless, readily confused with fighting. Even our language reflects the confusion, as well as the connection, between the two. The terms "boxing match" and "prize fight" are used almost interchangeably, as are the words "boxer" and "fighter."

Fighting is a direct antecedent of boxing. Perhaps other competitive sports also have roots in fighting activity, even if more remotely and less directly. Perhaps even competitive nonphysical games, such as chess and certain card games, may have attenuated connections to fighting. Just as is the case in fighting, these competitive games involve adversaries pitted in struggle for mastery, with advantage of some sort or other being sought through winning.

It would be an error to conclude, however, an equation between fighting and competitive sports and games. Neither the motives nor the feelings of

fighting combatants and sports competitors are necessarily the same. The connection I am drawing between fighting and competitive sports is not a functional but a developmental one, with each having separate goals, motives and emotions.

Over the years of childhood and youth, we children boxed often. We boxed in my back yard, in vacant lots and playgrounds. Like many kids, especially in poor neighborhoods, we even sparred playfully and in greeting, open-handed, usually. As a teenager, I boxed once in a while at YMCA gyms, and I achieved some degree of proficiency. In college I boxed on occasion in order to stay in condition. And later, in the Army, I worked out with various boxers. I was drawn somewhat to boxing situations, and I took pleasure in my boxing skills, but I never really enjoyed it. Boxing, I found, often provoked too much apprehension to be really enjoyable. I boxed mostly to establish to myself and to others that I had courage. If I weren't pushed by that motive, I would never have allowed my brother to persuade me once to enter the "Golden Gloves" with him.

I didn't enjoy hurting others, but the principal trouble with boxing is that it could hurt me too much. Boxing is too raw, too prototypical, too much like fighting. And, while in boxing the opponents are not necessarily hostile toward each other to begin with, I learned that strong angers can often be easily aroused, even in the most casual of workouts. Boxing contests, while one step forward from fighting, easily reversed their direction. Furthermore, boxing appeals to two types; one, the plodders like myself who needed to prove their strength and courage,and two, the hostile, bellicose guys who really like to beat up others.

So, while boxing served as some sort of compulsive ideal for me, I was never wholehearted in my pursuit. There were a number of sports I enjoyed more, such as wrestling and swimming, both of which I did a little in competition. But the sport I was really crazy about was football. As a youngster, football was always on my mind. I carry in my head to this day little, odd, trivial memory scraps about football heroes of the day, which warm me upon recollection. I had a true romance with football. I read every football story I could find in the public library and in every pulp magazine that came my way. I also wrote football stories, which bore similarity to those I read. In elementary school I was constantly organizing football teams, at least one every two or three weeks, and diagraming plays based on what I could pick up from the sports pages of the newspaper or from my older brother. While in the playing of football I may not have been any more advanced than my peers, I am sure that I was by far the greatest theoretician.

We had no adults to help us. There were no adult-sponsored leagues in those days to provide structure and assistance for football playing young children. Nor did we have protective equipment. But we kids were diligent,

interested and persistent, and we managed from fourth grade on to put teams together each autumn, and to organize more than impromptu games with children in other neighborhoods.

As I grew and became a teenager, my loftiest ambition, next to making it with a girl, would have been to make the high school football team. Both ambitions were intertwined, but equally farfetched. Being on the football team was the closest thing to salvation I could imagine. It would be the answer to nearly every problem of a self-confidence and social acceptability that I faced. It would give me physical confidence with other boys, especially the bigger and tougher ones, boost my sorely lacking confidence with girls, and pave the way for sexual acceptance by some admiring girl.

But, alas, salvation was not to be mine. I went out for football as a sophomore, but I was so timid about it that I was never issued my equipment. Compared physically to most of the boys on the team, I was still a kid, being hardly pubescent, and I felt intimidated. They were older, tougher, bigger, stronger and I knew it. Each succeeding year until graduation, I gave thought to trying out again, but that first experience had for the time undermined me, and I never did. Nonetheless, throughout my high school days and for a year or so beyond, I played football with organized neighborhood teams, with boys more equal to my own abilities.

By the time I started college some years after high school graduation, I was physically mature and, feeling more confident, I went out for football. I played both freshman and varsity football in college and enjoyed it enormously. Even though I was a good student and received recognition in other spheres as well, nothing did quite as much in boosting my self-eesteem as being on the football team and in being known as an athlete. Not that this was the way I thought I should feel but, in honesty, it was the way I felt. Yet, despite all of its positive meaning, I quit football after a year each of freshman and varsity play because, for personal reasons, I wanted to complete college in three years. It was a very difficult decision, even though a right one for me, but for many years the memory of the decision produced in me a tinge of sadness.

When I played football, especially in college, I often felt strong excitement at clashing and crashing with an opponent. There was a feeling about pitting my strength and force, speed and skill, against another that I liked. I liked to be reckless, and I found it exhilirating to be so caught up in the game that caution would give way to abandon. I found that I could lose myself, at least for short periods, in the activity, an experience that I identify with a soaring freedom. Sometimes, in play, I felt like I had no function other than to move obstacles, or to be one. Not that my enthusiasm was constant! It could be easily interrupted by being knocked on my rear. There were these jolting experiences and superior opponents who made me aware of my own limitations. But with all that, the playing of the game was very exciting, and it

is interesting that in the excitement of the game, I sometimes didn't feel my hurts and pains.

I was a fairly aggressive player but wasn't always aware of it. I obtained some insight into myself when on several occasions fellow players commented on the aggressiveness of my playing style in contrast to my manner off the field, which was more diffident and easy-going. I realized that football released me to be aggressive in a way that I could not ordinarily permit myself in social relations.

My football playing did not end in college; there was one more brief, crazy period of playing. During World War II the Infantry Division to which I belonged was holed up in Normandie for about a month prior to being committed to action, and somehow Company and Battalion football teams got organized. I think we played three games; they were the most reckless of games. I think most of us at least half-wished for a serious enough injury to keep us out of immediate combat. We played in a hilly, uneven pasture, studded with rocks and holes. We played without any protective equipment at all. The caliber of individual players was, of course, quite varied, but there were a number of ex-high school and college athletes among us, and our own particular team boasted an All-American from Ohio State.

I was 28 years of age when World War II ended, and I was discharged from service in the Army. For the next 15 years I participated very little in sports. I missed sports to some degree, but not very much. I'd feel some nostalgia for football in the autumn, but nothing difficult. Sure enough, at a picnic I would never sit out of a softball game. And several times a year, perhaps, a friend and I would play a little very awkward tennis. Actually I had little time for sports, what with graduate schools, earning a living, and trying to do a job as husband and father. Nor did I think of myself then as an ex-jock; nor as a deprived jock. Sports during those years seemed very peripheral in my life and I felt no urgency to alter that fact.

Much more difficult than my adjusting to a life without sports was adapting myself to sedentary work, which I had never done before. Prior to college I had done only manual work, most of it as a factory employee, and in college, besides dining hall employment, I had worked as a farm laborer. Also, Army service had entailed mostly highly physical activity and even after my discharge, before going back to graduate school, I briefly cut trees for a living. I enjoyed heavy physical labor, and to this day I seek out home projects of a physical nature, some of which my wife insists are of doubtful practical utility. I have always liked the work projects, physical ones in particular. Once, a few years ago, while I was absorbed in digging out a large twisted, octopus-like, stubborn and very resistive tree root, I had a fantasy that I was wrestling in a cave with a fierce and powerful monster. Of course I could not lose that match, but I like to amuse myself with such fantasies when I work alone on my projects.

When I returned to regular sports in my forties, it was not with any great anticipation of returning to an old love. Not at all. My falling in love with sports in my middle years was a slow process developing over a several-year period.

By my middle forties my formal education was completed and my prior economic problems were under control. I had completed a number of larger home improvement projects, and my children were more than half grown. My wife and I were freer of domestic concerns than previously and had more time available for other activities. I began to become more involved in community affairs, but also started to play tennis occasionally on weekends.

My involvement with volleyball, which became a very strong passion over the next several years, started at about the same time, and quite by chance. Our local Jewish Community Center established an informal recreational gym period for middleaged men. Those of us who showed up were too old for basketball, and we found calisthenics boring. Not knowing what else to do with ourselves in a gym, we played volleyball. Our play was mild and relaxed with a good deal of bantering and humor. We had a good deal of fun and some light exercise. My own inclination was to play a bit more intensely, but I felt constrained not to upset the tempo and mood of our play. Also I didn't want to be regarded as a showoff, so I held back.

Our volleyball continued on just about this same level for a month or two. About 12 to 18 men would show up weekly. We would bat the volleyball back and forth over the net, without much regard for the rules of the game, and with none for technique. We enjoyed the exercise and each other. The laughing and joking continued. But then, what happened over the next couple of months is an interesting phenomenon that I have seen many times since. Some dropped out, some men came less regularly, and the group dwindled to about eight to ten. But those of us who continued as regulars became more and more intense in our play. We continued to enjoy ourselves but also to extend ourselves more and more. Competition between us became keener, and we also became more concerned as to whether a ball landed in or out of bounds. We kept score more carefully and we argued more. We became more skillful, but because we lacked an instructor we failed to improve our form. We played harder and harder, and with greater and greater emotional involvement. And we played to win.

We also developed some better sense of teamwork as we played, and a feeling for the strengths and weaknesses of those with whom we played. Since there were so few of us we also developed some feelings of responsibiity to show up each time, and individually we tried to recruit others to our ranks, so that the group would not atrophy. By this time, Sunday morning volleyball had become quite important to us.

Our volleyball activity has continued for about 17 or 18 years now without a hiatus, despite the lack of any consistent professional leadership.

Attendance has varied considerably over the years. We have had as few as four show up and as many as 40 on a particular day. Over all the years, probably as many as 400 different men and several women have participated These days we have about 10 to 12 confirmed volleyball buffs, and of this group there are three who date our involvement back to the very beginning.

We have come to love the game and for a number of years have sought other outlets for playing it than the time regularly assigned us. We have formed a team and have sought opponents elsewhere. We have entered tournaments. And despite the rigidities that accompany aging for some of us, we have tried to improve our technqieus, and adapt to the ever-changing rules of American volleyball. Of the members of our group, I am much the oldest now, but I am also probably the most assiduous learner. I am also the most compulsive teacher and critic. I have read several books on volleyball, and whatever I learn I try to pass on to my colleagues.

Now and then, someone will join our ranks who had learned to play volleyball properly elsewhere and has acquired the basic skills of the game, which permits him to fit in easily with our level of play. But most newcomers to our games, even if they have played before, are unskilled and at a disadvantage in playing with us. In our early years we jocks tended to be too impatient with such players and scared them off, but even now that we have learned to be tolerant, our newcomers to the game still have a hard time of it psychologically, being quite self-conscious and too easily embarrassed by their shortcomings.

Some new players react apologetically and with chagrin and dismay to their errors and limitations. Occasionally some ex-athlete, as often as not a former basketball player, would become so depressed and angry with himself that he would drop out of the activity after one or two times. Then, there are those with defensive dispositions who in their over-sensitivity to criticism become absolutely resistive to any learning. To protect themselves from inadequacy feelings, they spurn all advice, and defiantly resist getting into the spirit of the game. The poorly coordinated nonathletic men also drop out quickly. They have difficulty in keeping up with the pace of our games and also feel discouraged and embarrassed.

Those who do persist and eventually join our ranks as volleyball jocks are not necessarily those with the most talent. While some natural athletic talent, in itself, encourages the newcomer to continue, it is not enough. Those who remain and become jocks are those who are as realistic as they are prideful. They are the men whose pride does not require instant proficiency and who can bear, at least temporarily, feelings of inadequacy. They are also people who, having sufficient confidence in their eventual ability to learn, can afford to be patient with themselves.

When I began to play volleyball I was close to my mid-forties. After the first few months I surprised and pleased myself with my quickness and jumping

ability. This realization was very encouraging to my efforts, although I like to think that I would have continued in any case. I had dieted and lost weight several years earlier and was now actually much lighter than I had been in college. I began to play volleyball and tennis more and more. I felt in good physical condition.

The more I played volleyball, the more engrossed in it I became. I had had no idea that the game involved skills, let alone that it was played by anyone other than casually. As a group, we began to understand that playing well involved skills, teamwork and strategies. All this we understood better as we formed a team and began to play other teams. Playing in tournaments elated me and, shades of my childhood, I sent away for rule books, and read and imparted instructional materials to my colleagues, just as I had diagrammed football tactics in grade school. I became self-appointed teacher and volleyball intellectual, roles that my colleagues regarded as a mixed blessing.

While I had always been, as I have indicated, a strong competitor, the nature of my play in both volleyball and tennis became progressively relentless. When I played volleyball, I would run and lunge for practically any ball. In volleyball, to make certain plays it is necessary to dive to the floor, and I would do this recklessly. I took pride in making an occasional spectacular shot, and in my durabiity in encounters with the floor. I acquired such a sufficient number of bruises that I became concerned. Now I wear elbow and knee pads for protection. I don't think that I played volleyball in my middle years any less avidly and relentlessly than I played football as a young man.

The same was true of my tennis playing. I've never been a good tennis player, but the more I played in middle age, the more relentless became my style of play. I chased every ball, even those too close to the fence, and those that meant risking a fall. When I served (first serves, only) I just had to put my entire strength into it. No matter the heat, I would play for hours. The more I sweated and ran, the more elated I would become. I took pride in outlasting others, but more germane to my pleasure was my strong, intense excitement at just struggling.

Sometimes, my relentless efforts scared me and on several occasions I discussed the matter with my physician, who was mostly reassuring. Even after I recovered from a bout of pericarditis, my physician was reassuring that playing just as hard as I wished was not contra-indicated. Not until my mid-50s when I developed an aortic valve narrowing were medical recommendations altered, and I was advised not to play competitively at all.

I have had no difficulty in giving up smoking, and no trouble in keeping my weight down, but limiting my sports activities is a very different matter. It has been extremely difficult. For a while I tried to just hit tennis balls against a wall, and then later to hit them back and forth with a good friend. But within a short time, I was back to playing regular games. I try to pace myself, and to

rest more between points, and to let the difficult ones go by. Despite the patience of my partners, my success in altering my style remains very limited.

In volleyball it is similar. My friends yell at me if I get too rambunctious in my play, and I try to remember not to pursue the difficult ones. Occasionally I'm controlled and sensible, generally after having scared myself, and I will sit out a few points or a game. But, at other times, I will try for a desperate save or a crashing spike shot.

Some Wednesday mornings, when I awake after a previous evening's volleyball, I feel stiff and tired and, a little sadly, I think that my volleyball days are just about over. By the time I have finished my coffee, those thoughts have evaporated, and I'm looking ahead to next Tuesday.

REFERENCE

Allport, G. *Becoming*. New Haven: Yale University Press, 1960.

II
SPORTS OBSERVED: ANALYSES OF SPECTATORS

9

The Function and Impact of Sports for Fans: A Review of Theory and Contemporary Research

Lloyd Reynolds Sloan
Howard University

INTRODUCTION

People have always flocked to the stands to watch the skilled play of others. Whatever has always brought the spectators to contests now regularly brings 70 million of them to the television screen for the moment's "big game" (Johnson, 1971). These 70 million cells that embody television's "Super Spectator" allow themselves to be bored, cajoled, seduced and frequently misled by professional advertising pitchmen in exchange for the privilege of watching a sporting event. This phenomenon is so reliable that sports television is fast becoming a self-perpetuating billion-dollar industry (Michener, 1976), frequently creating contests and even new "sports" to expand their market and presumably to satisfy viewer demands.

Sporting events frequently demand and readily receive even greater homage from the live spectator. Annually, millions of fans eagerly drive great distances and pay usurious admission prices to be allowed to stand through a basketball game or to sit in freezing rain and snow in a football stadium. For many, sports spectating is their only diversion and they spend considerable portions of their income in its pursuit (Michener, 1976; Roberts, 1976).

LLOYD REYNOLDS SLOAN, B.A., The University of Texas, M. A., and Ph.D., The Ohio State University (1972), is a social psychologist at Howard University. He enjoys white-water canoeing, scuba diving, skydiving, atypical research pursuits, elevated needs for stimulation and the various psychological hazards of being a first born. Related future plans include continued research on stimulation and achievement needs and their impact in diverse areas of social behavior including sports, leisure time, performance, and fundamental social affiliation processes in man and animal.

Why do they do it? What impact does sports have on spectators that it draws them so consistently, in spite of such costs, from other diversions and endeavors? Many possible answers to these rather encompassing questions have been suggested in the past. In this chapter, we consider those theories of involvement in sport and examine a series of recent experiments that empirically investigated the impact of sports, particularly winning and losing, upon the spectator.

THE SPECTATOR/THE FAN

Who is the spectator? In terms of demographic characteristics, we know that sport's viewers are predominantly male (Johnson, 1971) but increasingly less so. Although it has been suggested that the appeal of sports differs between the sexes (Thompkins, 1973), few regard the differences as anything other than a consequence of sex-discriminatory acculturation processes (Edwards, 1973). Beisser (1967) theorized that urban dwellers would attach themselves most strongly to sports and particular teams in order to satisfy the needs for belonging and identity that their deindividuated city could not. As it happens, however, rural areas exhibit as much or more interest in sports. Most other hypotheses dealing with general, personal or demographic characteristics seem no more impressive in their ability to predict who will or will not be a sports fan.

As our knowledge about the spectator grows, we well may discover that differences between individuals are far more important than those between groups in comprehending involvement in sports. It is certainly the case that participants in different sports tend to differ in a number of specific personality and dispositional characteristics (for review, see Chapter 4 in this volume; and Harris, 1973). It is certainly also probable that an individual potential spectator's personality and dispositions would influence the choice of sports or whether to ever become a spectator at all. That is, whatever needs are satisfied by watching sports might also be satisfied in other ways, by other activities for those who show little affinity for the sports' spectator's role. Thus, although all people are not sports fans, understanding the needs of involved spectators may well enhance our knowledge of broader human motives.

If people who do watch sporting events do so to satisfy a particular desire, then it is likely that only a few are merely spectators in its strict sense (i.e., watchers, observers). Novak (1976) contends that most sports viewers are not merely spectators, but rather are participants as are the true believers at the religious rituals to which Novak likens sporting events. A better word for the sports viewer might, therefore, be "fan," short for fanatic and descriptive of the enthusiastic devotee of a given diversion. Certainly the typical viewer falls

within the range of the two labels as they are commonly used. But just how involved do sports fans become?

John Lawther (1951) wrote conservatively that "the common people are wrapped up in sport enthusiasms. They have their favorite baseball team, their favorite basketball team and their favorite football team.... The community tends to become united in its sports enthusiasms and its endorsements of local teams [p. 150]." Today's observers indicate that this enthusiasm is still increasing. Michener (1976), Roberts (1976), Smith (1975), and many others have described innumerable fans whose only diversion in life was sport. When not watching it, they remember past games or plan for upcoming ones. For these people, sports is in fact, much more than diversion; it takes precedence over weddings, family, friends, employment, and in the case of team failure, inspired suicides and interpersonal controversies. To be sure, not many fans shoot themselves in the head because their football team fumbles too much as one Denver Bronco fan did in 1973, but they shoot one another all too frequently. Sports do have a deep influence on our lives, and that influence extends from the individual to collective lives at the local, national, and international levels as well.

The largest gathering by far, of any kind in Philadelphia (2 million), was drawn by a parade of the league champion Flyers hockey team. Washington D. C. operated at a fraction of its normal efficiency when the Redskins football team contended for the 1975 championship. When calls went "wrong," fans filed law suits and highly placed congressmen badgered sports commissioners for favorable decisions. Unfortunately, the consequences are not always so ludicrous.

We are all too familiar with riots following high school, college and professional sporting events. Gary Shaw (1973) aptly described many games being viewed as an invasion of the town by aliens to be repelled. If the home team couldn't do it the town's people frequently accomplished the task themselves, occasionally venting part of their anger at the losers as well. Notably, some of the victory celebrations have been as damaging as loser's riots. After Pittsburgh captured the World Series, the ensuing joy left 128 injured, almost 100 arrested and extensive property damage.

Perhaps the most startling examples of collective fan involvement have grown from international rivalries. When Team Canada lost to Russia's national hockey team in 1972 the consequences were described as a "national castration." A disputed call at a soccer game in Lima, Peru in 1964 led to a brawl in which 300 died. In 1971, 66 died in Glasgow following another soccer match. In 1969, the World Cup play-off series between already feuding Honduras and El Salvador precipitated within a week "The Soccer War" that left thousands of casualties.

Are fans involved? Are whole towns, states, or nations involved? There seems little doubt that the involvement is real, strong, and widespread and

that the goals, achievements and failures of sports teams are taken very seriously by the fans, perhaps in many cases, as seriously as they are by the sports' participants themselves.

The question of similarity between fan and participant feelings, attitudes and responses to sports is an important one. Many of the theories to be discussed below were created to account for the attraction of a sport to the participant. It is reasonable to theorize that if, as they appear to do, fan responses to sports parallels those of the participants, that many of these earlier theories should be somewhat applicable to the sport's fan as well as to the sport's participant. Let us recapitulate and examine briefly the apparent parallels that do exist between fan and participant in order to estimate the validity of generalizing these formerly participant-centered theories.

Apparently fan behaviors and feelings do parallel those of the participants in numerous ways. We have just seen a few examples of the extremes to which fans are elated by victory and crushed by defeat. They acquire longlasting and frequently bitter attitudes toward particular opponents. In much the same pattern as a team review and scouting report session, fans frequently "prepare" for the sport by ruminating over past games and predicting and discussing strategy for upcoming ones. They worry over injury reports and project their impact on games far in the future. Frequently fans even have economic as well as emotional stakes in the team's outcomes. In short, they feel and behave as though they were really associated with "their" team, perhaps in some stratified team-sports fan collective.

Most impressive of all of these parallels are perhaps the physical ones. Lawther (1951) described what he called "Spectatoritis" as follows:

> The enthusiastic spectator at an athletic contest is experiencing vicariously much of the joy of intense competition. He does get "stirred up" emotionally. Urinalysis of spectators reveals quantities of non-utilized sugar that have been released by excitement (adrenal gland stimulus) but not burnt up by exercise. The player burns up his extra sugar to furnish playing energy, but the fan discards whatever amount he does not utilize, in boisterous behavior.... The fan does go through a vigorous type of experience [p. 151].

Twenty years later, Corbin (1973) reported that numerous investigations had documented increased heart rate in spectators both during the game and in anticipation of it. He concluded that the vicarious participant "must personally maintain a fairly high level of fitness to prevent distortion of the balance of the sympathetic and the parasympathetic divisions of the nervous system... to maintain his own good health [p. 56]." We are all too well aware of the heart attacks that regularly occur during exciting games. Cardiologist Karpman (1976) has speculated that "emotional stress in spectators may well be as great or greater than the physical effort put out by the athletes they

watch... and their hearts are extraordinarily less capable of coping with tenseness than the players [p. 15]."

In all, fans seem to resemble participants in many ways, even in the physical exertion involved in preparing for and conducting the sporting event itself. It is reasonable, then, that we examine theories of participant involvement in sport in an effort to understand fan involvement. In light of the observed commonalities between participants and fans, it is not unreasonable to regard fan spectating as a kind of sport unto itself.

THE DEVELOPMENT OF THEORIES OF SPORTS

Before one can theorize about a phenomenon, adequate definitions of both concepts and events must exist in order to make the relevant boundaries and variables reliably identifiable to all concerned. Before we consider theory then, we should distinguish between the frequently confused and seemingly related concepts of play, recreation, games and sports.

Although some philosophers of sport disagree on some facets of what constitutes "play" (e.g., Caillois, 1961; Edwards, 1973; Huizinga, 1938; Weiss, 1969) most might agree with the following characteristics. Play is a fully voluntary activity set arbitrarily in time and place, terminable by the actor at any point. It is separate from ordinary life and has no purpose, importance or goal beyond the context of the play itself. If there are rules, they are constructed by the player for that event. Frequently it is an absorbing fantasy. Recreation also involves voluntary emersion in activities different from the everyday. It involves little necessary structure or fantasy and does have the singular purpose, as the name implies, of refreshing the actor in mind and/or body.

The game, like recreation, has goals. The goals of a game are, however, to obtain ends beyond the simple benefits of participation in the game. The game is not an end in itself, but a path to other desired ends through the resolution of competition. Games involve other people and may or may not be highly structured or seriously regarded.

Sport "to divert oneself" is today much more than that. Because all sport's rules, roles and behaviors are established formally and traditionally, sports require extensive preparation to fulfill the requirements of structured time, space and goal. Sports *always* involve physical exertion and thus only in sports are athletes found. Finally, sports participants always represent a group, thus making sport a business of serious purpose. Clearly, sport has no overlap with what fantasizing children do in play and little in common with the recreation of the solitary fisherman. Sports are most nearly like games in sharing the goal of victory and separated from games mainly in their degree of structure, history, serious consequence and required physical exertion. In

short, as much as anything else, sports are a form of occupation for the athletes who participate in them.

Sport, as characterized above, is the object of our inquiry. Considering the age and universal presence of sporting events, one might justifiably expect to find a great deal of well delineated theory and research readily available; but that is not the case. Where do the roots of sports research lie, and why is the empirical research in most areas of sport still so rudimentary?

The scientific study of sport has occurred primarily within sociology, psychology and to a considerably lesser extent in anthropology. Sociologists have for the most part directed their inquiries to questions of the functions of sports in the total context of social organization and society. Psychology has, on the other hand, been primarily concerned with the impact of sport on the individual, his or her development, and the motivations that influence the appeal of sports. Finally, some anthropologists have dealt with the content of games as a means to inferring and assessing the character of societies. Their techniques, long used to reflect on social norms and values in extinct societies, have only comparatively recently been turned to the analysis of modern societies as well.

The beginnings of inquiry into sport for sociology and psychology came primarily in the development of the former area about 100 years ago. Sport as a functioning component of social organization was initially addressed within the relatively undeveloped concept of "play". The theorizing of Groos (1898), McDougall (1918) and Spencer (1873), stimulated development of sport sociology and the differentation of the concept of "game" and finally "sport." With the works of Goffman (1959, 1961) and Veblen (1934), the role of sport extended from the development of the self to a reversion to barbarianism. While work in America was scattered, Huizinga (1938) and Caillois (1961) organized European theory to classify sports and their effects in many varied facets of social existence. Most recently, Loy and Kenyon (1969) and Edwards (1973) have tried to organize an overview of sport sociology with considerable success, and disappointingly have revealed that little empirical data collection has even been seriously attempted although theory continues to expand.

Although psychology's roots in concerns for sports phenomena lay with sociology's, they soon diverged. Psychological concerns soon turned to the interest and participation of the individual in sports and the motivations underlying them. Early progress suggested that play was part of a developmental process necessary for the growth and employment of function in many facets of the individual's repetoire. Psychodynamic notions of catharsis and group function contributed to accountings of adult as well as child play involvements. As sports psychology grew, play came to be seen as a learning and functional integration process for the developing child. The proposed educational functions of sports and play naturally generated

"problem-centered research" like Beisser's (1967), *The Madness in Sports,* which, in describing problems, addressed more directly the question of motivation in sports. Work like Beisser's and Ogilvie's and Tutko's (see Chapters 4 and 6 in this volume), helps to stimulate the currently seen, fledgling attempts to empirically address the theories that have waited so long to blossom or die in the light of data. These theories in some cases combine both sociological and psychological approaches into a truly social psychological address to the meaning and influence of sports.

It is important to note that the dearth of empirical research on sports derives not from neglect but from strong hindrance. Few professionals directly connected and concerned with sports have the training to pursue such research. Most scholars in other disciplines who do have the skills have, until recently, not regarded sports as a proper topic for study in part because of its formerly over-popularized recreational image. With that image it's not surprising that little research funding is available to encourage interdisciplinary research designed to overcome the preceeding problems. Most important, perhaps, is a problem propounded by Tutko (1973), and one certainly not limited to sports settings. Those in control of access to the sports arena guard it jealously against any intrusion which might threaten their orientations, operating policies or their simplistic and intuitive notions about sports. In short, if it doesn't seem likely to improve athletic performance, it is not valuable and remains an unallowable complication. Hopefully, the growth of a body of sports psychology with increasingly undeniable value will serve to dispel the beliefs that underly such restrictive practices.

THEORIES OF THE IMPACT AND FUNCTION OF SPORT

The general categories of sports theories that follow represent collections of both classical and contemporary theoretical approaches that are bound together by a common theme. Other specific schemes of theories of sport are easily found. I feel that the categories presented here are central, however, to most considerations of theory and constitute a simple but useful representation of their breadth. More detailed thought devoted to individual theories may be found in reviews by Ellis (1972), Harris (1973), and Weiss (1969) and in other chapters of this book.

For each category of theories, two factors will be important to note. First, we should be concerned with the degree to which these hypothesized mechanisms would have impact on spectator/fans as well as on formal sports participants. In each case the fan is thought possibly to be subject to his or her own experience of the phenomena, as distinct from the participant's, or to know the participant's experience vicariously. Although "spectators live

through a game in one way, and players in another" (Weiss, 1969, p. 164), it may well be that on many dimensions the differences are only quantitative ones.

The second point of special consideration will be the impact of the outcome of the event. For many theories, it is not merely the occurrence of the event but its consequence that should determine the responses of the spectators. Observed differences in the responses of "winners" and "losers" rather than just "fans" will allow us to make more critical distinctions between our theoretical formulations.

Finally, it is noteworthy that most, if not all, of these theories fall under the umbrella of Harris' (1973) extremely broad Somatopsychic Theory. In her treatise, Harris decries the conceptual separation of mind and body and marshalls evidence to suggest the integrated function of the various components of the organism. Harris' scheme generally states that attraction to sports is a consequence of reinforcing pleasures mediated by any of a number of factors ranging from activity and arousal to achievement and self concept needs that result from activity and sports involvement. Although this theory is so general that we do not attempt to draw specific predictions from it, we must certainly agree with the implication that many factors and possibly combinations of factors lie at the root of humanity's attraction to sports.

Salubrious Effects Theories

As the name implies, the theories grouped together here all suggest that, in some manner or other, activity or sports involvement is attractive because it provides a kind of pleasure and increased physical and mental well-being. Of these, the two best known historically are the Recreation Theory and the Diversion Theory.

According to the Recreation Theory, people restore and rejuvenate their energies to work and deal with life by playing. Fatigue and boredom are relieved by using the body physically in temporally novel ways. Except for notions analogous to that of man's need for stimulus variation (e.g., perhaps something like a need for response variation), there are no identified physiological bases for the reported effects.

The Diversion Theory might almost be thought of as a subset of the Recreation Theory. Diversion schemes specifically label play as an escape from work and the other tediums of life. It is seen as adding new dimensions to life and a very general change of pace generally regarded as contributing to the individual's well being. It does not, however, contain specific tenets as to the revitalization of personal energies in play as does the Recreation Theory. Possible mechanisms underlying each of these includes some form of stimulation seeking and the desire for the opportunity to make varied motor responses. We discuss stress and stimulation-seeking in a later section of the

chapter. The impact of kinesthetic satisfaction and the motor and mental facilitations of movement are perhaps the most promising of the theories suggesting attraction to sports for its physical benefits.

The concept of kinesthetic satisfaction is a complex one and many of its facets seem intangible because its mediators, and sometimes the meaning of its antecedents and consequences, remain elusive. Nonetheless, we are all familiar with "feeling good" about a physical act of performance, whether it takes the form of a complete act (a drive, kick, rally, etc.), or just a collection of movements that supply us with a complex of rich and varied sensations of kinesthetic feedback. Not infrequently, such feelings reportedly become exhilaration and joy that dominate all other feelings. The production of knowledge of this concept is complicated by the variously learned perceptions that attach meaning to an event for each individual. The individual's perceptions of his movements must be understood, therefore, in order to understand its meanings (Cratty, 1967).

Buehler (1973), Kreitler and Kreitler (Note 1), and Morris (1967) have all incorporated "the pleasure of function" into their outlooks on human involvements in activities of many varieties. Both children and adults tend to perform a (pleasurable) movement until satiated. When satiation is reached, other movements will be sought, employed and, in turn, be replaced with other variations and other combinations to prolong kinesthetic and other sensory pleasures.

Harris (1973) has reviewed the "feel-better" response that frequently follows participation. Active adults report a healthy tiredness, increased vigor and improved outlook following exercise and research has found them to be more energetic, ambitious, amiable and happier. Many of these correlational findings were confirmed in experimental studies in which increased fitness lead to increased self-confidence, happiness and relief from certain emotional and metabolic disorders. The pronounced effects of this "feel-better" response may well account for what has been termed "exercise addiction" in both man and animal. When regular exercisers could be convinced to give up exercise for research purposes, they experienced what seemed to be "exercise deprivation" (Baekeland, 1970). This deprivation has produced increased anxiety, sexual tension, affiliation needs and possible neuroses.

Undeniably, the aesthetic quality of movement and sports activities could contribute directly to the desirability of involvement in sports activity. A participant could well be aware kinesthetically of a movement beautifully performed. These considerations are dealt with in greater detail in a later, broader discussion of proposed aesthetic attractions in sport.

Winning, Losing, and Theoretical Effects on the Fans.   Based on the foregoing theories, Harris (1973) suggests that "much of the spectators' involvement can be explained by empathetic kinesthetic understanding they

have for the performer and their ability to relate to the performer because of this understanding [p. 179]." It may also be that the fan's own physical involvement as a spectator produces pleasurable kinesthetic stimulation (see also the following section).

None of these theories draws any distinct implications as to the effects of winning or losing at the sport on the spectators' or performers' attraction to sports involvement. Thus, outcome should be irrelevant for the predictions based on notions of salubrious effects.

Stress and Stimulation Seeking Theories

Klausner (1968) believes that individuals who do not experience tension, risk and stress in the normal course of life seek to create opportunities to fulfill their needs for stress in socially acceptable or unacceptable ways. It is Klausner's contention that only sports provide the means to create and experience those stresses in socially acceptable ways. All of the theories considered here, the seeking of risk, stress, arousal and stimulation, presume that some level of stress is sought by the organism and that when the obtained amounts fall below the desired, stress seeking increases. To be sure, the thresholds and patterns of stress vary between individuals (Kane, 1971; Petrie, Holland, & Wolk, 1963; Ryan, 1969) and the cultures that shape them, but it is presumed that all people have such homeostatic needs even though the thresholds may change with experience and age (Fenz & Epstein, 1969).

Sport then, is seen as a stressor which can be sought when a given amount of stress or stimulation is desired. More extreme risk in sport provides more stress, but, according to Rosenthal (1968), it is not approached in a foolhardy way. Fear and anxiety always remain, and only those who learn to control their fear and allow appropriate, self-testing risks experience the full euphoria that follows the dangerous situation.

A number of theories predict that eustress (pleasant stress) seeking phenomena will occur. Most suggest that insufficient stimulation is provided in everyday life. Elias and Dunning (1970), Frankl (1970), and Morris (1969) all suggest that modern society just has not enough exciting variability and that sport allows people to face desired challenges and experience wanted excitement and stimulation. Caillois (1961), Kenyon (1968), and Trippet (1969) conceptualize the stimulating events sought in sports as a "vertigo" or disequilibrium to be experienced in controlled doses as arousing drugs might be. Ellis (1972) actually specifies the desired effect as being physiological arousal of the body to match the situationally optimal level sought. Others (Bouet, 1969; Weiss, 1969) suggest that arousal is sought to allow expenditure of excess energy.

Winning, Losing, and Theoretical Effects on the Fans.   Notably, none of these theories attach any particular importance to the competitive outcome of

an event. In fact, several specify that it is the *process* of taking risk that provides the satisfactions sought, not the outcome of the risk. The same stimulation or stress is presumably produced in the event by the risks taken and sensations sought, whether or not the "game" is won.

Vicarious eustress may be sought from many sources, including observing and imitating others involved in sports. Harris (1973) notes that "competitive sports, contests of almost any nature, and performances staged for audiences have supplied and continue to supply eustress to participants and to millions of spectators alike [p. 112]." As evidence of the amount of energy generated vicariously, she cited the all too frequent riots which follow such events and performances, whether the favored team wins or loses.

Eustress may also be found in acting out the behaviors and emotions of others. Spectator sports may create such impact when a viewer experiences strong identification and acts out this simulation. The reader is reminded of having probably noticed quantum increases in touch football participation following (rather than preceeding) Saturday's game.

Finally, it is possible that the spectator seeks the arousal experienced by being involved with the crowd, in picking a team and risking failure in bad judgment, by cheering vigorously, and doubtless, by simply being a member of the crowd itself. Since the early work of LeBon (1896), behavioral scientists have recognized the intensification and simplification of emotions felt via social contagion and deindividuation in crowds (Milgram & Toch, 1969; Zimbardo, 1969). Even when cues to particular emotions are not present, simply being exposed to a large number of people causes arousal (Leiderman & Shapiro, 1964). It could be the case then, that the stress-stimulation-arousal seeking spectator is drawn not (only) by the vicarious stresses and experiences but by the real stresses of participation in the crowd. Such effects may well contribute to the attraction of sports, but cannot account for its entirety, for how could a crowd-participant explanation account for the interest of millions of separate television viewers?

Catharsis and Aggression Theories

In introducing this chapter, we noted several incidents of violence associated with sporting events and innumerable other such events no doubt have occurred. Could it be that aggressive actions are not just a consequence of observing sports, but might be the source of spectator attraction to athletic events? One presumed expert participant, Vince Lombardi, thought so. Referring to football, he affirmed that: "This is a violent sport. That's why crowds love it" (Michener, 1976, p. 421). What theoretical bases exist for believing that the aggressiveness of an event should make it attractive?

Without doubt the oldest and most persistent notions relating sport to aggression are those of catharsis, restraint, and sublimation, first strongly advanced by Aristotle. All versions of this concept suggest that catharsis or

reduction of aggression levels will occur either by participating in an aggressive act or vicariously through watching acts of aggression by others. This outlook is a central tenet of several theories including those of ethologists, Freudians, and others (Ardrey, 1966; Freud, 1955; Lorenz, 1966; Morris, 1967; Perls, 1969; Storr, 1970). They feel that man is driven by innate, instinctive aggressive energies which constantly grow. Thus they must be relieved periodically or erupt, producing catharsis in either case. Browne (1968) goes so far in relating sport to aggression as to claim that play is a learning form for adult aggression being comprised of many of the same dimensions as play evolves with age. There is, however, little data to suggest that this kind of vicarious catharsis actually occurs (cf. Bramel, 1969; Feshback & Singer, 1971).

Most psychological research has found that viewers of violence are actually more likely to behave aggressively *after* witnessing acts of violence (Berkowitz, 1970, 1975; Tannenbaum & Zillmann, 1975). Frustration-aggression observers (cf. Izenberg, 1968, 1972) and theorists (Berkowitz, 1969; Dollard, Doob, Miller, Mowrer, & Sears, 1939) suggest that those who have been angered by frustration are most likely to become hostile. Seeing acts of violence could then serve as cues to the appropriateness of the observer's own aggression. Spectator aggression could result, therefore, from witnessing events that: (1) made aggression seem justified or appropriate; (2) made a given target a more legitimate one for aggression; (3) made the viewer frustrated (the team lost) or aware of some earlier frustrations; and/or (4) simply reminded him or her of possible aggressive behaviors.

Another outlook on the relationship between viewing violence and subsequent aggression derives from social learning theory (Bandura, 1971, 1973). This position suggests that observers learn violent acts just by viewing them and that seeing them rewarded or punished will determine the extent to which they are inhibited or disinhibited and are displayed by the spectator.

Winning, Losing and Theoretical Effects on the Fans.   It is clear that all of these theories are strongly directed at the viewers of aggression and violence. Several even specify violence in sports as a variable that has impact on the viewer's consequent aggression. But what of the impact of one's favored team winning or losing?

Catharsis theories state that it is the viewing of violence that relieves aggressive tensions, so winning or losing should have little effect on the level of hostility in observers after the game. Watching should reduce aggressive tensions in all viewers. Frustration-aggression theories clearly would predict that watching one's team defeated would produce frustration since the goal of winning was blocked. Under the proper circumstances, then, losing would produce heightened aggressiveness in the spectator. Although winning should not produce frustration, it might enhance hostility somewhat by labeling the losers as deserving targets of violence. Finally, social learning positions

suggest that the strength of inhibitions against aggressive behavior might be reduced in all viewers simply by watching violence, thereby increasing the likelihood of subsequent aggression. In addition, it is possible that seeing violence bring a rewarding victory to one's preferred team should increase the likelihood of violence, while suffering (vicariously) the team's loss should inhibit hostile behaviors in the observers.

In one of the few existing field studies of the effects of sports on spectators, Goldstein and Arms (1971) pursued an answer to the preceding questions. Before and after the 1969 Army–Navy football game, interviewers administered a set of hostility scales (from Buss & Durkee, 1957) to male spectators. For comparison, the same measures were collected at a "competitive but nonaggressive" gymnastics meet. The investigators found that the average fan's hostility scores were higher after watching the combative football game than before, but that whether their team won or lost had no effect. In contrast, the nonaggressive gymnastics meet had no impact on its spectators. Goldstein and Arms concluded that their result generally supported disinhibition notions of the effects of viewing violence. Although popular catharsis theories received no support, the authors did note that hostility catharsis may require stronger, more direct aggression than that found in football.

Entertainment Theories

In this section we consider such notions of attraction to sports as the seeking of aesthetic and moral representation. Such theses may be readily collected under the broad generic concept of entertainment seeking. Entertainment, by definition, is the engaging of another's attention and/or occupying them pleasurably. Beisser (1967), Bouet (1968) Maslow (1970), and even Weiss (1969) have agreed that sport must be pursued, at least in part, for the pleasure it provides the individual, else it would cease to be of interest. By the implication of both theory and our own subjective feelings then, attraction to sport must be, at least in part, a consequence of its entertainment value. As such, we might well presume that many of the theoretical notions already discussed could fall generally under entertainment. Certainly the pleasure of kinesthetic sensation, stress, general stimulation, or aggressive experience could be loosely labeled as a kind of entertainment for the individual seeking it. The present discussion is limited to considerations of sources of entertainment derived from the content or meaning of the sports event. First, we reflect on some of the ways in which any content could *become* entertaining and then consider two content-dependent notions of the attraction of sports: aesthetics and the representation of moral values.

Presumably the processes of coming to find some things entertaining and others not, is composed of the same general elements as the processes of coming to like or be attracted to any individual or collection of people, objects

or institutions in one's environment. In the broadest sense, we are talking about the general process of socialization that begins in infancy and extends through life. Theories of socialization, attraction and attachment range from those based on genetics or innately initiated developmental processes to simple behavior learning theory. They differ in their mechanisms and the periods of life in which they have their major impact. However, all agree that the individual's environment, including parents, peers and culture, are critical elements in the direction of the socialization process. The role of a number of environmental agents is described by Edwards (1973) in portraying the introduction of the potential American sports fan as a young child to the world of sports. He describes the often observed collection of sports toys and clothing given even to infants. When mobility arrives, so do "junior" sports implements and travels to sporting events. Later in socialization the child comes to learn and then understand the "rules of the game" from guiding, encouraging adults, usually the parents, and to internalize whatever believed values and virtues are taught.

These observations are compatible with most theories of child socialization. Certainly innate theories like Freud's and Erikson's (1950) would happily accept the notion that young sports fans develop values and personalities as a function of parental actions and teachings during physiologically paced development. Likewise, cognitive-developmental theorists (cf. Kohlberg, 1969; Piaget, 1970) would readily support the thought that the acquisition of rule structure and moral concepts was a product of developmental and experiential processes. However, how do such theories account for the fact that many conversions to sports fandom occur in adults? Two positions posit mechanisms which operate as effectively in adults as in children.

Social learning theory was considered earlier as a mode of acquisition of aggressive behaviors or dimunition of inhibitions to aggression. Since the time of Watson (1925), learning has been theorized to account for socialization through processes of imitation, observational learning (Bandura & Walters, 1963), and reinforcement history (Skinner, 1971). Feeling that sports were entertaining or that they represented and taught certain moral or cultural values would then be learned as would any other response.

Zajonc's (1968) notion that familiarity leads to attraction and liking is even less complex. Simply by being exposed to sports and its trappings, we can come to like them, whatever our age. Quite a number of field and laboratory studies have shown this to be true of exposure to words, objects, pictures, people, public figures, products, roommates and attitudes and beliefs (cf. Baron & Byrne, 1977).

Regardless of the mechanism through which the content and meaning of sports may come to be attractive to us, most observers (cf. Michener, 1976; Novak, 1976) agree that they are and cite seemingly endless anecdotes in

support. Two particular aspects of sport thought to be specific elements of its attractiveness are aesthetics and sports' purported representation of life's moral values.

1. *Aesthetics*—pertaining to the beautiful, as separate from the moral or useful. In *The Ultimate Athlete*, George Leonard (1974) advances the thesis that there is a "dance" or beautiful skill to sports that we can appreciate even in losing a competition. Michener (1976) later echoed Leonard's notion that the aesthetic appreciation of skill in movement made sport an art form for many players and presumably for spectators as well. Why should sports be a source for aesthetic fulfillment? Miller (1970) feels that in some ways sport may be as play, an opportunity for freedom of experience and creative expression. Fromm (1941, 1955) has theorized that man has a need to become unique through creativity and Maslow (1968) lists as a growth motive the metaneed, aesthetics. The commitment to this aesthetic meaning varies among people but is particularly high in the creative (Barron, 1963a, 1963b, 1972), suggesting that others may be more likely to appreciate sports for nonaesthetic reasons. Little data is available to cast light on the role of aesthetics in sport.

2. Perhaps the most commonly held notion of the value of sport among laymen and scholars alike is that it builds character and prepares us for dealing with life's obstacles (cf. Harris, 1973; Weiss, 1969); consider for example the outlook of past national leaders: "Except for war, there is nothing in American life—nothing—which trains a boy better for life than football" (Robert Kennedy, in Clinch, 1973, p. 266); and sport "prepares young men for their roles as the future custodians of the Republic" (Douglas MacArthur, in Edwards, 1973, p. 150).

Miller (1970) suggests that our attraction to games and their rule structures may be precisely because they teach us of life by letting us witness life's values being portrayed. That is, the rules may share common origin with the moral underpinnings of life. Others (Loy & Kenyon, 1969) have, however, noted that the same sports are employed in this normative manner by members of very divergent politics and cultures, raising some question as to the utility of this outlook. In any case, sports have been thought to be attractive because they represent, express and teach values. Do they actually convey such values?

Edwards (1973) made personal assessments of many supposed facets of sport's value teachings and drew disappointing conclusions. The contribution of sports to the development of character, loyalty and altruism was labeled as "inconclusive," and others actually felt the contribution might be harmful (Ogilvie & Tutko, 1971). Cullen (1974), for example, found that violent rule violations by hockey players were viewed as relatively acceptable behavior by

fans and extremely acceptable by the players! These outlooks are more reminiscent of the original Olympic values than those idealized in modern sports creeds (Leonard, 1974). The claimed virtuous effects of sports on religiosity and nationalism were similarly unproved and athletes in general were regarded as neither more disciplined nor more prepared for life, than anyone else. Of course, sports still may be attractive because they *purport* to represent and teach life's ideals, even if in fact they do not do so.

Finally, it is worthy of note that a small group of writers feel that sport not only does not represent the game of life but that it should not and cannot if it is to be called sport. Novak (1976) feels that sport draws people because it resembles "primal symbols" and joyous religious participation—anything but the Calvinistic values of life.

Winning, Losing, and Theoretical Effects on the Fans.   If attraction to sports is a simple result of somehow coming to find sports entertaining or aesthetic or representative of life's values, then viewing sports should lift spectators' spirits regardless of winning or losing the game. Of course, it may be the case that we find ourselves "entertained" only when we win. Likewise, only our team's predominance could bring us cheer if the "value" we really want to see portrayed is "success." If we have been taught "the idolatry of victory" (Christenson, 1958), then what is sought in sport is not simply entertainment or a display of virtue, but accomplishment.

Achievement Seeking Theories

The idolatry of victory in sports (Christenson, 1958) is an undeniable fact. If there were ever any doubts, the following statements should dispel them:

> The winner is the only individual who is truly alive... Every time you win you are reborn; when you lose, you die a little [George Allen, in Michener, 1976, p. 42]. Defeat is worse than death because you have to live with defeat [Bill Musselman, in Michener, 1976, p. 42].

For years, the fact that success was of prime importance has been recognized and decried by philosophers (cf. Weiss, 1969) and idealizers (cf. Novak, 1976) of sport who frequently laid responsibility for the outlook at the feet of the Calvanistic Puritan tradition. The sport goal of individual achievement through competition is certainly consistent with the Calvinist traditions in America (Williams, 1970). However, this singular source of achievement orientation doesn't account for strong achievement norms in other cultures (Luschen, 1967). A better understanding of these phenomena could probably be obtained from theories of the general development and function of achievement needs in the individual, and such theories abound.

In studying the motivations of competitors, Maslow (1970) determined that the most centrally relevant of his heirarchy of needs were those for achievement and prestige. Similarly, Murray, et. al. (1938) concluded that the need for achievement was expressed as a desire for prestige, accomplishment, and overcoming obstacles. McClelland, Atkinson, Clark, and Lowell (1953) felt that the need derived from hedonistic pressures and developed into a competition with an individual standard of excellence. Others have agreed with the general "self-actualization" notion of motivation to achievement in sports, seeing it as an effort to expand one's capabilities (Morris, 1967), to acquire competence (Ellis, 1972), to achieve self-completion (Weiss, 1969), and to gain experience for mastery (White, 1963). Researchers in sports have found these theories to have some foundation. For example, Roberts, Arth, and Rush (1959) studied the games of 110 societies and found that most were exercises in mastery, and Ogilvie and Tutko (1963) found that social approval, achievement, and status concern were, indeed, basic to sport motives.

The preceding theory and data seem quite plausible and consistent in describing participants' probable motives for engaging in sports. How then could fans fulfill their achievement needs through their involvement with sports? My colleagues and I (Cialdini, Borden, Thorne, Walker, Freeman, & Sloan, 1976) have suggested that this might be accomplished if the fans could "bask in the reflected glory" of their victorious team.

Basking in Reflected Glory (BIRG): Winning, Losing, and Effects on the Fans.   It is not surprising that people should want to make others aware of their achievements. Why people try to emphasize their association with *someone else* who has been successful is less obvious. Perhaps people are intuitively aware of the effects of Heider's (1958) balance theory which suggests that association with a "positive" other will tend to make us appear more positive as well. We decided to examine the possibility that fans do BIRG by observing the rates at which school related apparel was worn following team wins and nonwins at seven universities with powerful football teams and enthusiastic fans. As predicted, students wore apparel which identified them with their school much more frequently on the day following a victory than they did following a nonwin. The wearing of apparel associated with other institutions did not vary, indicating that the results were not merely a consequence of increased sports-consciousness. These results, however, could be a result of generally increased attraction to the school rather than an attempt by individuals to enhance their personal prestige.

We felt we could separate these possibilities by giving the person a need to enhance personal prestige by causing him or her to fail or to be associated with failure, and then giving him or her a chance to BIRG a team's victory. This notion is much like Fromm's (1941, 1955) need for identity and

uniqueness. Fromm suggests people need a sufficient sense of identity and uniqueness and that if they could not obtain it individually through their own creative efforts, that they might seek and obtain some aspect of distinction by associating themselves with a positive other or group of others. Others agree that the needs to belong are very motivating (cf. Fromm, 1955; Maslow, 1968) and that the stronger the supplemental prestige requirements, the stronger the need for such positive associations (Beisser, 1967; Edwards, 1973; Lawther, 1951; Schafer, 1969).

In pursuit of the hypothesis that a failure should result in an increased tendency to BIRG, we contrived to allow students to use the pronouns "we" or "they" (referring to their school's team) to create or avoid an association with the team, immediately after the student had experienced personal success or failure. Calling the student as sport surveyors, we gave them a brief ambigous quiz and told them they had done "really well" or "not so well" and then asked them to tell us who won their school's last game. When the team had won (a desirable association) students who had just failed our test were much more likely to say "we won" than those who passed the test. When the school had lost, however, students made no increased attempt to associate themselves with the team. Thus, in sports as well as in other areas [e.g., social presentation (Schneider, 1969)], when people suffer a personal loss of prestige or esteem [or both, because they are related (Harvey, Kelly, & Shapiro, 1957)], they react by trying to enhance their image. Here they do it by trying to BIRG successful others. The same tendency to BIRG also was found when the subject was subjected to *de facto* association with another's failure. This indicates that such negative associations may damage one's self-perceived prestige as much as positive ones enhance it.

Thus far we have characterized BIRG behavior as one through which an individual may *choose*, at one's own option, whether or not to associate with another. If fans do, however, actually feel that they are a part of the team, then their freedom to associate or not could no longer be absolute. Instead, they would presumably only be able to *adjust* their degree of association with the team. This notion is consistent with the fact that we have not yet encountered any situation in which complete "BIRG"ing or denial of the association occurred or was even approximated. Thus, fan associations with sports may not provide simply the optional utility of BIRG, but may have some unavoidable consequences for the spectator both in victory and in defeat. Numerous writers feel that this is the case (e.g., Edwards, 1973; Izenberg, 1968, 1972; Lawther, 1951; Roberts, 1976; Weiss, 1969), and some feel that those consequences are very strong. Schafer (1969) suggests that fans identify strongly with a team because that team signifies an extension of their personal sense of self and that the impact of this voluntary relationship can be profound.

... by identifying with the team, the fan is afforded the chance to affirm his own worth and quality. But he does it at some risk. If his team wins, he feels good about himself... But, if his team loses, especially if it loses consistently, he too is a loser in his own eyes. Perhaps it is in this way that we can better understand why fans become so intensely concerned that their team win, and why attendance and interest fall off so markedly when a team consistently loses [p. 33].

Given that the consequences of association could be so great, how is it that fans' lives come to be so integrally involved with their teams?

We have already discussed several probable sources of the needs of belonging. These, coupled with such concepts as the simple need for affiliation (Schachter, 1959) and social comparison (Festinger, 1954), suggest that fan sports involvement, in part, satisfies needs to be with others, usually in some purposive group behavior. Pursuing the same general notion, that the group has a purpose, leads us to a second possibility. Fans may well believe that they have real impact on the team and its performance, if by no other means than acknowledging (sometimes) their support of the team. Most people who deal with sports generally argue that fans actually *do* have influence on the players (cf. Edwards, 1973; Lawther, 1951; and Roberts, 1976). Tutko and Richards (1971) conclude that although other social sources (parents, etc.) may have more long term effect, that during the game, fans probably predominate in influencing player emotions and motivations. The average fan may well know or believe this to be the case and thereby feel he or she makes a real contribution to the team's performance. It is worthy of note, however, that neither of the above hypotheses provides a completely convincing explanation for the often intense involvement displayed by isolated TV viewers far removed from both the team and the crowd.

It may be that teams "represent" their fans in a more remote manner not dependent upon physical proximity between them. This is certainly a common theme, well propounded by Paul Weiss (1969). He felt that the final stage in self completion in sport was to become a *representative* in a game; to function on behalf of, and thereby display the importance of, the organization represented. For Edwards (1973) this is a required aspect of the very definition of sport. Just as the player recognizes and lives the role of a representative, fans could well recognize and accept that player role as well. Thus, the team may actually represent some facets of a group or community.

Finally, it is possible that a member of a community or organization may have to live with a *de facto* association to a team simply because they are elements of the community. They may have to overtly accept the association as a result of normative pressures or comparative influences within the community (Schafer, 1969) or of possible complementary pressures from external "opposition" groups.

If in fact, fans do feel that they and their team are parts of a meaningful group, then the BIRG phenomenon may be only one facet of the relationship between sports and the nurturing of individual achievement feelings, prestige and self-esteem as a function of one's team's accomplishments. The fan who sees himself as a member of such a group would presumably be, therefore, subject to many of the same structural and dynamic influences as in any other group. Perhaps the most central of these structures, for the present concern, is that of cohesiveness or identification with the group. Success and failure have a great deal of impact on cohesiveness just as winning and losing had strong effects on the tendency to BIRG as it was described above. Cohesiveness, however, also mediates numerous aspects of group interaction and the individual's attitudes and feelings about the group and about himself. If a team's wins and losses had such consequences for the fans, then we could conclude that fan-team group relationship was more extensive than a simple desire to BIRG team victories. In short, if fan behavior resembles that of known groups, we can reasonably infer that fans perceive of themselves as group members, lending support to such assertions by the sports observers and theorists mentioned above. In addition, if fans are functionally members of the team group, then knowledge of group phenomena gleened from other research settings could greatly increase our ability to predict and understand the behavior of sports fans, including the formerly perplexing intensity and complexity of their involvement in sports.

THE EFFECTS OF WINNING AND LOSING ON COHESIVENESS AND GROUP-RELATED ATTITUDES

There is good reason to presume that collections of fans could come to see themselves as members of at least a loose-knit, tacitly recognized group. The fan conceivably could feel a very strong identity with the group, for such a group of fans could provide many characteristics known to enhance cohesiveness. Sports fans are certainly involved in an enjoyable activity, generally are congenial to their compatriots, and thus satisfy one antecedent of cohesiveness labeled pleasantness (Lott & Lott, 1965). It seems likely that they would also hold similar values and interests at least on issues relevant to the team, thus further increasing cohesiveness (Zander & Havelin, 1960). Threat from outside the group (e.g., from another team), also tends to increase cohesion (Sherif, Harvey, White, Hood, & Sherif, 1961), perhaps by making members more aware of their ingroup identity (Coser, 1956). Finally, we observed before that fans sought to identify with the team more when the team won. The phenomenon of goal achievement leading to cohesiveness has been well documented in other group types as well as in sports teams (Lott &

Lott, 1965; Peterson & Martens, 1973). Clearly, there are numerous reasons to believe that team fans could constitute a very cohesive group. The last of those phenomena mentioned also suggests that we could readily observe various levels of general cohesion by studying fans after team wins and team losses, just as we studied the BIRG tendency above. There are, however, many *consequences* of varied cohesiveness and group structure which could be examined in order to reflect on the existence of the proposed fan-team group (e.g., satisfaction, communication, cooperation, individual and group self-esteem, etc.; cf. Shaw, 1971). Based on these earlier findings, several predictions of fan responses were derived and investigated in two experiments at the University of Notre Dame.

Winning, Losing, and Inter-/Intra-Group Cohesiveness

Although fans may see themselves as sharing a group with their team, they must certainly distinguish between themselves and team members. That is, there should be subgroups within the fan-team group. It should, therefore, be possible for the fans to identify (be cohesive) primarily with their own subgroup, or with the fan-team group as a whole depending on personal needs. In a win, fans could emphasize identity with the whole but after a loss could lower their attachment to the team subgroup and distance themselves from it to avoid personal devaluation. The fan could make this discrimination most convincingly in interaction with another group member who was aware of and shared the distinctions within the subgroup structure. On the other hand, when interacting with someone outside the fan-team group (from outside the college or city) the primary distinction could well be between the outsider and the group as a whole, leaving the fans little opportunity to distinguish themselves from the fan-team group made more unitary in the other's eyes by the contrast between the interactants.

We examined this possibility by having experimenter-surveyors call systematically sampled students after won or lost basketball games to ask them how their school team did in the last game (Sloan, Note 2). The surveyors introduced themselves as representing the "Notre Dame Opinion Survey Center" or the "Midwest Opinion Survey Center" thereby labeling themselves as ingroup or outgroup members. Students' use of "we" or "they" pronouns in describing the win or loss was recorded as the measure of cohesiveness to the team or the total fan-team group (see Table 9.1). As predicted, the 161 fans (almost all students in the sample were fans) did not attempt to emphasize (BIRG), or deny association with the team after any games when called by the outgroup surveyor. When called by the ingroup surveyor, however, they significantly "distanced" themselves after a loss by referring to the team as "they" 82% of the time compared to only 58% of the time following winning performances.

TABLE 9.1
Subject's Identification With Team as a Function of Team Success and
Interviewer's Group Membership Status

		Subjects Response		
Caller Source		"We" (N)	"They" (N)	"We" (%)
Midwest survey	Win	18	25	42
	Loss	17	22	43
Notre Dame survey	Win	17	24	42
	Loss	7	31	18

Note: Subject's identification with the team was reflected by their use of first- vs. third-person pronouns in describing home basketball game outcomes following a victory or a loss. The calling interviewer's association, Notre Dame vs. Midwest Survey, determined the caller's respective ingroup vs. outgroup membership status with regard to the subject.

Thus, manipulating the intra- or inter-group relationship between interactants alters the fans' ability to casually alter the strength of their identity with the whole fan-team group in order to preserve their images after a team loss. Fans feel able to more easily separate themselves from the team in the eyes of another who shares their fan group membership than in the view of an outsider. It is noteworthy that Cialdini et al. (1976) had suggested that the fan might BIRG more in conversation with outsiders than with ingroup members and a tendency was observed in that direction. The reason proposed was that since the subject could claim the association (to a winner) more strongly than the outsider, that it would carry more prestige and therefore be a more sought-after identity. The data which supported this notion, however, came only from the subjects (about 13% of those responding) who in reporting the results of a win *and* a loss, shifted pronouns as BIRG hypotheses predict. It may well be the case that this small subgroup of the subjects may be those who feel least a part of, and least attached to, the fan-team group. They may use the association merely as a convenience to enhance their prestige through the simplest BIRG mechanisms but may not relate to team wins and losses as such personal victories and defeats as do others. We noted before that sports may serve vastly different purposes for some viewers, so perhaps we shouldn't be surprised at the existence of such a subgroup. Possibly these people just aren't as involved in sports and may not even be properly referred to as "fans." In the study reported above (Sloan, Note 2), the total fan group was sampled, including the other 87% who, in all likelihood, considered themselves more strongly involved in and a part of the total fan-team group. Naturally, these people would more likely be affected by the group structure and influence processes described above simply because they are more likely to perceive of themselves as group members.

We have seen that winning and losing effects cohesiveness with the team group, as does the fan's latitude to respond in identifying with the team. But what of the further consequences of varied cohesiveness? If fans really do belong to a meaningful group which experiences successes and failures, then fans' attitudes toward the group and their satisfaction with it should vary in addition to simple expressions of cohesiveness (e.g., Marquis, Guetzkow, & Heyns, 1951).

Winning, Losing, and Inter-/Intra-Group Influence on Evaluation of the Fan-Team Group

When the BIRG phenomena was first investigated by observing students' wearing of school related apparel after wins and losses (Cialdini et al., 1976), we were concerned that this phenomenon might simply be reflecting heightened attraction to their group and school. Further investigation confirmed that subjects were (also) seeking to enhance their prestige by making their association with the winning team more salient. If, however, fans feel that they are continuing members of the inclusive fan-team group, then such general phenomena as heightened attraction to the group following a win, should *also* occur. In order to pursue the notion that team wins and losses would influence evaluation of the group as well as cohesiveness, we once again resorted to the telephone survey technique.

Experimenter-surveyors called 569 student-fans following won or lost school football games. As in the preceding experiment, they asked respondents how the school did in their past football game, and how they would do in the next game. In addition to several filler items, the students were also asked to rank their school (Notre Dame) academically as an undergraduate institution. If the notion that student-fans feel themselves members of the group is supported by these data, then their evaluation of their group (institution) should differ following wins and losses. Because institutional prestige undoubtedly plays a part in its students' prestige and self-esteem, and would, therefore, be a valued student perception, this was thought to be a very conservative test of the general group evaluation hypotheses.

As in the preceding basketball centered surveys, students displayed increased cohesiveness after wins and decreased amounts after losses. In predicting the outcome of the next game to follow the recent win or loss, respondents replicated the earlier effects of the fan-surveyor group member relationship. In conversing with an ingroup surveyor, as compared to an outgroup surveyor, fans more readily identified (used pronoun "we") with the team following a win. In addition, they thought more students supported the team (i.e., also identified with the fan-team group) as they did. Following a loss, both effects significantly reversed.

Most importantly, predicted effects on general evaluation of the group-institution were observed (see Fig. 9.1). After a team loss, student estimates of their institution's academic rank dropped, but significantly less so in response to a surveyor from the same institution than to an outsider. Perhaps this should not be too surprising in light of the work of Tesser and his colleagues. They have consistently found that people are reluctant to transmit "bad news" or negative information to a person for whom it is relevant (cf. Johnson, Conlee, & Tesser, 1974). Once again, the results suggest strong support for the hypothesis that fans are functionally members of a fan-team group with which they identify to some extent.

We can summarize our findings regarding fan achievement seeking and personal involvement in sport in the following central conclusions. The BIRG (Cialdini et al., 1976) phenomenon seems to be very reliable. People do use associations with winning sports teams to enhance their prestige in others' eyes and very probably to increase self-esteem as well. They avoid such associations after a loss in order to protect their images. More is involved, however, than a superficial pragmatic tendency to BIRG and the fan's personal image maintenance. Other results considered here (Sloan, Note 2) suggest that in addition to optional associations and achievement consequences, sports may also provide some unavoidable ones to the fan. Many fans apparently feel that they actually belong to, are recognized as a part of, and perhaps somehow contribute to, an enduring fan-team group. As such, they must, to some extent, share the group's achievements and failures whether those consequences are desirable or not. This conclusion supports Edwards' (1973) contention that: "For the fan, it seems, outcomes on the athletic field are inextricably intertwined with outcomes in his own life [p. 272]." If fans do experience this kind of personal involvement with their teams, then some of the general theories of fan attraction to sports (e.g., Achievement, Aggression, and possibly, Stress and Stimulation), to which involvement is relevant, may be anticipated to be particularly central to

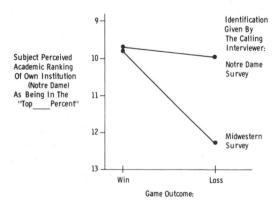

FIG. 9.1. Subject telephone ratings of their own institution (Notre Dame) as being in the "top __percent" academically for undergraduates, given as a function of the preceding game's outcome and the "ingroup" or "outgroup" membership of the caller.

understanding the impact of sports. The consequences of group dynamic processes are likely to be very relevant to several of our general theories, particularly Achievement Seeking, but are conceptually inconsequential for others (e.g., Salubrious Effects). Those other theoretical phenomena still may well affect sports' influence and attraction. Therefore, a continued investigation of the role of those theories may contribute to a more comprehensive understanding of the impact of sports on the fan.

A SOMEWHAT EMPIRICAL APPROACH TO THE EXAMINATION OF THEORY

Because of the nature of many of the theories of sport and the limitations (and advantages), imposed by naturalistic field research, the approach here is regarded as somewhat empirical. Several implications of, and reasons for, this approach are noteworthy.

First, and perhaps most compellingly, many of these general theories of sport are very loose knit in structure. Their antecedents and consequences are sometimes difficult to define and, therefore, hard to operationalize. Some mediating mechanisms are still nebulous even in hypothesized structure. A number are very basic in nature and only tenuous predictions concerning some situational variables can be made. For these theories, rather general, almost empirically derived factors and variables, may be productive and useful. Independent and dependent variables with intuitive theoretical face validity can be examined for their consistency with general predictions inferred from loosely structured theories. Even if the results produced by such an approach were not theoretically strong, at least empirical knowledge would be accrued to inspire elaboration of the inductive process.

If all the theories of sport were quite specific, the problems of experimental control and manipulation of some variables would remain. It is, for example, unlikely that sufficient sports exist to exemplify all combinations of even a handful of the characteristics of sports which could be of considerable importance in determining their appeal for the fan. Because we cannot readily create games, their structures, and outcomes, we can not precisely test many of our theories. Instead, we must use existing sports, natural settings and naturally occurring manipulations of factors thought to be of importance and then observe their consequences for the fan.

Finally, the theories aren't mutually exclusive and competitive. Any number of noncontradictory overlapping theories conceivably could be valid and may have additive or multiplicative influences on fan responses. For this reason we have to give particular attention to the major experimental factors of relevance to most of our theories and to their effects on patterns of responses that can discriminate between those theories.

In the remainder of this chapter, we consider the results of a series of studies designed to ascertain empirically the effects of viewing sports on spectators' moods, feelings and emotions. Because the sports vary in several characteristics and we examine spectator's responses following both team wins and losses, these results should provide useful, if not definitive, comparisons among the various general and situational theories of fans' attraction to sport.

A Methodology for Studying Fan Moods, Feelings, and Emotional Responses to Sport

In response to the need for broad sampling of responses, we employed a 16-item Mood Adjective Checklist (see Table 9.2) to examine fans reactions to the sporting event in a setting with considerable generality and realism. The checklist was administered by an interviewer as fans entered and left the sporting arena. Subjects in such situations might well be influenced by experimental demand (Orne, 1969), or other questionnaire hazards and distort their real feelings in responding. In order to provide convergent validity for the mood adjective data, fans were videotaped from a distance as they entered and departed. Their facial emotions were rated on five dimensions regarded by Ekman, Friesen, and Ellsworth (1972) as capable of being judged accurately and reliably.

Fans were observed at three types of sports events, basketball, football and boxing, which varied considerably in many aspects (e.g., overt aggression, risk of harm, speed, rule oriented structure, display of individual/group skill, ability to identify with the victor, and so forth). Naturally, such decidedly different types of events may draw quite different crowds, casting doubt on any rationale for comparing absolute levels of responding across types of sports. Presumably, however, the pre–post differences in patterns of response

TABLE 9.2
Adjectives Employed in All Mood Adjective Checklists

Angry	Hostile	Discouraged	Irritated
Frustrated	Sad	Upset	Tired
Happy	Satisfied	Pleased	Confident
Energetic	Benevolent	Calm	Tense

Note: Subjects were asked to, "indicate the extent to which each of these feelings apply to you *right now.*" They indicated their response by marking a unidirectional scale labeled "not at all," "somewhat," "considerably," and "extremely." Adjectives were selected to allow a broad range of influences to be reflected. An attempt was made to select diverse dimensions, at least some of which would have relevance to each separate theory. Some dimensions were favored in their frequency of representation in order to be more assured of sensitive sampling of them (e.g., satisfaction, displeasure).

to victory and loss can be meaningfully examined across sports to examine their degree of convergence in support of their mutual validity.

General Hypotheses of Theoretical Relevance

The following theory-inspired hypotheses are intended to be nonexhaustive; focusing only on the most central themes. The theories themselves are general, as are, therefore, their implications. More specific predictions correctly await more evolved and specific theories. Salubrious Effects Theories, as their name would seem to require, predict that after viewing sports, positive feelings should rise and prevail while anger, hostility and the like should become secondary (see Table 9.3). The hypothesized "feel better" response (cf. Harris, 1973), also predicts enhanced feelings of altruism and benevolence (Isen & Levin, 1972). If sports are rejuvenating, then the fan should feel more energetic as well. These theories suggest no differential effects from winning and losing or from sporting events of different natures.

Stress and Stimulation Seeking Theories suggest various possibilities for fan arousal, which may still be elevated after a game or may have dropped into a recovery phase. Either way, there should be observable change in experienced tension, energy, and the like. No changes due to winning or losing are predicted in any variable. However, it may well be that games within a sport that differ in their perceived difficulty may differ in their stressful or stimulating effects on the fans.

Catharsis and Aggression Theories clearly predict that watching violent sports, regardless of outcome, will decrease angry feelings and perhaps facilitate calm, pleasant ones. Social learning positions suggest that viewing will increase aggressiveness in all situations and certainly in a victorious game in which the fans' models are rewarded for their aggression rather than being punished by losing. Frustration–Aggression notions have no implications for a victory but a frustrating loss should increase anger and the like, and possibly tension, while diminishing feelings of happiness, particularly in more difficult or significant games.

Entertainment Theories uniformly predict increased pleasure, satisfaction and happiness, no matter what the game's outcome. Moral value notions of attraction to sports further suggest that benevolent, altruistic feelings also would be enhanced in fans following sporting events.

Achievement Themes natually emphasize the central importance of success and failure. When the team wins, pleasure and satisfaction should increase while frustrations and hostility would, if anything, abate. The reverse would be true of a team loss; satisfaction would drop as feelings of discouragement increased. All of these effects would be intensified in particularly difficult games which would tend to magnify the potential achievement possible. It is worthy of note that only two theories, Achievement and Frustration-

TABLE 9.3

Summarized Predictions of Sports Theories and Hypotheses

Theories	Variables[a]					Winning and Losing of Notable Theoretical Importance?
	Angry	Happy	Calm	Energetic	Benevolent	
Salubrious effects	↓	↑		↑	↑	No
Stress and stimulation seeking			← or →		No	
Aggression: Catharsis	↓					No
Social learning (possibly reversed in a loss)	↑					Possibly

246

					Yes/No
Frustration–aggression (effect *only* in a loss)	←→	→	→		Yes
Entertainment:					
General		←			No
Aesthetic		←			No
Moral value		←	←		No
Achievement win/loss	↓/←	↑/↓			Yes

[a]Note that only major elements within the 16-mood adjective dimensions are represented. As anticipated above, several adjectives appear to fall primarily on the same dimension.

Aggression, share predictions rather consistently. This should not be surprising since failure to achieve a goal is a reasonably good definition of frustration. Frustration–Aggression mechanisms make no predictions as to the effects of winning as do Achievement notions, and therefore, do not conflict. Thus, Frustration–Aggression hypotheses in this context might be seen as a subset of Achievement Theories of sport.

Certainly more extensive predictions could be made. For example, one might assume that benevolent feelings would increase whenever happiness and satisfaction did, or decrease whenever anger rose. Because our approach here is broad and general, more tenuous predictions have been omitted in order to place emphasis on central themes.

The Effects of Watching, Winning, and Losing on Fan's Moods, Feelings, and Emotions

We began our investigations by choosing a sport that seemed to exemplify a number of qualities of general theoretical concern, basketball. Basketball can be characterized as a game emphasizing skill, individual and team coordination and relatively moderate levels of overt violence. It is usually intensely competitive and stimulating and is played frequently enough to allow examination of both wins and losses in a constant setting (e.g., home games). Thus, basketball provides an appealing setting for such research.

Our trained team of interviewers approached 551 male and female home team fans in the corridors leading to the basketball arena and asked them to participate in a sports survey. Fans were asked a few questions concerning prior attendance and their investment in attendance, and after instruction, they then were given the adjective checklist to complete. Subjects' questions were resolved and they were thanked and released. Interviewing occurred for 20 minutes before and after the game. During that interval, interviewers approached and interviewed the next subject available near their station as soon as the preceding survey was completed. The survey was obviously short and the refusal rate was relatively low.

In addition to examining the effects of simply attending games, that is, observing the change in the average subject's moods and feelings from before to after the game, we were concerned with the effects of the game's outcome. Winning and losing are certainly the major categories of outcomes, but others are potentially possible. In fact, in our research (Sloan & Latronica, Note 3), basketball contests were accessible in such frequency and variety of circumstances that we were able to make a further theory-relevant distinction among games. That distinction was in terms of each game's subjectively perceived difficulty or significance.

Games within a sport are frequently perceived to vary in difficulty and it is likely that this would have effects on theoretical mediators of game impact

such as aggression, stimulation, aspects of entertainment perhaps, and certainly, achievement. The more difficult and significant games should be more stimulating and entertaining and would produce more achievement feelings in a win or more frustration in a loss. We set out to investigate this possibility by having a sample of 46 regular fans rate the eight home games in our data sample at the end of the regular season. Their ratings of the games they had witnessed gave us a reliable breakdown of games into three categories: easy wins (four games), difficult wins (two games), and difficult losses (two games). Obviously, there were few losses, and none were considered insignificant or easy. This categorization of the games was used as the multifaceted "game outcome" factor in analyzing our results. The other factor was, of course, the time, pre or post game, when the data was collected.

Basketball Game Outcome Effects on Fans' Reported Moods and Emotions.   The results of the experiment are displayed graphically in Fig. 9.2. Inspection of the patterns of results for the 16 mood adjectives immediately reveals several very clear-cut groups of variables which show the same influence of the experimental factors.

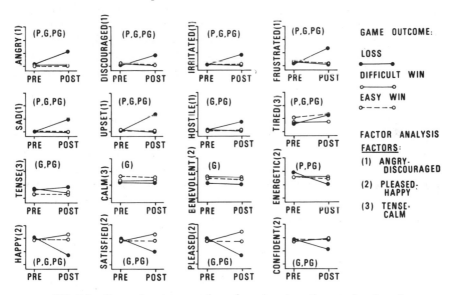

FIG. 9.2.   Pre- and post-game ratings of moods and emotions as a function of basketball home-game outcome. *Note:* All variables were rated on a four-point scale on which 1 = (bottom of each figure) = "not at all" and 4 = (top of each figure) = "extremely." The number representing the primary factor on which the variable loaded is in parentheses following the variable name. Letters within parentheses inside each figure indicate the factors that were significant for that variable: *P* = pre-post game; *G* = game outcome (loss, hard win, easy win); and *PG* = the interaction of factors *P* and *G*.

In order to discover whether these various moods and feelings were interrelated or actually were influenced by the experimental factors in similar ways, the mood variables were subjected to factor analysis. Thus, the within cell correlations among the variables were employed to determine the nature of the simple relationship between the mood adjectives when they were not differentially influenced by the factors in the experiment. The results were remarkably similar to those patterns so evident in Fig. 9.2. The 16 variables fit rather neatly into three factors: angry/discouraged (factor dimension #1 in Fig. 9.2); happy/pleased (#2 in Fig. 9.2); and calm/tense (#3 in Fig. 9.2). Only two were weakly represented on all dimensions—tired (#3) and benevolent (#2)—and they behaved irregularly across our experiments reported here.

Thus, instead of five general groups of variables suggested by the theories as being of central importance, subjects perceived the variables as falling on only three dimensions: anger, happiness, and calm. Thus implications regarding the validity or utility of the theories being considered here will be strongest when based on these three viable judgment continua.

Results and Implications. Contrary to implications drawn from Moral Value and Salubrious Theories, watching the game had no impact on spectator's feelings of benevolence. Absent were the simple main effects on calmness and tension and energy suggested by Stress-Seeking, Salubrious Effects and Catharsis notions. Instead, tension and energy followed the same patterns as did anger and happiness (respectively) described below. Tension did increase in a loss as predicted by the Frustration–Aggression Theory.

In contradiction to all theories except Achievement, Frustration–Aggression and possibly Social Learning, anger and happiness were differentially affected by wins and losses. Although the Social Learning Theory might predict different effects for wins and losses, its predictions run opposite to the results observed here. Anger (discouragement, etc.) increased after a loss and was seemingly nonexistent after a victory, while happiness (satisfaction, etc.) decreased in a loss and rose following a tough victory. Easy victories had little impact of any sort.

Only Achievement Theory predicts these anger-happiness results successfully. It should be noted that the Frustration–Aggression position also was upheld by these findings, but it makes predictions only for games which are lost, wherein frustration can be aroused. Thus, Frustration–Aggression can be subsumed functionally within the Achievement Theory and this seems reasonable on conceptual grounds as well. If achievement needs motivate the fans' attraction to sports and their identification with their team, then success must be a central objective just as for any other goal oriented group. Failure therefore should bring discouragement and frustration. Clearly then, Frustration–Aggression is a logical component of the Achievement Theory position, just as is the elation of victory.

The results indicate considerable support for Achievement/Frustration notions, strong opposition to Social Learning and Catharsis hypotheses, partial opposition to Entertainment and Salubrious Effect positions and more than anything else, null effects for Stimulation-Seeking Theories. Because these theories are broad and some are loose-knit, and because the methodology is somewhat new, caution should be exercised in drawing strong conclusions. Alternative explanations for these results and questions of their generality should be considered and we will now examine several obviously important ones.

One concern raised earlier questioned the accuracy of our subject-fans' reports of their feelings. Could it be that they were responding to demand characteristics (Orne, 1969) or social desirability or some similarly misleading cue? One way to investigate this possibility was to judge fan's emotions from their facial expressions which they presumably could not consciously or unconsciously bias as readily as they could a questionnaire response. In addition, of course, their facial emotions could be recorded when they did not know they were being observed for experimental purposes. This is precisely what we tried to do (Sloan & Marshall, Note 4). Our judges rated 209 basketball fans' emotional expressions, before and after the game, with moderate, albeit typical, interjudge reliability on dimensions of Happiness, Sadness, Anger, and Disgust/Contempt (Ekman et al., 1972). When these ratings were analyzed, the results were almost precisely the same as those for the similar variable when the subjects themselves reported their feelings. This convergent validation of our findings from two dramatically different sources allows us to have much greater confidence in the accuracy and meaningfulness of our measures, particularly the self-report measures, which are so central to the present research.

Other explanations for those results may be sought in the characteristics of the type of sport viewed and the characteristics' conceptual relationships to sport theories. In basketball, for example, Achievement/Frustration should be effective because victory is strongly sought and is easily recognized. Likewise, we should expect Entertainment theories to be influential, especially Aesthetics, because of the very obvious and frequent displays of physical skill and control. The success of Achievement notions and the failure of Entertainment Theories consequently seem more meaningful. But what of other theories? For example, perhaps the impact of Salubrious Effects and Stimulation-Seeking would increase in more arousing settings. Most notably, one could reasonably argue that a more overtly aggressive sport would be more likely to reveal the influences of Catharsis and Social Learning phenomena. In a sport in which aggressiveness and superior violence seems directly important for victory, fan aggressiveness should be a consequence, especially following a team win. Any sport of violence should produce catharsis effects, of course. In order to pursue these possibilities we embarked on a study of the football fan.

Football is undeniably violent, aggressive, and victory oriented as suggested earlier, thus satisfying many of the needed characteristics described above. Because winning seems to depend on successful aggression, Social Learning Theories' prerequisites should certainly be satisfied. Whether football at this institution is more fan-involving than basketball (vis á vis, Salubrious Effects and Stimulation-Seeking notions) is not documented, but seems subjectively to be the case even though the rate of game action may be perceived as slower.

Our method for collecting data was essentially the same as that for basketball. Interviewers contacted 321 home town fans as they entered or left the stadium immediately prior to or following the game. Thirty visiting opponent supporters were also interviewed and yielded analogous data not detailed here because of its limited quantity. Only two homes games, a simple win and a devastating loss, were examined for comparison to the results of the earlier basketball study.

Results and Implications.   Despite the fact that football differs on many dimensions from basketball, particularly on overt aggressiveness, the football results were almost identical to the comparable condition in the basketball studies, with two exceptions. Reported benevolence, which showed no changes in basketball, increased in a win and decreased in a loss, further supporting Achievement interpretations. Tension, which rose slightly after a loss in basketball, dropped slightly following a football defeat. Although the result might be taken as a modicum of support for Catharsis, it is contradicted by responses to all of the "anger" factor variables. The finding might be better explained by exhaustion due to successful Stress and Stimulation-Seeking or the trying fall weather in an outdoor stadium.

In summary then, we once again found that fans displayed feelings which indicated that they had sought to achieve a goal in the sporting event they watched. When their team won they were uplifted; when it lost they were discouraged, frustrated, and sad. They felt as though they themselves had strived for achievement and succeeded or failed. Again, it appears that the fans do believe themselves to be a part, along with the team, of a meaningful group in their lives.

For both football and basketball it appears that Achievement/Frustration concepts best account for the major responses of viewing fans. As in basketball, however, the predominance of Achievement phenomena does not imply that others are not present. Rather, other phenomena may simply be overpowered by the consequences of Achievement-Seeking. Therefore, one way to facilitate the observation of those hypothesized effects and reinforce our confidence in Achievement Seeking Theories simultaneously would be to investigate a setting which minimized fans' partisan involvement with competing participants. In such a situation, fans should not, to a great extent,

identify with, or share the achievement motives of, the interactants. They should presumably be subject to other proposed phenonmena. We sought and found a setting which approached these requirements fairly closely.

The final research setting was a "golden-gloves" type series of about a dozen short, three-round boxing matches conducted for the benefit of charity: the Notre Dame "Bengal Bouts". The subjects were 267 males and females, who were sampled as were the basketball fans in our earlier research. The amateur fighters had become contenders only within a few days of the fight, so little attachment had time to form. They were generally individual students representing themselves and so were well-known and/or identified with by only a small portion of the audience. Thus, the possibilities for sharing the success or defeat of a given boxer should have been small, and since each fight between near unknowns produced a winner and a loser, a fan's choices across the evening should be expected to balance out. In fact, the average fan picked winners 49% of the time; nearly chance success, possibly because so little was known about the boxers. Fans tried to pick only about 60% of the bouts, further suggesting the absence of knowledge of the participants.

The situation was, then, one in which little identification-mediated achievement was possible, while aggression and fan arousal and involvement in the bout itself were strong. Consequently, while other hypothesized phenomena should be quite active, achievement influences should be weak.

Results and Implications.   Because there was no single winner or loser to identify with, Achievement phenomena could not be factorially investigated. Positive correlations between number of winners picked and reported pleasure and confidence do suggest that achievement-seeking was still influential. Of importance to other theories were pre–post viewing changes in moods and emotions and very few such changes were observed.

Fans reported being tired after viewing and, considering their own vocal involvement, perhaps this isn't surprising. Seeking Stress and Stimulation should presumably lead to such excited behavior and eventually to fatigue. Simple predictions from Stimulation-Seeking theory are difficult to make, however, so this conclusion must be regarded with caution.

Hostility also increased after the bouts, but surprisingly did so only for female viewers. Females had seen less boxing prior to these bouts and could therefore have been more responsive to what they saw than were males. In support of that notion, females reported themselves as being more upset, irritated, tense, sad and tired both in anticipation of the bouts and following them than did males, suggesting that females were generally more aroused by the entire event. Perhaps, in that state, females were more susceptible to Social Learning phenomena and became slightly more hostile after viewing

hostility. Unfortunately, related variables did not show parallel effects. The often brutal consequences of the bout may well have served to inhibit viewers from expressing much aggression (cf. Goranson, 1970).

Most notably, there were no other changes. Although this was an incredibly violent and sometimes bloody affair, no Cathartic effects were observed. Although people were very much involved, shouting and jumping to their feet frequently, no Entertainment or Salubrious Effects predicted responses were observed. However, viewers appeared very much to have sought the exposure and to be enjoying themselves considerably.

Thus, the differences between the boxing setting and those of basketball and football in their effects on the fans appear to be rather telling in discriminating among theories. Although minor influences could possibly be attributed to other hypotheses, the major findings reflect on Achievement-Seeking. In basketball and football, strong identification with the team existed and extensive changes in mood and emotion occurred. Anger and sadness increased in a loss and happiness and satisfaction increased in victory. Although there was strong fan involvement in this boxing event, there was little personal identification with fighters who didn't represent the fans or their school against an opponent. There were no real opportunities for the fans to obtain enhanced esteem and prestige through association with a given winner, and fans showed little change in their moods and emotions as a result of viewing the bouts. Achievement-Seeking does seem to have a great deal of impact on the sports fan who is associated with or represented by a participant. When this association exists in the fan's perspective, then achievement-seeking is likely to be a central motivator of fans' attraction to sport. This boxing study reveals, however, that when borrowed achievements aren't readily available, fans are *still* drawn to sporting events; at least extremely stimulating and violent ones such as this.

CONCLUSIONS AND CONSIDERATIONS

In the preceding review of research relating to the impact of sports on the fan, one set of theoretical notions clearly dominated all others in its ability to predict and explain the empirical findings. Achievement-Seeking and its Frustration–Aggression subset, although broadly defined, successfully accounted for the occurrence and absence of the major effects observed in accord with the experimental factors which are hypothesized to produce them.

Early research pursuing the tendency to "Bask in Reflected Glory," to "BIRG," found that fans sought to associate themselves with a victorious sports team, to enhance their own esteem and prestige, particularly when they had recently suffered esteem damage. Worthy of note was the fact that some

fans always admitted their association with the team, even in a loss, suggesting a stronger bond to the team than mere momentary "BIRG-ing." Subsequent data supported hypotheses that fans actually feel they belong to a meaningful group with the team, by showing that they displayed responses typical of members of any group after success or failure, differentially denying the team and their school's prestige when conversing with in-and-out-group members following a loss. Thus, although fans may "BIRG" their team's victory for borrowed achievement, they also share the pain and very real consequences of its failures to achieve, because they preceive themselves as members of the team-group.

Findings supporting another implication of this prestige-oriented team-group membership further advance the Achievement-Seeking notion of sports' attraction and impact. A variety of moods and emotions changed as predicted following victories and defeats. However, these Achievement hypothesized changes occurred only when the fans actually identified with one of the participant-competitors and their representative clearly won or lost. When that was not the case, there was no self-perceived shared group membership, no possibility for substantial borrowing of achievement and hence no elation in victory or frustration in defeat.

Although Achievement-Seeking/Frustration–Aggression theories were roundly supported, other positions faired less well. There were only the smallest hints of Social Learning effects on aggression (and several reversals), and Catharsis notions were either not observed or were rejected. The frequent fever-pitch involvement of fans at these sporting events may subjectively serve as evidence for Stimulation-Seeking theories, but the most suggestive objective results could well have been the result of simple fatigue. Notably, only Achievement-Seeking accounts for all of the results recounted in preceding paragraphs. As interpreted here, only one of the other theories even makes distinctions between victories and defeats as having differential impacts and that solitary theory's predictions were generally contrary to the results.

The singular lack of success of these theories does not, however, warrant their outright rejection. The seminal research reviewed here does tap only a small portion of the realm of impact of sports. There are many reasons to suppose that other phenomena besides Achievement-Seeking may dominate the influence of sports in other circumstances. Fans at the boxing bouts described above, for example, were highly involved, even though there was no observed influence on their moods and emotions as there were in situations where achievement was possible. What mediated their involvement and what were its effects? Entertainment? Stimulation-Seeking? Achievement-Seeking Theory was predicted to be inapplicable there and apparently it was not, but we don't yet know enough about the influence, if any, of other theories to make many predictions from them. There are a number of viable possible

factors which could affect the effectiveness of the various hypothesized phenomena:

1. The theories may have vastly different or overlapping realms of influence. If they overlap, they may simply differ in magnitude or consequence and mask or cancel one another though they all have validity. They may vary in impact or applicability from situation to situation or from sport to sport as the situations and sports themselves differ on yet unidentified dimensions of relevance. Aesthetics, for example, may be important only in individual sports where skill is more easily discerned or in noncompetitive sports where aggressive competition and contrient interdependence prevail. Finally, it may be the case that some of these theories are only relevant to the understanding of "games," "recreation," and "play" rather than for the achievement themes that "contests" and "sports" inevitably include.

2. Just as there may be different theories for different sports, there may be different fans for different sports. People may vary in the source of their attraction to sports and needs they seek to satisfy by playing or watching. The results reviewed here may represent the relative importance of these for the average person but the weight of the phenomena may vary widely across spectators. In those studies virtually all of the spectators favored one team or the other and were greatly influenced by Achievement-Seeking. Perhaps other theories, such as aesthetics, would account for the behavior of more "pure" spectators who do not identify with a team, experience no victories or defeats and may actually go just to see a "good" game. Finally, it should be noted that theories which prove important for fans may not be very relevant for players who presumably experience more impact on all dimensions, particularly those with physical facets. Achievement-Seeking, however, seems to be a theme very relevant to players and fans alike.

3. We should recognize one other disconcerting possibility. It may well be that the impacts that sports have on the fans or participants could be quite different from the influences which attracted them initially. We may learn to love sports through repeated exposure, for example, but experience multifaceted consequences from our involvement. One solution to this limitation is to focus separately on sports' attraction and on sports' impacts just as we have focused mainly on sports' impact here. This inter-experiment convergent validation approach would enhance faith in our research conclusions of the underpinnings of sports.

Despite these three groups of ever-possible limitations to research in sports influences, the findings reviewed here seem substantial. A number of major theories of sport involvement appear to have little impact on sports fans. Fans do seem to be motivated by desires to achieve "vicariously" and within that display frustration and anger when their goal is denied them. Tutko and

Bruns (1976) have suggested that it is an American myth that "winning is everything" and that perhaps it is ideological for some people involved with sports. In the avid fans who were studied above, however, it appears the achievement of winning was a very real and predominant feature in their desires for sport. Perhaps Lombardi was wrong and winning wasn't the "only thing" for these fans, but there can be little doubt that for them, at least, winning seems undeniably to have been the most important thing.

People have always sought out sports and every sport has its fans. Modern sports activities have grown to tremendous proportions and the fans' fervor for them has grown at least as rapidly. In this chapter we have delineated several classes of the theories of sports' impact on the fan and have reviewed findings relevant to questions raised by many of those theoretical positions:

1. Salubrious Effects Theories predict increased positive feelings and a "feel better response" following sports involvement;
2. Stress and Stimulation-Seeking themes suggest changes in tension and energy;
3. Within the Aggression Theories, Catharsis predicts that viewing aggressive sports will decrease viewer aggression and that Social Learning implies the opposite. Frustration–Aggression suggests that anger will rise particularly when the favored team loses;
4. Entertainment notions see enhanced happiness and enjoyment as the major consequences of sports involvements; and finally,
5. Achievement-Seeking Theories predict anger in losses and happiness in victories and this thesis was the one most supported by the findings reviewed.

Fans were observed to emphasize their association with victorious teams to enhance their own esteem and prestige. More than that, they felt they actually belonged to a group with the team as was demonstrated by the influence victory and defeat had on their feelings about the group and the degree of their espousal or denial of it. The study of the impact of sports' outcomes on fan moods and emotions lent support to the earlier findings that: (1) fans sought achievement and esteem in sports victories; and (2) they apparently felt they inextricably belonged to the team-group since they were quite distressed in losses.

It was concluded that Achievement-Seeking was a major influence on the fans in situations where associations with the winner were plausible. Suggestions as to the viability of other phenomena were present also and it is possible that they may be of greater influence in the many facets of sports which are yet unexamined. Clearly, evolved theories and improved methodologies are needed before a relatively complete conceptualization of the possibly interrelated attractions and impacts of sports can be advanced.

Knowledge of sports' appeal and impact has great potential for explaining the meaning and use of that considerable and ever increasing portion of our lives when we can pursue that which we have not found in our work or our homes; when we choose to occupy our leisure and augment our lives by seeking involvement in sports, games, and play.

ACKNOWLEDGMENTS

The many who contributed to this research must be recognized. Particularly outstanding were the unflagging efforts of Carol Latronica, a competent and amiable researcher and supervisor/trainer of many "generations" of experimenters. Other associates who deserve special credit are Mark Borden, Elaine Marshall, Paul Schwieger, Alex Sloan, and the several dozen trained undergraduate experimenter/interviewers who actually braved encountering the fans before and after each game.

We were allowed to encounter the fans in appropriate settings through the kind permission and assistance of the directors and administrators of the Notre Dame Basketball Program, Bengal Bouts, and Athletic and Convocation Center. Their enlightened attitude toward sports research was exceptional. In the same vein, we thank the selfless Notre Dame teams and individual athletes who allowed us to complete our research designs by losing a few games. Without them, our own "research contests" could not have been won.

Finally, I must express my appreciation for the aid of the approximately 2000 Notre Dame fans and opponents who shared with us their feelings, moods, attitudes, and behaviors as data for these investigations. Whether hostile or happy, their contributions were very gratefully received.

REFERENCE NOTES

1. Kreitler, H., & Kreitler, S. *Movement and aging—psychologically viewed.* Paper presented at the International Symposium on Physical Activity and Aging, Tel-Aviv, October 1967.
2. Sloan, L. R. *The effects of team victories and defeats and "flexible" identification processes on fan cohesiveness and group related evaluations.* Unpublished manuscript, University of Notre Dame, 1976.
3. Sloan, L. R., & Latronica, C. *Fan self-reported moods and feelings before and after viewing basketball, football and boxing matches varying in outcome.* Unpublished manuscript, University of Notre Dame, 1977.
4. Sloan, L. R., & Marshall, E. J. *Fan facial emotional responses before and after watching, winning and losing in basketball and boxing matches.* Unpublished manuscript, University of Notre Dame, 1977.

REFERENCES

Allen, G. Cited in J. A. Michener, *Sports in America.* New York: Random House, 1976.
Ardrey, R. *The territorial imperative: A personal inquiry into the animal origins of property and nations.* New York: Atheneum, 1966.

Baekeland, F. Exercise deprivation. *Archives of General Psychiatry,* April 1970, *22,* 365.

Bandura, A. *Social learning theory.* Morristown, N.J.: General Learning Press, 1971.

Bandura, A. *Aggression: A social learning analysis.* Englewood Cliffs, N.J.: Prentice-Hall, 1973.

Bandura, A., & Walters, R. H. *Social learning and personality development.* New York: Holt, Rinehart & Winston, 1963.

Baron, R. A., & Byrne, D. *Social psychology: Understanding human interaction.* Boston, Mass.: Allyn & Bacon, 1977.

Barron, F. The needs for order and disorder as motivation in creative activity. In C. W. Taylor & F. Barron (Eds.), *Scientific creativity; its recognition and development.* New York: Wiley, 1963. (a)

Barron, F. *Creativity and psychological health: Origins of personality and creative freedom.* Princeton: Van Nostrand, 1963. (b)

Barron, F. *Artists in the making.* New York: Seminar Press, 1972.

Beisser, A. *The madness in sports.* New York: Appleton-Century-Crofts, 1967.

Berkowitz, L. The frustration–aggression hypothesis revisited. In L. Berkowitz (Ed.), *Roots of aggression.* New York: Atherton Press, 1969.

Berkowitz, L. The contagion of violence: An S–R mediational analysis of some effects of observed aggression. In W. J. Arnold & M. M. Page (Eds.), *Nebraska Symposium on Motivation.* Lincoln: University of Nebraska Press, 1970.

Berkowitz, L. *A survey of social psychology.* Hinsdale, Ill.: Dryden Press, 1975.

Bouet, M. *Signification du sport.* Paris: Éditions Universitaires, 1968.

Bouet, M. *Les motivations de sportif.* Paris: Éditions Universitaires, 1969.

Bramel, D. The attraction and reduction of hostility. In J. Mills (Ed.), *Experimental social psychology.* New York: Macmillan, 1969.

Browne, E. An ethological theory of play. *Journal of Health, Physical Education and Recreation,* September 1968, pp. 36–39.

Buehler, K. Cited in D. V. Harris, *Involvement in sport: A somatopsychic rationale for physical activity.* Philadelphia: Lea & Febiger, 1973.

Buss, A. H., & Durkee, A. An inventory for assessing different kinds of hostility. *Journal of Consulting Psychology,* 1957, *21,* 343–348.

Caillois, R. [*Man, play, and games*] (M. Barash, trans.). New York: Free Press of Glencoe, Inc., 1961.

Christenson, A. *The verdict of the scoreboard.* New York: American Press, 1958.

Cialdini, R. B., Borden, R. J., Thorne, A., Walker, M. R., Freeman, S., & Sloan, L. R. Basking in reflected glory: Three (football) field studies, *Journal of Personality and Social Psychology,* 1976, *34*(3), 366–375.

Clinch, N. G. *The Kennedy neurosis.* New York: Grosset & Dunlap, 1973.

Corbin, C. B. Among spectators, "trait" anxiety, and coronary risk. *Physician and Sports Medicine,* September 1973, *1*(2), 55–58.

Coser, L. A. *The functions of social conflict.* Glencoe, Ill.: Free Press, 1956.

Cratty, B. J. *Movement behavior and motor learning.* Philadelphia: Lea & Febiger, 1967.

Cullen, F. T. Attitudes of players and spectators toward norm-violation in ice hockey. *Perceptual and Motor Skills,* 1974, *38*(3), 1146.

Dollard, J., Doob, L., Miller, N., Mowrer, O., & Sears, R. *Frustration and aggression.* New Haven: Yale University Press, 1939.

Edwards, H. *Sociology of sport.* Homewood, Ill.: Dorsey, 1973.

Ekman, P., Friesen, W. V., & Ellsworth, P. *Emotion in the human face.* New York: Pergamon Press, 1972.

Elias, N., & Dunning, E. The quest for excitement in unexciting societies. In G. Luschen (Ed.), *The cross-cultural analysis of sport and games.* Champaign, Ill.: Stipes, 1970.

Ellis, M. J. *Why people play.* Englewood Cliffs, N.J.: Prentice-Hall, 1972.

Erikson, E. H. *Childhood and society.* New York: Norton, 1950.

Fenz, W. D., & Epstein, S. Stress: In the air. *Psychology Today,* September 1969, pp. 27–59.

Feshback, S., & Singer, R. *Television and aggression.* San Francisco: Jossey-Bass, 1971.

Festinger, L. A theory of social comparison processes. *Human Relations,* 1954, *7,* 117–140.

Frankl, V. E. The case for tension. *The Pittsburgh Press,* April 12, 1970.

Freud, S. Beyond the pleasure principle (in Vol. 18), and Civilization and its discontents (in Vol. 21). In J. Strachey (Ed.), *The standard edition of the complete psychological works of Sigmund Freud.* London: Hogarth, 1955.

Fromm, E. *Escape from freedom.* New York: Holt, Rinehart & Winston, 1941.

Fromm, E. *The sane society.* New York: Rinehart, 1955.

Goffman, E. *The presentation of self in everyday life.* New York: Doubleday, 1959.

Goffman, E. *Encounters.* Indianapolis: Bobbs-Merrill, 1961.

Goldstein, J. H., & Arms, R. L. Effects of observing athletic contests on hostility. *Sociometry,* 1971, *34*(1), 83–90.

Goranson, R. E. Media violence and aggressive behavior: A review of experimental research. In L. Berkowitz (Ed.), *Advances in experimental social psychology.* New York: Academic Press, 1970.

Groos, K. *The play of animals.* New York: Appleton, 1898.

Harris, D. V. *Involvement in sport: A somatopsychic rationale for physical activity.* Philadelphia: Lea & Febiger, 1973.

Harvey, O. J., Kelly, H. H., & Shapiro, M. M. Reactions to unfavorable evaluations of self made by other persons. *Journal of Personality,* 1957, *25,* 393–411.

Heider, F. *The psychology of interpersonal relations.* New York: Wiley, 1958.

Huizinga, J. *Homo ludens: A study of the play-element in culture.* Boston: Beacon Press, 1938.

Isen, A. M., & Levin, P. F. Effects of feeling good on helping: Cookies and kindness. *Journal of Personality and Social Psychology,* 1972, *21,* 384–388.

Izenberg, J. *The rivals.* New York: Holt, Rinehart & Winston, 1968.

Izenberg, J. *How many miles to camelot: The all-American sports myth.* New York: Holt, Rinehart & Winston, 1972.

Johnson, R., Conlee, M., & Tesser, A. Effects of similarity of fate on bad news transmission: A reexamination. *Journal of Personality and Social Psychology,* 1974, *24,* 26–32.

Johnson, W. O., Jr. *Super spectator and the electric lilliputians.* Boston: Little, Brown, 1971.

Kane, J. E. Personality, arousal and performance. *International Journal of Sport Psychology,* 1971, *2,*(1).

Karpman, H. Cited in M. Roberts, *Fans! How we go crazy over sports.* Washington, D. C.: New Republic Book. 1976.

Kennedy, R. Cited in N. G. Clinch, *The Kennedy neurosis.* New York: Grosset & Dunlap, 1973.

Kenyon, G. S. A conceptual model for characterizing physical activity. *Research Quarterly,* 1968, *39,* 96–105.

Klausner, S. Z. Empirical analysis of stress-seekers. In S. Z. Klausner (Ed.), *Why man takes chances.* Garden City, N.J.: Anchor Books, Doubleday, 1968.

Kohlberg, L. Stage and sequence: The cognitive-developmental approach to socialization. In D. Goslin (Ed.), *Handbook of socialization theory and research.* Chicago: Rand McNally, 1969.

Lawther, J. D. *Psychology of coaching.* New York: Prentice-Hall, 1951.

LeBon, G. *The crowd.* London: Ernest Benn, 1896.

Leiderman, P. H., & Shapiro, D. (Eds.). *Psychobiological approaches to social behavior.* Stanford, Calif.: Stanford University Press, 1964.

Leonard, G. *The ultimate athlete.* New York: Viking, 1974.

Lorenz, K. *On aggression.* New York: Harcourt, Brace & World, 1966.

Lott, A., & Lott, B. Group cohesiveness as interpersonal attraction: A review of relationships with antecedent and consequent variables. *Psychological Bulletin,* 1965, *64,* 259–309.

Loy, J. W., & Kenyon, G. S. *Sport, culture and society.* New York: Macmillan, 1969.

Luschen, G. The interdependence of sport and culture. *International Review of Sports Sociology.* Warsaw: Polish Publishers, 1967.

MacArthur, D. Cited in H. Edwards, *Sociology of sport.* Homewood, Ill.: Dorsey, 1973.

Marquis, D., Guetzkow, H., & Heyns, R. A social psychological study of the decision-making conference. In H. Guetzkow (Ed.), *Groups, leadership, and men.* Pittsburgh: Carnegie Press, 1951.

Maslow, A. H. *Toward a psychology of being* (2nd ed.). New York: Van Nostrand, 1968.

Maslow, A. *Motivation and personality.* New York: Harper & Row, 1970.

McClelland, D. C., Atkinson, J. W., Clark, R. A., & Lowell, E. L. *The achievement motive.* New York: Appleton-Century-Crofts, 1953.

McDougall, W. *Social psychology.* New York: J. W. Luce & Co., 1918.

Mead, G. H. *Self and society.* Chicago: University of Chicago Press, 1934.

Michener, J. A. *Sports in America.* New York: Random House, 1976.

Milgram, S., & Toch, H. Collective behavior: Crowds and social movements. In G. Lindzey & E. Aronson (Eds.), *Handbook of social psychology* (2nd ed.). Reading, Mass. Addison-Wesley, 1969.

Miller, D. L. *Gods and games: Toward a theology of play.* New York: World, 1970.

Morris, D. *The naked ape.* New York: McGraw-Hill, 1967.

Morris, D. *The human zoo.* New York: Dell, 1969.

Murray, H. *Explorations in personality.* New York: Oxford University Press, 1938.

Musselman, B. Cited in J. A. Michener, *Sports in America.* New York: Random House, 1976.

Novak, M. *The joy of sports.* New York: Basic Books, 1976.

Ogilvie, B., & Tutko, T. A. A psychologist reviews the future contribution of motivation research in track and field. *Track and Field News,* September 1, 1963.

Ogilvie, B., & Tutko, T. A. Sports don't build character. *San Francisco Chronicle,* September 23, 1971 (*Psychology Today,* October 1971, pp. 60–63.)

Orne, M. T. Demand characteristics and the concept of quasi-controls. In R. Rosenthal & R. L. Rosnow (Eds.), *Artifact in behavior research.* New York: Academic Press, 1969.

Perls, F. S. *Ego, hunger, and aggression.* New York: Random House, 1969.

Peterson, J. A., & Martens, R. Success and residence affiliation as determinants of team cohesiveness. *Research Quarterly,* 1973, *43,* 62–76.

Petrie, A., Holland, L., & Wolk, I. Sensory stimulation causing subdued experience: Audio-analgesia and perceptual augmentation and reduction. *Journal of Nervous and Mental Disease,* 1963, *137,* 312–321.

Piaget, J. Piaget's theory. In P. H. Mussen (Ed.), *Carmichael's manual of child psychology* (3rd ed.). New York: Wiley, 1970.

Roberts, J., Arth, M., & Rush, R. Games in culture. *American Anthropologist,* 1959, *61,* 597–602.

Roberts, M. *Fans! How we go crazy over sports.* Washington, D.C.: New Republic Book Co., 1976.

Rosenthal, S. R. Risk exercise revisited. *Polo,* 1968.

Ryan, E. D. Perceptual characteristics of vigorous people. In R. C. Brown, Jr. & J. B. Cratty (Eds.), *New perspectives of man in action.* Englewood Cliffs, N.J.: Prentice-Hall, 1969.

Schachter, S. *The psychology of affiliation.* Stanford, Calif.: Stanford University Press, 1959.

Schafer, W. E. Some sources and consequences of interscholastic athletics. In G. S. Kenyon (Ed.), *Sociology of sport.* Chicago: Athletic Institute, 1969.

Schneider, D. J. Tactical self-presentation after success and failure. *Journal of Personality and Social Psychology,* 1969, *13,* 262–268.

Shaw, G. *Meat on the hoof.* New York: Dell, 1973.

Shaw, M. *Group dynamics: The psychology of small group behavior.* New York: McGraw-Hill, 1976.

Sherif, M., Harvey, O., White, B., Hood, W., & Sherif, C. *Intergroup conflict and cooperation: The robbers cave experiment.* Norman: Institute of Group Relations, University of Oklahoma, 1961.

Skinner, B. F. *Beyond freedom and dignity.* New York: Vintage, 1971.

Smith, M. D. Sport and collective violence. In D. W. Ball & J. W. Joy (Eds.), *Sport and the social order.* Reading, Mass.: Addison-Wesley, 1975.

Spencer, H. *The principles of psychology.* New York: Appleton, 1873. (Cited in H. C. Lehman & P. A. Witty, *The psychology of play activities.* New York: A. S. Barnes, 1927).

Storr, A. *Human aggression.* New York: Atheneum, 1970.

Tannenbaum, P. H., & Zillmann, D. Emotional arousal in the facilitation of aggression through communication. In L. Berkowitz (Ed.), *Advances in experimental social psychology.* New York: Academic Press, 1975.

Thompkins, W. G. Cited in H. Edwards, *Sociology of sports.* Homewood, Ill.: Dorsey, 1973.

Trippett, F. A special report on the way you play: The ordeal of fun. *Look,* July 29, 1969, pp. 24–34.

Tutko, T. Cited in H. Edwards, *Sociology of sport.* Homewood, Ill.: Dorsey, 1973.

Tutko, T. A., & Bruns, W. *Winning is everything and other American myths.* New York: Macmillan, 1976.

Tutko, T., & Richards, J. W. *Psychology of coaching.* Boston: Allyn & Bacon, 1971.

Veblen, T. *Theory of the leisure class.* New York: Modern Library, 1934.

Watson, J. B. *Behaviorism.* New York: W. W. Norton, 1925.

Weiss, P. *Sport: A philosophical inquiry.* Carbondale and Edwardsville: Southern Illinois University Press, 1969.

White, R. Ego and reality in psychoanalytic theory: A proposal regarding independent ego energies. Monograph II, *Psychological Issues* (Vol. 3). New York: International Universities Press, 1963.

Williams, R. M., Jr. *American society.* New York: Knopf, 1970.

Zajonc, R. B. Attitudinal effects of mere exposure. *Journal of Personality and Social Psychology Monograph Supplement,* 1968, *9,* 1–27.

Zander, A., & Havelin, A. Social comparison and interpersonal attraction. *Human Relations,* 1960, *13,* 21–32.

Zimbardo, P. G. The human choice: Individuation, reason, and order versus deindividuation, impulse, and chaos. In W. J. Arnold & D. Levine (Eds.), *Nebraska Symposium on Motivation.* Lincoln: University of Nebraska Press, 1969.

10 Aggression and Sport

George Gaskell
*London School of Economics
and Political Science*

Robert Pearton
*St. Mary's College
University of London*

INTRODUCTION

In this chapter, for which we take equal responsibility, we have interpreted "aggression and sport" more widely than in the typical literature, where it is interpreted as the study of aggression with sport. Although we, too, analyze aggression within sport, we broaden the discussion to encompass aggression around sport, because it appears to us that not only are these two aspects essentially interrelated but that much of the current social concern stems from the increasing use of sport situations as the loci for violence. We have found it necessary to question some of the assumptions and clarify some of the concepts that have been used in both the experimental and theoretical approaches to aggression. We are also concerned with the importance of sport as a social phenomenon worthy of serious attention by social scientists, and we discuss some of the methodological consequences that this implies.

GEORGE GASKELL is lecturer in social psychology at the London School of Economics and was a member of the Open University Course Team for Social Psychology. Articles published by Dr. Gaskell have been on various topics including decision making, interpersonal perception, leisure, vandalism, and group dynamics. He was academic director of a television program on soccer hooliganism for the Open University.

ROBERT PEARTON is Senior Lecturer at St. Mary's College, University of London, with special responsibility for University Courses in the sociology of sport. Dr. Pearton is a founder member of the B.S.A. Study Group on Leisure and Recreation and a member of the British Physical Education Association Study Group of Sociology of Physical Education. He is a former international sportsman.

History suggests that violence is one of the most ubiquitous characteristics of man. In the 20th century, there has been an escalation in the scale of wars to a global level and a sophistication of weaponry such that the capacity to annihilate humanity lies in the throw of a switch. And yet a broad historical perspective indicates that, in many aspects of day-to-day living, societies are now less violent than in earlier times. The decline in levels of interpersonal violence is part of a civilizing process. This has at the same time increased peoples' sensitivity and changed their standards and expectations, so that recent increases in various forms of crime, and the infiltration of violence into areas of life traditionally regarded as protected, have generated the current concern with the problem of violence and destruction. Zimbardo (1969) makes the point that even God is no longer sacrosanct, having observed some 67 churches and synagogues in one area of New York City vandalized in a period of 6 months.

Historical analysis suggests that sport has been influenced by the civilizing process. The violence that once characterized football and the prize fights has become unacceptable, and a whole range of sports emphasizing skill and dexterity rather than brute strength has evolved. Sport is now popularly conceived of as being both socially and personally beneficial and an area in which violence has come to have no place. The central ideology of the Olympic Movement, for example, is that sport makes for peace, engendering greater levels of goodwill and international understanding. In the words of Philip Noel-Baker (1964), "[international sport] has become a powerful influence for the better international understanding by which alone stable peace may one day be established [p. 3]." The 1200 years of uninterrupted competition in the Ancient Olympic Games contrasts starkly with the checkered history of the Modern Games—80 years old, twice cancelled because of world war, and increasingly penetrated by violence or the consequences of violence to the point that protection of the competitors at the Montreal Olympics involved the Canadian armed forces in their biggest operation since the end of World War II. The activities of extremists and terrorists against which this security operation was mounted are not simply news items from some distant parts of the world. From Rome to Rio, from Bonn to Bogota, political and revolutionary violence is an established aspect of crime. Urban guerilla activities in the United Kingdom—in the form of political assassination, the bombing of public places, kidnapping, and sectarian murder—make violence and its impact a feature of everyday life. The baggage check, weapon detector, and body search, experiences that until even recent times would have surprised an international air traveller, are now part of the domestic scene.

As yet, much of the alarm about violence in society is the result not solely of the activities of political extremists and professional criminals but of violence among the general populace and particularly among the young. Many people

are concerned, because this violence seems motiveless, because it seems to have grown despite higher levels of material wealth, and because of the facility with which society appears to accept and adjust to it. Furthermore, sophisticated forms of communication, particularly television, bring both local and international incidents into the homes of millions and serve to heighten sensitivity.

In the United Kingdom, rates for some crimes increased consistently throughout the 1960s. The most dramatic increases were in juvenile offenses, including theft, drunkenness, vandalism, and robberies with violence, which increased 2½-fold during the decade. In 1974, deliberately started school fires cost £5 million in insurance payouts, and in the Inner London Education Authority area alone, the bill for replacing and repairing the objects of school vandalism was £2.2 million. The wanton destruction of property, particularly public property in the form of pay phones, bus shelters, and train seats, has been frequently highlighted in the media as fuel for a campaign for stronger sanctions.

In other ways, though, the media put across a very different kind of message in which violence is normalized and aggression pays off. Our daily television diet is liberally spiced with gunfights, car smashes, punch-ups, extortion, and gratuitous terror in which even the good guy has to kill to win—and kill with an emotional detachment such that the enjoyment of his next drink, joke, or night on the town is unimpaired. The big screen, in the name of cinema verité, offers us more and more violence, blood and guts, and a glimpse into our future—with films like *Rollerball*, in which killing becomes a game between athletes, and *Death Race 2,000*, in which the killing is unhampered by rules—because the victims are ordinary pedestrians on the streets. Increases in juvenile crime, in vandalism and violence, appear to be a feature of other industrialized societies. Zimbardo gives a number of examples from the United States and sets out in his paper the statistics for New York City. Many European countries both West and East have also reported sharp increases in delinquency during the last decade.

Nowhere has the media campaign against juvenile crime in the United Kingdom been more forcibly stated than in the condemnation of soccer hooliganism, the rowdy destructive and occasionally violent behavior of young supporters. In other ways, too, violence in and around sport is giving increasing cause for concern. Serious on-pitch offenses in the Football League increased by over 75% between 1960 and 1970 and led subsequently to the "referees clampdown" of 1971. Officials of the Amateur Rugby Union are concerned about the encroachment of gratuituous violence into a game already finely balanced between vigorous physical contact and aggression, and a game, too, in which the balance has always depended ultimately upon the self-restraint of the players. In South America, soccer riots have led to the electrification of fences to keep the crowds from the players, but even electric

fences could not have prevented the "soccer war" between Honduras and El Salvador that followed a World Cup qualifying match between the two countries in 1972. International cricket conferences meet in an attempt to regulate the use of body line bowling, following a test match incident in New Zealand in 1975 in which a delivery deliberately aimed at the body of a New Zealand batsman hit him just underneath the heart. Only emergency medical treatment saved his life.

In January, 1975, the increasing violence of professional ice hockey was marked by the first criminal proceeding in the United States against a sportsman for conduct performed within the playing area. Forbes, a member of the Boston Bruins, was indicted for aggravated assault with a dangerous weapon. The events leading to the indictment were as follows. Forbes checked Boucha, of the Minnesota North Stars, against the boards with his elbows up, and Boucha retaliated by punching Forbes. During the 7-minute penalty, the players exchanged remarks and on returning to the ice, Forbes took a swing at Boucha, who was hit with the butt end of the stick and fell to the ice, covering his seriously injured face. Forbes leapt on Boucha and punched him until the two were separated. Boucha needed 25 stitches to close the stick-inflicted wound, and surgery was performed to repair a fracture in the floor of his right eye socket.

The current focus of attention upon sport must be seen partially as a reaction against the violation of an area of social life traditionally regarded as a totally inappropriate context for violence. It is, too, the consequence of a growing realization that sport is ill-equipped to deal with violence and to administer effective sanctions. This is the point that emerges from the ice hockey incident already mentioned. Kuhlmann (1975), writing in the *Wisconsin Law Review,* argues that although a certain amount of physical injury will inevitably result from ice hockey games, it can usually be controlled effectively within the sport, in the context of the rules. However, where violence results in serious injury, the sanctions of the sport are ineffective. They do not offer appropriate compensation, nor do they act as a deterrent. In other words, rules that suspend those of the "real world" are not powerful enough to deal with "real-world" transgressors. The answer, says Kuhlmann, may be prosecution in the courts not only for the guilty player but for the coach and employer, who may be criminally responsible through conspiracy statutes. "Perhaps," Kuhlmann (1975) suggests, "the limit of tolerable violence in sports has been reached [p. 790]."

SOCIAL SCIENCE AND SPORTS VIOLENCE

Not surprisingly, hand-in-hand with the escalation of violence in our times has grown the belief that social science has an important contribution to make towards solving the problem; and one can readily identify this as part of a

wider movement toward the problem-solving and policy-making role of the social sciences in an industrial society. The study of aggression has occupied scholars from a wide range of disciplines, and theoretical proposals on the origins, causes, control, and release of aggression cover an equally wide spectrum.

The majority of the empirical research is, however, psychological in nature and has consequently focused upon the individual. A simple laboratory experiment of this kind involves two conditions. Subjects are either shown a film of a brutal boxing match or a film of an exciting track race. Following this, the subjects take part in an apparently unrelated experiment on learning. Here the experimenter asks the naive subject to act as the teacher and to give electric shocks to a learner (a confederate of the experimenter) each time he or she makes a mistake. Of course, no shocks are actually given, but the naive subject does not know this. When the learner makes a mistake, which is regularly, the teacher can select any one of 10 levels of intensity of shock. The duration and intensity of the shock are recorded and taken as operational measures of aggression. Typically, those who have watched the boxing match administer more intense and longer shocks than those who watched the track race. Thus it is concluded that watching aggression leads to increased aggression. A number of modifications on this basic theme have been used. In one, subjects are made to feel angry by receiving apparently gratuitous insults from a technician; in another, they receive shocks themselves. Following these provocations, they view either the aggressive or neutral film and then administer shocks to the person who annoyed them. The purpose of these experiments is to isolate the variables that are thought to be causally related to aggressive behavior and to produce a situation with maximum impact on the subjects such that the predictions of rival theories can be tested. All too often, however, the manipulations are assumed to make people angry and the measures assumed to be indicants of aggression.

Although it is not our intention to denigrate the efforts of laboratory researchers, we feel it is important to point out that the study of aggression in real-life situations has been seriously neglected. No research design that simply places subjects in artifical environments and requires them to convert stimulus inputs into measurable outputs can be generalized to real-life situations, when the situation, and the principle that the individual is actively interpreting that situation, are not part of the equation. It is our contention that there is a need for more research in natural settings (cf. Webb, Campbell, Schwartz, & Sechrest, 1966). The consequence of such an orientation is (1) a greater stress upon interpersonal behavior in everyday group activities, and (2) an attempt to see the situation as the social actor sees it, thereby emphasizing social-psychological and sociological perspectives.

It is in that context that we view the importance of the study of aggression and sport. Despite a serious lack of interest in sport as an area for investigation on the part of social scientists, it has much potential for fruitful

and consequential research. Its neglect by social scientists is due largely to the belief that sport is outside real life, trivial and unrelated to more important social phenomena. This nominalistic bias is reinforced by more pervasive social philosophies that accord physical activity an inferior status to cerebral and aesthetic. Social science, which in its development into a number of disciplines of academic respectability has proved to be somewhat conservative in perspective, has duly focused attention upon what its exponents have viewed as the serious, the weighty, and the problematic in society.

Yet sport is among the most universal and pervasive of activities, of central importance in the lives of millions of people, be they participants or spectators, and, as this analysis of aggression and sport will show, interpenetrating many other areas of life at both personal and societal levels. This is not the place for a lengthy justification for the study of sport, which has been presented elsewhere (cf. Dunning, 1971; Loy & Kenyon, 1969; Weiss, 1971). Our point is that the serious study of sport is justified not only by its importance in our society and the wide range of problematic issues it encompasses but by the opportunity it offers the social scientist to undertake research in natural settings. The idea that sport is unreal, self-contained, and frivolous is, we would suggest, the result of an overtrivialized treatment by social scientists, a consideration of its surface features only, and a neglect of its symbolic dimensions. It is precisely because, in controlled and microcosmic ways, sport and what goes on in sport represents the real business of living that it has such potential. This, as we have suggested, has methodological consequences. It means that we must forsake the rigor and reliability of the laboratory in favor of the complexity of the actual settings in which sport takes place.

Another value-bias that permeates sport is the long-standing conviction that sport is good, and, as we have suggested, this is not only built into Olympic ideology at international level but pervades sport at every level. It is, for example, absolutely central to the rationale of sport programs in education; and as we show in our analysis of soccer hooliganism, there is a great reluctance from within sport to accept that sport may in some ways be associated with socially unacceptable behaviors. We have observed elsewhere (Pearton & Holliday, Note 1) that more battles may have been started on the playing fields of Eton than were ever won there. The belief that sport yields only positive benefits must be regarded problematically and the concept of sport, itself, viewed in more discriminating ways.

Much confusion surrounds the concepts of aggression and sport. There is a sense in which sport may be used as a generic, all-embracing term, as befits its institutionalized status. Under the umbrella of sport as an institution are a whole range of activities that have common characteristics. Thus, sports may be defined as rational playful activities characterized by gross muscular movement, competition, agreed-upon rules and criteria for deciding a winner.

While there are many activities which display these characteristics, there are important ways in which they are very different. It would seem relevant to distinguish between combat sports, contact sports, and noncontact sports. Boxing, it is clear, offers more opportunity for aggression than football, and football more opportunity than volleyball. The distinction between individual and team sports is also important and particularly in the context of the spectator. Heinila (1970) and Kleinman (Note 2) suggest, for example, that ingroup identification and outgroup rejection are stronger among sports crowds watching teams than those watching individual competitors.

Another important distinction that should be applied is the level at which the actual game is played. We can clearly recognize a kick about in the park as football, and a sandlot game as baseball, but they represent low levels of rule enactment and enforcement and a high proportion of intrinsic satisfaction. Conversely, the World Cup Final and the final match of the World Series involve rigid rule enforcement, formal organization and considerable extrinsic rewards. We can regard these examples as the polarities on a continuum of games within each sport, in this case the sports of football and baseball—a continuum on which any particular game should be located in an analysis of sport and aggression. It does seem to us, for example, that the professional foul in soccer was born at top level in the English Football League and was the child of the legal decision to abolish maximum wages for players, thus increasing dramatically the extrinsic rewards to be had at top levels of play. Such considerations are essential in an analysis of aggression and sport.

We define aggression as "behavior in which there is intention to injure another." It is the resultant of a number of forces acting both within and upon the individual at the same time. These are:

1. Instigation—a drive or motivation toward the performance of aggressive behavior;
2. Inhibition—tendencies within the individual against aggression but also perhaps toward some positive, nonaggressive act; and
3. Situational factors—the immediate environmental circumstances that may serve to facilitate or inhibit aggression.

Most theorists would agree with a simple model of aggression that proposes that aggression is the result of two sets of opposing motivational forces—on the one hand, the personal and situational factors that facilitate aggression, and on the other, the personal and situational factors that inhibit aggression. However, most theorists would certainly disagree as to the relative importance of each of these contributory forces, and, more fundamentally, as to the nature of each. The intention to aggress may exist in the absence of overt behavior, and indeed, this is an important dimension of instigation

analysis. However, our central concern as social scientists is with overt behavior. This definition encompasses aggression against a nonhuman or an inanimate object if the intention is injury to a person, because the intention may not be "successfully" realized or may be displaced or sublimated. Not included in our definition of aggression are acts that cause pain but in which the intention to do harm is lacking, as in surgery or in accidents.

This definition also clarifies the two factors that cause a great deal of semantic confusion in the literature on sport and aggression: namely, motivation and physical contact. Despite the popular notion that the player with a strong desire to win is an "aggressive player," a high level of motivation is not itself evidence of aggressiveness. Neither is vigorous physical contact of the kind that characterizes many sports aggressive unless it has, as an objective, deliberately intentioned injury. A strong tackle in football is not aggressive. "Going over the ball" intentionally to strike one's opponent's shins is. In fact, all sports have rules circumscribing the use of physical contact and penalizing not only aggressive play but unintentioned breaches of the rules that result from clumsiness, mistiming, etc. An analysis of aggression and sport will clearly have to take account of such distinctions.

THEORETICAL ANALYSES OF
AGGRESSION AND SPORTS

What theories have been formulated to explain aggression and what are their implications for sport? There are two basic themes concerning the origins of aggression. On the one hand, aggression is viewed as instinctive and inevitable; on the other hand, it is considered to be the result of learning and a product of the environment. Popular with the layman is the instinctive, or biological view that is championed by the ethologists Lorenz (1966) and Ardrey (1966). They claim, on the basis of extensive animal studies, that since aggression, like other animal behaviors, is instinctive and a requirement of species survival, and since man evolved from the lower animals, then instigation to aggression must be an instinct in man too.

Inhibition is similarly instinctive, but whereas in animals inhibitory processes are regulators of aggression such that conspecific injury is rare, in the human race the rapid evolution of technological prowess, and in particular the development of sophisticated weapons, have resulted in capacities to aggress overriding the instinctive inhibitions. Man, consequently, has become the "killer ape"—the only regular and habitual killer of his own species.

Since aggression is instinctive, it must have an outlet, otherwise it will build up like steam in a boiler. Because man's regulating equipment has not kept pace with his aggression, society must find periodic outlets that will serve as

social safety-valves. This rather pessimistic view of humanity has great popularity, partly because of the most readable accounts of the ethologists' work, but partly, no doubt, because our history does rather seem to confirm the validity of the argument. It would seem that the idea that "man is doomed by his genes" has much appeal as an alternative to examining one's conscience, accepting responsibility for one's actions and applying self-control.

There have been a number of criticisms of the ethological argument. There is a large body of evidence showing that animal behaviors are not solely determined by biological factors, and that even instinctive behavior patterns depend upon the presence of appropriate external stimuli for their expression. There is much controversy over the extent to which animals are instinctively aggressive. Binford (1972), Montagu (1968) and Russell (Note 3) have argued that ethologists have very little supportive evidence from animal studies in natural settings and that aggression in captivity is related to crowding and the consequent breakdown of the social order.

There is concern, too, at the extrapolation of results of ethological studies to humans. To argue, for example, that home ownership fulfills a similar function in a person as territoriality in animals entails a conceptual leap that many behavioral scientists are hesitant to make. Moreover, in the context of aggression, there is clear evidence of great diversity among human cultures, and even of nonviolent cultures, "appollonians," as Benedict (1924) called them. It is apparent that environmental factors cannot be ignored. Goldstein (1975) concludes his review of the evidence thus: "to argue that, because man can behave like lower organisms, this is the way he must behave, is fallacious [p. 5]."

The emphasis upon biological aspects of aggression has received some support from organic scientists working on brain stimulation and resultant physiological change. It is widely accepted that anger has recognized physiological concomitants, including increased activity in the lateral hypothalamus of the brain, increased secretion from the adrenal glands and a rise in systolic blood pressure—the body, in other words, becomes physiologically aroused. Research on electrical and chemical brain stimulation suggests that, in both animals and man, aggression can be artifically stimulated, and some authors have taken this evidence as proof that aggression is therefore only a matter of biology. In a similar vein, the "XYY Syndrome"—that is, the presence of an additional Y chromosome in an above-average proportion of criminally violent males—has been proposed as evidence of biological determinism. The argument is susceptible to the same criticisms that are leveled at the ethologists. The fact that there is an observed physiological process at work says nothing about the factors that cause its activation.

While the recent work of ethologists has restated the biological basis of aggression, it was formerly proposed by Freud who saw aggression as a manifestation of the death instinct, that, along with eros, the life instinct, is responsible for human motivation. This view of aggression has been developed by a number of psychoanalysts who have reached conclusions similar to those of Lorenz about the importance, for personal and societal safety, of period discharges of aggression. However, psychoanalysis departs from the ethological argument with respect to inhibition. Inhibitions are developed out of interaction with the environment; for the individual as the result of early familial relationships and the subsequent development of the superego, and societally as the result of enculturation. It is not possible to rid man of his aggressive impulses but they may be diverted and channeled so that man will not inevitably behave destructively. It becomes, of course, very difficult to test a theory like this. It shares with the ethological theory the idea that aggression is genetically part of us and has the appeal of both simplicity and generality, but it is not susceptible to empirical test.

In contrast to the instinct theories, the "frustration–aggression hypothesis" proposed by Dollard et al. (1939) emphasizes the role of acquired drives and motives in aggressive behavior and, consequently, has generated much interest among behavioral scientists. In its original form the theory proposed that aggressive activity was always the consequence of frustration—a condition that results from interference with a personal objective—and, conversely, that such frustration will always result in an arousal of the desire to aggress. This desire to aggress need not be manifested in aggressive behavior since it is essentially an internal mechanism. Moreover, the likelihood of punishment serves to inhibit aggression toward the source of frustration. However, the aggression is not destroyed, it is displaced, delayed or disguised. Your boss gives you a rough day—you go home and kick the dog, because aggressing against your boss is inhibited by the chance that you might lose your job. This is but one of the ways of venting aggression on something or somebody who can't retaliate. This, the early theorists termed "displacement": a change in the form of aggression. Having aggressed, either directly or indirectly, against the source of frustration, the person experiences a reduction in the drive to aggress. The frustration–aggression hypotheses have been much criticized and have subsequently been modified in a number of ways. While many advocates of the theory regard frustration as the necessary antecedent of aggression, research has shown that attack, physical pain, or noxious stimulation can also lead to aggression because, in a similar way to frustration, these increase arousal. Since frustration is not the sole antecedent of aggression but merely one in a list, the original theory loses much of its power. Despite the fact that little research has been done on sources of frustration, researchers still feel safe in invoking its existence arguing that "he must have been frustrated, because he behaved aggressively."

While the frustration–aggression hypothesis assumes that aggression is the consequence of certain environmental conditions, it shares with the ethological and psychoanalytic perspectives the view of aggression as general and inevitable. For Lorenz and Freud, the instigation to aggress is instinctive, for Dollard and his associates, it is seen as a drive that once aroused, must have an outlet. All three theories predict that an act of aggression serves to reduce the drive. This is the principle of catharsis. Furthermore, it is held that through displacement, aggressive behavior may be channeled, diverted and controlled. It is in this context that the importance of sport as an agency for personal and social control is held to lie. Since sport is an ideal way to let off steam, it is argued that sport is cathartic, a safety valve, through which aggression may be channelled in harmless ways. Consequently, those popular sports that stress competition and entail vigorous physical contact are generally thought to serve highly desirable societal objectives. It is also claimed that witnessing such sports produces, by empathy, the same results so that the more aggressive the event the healthier it is considered to be (see Chapter 11, by Zillmann et al.). This was the purpose of the Roman arena, and could be the rationale of bullfighting, and of trends in the media to which we have already referred. For Lorenz, the principal value of competitive sport lies in its capacity to stand in place of "that most indispensable and, at the same time, most dangerous form of aggression... collective militant enthusiasm [p. 242]." International representative sport is therefore a "war without weapons" but a war in which both victory and defeat are symbolic— even the loser lives to fight another day. In the words of Storr (1968), "rivalry between nations in sport can do nothing but good [p. 132]." At a more domestic level, Gerth and Mills (1954) consider that "great volumes of aggression are cathartically released by crowds of spectators cheering their favorite stars of sport—and jeering the umpire [p. 63]." Competitive sport is for man an important arena for ritualized aggression.

In order to support this view it has to be accepted that involvement in sport, either directly as competitors or vicariously as supporters, makes people less aggresssive. But surely sport's capacity to serve as catharsis would be limited to those activities where some form of aggression occurs. However, as we have already pointed out, aggression in sport is highly prescribed by the rules. Opportunities to aggress regularly in sport are not common and many of the claims for the potential for sport to serve in this manner must be ascribed in the first instance to conceptual confusion. Nevertheless, having made that point we can still ask whether physical contact, or some other aspect of the sport situation, may produce catharsis, through the process of displacement. Certainly this is assumed in the theoretical perspectives to which we have referred. This, of course, amounts to a dramatic change in the concept of displacement. In its original form the concept referred to object displacement —that is, to the possibility that aggression could be diverted towards another

object. In putting the case for catharsis through sport though, what is being proposed is that aggression can be "displaced" onto nonaggressive activity, which will then serve to reduce the drive. That is the kind of conceptual ambiguity that characterizes much of the theoretical underpinning of aggression. It is because of the circularity of much of the argument that such convenient modification can be made, without seeming to endanger the original thesis.

Furthermore, since sport is, by definition, competitive, doesn't sport have a built-in capacity to frustrate? This question is worth posing in terms of sport generally since winning always presupposes somebody else losing, but it is worth asking, too, in more discriminating ways. For example, the manner in which the result was achieved may be important. Losing may be a cause for frustration through loss of self-esteem, but it may be greater when there is a strong expectation of success, or stronger still when success seems to have been "stolen" by a bad refereeing decision, a lucky shot, or a deflection. The likelihood of frustration may be even greater at upper levels of competition which may, as we have suggested, involve significant amounts of personal or national investment, or where success results in considerable extrinsic rewards. It is one of our observations, for example, that soccer hooliganism is positively correlated with league status, and while we do not suggest that other factors need not be considered, it is an important relationship to account for.

There have been a number of laboratory experiments on competition, defeat, and counteraggression. Gaebelin and Taylor (1971) suggest that while competition increases the readiness of participants to respond aggressively, aggressive behavior depends upon specific situational stimuli. Ryan (1970) found that defeated subjects were more likely to aggress than winners, but Taylor and Epstein (1967) found no relationship between victory or defeat and aggression. We would emphasize again the need to assess sport in a more discriminatory way. In testing the hypothesis, for example, that vigorous physical activity produces catharsis, it would seem reasonable to distinguish between contact and noncontact sports. Unfortunately, distinctions of this kind do not typify the laboratory settings which characterize most of the research and not surprisingly, therefore, results of experiments on sport as catharsis are conflicting. In fact, there is evidence to suggest that vigorous physical contact and aggression are positively correlated.

Such a finding is consistent with Bandura and Walters' (1963) thesis that aggressive responses are learned like any other social behavior. In the social learning theory, aggression is the consequence, not of an instinct, or innate disposition, but of observing and imitating others, and especially those of high status. Aggression is related to the prevalence of aggressive models, the extent to which their behavior is condoned and the degree to which its imitation is rewarded. Learning aggressive behaviors is, therefore, part of the

socialization process and parents and peers are important models. Other subtle factors of a pervasive nature may also be influential such as trends in the media, war games and toys, and aspects of the teaching of history. As a result of these processes, the balance of which will vary according to the cultural milieu, an individual may learn to respond aggressively or nonaggressively to particular stimuli, including frustration. While aggression may, in some instances, be the learned response to frustration, it need not be so. Furthermore, aggression may occur not only without anger but also in the absence of frustration (e.g., soldiers in training). Such aggression Buss (1961) defines as instrumental to distinguish it from self assertive reactions where anger and arousal are typically associated.

Social learning theory does not embrace the principle of catharsis as drive reduction. Far from channelling aggression in harmless ways, aggressive acts and displays serve to normalize, heighten, and reinforce aggressive behavior. This has been forcefully demonstrated by Bandura (1965) in a series of studies on childrens' imitation of adult aggression. In front of children an adult verbally and physically assaulted a large inflatable doll. One group of children saw the adult rewarded while another group saw the adult punished. When the children played with the doll the former group imitated the aggressive behaviors but the latter group did not. However, when an inducement was offered for copying the models all the children showed a high level of imitation. Thus a distinction between learning and performance must be drawn. All the children learned the aggressive behaviors but those who saw the model punished were inhibited from performing in an aggressive way until they themselves were rewarded for so doing. It was also apparent that the children did not confine themselves to mere imitation but invented new and creative forms of aggression. Some aspects of sport have the potential to heighten aggression, especially where the violation of rules meets with approval and success. It is in this context that the increase in violent play that has characterized a number of sports gives cause for concern. Such violence not only contaminates sport itself but may also spill over to other behaviors. This may apply not only to the participant but also to the spectator since closely witnessing contest sports will tend to raise rather than lower levels of personal excitement or arousal.

A combination of arousal and aggressive modeling may be an even greater stimulus for aggression. Berkowitz (1962) has drawn from the theories of frustration–aggression and social learning and stresses the importance of both frustration and environmental factors. In his thesis, the likelihood of aggression is a joint function of the person's internal readiness to aggress and the presence of external cues that elicit the aggression and provide a target These assumptions have been tested by Berkowitz and Geen (1966) using procedures outlined previously. Subjects were either angered or treated neutrally and then shown films of either a brutal boxing match or an exciting

track race. In addition, an attempt was made to manipulate the cue value of the provocateurs by naming one of them after a character in the boxing match. The combined effects of anger, aggressive modeling from the film and aggressive labeling produced the highest level of aggression.

Berkowitz, too, questions the cathartic value of aggression. While an angered person may feel better after lashing out, this very act will tend to increase the probability of subsequently behaving in a similar way, since the target's cue value for aggression will have increased. The balance of evidence from theories of aggression is that sports involvement may heighten arousal, produce instances of aggressive behaviors and their reward, and provide a context in which the emulation of such behaviors is condoned. Thus, the idea that sport moderates levels of personal aggression must be ranged against the possibility that it may serve to foster aggressive behavior.

It is because the catharsis hypothesis was formulated in such a specific way and then subsequently invoked to mean all things to all men that its utility as a concept has been vitiated. Yet, we would contend that its unnecessarily narrow interpretation by theorists as the counter to arousal and excitement masks its potential value. The earliest formulation of the catharsis concept may be attributed to Aristotle who embodies in his theory of leisure the notion that music and tragedy have purging and curative effects that can restore mental balance and well-being in a way similar to that produced physiologically by medicine. However, for Aristotle, this potential was two-way, not only functioning as an outlet for the harmful and the undesirable or as a calming effect in the case of overexcitement, but as a means of lifting depression, stimulating excitement and creating pleasure. Man might be safely brought down from the dizzy and dangerous heights but could also be brought up from the dismal and equally dangerous depths. Excitement, stimulation, and pleasure were regarded as just as important as restraint and tension release, at least to men of Aristotle's day. Post-Hellenic civilization, with its strong prescription of puritanism, suggests not so much a change in the fundamental nature of man but a change in perspective; a partially obscured view that saw only the harmful effects of excitement and pleasure-seeking. This perspective, deep-rooted in our dominant philosophies, is apparent in the scientific bias evident in the literature. Physiological studies have focused almost entirely on the effects of tension build-up through deprivation of desired objectives—on unpleasurable kinds of excitement, while, until recently psychologists have similarly viewed tension as harmful and a condition to be avoided. The sociological perspective has been to juxtapose work with leisure, and in viewing the former as the necessary, worthwhile and ennobling activity of life, it has reduced the latter to a position of dependency; as rest, recuperation or diversion from work.

Elias and Dunning (1970) in their paper entitled "The Quest for Excitement in Unexciting Societies," take up the Aristotelian concept of catharsis and

suggest its relevance to modern industrial societies. Modern industrial society is unexciting, they suggest, in necessitating degrees of restraint and levels of interdependence such that spontaneous and elementary excitement have been progressively restricted. It is in these circumstances that the compensatory function of play–excitement has increased. Societally and personally, excitement generated in this way has beneficial effects and is harmless because, although the physiological effects of "mimetic" excitement are the same as those of excitement generated in real-life situations, the psychological and social consequences are different. According to Elias and Dunning (1970): "In serious excitement men are liable to lose control of themselves and become a threat. Mimetic excitement is socially and personally without danger and can have a cathartic effect (p. 41)." Catharsis, then, is the result of tension—arousal as well as tension-reduction. Elias and Dunning illustrate their analysis with reference to the effects of watching football. In doing so they make a case for sport as a natural and advantageous source of knowledge, because these aspects of the game which make for mimetic excitement are most easily observed. Watching football allows for the opportunity to build up tension pleasurably through a process of interaction between players and spectators. Kaelin (1968) makes a similar point: The "well-played game" is the result of "building up tension, sustaining and complicating and ultimately releasing the percipient into a state of peace (p. 26)." Structural variations between sports give them different capacities for generating such excitement and within any particular sport there are specific situational factors that make some games and encounters more arousing than others, such as the importance of the contest, or the extent to which spectators identify with the players. It is a matter for further research to investigate more fully the features that determine this cathartic potential (see Chapter 11).

In reviewing the empirical evidence on aggression and sports, it is pertinent to draw a distinction between the participant and the spectator. There is, however, a paucity of substantial empirical evidence on either topic, a paucity that attests to the contempt for academic studies in this area. We have already argued for the more serious treatment of sport and, in presenting this review, we discuss further avenues of research that might prove useful.

The psychometric approach has dominated studies of the sports participant and the search for the personality profile of the successful sportsman has been a dominant interest of psychologists. The underlying assumption of this research is not dissimilar to early social psychological investigation of leadership, which was based on the idea that leaders possess a unique and characteristic personality style. It was thought that if this personality could be isolated and described, using psychological testing, then in future, leaders could be selected on the basis of their possession of these important traits. In this way, industry, government and the armed forces

could ensure that the most competent took positions of authority. In some 1500 studies of leaders and followers, Gibb (1947) found few consistently differentiating personality traits. Leaders appear to be slightly more intelligent and better adjusted than followers but little else. While many believe that the skills of leadership are innate, psychological research has been unable to substantiate this prevalent view.

In sports psychology, a similar argument has lead to attempts to isolate the personality of the successful participant, and there have been a large number of studies comparing successful with less successful competitors. In general terms, a personality profile of the successful sportsman has emerged in which he is described in terms of persistence, dominance, conscientiousness, extraversion and aggression. Using a wide variety of personality inventories, including Cattell's 16 P.F. (1957), Ogilvie and Tutko (1964) have studied Olympic swimmers, track athletes, volleyball players, motor racing drivers and many other top level competitors. In terms of the 16 P.F. results, successful sportsmen were high on factor E (dominance), F (surgency), I (toughmindedness)—indicating general aggressiveness—and on C (stability), O (confidence) and Q_2 (self sufficiency). In England, Kane (1970) has corroborated many of these findings and concludes that they allow for a working description of the sportsman as a stable and aggressive extrovert. But in drawing this conclusion, Kane points to the problematic nature of this type of research. Does long-term engagement in sport in some way shape the athlete's personality or does success depend in large measure on the possession of certain inherited personality characteristics? As with all correlational studies, the direction of causation is equivocal. If aggression is a characteristic of the successful sportsman, is this due to a diet of intensive training and competition, or is it, in some way, part of the general personality profile developed before entering the world of sports? Ogilvie and Tutko (1971) can find no empirical support for the contention that sports participation molds character and conclude that their findings reflect the ruthless selection process that occurs in sports. If you have not got the appropriate personality, then you will never make it to the top. Ismail and Tratchman (1976) champion the alternative view and propose a general thesis that personality can change as a result of confronting a difficult challenge and overcoming it. In a study of unfit university staff, they found small changes in personality, measured by the Cattell 16 P.F., after a one month's intensive physical exercise program. However, while the thesis is interesting, their research methodology is so questionable that little credence can be given to their results. Until more sophisticated designs for research are used, the answer to the problem of sport and personality will remain unresolved. It does seem hard to believe that a particular personality type is the basis for success in sports. In fact, Kane acknowledges that there are differences in sports motivation between those in individual and team games and between

the sexes. Kenyon (1969) suggests that men seek out competition, risk-taking, exertion and ascetics while women emphasize social motivations, including social interaction, aesthetics and beauty. These findings are complemented by studies in social psychology on coalition formation in the triad, which clearly demonstrate that cooperation is the dominant strategy for women and fairness an important value, but for men competition is paramount regardless of any higher-order moral values (see Caplow, 1968).

The distinction between competitiveness and aggressiveness is an important one, and one that has lead to much confusion. Many wrongly assume that the person who is highly competitive is ipso facto aggressive. Just because successful sportsmen are high on dominance and toughmindedness does not necessarily imply, as Ogilvie and Kane contend, that they are generally more aggressive. It seems more likely that such traits are associated with competitiveness rather than intention to do harm to others.

Another source of confusion arises from attempts to understand players' behavior without considering the rules and strategies of the particular sport. In a study of German football teams, Volkamer (1971) suggests that "aggressive acts" (e.g., personal fouls) are more likely to occur when a team is losing, playing away from home, or occupies a low position in the league, when the score is low; and when a high-ranking team meets a low-ranking team. He cites the frustration–aggression hypothesis to account for these findings. However, all but the last condition are predictable without recourse to such a theoretical model. In any team game involving contact the defensive players are there to prevent the opposition from scoring. In professional soccer the unchivalrous professional foul is now part of the successful defender's repertoire. A team occupying a low position in the league is, comparatively, a losing team and losing teams generally play more defensive football than winning teams. Similarly, low scoring games imply an emphasis upon defensive football. In this latter respect the paucity of goals in European, and particularly Italian, football is attributed to the sophistication of defensive tactical methods. It is part of the strategy of professional football teams to play defensively away from home—to play for a draw. In other words, fouling may be related to defensiveness without recourse to the frustration–aggression hypothesis. Winkler (Note 4) has collected statistics for a number of years which indicate that over 75% of fouls are committed by defenders, but that in the penalty area, the most vital in defense, fouls by attackers outnumber those by defenders 20:1. This is the consequence of the utility of sanctions; giving away a free kick is not considered a severe enough sanction to prevent a foul, but giving away a penalty shot is. Fouling can be explained entirely by the strategies and rules of the game. Other research has investigated the relationship between the players' personality and their conduct on the field. Russell (1974), in a study of Canadian ice hockey, shows that defensive players are more Machiavellian (i.e., manipulative) in

interpersonal style than forwards and are also slightly more aggressive (although this latter correlation did not reach significance). However, behavioral differences between attackers and defenders in ice hockey may be related to patterns of play, as in football. It is clear that an analysis of behavior in any sport must recognize the importance of rules and tactics. All too often one reads of top soccer players being incapacitated in the first few minutes of the game, at times presumably on the specific instruction of the coach, of unskilled boxers making up for lack of skill by head butting and eye gouging, and ice hockey teams like the Philadelphia Flyers, who by their own admission are lacking in skills and resort to physical violence in attempts to draw crowds and pulverize the opposition. Such incidents cannot be attributed to personality defects of the players; they are a conscious and intentional strategy on the part of the individual and team to succeed by intimidation and violence.

Any attempt to link personality and sports participation is bedeviled by limitations in both the theory and measurement of personality. If a personality trait is a consistent and enduring characteristic of an individual, what does it mean to obtain a high score on aggressiveness? Is the person moderately aggressive all the time or perhaps twice as aggressive half the time? Moreover, the relationship between "what we say and what we do" (Deutscher, 1973) is problematic in social science; and, in the context of aggression research, there is little evidence to link measures of either personality or attitudes to overt aggressive behavior. Because there is no substantial evidence that sportsmen are more aggressive outside the sports arena, we contend that what aggression there is, is situation specific and probably more determined by the competitive nature of the situation and the strategies of play than by personality predisposition. We therefore consider that the search for the personality correlates of sports performance is of limited value.

Thus far, we have concentrated our analysis on top level sportsmen which inevitably ignores the vast majority of people who are involved in sports as a pastime. Nevertheless, we must not underrate the importance of understanding and controlling aggression at upper levels of performance, for it is here that standards of behavior are set. As social learning theory would predict, those at the pinnacle are the high status models for countless others, and we would suggest that there is probably a one-way influence process down the hierarchy of participation. We have already noted that financial and commercial pressures on officials and players alike make overtly aggressive behaviors on the field of play and in the arena an almost legitimate activity— especially when the players get away with it. Now while aggression in sport is not well documented, it is certainly not just a phenomenon of the 1960s and 1970s. What has changed dramatically, however, is the relationship between performers at the top and those at other levels. We believe that through

commercial activities, radio, television, and the action replay, the elites unintentionally wield more and more influence upon playing standards. The overt behavior of top-level performers is transmitted to larger and larger audiences. Thus it is that the professional foul is copied at school-boy level in a context divorced from the pressures that fostered it. It is not only the style of play that is copied here but the explicit rationale for participation—the pursuit of success.

Many have emphasized the importance of competitiveness, because, like Lorenz, they see it as "an essential part of the life preserving organization of instincts"; fighting for survival is seen as part of the evolutionary process of self-preservation. Others have argued for it on the basis of its contribution to the development of character. In many ways, success in society is equated with beating others and winning becomes an end in itself. But such an emphasis devalues cooperative action, which may well be a fundamental condition for human development (cf. G. H. Mead, 1934). It has been argued by Bronfenbrenner (1970) that Western societies give insufficient emphasis to cooperation in socialization. Although sport is competitive, cooperation is an important dimension of participating and this is particularly true for the majority of sportsmen and women who have neither the ability nor the inclination to become top level performers. For them it is the journey not the arrival that matters. If Lombardi's dictum that "winning isn't everything—it's the only thing" provides the rationale for sports participation, then many of the potential benefits to the individual will be missed. This is a matter particularly germane to schools in which the educational values of sport held to accrue from playing, however badly, are being overtaken by that of winning, thus making sport at the top level the appropriate model. The use of sport as an important medium for school prestige has lead to a concentration upon successful teams and the talented performer to the exclusion of the less able. The same shift in values is evident at the junior school level where success-dominated sports have increasingly infiltrated physical education programs; witness the growth in junior football, little league baseball, and biddy basketball. The benefits of physical education lie in providing all pupils the opportunity for vigorous physical activity, improvement of skill, cooperation with others in the performance of group tasks, and competing in controlled situations. These will be rendered less effective by too great an emphasis on winning. To encourage participation at all levels, there must be a greater choice of activities including those in which performance can be assessed not only in terms of winning but of improving personal standards. Sports have an important place in physical education since they bring people together in peaceful and enjoyable activities where habits of nonaggression and of winning and losing gracefully may be developed. Furthermore, sports are significant aspects of social life and participation provides an important entré to popular culture.

RESEARCH ON
OBSERVING SPORTS

We now discuss the research that, directly or indirectly, analyzes the impact upon the individual of watching sports. We have already indicated that evidence does not support catharsis as it has generally been defined, and we have discussed the influential social learning theory and the research which demonstrates that those watching scenes of aggression may emulate the model's aggression. However, there has not been a full test of this theory in a sports context. We examine in some detail research into soccer hooliganism that not only demonstrates alternative methodologies to laboratory experiments but also shows that aggression must be considered in a much broader social context.

It is apparent, as we suggested previously, that aggression must be viewed problematically, even in the laboratory. Berkowitz and Alioto (1973) have demonstrated that the observer's interpretation of an event involving aggression affects his or her subsequent behavior. If a filmed boxing match was defined as an aggressive encounter, in which the victor wanted to injure his opponent, rather than a clean fight between professionals, then subjects were more aggressive (i.e., gave more electric shocks) to a tormentor. Thus, viewing what is believed to be the deliberate infliction of harm produces a more aggressive reaction.

Many of these laboratory results must be interpreted with caution, particularly in the context of their generality, or relevance, to nonlaboratory situations. In the study referred to, the authors had to conclude that "the findings were not as impressive as we had hoped." In fact, differences in the amounts of aggression that followed the two conditions were trivially small. Furthermore, differences in aggressive behavior following aggressive and nonaggressive films were largely insignificant. In many experiments small but statistically significant differences in such measures as the length of time subjects press the shock button are interpreted as convincing evidence of heightened aggression. There is a world of difference between statistical and psychological significance. Unless more convincing findings come from such studies on viewing aggression, the utility of such research is open to question.

Berkowitz and Alioto do raise an important issue concerning the way in which a particular act comes to be defined as aggressive. Is there a consensus among spectators as to what constitutes an aggressive act in a sport situation? This obviously hinges on the spectators' interpretation of the players' intentions and on the events that lead up to a particular incident. Hastorf and Cantril (1954), in an ingenious study, have shown that the definition of an aggressive act is highly problematic and that there is little agreement among supporters of opposing teams as to what constitutes legitimate and illegitimate physical contact. Their research followed an end-of-season football game

between Princeton and Dartmouth in which the Princeton star player was carried off with a broken nose and concussion. Subsequently a Dartmouth player's leg was broken. After the match, which Dartmouth won, a controversy broke out as to who had instigated the hostilities, and accusations began to fly. During the weeks after the game, Hastorf and Cantril interviewed some 324 students from both colleges. Those supporting Princeton, the losers, were bitter. Nearly all judged that the game had been "rough and dirty," 86% thought that Dartmouth had started the trouble, and only 11% considered that both teams were to blame. The Dartmouth supporters held quite a different view. Over 50% judged the game as "fair," only 36% thought that their team was to blame, and the majority, 53% considered both teams equally responsible. The findings fall into a predictable pattern and demonstrate the problematic nature of defining aggressive acts. In general, people condone aggression of which they approve, relabeling it as assertiveness, and criticize those whose aggressive behavior displeases them. A systematic account of this phenomenon has been provided by Mann (1974), who has demonstrated that supporters of losing teams typically attribute defeat to external factors such as referee bias, bad luck, or the opposition's dirty play, rather than their own team's incompetence. Hastorf and Cantril's research is of great value since it is one of the few studies that attempts to get to grips with an actual incident and to elucidate the subjective nature of aggression. If we are concerned with aggression in real life we must understand what constitutes an aggressive episode. The showing of a boxing match in a laboratory is presumed to demonstrate aggression— whether the subjects view it as such is open to question.

In another field study, Goldstein and Arms (1971) used two sports contests to evaluate the catharsis, social learning, and frustration-aggression hypotheses. There were two situations: an Army versus Navy football match which the researchers defined as aggressive, and a gymnastics competition, defined as nonaggressive. Levels of hostility in spectators were measured before and after the two contests using a questionnaire devised by Buss and Durkee (1957). There were 28 questions measuring various aspects of hostility. In a comparison of before-game and after-game hostility, Goldstein and Arms showed that while there was no increase in hostility after the gymnastics competition, there was a significant increase following the football game. They also found that regardless of team support (i.e., preferring either the Army or the Navy) all the spectators at the football game became more hostile. Goldstein and Arms concluded that there was no evidence for either drive reducing catharsis—of the "Lorenz" type—or for aggression resulting from frustration. There was evidence that observing a sports game with physical contact reduces peoples' inhibitions against aggression and that this reduction in inhibition leads to increased verbal hostility.

The idea that viewing an arousing competition leads to a reduction of inhibition against normally unacceptable behaviors is an interesting one, and one that can readily be seen in everyday life. Thus, after motor racing events, many spectators leave the car parks in a manner reminiscent of the drivers on the track. However, one must be careful not to over-interpret experimental findings. Goldstein and Arms relied only on verbal responses to a questionnaire and whether increased verbal hostility in response to such a questionnaire would be translated into other types of aggression is, as we have already suggested, open to question. There is an alternative explanation for their findings. In a crowd, people can act in ways they would not contemplate at home or at work. This may be because the mood of the crowd has an infectious quality to which individuals are sensitive because they are anonymous. The nature of the sports event gives rise to such behaviors. Cheering, voicing one's opinions, arguing with other spectators and shouting at the referee and players, are commonplace activities in which even the most placid may join. The spectator enters a sphere of unreality in which the rules of everyday life are temporarily suspended and each spectator may equally voice opinions, judge excellence, and recognize no higher authority.

SOCCER HOOLIGANISM

It is in the context of these broader issues that some important research into aggression among sport's spectators has been undertaken. This research has paralled the concern of the media, the courts, and the public over the apparently ever increasing incidents of aggression among spectators at football matches in the United Kingdom. Football is the national game. Every Saturday from August through April, crowds of up to 60,000 assemble to watch each match and over 1 million watch football every weekend. Coverage of football is a major feature of both the newspapers and television. Practically every Saturday throughout the season, the media features another grim episode of what has become a national problem—soccer hooliganism. This involves activities within the soccer ground such as attacks on other spectators and the police and invasions of the pitch, as well as activities associated with travel to and from the match such as breaking up trains, smashing shop windows, and further clashes with the police. Although incidents of actual violence are rare, there is much criminal behavior. In the public's mind, soccer hooligans have replaced mods and rockers, hell's angels, and disruptive students as the current example of the malaise of youth. Magistrates pontificate regularly on the evils of these activities, and the media call for ever-increasing fines and sentences to be meted out to the offenders.

Undoubtedly, although episodes of hooliganism are not merely a feature of the last 5 years, concern over the problem has grown dramatically. Until

recently, soccer hooliganism attracted little attention from social scientists, and both the description and explanation have been monopolized by the pundits in the media. An analysis of their assessment over the last year indicates a high degree of agreement as to the diagnosis and cure of the problem. Soccer hooliganism is seen as aggressive and antisocial, perpetrated by adolescents who are not really interested in the game and concentrated in a small hard core of troublemakers in the crowd—the potentially criminal elements. It is argued that if these renegade individuals could be excluded from the ground and perhaps reformed in some penal way, then the football terraces would be safe for the vast majority of spectators who come only to watch and enjoy the game. As to the origin of this behavior, many blame the lack of discipline in the family and in schools, or the permissive society generally.

One might wonder why it is that social scientists have been so reluctant to investigate such an apparently important social problem. One of the main reasons is that it is a complex phenomenon for which no current methodology is readily available. Obviously, it would be rather difficult to carry out an experiment on a soccer crowd in vivo, and totally unrealistic to simulate a soccer crowd, with say 50 randomly selected subjects, in the laboratory. Furthermore, laboratory experimentation involves the isolation and manipulation of a limited number of known and controllable variables. In the context of soccer crowds and aggression, we neither know what the salient variables are, and even if we did, it might not be possible to control them. In any science, description must precede explanation. Hypotheses tested in vacuo are likely to be a waste of time and explanations based on hunches, prejudices, or opinions expressed in the media tend to be rather less than adequate. Unless there is some basic analytic description of the phenomenon, it is very difficult to assess the problem or the adequacy of a proposed explanation. There are far too many moralistic reformers about, particularly in the context of sport, without social scientists joining their ranks and preaching from a pseudo-scientific platform!

Before looking at two examples of research in spectator aggression, let us briefly consider the explanations that have been put forward to account for hooliganism. These are not alternatives to the general aggression theories, rather they are more specific attempts to account for a particular issue. Ultimately, an understanding of soccer hooliganism must involve some aspects of aggression theory but, for the present, the utility of these broader approaches is difficult to assess since each of them can account for the phenomenon ex post facto.

The genetic or psychometric explanations of aggression are popularly cited. It is held that individuals in the crowd suffer from a mental or psychological abnormality and commit almost psychopathic acts of violence. Such an analysis is echoed by the one-time captain of England, Bobby Moore

writing in a British national newspaper: "You've heard them. You've seen how they carry on, tainting the name of the game. I'll never understand their mindless mentality.... I've a simple message to that moronic minority who don't go to watch football and its great players, but go to fight, throw missiles at the police, invade the pitch, and make an utter nuisance of themselves. Clear Off!" Harrison (1974) found some evidence to support this position in his study of Cardiff City Football Club. He found that the leader of a gang of 14- to 16-year-olds was a 26-year-old mental retardate. What he lacked in mental ability was compensated by his size and strength. His mother is reputed to have hidden his "bovver boots" to prevent his committing aggressive and violent acts, and he describes himself, as he puts his boots on as looking forward to kicking and injuring others. Advocates of the above explanation would probably ascribe to a link between personality and criminality and support the psychological testing of at least the younger spectators in an attempt to identify the undesirable elements. But testing of convicted soccer hooligans has failed to isolate a general personality attribute that might account for their behavior (Walshe-Brennan, 1975).

Some sociologists believe that hooliganism is part of the more general delinquent and vandalistic tendencies of youth and thus no more than a currently fashionable example of the general social malaise. The current concern arises from the belief that sports should be free of such negative aspects. It is for this reason that sports administrators have been reluctant to acknowledge that hooliganism may now be an integral part of the sport, and to sponsor relevant research. Others suggest that hooliganism is related to the increased professionalization of the game and the consequent distancing of the players from the supporters (Taylor, 1971). Identification with the club is seen as an important way of maintaining a sense of belonging and group identify. Football is a sport with very strong industrial working-class origins. The majority of successful clubs are located in the northern centers of manufacturing industry. The football team is evocative of the working-class community and support for the team an acceptably masculine way of expressing community solidarity. Hooliganism is a result of demonstrating support for the team in a culture where masculine assertiveness and physical toughness are valued attributes.

Another explanation may be couched in terms of what we have labeled the risqué shift. In many groups, there are institutional opportunities to behave in not only outrageous and normally unacceptable ways but ways that would be completely reprehensible if viewed in a different light. These risqué activities are both satisfying and enjoyable for the participants and give them a "lift" from the routine of everyday life. Overdrinking, illicit drugs, office parties, motor rallying, jollities after rugby, continental holidays, and anything from fancy-dress to wife swapping parties are among activities of this kind. But for the working-class boy living in an urban center, there are few such

opportunities, and the football ground is one of the few places where he can get away from supervision and have some fun literally "knocking-about" with his mates. Interestingly, almost all convicted soccer hooligans live with their parents.

One issue that has not been aired, to our knowledge, is the impact of televised sports coverage on soccer hooliganism. During the football season at least four games are presented on television each week. Every interesting sequence of play is repeated on action replay, and all incidents of hooliganism monitored closely. This increased coverage may have two effects. Firstly, it may actually normalize hooliganism and, in presenting the worst examples, both encourage the attendance of roughnecks and set the standards of behavior for other spectators. Secondly, it is probably the case that one can see more football in one's armchair at home than at the match. In order to justify the effort of getting to a match and paying a moderate entrance fee, spectators may feel that the added ingredients of excitement provided by hooliganism lengthen the period of enjoyable arousal and make up for the effort of attending. Although these are speculations, we do believe that a more thoughtful and somewhat less moralistic and inquisitorial approach on the part of the media would be of benefit.

These explanations are neither comprehensive, nor mutually exclusive. Most are based on speculation rather than on an investigation of what actually happens at football grounds. We feel that the investigation of soccer hooliganism is typical of the challenge that the serious study of sport presents to social scientists. The problem is important socially, contains many complex sociological and psychological parameters, and is fairly common-place. The issue confronting the interested social scientist is that no particular methodology suggests itself as suitable for such an investigation. We think that many sport situations would present such a problem, and the various ways of investigating soccer hooliganism that we discuss below may be more generally relevant.

There are a number of alternative ways in which hooliganism could be studied that would enable the researcher to build up a picture, or description of the situation. First, a systematic survey of archival data in which the incidence and extent of hooliganism would be correlated with other variables such as the size of crowd, the number of fouls and disputed penalties, the position of the team in the football league and the extent to which "home" or "away" supporters are involved. Such a systematic survey, backed up with appropriate analyses, would throw some light on the relationship between hooliganism and such variables. It could be established whether it has increased significantly over the last 50 years and what effect various counter-hooliganism measures have had. Such a survey might throw up interesting lines for further investigation. The potential for archival material is underlined by the research of Russell and Drewry (1976) on crowd size,

competitiveness and aggression in which they showed that aggression in ice hockey was related to league standing and match score.

Second, in-depth interviews or a questionnaire on a sample of convicted soccer hooligans and on a matched (i.e,, equivalent) sample of nonhooligan football supporters may be utilized. Such factors as background, education, intelligence and personality variables could be measured along with more qualitative material. A comparison could be made between the two samples to see whether particular variables differentiated the two groups. During the interview it would be important to find out the hooligans' explanation for their behaviors. Do they see it as mindless vandalism or would their accounts suggest something else?

Third, an investigation might involve participant observation techniques that were used by the researchers whose work will be discussed later. Participant observation involves repeated genuine social interaction on the scene with the subjects themselves, as part of the data-gathering process. It is rather like an in-depth interview conducted over a long period of time in which the researcher not only monitors what is going on, but attempts to understand what it means to the people involved. Participant observation is mainly a descriptive methodology not normally used in theory testing. Essentially the researcher participates in the daily lives of the people under study, listening to what is said, watching what is done, and questioning them over a period of time. As a technique, it is one of the most controversial in the social sciences. Its reliability is very much open to question since the results of such research are qualitative; it depends largely on the ingenuity of the researcher; and no formalized methods are set down. Furthermore, by his very presence the observer may affect that which he is measuring and may tend to observe what he expects to find. With such problems, why do researchers choose to use it? La Piere (1934) suggested the reason 40 years ago in explaining the all too prevalent use of the questionnaire:

> The questionnaire is cheap, easy and mechanical. The study of behavior is time consuming, intellectually fatiguing and depends for its success on the ability of the investigator. The former gives quantitative results, the latter mainly qualitative. Quantitative measures are quantitatively accurate, qualitative evaluations are always subject to errors of judgment. Yet it would seem far more worthwhile to make a shrewd guess regarding that which is essential rather than to accurately measure that which is likely to prove quite irrelevant [p. 237].

For many phenomena on which our basic understanding is limited, particularly those of a complex nature, La Piere's comment is particularly pertinent. Occasionally too high a value is placed on reliability (i.e., consistency of measurement) at the expense of validity (i.e., getting at that which is important and theoretically significant). In a research program, knowledge of a cumulative nature is sought and it is often necessary to break

with certain tenets of the experimental method in the early stages in order that a basic insight may be gained. Derivations and implications from such nonquantitative research can always be investigated thoroughly later on.

Corrigan (1977) has used participant observation techniques in an attempt to understand some aspects of working class youth culture. He was working in Sunderland where an integral part of the youth culture was the Saturday afternoon football game. Sunderland Football Club enjoys massive and consistent support from the local community and, as with most clubs, it experiences some episodes of hooliganism. The fortunes of the club greatly influence the local community and are a major conversation topic. After a disappointing performance, production in the local factories decreases while the post mortem is held. In his research, Corrigan emphasizes that the match itself must not be taken out of the context of Saturday, and that Saturday is a special day in the week for the working-class youth. In a rather monotonous week in which school, or work, provide little satisfaction, Saturday is the one day when something exciting and remarkable may happen. A good game or an unusual incident gives the boys something to talk about for the rest of the week. Hence, on Saturday, situations are engineered, and experiences created. This is very much a group activity, for it is in the group that the individual achieves a sense of identity. The day begins at 11:00 in the morning and goes on into the evening, well after the match has ended. The game is the focus of the day but it is not only the football that is enjoyed. During the morning the youths meet up, drink coffee, exchange views on their team and the opposition, and reminisce about previous encounters. Many of the fans are exceedingly knowledgeable about the game. At one o'clock they drift towards the ground in groups. Meetings with opposing fans may turn into a scuffle, accompanied by cat calls and abuse until the fracas is broken up by the police. In the ground, singing and chanting help to build up the atmosphere. The event is much more than the match, Saturday is a day for creating something out of nothing that will be noteworthy and remarkable. Corrigan believes that most groups contain one boy, "the nutter," who is significant because he demonstrably breaks the law and thereby generates many tales of daring and bravado. The others do not follow his lead through fear of arrest. Corrigan does not think that the nutter is necessarily different in background from the average supporter, but is someone who perhaps used to be a scapegoat, or was on the periphery of the group, and who now attempts to gain acceptability by excessive behavior.

Thus Corrigan's analysis extends the picture to the entire social milieu of the working-class boy. If there is a solution to hooliganism, it is to be found in the relationship between the boys and the social institutions that form a major part of their lives. Aggression in this situation cannot be understood in terms of simple stimulus–response relationships. The activities on the pitch do influence the fans; they are there to watch a match, but their behavior is influenced by many other factors. We encounter here the problematic nature

of aggression. What the public defines as aggressive, mindless, and deplorable, is not seen as such by the boys themselves. To them it is entertaining, daring, and an essential part of the Saturday spectacular that provides a welcome relief from the monotony of provincial life. In proposing this view, we are not condoning violent acts; far from it. We do consider, however, that unless these activities are more fully understood, scientists will have little chance of usefully contributing to the debate. Of course, Corrigan's methodology is highly questionable and his thesis lacks a theoretical framework. In the context of theory, Elias and Dunning's writings suggest a possible unifying concept. On method, it is our view that such research as this should be viewed in the context of an ongoing program. If it leads to a better understanding and perhaps to further work of a more quantitative nature, then it is well justified.

The research of Marsh (1975, 1976) is complementary to that of Corrigan. Working independently at the ground of Oxford United Football Club, Marsh has used a modified ethological appproach in his attempts to understand the meaning of crowd behavior at fooball matches. This inevitably involves aggressive incidents. While the detached observer might consider the singing, chanting, flag waving and scuffling with opposing fans as activities quite separate from the game and largely irrelevant, Marsh, having spent more than a season with the Oxford supporters, comes to a different conclusion. He considers these bizarre activities to be imbued with meaning, regulated by complex rules, and an integral part of supporting a football team and enjoying a game.

He begins his analysis by suggesting that soccer, a game played by men, and watched by boys and men, is a contemporary example of the phenomenon of male bonding. Marsh quotes the work of Tiger (1969) in suggesting that such bonding was originally a prerequisite of hunting but is now manifested in social and leisure activities. While hunting was characterized by aggression and violence, the football game involves only "ritual violence." This refers to the outcome of aggression contained within symbolic behavior, or a rule-governed framework. This is not dissimilar to Beisser's (1967) more general analysis in which he suggests that the traditional qualities associated with manliness, such as strength, agility and endurance, are no longer relevant in modern industrial society. Sport, according to Beisser, allows men to maintain their identity by the unproductive and socially harmless display of these traditional qualities.

It would seem to us that many of the activities associated with soccer hooliganism are attempts by working-class youth to demonstrate, in ritual fashion, the traditional qualities of physical toughness and assertiveness. Improvements in working-class living and working conditions have led to a situation in which young people are no longer as tough as preceding generations, and in which the daily requirements of life do not demand that

they be so. Nevertheless, such qualities remain prized attributes. Thus, hooliganism may be seen as a way of demonstrating them within the security of a group.

Both Marsh and Corrigan stress the fact that, though confrontation between groups of opposing supporters involve many people, few actually get hurt. According to Marsh, the reason serious injury is so infrequent is that the ritualized aggression, the threat and counter threats, are acknowledged by all to be acceptable within a prescribed framework of rules. On a typical day, the spectators assemble in their particular territories behind each goal, an hour or two before the match. The police helpfully reinforce this division by channelling the fans of the opposing teams to the appropriate part of the ground. Once a good number of fans are established, the mock battle commences with chanting, taunting and flag waving; each group trying to make the greatest impression with its display. Songs like "You'll never walk alone" or sometimes "You'll never walk again" are sung after the fashion of a Welsh choir but with the added ingredient of colorful team scarves held horizontally and rocked to the beat. The spectacle is impressive even to the uncommitted and the atmosphere is exciting. Originally such activities were restricted to the 90 minutes of play when supporters attempted to "lift" or congratulate their team. Now it typically begins before the match, reaching a crescendo when the teams emerge or a goal is scored. During the interval, and occasionally in the match itself, when an incident occurs or a bad foul goes unpenalized, cries such as "aggro" erupt and possibly a foray of the "braves" is initiated against the opposition's territory. The youngest boys look on with admiration as reputations are made by their seniors. The whole spectacle is observed passively by those with established reputations who only intervene if things get out of hand or a good battle is in the offing.

In Marsh's view, these are not necessarily undesirable activities but have an important social function. In common with the ethologists, he believes in the inevitability of aggression and in the need for society to provide appropriate channels for its harmless dissipation. Whereas the aggression of mugging and street violence is nonritualized and socially harmful, at the football match few are unaware of the tacitly held rules. People know when an encounter contains ritual conflict; they know what to anticipate and what response to make. Only when the ritual breaks down does the situation deteriorate and then the fans admit to fear. A good example of this ritualized aggression was presented inadvertently on the television. At one particular game, a fight broke out between opposing fans and play was held up while the police attempted to restore order. During this period fans could be seen "kung-fu kicking" other people. This, according to the media, was one of the worst episodes yet. But on closer inspection of the film, it was quite apparent that the kung-fu kicks were aimed at a point in mid-air some 2 or 3 feet away from the "target." In the 10-minute battle, the most serious assault occurred when

various youths were pushed to the ground. Of course, this rough and tumble interrupted the game and could potentially have been violent, but to condemn it out of hand as mindless hooliganism is to miss the subtlety and the complexity of the situation.

Although Lorenz sees the value of sports in combating militant chauvinistic ethnocentrism, Marsh takes a somewhat different view. He considers that some form of aggression in ritual form provides an alternative to other more serious and less desirable activities. In the football ground the opposing supporters are not united in their appreciation of the event, far from it—they are divided by their team loyalties but tied by the tacitly held rules of the game of supporting. Some may not agree with Marsh's views on male bonding or on the inevitability of aggression between men, but we find his description of crowd behavior both subtle and constructive. In analyzing the way implicit rules govern crowd behavior, he parallels Corrigan in the contention that spectator hooliganism can only be understood in a wider context. It is a phenomenon located in a complex rule structure and forms an integral part of the activities of the week. Certainly the research methods used by Marsh and Corrigan are much less reliable than those of the typical laboratory or psychometric study, the sample sizes prohibit confident generalizations and it is apparent that many aspects of hooliganism, particularly the infrequent violent episodes or more frequent breaking up of shops or trains, are still not understood. But we consider that this work has, at least, laid the foundations for further research, showing that nonexperimental methods can be valuable in providing the basic analytic description of the situation necessary before the specific investigations can be sensibly conducted. Such an orientation has been successful elsewhere (e.g., Taylor, Walton, & Young, 1976). As these methods appear to be useful in understanding spectator behavior, perhaps asking athletes and sportsmen about aggression and their reactions to it would be a useful inroad to the analysis of aggression and the sports participant.

CONCLUSION

Many of the implications of this discussion are incorporated in the text. However, we would particularly like to reiterate a number of considerations relevant to further research. There is a need for a more serious attempt to understand sport and its social significance. This involves viewing sport in discriminating ways. Sport, itself, must be analyzed so that important differences in its structure are fully reflected. Furthermore the benefits held to accrue from sports involvement must be regarded problematically. There is also a general need to be more precise about the meaning and conceptualization of aggression. This is particularly germane to an analysis of sport where

many activities are inappropriately labeled aggressive. Too often the positivistic approach to aggression and the generic approach to sport, which characterize much of the literature, fail to uncover and account for the subleties of meaning that are essential to a fuller understanding of the nature of sport and aggression.

REFERENCE NOTES

1. Pearton, R. E., & Holliday, F. M. *Physical education in England since 1945.* Unpublished manuscript, St. Mary's College, University of London, 1969.
2. Kleinman, S. *A study to determine the factors that influence the behavior of sports crowds.* Unpublished doctoral dissertation, Ohio State University, 1960.
3. Russell, W. *Population control in animal and man.* Paper presented to the Social Psychology Section, British Psychological Society, September 1972.
4. Winkler, T. Communication presented at the seminar meeting of the British Sociological Association, Study Group on Sport, 1971.

REFERENCES

Aristotle [*Politics*] (B. Jowett, trans.). Oxford: Oxford University Press, 1905.

Ardrey, R. *The territorial imperative.* New York: Dell, 1966.

Bandura, A. Influence of model's reinforcement contingencies on the acquisition of imitative responses. *Journal of Personality & Social Psychology,* 1965, *1,* 589–595.

Bandura, A., & Walters, R. H. *Social learning and personality development.* New York: Holt, Rinehart & Winston, 1963.

Beisser, A. *The madness in sports.* New York: Appleton-Century-Crofts, 1967.

Benedict, R. *Patterns of culture.* Baltimore: Penguin, 1924.

Berkowitz, L. *Aggression: A social psychological analysis.* New York: McGraw-Hill, 1962.

Berkowitz, L. Aggressive cues in aggressive behaviors and hostility catharsis. *Psychological Review,* 1964, *71,* 104–122.

Berkowitz, L., & Alioto, J. T. The meaning of an observed event as a detemimant of its aggressive consequences. *Journal of Personality & Social Psychology,* 1973, *28,* 206–217.

Berkowitz, L., & Geen, R. G. Film violence and the cue properties of available targets. *Journal of Personality & Social Psychology,* 1966, *3,* 525–530.

Binford, S. Apes and original sin. *Human Behavior,* 1972, *1*(6), 64–71.

Bronfenbrenner, U. *Two worlds of childhood: U.S. and U.S.S.R.* New York: Russell Sage Foundation, 1970.

Buss, A. H., & Durkee, A. An inventory for assessing different kinds of hostility. *Jounal of Consulting Psychology,* 1957, *21,* 343–348.

Buss, A. H. *The psychology of aggression.* New York: Wiley, 1961.

Caplow, T. *Two against one: Coalitions in triads.* Englewood Cliffs, N.J.: Prentice-Hall, 1968.

Cattell, R. B. *Handbook. Sixteen personality factor questionnaire.* Urbana, Ill. Institute for Personality and Ability Testing, Champaign, 1957.

Corrigan, P. *Schooling the smash street kids.* London: Macmillan, 1977.

Deutscher, I. *What we do/What we say: Sentiments and acts.* Glenview, Ill.: Scott, Foresman, 1973.

Dollard, J., Doob, L., Miller, N., Mowrer, O., & Sears, R. *Frustration and aggression.* New Haven, Conn.: Yale University Press, 1939.

Dunning, E. *The sociology of sport.* London: Cass, 1971.

Elias, N., & Dunning, E. The quest for excitement in unexciting societies. In G. Lushchen (Ed.), *A cross-cultural analysis of sports and games.* London: Stipes, 1970.

Freud, S. *Beyond the pleasure principle.* London: Hogarth, 1948.

Gerth, H., & Mills, C. W. *Character and social structure.* London: Routledge & Kegan Paul, 1954.

Gibb, C. A. The principles and traits of leadership. *Journal of Abnormal & Social Psychology,* 1947, *42,* 267–284.

Gaebelin, J., & Taylor, S. P. The effects of competition and attack on physical aggression. *Psychonomic Science,* 1971, *24,* 65–66.

Golstein, J. H. *Aggression and crimes of violence.* New York: Oxford University Press, 1975.

Goldstein, J. H., & Arms, R. L. Effects of observing athletic contests on hostility. *Sociometry,* 1971, *34,* 83–90.

Harrison, P. Soccer's tribal wars. *New Society,* 1974, *29,* 602ff.

Hastorf, A. H., & Cantril, H. They saw a game: A case study. *Journal of Abnormal & Social Psychology,* 1954, *44,* 129–134.

Heinila, K. Notes on inter-group conflict in sport. In G. Luschen (Ed.), *A cross-cultural analysis of sports and games.* London: Stipes, 1970.

Hokanson, J. E. Psychophysiological evaluation of the catharsis hypothesis. In E. I. Megargee & J. E. Hokanson (Ed.), *The dynamics of aggression.* New York: Harper & Row, 1970.

Ismail, A., & Tratchman, L. Jog your personality into shape. *Psychology Today,* 1976, *2*(8), 24–28. (U.K. edition)

Kaelin, E. F. The well-played game: Notes toward an aesthetics of sport. *Quest Monographs,* May 1968, 16–28.

Kane, J. Personality and physical abilities. In G. Kenyon (Ed.), *Contemporary psychology in sport.* Chicago: Athletic Institute, 1970.

Kenyon, G. S. A conceptual model for characterizing physical activity. In J. W. Loy & G. S. Kenyon (Eds.) *Sport, culture and society.* New York: Macmillan, 1969.

Kuhlmann, W. Violence in professional sports. *Wisconsin Law Review,* 1975, *3,* 771–790.

La Piere, R. T. Attitudes vs. actions. *Social Forces,* 1934, *13,* 230–237.

Lorenz, K. *On aggression.* New York: Harcourt, Brace & World, 1966.

Loy, J., & Kenyon, G (Eds.). *Sport, culture and society.* London: Macmillan, 1969.

Mead, G. H. *Mind, self and society.* Chicago: University of Chicago Press, 1934.

Mann, L. On being a sore loser; How fans react to their team's failure. *Australian Journal of Psychology,* 1974, *26,* 37–47.

Marsh, P. Understanding aggro. *New Society,* 1975, *32*(652), 7–9.

Marsh, P. Careers for boys, nutters, hooligans and hardcases. *New Society,* 1976, *36*(710), 346–348.

Montagu, M. F. A. *Man and aggression.* New York: Oxford University Press, 1968.

Morton, H. *Soviet sport.* New York: Collier, 1963.

Noel-Baker, P. Sport and international understanding. In E. Jokl & E. Simon (Eds.), *International research in sport and physical education.* Springfield, Ill.: C. C. Thomas, 1964.

Ogilvie, B. C., & Tutko, T. A. *Problem athletes and how to handle them.* London: Pelham, 1966.

Ogilvie, B. C., & Tutko, T. A. Sport: If you want to build character, try something else. *Psychology Today,* 1971, *5*(5), 61–63.

Russell, G. W. Machiavellianism, locus of control, aggression, performance and precautionary behaviour in ice hockey. *Human Relations,* 1974, *27,* 825–837.

Russell, G. W., & Drewry, B. R. Crowd size and competitive aspects of aggression in ice hockey: An archival study. *Human Relations,* 1976, *29,* 723–735.

Ryan, E. D. The cathartic effect of vigorous motor activity on aggressive behavior. *Research Quarterly*, 1970, *41*, 542–551.

Storr, A. *Human aggression*. New York: Atheneum, 1968.

Taylor, I. R. Soccer consciousness and soccer hooliganism. In B. Cohen, ed., *Images of deviance*. Baltimore: Penguin Books, 1971.

Taylor, I., Walton, P., & Young, J. *New directions in criminology*. London: Routledge & Kegan Paul, 1976.

Taylor, S. P. & Epstein, S. Aggression as a function of the interaction of the sex of the aggressor and the sex of the victim. *Journal of Personality*, 1967, *35*, 474–486.

Tiger, L. *Men in groups*. London: Nelson, 1969.

Tinbergen, N. *The study of instinct*. Oxford: Clarendon, 1951.

Volkamer, M. Zurur aggressivitat in Konkumenz—orientierten sozialen. *Sport Wissenschaft*, 1971, *1*, 68–76.

Walshe-Brennan, K. Football hooliganism. *Nursing Mirror*, November 1975, pp. 46–49.

Webb, E. J., Campbell, D. T., Schwartz, R. F., & Sechrest, L. *Unobtrusive measures: Nonreactive research in the social sciences.* Chicago: Rand McNally, 1966.

Weiss, P. *Sport; A philosophical inquiry*. London: Arcturns, 1971.

Zimbardo, P. G. The human choice: Individuation, reason and order vs. deindividuation, impulse and chaos. In W. Arnold & D. Levine (Eds.), *Nebraska Symposium on Motivation* (Vol. XVII). Lincoln: University of Nebraska Press, 1969.

11 The Enjoyment of Watching Sport Contests

Dolf Zillmann
Indiana University

Jennings Bryant
University of Massachusetts

Barry S. Sapolsky
Florida State University

INTRODUCTION

This chapter addresses the phenomenon of spectatorship in sports, not of active sports participation. Surprisingly, this phenomenon, in spite of its obtrusiveness in ancient and contemporary culture generally, and in the so-called mass media of communication in particular, has received very little attention in modern psychology. Grand speculations are abundant, but systematic research into the factors that created and sustain the societal phenomenon in question is rare, if at all existent. There seem to be reasons for such negligence, and we will make efforts to disclose them. We look into what appears to be a stigmatization of the sports spectacle, and we discuss the many proclamations of ill effects of spectatorship. But we also look at proposals of beneficial consequences. Most of all, however, we concern ourselves with the enjoyment audiences apparently derive from watching sport contests, regardless of other effects such preoccupation may produce. We propose numerous factors that potentially contribute to the enjoyment of watching sport contests, and we present recent research findings pertinent to our

DOLF ZILLMANN is Professor of Communication and Director of the Institute for Communictation Research at Indiana University. JENNINGS BRYANT is Assistant Professor in the Department of Communication Studies at the University of Massachusetts, and BARRY S. SAPOLSKY is Assistant Professor in the Department of Mass Communication at Florida State University. The authors developed and pursued their interest in sportsfanship as they collaborated on various projects in the psychology of entertainment at the Institute for Communication Research at Indiana.

proposals. It is hoped that our theoretical suggestions, together with the initial research evidence, will stimulate a new interest in the psychology of this ubiquitous phenomenon of sports spectatorship and maybe help to remove some of the stigma attached to studying it.

PARTICIPATION VERSUS SPECTATORSHIP

Much good has been said about active participation in sports. The medical value of vigorous activities, which the engagement in sports competition usually requires, has long been recognized. This value is not in doubt at all (cf. Johnson & Buskirk, 1974; Plessner, Bock, & Grupe, 1967), and programs promoting physical fitness and, ultimately, good bodily health through the participation in sports appear to be founded on strong, compelling evidence.

In contemplating the laudatory implications of active sports participation, many educators have gone far beyond medical considerations, however. For some time, physical educators accepted a view known as "mind–body unity" (cf. Layman, 1972) which led them to suggest that a healthy body could house only a healthy mind. This suggestion of a close relationship between physical and mental health has been with us ever since. Most modern educators would probably acknowledge that, although the relationship is not a necessary one, it does exist in general terms. Interestingly, such beliefs endure in the absence of an adequate theoretical foundation. A psychological or psychophysiological mechanism linking physical and mental health has not been uncovered, and correlational data (e.g., Gordon, Rosenberg, & Morris, 1966; Morgan, 1968, 1970) are only suggestive of a connection. It is only recently that a mechanism for the assumed linkage between physical fitness and mental health, or more accurately, between cardiovascular fitness and emotionality has emerged (cf. Zillmann, Johnson, & Day, 1974a; Cantor, Zillmann, & Day, 1978).

Regardless of the consideration of physical fitness, it is widely held that the participation in sports activities reduces tension and controls aggressiveness. These beliefs often take the form of truisms. Joggers, for example, tend to insist that without their exercise they would be more susceptible to emotional problems—outbursts and depressions alike. And some professional football players have given the impression that they "would kill people" if they couldn't be out there on the field leveling their fellow players. For the most part, such beliefs derive from the speculative writings of Freud (e.g., 1940, 1946a, 1946b, 1950) and his followers, notably Adler (1927), who viewed vigorous, competitive action as a means of redirecting "instinctive" forces, primarily forces of a destructive nature. In this view, people maintain their sanity, so to speak, only as they manage to rechannel their aggressive impulses, accepting substitute targets and substitute activities, but nonethe-

less obtaining "catharsis," that is, a purgation of their destructive urges. These Freudian thoughts on the mental-health value of discharging destructive energy in comparatively innocuous ways have been propagated by uncounted writers of a psychoanalytic orientation. But it is the ethologist Lorenz (1963) who, more than others, has pondered their implications for sports. Lorenz views competitive sports as "ritualized aggression" through which actual aggression can be curbed. Participation in sports activities, especially in the context of competition and contests, is viewed as the dynamic through which potentially destructive energy is discharged, and the repeated discharge, in turn, is viewed as counteracting the continuous, spontaneous build-up of aggressive forces that would ultimately reach intolerable levels. Sports participation, then, is seen as a means through which violent outbursts are held in check, both at the individual and at the social level. So confident was Lorenz in his reasoning regarding these mechanics that he projected sports competition as the primary preventive for war, a belief that has also been expressed by Storr (1968). Such high hopes are not encouraged, however, by the available research evidence. Data on the cathartic discharge of hostile inclinations through some form of substitute response are largely negative (cf. Quanty, 1976), and the view that catharsis could be obtained through physical activities, especially through sports competition, is severely challenged by the findings. Vigorous pounding, for example, was found to enhance rather than to reduce hostile expressiveness (Hornberger, 1959). Similarly, strenuous physical exercise, bicycling, was found to further rather than diminish aggressive behavior in annoyed persons (Zillmann & Bryant, 1974; Zillmann, Katcher, & Milavsky, 1972). A study that involved the element of competition (both winning and losing associated with vigorous physical activity) in addition to noncompetitive physical exercise and a no-exercise control again failed to show any kind of catharsis (Ryan, 1970). Even the direct engagement in a competitive and aggressive sport, football, produced results counter to catharsis. High school football players exhibited an increase in hostile inclinations after playing the game, this being in contrast to no change in such inclinations in physical education students who were engaged in a variety of activities (Patterson, Note 1). The comparison of aggressiveness in athletes and in nonathletes does not change this picture. Contact-sport athletes, because they have frequent occasion to discharge violent urges, should be comparatively nontense and hard to provoke. The opposite proved correct. Contact-sport athletes responded more rather than less aggressively to provocation than did either noncontact-sport athletes or nonathletes (Zillmann, Johnson, & Day, 1974b). In the light of these findings, the participation in competitive, aggressive sports, which is the type of sports that has been considered to hold the greatest promise for the cathartic discharge of destructive inclinations, may more rightfully be viewed as a disinhibition training that ultimately promotes violent reactions.

Notwithstanding apparently untenable claims concerning the participation in sports as a means to subdue violence in society, the active involvement with sports has been encouraged as a form of play with great recreational value (e.g., Godbey & Parker, 1976; Menninger, 1948). Along with other play activities, participation in sports is considered an antidote to the stress of labor (cf. Dumazedier, 1967; Kaplan, 1960). Disregarding professionalism in sports, the engagement in sports activities is free from the compulsion of labor. A person may hike, jog, swim, play tennis or baseball if he or she pleases and as he or she pleases. And if he or she suffers from the restrictiveness of his or her working conditions, he or she is free to pick an activity associated with minimal constraints, such as scuba diving, horseback riding, or gliding. These and similar activities are viewed as capable of involving the participants to a degree that they forget their worries and consequently experience a relaxation of tensions, even in physiological terms. Participation in sports, as Dumazedier (1964) sees it, can readily serve the three functions of leisure that he has proposed: (1) *relaxation*, which relieves the fatigue caused by the activities of daily life; (2) *recreation*, which relieves the boredom of daily life; (3) *free development*, which provides relief from specialization. But while such an analysis of sports activities that could serve a recreational function seems to favor noncompetitive, nonvigorous, and nondemanding engagements, the elements of competition and challenge, of skill and mastery, have also been implicated with recreational value (cf. Cozens & Stumpf, 1953; Kenyon, 1970; Loy & Kenyon, 1969). Competition is said to promote comradery and friendship, and the mastery of general and unique motor skills, attained through disciplined training, is seen as an important factor in character formation. However, regardless of accomplishments at the personality level, active participation in sports has generally been assumed to relax and to recreate. The person's mental and physical capacities are seen as being restored: Through the engagement in sports, the person is rejuvenated and recovers from the energy-draining experience of daily duties. And as social philosophers (e.g., von Krockow, 1974) have observed, participation in sports, for the better or worse, ultimately serves modern industrial society in that it restores the person's capacity to work. A possible exception in the recreational function of participation in sports concerns activities that entail great challenges. As many cases attest (cf. Klausner, 1968), within the context of sports people can readily become obsessed with daring endeavors and pursue them whether or not this proves relaxing. In fact, many sports obsessions are reportedly practiced for the declared purpose of obtaining the experience of stress.

Independent of physical and recreational benefits from the active involvement in sports, educators have always stressed that such participation teaches "a sense of fairness." Competitive games are characterized by sets of well-defined rules (cf. Sutton-Smith, 1969, 1971), and any transgression of

these rules is readily recognized by participants and onlookers. Cultures have generally provided for the strict observation of "the rules of the game," and rule violations are met with prompt disapproval by participants and spectators alike. Children quickly learn to compete within the rules and to brand any violation as unfair. A sense of fairness is thus essentially forced through social reproach. Put negatively, it is taught through punishment. In defense of playful competition it could be argued, however, that the punishment involved is generally trivial: At the initial stages it would be the discontinuation of a pleasureable activity. Be this as it may, engagements in competitive sports convey and reinforce the moral notion of fairness. Such an educational accomplishment may be viewed as meritorious, but it should not be seen as unique to sports competition. It clearly accrues to rule-governed competitive play behavior in general (cf. Sutton-Smith & Roberts, 1964).

A potential benefit of participation in sports, which is uniquely associated with sports competition, has recently been pointed out by Scott (1970). Scott proposed that vigorous, physical competition induces intense emotional reactions such as fear and anger which the participant cannot express at the time; these emotions then dissipate, however, an experience that teaches the participant to cope with aversive emotional states. We have taken a similar position (Zillmann, Johnson, & Day, 1974b) and have gone so far as to suggest that one of the most significant benefits of active sports competition is attainable through the experience of defeat: In the heat of competition, a player may feel intensely frustrated, humiliated, angry, or depressed yet can neither come out hitting the opponents nor run away from them. Characteristically, the player may not even display his or her feelings. Within the confines of strict rules, the player just has to serve the next ball, try for another basket, take on the next batter, or simply line up again with his or her teammates. If the player might normally throw a temper tantrum, the emotional flares must be held back. As play continues, these flares should dissipate, and this experience of having contained the urges of an outburst, in the face of extreme levels of excitation, may prove a most valuable training in the control of impulsive emotional reactions.

In summary, then, participation in sports has been said to: (1) promote physical fitness and health; (2) produce mental benefits of fitness; (3) help to control aggressive behavior; (4) have recreational value (in that it relaxes tensions, relieves from boredom, and in contrast to labor provides free personal development); (5) teach a sense of fairness; and (6) serve the control of disapproved impulsive emotional behaviors.

We have pointed out that some of these propositions are questionable, at least in the general form in which they are usually presented, and others (e.g., Sutton-Smith, 1971) have stressed the need for research to determine the validity of many beliefs regarding the implications of active sports participation. These qualifying remarks do not change the fact, however, that

participation in sports is widely, if not universally hailed as having a wealth of beneficial effects—and virtually no undesirable side effects.

The situation is totally different when sports *spectatorship* is being considered. The discussion of spectatorship amounts to a nearly universal condemnation of the phenomenon. Moral arguments abound. Characteristically, they are contained in anthropological and sociological speculations, and they are applied in a rather roundabout manner. Predictive psychological theory is conspicuously absent, and value-independent, descriptive sociological accounts have only recently been published (e.g., Kenyon, 1969). Most, if not all of the projected benefits of active participation in sports have been declared unattainable through spectatorship. Sitting in the bleachers or in front of a television set obviously does nothing for physical fitness. Spectatorship, then, is devoid of the benefits of fitness: bodily health and its positive mental concomitants. Along with other forms of entertainment, it has been viewed as a useless activity, a "waste of time" (e.g., Lazarsfeld & Merton, 1948). Worse yet, it has been viewed as an activity that mobilizes the baser instincts of people. We are reminded of the spectator's blood lust in enjoying gladiatorial combat in Rome, of medieval dueling contests, or of animal torment as featured in bull fights. There is little doubt that spectators have been vicious at times. It is reported, for example, that spectators of dueling contests in 16th-century Italy were disorderly and had to be contained with threats of penalty. According to Bryson (1938), it was customary before the combat for the herald to make a proclamation warning the spectators about stiff penalties for such offenses as bearing arms or entering the dueling field. Some offenses resulted in the confiscation of property, and others were corporal, such as the amputation of a hand by the stroke of a sword. But while the Medici and the Borgias tried to subdue yelling and spitting on the part of the audience, other cultures have permitted and even ritualized intense emotional displays. Ellis (1829) reported that in many Polynesian cultures brutal wrestling matches were preceded by spectator partisans who engaged in exchanges of most derisive and insulting chants, and that, as soon as one of the wrestlers was incapacitated, the crowd broke out in a most violent frenzy. But one need not resort to historical notes to find illustrations of uncontrolled or questionable spectator behavior. In 1964, a soccer match in Lima, Peru, triggered a riot in which about 300 persons were killed and about 500 were severely injured, and diplomatic relations between El Salvador and Honduras were broken off because of disturbances over soccer (Lever, 1969). In the United States, bedlam ensued in Pittsburgh when the Pirates won the 1971 World Series of baseball: There was "a wave of destruction, looting, sex in the streets" (AP release), along with numerous hospitalizations. On other occasions, and in different sports, the fans raided the playing field and attacked players (Fimrite, 1974), bombarded referees with bottles, and "streaked" through stadiums. If these are relatively rare incidents, the crowds

drawn to professional wrestling matches or other "sports spectaculars" are regulars. Apparently, there is an audience for seemingly vicious fighting (cf. Stone, 1958), for motorcycle jumps across shark-infested waters, for rope-walking gorge crossers, and the like (cf. Severn, 1974). It seems that death-defying acts, whether they require great motor skills or not, have always been marveled at (by those who do not consider them outright stupid). And while a ready-made rationalization for the enjoyment of such spectacles is provided in the admiration of courage, some spectators have left little doubt that, occasionally at least, they would have liked to see the mishap rather than "another perfect plunge through the flaming rings."

Taken together, the spectator's image is not a positive one. Spectators have been depicted as passive and lazy (the proverbial corpulent beer drinker in front of the TV set), as insensitive and cruel, and as eagerly awaiting a display of violence and disaster. In addition, they have been pictured as ready to take violent action themselves.

The "principal" differences between the sports participant and the sports spectator have been detailed by numerous writers. In a paper entitled the "Social psychology of the spectator" (a more appropriate title would have been "The Morality of Sports Participation and the Immorality of Sports Spectatorship"), Howard (1912) describes spectatorship as bad and partisan-ship as evil. Participation, in contrast, is good. Involvement in play is said to excite joyous emotions, and these pleasurable emotions are seen by Howard as building up energy and as restoring the "capacity for straight thinking [p. 42]" and, ultimately, for work. The "mob-mind of the athletic spectator," on the other hand, succumbing to "the elemental gaming and struggle-instinct of the human animal [p. 43]," produces disagreeable emotions, and these emotions are said to tear down and diminish energy. Given such a clear-cut value difference, Howard condemned watching and advocated action in no uncertain terms: "Let the apostle of social righteouness break into Satan's monopoly [p. 41]!"

Others have refrained from using such dramatic language, but have drawn distinctions and have set up parallels that forecast great drama: the decline of cultures in which spectatorship flourishes. Stone (1958) distinguished between play and dis-play, a conceptual differentiation parallel to that between participation and spectatorship. In terms of this nomenclature, he viewed ancient Greece as a culture of play and glory. He viewed Rome as the decadent culture of dis-play and vainglory. Play or participation in sport, as in the initial Olympic Games, is seen as ennobling the players. The spectacle, in contrast, is said to be "inherently immoral and debasing [p. 262]." Stone proposed that, as spectatorship comes to dominate over participation, the spectator places demands on spectacular play, thereby creating the spectacle. In this regard, he said, the spectator should be viewed "as an agent of destruction as far as the dignity of sport is concerned [p. 262]." Most

importantly, however, Stone pointed to the parallel between contemporary U.S. culture and Roman decadence, and he urged to look for ways of bringing the dignity of the play (or participation) to the dis-play (or spectatorship). More recently, Beisser (1967) has taken a similar stand; he stressed that, next to the Roman Empire in the period of decline, "the United States is the second great nation in history to spend great amounts of time and resources in elaborately producing spectator sports [pp. 13–14]." The message is clear. Beware of the spectator!

Ironically, while the obtrusive misbehavior of sports spectators deeply troubled some writers, others detected merit in the preoccupation and fascination with rough-and-tumble play. The concept of catharsis is again of central importance. But in considering spectatorship, the discharge of aggressive impulses obviously cannot come through an assault upon a substitute target, nor through substitute vigorous activities. Acts of physical aggression are characteristically not performed by the spectator—as he or she watches a sports contest. Such acts can only be performed "in fantasy" or *vicariously*. The spectator can "go with the action," and it has been presumed that this process can be intense enough to provide the spectator with some of the benefits of the real action. This view that a cathartic relief from destructive urges can be attained through the "vicarious participation" in vigorous and aggressive sports competition, with its roots in Greek philosophy and in Freudian reasoning, has been popularized by Dollard, Miller, Doob, Mowrer, and Sears' influential publication (1939), on *Frustration and Aggression*. Feshbach (1961, 1970) further promoted this notion of "symbolic" catharsis. But Lorenz (1963), again echoed by Storr (1968), applied it specifically to sports spectatorship. He considered the spectator's "enthusiastic involvement" with sports, especially with sports competition that has the general characteristics of "ritualized combat," to be a sufficient condition for catharsis to occur. There resides a vindication for sports spectatorship in this speculation. It makes the violent sports spectacle a valuable control mechanism for violence in society. The rougher, the better. And if spectators run amok at times and display behavior characteristics that are generally reproached, it would seem that we only witness catharsis at work, and we are spared of what might have happened had this opportunity for catharsis not been provided.

A wealth of pertinent research findings does not bear out such projections. Turner (1970) and Goldstein and Arms (1971) studied the effects of attending wrestling matches, football games, basketball games, and track meets on hostile expressiveness. They found that spectators became more rather than less abusive after attending combat-like, aggressive contests. Due to coincidence (in research on media violence, films of prize-fights were frequently employed as aggressive materials), much is known about the impact on aggressive behavior of watching boxing matches. This work, which

has been reviewed elsewhere in considerable detail (e.g., Berkowitz, 1965; Geen, 1976; Tannenbaum & Zillmann, 1975) shows with impressive consistency that watching boxing increases rather than decreases aggressive behavior in annoyed males. And although different investigators favor different explanations for this aggression-facilitating effect of exposure to "ritualized aggression," it is clear that there is no cause to perpetuate beliefs in symbolic catharsis. In the face of the research evidence, Lorenz has reassessed the situation. He recently acknowledged that he now has "strong doubts whether watching aggressive behavior even in the guise of sport has any cathartic effect at all" (Evans, 1974, p. 93). The promise of catharsis through spectatorship has thus faded away, and with it the possibility of a broad beneficial effect of watching sport contests.

IN DEFENSE OF SPORTSFANSHIP

For the most part, the case against sports spectatorship has been based upon the obtrusive behavior of rather small subpopulations. Yes, some spectators have taken a liking to the bizarre and the violent. And yes, some have conducted themselves very poorly. But such preferences and such conduct should not be treated as frequent, as typical, much less as dominant. Dubious taste and misconduct are the exception. This should be very clear when one considers the vast numbers of fans. The incidence of watching a sport contest runs into the billions every year (e.g., Beisser, 1967; Johnson, 1971). Millions across the country and around the world watch sports events every week, live or on television. And yet, there are only a few cases of obtrusive misconduct. We should not lose sight of the fact that the typical sports fan manages his or her emotions admirably. He or she may yell and stomp the ground but, after the game, he or she usually will be no more vicious than after an exciting movie or a stimulating concert. And by the same token, the types of sports that attract millions of spectators time and time again are generally not stunts in which people put themselves on fire or hurl themselves across canyons. Instead, popular sports feature highly developed but nonetheless basic motor skills: speed, agility, balance, accuracy, strength, and endurance. The most popular sports (e.g., baseball, football, basketball, soccer, and tennis) are, in fact, built around skills that nearly everybody masters: carrying, throwing, kicking, catching, or hitting a ball. In general, then, sports spectatorship appears to pay homage to commonly practiced skills rather than to foolhardiness evidenced in reckless action.

All this is not to whitewash the spectator image. As acknowledged earlier, audiences can be attracted to obscure events in what has been called a "carnival of sports" (Severn, 1974). And it is quite conceivable that even large audiences take pleasure in seeing rather rough and violent action, as

uncounted observers of sports crowds have suggested. We would like, however, to point out the need to correct for the distortions that have come with undue attention to the obtrusive reactions of fans attracted to obscure "sports events."

An unprejudiced look at sports spectatorship at large reveals that sports spectatorship may have many of the benefits of active participation in sports. No doubt, as stated earlier, the benefits of physical fitness do not exist for spectatorship. It could also be argued that the element of mastery regarding motor skills is unattainable. The participant in sports can develop skills and enjoy his or her accomplishments, but the spectator can not. The spectator may not be at a critical loss, however, because most skills in question have little if any practical merit. Throwing the javelin over a respectable distance, for example, or having a good ratio of sinking baskets from the free-throw line, in and of itself, may be viewed as trivial mastery. On the other hand, if such mastery enhances a person's self-esteem and even gives him or her the admiration of others, especially of his or her same-sex and opposite-sex peers, participation in sports must be considered to have personal value that cannot be matched by spectatorship.

Regarding the cathartic release of pent-up destructive impulses, both sports participation and sports spectatorship appear to have been erroneously credited with great accomplishments. As the research findings referred to earlier suggest, and counter to common belief, neither involvement delivers catharsis. And while some advocates of the catharsis doctrine now feel that just watching sports "combat" might not suffice (cf. Evans, 1974), but still maintain that participating in it would, there is no evidence which would compellingly support the view that, regarding catharsis, looking-on is "less beneficial" than acting-out.

In discussing recreational value, sports spectatorship certainly meets all the criteria of a beneficial leisure activity. Just as active participation in sports does, spectatorship relieves from boredom, relaxes tensions, and provides for personal development (cf. Dumazedier, 1964, 1967). In contrast to active participation, these benefits are within the reach of nearly everyone. Recreation through spectatorship permits the development of diverse interests. It comes at a low cost in effort, and it requires minimal skills. The benefits of spectatorship are accessible to those who would do poorly and only be frustrated and annoyed by active participation in sports programs. They are accessible to the weak and the ill, and to those too old to exert great amounts of energy. Spectatorship even promotes comradery and feelings of institutional, communal, or national solidarity. As the players are bonded through "the thrill of victory and the agony of defeat," so too are the spectators who, with their friends and acquaintances, rejoice in the victory and suffer torment from the defeat of the person or the team of their school, their college, their town, or their country—or so it seems. If spectators indeed share (to some degree) the apprehension, the anguish, the joy, the pride, or the

humiliation of the teams they affiliate with, the experience should bond together those who confess to the same affiliation. This condition for the experience of solidarity is generally met for people who interact frequently. People "root for the home team." Friends attending a game or watching it on television share their pleasures and pains. They cheer and hate together. In that, sportsfanship is principally not different from actual participation. Differences of degree may well exist, however. It is conceivable that winning or being defeated in sport contests produces degrees of cohesion for the players that the spectators' feelings of solidarity cannot match. But it appears that sportsfanship can unite and provide feelings of belongingness that are beneficial to the individual and to the social setting in which he or she lives. Unfortunately, the specific social consquences of enthusiastic spectatorship, for the most part, are yet to be determined. There are grounds for the expectation of beneficial effects. But these effects should be considered with due modesty. It would seem that they are carried much too far when sports spectatorship is projected as the "cement of democracry" (Cozens & Stumpf, 1953).

In all, there is little doubt that sports spectatorship has great recreational value. Under the assumption that people do not seek out boredom, the enormously large audiences drawn to sport contests attest to their boredom-relieving function. Relief of tension is in evidence for noncombatant yet competitive sports. It has been shown (Bryant & Zillmann, 1977) that exposure to this type of sport relaxes annoyance-induced physiological arousal and reduces motivated and displaced hostile behavior. Exposure to aggressive sports did not have these consequences, however. But here, it should be recalled, the failure to observe relaxation is the same as for the actual engagement in aggressive sports. The solidarity-enhancing function of spectatorship has recently been demonstrated (Cialdini, Borden, Thorne, Walker, Freeman, & Sloan, 1976). It was found that people unite mainly behind winning performances: Affiliation with winning teams is obtrusively expressed, presumably in hopes for a rub-off of glory.

If participation in sports teaches a sense of fairness, so does sports spectatorship. In fact, competitive sport, even competitive professional sport, can be viewed as a model through which fairness is most effectively taught. Great performances within the rules of the game are praised and any transgression is promptly punished. In basketball, for example, transgressions are marked by the referee's whistle and transgressors are singled out and made to identify themselves by raising their hand. Flagrant transgressors are ejected from the game, and those who suffered from transgressions are awarded "penalty shots." Sports spectatorship is apparently a most popular forum in which the concepts of fairness and justice are continuously being taught through social learning (cf. Bandura, 1969, 1971).

Sports spectatorship can even be considered to teach the control of heterodox impulsive emotional behavior—similar to the actual participation

in sports, but conceivably to a lesser degree. Regarding spectators who are closely affiliated with their team (the so-called loyal fans), it must be a trying experience for them to see their favorites go down in humbling or humiliating defeat. We know of fans who take large doses of tranquilizers to be prepared for the eventuality of their team's defeat. Witnessing such defeats apparently can produce intensely noxious states. Yet, under the assumption that spectators generally do not resort to drugs to master their emotional disturbances, it would seem that they control their emotions very effectively. The repeated experience of disappointment resulting from witnessing the defeat of a supported team may well function as training in coping with adverse emotional reactions. In fact, sports spectatorship may serve this function better than sports participation. Regarding the opportunity to act out frustrations, it can be argued that the spectator is far more restricted than the player. The principle of passive inhibition (cf. Scott, 1958), then, applies more directly to spectatorship. The acutely irritated and annoyed spectator, in the bleachers or at home, cannot change the course of events in the game. He or she can moan and yell complaints but cannot turn matters his or her way through hostile or aggressive action. He or she can only wait out the disturbance—wait for his or her emotions to dissipate. These are exactly the conditions required for passive inhibition. Nonaggressive habits are acquired through the performance of nonaggressive reactions. Or put more affirmatively, coping with irritations is learned through waiting out irritations. Again, the extremely rare errant reaction of fans (e.g., the bottle thrown at the referee) should be seen in its proper perspective. It should also be noted that aggressive outbursts are more frequent in those who play than in those who watch the game.

Up to this point, we have discussed the merits of sports spectatorship in terms of the merits of participation in sports. We have argued that sports spectatorship is capable of producing many, though clearly not all, of the benefits accruing to participation. Now we turn to benefits of spectatorship that participation cannot produce or can only offer to a lesser degree.

The fact that any particular sport contest involves only a relatively small number of people, whereas spectatorship is virtually unrestricted numerically, may seem trivial but actually is of great importance. Players of the game may have much to revel about, but any such revelry is quite meaningless to outsiders. Spectatorship expands the social experience of revelry to a point where it creates a new social phenomenon. A game can be "the talk of the town." It can be a national event, such as the Superbowl or the World Series. It even can be a global affair, such as in the Olympic Games. The electronic and printed media let millions share every major sports event. The media prepare the spectators for the contests, give the "play-by-play" accounts, and provide them with instant appraisals of performances and performers (cf. Johnson, 1971). Apprehensions about a contest can be shared a millionfold.

But more importantly, millions can share in the revelry of a victory or the humiliation of a defeat. Sports events become conversation topics that can help establish social contacts and further existing ones. In the office, for example, one can readily promote good relations (with secretaries and colleagues alike) by dropping comments about yesterday's basketball game, and one can possibly make friends on the plane by "talking pro-football" with a fellow passenger. But sports is not just a handy conversation topic alongside many others, such as fashion, the movies, or dirty jokes (cf. Mendelsohn, 1966). It seems more universally employable. But equally important, it appears to be a low-risk topic. Sparing the careless display of loyalty to a possibly resented team and of contempt for all others, talking sports is relatively noncontroversial. Jokes can prove to be offensive, and views on movies can meet with disapproval as much as views on politics. In contrast, great performances in sports are often unquestionable. It is almost inconceivable that marveling at the Olympic performance of Dorothy Hamill at Innsbruck or Nadia Comaneci at Montreal could prompt vehement disapproval from anyone. And in the face of several rushing records, who could argue with someone who describes O. J. Simpson as a good running back? Reveling in unquestionably great competitive sports performances, then, is a rather risk-free enjoyable social exercise. The enormous popularity that sport enjoys as a topic for conversation (Stone, 1969) would seem to corroborate this view.

Sportsfanship is a low-risk proposition in yet another way. Obviously, in competition not everyone can be a winner. Losing is largely unavoidable, and for the most part, it is a disturbing, if not a painful experience for the participants involved. Not so for the spectator. Although spectators tend to enjoy the victory of their team as if it were their own, they manage to give the team full credit for defeat. There is no personal sting in the defeat. No personal pride is lost. As the findings reported by Cialdini et al. (1976) show, spectators think about victory in terms of the inclusive "we" and about defeat in terms of the exclusive "they." Such a cognitive maneuver on the part of the spectator assures the enjoyment of victory, but circumvents the agony of defeat. Thus, while the sports participant, being unable to attribute a loss to the actions of others, has to take the full blow of defeat, the spectator enjoys the protection of a "defense mechanism." This mechanism, it should be noticed, amounts to an entirely appropriate interpretation of events. Unlike the mechanics governing the phenomenon of sharing the glory of victory, it is not based on misaccreditation.

Last but maybe not least, it should be mentioned that sportsfanship does not present a health hazard. Active participation in sports is unquestionably of enormous value in promoting physical fitness and bodily health, but it also places the participant at risk, low and acceptable as this risk may be, of pulling muscles, twisting ankles, and breaking bones. In contrast, whatever benefits

sports spectatorship has to offer, they can be attained without risk of injury or pain. Sportsfanship is safe in a physical sense.

But independent of all these beneficial characteristics that sports spectatorship may have in comparison to active sports participation, the phenomenon of euphoria in sportsfanship should be of interest in its own right. This is to say that the enjoyment people all over the world apparently derive from watching sport contests is worthy of investigation, regardless of other benefits or the lack thereof. If spectatorship produced no effects other than enjoyment, and even if such enjoyment were branded as "superficial," it would still be an experience of some value and preferable to many others. As it turns out, sports spectatorship, for the most part, is a rather harmless, risk-free affair with beneficial consequences. But if it were not, if it were an activity that defies the concept of mental health or the like, we would still have to make an effort at understanding the pleasures that sportsfanship provides. What attracts the fans to the games? What is it within a contest that they enjoy? What enhances and what impairs enjoyment? In short, what are the factors that govern and control the enjoyment of sport contests? We will now turn to the analysis of these factors.

EXPLORING THE SPECTATOR'S AFFECTIVE REACTIONS

As has been indicated earlier, much speculation has gone into the phenomenon of joyful sports spectatorship. Pseudo and grandiose explanations are plentiful. Many investigators have apparently been content with simply labeling the phenomenon to be explained. They have presented sport contests as "rituals" (e.g., Storr, 1968) and as "rites" (e.g., Beisser, 1967). Such characterizations may point out interesting parallels between earlier and contemporary cultures, but they certainly do not explain why these rituals and rites exist and why they are so popular. The description of the annual football craze in America, for example, as an "American masculinity rite" merely restates the existence of the football craze, but it does not aid in our understanding of this craze. Description, no matter how suggestively presented, is not to be confused with explanation. There are grand speculations, however, that cannot readily be dismissed as pseudo-explanations. The enjoyment of competition, especially of aggression-laden competition, can be projected, for instance, on the basis of Lorenz' (1963) concept of ritualized aggression. If, following Lorenz, one were to assume that (1) destructive energy spontaneously builds up in the organism, (2) the performance of aggressive acts reduces such energy to tolerable levels, a process that is pleasantly experienced, (3) the performance of competitive actions also serves this pleasing outlet function, and (4) even merely

witnessing competitive actions serves this function, one seems to have accounted for the popularity of sports—doing and viewing. Fry (Note 2) has recently presented a similarly universal rationale. He suggested that the human organism, which was built to meet and withstand considerable stress in the fight for survival, has been more and more deprived of challenges. Sports competition provides substitute challenges that can be met head-on in direct engagements, or "from a distance" through the spectator's vicarious involvement. While the two views critically differ with regard to the function that the involvement with sports is to serve (outlet-relief vs. stress-seeking), they are both biologically oriented. People, in short, need sport because of their biological constitution, and they enjoy it because it satisfies a biological need. This type of proposal is unquestionably fundamental and possibly intriguing. But independent of potential appeal, it is problem-laden as an explanation. Enjoyment of sport contests can be made to appear plausible, but the account of enjoyment is *post hoc.* Characteristically, the account cannot be faulted. It cannot be put to the test. Since its possible falsehood cannot be evaluated, it cannot be considered valid either. Another difficulty arises from the fact that, while the different rationales make the enjoyment of sports appear equally plausible, the accounts are based on incompatible assumptions. Enjoyment has been "explained" through both stress relief and stress-seeking. This creates a situation in which one account challenges the other, without the possibility of a reconciliation. Furthermore, a principle problem is to be seen in the involvement of far-reaching assumptions that are not only highly arbitrary, but conflict with much recent research evidence. The assumption that watching sport contests relieves biologically founded destructive impulses, for example, may well help to make the phenomenon of sportsfanship appear plausible, but in the light of the nonsupportive research evidence discussed earlier, one would have to conclude that such an assumption is highly misleading, causing more damage than good.

Generally speaking, it appears that broad notions such as those presented above are suggestive at best. They are sufficiently vague so as to effectively elude decisive testing, and since their appropriateness cannot really be determined, they do not explain anything in the sense of accurate prediction. Also, they are usually so broad that almost all specific aspects of the enjoyment of sport contests remain yet to be made to appear plausible.

In the following sections, we take the position that understanding the enjoyment of sport contests can best be furthered by the advancement of more specific, testable proposals. In recognition of the complexity of the phenomenon of sportsfanship, we avoid round-about universal proposals, and we instead attempt to explain the various salient aspects of the enjoyment of sports, one at a time. It is hoped, of course, that as we come to understand the various facets of sports spectatorship, we will successively advance our understanding of the phenomenon at large. Below, we develop various

rationales regarding the spectator's affective reactions, and we present and discuss recent research findings pertaining to them.

Disposition Theory of Sportsfanship

The enjoyment of watching sport contests, as everyone who has observed it in others will acknowledge, is not a simple function of the athletes' display of excellence in motor and/or strategic skills. It apparently depends, to some extent at least, on the particular person displaying such excellence, and on the particular team to which this person belongs. People applaud great play on the part of their favorite athletes and teams. The same excellence, the same mastery of skills, seems to be far less appreciated, possibly even deplored, when it is exhibited by disliked athletes or resented teams. In short, the spectator's disposition toward a player or a team appears to determine the degree to which he or she will enjoy or deplore great and poor play. The spectator should rejoice with every move his or her favored party makes toward victory and should suffer disappointment whenever the opposing party places victory in jeopardy. Spectators are known "to root" for players and teams, hoping and wishing that their party will succeed in defeating the opposition. By the same token, spectators appear to wish that the players and teams they dislike be defeated, and they seem to take pleasure in seeing the opposition humiliated and "destroyed." The indicated dynamics are those of the disposition theory of mirth (Zillmann & Cantor, 1976), a general model from which the spectator's affective reactions to the events in a sport contest can readily be predicted.

In principle, the disposition theory of mirth asserts "that loss of value inflicted upon our enemies and gain of value obtained by our friends is appreciated, and that gain of value obtained by our enemies and loss of value inflicted upon our friends is deplored" (Zillmann & Cantor, 1976, p. 113). The specific application of this model to the appreciation of sport contests results in the following propositions:

1. Enjoyment derived from witnessing the success and victory of a competing party increases with positive sentiments and decreases with negative sentiments toward that party.
2. Enjoyment derived from witnessing the failure and defeat of a competing party increases with negative sentiments and decreases with positive sentiments toward that party.

There are two mirth-promoting dispositional conditions, then, whose contributions can be assumed to combine additively. The optimal condition for enjoyment is the contest in which an intensely liked player or team defeats an intensely disliked opponent. Other things equal, the worst condition for

enjoyment is provided in the reverse situation. The confrontation of two equally liked or disliked parties is obviously a mixed blessing. The dispositional forces that enhance enjoyment are counteracted by those impairing it, and enjoyment is consequently held to a comparatively low level. In this context, disappointment can be treated as the inverse of enjoyment. A contest in which an intensely liked player or team "is beaten" by an intensely disliked opponent obviously constitutes the optimal condition for disappointment. Finally, it should be noticed that the model predicts minimal enjoyment (or disappointment) for the case in which the spectator is not dispositionally involved. Indifference toward players and teams is expected to produce flat affective reactions, if it produces affective reactions at all.

Applied to sports spectatorship, the disposition model may sound plausible because it accords well with introspective accounts. One "loves" some teams and "hates" others. One also recalls the euphoria of seeing one's home team beat a resented rival and the trying experience of the reverse. Notwithstanding such supportive intuitive appraisals, we recently conducted several investigations to determine the validity of predictions from the disposition model. We explored dispositional factors in the appreciation of football, basketball, and tennis.

A first study probed the implications of dispositions toward professional football teams. In a large-enrollment introductory communications course at Indiana University, a survey was administered that assessed the liking and disliking of various competitive sports, players, and teams. Included was football and all professional football teams. The analysis of dispositions toward teams showed a strong differentiation for the Minnesota Vikings and an adequate one for the St. Louis Cardinals: The Vikings were intensely liked by some and intensely disliked by others; the Cardinals were liked and disliked, but to a lesser degree. Additionally, many subjects were indifferent toward the one or the other team. On the basis of these dispositional data, a factorial design was created, with negative, neutral, and positive dispositions toward the Vikings and negative, neutral, and positive dispositions toward the Cardinals being the two cross-varied factors. One month after the survey, and ostensibly entirely unrelated to it, subjects watched a live-televised regular-season game between these teams. They rated their enjoyment of every play on a scale ranging from "disliked it a lot" (–50) to "liked it a lot" (50). In the data analysis, plays of the same kind (i.e., successful or unsuccessful runs, short or long passes, field-goal attempts, etc.) were combined for each team. Subjects also rated their enjoyment of the entire game. The game itself was a close contest won by the Vikings (28–24).

The findings generally agree with the predictions from disposition theory. As can be seen from Table 11.1, a positive disposition toward a team tended to enhance the appreciation of offensive plays successfully executed by that team. But while a negative disposition toward a team tended to impair such

TABLE 11.1
Viewers' Appreciation of Plays in Professional Football
as a Function of Disposition Toward Teams[1]

| | Disposition | | | | | |
| | Toward Team A (Vikings) | | | Toward Team B (Cardinals) | | |
Type of Play	Negative	Neutral	Positive	Negative	Neutral	Positive
Successful run[2] by team A	-2^a	8^b	9^b	9	3	3
Successful run by team B	15	14	11	11^a	12^a	17^b
Successful pass[3] by team A	-4^a	11^b	14^b	14	5	2
Successful pass by team B	25	26	20	19^a	23^{ab}	29^b

Note: Letter superscripts indicate significant main effects for disposition toward teams. Means having no letter in their superscripts in common differ significantly at $p < .05$ by Newman-Keuls' test.

[1]Minnesota Vikings vs. St. Louis Cardinals at St. Louis. Regular game of the 1974 season as broadcast by ABC's Monday Night Football.

[2]A successful run is defined as a run on which at least 3.3 yards are gained or which results in a first down or a score.

[3]Only long passes are considered here. A successful long pass is defined as a completed forward pass that travels at least 10 yards across the line of scrimmage to the point of reception.

appreciation, it dropped to nonappreciation and disappointment only in the case of intensely negative sentiments toward the team. For the teams under consideration, only the Vikings met this condition. With regard to defensive plays, a somewhat different picture emerges. Theoretically, successful defense is equivalent to the opposition's unsuccessful offense. For example, a person rooting for Team A certainly should enjoy seeing this team progress toward victory, but he or she should equally enjoy seeing Team B stagnate, presumably because of good defense on the part of Team A. Appreciation tended to follow this line of reasoning (the differences between means generally accord with it), but the differentiations failed to be reliable. An explanation for this lack of a corresponding inverse appreciation between offensive and defensive play can be offered in attributional terms: The spectator may readily credit the offense with the successful execution of an offensive play; in contrast, as the opposition fails to be successful with an offensive play, he or she may give some credit to excellent defense but may also attribute it to ineptness in the opposition's offense. Even a spectacular interception, for example, can be viewed as partly the fault of the quarterback.

Enjoyment of the entire game was as predicted. Not surprisingly, with the Vikings winning the contest, appreciation was nearly nonexistent (M = 4) in those who both "hated" the Vikings and "loved" the Cardinals. It was much higher in all remaining conditions. It was unexpectedly high (M = 39) for those who disliked both teams.

Enjoyment of the outcome specifically was again as predicted. Maximal enjoyment (M = 19) was found in those who both liked the Vikings and disliked the Cardinals. Maximal disappointment (M = –33) was observed in those who both disliked the Vikings and liked the Cardinals. Viking haters considered the outcome significantly more a result of luck than did Viking fans or those who were indifferent toward this team. The perception of football skills was not affected by disposition, however.

All dispositional effects reported were obtained for both sexes. The only sex difference observed in the entire investigation concerned excitement about the game. Male viewers rated the game as significantly more exciting than female viewers (M = 29 and M = 18, respectively).

The dispositional mediation of the enjoyment of sport contests appears to be most obtrusively displayed in the cheers and moans of large crowds. Under the rather safe assumption that a crowd roots for the home team, successful offensive plays on the part of the home team should produce roars of applause, and unsuccessful offensive attempts should yield moans of disappointment. The reverse should be true for the crowd's reactions to the visiting team's play.

To secure these effects, we conducted another investigation on the enjoyment of watching football. We selected college contests in which there could be little doubt about the team the crowd would favor: Tufts University vs. Amherst College at Amherst and Bowdoin College vs. Amherst College at Amherst. The crowd's vocal reactions were recorded during the contest. The play-by-play reactions, in random order, were later presented to judges who were naive about the plays and the teams. The judges evaluated every vocal reaction in terms of the degree of enjoyment or disappointment they could detect in it. The scores were then related back to the specific types of plays of the home or visiting team.

The Bowdoin vs. Amherst game proved to be a lopsided contest with Amherst winning 42–7. The findings presented in Table 11.2 are those from the Tufts vs. Amherst game, a very close contest won by Tufts (18–17). The data from the lopsided game are essentially the same as those presented. The closer contest yielded somewhat stronger differentiations, however.

In contrast to the earlier investigation on the enjoyment of televised professional football, these data on live attendance do show the symmetry of enjoyment and disappointment that the disposition model predicts. Failing plays of the visiting team were nearly as much applauded as successful plays of the home team, and failing plays of the home team were nearly as much

TABLE 11.2
Viewers' Appreciation of Plays in College Football
as a Function of Affiliation With Teams[1]

	Affiliation	
Type of Play	Positive (Home Team)	Negative (Visiting Team)
Successful run[2]	6.9^d	-5.0^a
Successful pass[3]	6.0^d	-3.6^{ab}
Unsuccessful run	-1.0^b	2.3^c
Unsuccessful pass	-4.2^{ab}	5.0^{cd}

Note: Appreciation was measured from audio-recordings of the crowd's reactions to the plays. Two coders, blind with regard to teams and plays, judged the degree to which a reaction expressed enjoyment (10) or disappointment (-10). Coder reliability was .88. Means having no letter in their superscripts in common differ at $p < .05$ by Newman-Keuls' test.
[1]Tufts University vs. Amherst College at Amherst, Massachusetts, 1976.
[2]A successful run is defined as a run on which at least 3.3 yards are gained or which results in a first down or a score.
[3]A successful pass (long and short combined) is defined as any completed forward pass.

deplored as successful plays of the visiting teams. In fact, the symmetry of enjoyment and disappointment is so strong that it severely challenges the view that it is athletic greatness (no matter who displays it) that is being applauded by the college-game crowds. A pass completion by the visiting team, for example, if it was not perceived as "a lucky shot," may have been acknowledged as "good football." But as the data show, it did not spark applause or cheers. And by the same token, a passing play "going nowhere" for the visitors caused a level of enjoyment comparable to that associated with the display of good athletic skills in the successful offensive plays by the home team.

The fact that the data on college football corroborate the predictions from the disposition model more decisively than those on professional football can be explained in several ways. First, it can be argued that the requirement to rate the enjoyment of individual plays (in the pro-football game) may have fostered a more critical appraisal. In an effort to see matters "objectively," subjects may have subdued their dispositional bias to some extent. No such constraint is present in the cheer-and-moan data. The raters, in failing to record much disappointment, may also have yielded to the idea that watching professional football is supposed to be enjoyable. Second, it has often been suggested that college contests generate more excitement than professional encounters because of far greater involvement on the part of the crowd. This greater degree of involvement translates into more pronounced positive and

negative dispositions toward the teams, which should ultimately produce more intense reactions of enjoyment and of disappointment, together with a more distinct separation between the two. Finally, the observed extreme differentiation in the crowd reactions could be due to social facilitation (cf. Zajonc, 1965). It is conceivable that the immediate presence of many co-acting others stimulates the expression of euphoria and, maybe more importantly, disinhibits the expression of dysphoria.

Further evidence of the dispositional mediation of the enjoyment derived from watching sport contests comes from an investigation of basketball. We secured the cooperation of large numbers of subjects, all affiliated with Indiana University, in obtaining ratings of their reactions to play leading to the scoring of baskets in the championship game of the 1976 Olympic Games in Montreal, Canada. Subjects were prepared to rate basket-by-basket play and permitted to watch the game under "natural conditions" (i.e., at home or anywhere, alone or in the company of others). We hoped that the final game, as in the 1972 Munich games, would confront Russia and the United States. But Russia was eliminated by Yugoslavia, and the championship game thus featured Yugoslavia vs. the United States. The game was not televised in extenso. The data, then, derived from only those portions of the game which ABC elected to broadcast. The analysis of the scores by plays was analogous to that in the football studies discussed earlier.

As Table 11.3 shows, plays resulting in baskets scored by Yugoslavia were not enjoyed. Female viewers actually responded with mild disappointment. In sharp contrast, plays that produced baskets for the American team were predictably applauded with considerable intensity. The findings reveal yet

TABLE 11.3
Viewers' Appreciation of Scoring Plays in Olympic Basketball Competition
as a Function of Affiliation With Players[1]

	Affiliation		
Sex of Viewer (I.U. Students)	Highly Positive (I.U. Player)	Positive (Non I.U., U.S. Player)	Negative (Yugoslav Player)
Male	75[c]	59[b]	3[a]
Female	79[c]	64[b]	-4[a]
Sex of Viewer Combined[2]	77[c]	61[b]	0[a]

Note: Means having different letter superscripts differ significantly at $p < .05$ by Newman-Keuls' test.
[1]United States vs. Yugoslavia in the championship game at the 1976 Olympic Games in Montreal, Canada, as broadcast by ABC.
[2]Weighted means.

another and maybe more interesting dispositional consequence, however. Two players on the American team were local basketball heroes: Scott May and Quinn Buckner, both members of the 1976 NCAA Basketball Championship Team of Indiana University. Regarding their scoring plays, the disposition model predicts extreme enjoyment reactions because of intensely favorable dispositions. Under the assumption that the baskets scored by these two players were no more spectacular than those scored by the other members of the American team, the fact that they nonetheless sparked more intense mirthful reactions again attests to the dispositional mediation of the enjoyment derived from watching sport contests.

In the discussed investigations it was assumed that the liking or disliking of a team does not covary with behavioral characteristics that would systematically affect enjoyment. It was considered unlikely, for example, that Viking-lovers are generally cheerful and Viking-haters generally sad people, or vice versa. To avoid such assumptions altogether, dispositions cannot be sampled, but have to be manipulated. We have attempted such manipulations, but our attempts have been quite unsuccessful. In an investigation of the appreciation of watching tennis, we tried to create favorable and unfavorable dispositions toward Bjorn Borg and Ilie Nastase. Subjects read especially prepared clippings ostensibly taken from sports magazines. The clippings pictured Borg either as a nice young man or as a money-grabbing, heartless exploiter of girl fans. Similarly, Nastase was pictured either as a misunderstood, unduly criticized, and actually kind person or as a truly obnoxious guy unable to control his temper in his personal life as well as on the court. Subjects were not taken by such manipulatory efforts. Apparently, these players are far too well known to change perception of them with a magazine article.

In this investigation of tennis we succeeded, however, in manipulating the game itself. A relatively unimportant match between the players in question (at the 1976 World Invitational Tennis Classic), televised by ABC, was taped and edited in such a way that it was won either by Borg or by Nastase. The number of games won and lost by either player was kept constant, with wins and losses reversed so as to fix the outcome of the match. Subjects rated their enjoyment of every game and of the match itself. At this point we have to return to the ineffectiveness of the disposition manipulation. No matter how Borg was depicted, he was liked, and more so than Nastase. Seeing Borg defeat Nastase was thus predictably more enjoyed than seeing the reverse, regardless of feelings toward Nastase. The effects of rooting are more strongly demonstrated in the comparison of a match won versus a match lost by a disliked Nastase. Taking the appreciation data across games won and lost, subjects deplored seeing nasty Nastase defeat Borg ($M = -2.3$), and they enjoyed witnessing his defeat at the hands of Borg ($M = 2.4$), the difference in appreciation being highly significant.

Taken together, the reported findings show that: (1) affective dispositions toward players and teams, both positive and negative, do indeed exist in the audience at large; and (2) these dispositions determine the appreciation of events in sport contests and, ultimately, the appreciation of contests altogether to a very high degree. They leave no doubt that people "have feelings about athletes," and that they enjoy or despise events and outcomes in accord with their feelings. It remains to be seen, however, exactly what function these dispositions serve and how they develop. Why do people affiliate with some players or teams and not with others? Why and how do they grow fond of some athletes and come to resent others?

The phenomenon yet to be adequately explained is that of the loyal local fan. Why do people tend to cheer for their home team, regardless of athletic excellence? Is it the need to feel a sense of solidarity with a local community? Or is it a matter of social control that rewards conformity and punishes deviancy? The latter may be the case in crowd behavior, but it is difficult to see how such control could exert itself in television and radio audiences. Could it be that the conversation value of a sport contest, as discussed earlier, is a sufficient incentive condition for the spectator to back the local team? But even a viable explanation of the local-fan phenomenon would not fully answer the question of rooting regarding the individual athlete. To be sure, if Jimmy Connors, for example, competes as an American against an opponent who represents a foreign country, say Spain, the local-fan phenomenon simply extends to the national level. But what if Connors meets another American to fight for the big money? The local-fan phenomenon suddenly no longer applies. While, in all likelihood, Connors would enjoy the support of some well-wishers, there would be many others who hope for his destruction. Conceivably, there are those who decide to root for the party most likely to win. This decision not only favors athletic excellence (in the long run) but assures maximal psychological benefits: There is more to cheer about during a contest and more glory to bask in later. Yet, in defiance of such promise, uncounted sports fans insist that what they enjoy more than anything is seeing David destroy Goliath. There appear to be both types of fans, those who play it safe and root for the champion, and those who take chances and root for the daring challenger. But while topdog and underdog rooters may consitute most interesting personality types, rooting seems to take many other orientations as well. Fans may wish that victory come to the attractive, the humble, and the kind athlete, and they may wish that defeat come to the greedy, the arrogant, and the insensitive athlete. With the exception of the social phenomenon of local sportsfanship, it is conceivable that the dynamics of rooting are a specific manifestation of the general dynamics of affect. This is to say that the affective dispositions that make for rooting in the enjoyment of sports, are formed and modified just as any other disposition. Nice people are considered deserving of reward, bad people of punishment (cf. Zillmann

& Bryant, 1975; Zillmann & Cantor, 1976). When the little that is known about Borg, for example, makes him appear a nice guy, he should be perceived as deserving of a victory over nasty Nastase. And if Nastase blatantly insults and offends his opponent, his defeat, in bringing justice to the situation, should become a pleasureful event for nearly everybody looking on.

The Human Drama in Sport Displays

Many of those who have addressed the phenomenon of sports spectatorship (e.g., Beisser, 1967; Johnson, 1971) have described the sport contest as a battle. They have depicted athletic competition as a furious struggle, not as a game in which emotionally detached players try to determine who does best on a particular motor task. In fact, most writers have implied, if not explicitly proposed, that the element of struggle is a necessary ingredient of the popular sport event.

It would appear, indeed, that the spectator expects a contest to be a "hard fought battle" rather than a playful show of athletic skills. Again, it is not the mastery of particular skills per se that is the sole object of attention. The spectator appears to pay close attention to the circumstances of a competitive performance, especially to the motivational circumstances. Accurate passing in football, for example, may well be applauded in a preseason game, but the same performance should produce great happiness or great disappointment, dependent upon whose side the spectator supports, in a decisive late-season game from which only one team can proceed to the play-offs. Great incentives (i.e., the big money in professional sports, the entry in the record books in sports where money is not a dominant force, or the admiration that comes with the victory over a strong competitor) and punitive consequences (i.e., the annoyance of seeing the opponents collect the incentives and the social humiliation that comes with defeat) are apparently believed to spur the competitive spirits and, ultimately, to make the sport contest a forum in which genuine human conflict can unfold, all within strictly defined limits. It appears that watching sport contests can produce intense positive and negative affective reactions only when the contest is perceived as a clash of human emotions. Great fortunes must be at stake, and there must be the threat of impending disaster. The conditions here are actually very similar to those that make for great drama. The threat of impending disaster, for example, produces suspense in watching a sport contest just as it does in a suspense movie. And as appreciation of drama tends to increase with the degree of suspense (cf. Zillmann, Hay, & Bryant, 1975) so presumably does the appreciation of sport contests. Seeing a liked player struggle with a tough rival not only should be more suspenseful, but should also liberate more enjoyment than the safe play against a weak opponent. But independent of

tensions during a match and their effect on the affective reactions to the final outcome, there can be little doubt that the elements of human drama surrounding a sport contest are salient factors in the determination of the spectator's enjoyment or disappointment.

On the basis of the above reasoning, we propose that the enjoyment of watching sport contests is partly a function of the degree to which a contest is perceived as involving human conflict. Generally speaking, appreciation should increase with the intensity of perceived conflict. Highly motivated, fierce competition should produce more enjoyment in the spectator than haphazard rivalry and "lack of determination." The apparent expectation is that the competitor make an all-out effort to win—that he "fight his guts out," so to speak. Only under these circumstances does it become meaningful to talk in terms of the popular concepts of "the thrill of victory" and "the agony of defeat." Only a hard fought battle produces the affect intensity of triumph, and only the fully committed competitor suffers agonies.

We have recently put this proposal to the test. In a study on the enjoyment of watching tennis, we have manipulated the sportscasters' commentary on identical play. Three versions were created:

1. A sportscaster gave the play-by-play account; the comments were strictly descriptive of the visible play, with ample pausing between comments.
2. In addition to the commentary provided in (1), two reporters provided information about the players, especially about feelings they had for one another; specifically, they were described as the best of friends.
3. In addition to the commentary provided in (1), the two additional sportscasters presented the players as embittered rivals who felt intense hatred for one another and sought to destroy and humiliate their opponent.

The sportscast was thus identical regarding the play itself and the descriptive commentary thereof. It differed only in that the match was made to appear as a friendly contest in the one treatment condition and a fierce battle in the other. To assure that the actual relationship between the players was unknown to the audience, we selected a match between Grand Masters with whom our subjects, college undergraduates at the University of Massachusetts, were not familiar.

The findings are presented in Table 11.4. As can be seen, the data show compellingly that the perception of fierceness in competition enhances the enjoyment of watching a sport contest. Tense and hostile play not only proved to facilitate enjoyment, but made the entire contest more exciting, more involving, and more interesting to the audience. All these effects were obtained for both male and female viewers.

TABLE 11.4
Viewers' Appreciation of Tennis as a Function of Perceived Dispositions
of the Players Manipulated through Commentary[1]

Dependent Measure	Reported Relationship Between Players		
	No Particular Relationship Specified	Personal Friendship, Mutual Admiration	Bitter Rivalry, Mutual Hatred
Appreciation of Play:			
Enjoyable	17[a]	18[a]	34[b]
Exciting	11[a]	10[a]	19[b]
Involving	13[a]	14[a]	25[b]
Interesting	13[a]	18[a]	30[b]
Perception of Players:			
Hostile	8[a]	1[a]	40[b]
Tense	9[a]	6[a]	22[b]
Competitive	17[a]	14[a]	39[b]

Note: Comparisons are within measures only. Means having different letter superscripts differ significantly at $p < .05$ by Newman-Keuls' test.

[1]Sven Davidson vs. Torbin Ulrich, 1976 Almaden Grand Masters as broadcast by PBS.

Potentially there are many factors which, when appropriately manipulated, can enhance the apparent intensity of rivalry in a sport contest. Winning for the sheer glory of winning may leave many unconvinced of claims of a "real battle." In our society, playing for money removes any doubts about the determination to win. And the so-called big money convinces anybody that the players will fight, especially in the winner-take-all type situation. But there are more direct indices of the sincerity of competition.

Probably the most archaic index of high competitiveness is the willingness to exert large amounts of energy in vigorous and vicious play, particularly when such play occurs in defiance of mutually inflicted pain and injury. Rough and aggressive play "proves" intense competition. It stands for human conflict at the gut level. In short, it stands for high drama. In football, for example, stopping the forward progress of a running back by pushing him backwards is a play that fails to exhibit competitive intensity, regardless of how effective it may have been as a defensive move. In contrast, competitive intensity is obvious and undeniable in the bone-crushing tackle that "levels" the ball carrier. Or in basketball, the dunk viciously scored "with authority" leaves no doubt that the dunker is there to fight. A lay-up does the same damage to the opponent, but is far less exhibitive of competitive intensity.

This reasoning suggests that roughness and aggressiveness of play, within the confines of the rules of the game, will facilitate the enjoyment of watching

sport contests not because it provides a vicarious outlet for aggressive urges (the much-proposed mechanism not evidenced by pertinent research findings), but because it assures the viewer a high degree of competitiveness—human drama and all.

We have explored the enjoyment of rough play in various investigations. In a study of professional football, a large number of plays were extracted from numerous televised games and arranged in random order. After the degree of roughness involved in each play was secured by a pretest, subjects rated their enjoyment of every play in this sequence. As Table 11.5 shows, very rough play was enjoyed to a substantially higher degree than play associated with lower levels of roughness. This special appreciation of aggressive play is most pronounced for male viewers. It is comparatively weak in females.

Another study probed the effects of rough play in professional ice hockey. Especially rough and not-so-rough portions of play were selected, and their properties ascertained in a pretest. When shown without the broadcast commentary, rough play again produced more favorable evaluations. This can be seen in Table 11.6. The presence of the commentary, however, proved to alter perception of play in rather crucial ways. It proved powerful enough to affect the perception of roughness itself. Normal play described as rugged appeared rougher to the viewer than actually rough play. And as a consequence of this shift in perception, not-so-rough play that appeared

TABLE 11.5
Viewers' Appreciation of Plays in Professional Football as a
Function of Degree of Roughness Involved[1]

Sex of Viewer	Degree of Roughness[2]			Degree of Roughness Combined
	Low	Medium	High	
Male	$11^{a,A}$	$16^{ab,A}$	$31^{b,B}$	19_B
Female	$5^{a,A}$	$4^{a,A}$	$15^{a,A}$	8_A
Sex of Viewer Combined	8^a	10^a	23^b	

Note: Means having different lower-case letter superscripts differ significantly at $p < .05$ by Newman-Keuls' test (horizontal comparisons). Means having different upper-case letter superscripts differ significantly at $p < .05$ by Cochran's test (vertical comparisons). The subscripted means differ by F test.

[1]The plays were taken from numerous games of the 1976 season. The games were broadcast by various networks.

[2]The degree of roughness of the various plays was determined in a pretest. All levels differ significantly from one another ($p < .05$ by Newman-Keuls' test).

TABLE 11.6
Viewers' Appreciation of Professional Ice Hockey as a Function of Degree of
Roughness Involved and of Commentary Stressing Roughness[1]

Dependent Measure	Normal Play		Rough Play	
	No Commentary	Commentary[2]	No Commentary	Commentary[2]
Appreciation of Play:				
Enjoyable	39[a]	54[a]	43[a]	40[a]
Entertaining	35[a]	54[c]	44[b]	38[a]
Perception of Play:				
Action-packed	66[b]	70[b]	69[b]	54[a]
Enthusiastic	60[a]	76[b]	75[b]	74[b]
Rough	39[a]	67[d]	61[c]	47[b]
Violent	28[a]	62[c]	58[c]	41[b]

Note: Means having different letter superscripts differ at $p < .05$ by Newman-Keuls' test.
[1]Boston Bruins vs. Detroit Redwings at Detroit. Regular game of the 1976 season as broadcast by the Boston Bruins Network.
[2]The commentary was that of the original broadcast. It thus was different for normal and for rough play. Regarding roughness of play, it proved significantly different: The commentary associated with normal play contained a larger number of references to the roughness of play ($p<.05$ by chi-square test) than did the commentary associated with rough play.

rough was appreciated as if it were truly rough play. Interestingly, in stressing roughness of play when play was not so rough, the sportscasters behaved as though they had to make up for a deficit in roughness of play. In other words, they behaved as if they had to add drama when drama was low. When play was rough, there was apparently no need to add to the unfolding drama (cf. Comisky, Bryant, & Zillmann, 1977).

The interest in sports competition as high drama is most obtrusively served by the so-called mass media. The electronic and the printed media alike not only dedicate great portions of time and space to sports coverage as such, but report in great detail about players and teams, about the circumstances of contests, about the history of personal, team, or fanship rivalries, mutual dislikes of coaches, etc. Coverage of the contest itself is by no means an exercise in descriptive reporting. Much commentary on play apparently seeks to create an awareness of the dramatic elements of a contest, presumably to enhance appreciation of the contest as drama. In a representative content analysis we conducted on the coverage of professional football by American television, we observed that about 26% of all statements made in the commentary serve the dramatization of the contest. This amounts to about 265 statements per contest. Most of this drama-serving commentary amounts to praise. Competitive strength is emphasized in about 130 statements per game. Derogatory comments are also made, but they are comparatively rare (about 26 per game). But dramatization is also achieved on the screen itself.

The camera singles out those who return to the bench in glee and those who seethe in anger. It shows the jubilant and the injured, and it dwells on the face of the infuriated coach. Per televised football game, the screen features "the thrill of victory" in about 11 dramatic shots and "the agony of defeat" in about 13 (cf. Bryant, Comisky, & Zillmann, 1977).

Social Facilitation

It is generally taken for granted that watching a sport contest alone is less enjoyable than watching it in the company of friends, or in the midst of a cheerful crowd. Those who have sought to explain this truism have often alluded to a transformed state of mind created by the very presence of others. They have cited LeBon's (1896) proposal that people in a crowd become highly vulnerable to suggestion: Their rational skills deteriorate, and their emotional responsiveness increases. As a consequence, the people are readily taken by the expression of emotion surrounding them. Expressed enjoyment or disappointment carries over to them, and affective reactions are more intense than in the absence of the suggestive crowd behavior. Zajonc (1965) has provided a rationale that makes essentially the same predictions. The emotion-enhancing effect of the presence of others, referred to as social facilitation, is not viewed as the result of emotional suggestiveness, however. It is said to result from the fact that the presence of others arouses a person. It is this socially induced arousal that is implicated with the intensification of affective experiences. Further rationales could readily be developed. It could be argued, for example, that enjoyment or disappointment is enhanced through empathy. More specifically, it can be seen as being enhanced through the liberation of affect that is classically conditioned to the expression of emotion in others (cf. Bandura, 1969; Zillmann & Cantor, 1977). Counter-proposals are not espoused by anybody, but could be based on distraction occasioned by the crowd's behavior.

The notion of the social facilitation of the enjoyment of watching sport contests was empirically evaluated in the investgation of Olympic basketball described earlier. Subjects watched the United States versus Yugoslavia championship game alone, with just one other person, in a small group, or in a larger crowd-like group. Table 11.7 displays the enjoyment ratings of plays leading to scores either for the United States or the Yugoslav team. Considering all plays together, the social conditions for viewing had no appreciable effect. This might have been expected because the predicted facilitation of enjoyment (of U.S. scores) and disappointment (opponent scores) should have been symmetrical and thus, ideally, led to the absence of an overall effect for social conditions. But a look at the enjoyment of U.S. scoring plays and the disappointment of Yugoslavian scoring plays does not reveal the predicted symmetry. Enjoyment of U.S. baskets simply did not

TABLE 11.7
Viewers' Appreciation of Scoring Plays in Olympic Basketball Competition
as a Function of Social Conditions[1]

	Social Condition for Viewing			
Team Scoring	Alone	With Another Person	In a Small Group (2-4 Persons)	In a Larger Group (5 and More Persons)
United States	61[c]	63[c]	70[c]	61[c]
Yugoslavia	2[ab]	−10[a]	−11[a]	21[b]
Both Teams Combined[2]	39[a]	36[a]	40[a]	46[a]

Note: Means having different letter superscripts differ significantly at $p < .05$ by Newman-Keuls' test.
[1]United States vs. Yugoslavia in the championship game at the 1976 Olympic Games in Montreal, Canada, as broadcast by ABC.
[2]All means are weighted by the number of scoring plays by the respective teams.

show a social-facilitation effect, and the enjoyment or disappointment associated with Yugoslavian baskets is opposite to the expected effect. The social-facilitation argument is thus in no way supported by the findings (cf. Sapolsky & Zillmann, 1978). Surprisingly, it is the large-group or crowd condition that produced the unexpected results. Without this condition, the pattern of means is at least consistent with predictions. The crowd condition, however, clearly failed to enhance enjoyment of U.S. baskets as it should have. More surprisingly, it not only failed to further the disappointment over Yugoslavian scoring plays, but actually caused considerable enjoyment of such plays. This latter finding is puzzling. It challenges the social-facilitation argument. Disappointment should have caught on, and viewers should have more intensely deplored the plays in question. One might be inclined to return to Le Bon's claim that cognitive skills are retarded as a person joins a crowd, and that jubilation is indiscriminately applied. But such a view conflicts not only with common observation (even the most excited crowd apparently manages to separate the play of the home team from that of the visitors), but also with the data at hand. Only if jubilation over U.S. baskets would have been particularly pronounced, which it was not, would there be reason to expect a spill-over into opposition play. It appears that the unexpected finding can be more readily explained as an effect of social control, or more accurately, of the relaxation of social control in the crowd condition. Scoring plays against the United States, no matter how marvelously executed, could not be applauded in the presence of friends and acquaintances because these persons exerted social control. Such cheering would have suggested that the person roots for the foreign team—obviously a socially improper reaction. Scoring plays against the U.S. team were thus predictably deplored under

these circumstances. The discussed social control does not apply, or it applies to a lesser degree, to viewing in solitude and, apparently, to viewing as a comparatively anonymous member of a crowd. In either of these viewing conditions, the spectators are not held as much accountable for their "deviant" affective reactions as they are in the company of people who know them well. As a result, they are free to applaud great athletic performances by an opposition team—at least as long as such performances do not place in jeopardy the victory of the team they support. The dispositional bias in the appreciation of play is, of course, not in question. Even in the crowd condition it is clearly in evidence.

In the light of these findings, one should refrain from treating the social facilitation of the enjoyment of watching sport contests as a truism. The presence of others appears to mediate such enjoyment in a more complex fashion than is suggested by the popular arguments that have been entertained.

Uncommon, Risky, and Effective Play

The enjoyment derived from witnessing events in the context of play has been linked to the surprise value of these events (cf. Berlyne, 1960, 1969). Uncommon, unexpected, and uncertain events are said to hold greater promise for being appreciated than common, expected, and certain events. Common and certain events convey little novelty and hence constitute comparatively dull affairs. Uncommon and unexpected events, in contrast, carry considerable novelty. They take the viewer by surprise, and they thus constitute interesting and possibly exciting affairs. Characteristically, these propositions are drawn from information theory (Shannon & Weaver, 1949; Wiener, 1961), a mathematical theory in which statistical unpredictability is equated with amount of information. To be sure, information theory is, for the most part, not directly applied, but used as an analog in the speculations regarding surprise and reactions thereto. Amount of information, that is, statistical unpredictability, is taken to index novelty and surprise. In Bense's (1954, 1956, 1958, 1960) mathematical theory of aesthetics, it becomes a measure of aesthetic appeal. Bense applied his theoretical model to the enjoyment of watching sport contests specifically, arguing that it is the unpredictability of the sports event, the uncertainty about the outcome, that makes for the excitement of sports spectatorship and ultimately for the enjoyment of sport contests. In his view, it is the element of true unpredictability that favors sports spectatorship, especially regarding contests, over other forms of entertainment in which the unpredictability of events is artificial and comparatively low.

The argument certainly holds intuitive appeal. Contests are often described as becoming boring as soon as the outcome is no longer in doubt and the

contest becomes lopsided. Close contests, as their frequent characterization as "barn-burners," "cliff-hangers," "heart-stoppers," and "nail-biters" suggests, can provide a thrill of excitement that is difficult to match with action-dramas whose outcomes have become quite predictable (cf. Mendelsohn, 1966). But the argument can also be questioned on intuitive grounds. The very phenomenon of rooting would tend to challenge the generality of the enjoyment-through-unpredictability formula. The loyal fan may greatly enjoy pleasant surprises, but not surprise per se. And the excitement of a "cliff-hanger" may only be enjoyed in retrospect after the supported team managed to eke out a victory. A close contest resulting in the defeat of the supported team gives little cause for jubilation. As in the case of unresolved suspense (cf. Zillmann, Hay, & Bryant, 1975), high degrees of residual excitation are not channeled into euphoria (because such a reaction is without cognitive basis), and the spectator should leave in distress. Additionally, as the findings of the entirely lopsided Bowdoin versus Amherst football game reported earlier suggest, one-sided contests can stir up considerable excitement as long as the supported team is winning. Greatly lacking unpredictability, the loyal Nebraska fans, for example, presumably nonetheless thoroughly enjoyed seeing their highly rated football team not just defeat, but trample and humiliate an unheralded Indiana team.

All this is to say that the degree to which an event in sports is unpredictable and takes the spectator by surprise does not necessarily trigger a proportional degree of mirth. Rather, it is likely that the surprise value of play merely modifies the affective reactions determined by the spectator's dispositions toward players and teams: Novel, innovative, and surprising play, especially when it proves effective, may be more appreciated than equally effective familiar play of a supported player or team; if displayed by the opposition, unpredictable play should lead to less rather than to greater appreciation. This probable interaction should be recognized in the study of the effects of unpredictable play on enjoyment.

Regarding specific play, the uncertainty rationale can be applied in at least two principal ways. First, a play can be uncertainty-laden in that it is rarely used and thus comes unexpected when it comes. The more often a play is used, the more it is expected and the less it surprises. The frequency, then, with which particular plays are being employed determines the degree to which they should cause surprise and enjoyment. According to this reasoning, enjoyment of a play should be inversely proportional to the frequency of its past usage. In football, for example, the run is more frequently used than the short pass which, in turn, is more frequently used than the long pass. Across dispositions toward players and teams, and across a great many plays differing in their individual manifestations, the long pass should thus be more appreciated than the short pass, and the short pass should be more appreciated than the run. This is indeed the case. Our initial study on the enjoyment of professional football shows successfully completed long passes

(M = 23.2) to be more enjoyed than successfuly completed short passes (M = 15.4) which, in turn, were more enjoyed than successful runs (M = 8.8). This assessment may be highly confounded with the appreciation of greater and lesser skills involved in the plays. Such possible confoundings are not an issue, however, in the reactions to unsuccessfully attempted plays of the kind in question. Unsuccessful attempts resulted nonetheless in the same differentiation: 5.5 for the long pass, 1.6 for the short pass, and 0.4 for the run. Interestingly, a relatively rare play, the long pass, was nearly as much appreciated when it failed as a relatively frequent play, the run when it succeeded.

Second, a play can be uncertainty-laden in that it entails a high risk of failure. A safe play assures the accomplishment of its objective with near certainty. A risky play provides no such assurance; on the contrary, the likelihood of success slips down toward that of failure, with the .5-ratio defining maximal uncertainty about a play's outcome. Plays associated with a success ratio substantially below .5 are not just very risky, but somewhat foolhardy. Failure becomes predictable, and there is little surprise in this outcome. If, however, a player or team manages to pull off a play considered unlikely to succeed, the highly unpredictable has happened and may be celebrated as gutsy play—play in defiance of the odds. In short, this reasoning leads to the prediction that, while safe play, in the long run, is dull and unexciting, risky play is enjoyable. Enjoyment of successful play should be proportional to the risk of failure involved.

We have explored the discussed relationship between uncommonness, riskiness, and enjoyment of play in a correlational study on football. Effectiveness of play was an additional factor in this investigation. This latter factor was included to determine the degree to which enjoyment of play is simply a function of the supported team's progress toward the ultimate goal: victory.

Subjects rated, where applicable, the following characteristics of nearly all conceivable and carefully described plays in the game of football:

1. The average frequency of a play's successful or unsuccessful use by a team in a game, serving as the measure of commonness or uncommonness, respectively.
2. The failure percentage (i.e., the percentage of unsuccessful execution), serving as a first measure of riskiness.
3. The turnover percentage, serving as a second measure of riskiness.
4. The average gain of yardage, serving as a measure of effectiveness.
5. The degree of enjoyment or disappointment associated with seeing the play in question successfully executed by a liked team.

The findings for all commonly employed offensive plays of football are summarized in Fig. 11.1. The results on the second measure of riskiness were

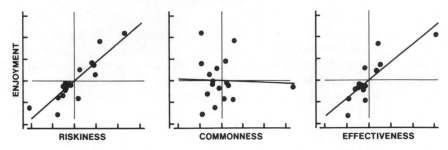

FIG. 11.1.   Enjoyment of offensive plays in football as a function of riskiness, commonness, and effectiveness of play. The data are presented in z-scores. For *riskiness,* $r = .90$, $\beta = .87$, variance accounted for $= 76\%$; for *commonness,* $r = -.11$, $\beta = -.05$, variance accounted for $= .2\%$; and for *effectiveness,* $r = .81$, $\beta = .81$, variance accounted for $= 65\%$. The multiple-regression analysis involving all three predictor variables yielded $R = .91$.

deleted from presentation because they were entirely redundant with those of the first measure.

As can be seen from the figure, the enjoyment of a play can be predicted with considerable accuracy on the basis of the risk of failure it entails. The very long pass or "bomb" was considered the riskiest play (60% failure). It also was the play most enjoyed. In contrast, the extra-point kick after a touchdown and the quarterback sneak were considered the safest plays (12% and 27% failure, respectively). These plays were those enjoyed the least. A typical high-risk play was the reverse (45% failure, $z = .92$), which was also highly enjoyed ($z = .70$). With the exception of the short pass over the middle, all plays associated with an above-par risk (positive z-score) were also above-par appreciated. The data, then, corroborate the proposition of proportionality between risk and enjoyment in the appreciation of plays successfully executed by a liked team. The gutsy call apparently demands the spectator's respect.

A look at the commonness of play, however, fails to support the uncertainty-oriented reasoning. The frequency with which a play is used proved to be entirely unrelated to enjoyment. The run is very, very common ($z = 3.39$) and enjoyed somewhat below par ($z = -.32$). The short sideline pass is similarly enjoyed ($z = -.38$) but is far less frequently employed ($z = -.15$). On the other hand, the bomb is about as uncommon ($z = -.85$) as the reverse ($z = -.87$), yet both plays are quite differently enjoyed ($z = 2.19$ and $z = .70$, respectively). In short, the findings call into question the view that audiences applaud uncommon, rarely employed and hence relatively surprising plays, and that they abhor plays that are used over and over again.

There is, however, an unexpectedly strong relationship beteen yardage gained and appreciation of play. In the analysis, kicking plays (i.e., extra points and field goals) were removed because gain of yardage does not meaningfully apply. Appreciation of the remaining offensive plays could be

rather accurately predicted on the basis of yardage gained. The bomb, the play most enjoyed, is the obvious big yard-gainer ($z = 3.13$). The plunge and the quarterback sneak (for both, $z = -.90$) are the lowest-yardage plays, and their enjoyment is far below par ($z = -.89$ and $z = -1.65$, respectively). The common run produces below-par yardage ($z = -.62$) and also below-par enjoyment ($z = -.43$). As more yardage is gained in a break-away run ($z = .41$), appreciation increases along with the yardage ($z = 1.69$). According to these results, the plays applauded are "the plays that work." The more effective they are, the more enjoyment they stimulate—regardless of other considerations.

The relationship between riskiness of play and enjoyment is highly redundant with that between effectiveness of play and enjoyment ($r = .90$). Risky play, if it succeeds, obviously produces good yardage. There is thus little to be gained from combining these predictor variables ($R = .90$). Commonness of play proved negatively related to riskiness ($r = -.27$) and to effectiveness ($r = -.29$). The involvement of this predictor variable in multiple-regression predictions again failed to improve prediction appreciably. The thrust of the findings, then, is that the appreciation of offensive plays in football is a simple function of either risk or effectiveness of play.

CONCLUDING REMARKS

In the foregoing discussion we have presented rationales and findings that implicate the influence of a variety of factors on the enjoyment derived from watching sport contests. It is hoped that the factors discussed include those that are critically involved in the determination of enjoyment. Affective disposition toward players and teams appears to be a determining factor of overriding importance. But we certainly have not exhausted all conceivable contributing factors. In the exploration of enjoyment-producing aspects of play, for example, aspects such as a play's aesthetic appeal or its apparent vigor could have been included. The strategy issue has been entirely neglected. A high-risk play, for example, can be foolish at times and "good strategy" at others. Finally, several rationales we applied to the play-by-play action could have been applied, directly or in modified form, to games at large. The reasoning on the likelihood of outcomes is a case in point. The spectator's assessment of "the odds" for the party he or she roots for to win appears to affect appreciation greatly and in a highly predictable way. At Indiana, for example, a loss to Ohio State's superior football team by less than 14 points has lately been celebrated as if it were a victory, and a close contest with Purdue won by the basketball championship team was detested like a defeat. Obviously, much remains to be explored. The most important task of those that demand our attention, however, should be the construction of a coherent theoretical model that integrates the various seemingly unrelated rationales presently entertained.

ACKNOWLEDGMENTS

The reported empirical investigations into the affective consequences of witnessing aggressive behavior in sport contests were supported in part by Grant SOC75-13431 from the National Science Foundation to Dolf Zillmann.

REFERENCE NOTES

1. Patterson, A. H. *Hostility catharsis: A naturalistic quasi-experiment.* Paper presented at the annual convention of the American Psychological Association, New Orleans, September 1974.
2. Fry, W. F., Jr. *Popular humor in American politics.* Paper presented at the annual convention of the American Psychological Association, Washington, D.C., September 1976.

REFERENCES

Adler, A. *Understanding human nature.* Garden City, N.Y.: Garden City Publ. Co., 1927.

Bandura, A. *Principles of behavior modification.* New York: Holt, Rinehart & Winston, 1969.

Bandura, A. (Ed.). *Psychological modeling: Conflicting theories.* Chicago: Aldine, 1971.

Beisser, A. R. *The madness in sports: Psychosocial observations on sports.* New York: Appleton-Century-Crofts, 1967.

Bense, M. *Aesthetica: Metaphysische Beobachtungen am Schönen.* Stuttgart: Deutsche Verlags-Anstalt, 1954.

Bense, M. *Ästhetische Information.* Krefeld: Agis, 1956.

Bense, M. *Ästhetik und Zivilisation: Theorie der ästhetischen Kommunikation.* Krefeld: Agis, 1958.

Bense, M. *Programmierung des Schönen: Allgemeine Texttheorie und Textästhetik.* Krefeld: Agis, 1960.

Berkowitz, L. The concept of aggressive drive: Some additional considerations. In L. Berkowitz (Ed.), *Advances in experimental social psychology* (Vol. 2). New York: Academic Press, 1965.

Berlyne, D. E. *Conflict, arousal, and curiosity.* New York: McGraw-Hill, 1960.

Berlyne, D. E. Laughter, humor, and play. In G. Lindzey & E. Aronson (Eds.), *The handbook of social psychology* (Vol. 3, 2nd ed.). Reading, Mass.: Addison-Wesley, 1969.

Bryant, J., Comisky, P., & Zillmann, D. Drama in sports commentary. *Journal of Communication,* 1977, *27*(3), 140–149.

Bryant, J., & Zillmann, D. The mediating effect of the intevention potential of communications on displaced aggressiveness and retaliatory behavior. In B. D. Ruben (Ed.), *Communication yearbook 1.* New Brunswick, N.J.: Transaction, International Communication Association, 1977.

Bryson, F. R. *The sixteenth-century Italian duel.* Chicago: University of Chicago Press, 1938.

Cantor, J. R., Zillmann, D., & Day, K. D. Relationship between cardiorespiratory fitness and physiological responses to films. *Perceptual and Motor Skills,* 1978, *46*, 1123–1130.

Cialdini, R. B., Borden, R. J., Thorne, A., Walker, M. R., Freeman, S., & Sloan, L. R. Basking in reflected glory: Three (football) field studies. *Journal of Personaity and Social Psychology,* 1976, *34*, 366–375.

Comisky, P., Bryant, J., & Zillmann, D. Commentary as a substitute for action. *Journal of Communication,* 1977, *27*(3), 150–152.

Cozens, F. W., & Stumpf, F. S. *Sports in American life*. Chicago: University of Chicago Press, 1953.

Dollard, J., Doob, L. W., Miller, N. E., Mowrer, O. H., & Sears, R. R. *Frustration and aggression*. New Haven, Conn.: Yale University Press, 1939.

Dumazedier, J. The point of view of a social scientist. In E. Jokl & E. Simon (Eds.), *International research in sport and physical education*. Springfield, Ill.: C. C. Thomas, 1964.

Dumazedier, J. *Toward a society of leisure*. New York: Free Press, 1967.

Ellis, W. *Polynesian researches, No. 1*. London: Fisher, Son, & Jackson, 1829.

Evans, R. I. A conversation with Konrad Lorenz about aggression, homosexuality, pornography, and the need for a new ethic. *Psychology Today*, 1974, *8*(6), 82–92.

Feshbach, S. The stimulating versus cathartic effects of vicarious aggressive activity. *Journal of Abnormal and Social Psychology*, 1961, *63*, 381–385.

Feshbach, S. Aggression. In P. H. Mussen (Ed.), *Carmichael's manual of child psychology* (Vol. 2). New York: Wiley, 1970.

Fimrite, R. Take me out to the brawl game. *Sports Illustrated*, 1974, *40*(24), 10–13.

Freud, S. Vorlesungen zur Einführung in die Psychanalyse. In *Gesammelte Werke* (Vol. 11). London: Imago, 1940. (Originally published, 1917.)

Freud, S. Triebe und Triebschicksale. In *Gesammelte Werke* (Vol. 10). London: Imago, 1946. (Originally published, 1915.) (a)

Freud, S. Zeitgemässes über Krieg und Tod. In *Gesammelte Werke* (Vol. 10). London: Imago, 1946. (Originally published, 1915.) (b)

Freud, S. Warum Krieg? In *Gesammelte Werke* (Vol. 16). London: Imago, 1950. (Originally published, 1933.)

Geen, R. G. Observing violence in the mass media: Implications of basic research. In R. G. Geen & E. C. O'Neal (Eds.), *Perspectives on aggression*. New York: Academic Press, 1976.

Godbey, G., & Parker, S. (Eds.). *Leisure studies and services: An overview*. Philadelphia: Saunders, 1976.

Goldstein, J. H., & Arms, R. L. Effects of observing athletic contests on hostility. *Sociometry*, 1971, *34*, 83–90.

Gordon, H. L., Rosenberg, D., & Morris, W. E. Leisure activities of schizophrenic patients after return to the community. *Mental Hygiene*, 1966, *50*, 452–459.

Hornberger, R. H. The differential reduction of aggressive responses as a function of interpolated activities. *American Psychologist*, 1959, *14*, 354.

Howard, G. E. Social psychology of the spectator. *American Journal of Sociology*, 1912, *18*, 33–50.

Johnson, W. O., Jr. *Super spectator and the electric Lilliputians*. Boston: Little, Brown, 1971.

Johnson, W. R., & Buskirk, E. R. (Eds.). *Science and medicine of exercise and sport* (2nd ed.). New York: Harper & Row, 1974.

Kaplan, M. *Leisure in society: A social inquiry*. New York: Wiley, 1960.

Kenyon, G. S. (Ed.). *Aspects of contemporary sport sociology*. Chicago: Athletic Institute, 1969.

Kenyon, G. S. (Ed.). *Contemporary psychology of sport*. Chicago: Athletic Institute, 1970.

Klausner, S. Z. (Ed.). *Why man takes chances: Studies in stress-seeking*. Garden City, N.Y.: Anchor Books, 1968.

Krockow, C. von. *Sport: Eine Soziologie und Philosophie des Leistungsprinzips*. Hamburg: Hoffman & Campe, 1974.

Layman, E. M. The contribution of play and sports to emotional health. In J. E. Kane (Ed.), *Psychological aspects of physical education and sport*. London: Routledge & Kegan Paul, 1972.

Lazarsfeld, P. F., & Merton, R. K. Mass communication, popular taste and organized social action. In L. Bryson (Ed.), *The communication of ideas: A series of addresses*. New York: Harper, 1948.

LeBon, G. *The crowd: A study of the popular mind.* London: Benn, 1896.

Lever, J. Soccer: Opium of the Brazilian people. *Trans-Action,* 1969, *7*(2), 36–43.

Lorenz, K. *Das sogenannte Böse: Zur Naturgeschichte der Aggression.* Wien: Borotha-Schoeler, 1963.

Loy, J. W., Jr., & Kenyon, G. S. (Eds.). *Sport, culture, and society: A reader on the sociology of sport.* London: Macmillan, 1969.

Mendelsohn, H. *Mass entertainment.* New Haven, Conn.: College & University Press, 1966.

Menninger, W. C. Recreation and mental health. *Recreation,* 1948, *42,* 340–346.

Morgan, W. P. Fact and fancy concerning psychological and sociological benefits for physical exercise and formal physical education: General psychological considerations. *Journal of Health, Physical Education and Recreation,* 1968, *39,* 26–28.

Morgan, W. P. Physical fitness correlates of psychiatric hospitalization. In G. S. Kenyon (Ed.), *Contemporary psychology of sport.* Chicago: Athletic Institute, 1970.

Plessner, H., Bock, H. E., & Grupe, O. (Eds.). *Sport und Leibeserziehung: Sozialwissenschaftliche, pädagogische und medizinische Beiträge.* München: Piper, 1967.

Quanty, M. B. Aggression catharsis: Experimental investigations and implications. In H. G. Geen & E. C. O'Neal (Eds.), *Perspectives on aggression.* New York: Academic Press, 1976.

Ryan, E. D. The cathartic effect of vigorous motor activity on aggressive behavior. *Research Quarterly,* 1970, *41,* 542–551.

Sapolsky, B. S., & Zillmann, D. Enjoyment of a televised sport contest under different social conditions of viewing. *Perceptual and Motor Skills,* 1978, *46,* 29–30.

Scott, J. P. *Aggression.* Chicago: University of Chicago Press, 1958.

Scott, J. P. Sport and aggression. In G. S. Kenyon (Ed.), *Contemporary psychology of sport.* Chicago: Athletic Institute, 1970.

Severn, B. *A carnival of sports: Spectacles, stunts, crazes, and unusual sports events.* New York: McKay, 1974.

Shannon, C. E., & Weaver, W. *The mathematical theory of communication.* Urbana: University of Illinois Press, 1949.

Stone, G. P. American sports: Play and dis-play. In E. Larrabee & R. Meyersohn (Eds.), *Mass leisure.* Glencoe, Ill.: Free Press, 1958.

Stone, G. P. Some meanings of American sport: An extended view. In G. S. Kenyon (Ed.), *Aspects of contemporary sport sociology.* Chicago: Athletic Institute, 1969.

Storr, A. *Human aggression.* New York: Atheneum, 1968.

Sutton-Smith, B. The two cultures of games. In G. S. Kenyon (Ed.), *Aspects of contemporary sport sociology.* Chicago: Athletic Institute, 1969.

Sutton-Smith, B. Play, games, and controls. In J. P. Scott & S. F. Scott (Eds.), *Social control and social change.* Chicago: University of Chicago Press, 1971.

Sutton-Smith, B., & Roberts, J. M. Rubrics of competitive behavior. *Journal of Genetic Psychology,* 1964, *105,* 13–37.

Tannenbaum, P. H., & Zillmann, L. Emotional arousal in the facilitation of aggression through communication. In L. Berkowitz (Ed.), *Advances in experimental social psychology* (Vol. 8). New York: Academic Press, 1975.

Turner, E. T. The effects of viewing college football, basketball and wrestling on the elicited aggressive responses of male spectators. In G. S. Kenyon (Ed.), *Contemporary psychology of sport.* Chicago: Athletic Institute, 1970.

Wiener, N. *Cybernetics: Or control and communication in the animal and the machine* (2nd ed.). New York: Wiley, 1961.

Zajonc, R. B. Social facilitation. *Science,* 1965, *149,* 269–274.

Zillmann, D., & Bryant, J. Effect of residual excitation on the emotional response to provocation and delayed aggressive behavior. *Journal of Personality and Social Psychology,* 1974, *30,* 782–791.

Zillmann, D., & Bryant, J. Viewer's moral sanction of retribution in the appreciation of dramatic presentations. *Journal of Experimental Social Psychology*, 1975, *11*, 572–582.

Zillmann, D., & Cantor, J. R. A disposition theory of humor and mirth. In T. Chapman & H. Foot (Eds.), *Humor and laughter: Theory, research, and applications.* London: Wiley, 1976.

Zillmann, D., & Cantor, J. R. Affective responses to the emotions of a protagonist. *Journal of Experimental Social Psychology*, 1977, *13*, 155–165.

Zillmann, D., & Hay, T. A., & Bryant, J. The effect of suspense and its resolution on the appreciation of dramatic presentations. *Journal of Research in Personality*, 1975, *9*, 307–323.

Zillmann, D., Johnson, R. C., & Day, K. D. Attribution of apparent arousal and proficiency of recovery from sympathetic activation affecting excitation transfer to aggressive behavior. *Journal of Experimental Social Psychology*, 1974, *10*, 503–515. (a)

Zillmann, D., Johnson, R. C., & Day, K. D. Provoked and unprovoked aggressiveness in athletes. *Journal of Research in Personality*, 1974, *8*, 139–152. (b)

Zillmann, D., Katcher, A. H., & Milavsky, B. Excitation transfer from physical exercise to subsequent aggressive behavior. *Journal of Experimental Social Psychology*, 1972, *8*, 247–259.

12

Sports Crowds Viewed from the Perspective of Collective Behavior

Leon Mann
*The Flinders University
of South Australia*

INTRODUCTION

The growing interest in sport as a field of research inquiry means that inevitably attention must be directed to the consumers of organized sport— the sports fan in his or her public role as a member of a spectator crowd. The expansion of spectator sport as a major leisure-time activity has produced changes in the ideology and practice of sport. This in turn has been accompanied by the appearance of a variety of crowd phenomena that make the sports crowd an important subject in its own right. Here we examine the sports crowd as an aspect of collective behavior and discuss how the conduct of spectators before, during, and after the event can be affected by their belonging to a crowd. What is the relevance of the study of sports crowds? Why is the field important?

The sports crowd can be regarded as a regular, scheduled gathering of groups of partisan followers and interested observers whose behavior is more or less predictable. Blumer (1946) classified spectators at sports events as a "conventionalized crowd." The conventionalization of sports crowds raises interesting questions relating to recruitment into the sports crowd and how norms governing spectatorship are developed and learned. Also members of sports crowds are frequently participants in other related forms of collective

LEON MANN is Professor of Psychology at The Flinders University of South Australia. He is author of *Social Psychology* and (with Irving Janis) of *Decision Making.* He has taught at Harvard, Melbourne, and Sydney Universities.

behavior. Spectators will have been part of a commuter crowd en-route to the event, may have waited in long queues for admission, and may become part of an expressive, victory crowd. The sports crowd transforms readily into a destructive crowd (a riot), an acquisitive crowd (an entry stampede), an escape crowd (an exit panic), all potentially disastrous. The links between the conventional sports crowd and other less regular crowd types make it especially important to students of collective behavior interested in the dynamics of transformation and change in the conduct of the person-in-the-crowd. Appreciation of the close connection between sports crowds and a host of other collective forms also serves as a corrective to the tendency to focus almost exclusively on collective violence in sport (cf. Ingham & Smith, 1974).

The sports crowd, in its diverse forms, represents a challenge to the major theories of collective behavior. All theories are put to the test in predicting and explaining the conduct of spectator crowds. The sports crowd is not merely a large aggregate of individuals acting out a set of predetermined responses in parallel. The fact of aggregation, in large and small assemblies under conditions of emotional arousal and tension, comes to influence behavior, both directly—through social pressure, coercion, modeling of others' behavior—and indirectly—through noise, competition, and physical fatigue. The basic theoretical questions of interest to collective behavior theorists are listed in the following section, where their relevance to the sports crowd is discussed (see p. 339ff). The sports crowd is also of applied significance, as it represents a setting where principles of crowd maintenance and control are frequently put into practice, often, as we shall see, with disastrous results.

Although the sports crowd is a suitable and convenient vehicle for the investigation of a variety of psychological phenomena, its research potentialities have been largely ignored. An early exception is Hastorf and Cantril's (1954) classic study of the distorted perceptions of sports fans. There is some indication, however, of a growing awareness of the research potential of the sports crowd for testing general psychological hypotheses about aggression (Goldstein & Arms, 1971) and reference group identification (Mann, 1974a; Cialdini *et al*, 1976). The sports crowd has many characteristics that make it ideal for conducting systematic, controlled field research. It is *scheduled:* Accordingly, the investigator can prepare the research instruments in advance. The *location* or venue is known: Therefore, the investigator can make careful observations and records of individual spectators. The crowd is essentially *stationary* and *captive,* enabling accurate and representative area sampling. And although no two episodes are exactly alike, sports events occur with sufficient regularity to enable replication and the gathering of large quantities of data.

THE "WHOLE CROWD" PROBLEM

For convenience we refer to the sports crowd in much the same way as it is convenient to refer to the protest crowd. The use of this term immediately suggests that the crowd *as a whole* can be described and explained as if it constituted a uniform entity. This is not intended; on occasion there are crowds in which members are uniform and identical in their conduct. Ticket lines, for example, consist of people all of whom are performing the identifying behavior, that is, waiting in an orderly queue. In some panics, all of the spectators appear to behave in a uniform, "selfish" manner. In most crowds, and this includes sports crowds, the entire assembly does not behave in a uniform or continuously homogeneous fashion. At a typical sports event, there are rival groups of spectators, some of whom are highly involved, others less interested. Many spectators are there as "neutral," nonpartisan spectators. Some are there to sell programs or refreshments and some to keep order. But for convenience, all are labeled together as a sports crowd. The crowd, then, is not a single entity with a uniform membership, all thinking and doing the same thing. It is comprised of separate individuals, often of many small groups, who develop and carry the crowd's standards. To understand the crowd it is essential to take account of *individual* responses and patterns of *group* interaction and influence. In brief, psychologists and social psychologists can contribute a great deal to a field that has been traditionally designated as a sociological domain.

We cannot, however, generalize all sports crowds. Obviously, various spectator sports draw different kinds of fans. Tennis, polo, professional wrestling, football, and roller ball appeal to rather different people, and norms and standards regarding spectator conduct differ widely across these sports. The conclusions drawn from data on one or two spectator sports (most frequently football) will not necessarily hold for all other spectator sports.

BASIC THEORETICAL QUESTIONS

Collective behavior theory has been concerned with four basic issues, which relate to: (1) the essential characteristics of crowd behavior; (2) changes that occur in the person who belongs to a crowd; (3) mechanisms that explain such changes; and (4) the role of social conditions involving conflict and strain in collective behavior. These issues have been debated keenly with respect to riots, civil disturbances, and panics—forms that challenge or disrupt the social order. It is possible that an analysis of sports crowds could contribute something to the discussion of these issues:

1. The dominant stereotype of crowds stemming from LeBon's (1895) influential treatise is that they are irrational, uncontrolled, and violent. Journalistic accounts of sports crowds tend to invoke the same negative image. Couch (1968) and Turner and Killian (1972), however, have attempted to refute the traditional viewpoint of crowd irrationality, arguing that crowds are regulated by norms, are no less rational than individuals, and act on the basis of careful weighing of alternatives. Considering the mammoth number of sports crowds each year at which spectators are orderly and restrained, it is erroneous to present a uniformly negative image of the sports crowd. Systematic records of sports violence and disorder would assist in further examination of the accuracy of the stereotype.

2. Some theorists, such as LeBon (1895), argued that there is a radical *transformation* in individual conduct as a consequence of membership in a crowd. In a Jekyll-Hyde metamorphosis, the independent rational person becomes an irrational destructive being. Allport (1924) and Freud (1921) held that although people in the crowd are uninhibited, this represents an essential continuation, a manifestation of underlying impulses which are released or intensified in the crowd. Within sports crowds, there appears to be evidence for both views. There are accounts of apparently respectable citizens losing all self-control in the excitement of a sports event (Harrington, 1968). Sports violence can also be traced to groups of violence-prone youths who come armed for trouble, and go into action shielded by the anonymity of the crowd. Whether spectators become radically transformed in crowds or merely express underlying impulses, has important implications for principles of crowd control.

3. The key problem of collective behavior theory is to explain changes that occur in individual conduct in crowd situations. Three classic theoretical viewpoints—contagion theory, convergence theory, and emergent norm theory, each postulate distinct social influence mechanisms responsible for behavioral changes that occur in a crowd. Contagion theory holds that through a process of suggestion (LeBon, 1895), milling (Blumer, 1946) and imitation (Wheeler, 1966) a mood or idea spreads from person to person in a crowd until most, if not all, members begin to act in an uninhibited manner. Deindividuation theory (Zimbardo, 1969), a variation of contagion theory, argues that the mechanisms explaining uninhibited behavior in crowds are anonymity, arousal, and similarity of dress. Convergence theory attributes apparent changes that occur when an individual joins a crowd to the process of social facilitation, an intensification of pre-existing responses when in the presence of others (Allport, 1924). Emergent norm theory (Turner & Killian, 1972) maintains that crowd membership produces changes in individual behavior through the emergence of new group norms and pressure to conform to them.

Each of these theories provides guidelines for investigating sports crowds and can be tested in reference to them. According to contagion theory, the spread of booing, slow clapping, and bottle throwing, should occur most readily when the act is initiated by a high status model in a large, anonymous crowd. Deindividuation theory would lead to the prediction that most foul language and bottle throwing would be found at night games, because darkness provides a cover of anonymity, although Harrington (1968) found no evidence for this in British soccer violence. According to the social facilitation principle, the most energetic applause and jeering should be found in large sports crowds. The emergent norm theory leads the investigator to look for evidence of the establishment of standards of conduct enforced by social sanctions in queues and crowds.

All of these social influence mechanisms can operate simultaneously or sequentially in crowds. For example, all theories postulate that crowd size is a factor that instigates and enforces behavior change: deindividuation (because of greater anonymity), social facilitation (because of greater arousal), emergent norm theory (because of greater pressure to conformity). The theories do make different predictions, however, relating to the variable of crowd composition. For example, contagion and deindividuation theories predict that most destructiveness occurs in crowds of anonymous strangers, while emergent norm theory predicts that once a proaggression norm has been established, most destructiveness will occur when crowd members are fully identifiable to one another.

4. A final issue is the part played by societal factors, such as social conflict and strain, in the production of collective behavior. Smelser (1962) holds that all collective behavior—riots, panics, crazes, and social movements—are a response to underlying social strains, tensions, or grievances. This raises several questions about sports crowds. Is it always necessary to invoke social conditions to explain crowds properly? Marx (1970) maintains that some forms of collective violence, such as sports victory riots, are "issue-less," in that they are not caused by strain or grievance. What are the appropriate crowd control measures if strain and grievances are essential components of any outburst involving sports spectators? The implication is that attention should be directed toward the prevention or remediation of social factors that cause strain and grievance, and away from punitive measures. This is the argument made by Taylor (1971), who views spectator hooliganism at British soccer games as the inevitable consequence of strain and alienation between young working-class supporters and professional, middle-class team management.

Smelser's (1962) model of collective behavior is important for other reasons. It is one of the few theories offering a systematic approach to the analysis of collective episodes, as it specifies the conditions that are necessary

and sufficient to produce all major forms of collective behavior—structural conduciveness, strain, a generalized belief, a precipitating factor, mobilization for action, and weak social control. The logic of the model for sports crowd episodes is that they are the end product of a complex set of sociological and psychological factors. Unfortunately there have been no direct tests of Smelser's theory as it relates to sports crowds, although several writers have drawn on the model as a framework for analysing social structural factors in sport.

The four basic issues are points of departure for discussion of the collective behavior perspective on sports crowds. We return to some of these issues later when we come to an analysis of various sports-related crowd forms—ticket queues, entry and exit panics from stadiums, riots, and postgame assembly. First, however, a brief detour to introduce several dimensions of crowds that are important in the analysis of crowd forms.

CROWD DIMENSIONS AND CROWD DYNAMICS

Crowd dimensions are identified for several reasons: to provide a framework for precise description; as a conceptual tool for deriving hypotheses linking variations in crowd structure to crowd conduct (an example is the effect of crowd size on spectator disinhibition—see above), as a guide to investigators who must take into account factors such as boundaries and density when working in the crowd. Five dimensions are listed corresponding to observable, measurable features of the sports crowd—size, density, noise, seated-standing, and composition. Other crowd dimensions could be considered (e.g., polarization, zones, etc.), but they are of less relevance here (for a general discussion of dimensions of crowd behavior, see Milgram & Toch, 1969).

Crowd Size

This dimension is probably the most important for analysing the sports crowd. A number of major theoretical and applied questions relate to crowd and audience size (see the foregoing):

1. What differences are found between large and small crowds? Irresponsible conduct is more likely to be found in large crowds. In large crowds communication is weak and primitive. Members develop feelings of power and legitimacy to act and to resist authority. A feeling of invulnerability emerges (because members are relatively anonymous), and there may be a tendency to diffuse responsibility.

2. Social influence on individual members may be a function of crowd size.

Several models postulate that the crowd's impact on the individual member, especially pressures on the individual to conform, will be greater in large crowds than in small (cf. Latané, 1976; Mann, 1976). No systematic work has been conducted on sports crowd size and its effects on spectators. Turner (1968) has reported an increase in frequency of aggressive responses on projective tests following a football and a basketball game attended by large crowds but no increase following a wrestling match attended by a small crowd. There is inconclusive evidence that large crowds are associated with fiercer competition and aggression in players (Harrell & Schmitt, 1973). Russell and Drewry (1976) tested the relationship between crowd size and player aggression by means of an archival analysis of the records of 60 Canadian ice hockey games played over two seasons. At each game an official estimated crowd attendance and collected data on player aggression. In one season a nonsignificant correlation occurred between crowd size and player aggression ($r = -.16$) but in the second season the correlation was positive and significant ($r = +.36$). The crowds were, however, quite small (range 15–350). It is possible that a stronger relationship would be found for national league games played before larger crowds.

A connection between large crowds and spectator violence can be assumed if player aggression in turn produces aggressive crowd reactions. This, of course, could also be due to several other factors:

1. In large crowds there would be greater probability of uncontrolled, violent spectator types.
2. In large crowds there are more opportunities for encountering frustration (for example, in obtaining services, getting a good view of the game, etc.).
3. In large crowds there will be more noise, closer body contact and, in general, greater arousal, which is a factor in producing aggression (Berkowitz, 1972).
4. In large crowds there is greater anonymity of spectators from authority (and therefore a cover for the violence-prone) and greater deindividuation (weakened sense of identity), which is a factor in disinhibited aggressive and sexual behavior (cf. Zimbardo, 1969).

Crowd Density

The interperson distance between people in queues and crowds may be a factor contributing to breakdown of order before and during sports events. There are national and cultural differences in tolerance for interpersonal distance and density (Hall, 1966). The relatively high incidence of entry stampedes, rumors, and violence at sports events in Latin America could be due partly to the high levels of crowd density tolerated. Any sudden

movement in part of the crowd to get in or out of the stadium reverberates dramatically throughout the rest of the crowd and can spell disaster.

Crowd Noise

Spectators communicate to each other and to players by shouting encouragement, singing and chanting. The crowd's response to a play or a decision contributes to the general noise level. The chanting of simple slogans is a means of voicing support and binding spectators to each other. It is also the main channel for defining and communicating shared ideas. In 1968, Viv Richards, a young West Indian playing his first game in first-class cricket was given out erroneously, in the view of many spectators. The crowd erupted and poured onto the field. Soon the cry went up. "No Viv, no match! no Viv, no match!" The umpires took the message and recalled Richards to bat. In British football a kind of ritualized verbal warfare is waged; opposing groups of fans chant obscene and menacing slogans to intimidate opposing players and spectators (Marsh, 1975). Analysis of the content of chants and songs, who initiates them, and who takes them up, could provide some measure of the growth and spread of crowd moods (see Chapter 10, this volume). At U.S. baseball games, spectators are stimulated by orchestrated sources—trumpets, electric organs, coordinated chants ("Go-go-go-"). Crowd noise, an index of arousal and excitement, can also be an instigator of *further* arousal, which according to several theories (Zimbardo, 1969; Berkowitz, 1972) is a condition for uninhibited and aggressive behavior. Geen and O'Neal (1976) report that loud noise facilitates the expression of aggression; however it is important to separate the specific aversive effects of noise from its more general arousal properties. Several mini-experiments to test the effects of crowd noise on individual spectators can be suggested. Do deaf spectators become as aroused as normal-hearing spectators at sports events? Would arousal be reduced in a group of spectators who were made to wear high quality earphones which shielded out crowd noise? Among home viewers, is arousal less if the sound of a televised game is turned off? (The broadcaster's "excited" voice is another variable here.)

The first three dimensions—size, density, and noise,—are closely, but not invariably, interrelated. A large, noisy, densely packed crowd provides the optimal conditions for disinhibited behavior. Size, density and noise, however, are *mediating* variables; the reason why a large crowd has been attracted to the event is a prior factor in spectator behavior.

Seated/Standing

Whether the crowd is seated or standing, may have implications for panic and violence. Crowds which are seated tend to be passive and orderly. Stadiums in the United States usually seat all spectators and this may explain why there is

a relatively low level of crowd disorder *at* American sports events (*post*event disorder could be a different matter). Standing crowds tend to be active. People shift from foot to foot, if restless "mill around" and obstruct others. There is greater scope for giving and taking offense in a standing crowd where personal territory and space is not clearly demarcated. A standing crowd is freer to act, to hurl objects. In a crush it is more likely to sway and fall, causing wholesale panic. The terrible crushes at Bolton, United Kindgom, in 1945, and Ibrox Park, Glasgow, in 1971, in which many spectators died as they pushed for a vantage point, occurred on the "terrace" sections of the stadium where the crowd was standing. A testable hypothesis is that crowd violence (fights, bottle throwing, invasion of the field) is more likely to occur among standing spectators. (An adequate test requires, of course, the control of obvious extraneous variables, such as social class and age of spectator in standing and seated areas of the stadium.)

Crowd Composition

The characteristics of spectators has significance for testing several theories of sports crowd violence, especially convergence theory (riff-raff theory). The sports crowd consists of many subgroups— partisan spectators and neutral observers, fanatic supporters who follow their team everywhere, to those attending their first match, spectators who have come in large groups of friends hours, sometimes days before the event, and those who have come alone. To speak of an undifferentiated sports crowd is therefore a gross distortion. Roles and tasks of particular spectators—such as cheer leaders— may be determined before the event. Where the crowd consists substantially of groups who arrive together bringing their existing norms, the individual is likely to follow his or her group's norms. The group will then *mediate* or confer resistance to the crowd's impact on the individual, depending upon whether the group's norms are consistent with or opposed to those of the crowd. For example, a group of nuns at an ice hockey game would be unlikely to engage in abuse of the referee; a nun alone, especially if dressed in civilian garb, would be more likely to join in a storm of abuse. The role of the group as an initiator and carrier of queue culture is considered later.

CROWD FORMS RELATED TO SPORTS

The taxonomic tradition in collective behavior has led to a refined classification of crowd forms and the identification of new types (Marx & Wood, 1975). The taxonomic tradition should be extended to sports-related crowds for two reasons: First, to demonstrate the wide variety of crowd forms associated with sports events—queues, panics, riots, postgame assemblies. Second, an accurate description of sports crowds requires that this be done

for principal types separately to test whether some, most, or all are typically uncontrolled and irrational, as suggested by the traditional stereotype. We shall review several major crowd forms associated with sports events, commencing with queues of football fans.

QUEUES AT SPORTS EVENTS

Marathon queues are an important source of information about sports fans because:

1. They provide a direct measure of the depth of involvement—the extent to which fans are prepared to spend time and money to get tickets to watch their team. The most loyal and committed fans are those who wait in long lines for tickets, for days and sometimes for weeks.

2. They give an indication of the conduct of the sports fan in a collective situation prior to the sports event, and prior to the excitement, triumph or disappointment. This information can be useful in testing collective behavior theory. If, as convergence theory postulates, crowd behavior is merely an intensification of individual predispositions, then these same predispositions—to compete, to be aggressive, etc.—should be manifest to some extent in the pregame collectivity, such as a queue.

Long, marathon queues for tickets to sports events turn out to be one of the most ordered forms of collective behavior. Field studies of marathon, overnight queues for Australian football games (Mann, 1970) reveal that highly cooperative norms emerge to regulate place-keeping, butting-in, and brief absences from the queue. Such orderliness is not altogether surprising in a club ticket line as common allegiance to the Club provides a basis for cooperation. However, a high level of cooperation and orderliness was also found in the multiple queues outside the Melbourne Football Stadium, even though the queuers were supporters of 12 different clubs, some of them bitter rivals.

The queuers are, of course, not a cross section of the spectators who get to see the game. They are the most dedicated to football and the least dedicated to work. Fans who spend days waiting in a cold queue seem to have few other pressing claims on their time. In the Melbourne football queues, the typical queuer was male, under 25, living in a working-class suburb, and an absentee from work.

The key to the emergence and maintenance of orderly and cooperative norms in the queue lies in the fact that most queuers wait together with a small group of friends (we have noted earlier the significance of the group as a mediating unit between the crowd and the individual). Queues that are

composed of family groups and groups of acquaintances rather than aggregates of lone strangers are better able to forge norms and enforce conformity to them. For example, in the Melbourne queues very little queue-jumping occurred in lines composed of well-knit groups because there was a strong sense of community that enabled people to spot intruders and close ranks against them. Thus, only rarely did violence break out in the Melbourne queues.

The presence of well-knit groups in the queue forms the basis of a major feature of queue life—the shift system that regulates leaves of absence from the queue. When queues last for several days, it is unreasonable to expect everyone to stand in line continuously, but the queue must be maintained and order of priority must be recognized. The Melbourne queues handled the problem of leave of absence by devising a shift system in which members of groups spelled one another, each spending one hour "on" to every 3 hours "off." (Another acceptable method was to leave an item of property as a temporary place marker.)

We found that a queue tradition had evolved in the Melbourne football queues. Many of the fans were "veterans" who looked forward to their annual marathon wait for tickets. Originally they had turned out to wait in line simply because they had no alternative means of getting tickets. But over the years, the lines had become a cherished ritual. Queue veterans regarded the activity as an annual adventure, offering excitement and diversion in an otherwise routine existence. The carnival atmosphere of gossip, conviviality, drinking, and card-playing, was evidence of this. Queuing serves to bind the fan's dedication and commitment to the team. To have waited through several cold, wet days for a pair of tickets enhances the value of the game and of the team.

The significance of these field studies of football queues is that they show, contrary to contagion theory (LeBon 1895), that a crowd does not reduce its participants to a uniform level of irrational, uncontrolled behavior. If anything, collectivities of this kind composed of dedicated fans, demonstrate an impressive capacity to maintain an orderly social system for regulating individual behavior. Such well-regulated, normative conduct, emerging from those assembled, is consistent with emergent norm theory (Turner & Killian, 1972).

The Optimistic Queuer

A member of the sports queue who deserves special mention is the optimistic latecomer, the person who continues to wait in line even though there are many more people ahead than there are tickets available (Mann & Taylor, 1969). Optimistic latecomers were found in all of the Melbourne football queues. One explanation for this phenomenon is the wish fulfilment

hypothesis; the desperate latecomer subconsciously underestimates numbers ahead in order to justify participation in an almost futile activity. Other explanations are possible, such as a self-selection bias, the latecomers who stay and wait being the worst judges. Two points can be made about optimistic latecomers. First, that despite their bitter disappointment when inevitably the tickets ran out, the Melbourne queuers did not become violent. (Similarly, 10,000 Oakland Raider fans who waited for half a day for Superbowl tickets on December 29, 1976, and missed out, showed no violence.) Second, given the possibility that latecomers could become angry if disappointed, it is surprising that officials rarely feel obliged to inform and turn them away, an example of irresponsible attitudes to crowd control.

PANICS

Another stereotype of the sports crowd is of a selfish mob competing for entry, space and exit in a stadium. The occasional stampedes and crushes that occur at sports events are cited as evidence of the essential irrationality of the spectator. The outside observer, with the benefit of hindsight, is able to regard a stampede as irrational. In many, if not most, cases, entry and exit panics can be blamed on the ignorance of authorities and officials who create the physical conditions for panic.

Entry Panics

Entry panics occur at sports events when individuals who fear they are in danger of missing out push and trample others in an attempt to gain service or entry. Entry panics reflect the breakdown or disintegration of the queue principle. An orderly, well regulated queue or crowd of people (the line might be implicit) seeking a scarce commodity or access to a public place, becomes impatient or fearful of missing out and begins to push and compete for priority or quicker service.

Entry panics are due to the build-up of large crowds. Access to the stadium is too narrow to enable rapid entry, or space within the stadium is too limited to permit entry for everyone. A crush builds up and those at the head near the entrances and turnstiles are trampled. (In the Bolton, U. K. football stadium crush, March 1945, 85,000 fans turned up and crammed into a stadium that could accommodate only 50,000. Here the crush occurred in the stadium.)

Entry panics at sports events are rare: exit panics (see below) are more common. Here are some recent examples of entry panics that occurred outside sports arenas:

—*Sutherland, United Kingdom:* On March 4, 1964, a 15-year-old girl and a 45-year-old man died and 80 people were injured when a crowd of more than 100,000 struggled to gain entry into a soccer field with room for only 62,000.

— *Kwangju, South Korea:* On October 6, 1965, 14 people were killed in a stampede as thousands tried to enter a filled sports stadium.

— *Bukavu, Congo:* On October 6, 1969, 27 football fans died and 107 were injured when a crowd stampeded outside a football stadium in Bukavu, Western Congo. The authorities had insisted that the crowd wait outside the stadium until the arrival of President Mobutu. Shortly before his arrival, authorities allowed the crowd to begin moving through the gates. A stampede started, and hundreds were trampled.

— *Calcutta, India:* On December 16, 1969, six people were trampled to death and over 50 were injured in a seething mass of 20,000 cricket fans in a stampede outside the ticket office at the Eden Gardens ground, where people had been waiting all night to buy tickets for a cricket match between India and Australia.

— *Cairo, Egypt:* On February 19, 1974, 49 people were killed and 47 injured in a stampede when thousands of fans crashed through the iron gates of Zamalek stadium minutes before the scheduled start of a game between the Zamalek soccer club and a visiting Czech team. The game, planned for Cairo stadium, had sold 100,000 tickets. At the last minute, the organizers switched the match to Zamalek Stadium, which has a capacity of only 45,000 but is closer to the city center. One hour before the scheduled start, 80,000 had crammed into the stadium. Thousands were left outside. Egyptian authorities in another last-minute decision decided not to televise the game, sending thousands more fans to the stadium in search of tickets. As fans broke through the stadium gates and poured into the stadium, many fell and were trodden underfoot.

The key to the prevention of an entry panic is an understanding of the mechanisms that serve to maintain order and control in an acquisitive crowd. In entry panics, disorder occurs through the breakdown of the norm of nonpushing. People at the rear seek to gain entry or service more rapidly. To prevent the impatience of some from transforming a queue or orderly crowd into a wild stampede, several simple precautions are necessary. Authorities have the prime responsibility for anticipating the build-up of a crowd and for regulating and controlling it. A sufficient number of ticket boxes and service counters for the sale of the commodity must be provided; additional police and attendants must be on hand to control the crowd and turn people away at some point if the stadium or building has reached capacity. Sufficient entrances must be provided to enable easy entry into the stadium and prevent the build up of large impatient knots of people. The tragedy at the Bukavu football stadium in the Congo would not have occurred if officials at the stadium had acted sensibly and permitted the crowd to enter as they arrived and not required them to wait outside. The disaster at Zamalek stadium in Cairo would not have occurred if officials had not arbitrarily switched venues and compounded their error by failing to televise the game. The crush and

stampede outside the Sutherland football stadium in England and the Eden Gardens ground in India would most probably have not occurred if a sufficient number of police and officials had been on hand to control crowds and turn away latecomers.

But even when officials are negligent or are caught unprepared, it is remarkable that the crowd itself is sometimes able to act to reestablish order in the face of imminent panic. Here is an example of how a conspicuous, vocal minority can establish and reinforce a norm of orderliness in a crowd verging on a state of panic (Chakotin, 1941):

> In Paris we were once witnesses of a terrible situation: The neighbourhood of the Velodrome d'Hiver (Winter Sports Stadium) was densely crowded for a big race. There were two narrow entrances, and no police to be seen. The crowd rushed to the entrances, and the pressure seemed to be threatening suffocation for many victims. But suddenly some of the crowd began to shout rhythmically, 'Don't push! Don't push!' and the shout was taken up and chanted in chorus by the whole multitude. The result was marvellous: order was restored, the pressure reduced; a collective inhibition had spread through the minds of the whole throng [pp. 43-44].

This example, incidentally, illustrates how a crowd can regulate its own conduct when things seem to be getting out of hand by expressing itself in a simple, direct way. To attempt to shout a complex set of instructions would be useless because the message would be confused or drowned among the cries of those in distress. A simple message like "Don't push!" repeatedly chanted in unison carries to those at the rear and saves the day.

I too was witness to a *near* entry panic at Boston Garden in 1969 when tickets for the National Hockey League Playoffs went on sale. Because of an absence of barriers, the crowd surged around ticket windows, and there was no way for people who had obtained their tickets to work their way free. The Boston police with true initiative plunged into the crowd and formed a human chain, picking up customers as they received their tickets and passing them bodily overhead from policeman to policeman until they were safely ejected out of the crowd.

Exit Panics

The most frequent and probably the most deadly form of panic is the exit panic. Exit panics are triggered off when a threat or danger arises in a confined area from which the possibility of escape is severely restricted by the limited number or narrowness of the exits. The threat in a sports stadium may be fire, an explosion, tear-gas fired by the police or the building's imminent collapse. In many such incidents the greatest loss of life is not due to the immediate threat itself but to the maladaptive reactions of terrified people

who trample others and coincidentally block the exits in their frantic efforts to escape. Loss of life through trampling in a sports stadium means that people have failed to form a rudimentary "queue" or order of priority for escape and have failed to adhere to the norm of nonpushing. A partial list of some of the worst exit panics at sports events shows that most occur in Latin American countries:

—*Buenos Aires Soccer Stadium:* In July 1944, eight died and 80 were injured in an exit panic.

—*Lima, Peru, Soccer Stadium:* On May 24, 1964, 300 soccer fans died in an exit panic at the match between Peru and Argentina. Argentina was leading 1–0 when 2 minutes before the end a Peruvian player broke through and scored. The referee disallowed the goal because of rough play. The crowd of more than 45,000 voiced their disapproval and some spectators leapt over the barriers to attack the referee. The referee then suspended the game, but more and more fans crashed through the barriers and onto the pitch. The police then fired their revolvers and fired teargas, panicking the crowd.

—*Jalapa, Mexico:* On November 30, 1964, 24 were killed as 5000 panicked and stampeded out of the stadium.

—*Buenos Aires Soccer Stadium:* On June 23, 1968, 71 died and 130 were injured. The stampede was started by hooligans who tossed burning newspapers at spectators on a winding staircase leading from the stadium.

—*Salvador, Brazil Soccer Stadium:* On March 6, 1971, 3 were killed and 800 injured in a stampede sparked by a minor explosion in the stadium's lighting system. Spectators who shouted "The stadium is falling down!" triggered the panic.

—*Westbury, New York:* 1971. 37 people were injured at Roosevelt racecourse in a stampede that started after a soft-drink machine made gurgling noises.

—*Teresina, Brazil:* August 29, 1973. Four people died and 100 were injured seriously when the crowd in a new football stadium panicked and rushed for the exits after a false alarm that the grandstands were collapsing.

The crowd in panic seems selfish, nonadaptive, and irrational. But we are referring to the total effect of the interdependent behavior, not the conduct of individual crowd members. When people are unfamiliar with the general layout of the stadium, and smoke and fumes blind their view of the exits, or in confusion they are unable to monitor the effects of their behavior on others, it is meaningless for an observer after the event to characterize their behavior as selfish and irrational. Turner and Killian (1972) make this point very well in insisting that one must look at the definition of the situation from the viewpoint of a participant.

Exit panics can be prevented, or at least the magnitude of their effects reduced, if measures are taken to maintain order or initiate an order of

priority for escape. Specific measures are of course governed by the setting and the nature of the threat. There are regulations that govern modern buildings and public places: Doors must open outwards, exits must be clearly labeled, stairways must meet certain specifications. Unfortunately many arenas and stadiums are still not "panic proof" (next time you are in a stadium appraise it from the viewpoint of its panic potential).

Two general observations can be made about entry and exit stampedes at sports events:

1. The fact that panics occur at sports events does not necessarily reflect adversely on spectator conduct. Very often the breakdown in order is due to ignorant or irresponsible police and officials who fail to exercise proper control or who overreact to crowd actions.

2. The relatively high incidence of sports panics in Latin American countries needs some explanation. Cultural factors relating to public order, tolerance for crowding in public places, as well as social strain and tension ("panicky" reactions to ambiguous stimuli) may help explain the striking incidence of panic in some Latin American countries. (For a discussion of cultural factors in sports crowds, see pp. 364–365.)

CLASSIFYING SPORTS RIOTS

A major concern of collective behavior is the development of a typology of crowds. The taxonomic tradition (cf. Marx & Wood 1975) has led to the identification of new forms (e.g., baiting crowds, apathetic bystander crowds) and to the making of finer distinctions between old forms (e.g., entry versus exit panics). Following the ghetto and antiwar disturbances of the 1960s, crowd typologies were extended to allow a finer classification of riots (e.g., communal versus commodity riots, Janowitz, 1968; instrumental versus "issueless" riots, Marx, 1970). The usefulness of crowd typologies depends on how they are used in theory building and in explanation. In this section we distinguish between different types of sports riots to show that the usual stereotype of the sports riot, as a wild, uncontrolled outburst following defeat, is not the major or only form.

A distinction can be made between five types of riots, based on the apparent, dominant characteristic of the rioters. The types are labeled: frustration, outlawry, remonstrance (protest), confrontation, and expressive, forming the handy mnemonic FORCE. The FORCE typology can be applied to sports (see Table 12.1). The rationale is to avoid the error of treating sports riots as if all episodes fitted a single, monolithic pattern, and to avoid the error of generalizing to all sports riots on the basis of a distinct, highly salient type, such as spectators who rampage in defeat. The accurate classification of a riot

TABLE 12.1
A Sports Riot Typology

Type			Relevant Theoretical Formulations	Likely Activity or Targets
Frustration	{	(a) deprivation (b) felt injustice	aggression theory and variations	Attack source or symbol of frustration (stadium, property, officials, referee, players)
Outlawry			(a) Social contact and strain	Attack authority
			(b) Convergence theory (riff-raff version)	Attack property, intimidate supporters of other team
Remonstrance (protest)			Theory of social movements	Attempt disruption of event; challenge authority
Confrontation			Social conflict and strain	Attack rival group
Expressive	{	victory defeat	Contagion and deindividuation theories	General disinhibited conduct

may have implications for understanding: (1) the causes of the outburst (whether predominantly social–systemic or individual–reactive); (2) its relationship to the sports event (prior, during, or after); (3) the kinds of riot participants (the criminal element or the most outraged); and (4) the most likely targets of violence (the referee, supporters of the other team, property).

The FORCE typology is based mainly on analyses of case materials and archival records (such as *New York Times Index*). It is probable that other, perhaps more heuristic classifications, could be evolved. It is also possible that some outbursts will not fit neatly into a single category, representing "mixed" types, or episodes in which several different, interconnected events occur.[1] Before we discuss the typology it should be noted that sports riots, at least those rated newsworthy by the national media, are not very common. Lewis (Note 1) found 245 sports riots after combing seven national U.S. newspapers for the years 1960–1972. My own count from the *New York Times Index* 1950–1974 is 62 sports riots, 48 of them associated with soccer or

---

[1]There have been other attempts to classify sports riots—Lang (1970) and Lewis (Note 1).

football. Admittedly, the U.S. press does not report every major outburst that occurs in sports—indeed the coverage probably falls well below 10%. The point, however, is that sports-related violence draws considerable attention when it occurs, but given the thousands of matches that are held every year, such violence is not common.

Frustration

On March 17, 1974, in Honduras, thousands of fans burned down the soccer stadium. They were angry because officials had suspended two matches on the grounds that the crowd was too large for the stadium.

In Lima, Peru, 1964, fans swarmed onto the soccer pitch and attempted to lynch the referee following a disallowed goal that would have enabled the national team to tie with Argentina.

In both these examples, bitterly disappointed fans retaliated for what they regarded as an illegitimate or unacceptable action—a capricious decision to deprive them of their sport or an erroneous decision to penalize their team and threaten it with defeat. Violence erupted because the fans were disappointed or frustrated in their expectation that holding a ticket entitled them to see a game, or that the game would be refereed fairly and judiciously. I use the term *frustration* riots for hostile outbursts that follow any action that blocks or disappoints a legitimate expectation about the availability, rules, and adjudication of the game.

Not all violence in sports stems from spectator frustration (see below). The "strong form" of frustration–aggression theory, that frustration always leads to some form of aggression and that aggression is always caused by frustration (Dollard et al., 1939) is no longer given much credence. However, a link between frustration and aggression has been established empirically, and it is a connection that appears in a particular type of sports riot. Actually, *two* subtypes are identified corresponding to the source of the frustration:

1. *Deprivation.* When fans are deprived of a service (e.g., access to the stadium is blocked, the game is a fake), they experience frustration. Frustration, and therefore aggression, is likely to be most intense when deprivation is most severe and appears most illegitimate or arbitrary (cf. Brown & Herrnstein, 1975). We can understand the sheer frustration of the Egyptian fans who tore down the gates of Zamalek Stadium (see pp. 349–350). They held tickets but were refused admission when, for no good reason, the game was moved to a smaller stadium. The link between frustration and aggression has been elaborated by a number of scholars (e.g., Bandura, 1973; Berkowitz, 1972) and has been applied to civil disorders in the light of the ghetto riots of the 1960s. Frustration can be the result of *absolute*

or *relative* deprivation of needs and expectations. Frustration is generated by the realization that legitimate needs and expectations are not being met. A crowd that has waited all night outside a stadium learns that tickets to the game have already been allotted. Fans who have waited for hours find that latecomers are admitted to the best seats. A highly rated boxing championship turns out to be a farce in which two unfit boxers spar at one another. We are using deprivation here in a different way from the political scientists and sociologists (Davies, 1971; Gurr, 1970), whose concept of deprivation relates to quality of life. However, if people value highly a commodity such as sport, disappointment encountered in satisfying this need can elicit as much hostility as deprivation of food, transport, and shelter. Thus we would expect the target of hostility to be the source or symbol of the frustration—authority, the players, the referee.

2. *Perceived injustice.* Sports riots frequently are precipitated by a referee's decision—to award a penalty or to disallow a goal at a crucial point of the game, when the decision virtually ensures defeat. Referees can be inconsistent and unjust in their rulings: A player is brutally felled and the referee does nothing; a penalty is awarded but no infringement has occurred. But spectators generally tend to distort what they see, especially when the incident is ambiguous (cf. Hastorf & Cantril, 1954; Mann, 1974a). Felt injustice relates to a faulty or arbitrary decision during the game. The panic and riot in Lima, Peru, May 1964, was sparked off by the referee's decision to disallow the Peruvian goal because of rough play. Several serious Italian soccer riots have been triggered by disputed decisions. (The reactions of players to a referee's decision can also "fire" a crowd.) Sometimes the grievance that leads to the riot occurs before the game. The Montreal hockey riot, 1955 (Lang & Lang, 1961), began when enraged Montreal Canadian's fans attempted to storm the box of the President of the National Hockey League during a game between Montreal and Detroit. Several days before the game, "Rocket" Richard, the Canadian's star player had been suspended by the League President for fighting.

Outlawry

British soccer matches have been marred by "soccer hooliganism," a term that describes the conduct of thousands of young fans who smash subway trains on their way to and from the game, threaten or fight with opposing fans, and rampage through the streets near the stadium. Manchester United and Glasgow Rangers fans have achieved notoriety for their violence. Rarely does the violence escalate to the point where spectators are killed or seriously injured (cf. other sports riots). The soccer hooligan subculture has been analyzed by a number of British sociologists (Harrington, 1968; Taylor, 1971; Marsh, 1975). All agree that there is an identifiable group of young,

unemployed or underprivileged fans who are involved in soccer violence, but they disagree on the causes (see the following). The game, therefore, becomes an opportunity for the delinquent gang to assemble and engage in threatening or destructive acts. To a large extent the game itself and its outcome are incidental to the violence.

Convergence theory could be invoked to explain soccer hooliganism. It asserts that the unfolding of a hostile outburst is virtually predetermined by the kinds of people who gather and their latent predispositions. All that is required is some stimulus or incident to enable those predisposed to violence to reveal their true selves and do what they really want. One variation of convergence theory is the "riff-raff" theory; crowd violence is simply the work of the violence-prone, criminal elements and malcontents in the community who congregate to act out their antisocial tendencies. Harrington (1968) reports statistics on 497 convicted British soccer hooligans, 60% of whom had prior convictions: "The nature and number of previous offences suggest that those with a criminal record and violent propensities may not infrequently use the football ground as a social situation in which to express their anti-social tendencies [p. 14]." Many soccer hooligans carry knives, hammers, sticks, spikes, choppers, and powdered pepper—indicating a preparedness to threaten or engage in violence. Marsh (1975) maintains that much of the violence is "ritualized" (i.e., rarely is physical injury inflicted); the idea is to threaten and intimidate rival fans, not injure them. However, this does not explain the damage done to trains and other property before and after soccer matches. In acting-out anti-social tendencies, a cohesive mob within the crowd may select rival fans or police and officials for its targets. It is not only a British phenomenon. Soccer hooliganism has been reported in Italy and in Russia.

Remonstrance

A third type of spectator outburst is based on political protest or remonstrance. A section of the crowd uses the sports event as an arena to express a political grievance or to advance an ideology. As sport becomes more politicized, an instrument in international relations, organized protest, and demonstrations have moved into the sports arena. The most prominent example is the series of protest riots against the 1970–1971 tours of Britain and Australia by South African sports teams. Attempts to disrupt games played by South African rugby and cricket teams involved thousands of demonstrators who invaded the field of play, hurled smoke bombs, blew whistles and battled the police. Disruption was the tactical weapon of a social movement whose aim was to expose apartheid and racial discrimination in the selection of South African sports teams. These demonstrations, carefully

planned and organized, were an attack against a political ideology (Hain, 1971). The demonstrators sought not only to disrupt the event, but also to provoke the police and authorities into overreaction so as to draw maximum publicity to their cause.

Confrontation

Competition is inherently a breeding ground for conflict (Deutsch, 1973; Sherif et al, 1961). When the competing parties in sport are groups with a history of smoldering hostility and resentment, intergroup violence frequently erupts between rival bands of supporters. The most famous case is that of the war between the neighboring countries of El Salvador and Honduras that broke out in August 1969. The war has been traced to a soccer match between the two countries (Lever, 1969), although it is more probable that the match was the precipitating incident, following months of protracted tension between the two countries. In June 1969, Salvador beat Honduras 3–0 in Salvador. Apparently this led Honduran crowds to attack Salvadoreans living in the country, forcing at least 10,000 to flee for their lives. Relationships deteriorated, and by August both countries were at war.

In sports contests between teams representing rival national, regional, ethnic or religious groups, supporters tend to regard the outcome as a test of their group's worth and standing. Confrontation riots may occur during the contest (especially if there is animosity between players) but are more likely after the game, when rival groups insult and jostle each other while leaving the stadium. Thus the sports event is an opportunity for preexisting conflicts and tensions to become exacerbated and break out in the open. It is the losing group, whose prestige has been undermined, that is more likely to provoke hostilities, but the winner's fans in their excitement may also attack. In 1967, jubilant Czechoslovak youths ransacked the Prague offices of the Russian airline after their team beat the Russians in hockey.

A number of examples illustrate the role of national, religious and tribal conflicts in sports riots. In May 1953, Hungary defeated Italy in a soccer match in Rome. After the game a clash occurred between rival groups of spectators. Soccer games between the Glasgow Rangers (a Protestant team) and Celtics (a Catholic team) are notorious battlegrounds. In Papua New Guinea, in 1972 and again in 1973, football matches between regional teams led to intertribal warfare. Soccer matches between rival regions in Italy and in Brazil frequently end in violence. In Porto Alegre, Brazil, in October 1973, 300 fans armed with knives and guns joined players fighting on the field in a match between two provincial teams. Interracial violence frequently occurs following basketball games in the U.S. between high schools from black and white areas. To understand outbursts of intergroup hostility in sport, it is

essential to take account of the meaning of group identification for team supporters and the nature of preexisting strains and resentments between groups.

Expressive

A category of sports riots can be reserved for violent outbursts that appear to be almost entirely expressions of extreme euphoria (in victory) or deep depression or anger (in defeat). Expressive riots are *post*game phenomena. They differ from frustration riots in that the disappointment (in the case of defeat) is not based on legitimate expectations that have been arbitrarily or capriciously thwarted. It is tempting to regard expressive riots as a wastebasket category for episodes that do not fit neatly elsewhere. I maintain, however, that there is a distinct category of expressive sports riots (although *all* riots are expressive to the extent that emotions are aroused.)

Expressive riots are due to extreme emotional arousal that leads to a loss of normal restraint. The person is no longer inhibited from engaging in wild, antisocial behavior. When a person is highy aroused, either through intense joy, grief, anger or fear, rational processes that regulate conduct are suspended, opening the way for uninhibited behavior. According to this general arousal hypothesis, the magnitude of arousal, not the kind of emotion, produces disinhibition. Since there is a general lowering of inhibitions, extreme arousal can trigger a variety of impulsive actions—sexual, exhibitionistic, infantile, and aggressive. The extreme elation that folows a heady victory can produce the same kind of mayhem ordinarily associated with bitter, unexpected defeat. A notorious "victory" riot that illustrates this point occurred in Pittsburgh, October 1971, following the Pittsburgh Pirates' win in the World Series. The *New York Times* (Oct. 18, 1971) reported a boisterous celebration of 100,000 people that rapidly got out of hand. Fires were set, cars overturned, telephone booths ripped apart. Some people danced nude in the streets, and at least a dozen rapes were reported. Hundreds were arrested and many were injured. A less spectacular "celebration riot" occurred in Barcelona, Spain, in May 1972, when thousands of Scottish fans invaded the pitch after their team, Glasgow Rangers, won the European Cup-winners final. After the game, inebriated Scotsmen drifted around the streets in a celebration that left 97 spectators and eight police injured. In the Pittsburgh and Barcelona "riots," alcohol contributed to loss of inhibitions. A third, but unique, example of a victory riot was the 1967 incident in which exuberant Czechoslovak youths ransacked the Prague offices of Aeroflot, the Russian airline, following the Czech hockey team's win over Russia in the world hockey championships. Earlier that year, the Russian army had suppressed a Czech attempt to liberalize their own government. The Czechoslovakian fans, in their elation, were clearly making a political point

(cf. confrontation riots). This example shows that victory riots can be issue-related, consistent with Smelser's (1962) model and contrary to Marx's (1970) claim that they are "issue-less."

Expressive crowds are usually unstable. They tend to be formally leaderless, have few guidelines and the emotions of participants may escalate to the point where other emotions take over. This would appear to go against the emergent norm principle that the limits of permissible conduct are implicitly defined in crowds (Turner & Killian, 1972, p. 100). Turner and Killian explain, however, that the expressive crowd becomes transformed into an acting, hostile crowd if it develops a sense of power to legitimize actions and if its activities are blocked or interfered with. For example, when police move to disperse people or arrest a few drunken members, the victory crowd may turn ugly. But even when there is no interference, intense emotional arousal, such as delirium that accompanies a spectacular victory, can produce virtually the same conduct found in a race riot.

Riots in defeat have a strong "sore-loser" component. Extreme anger or depression following the defeat of one's team may lead to a loss of control. Many sore loser riots occur after high school sports contests. The following example is typical. In December 1974, a crowd of Florida high school students, upset over their school's loss in a football playoff game, vandalized the game site and pelted authorities with rocks. The disturbance erupted after one team won 15–13 in the final seconds on a 30-yard field goal. It is not only a close, last-minute loss that brings out the "sore-loser" rioter. In Guatemala City in February 1977, five people were killed when local soccer fans, angered after their home town club lost 6–3 to an army team, attacked the winning players with machetes. "Sore-loser" targets may be anything conspicuous—the stadium, officials, own team, other team, opposing fans, stores, or buses. Since the fan is able to attribute the loss to almost anything, anger can be directed at any target.

MILD "SORE-LOSER" REACTIONS

A mass outpouring of crowd violence is, however, not the usual response to a team's loss, and when it does occur it may involve only a subgroup of spectators. It is likely that those engaged in violence are those who earlier judged that the team had been treated in a grossly unfair manner by the referee or the opposition (cf. frustration riots). Spectators perceive and interpret a game in line with their team loyalties. For example, Hastorf and Cantril (1954) conclude that team loyalty operates during a game, filtering and shaping what is perceived—only the fouls committed by the other team are spotted, those committed by one's own are not seen. Mann (1974a) has pointed to distortions of judgment found after the game to rationalize and

reduce the bitterness of defeat: beliefs that the loss was due to bad luck or poor umpiring, that the opposing team "played dirty" and yet received more beneficial penalties. Not all loser's fans misperceive or rationalize in this way—indeed only a minority when the game's outcome is decisive.

Although distortion and rationalization might soothe the bruised pride of some fans, they can fuel the ire of others. If the game is close and bitterly fought, cumulative misperceptions and rationalizations could elicit generalized hostile beliefs, which, according to Smelser (1962), are a necessary component of riots. It could be a good idea to display on the scoreboard the actual statistics of fouls and penalties so as to prevent the potential dangers of "sore-loser" distortions.

Research on sore-losers has been extended by two students at Flinders University. Jennings (Note 2) examined the closeness of the game on the losers' tendency to distort and rationalize. Spectators were interviewed at eight Australian rules football games. The margin of defeat ranged from two points (the closest) to 56 (the widest). As predicted, the closer the game, the greater the tendency of loser's fans: (1) to distort the number of "free kicks" (penalties) awarded; (2) to attribute the loss to bad luck or poor umpiring; and (3) to perceive dirty play by opponents. Belcher (Note 3) investigated whether "sore-loser" reactions can be detected *during* a game. [Mann's (1974a) research had been limited to postgame reactions, which, of course, could be interpreted as conscious rationalizations rather than misperceptions.] Basketball fans were interviewed at half-time and again at the end of the game. At the half, 56% of the trailing team's fans (versus 19% of the leading team's fans) attributed the score to luck or poor umpiring. In the second half, the team trailing at half-time gained the lead and went on to win by two points; 76% of the loser's fans (versus 42% of the winner's fans) attributed the victory to luck or poor umpiring. This study shows that distortion and misperception occur both during and after a game, although reactions tend to be sharper at the end. The significance of distortions that occur during a contest is that they may fuel emotional reactions that underlie crowd violence *during* a game.

To summarize this section: Five types of sports riots have been classified on the basis of participants' dominant or salient characteristics. Rioters may seek to: (1) retaliate for an illegitimate, frustrating decision; (2) "act out" hostile needs; (3) stage an ideological protest; (4) confront a hated rival group; and (5) release and express inhibited impulses. The schema is not meant to be exhaustive or predictive. Rather, it is intended as a starting point for a discussion of what constitutes a sports riot, together with a specification of the associated psychological mechanisms, the kinds of participants involved, and their usual targets. The schema, based on analysis of materials collected from the *New York Times Index,* could be refined on the basis of more detailed accounts and further conceptual analysis.

THE AGGRESSIVE EFFECTS OF VIEWING SPORT

The schema identified five types of sports violence that occur under exceptional circumstances:

1. A group of fans strongly believe that their team has been cheated.
2. Gangs of delinquent elements predisposed to violence act out their hostilities.
3. A protest movement attempts to stage a demonstration.
4. Long-smoldering conflict between rival groups erupts into open hostiilty.
5. Under intense emotional arousal, fans lose self-control and become uninhibited.

These are rare occurrences. A much more common feature of sports events is the happy or disappointed fan who shows little aggressive or disruptive behavior. The question arises as to whether beyond *specific* conditions which give rise to crowd violence (see Table 12.1) there are *general* factors associated with spectator sport which promote uninhibited behavior. Is there something about attending or viewing any sports event that arouses the spectator, elicits aggressive feelings and primes him to act in a violent manner?

There is something about the conditions under which spectating takes place and about the content of what is viewed that prepares the ground for sports violence. Three elements associated with contact sports contribute to aggressive tendencies among spectators (see Table 12.2):

1. The spectator is immersed in a crowd;
2. The spectator views a display of ritualized (occasionally nonritualized) aggression;
3. The spectator suffers (or enjoys) the outcome of loss (or victory);

TABLE 12.2
Predictions about the Likelihood of Aggressive Tendencies
Being Produced by Viewing a Sports Contest

Element	Factor	Spectator Alone			Spectator in Crowd		
		Loser	*Winner*	*Neutral*	*Loser*	*Winner*	*Neutral*
Crowd	General arousal	no	no	no	yes	yes	yes
Player aggression	Modeling-disinhibition	yes	yes	yes	yes	yes	yes
Game outcome	Frustration	yes	no	no	yes	no	no

Consider each of these elements in turn: crowd factors, player conduct, and outcome of game:

1. The spectator is aroused by the conditions of viewing a game—as a participant in a large, noisy, densely packed crowd. Zimbardo (1969) and Greenacre (1973) refer to the state of "deindividuation," a state of diminished self-awareness and self control produced by being immersed in a large, constricted crowd. Deindividuation leads to a weakening of inner restraints and contributes to the expression of aggression. Berkowitz's (1972) revision of frustration–aggression theory, which gives a central role to emotional arousal in the priming of aggression, would also posit that a host of crowd-related factors—noise, chanting, bodily contact—could "excite" the spectator and facilitate aggression.[2]

2. Another factor contributing to spectator aggression is observation of player aggression and misconduct. Social learning theorists (e.g., Bandura, 1973) emphasize that aggression is learned and facilitated by modeling cues. Goldstein and Arms (1971) argue that observation of a violent game such as football has a general disinhibiting effect and this explains the pre- to postgame increase in aggressive feelings among *all* spectators[3] (see also Turner, 1968). According to this approach the more spiteful and vicious the play, the greater the likelihood of spectator aggression.

3. A third contributing factor to spectator aggression is the *outcome* of the game.

Classic frustration–aggression theory would predict that fans of the losing or beaten team would show aggressive tendencies. The literature provides no evidence to support this hypothesis (cf. Goldstein & Arms, 1971). However, a revised hypothesis, which relates loser aggression to close, unexpected defeat, could possibly gain empirical support.

Identification of crowd, player, and outcome factors as antecedents of aggression leads to several differential predictions about spectator aggression as well as recognition that each factor should be systematically varied to gain an understanding of spectator behavior. Table 12.2 sets out a number of predictions that follow from an analysis of the three elements. The table suggests that:

---

[2]It should also be noted that crowd variables function not only to *arouse* the spectator. Being in a crowd *facilitates* and energizes the dominant mood or response (Allport, 1924; Zajonc, 1965). Being in a crowd also *enables* the spectator, if motivated, to act aggressively, as the crowd provides a cover of anonymity (cf. Zimbardo, 1969). Certain aggressive acts can only be accomplished by a crowd (e.g., tearing down the goal posts), and the crowd enables diffusion of responsibility for antisocial acts.

[3]Goldstein and Arms' results are also consistent with the crowd arousal hypothesis.

1. An increase in aggression is most likely and should be strongest if the spectator is in a large crowd, has observed extreme player aggression and his team has lost heavily.

2. Aggression is least likely and should be weakest if the person views the game alone, is a neutral (non) supporter or is a fan of the winner.

3. An *increase* in aggression among lone viewers, or among winning and neutral fans, would be incompatible with arousal theory and frustration theory, respectively.

4. A *decrease* in aggression among fans viewing a vicious game would embarrass modeling-disinhibition theory.

We have attempted to point out how the three approaches emphasize rather different factors associated with spectator aggression. All, however, are complementary; in some hostile outbursts, all three factors could be operating, and this is likely to be the case in any of the most spontaneous riot types—frustration, confrontation, and expressive riots.

POSTEVENT ASSEMBLING

Another crowd form related to sport is the coming together of large groups of fans after the game. Postgame assembling indicates that powerful feelings stirred by the event can persist for a considerable time after the game is over. In 1966, the Italian soccer team which had been unexpectedly defeated by North Korea in the World Cup returned home to an airport reception of abuse and tomatoes. In 1973, more than 2000 irate Iranian fans gathered at Teheran airport to jeer the arrival of their national soccer team which had lost 0–3 to Australia two days earlier. The Iranian fans had confidently expected a win over Australia. The prime location for postgame fan convergence is the airport. The media play an important role in sending "assembling instructions" about when and where the crowd should congregate (McPhail & Miller, 1973). McPhail and Miller investigated one "assembling process" in which 4000 students gathered at a Southern airport to meet the arrival of a university basketball team that had scored an upset victory over a nationally ranked, traditional rival. They questioned a large sample of students regarding their participation in the airport gathering. A number of variables determined whether fans converged on the airport or not (e.g., whether they had heard the broadcast, and access to transport). Attendance at prior home games correlated + .42 with being at the airport, which suggests that involvement as a fan predisposes the person to assemble in support of the team even when it is not engaged in a contest. During the airport welcome, a "riot" broke out in which there was looting and property damage, police use of tear gas and several arrests—an example of the dynamic interconnection

between crowd forms. McPhail and Miller's study is a nice illustration of how the unscheduled sports crowd can be used as a vehicle for the investigation of general collective behavior processes.

THE CULTURE FACTOR

To understand collective behavior in sport, a cross-cultural perspective is imperative. One may ask in general whether the *forms* and *meanings* of collective behavior differ across national cultures (Mann, 1974b) and this question can usefully be asked of collective episodes involving sport. It appears that some crowd forms occur more frequently in some countries than in others. Riots and panics at sports stadiums are more commonly found in Latin American countries than elsewhere. The *New York Times Index* lists 48 football riots from 1950 to 1974; Latin American countries and Italy were the most frequent locations.

For any form, the *meaning* underlying the episode may vary considerably across cultures. A sports riot involving regional groups may take on a strong political flavor in a newly emergent country, such as Papua New Guinea. In other countries, spectator violence can be an indirect expression of social alienation and conflict (cf. Taylor, 1971). In an economically and socially disadvantaged region, allegiance to a team may have quite different significance—as a major source of pride and social esteem—from team allegiance in a large urban center where sport is merely another leisure-time activity.

The apparent variations in forms and meanings of sports crowds across countries can be traced to at least three factors:

1. Current levels of political and systemic frustration that create the climate and atmosphere for crowd action (cf. Smelser, 1962). Under social strain people become less trusting of authority, more competitive, more anxious, more extreme in reactions. The threshold for collective violence and dislocation is then lowered, especially wherever large crowds gather, such as at sports contests.

2. Cultures differ in norms relating to respect for order, tolerance for expression of emotion (including aggression), and recognition of the prior rights of others to service (Hall, 1966; Mann, 1970). The sports stadium is a setting where these norms and values gain expression.

3. There are national differences associated with what might be termed "physical-conduciveness" to collective behavior. In poor, overpopulated countries, large crowds gather in small, inadequate arenas. In Latin American countries, there is considerable tolerance for crowding and close interpersonal distance. These spatial–ecological factors can become antecedents of panic, disorder and rumor.

In general, we would expect to find a close relationship between countries high on these dimensions and the frequency and severity of sports crowds (cf. Chapter 3, this volume). Sipes (1973) compared 10 warlike societies (e.g., Tibetans) and 10 peaceful societies (e.g., Hutterites) and found that almost all of the warlike societies but few of the peaceful societies had combative sports. The conclusion is that combative sport reinforces aggression in a culture. The question arises as to whether combative sport is also likely to encourage spectator violence. There are some leads but no systematic evidence to suggest this is the case. Lewis (Note 1) listed 245 sports riots reported in seven national U.S. newspapers 1960-1972. Riots most frequently occurred at contests involving combative sports: football ($n = 61$), baseball ($n = 58$), basketball ($n = 46$), ice hockey ($n = 29$), and boxing ($n = 19$). Baseball is, of course, a noncombative sport; for an explanation of the high incidence of baseball riots it is necessary to go beyond the simple aggression-reinforcement hypothesis.

CONCLUSION

We listed earlier the contributions an analysis of sports crowds could make for collective behavior theory. We now conclude by indicating the possible contributions of a collective behavior perspective in sport for development of the fields of sports psychology and sociology.

The collective behavior perspective means that a much wider array of crowd phenomena than collective violence are encompassed within the field. We refer to mass behavior such as queues, entry and exit panics, protest demonstrations, post game convergence and assembly. This could be extended further to encompass other aspects of collective behavior in sport: social movements that seek reform in sport or use sports contests as an occasion for political protest; "crazes," such as epidemics of "streaking" at spectator sports (Evans & Miller, 1975); public opinion about changes in the nature of sport; and the role played by spectator sport as a safety valve in the social order. Another problem requiring attention is, of course, the effect of the crowd on players and how crowd stimuli influence their performance and conduct.

The collective behavior perspective also means a different focus in the analysis of spectator conduct. Rather than viewing the crowd as a mere aggregate of spectators reacting to what is happening on the field, the focus changes to the crowd as a social group in its own right. Consideration is then given to the effect of crowd members on each other, how spectators interact and influence each other within the crowd. This leads, in turn, to an examination of group factors that determine individual spectator reactions— anonymity, social facilitation, conformity pressures, norm emergence, diffusion of responsibility, communication patterns, and so on. Although this perspective recognizes the role played by individual processes such as

perceptual distortion, rationalization, attitudes, motivations, and impulses, it extends and broadens the scope to encompass group and societal factors as determinants of spectator behavior at sports events.

ACKNOWLEDGMENTS

Preparation of this chapter was aided by support from the Australian Research Grants Committee for a project on Studies in Crowd Behavior.

REFERENCE NOTES

1. Lewis, J. M. *Sports riots: Some research questions.* Paper presented at the American Sociological Association Meetings, San Francisco, August 1975.
2. Jennings, G. *The effect of closeness in scores on the reactions of football supporters.* Unpublished manuscript, Flinders University, 1974.
3. Belcher, J. *The basketball match: Sore losers?* Unpublished manuscript, Flinders University, 1976.

REFERENCES

Allport, F. H. *Social Psychology.* Boston: Houghton Mifflin, 1924.

Bandura, A. *Aggression: A social learning analysis.* Englewood Cliffs, N.J.: Prentice-Hall, 1973

Berkowitz, L. Frustrations, comparisons, and other sources of emotional arousal as contributors to social unrest. *Journal of Social Issues,* 1972, *28,* 77–91.

Blumer, H. Collective behavior. In A. M. Lee (Ed.), *Principles of sociology.* New York: Barnes & Noble, 1946.

Brown, R., & Herrnstein, R. J. *Psychology.* Boston: Little, Brown, 1975.

Chakotin, S. *The rape of the masses.* London: Routledge & Kegan Paul, 1941.

Cialdini, R., Borden, R. J., Thorne, A., Walker, M., Freeman, S., & Sloan, L. Basking in reflected glory: Three (football) field studies. *Journal of Personality and Social Psychology,* 1976, *34,* 366–375.

Couch, C. J. Collective behavior: An examination of some stereotypes. *Social Problems,* 1968, *15,* 310–322.

Davies, J. C. (Ed.). *When men revolt and why.* New York: Free Press, 1971.

Deutsch, M. *The resolution of conflict: Constructive and destructive processes.* New Haven, Conn.: Yale University Press, 1973.

Dollard, J., Miller, N. E., Doob, L. W., Mowrer, O. H., & Sears, R. R. *Frustration and aggression.* New Haven, Conn.: Yale University Press, 1939.

Evans, R. R., & Miller, J. L. Barely an end in sight. In R. R. Evans (Ed.), *Readings in collective behavior* (2nd ed.). Chicago: Rand McNally, 1975.

Freud, S. *Group psychology and the analysis of the ego.* London: Hogarth, 1921.

Geen, R. G., & O'Neal, E. C. (Eds.). *Perspectives on aggression.* New York: Academic Press, 1976.

Goldstein, J. H., & Arms, R. L. Effects of observing athletic contests on hostility. *Sociometry*, 1971, *34*, 83–90.

Greenacre, P. Crowds and crisis: Psychoanalytic considerations. In R. Eissler (Ed.), *The psychoanalytic study of the child* (Vol. 27). New York: Quadrangle Books, 1973.

Gurr, T. R. *Why men rebel*. Princeton, N.J.: Princeton University Press. 1970.

Hain, P. *Don't play with Apartheid*. London: Allen & Unwin, 1971.

Hall, E. T. *The hidden dimension*. New York: Doubleday, 1966.

Harrell, W. A., & Schmitt, D. R. Effects of a minimal audience on physical aggression. *Psychological Reports*, 1973, *32*, 651–657.

Harrington, J. A. *Soccer hooliganism: A preliminary report*. Bristol, England: Wright, 1968.

Hastorf, A. H., & Cantril, H. They saw a game: A case study. *Journal of Abnormal and Social Psychology*, 1954, *49*, 129–134.

Ingham, A. G., & Smith, M. D. Social implications of the interaction between spectators and athletes. *Exercise and Sport Sciences Review* 1974, *2*, 189–224.

Janowitz, M. *Social control of escalated riots*. Chicago: University of Chicago Center for Policy Studies, 1968.

Lang, G. E. Riotous outbursts in sports events. *Sociological Abstracts*, 1970, *18* (5), 820.

Lang, K., & Lang, G. E. *Collective dynamics*. New York: Crowell, 1961.

Latané, B. Theory of social impact. *Proceedings of the 21st International Congress of Psychology*. Paris, France, 1976.

LeBon, G. *The Crowd: A study of the popular mind*. London: Unwin, 1895.

Lever, J. Soccer: Opium of the Brazilian people. *Trans-action*, 1969, *7*(2), 36–43.

Mann, L. The social psychology of waiting lines. *American Scientist*, 1970, *58*, 390–398.

Mann, L. On being a sore loser: How fans react to their team's failure. *Australian Journal of Psychology*, 1974, *26*, 37–47. (a)

Mann, L. Cross national aspects of riot behavior. In J. Dawson & W. Lonner (Eds.) *Readings in cross-cultural psychology*. Hong Kong: University of Hong Kong Press, 1974. (b)

Mann, L. Social influence in the crowd. *Proceedings of the 21st International Congress of Psychology*. Paris, France, 1976.

Mann, L., & Taylor, K. F. Queue counting: The effect of motives upon estimates of numbers in waiting lines. *Journal of Personality and Social Psychology*, 1969, *12*, 95–103.

Marsh, P. Understanding aggro. *New Society*, 1975, *35*, 7–9.

Marx, G. T. Issueless riots. *Annals of American Academy of Political and Social Sciences*, 1970, *391*, 21–33.

Marx, G. T., & Wood, J. L. Strands of theory and research in collective behavior. In A. Inkeles (Ed.), *Annual review of sociology*, 1975 (Vol. 1). Palo Alto, Calif.: Annual Reviews, Inc., 1975.

McPhail, C., & Miller, D. The assembling process: A theoretical and empirical examination. *American Sociological Review*, 1973, *38*, 721–735.

Milgram, S., & Toch, H. Collective behavior: Crowds and social movements. In G. Lindzey & E. Aronson (Eds.), *Handbook of social psychology* (2nd ed.) (Vol. 4). Reading, Mass.: Addison-Wesley, 1969.

Russell, G. W., & Drewry, B. R. Crowd size and competitive aspects of aggression in ice hockey: An archival study. *Human Relations*, 1976, *8*, 723–735.

Sherif, M., Harvey, O., White, B., Hood, W., & Sherif, C. *Intergroup conflict and cooperation. The robbers cave experiment*. Norman: University of Oklahoma, Institute of Group Relations, 1961.

Sipes, R. G. War, sports and aggression: An empirical test of two rival theories. *American Anthropologist*, 1973, *75*, 64–86.

Smelser, N. *Theory of collective behavior*. New York: Free Press, Glencoe, 1962.

Taylor, I. R. Soccer consciousness and soccer hooliganism. In S. Cohen (Ed.), *Images of deviance*. Middlesex, England: Pelican, 1971.

Turner, E. T. The effects of viewing college football, basketball and wrestling on the elicited aggressive responses of male spectators. In G. S. Kenyon (Ed.), *Contemporary psychology of sport*: Proceedings. Rome, Italy: International Society of Sport Psychology, 1968.

Turner, R. H., & Killian, L. M. *Collective behavior*. Englewood Cliffs, N.J.: Prentice-Hall, 1972.

Wheeler, L. Toward a theory of behavioral contagion. *Psychological Review*, 1966, *73*, 179–192.

Zajonc, R. B. Social facilitation. *Science*, 1965, *149*, 269–274.

Zimbardo, P.G. The human choice: Individuation, reason, and order versus deindividuation, impulse and chaos. In W. Arnold & D. Levine (Eds.), *Nebraska Symposium on Motivation* (Vol. 17). Lincoln: University of Nebraska Press, 1969.

III

FACTORS THAT INFLUENCE THE OUTCOME OF SPORTS COMPETITION

13 A Resistant Analysis of 1971 and 1972 Professional Football

Frederick Mosteller
Harvard University

INTRODUCTION

In making football schedules, it inevitably turns out that some teams have a stiffer schedule than others. It is a curse of professional football that, unlike baseball, not only do the same teams not play one another repeatedly, but in a given season some teams do not play others at all. In 1971 and 1972 there were 26 teams in the major professional conferences but the schedule had 14 games. Each team played three or four teams twice in the 1971 and 1972 schedule and six or eight other teams once each. Imbalances occur and one cannot evaluate them until the season is completed.

In the analysis presented here, we adjust for the effect of teams playing schedules of unequal difficulties to see how the teams compare after such adjustments are made. Our adjustment process is not quite the usual one. We have employed what can be called a resistant analysis. The averages we employ are based on trimeans. Essentially, trimeans are the weighted average

FREDERICK MOSTELLER took his doctorate in mathematics, specializing in statistics, from Princeton University, where he also taught. In 1946, he came to Harvard in the Department of Social Relations, and in 1957, he joined the newly formed Department of Statistics, which he initially chaired. His research contributions have been primarily in statistical theory and in the social and medical areas. His sports publications have dealt with analyses of collegiate and professional football scores and of the outcome of baseball's World Series. His own active participation in sports is confined to ping pong, but he is a TV fan of every form of sports, especially football, baseball, basketball, golf, track, field, gymnastics, swimming, diving, skating, and billiards.

of the quartiles of the data and the median, the latter being given double weight. In the case of samples of size 14 and the length of the basic football season, the quartiles are the scores, four in from each end of the ordered scores and the median is the average of the seventh and eighth scores. Tukey (1977) calls the quartiles "hinges."

The purpose of using trimeans as the averages in this analysis is to prevent very unusual scores from having much effect. Occasionally, a team may "take off" and score a great many points against some other team that is rather demoralized for the day. Or, in the struggle to win an otherwise tight game, a team may lose very much more badly than it would have deserved. Unless this is a regular habit, one or two of these extreme results would not be much reflected in the trimean. Resistant means give strong indications of the position of the center of a distribution without allowing occasional wild observations to have much influence. It might be thought that they have no influence, but they do have some, because if three wild observations occur, the fourth observation enters the trimean calculation; whereas were it not for the wild ones, a smaller observation would likely have entered. In using this sort of analysis, there is no pretense that the statistics "know" which are the wild ones and which are not. Instead, the statistical program is designed to cope with wild observations systematically as a matter of course, rather than depending upon recognizing which are "wild."

We have broken up the problem into two parts—offensive scoring and defensive scoring. This is a convenience in handling the data, but the words "offensive" and "defensive" should not be overinterpreted. Frequently the defensive team scores for its own side and the offensive team will then have allowed a score against its own defensive team. This will contribute to what we will call the "offensive score." Hence, although it is convenient to speak in terms of offense and defense, the interpretations cannot be limited to the divisions of the team with those names.

Table 13.1 shows the schedule and scoring for the regular 1971 and 1972 seasons. The key summary tables are Tables 13.7 and 13.10, which give our final results. We begin with Table 13.1, construct Tables 13.2 through 13.6, and then move these results to Tables 13.7 and 13.8. Table 13.9 is fundamental for Table 13.10, a venture separate from the main thread.

OFFENSIVE SCORING

Each team has a trimean of scores made against it by its opponents—that is, the "average" score its "defense" lets through, also called a *resistant average*. Consider the teams on the Atlanta Falcons' 1971 schedule. The stem-and-leaf plots for Atlanta's scores and its opponents' scores are:

Atlanta Scored		The 14 Opponents Scored Against Atlanta	
0	3799	0	66
1	67	1	347
2	004488	2	00114446
3	18	3	
		4	1

Offense		Defense	
Hinge	9	Hinge	14
Median	20	Median	20.5
Hinge	28	Hinge	24
Trimean	19.25	Trimean	19.75

Thus Atlanta scored 3, 7, 9, 9, 16, 17, 20, 20, 24, 24, 28, 28, 31, and 38 points. The hinges are the fourth observations in from each end of the distribution. The trimean is $\frac{1}{4}[9 + 28 + 2(20)] = 19.25$.

Table 13.2 shows the stem-and-leaf and the summary statistics for the offensive scores in the 14 games for each team and each of its 14 opponents' scores (the original team's defensive score or points given up).

Next we build Table 13.3, based on the opponent's opponents. For example, in 1971 Atlanta played Team 11 (San Francisco) first. From Table 13.2, San Francisco scored a trimean of 21 against its opponents and they scored a trimean of 16.75 against San Francisco. We build Table 13.3 line by line for each team on Atlanta's schedule. We now sum the columns of Table 13.3 to get the opponents' total offensive strength and their total defensive strength. For Atlanta these were 279.25 and 270.25, respectively. This tells us the total score an "average" team might be expected to make against this schedule and the total points it is expected to give up.

In going from Table 13.3 to Table 13.5, the opponents' offense total corresonds to the original team's (say Atlanta's) expected defense score. And the opponents' defense total corresponds to the original team's offensive expected total.

We can then take the trimean from Table 13.2 for the Falcons and multiply by 14 to see what sort of offensive "average" they actually got (Table 13.5). When we do this, it turns out that an average team would score 270.25 points during the season against the Falcons' schedule. The Falcons had a trimean of 19.25 and so they scored 14 × 19.25 or 269.5. Thus they were only 0.75 point short over the whole season of what they might have been expected to score. We make similar calculations for the offense of every team. Many, of course, are not close to zero. For example, in 1971 Dallas got a net advantage of 88

TABLE 13.1a
Scores of Games (1971)[a]

1. ATLANTA	2. CHICAGO	3. DALLAS	4. DETROIT	5. GREEN BAY	6. LOS ANGELES
11 H 20 17	25 H 17 15	14 A 49 37	7 H 13 16	8 H 40 42	9 A 20 24
6 A 20 20	7 A 20 17	10 A 42 7	22 A 34 7	18 H 34 13	1 H 20 20
4 A 38 41	6 A 3 17	13 H 16 20	1 H 41 38	17 H 20 17	2 H 17 3
12 H 9 26	9 H 35 14	8 H 20 13	5 H 31 28	4 A 28 31	11 A 20 13
6 H 16 24	11 A 0 13	9 A 14 24	19 A 31 7	7 H 13 24	1 A 24 16
9 H 28 6	4 A 28 23	22 H 44 21	2 H 23 28	6 A 13 30	5 H 30 13
15 A 31 14	3 H 23 19	2 A 19 23	5 A 14 14	4 H 14 14	21 H 14 20
17 A 9 6	5 H 14 17	12 A 16 13	18 A 24 20	2 A 17 14	16 A 17 24
8 H 17 21	13 H 16 15	10 H 20 7	6 H 13 21	7 A 0 3	4 A 21 13
5 H 28 21	4 H 3 28	13 A 13 0	2 A 28 3	1 A 21 28	11 H 17 6
7 A 7 24	21 A 3 34	6 H 28 21	20 H 32 21	9 H 21 29	3 A 21 28
24 H 24 13	18 A 3 6	23 H 52 10	10 H 20 23	12 A 16 16	9 H 45 28
11 A 3 24	5 A 10 31	8 A 42 14	7 A 10 29	2 H 31 10	13 H 24 38
9 A 24 20	7 H 10 27	12 H 31 12	11 A 27 31	21 A 6 27	25 A 23 14

7. MINNESOTA	8. NY GIANTS	9. NEW ORLEANS	10. PHILADELPHIA	11. SAN FRANCISCO	12. ST.LOUIS
4 A 16 13	5 A 42 40	6 H 24 20	17 A 14 37	1 A 17 20	13 H 17 24
2 H 17 20	13 H 3 30	11 H 20 38	3 H 7 42	9 A 38 20	23 H 17 10
14 H 19 0	12 A 21 20	19 A 13 13	11 H 3 31	10 A 31 3	8 H 20 21
10 A 13 0	3 A 13 20	2 A 14 35	7 H 0 13	6 H 13 20	1 A 26 9
5 A 24 13	16 H 7 31	3 H 24 14	24 A 10 34	2 H 13 0	13 A 0 20
16 H 10 3	10 A 7 23	1 A 6 28	8 H 23 7	12 A 26 14	11 H 14 26
8 A 17 10	7 H 10 17	13 A 14 24	18 H 17 16	22 H 27 10	14 A 28 23
11 H 9 13	26 H 35 17	24 H 21 21	13 A 7 7	7 A 13 9	3 H 13 16
5 H 3 0	1 A 21 17	11 A 26 20	3 A 7 20	9 H 20 26	26 A 17 20
9 A 23 10	25 A 13 17	7 H 10 23	12 A 37 20	6 A 6 17	10 H 20 37
1 H 24 7	12 H 7 24	5 A 29 21	13 H 13 20	23 A 24 21	8 A 24 7
26 A 14 30	13 A 7 23	6 A 28 45	4 A 23 20	20 H 17 26	5 H 16 16
4 H 29 10	3 H 14 42	15 H 17 21	12 H 19 7	1 H 24 3	10 A 7 19
2 A 27 10	10 H 28 41	1 H 20 24	8 A 41 28	4 H 31 27	3 A 12 31

13. WASHINGTON	14. BUFFALO	15. CLEVELAND	16. BALTIMORE	17. CINCINNATI	18. DENVER
12 A 24 17	3 H 37 49	19 H 31 0	23 H 22 0	10 H 37 14	21 H 10 10
8 A 30 3	21 H 14 29	16 A 14 13	15 H 13 14	25 A 10 21	5 A 13 34
3 A 20 16	7 A 0 19	24 H 20 34	22 A 23 3	5 A 17 20	20 H 3 16
19 H 22 13	16 H 0 43	25 H 27 17	14 A 43 0	21 H 13 23	24 H 16 27
12 H 20 0	23 A 17 28	17 A 27 24	8 A 31 7	15 H 24 27	26 H 20 16
20 A 20 27	26 A 3 20	18 H 0 27	7 A 3 10	24 A 27 31	15 A 27 0
9 H 24 14	12 H 23 28	1 H 14 31	25 H 34 21	19 A 6 10	10 A 16 17
10 H 7 7	21 A 0 34	25 A 9 26	6 H 24 17	1 H 6 9	4 H 20 24
2 A 15 16	22 H 33 38	20 A 7 13	23 A 14 13	18 A 24 10	17 H 10 24
3 H 0 13	23 H 7 20	22 H 27 7	21 A 14 17	19 H 28 13	20 A 10 28
10 A 20 13	22 H 27 20	19 A 37 24	24 A 37 14	26 H 31 0	25 A 22 10
8 H 23 7	16 A 0 24	17 H 31 27	14 H 24 0	15 A 27 31	2 H 6 3
6 A 38 24	19 H 14 20	9 A 21 17	21 H 14 3	25 H 13 21	26 A 17 45
15 H 13 20	20 A 9 22	13 A 20 13	22 H 17 21	23 A 21 35	24 A 13 31

19. HOUSTON	20. KANSAS CITY	21. MIAMI	22. NEW ENGLAND	23. NY JETS	24. OAKLAND
15 A 0 31	26 A 14 21	18 A 10 10	24 H 20 6	16 A 0 22	22 A 6 20
20 H 16 20	19 A 20 16	14 A 29 14	4 H 7 34	12 A 10 17	26 A 34 0
9 H 13 13	18 A 16 3	23 H 10 14	16 H 3 23	21 A 14 10	15 A 34 20
13 A 13 22	26 H 31 10	17 A 23 13	23 H 20 0	22 A 0 20	18 A 27 16
4 H 7 31	25 H 38 16	22 H 41 3	21 A 3 41	14 H 28 17	10 H 34 10
25 A 16 23	13 H 27 20	23 A 30 14	3 A 21 44	21 H 14 30	17 H 31 27
17 H 10 6	24 A 20 20	6 A 20 14	11 A 10 27	26 A 21 49	20 H 20 20
22 A 20 28	23 A 10 13	14 H 34 0	19 H 28 20	20 H 13 10	9 A 21 21
24 A 21 41	15 H 13 7	25 H 24 21	14 H 38 33	16 H 13 14	19 H 41 21
17 A 13 28	18 H 28 10	16 H 17 14	15 A 7 27	14 A 20 7	26 H 34 33
15 H 24 37	4 A 21 32	2 H 34 3	14 A 20 27	11 H 21 24	16 H 14 37
25 H 29 3	11 A 26 17	22 A 13 34	21 H 34 13	3 A 10 52	1 A 13 24
14 A 20 14	24 H 16 14	16 A 3 14	23 A 6 13	22 H 13 6	20 A 14 16
26 H 49 33	14 H 22 9	5 H 27 6	16 A 21 17	17 H 35 21	18 H 21 13

25. PITTSBURGH	26. SAN DIEGO
2 A 15 17	20 H 21 14
17 H 21 10	24 H 0 34
26 H 21 17	25 A 17 21
15 A 17 27	20 A 10 31
20 A 16 38	18 A 16 20
19 H 23 16	14 H 20 3
16 A 21 34	23 H 49 21
15 H 26 9	8 A 17 35
21 A 21 24	12 H 20 17
8 H 17 13	24 A 33 34
18 H 10 22	17 A 0 31
19 A 3 29	7 H 30 14
17 A 21 13	18 H 45 17
6 H 14 23	19 A 33 49

[a]The first number is the opponent's code; H indicates game played at team's home (A, away); the next number is the team's score; the last number is the opponent's score.

374

TABLE 13.1b
Scores of Games (1972)[a]

1. ATLANTA

Opp	H/A	Team	Opp
2	A	37	21
22	A	20	21
6	H	31	3
4	H	23	26
9	A	21	14
5	A	10	9
11	H	14	49
6	A	7	20
9	H	36	20
13	A	13	24
18	H	23	20
19	H	20	10
11	A	0	20
20	H	14	17

2. CHICAGO

Opp	H/A	Team	Opp
1	H	21	37
6	H	13	13
4	H	24	38
5	A	17	20
15	A	17	0
7	H	13	10
12	A	27	10
4	A	0	14
5	H	17	23
11	H	21	34
17	H	3	13
7	A	10	23
10	A	21	12
24	A	21	28

3. DALLAS

Opp	H/A	Team	Opp
10	H	28	6
8	A	23	14
5	A	13	16
25	H	17	13
16	A	21	0
13	A	20	24
4	H	28	24
26	A	34	28
12	H	33	24
10	A	28	7
11	H	10	31
12	A	27	6
13	H	34	24
8	H	3	23

4. DETROIT

Opp	H/A	Team	Opp
8	H	30	16
7	H	10	34
2	A	38	24
1	A	26	23
5	H	23	24
26	H	34	20
3	A	24	28
2	H	14	0
7	A	14	16
9	H	27	14
23	H	37	20
5	A	7	33
14	A	21	21
6	A	34	17

5. GREEN BAY

Opp	H/A	Team	Opp
15	A	26	10
24	H	14	20
3	H	16	13
2	H	20	17
4	A	24	23
1	H	9	10
7	H	13	27
11	H	34	24
2	A	23	17
19	A	23	10
13	A	16	21
4	H	33	7
7	A	23	7
9	A	30	20

6. LOS ANGELES

Opp	H/A	Team	Opp
9	H	34	14
2	A	13	13
1	A	3	31
11	H	31	7
10	A	34	3
17	H	15	12
24	A	17	45
1	H	20	7
18	H	10	16
7	H	41	45
9	A	16	19
11	A	26	16
12	A	14	24
4	H	17	34

7. MINNESOTA

Opp	H/A	Team	Opp
13	H	21	24
4	A	34	10
21	H	14	16
12	H	17	19
18	A	23	20
2	A	10	13
5	A	27	13
9	H	37	6
4	H	16	14
6	A	45	41
25	A	10	23
2	H	23	10
5	H	7	23
11	A	17	20

8. NY GIANTS

Opp	H/A	Team	Opp
4	A	16	30
3	H	14	23
10	A	27	12
9	H	45	21
11	A	23	17
12	H	27	21
13	H	16	23
18	H	29	17
13	A	13	27
12	A	13	7
10	H	62	10
17	A	10	13
21	H	13	23
3	A	23	3

9. NEW ORLEANS

Opp	H/A	Team	Opp
6	A	14	34
20	H	17	20
11	H	2	37
8	A	21	45
1	H	14	21
6	H	3	34
11	A	20	20
10	H	21	3
7	A	6	37
1	A	20	36
4	A	14	27
6	H	19	16
23	A	17	18
5	H	20	30

10. PHILADELPHIA

Opp	H/A	Team	Opp
3	A	6	28
15	H	17	27
8	H	12	27
13	A	0	14
6	H	3	34
20	A	21	20
9	A	3	21
12	H	6	6
19	A	18	17
3	H	7	28
8	A	10	62
13	H	7	23
2	H	12	21
12	A	23	24

11. SAN FRANCISCO

Opp	H/A	Team	Opp
26	H	34	3
14	A	20	27
9	A	37	2
6	A	7	31
8	H	17	23
9	H	20	20
1	A	49	14
5	A	24	34
16	H	24	21
2	A	34	21
3	A	31	10
6	H	16	26
1	H	20	0
7	H	20	17

12. ST. LOUIS

Opp	H/A	Team	Opp
16	A	10	3
13	A	10	24
25	H	19	25
7	A	19	17
13	H	3	33
8	A	21	27
2	H	10	27
10	A	6	6
3	A	24	33
8	H	7	13
21	A	10	31
3	H	6	27
6	H	24	14
10	H	24	23

13. WASHINGTON

Opp	H/A	Team	Opp
7	A	24	21
12	H	24	10
22	A	23	24
10	H	14	0
12	A	33	3
3	H	24	20
8	A	23	16
23	A	35	17
8	H	27	13
1	H	24	13
5	H	21	16
10	A	23	7
3	A	24	34
14	H	17	24

14. BUFFALO

Opp	H/A	Team	Opp
23	H	24	41
11	H	27	20
16	H	0	17
22	H	38	14
24	A	16	20
21	A	23	24
25	H	21	38
21	H	16	30
23	A	3	41
22	A	27	24
15	A	10	27
16	A	7	35
4	H	21	21
13	A	24	17

15. CLEVELAND

Opp	H/A	Team	Opp
5	H	10	26
10	A	27	17
17	H	27	6
20	H	7	31
2	H	0	17
19	A	23	17
18	A	27	20
19	H	20	0
26	A	21	17
25	H	26	24
14	H	27	10
25	A	0	30
17	A	27	24
23	A	26	10

16. BALTIMORE

Opp	H/A	Team	Opp
12	H	3	10
23	H	34	44
14	A	17	0
26	H	20	23
3	H	0	21
23	A	20	24
21	H	0	23
22	A	24	17
11	A	21	24
17	A	20	19
22	H	31	0
14	H	35	7
20	A	14	24
21	A	0	16

17. CINCINNATI

Opp	H/A	Team	Opp
22	A	31	7
25	H	15	10
15	A	6	27
18	H	21	10
20	A	23	16
6	A	12	15
19	H	30	7
25	A	17	40
24	H	14	20
16	H	19	20
2	A	13	3
8	H	13	10
15	H	24	27
19	A	61	17

18. DENVER

Opp	H/A	Team	Opp
19	H	30	17
26	A	14	37
20	H	24	45
17	A	10	21
7	H	20	23
24	A	30	23
15	H	20	27
8	A	17	29
6	A	16	10
24	H	20	37
1	A	20	23
20	A	21	24
26	H	38	13
22	H	45	21

19. HOUSTON

Opp	H/A	Team	Opp
18	A	17	30
21	A	13	34
23	H	26	20
24	H	0	34
25	A	7	24
15	H	17	23
17	A	7	30
15	A	0	20
10	H	17	18
5	H	10	23
26	A	20	34
1	A	10	20
25	H	3	9
17	H	17	61

20. KANSAS CITY

Opp	H/A	Team	Opp
21	H	10	20
9	A	20	17
18	A	45	24
15	A	31	7
17	H	16	23
10	H	20	21
26	A	26	14
24	H	27	14
25	A	7	16
26	H	17	27
24	A	3	26
18	H	24	21
16	H	24	10
1	A	17	14

21. MIAMI

Opp	H/A	Team	Opp
20	A	20	10
19	H	34	13
7	A	16	14
23	A	27	17
26	H	24	10
14	H	24	23
16	A	23	0
14	A	30	16
22	H	52	0
23	H	28	24
12	H	31	10
22	A	37	21
8	A	23	13
16	H	16	0

22. NEW ENGLAND

Opp	H/A	Team	Opp
17	H	7	31
1	H	21	20
13	H	24	23
14	A	14	38
23	H	13	41
25	A	3	33
23	A	10	34
16	H	17	24
21	A	0	52
14	H	24	27
16	A	0	31
21	H	21	37
9	A	17	10
18	A	21	45

23. NY JETS

Opp	H/A	Team	Opp
14	A	41	24
16	A	44	34
19	A	20	26
21	H	17	27
22	A	41	13
16	H	24	20
22	H	34	10
13	H	17	35
14	H	41	3
21	A	24	28
4	A	20	37
9	H	18	17
24	A	16	24
15	H	10	26

24. OAKLAND

Opp	H/A	Team	Opp
25	A	28	34
5	A	20	14
26	H	17	17
19	A	34	0
14	H	28	16
18	H	23	30
6	H	45	17
20	A	14	27
17	A	20	14
18	A	37	20
20	H	26	3
26	A	21	19
23	H	24	16
2	H	28	21

25. PITTSBURGH

Opp	H/A	Team	Opp
24	H	34	28
17	A	10	15
12	A	25	19
3	A	13	17
19	H	24	7
22	H	33	3
14	A	38	21
17	H	40	17
20	H	16	7
15	A	24	26
7	H	23	10
15	H	30	0
19	A	9	3
26	A	24	2

26. SAN DIEGO

Opp	H/A	Team	Opp
11	A	3	34
18	H	37	14
24	A	17	17
16	A	23	20
21	A	10	24
4	A	20	34
20	H	14	26
3	H	28	34
15	H	17	21
20	A	27	17
19	H	34	20
24	H	19	21
18	A	13	38
25	H	2	24

[a]The first number is the opponent's code; H indicates game played at team's home (A, away); the next number is the team's score; the last number is the opponent's score.

TABLE 13.2a
Stem-and-Leaf Plots (1971) for Each Team's Scores and Its Opponent's Scores

Teams 1–9

1 ATLANTA	2 CHICAGO	3 DALLAS	4 DETROIT	5 GREEN BAY	6 LOS ANGEL.	7 MINNESOTA	8 NY GIANTS	9 N ORLEANS
0|3799 1|67 2|004488 3|18	0|03333 1|00467 2|038 3|5	1|34669 2|008 3|1 4|2249 5|2	1|0334 2|03478 3|1124 4|1	0|06 1|33467 2|0118 3|14 4|0	1|4777 2|00011344 3|0 4|5	0|39 1|0346779 2|34479	0|37777 1|0334 2|118 3|5 4|2	0|6 1|03447 2|00144689

	1	2	3	4	5	6	7	8	9
Hinge	9	3	16	14	13	17	13	7	14
Median	20	12	24	25.5	18.5	20.5	17	13	20
Hinge	28	20	42	31	28	24	24	21	24
Trimean	19.25	11.75	26.5	24	19.5	20.5	17.75	13.5	19.5

Opponents:

1	2	3	4	5	6	7	8	9
0|66 1|347 2|00114446 3| 4|1	0|6 1|34557779 2|378 3|14	0|077 1|02334 2|01134 3|7	0|377 1|46 2|0113889 3|18	0|3 1|034467 2|4789 3|01 4|2	0|36 1|33346 2|004488 3|8	0|00037 1|0000333 2|0 3|0	1|7777 2|00334 3|01 4|012	1|34 2|001113448 3|58 4|5

	1	2	3	4	5	6	7	8	9
Hinge	14	15	10	14	14	13	3	17	20
Median	20.5	17	13.5	21	20.5	18	10	23	22
Hinge	24	27	21	28	29	24	13	31	28
Trimean	19.75	19	14.5	21	21	18.25	9	23.5	23

Teams 10–18

10 PHILA.	11 SAN FRAN.	12 ST.LOUIS	13 WASH.	14 BUFFALO	15 CLEVELAND	16 BALTIMORE	17 CINCINNATI	18 DENVER
0|03777 1|03479 2|33 3|7 4|1	0|6 1|33377 2|04467 3|118	0|07 1|2346777 2|00468	0|07 1|35 2|00002344 3|08	0|0000379 1|447 2|37 3|37	0|079 1|44 2|001777 3|117	0|3 1|34447 2|2344 3|147 4|3	0|66 1|0337 2|144778 3|17	0|36 1|00033667 2|0027

	10	11	12	13	14	15	16	17	18
Hinge	7	13	13	15	0	14	14	13	10
Median	13.5	22	17	20	11.5	20.5	22.5	22.5	14.5
Hinge	23	27	20	24	23	27	31	27	20
Trimean	14.25	21	16.75	19.75	11.5	20.5	22.5	21.25	14.75

Opponents:

10	11	12	13	14	15	16	17	18
0|777 1|36 2|00008 3|147 4|2	0|0339 1|047 2|0001667	0|79 1|0669 2|001346 3|17	0|0377 1|3334667 2|047	1|9 2|000024889 3|48 4|39	0|07 1|33377 2|44677 3|14	0|000337 1|034477 2|11	0|09 1|0034 2|01137 3|115	0|03 1|00667 2|14478 3|4 4|5

	10	11	12	13	14	15	16	17	18
Hinge	13	9	16	7	20	13	3	10	10
Median	20	18.5	20	13.5	26	20.5	11.5	20.5	19
Hinge	31	21	24	17	34	27	17	27	27
Trimean	21	16.75	20	12.75	26.5	20.25	10.75	19:5	18.75

Teams 19–26

19 HOUSTON	20 KAN. CITY	21 MIAMI	22 N ENGLAND	23 NY JETS	24 OAKLAND	25 PITT.	26 SAN DIEGO
0|07 1|033366 2|00149 3| 4|9	1|03466 2|0012678 3|18	0|3 1|0037 2|03479 3|044 4|1	0|33677 1|0 2|000118 3|48	0|00 1|0033344 2|0118 3|5	0|6 1|344 2|0117 3|14444 4|1	0|3 1|045677 2|1111136	0|00 1|0677 2|001 3|033 4|59

	19	20	21	22	23	24	25	26
Hinge	13	16	13	7	10	14	15	16
Median	16	20.5	23.5	20	13.5	24	19	20
Hinge	21	27	30	21	21	34	21	33
Trimean	16.5	21	22.5	17	14.5	24	18.5	22.25

Opponents:

19	20	21	22	23	24	25	26
0|36 1|34 2|02388 3|1137 4|1	0|379 1|0034667 2|001 3|2	0|0336 1|03444444 2|1 3|4	0|06 1|337 2|03777 3|34 4|14	0|67 1|00477 2|0124 3|0 4|9 5|2	0|0 1|0366 2|0001147 3|37	0|9 1|033677 2|23479 3|48	0|3 1|4477 2|011 3|11445 4|9

	19	20	21	22	23	24	25	26
Hinge	14	10	6	13	10	16	13	17
Median	25.5	15	14	25	18.5	20	19.5	21
Hinge	31	20	14	33	24	24	27	34
Trimean	24	15	12	24	17.75	20	19.75	23.25

TABLE 13.2b
Stem-and-Leaf Plots (1972) for Each Team's Scores and Its Opponents Scores

	1 ATLANTA	2 CHICAGO	3 DALLAS	4 DETROIT	5 GREEN BAY	6 LOS ANGEL.	7 MINNESOTA	8 NY GIANTS	9 N ORLEANS
	0|07	0|03	0|3	0|7	0|9	0|3	0|7	1|0333466	0|26
	1|0344	1|033777	1|037	1|044	1|3466	1|0345677	1|004677	2|33779	1|0444779
	2|00133	2|111147	2|0137888	2|13467	2|033346	2|06	2|1337	3|	2|00011
	3|167		3|344	3|04478	3|034	3|144	3|47	4|5	
						4|1	4|5	5|	
								6|2	
Hinge	13	13	17	14	16	14	14	13	14
Median	20	17	25	25	23	17	19	19.5	17
Hinge	23	21	28	34	26	31	27	27	20
Trimean	19	17	23.75	24.5	22	19.75	19.75	19.75	17

Opponents:

	0|39	0|0	0|0667	0|0	0|77	0|377	0|6	0|37	0|3
	1|047	1|002334	1|346	1|4667	1|000377	1|234669	1|0033469	1|02377	1|678
	2|00001146	2|0338	2|344448	2|0013448	2|001347	2|4	2|00334	2|113337	2|0017
	3|	3|478	3|1	3|34		3|14	3|	3|0	3|04677
	4|9					4|55	4|1		4|5
Hinge	14	12	7	16	10	12	13	12	18
Median	20	17	19.5	20.5	17	16	17.5	19	24
Hinge	21	28	24	24	21	31	23	23	36
Trimean	18.75	18.5	17.5	20.25	16.25	18.75	17.75	18.25	25.5

	10 PHILA.	11 SAN FRAN.	12 ST. LOUIS	13 WASH.	14 BUFFALO	15 CLEVELAND	16 BALTIMORE	17 CINCINNATI	18 DENVER
	0|0336677	0|7	0|3667	1|47	0|037	0|007	0|0003	0|6	1|0467
	1|02278	1|67	1|000099	2|1333444447	1|066	1|0	1|07	1|2234579	2|000014
	2|13	2|000044	2|1444	3|35	2|1134477	2|0136677777	2|00014	2|134	3|008
		3|1447			3|8		3|145	3|01	4|5
		4|9						4|	
								5|	
								6|1	
Hinge	6	20	7	23	10	10	3	13	17
Median	8.5	22	10	24	21	24.5	20	18	20
Hinge	17	34	21	24	24	27	24	24	30
Trimean	10	24.5	12	23.75	19	21.5	16.75	18.25	21.75

Opponents:

	0|6	0|023	0|36	0|037	1|477	0|06	0|007	0|377	1|037
	1|47	1|047	1|347	1|033667	2|014478	1|007777	1|0679	1|000567	2|11333479
	2|011347788	2|011367	2|345777	2|0144	3|058	2|0446	2|133444	2|0077	3|77
	3|4	3|14	3|133	3|4	4|11	3|01	3|	3|	4|5
	4|						4|4	4|0	
	5|								
	6|2								
Hinge	20	10	14	10	20	10	10	10	21
Median	23.5	20.5	24.5	16	25.5	17	20	15.5	23
Hinge	28	26	27	21	35	24	24	20	29
Trimean	23.75	19.25	22.5	15.75	26.5	17	18.5	15.25	24

	19 HOUSTON	20 KAN. CITY	21 MIAMI	22 N ENGLAND	23 NY JETS	24 OAKLAND	25 PITT.	26 SAN DIEGO
	0|00377	0|37	1|66	0|0037	1|06778	1|47	0|9	0|23
	1|0037777	1|0677	2|0334478	1|03477	2|0044	2|001346888	1|036	1|034779
	2|06	2|004467	3|0147	2|11144	3|4	3|47	2|34445	2|0378
		3|1	4|		4|1114	4|5	3|0348	3|47
		4|5	5|2				4|0	
Hinge	7	16	23	7	17	20	16	13
Median	11.5	20	25.5	15.5	22	25	24	18
Hinge	17	26	31	21	41	28	33	27
Trimean	11.75	20.5	26.25	14.75	25.5	24.5	24.25	19

Opponents:

	0|9	0|7	0|000	1|0	0|3	0|03	0|023377	1|477
	1|8	1|044467	1|00033467	2|0347	1|037	1|4466779	1|05779	2|0011446
	2|000334	2|0113467	2|134	3|113478	2|0446678	2|017	2|168	3|4448
	3|00444			4|15	3|457	3|04		
	4|			5|2				
	5|							
	6|1							
Hinge	20	14	10	24	17	14	3	20
Median	23.5	18.5	13	32	25	17	12.5	22.5
Hinge	34	23	17	38	28	21	19	34
Trimean	25.25	18.5	13.25	31.5	23.75	17.25	11.75	24.75

TABLE 13.3a
Trimeans for the Season (1971) by the Opponents of the Team Given at the Head[a]

1. ATLANTA — Opponents

Code no.	Off.	Def.
11	21.	16.75
6	20.5	18.25
4	24.	21.
12	16.75	20.
6	20.5	18.25
9	19.5	23.
15	20.5	20.25
17	21.25	19.5
8	13.5	23.5
5	19.5	21.
7	17.75	9.
24	24.	20.
11	21.	16.75
9	19.5	23.
	279.25	270.25

2. CHICAGO — Opponents

Code no.	Off.	Def.
25	18.5	19.75
7	17.75	9.
6	20.5	18.25
9	19.5	23.
11	21.	16.75
4	24.	21.
3	26.5	14.5
5	19.5	21.
13	19.75	12.75
4	24.	21.
21	22.5	12.
18	14.75	18.75
5	19.5	21.
7	17.75	9.
	285.5	237.75

3. DALLAS — Opponents

Code no.	Off.	Def.
14	11.5	26.5
10	14.25	21.
13	19.75	12.75
8	13.5	23.5
9	19.5	23.
22	17.	24.
2	11.75	20.
12	16.75	20.
10	14.25	21.
13	19.75	12.75
6	20.5	18.25
23	14.5	17.75
8	13.5	23.5
12	16.75	20.
	223.25	283.

4. DETROIT — Opponents

Code no.	Off.	Def.
7	17.75	9.
22	17.	24.
1	19.25	19.75
5	19.5	21.
19	16.5	24.
2	11.75	19.
5	19.5	21.
18	14.75	18.75
6	20.5	18.25
2	11.75	19.
20	21.	15.
10	14.25	21.
7	17.75	9.
11	21.	16.75
	242.25	255.5

5. GREEN BAY — Opponents

Code no.	Off.	Def.
8	13.5	23.5
18	14.75	18.75
17	21.25	19.5
4	24.	21.
7	17.75	9.
6	20.5	18.25
4	24.	21.
2	11.75	19.
7	17.75	9.
1	19.25	19.75
9	19.5	23.
12	16.75	20.
2	11.75	19.
21	22.5	12.
	255.	252.75

6. LOS ANGELES — Opponents

Code no.	Off.	Def.
9	19.5	23.
1	19.25	19.75
2	11.75	19.
11	21.	16.75
1	19.25	19.75
5	19.5	21.
21	22.5	12.
16	22.5	10.75
4	24.	21.
11	21.	16.75
3	26.5	14.5
9	19.5	23.
13	19.75	12.75
25	18.5	19.75
	284.5	249.75

7. MINNESOTA — Opponents

Code no.	Off.	Def.
4	24.	21.
2	11.75	19.
14	11.5	26.5
10	14.25	21.
5	19.5	21.
16	22.5	10.75
8	13.5	23.5
11	21.	16.75
5	19.5	21.
9	19.5	23.
1	19.25	19.75
26	22.25	23.25
4	24.	21.
2	11.75	19.
	254.25	286.5

8. NY GIANTS — Opponents

Code no.	Off.	Def.
5	19.5	21.
13	19.75	12.75
12	16.75	20.
3	26.5	14.5
16	22.5	10.75
10	14.25	21.
7	17.75	9.
26	22.25	23.25
1	19.25	19.75
25	18.5	19.75
12	16.75	20.
13	19.75	12.75
3	26.5	14.5
10	14.25	21.
	274.25	240.

9. NEW ORLEANS — Opponents

Code no.	Off.	Def.
6	20.5	18.25
11	21.	16.75
19	16.5	24.
2	11.75	19.
3	26.5	14.5
1	19.25	19.75
13	19.75	12.75
24	24.	20.
11	21.	16.75
7	17.75	9.
5	19.5	21.
6	20.5	18.25
15	20.5	20.25
1	19.25	19.75
	277.75	250.

10. PHILADELPHIA — Opponents

Code no.	Off.	Def.
17	21.25	19.5
3	26.5	14.5
11	21.	16.75
7	17.75	9.
24	24.	20.
8	13.5	23.5
18	14.75	18.75
13	19.75	12.75
3	26.5	14.5
12	16.75	20.
13	19.75	12.75
4	24.	21.
12	16.75	20.
8	13.5	23.5
	275.75	246.5

11. SAN FRANCISCO — Opponents

Code no.	Off.	Def.
1	19.25	19.75
9	19.5	23.
10	14.25	21.
6	20.5	18.25
2	11.75	19.
12	16.75	20.
22	17.	24.
7	17.75	9.
9	19.5	23.
6	20.5	18.25
23	14.5	17.75
20	21.	15.
1	19.25	19.75
4	24.	21.
	255.5	268.75

12. ST. LOUIS — Opponents

Code no.	Off.	Def.
13	19.75	12.75
23	14.5	17.75
8	13.5	23.5
1	19.25	19.75
13	19.75	12.75
11	21.	16.75
14	11.5	26.5
3	26.5	14.5
26	22.25	23.25
10	14.25	21.
8	13.5	23.5
5	19.5	21.
10	14.25	21.
3	26.5	14.5
	256.	268.5

13. WASHINGTON — Opponents

Code no.	Off.	Def.
12	16.75	20.
8	13.5	23.5
3	26.5	14.5
19	16.5	24.
12	16.75	20.
20	21.	15.
9	19.5	23.
10	14.25	21.
2	11.75	19.
3	26.5	14.5
10	14.25	21.
8	13.5	23.5
6	20.5	18.25
15	20.5	20.25
	251.75	277.5

14. BUFFALO — Opponents

Code no.	Off.	Def.
3	26.5	14.5
21	22.5	12.
7	17.75	9.
16	22.5	10.75
23	14.5	17.75
26	22.25	23.25
12	16.75	20.
21	22.5	12.
22	17.	24.
23	14.5	17.75
22	17.	24.
16	22.5	10.75
19	16.5	24.
20	21.	15.
	273.75	234.75

15. CLEVELAND — Opponents

Code no.	Off.	Def.
19	16.5	24.
16	22.5	10.75
24	24.	20.
25	18.5	19.75
17	21.25	19.5
18	14.75	18.75
1	19.25	19.75
25	18.5	19.75
20	21.	15.
22	17.	24.
19	16.5	24.
17	21.25	19.5
9	19.5	23.
13	19.75	12.75
	270.25	270.5

16. BALTIMORE — Opponents

Code no.	Off.	Def.
23	14.5	17.75
15	20.5	20.25
22	17.	24.
14	11.5	26.5
8	13.5	23.5
7	17.75	9.
25	18.5	19.75
6	20.5	18.25
23	14.5	17.75
21	22.5	12.
24	24.	20.
14	11.5	26.5
21	22.5	12.
22	17.	24.
	245.75	271.25

17. CINCINNATI — Opponents

Code no.	Off.	Def.
10	14.25	21.
25	18.5	19.75
5	19.5	21.
21	22.5	12.
15	20.5	20.25
24	24.	20.
19	16.5	24.
1	19.25	19.75
18	14.75	18.75
19	16.5	24.
26	22.25	23.25
15	20.5	20.25
25	18.5	19.75
23	14.5	17.75
	262.	281.5

18. DENVER — Opponents

Code no.	Off.	Def.
21	22.5	12.
5	19.5	21.
20	21.	15.
24	24.	20.
26	22.25	23.25
15	20.5	20.25
10	14.25	21.
4	24.	21.
17	21.25	19.5
20	21.	15.
25	18.5	19.75
2	11.75	19.
26	22.25	23.25
24	24.	20.
	286.75	270.

19. HOUSTON — Opponents

Code no.	Off.	Def.
15	20.5	20.25
20	21.	15.
9	19.5	23.
13	19.75	12.75
4	24.	21.
25	18.5	19.75
17	21.25	19.5
22	17.	24.
24	24.	20.
17	21.25	19.5
15	20.5	20.25
25	18.5	19.75
14	11.5	26.5
26	22.25	23.25
	279.5	284.5

20. KANSAS CITY — Opponents

Code no.	Off.	Def.
26	22.25	23.25
19	16.5	24.
18	14.75	18.75
26	22.25	23.25
25	18.5	19.75
13	19.75	12.75
24	24.	20.
23	14.5	17.75
15	20.5	20.25
18	14.75	18.75
4	24.	21.
24	24.	20.
14	11.5	26.5
	268.25	282.75

21. MIAMI — Opponents

Code no.	Off.	Def.
18	14.75	18.75
14	11.5	26.5
23	14.5	17.75
17	21.25	19.5
22	17.	24.
23	14.5	17.75
6	20.5	18.25
14	11.5	26.5
25	18.5	19.75
16	22.5	10.75
2	11.75	19.
22	17.	24.
16	22.5	10.75
5	19.5	21.
	237.25	274.25

22. NEW ENGLAND — Opponents

Code no.	Off.	Def.
24	24.	20.
4	24.	21.
16	22.5	10.75
23	14.5	17.75
3	26.5	14.5
11	21.	16.75
19	16.5	24.
14	11.5	26.5
15	20.5	20.25
14	11.5	26.5
21	22.5	12.
23	14.5	17.75
16	22.5	10.75
	274.5	250.5

23. NY JETS — Opponents

Code no.	Off.	Def.
16	22.5	10.75
12	16.75	20.
21	22.5	12
22	17.	24.
14	11.5	26.5
21	22.5	12.
26	22.25	23.25
20	21.	15.
16	22.5	10.75
14	11.5	26.5
11	21.	16.75
22	17.	24.
17	21.25	19.5
	275.75	255.5

24. OAKLAND — Opponents

Code no.	Off.	Def.
22	17.	24.
26	22.25	23.25
15	20.5	20.25
18	14.75	18.75
10	14.25	21.
17	21.25	19.5
20	21.	15.
9	19.5	23.
19	16.5	24.
26	22.25	23.25
16	22.5	10.75
1	19.25	19.75
20	21.	15.
18	14.75	18.75
	266.75	276.25

25. PITTSBURGH — Opponents

Code no.	Off.	Def.
2	11.75	19.
17	21.25	19.5
26	22.25	23.25
15	20.5	20.25
20	21.	15.
19	16.5	24.
16	22.5	10.75
15	20.5	20.25
21	22.5	12.
8	13.5	23.5
18	14.75	18.75
19	16.5	24.
17	21.25	19.5
6	20.5	18.25
	265.25	268.

26. SAN DIEGO — Opponents

Code no.	Off.	Def.
20	21.	15.
24	24.	20.
25	18.5	19.75
20	21.	15.
18	14.75	18.75
14	11.5	26.5
23	14.5	17.75
8	13.5	23.5
12	16.75	20.
24	24.	20.
17	21.25	19.5
7	17.75	9.
18	14.75	18.75
19	16.5	24.
	249.75	267.5

[a]Defense means points allowed, and offense means points made.

TABLE 13.3b
Trimeans for the Season (1972) by the Opponents of the Team Given at the Head[a]

1. ATLANTA

Code no.	Off.	Def.
2	17.	18.5
22	14.75	31.5
6	19.75	18.75
4	24.5	20.25
9	17.	25.5
5	22.	16.25
11	24.5	19.25
6	19.75	18.75
9	17.	25.5
13	23.75	15.75
18	21.75	24.
19	11.75	25.25
11	24.5	19.25
20	20.5	18.5
	278.5	297.

2. CHICAGO

Code no.	Off.	Def.
1	19.	18.75
6	19.75	18.75
4	24.5	20.25
5	22.	16.25
15	21.5	17.
7	19.75	17.75
12	12.	22.5
4	24.5	20.25
5	22.	16.25
11	24.5	19.25
17	18.25	15.25
7	19.75	17.75
10	10.	23.75
24	24.5	17.25
	282.	261.

3. DALLAS

Code no.	Off.	Def.
10	10.	23.75
8	19.75	18.25
5	22.	16.25
25	24.25	11.75
16	16.75	18.5
13	23.75	15.75
4	24.5	20.25
26	19.	24.75
12	12.	22.5
10	10.	23.75
11	24.5	19.25
12	12.	22.5
13	23.75	15.75
8	19.75	18.5
	262.	271.25

4. DETROIT

Code no.	Off.	Def.
8	19.75	18.25
7	19.75	17.75
2	17.	18.5
1	19.	18.75
5	22.	16.25
26	19.	24.75
3	23.75	17.5
2	17.	18.5
7	19.75	17.75
9	17.	25.5
23	25.5	23.75
5	22.	16.25
14	19.	26.5
6	19.75	18.75
	280.25	278.75

5. GREEN BAY

Code no.	Off.	Def.
15	21.5	17.
24	24.5	17.25
3	23.75	17.5
2	17.	18.5
4	24.5	20.25
1	19.	18.75
7	19.75	17.75
11	24.5	19.25
2	17.	18.5
19	11.75	25.25
13	23.75	15.75
4	24.5	20.25
7	19.75	17.75
9	17.	25.5
	288.25	269.25

6. LOS ANGELES

Code no.	Off.	Def.
9	17.	25.5
2	17.	18.5
1	19.	18.75
11	24.5	19.25
10	10.	23.75
17	18.25	15.25
24	24.5	17.25
1	19.	18.75
18	21.75	24.
7	19.75	17.75
9	17.	25.5
11	24.5	19.25
12	12.	22.5
4	24.5	20.25
	268.75	286.25

7. MINNESOTA

Code no.	Off.	Def.
13	23.75	15.75
4	24.5	20.25
21	26.25	13.25
12	12.	22.5
18	21.75	24.
2	17.	18.5
5	22.	16.25
9	17.	25.5
4	24.5	20.25
6	19.75	18.75
25	24.25	11.75
2	17.	18.5
5	22.	16.25
11	24.5	19.25
	296.25	260.75

8. NY GIANTS

Code no.	Off.	Def.
4	24.5	20.25
3	23.75	17.5
10	10.	23.75
9	17.	25.5
11	24.5	19.25
12	12.	22.5
13	23.75	15.75
18	21.75	24.
13	23.75	15.75
12	12.	22.5
10	10.	23.75
17	18.25	15.25
21	26.25	13.25
3	23.75	17.5
	271.25	276.5

9. NEW ORLEANS

Code no.	Off.	Def.
6	19.75	18.75
20	20.5	18.5
11	24.5	19.25
8	19.75	18.25
1	19.	18.75
11	24.5	19.25
10	10.	23.75
7	19.75	17.75
1	19.	18.75
4	24.5	20.25
6	19.75	18.75
23	25.5	23.75
22	14.75	31.5
5	22.	20.25
	283.25	283.5

10. PHILADELPHIA

Code no.	Off.	Def.
3	23.75	17.5
15	21.5	17.
8	19.75	18.25
13	23.75	15.75
6	19.75	18.75
20	20.5	18.5
9	17.	25.5
12	12.	22.5
19	11.75	25.25
3	23.75	17.5
8	19.75	18.25
13	23.75	15.75
2	17.	18.5
12	12.	22.5
	266.	271.5

11. SAN FRANCISCO

Code no.	Off.	Def.
26	19.	24.75
14	19.	26.5
9	17.	25.5
6	19.75	18.75
8	19.75	18.25
9	17.	25.5
1	19.	18.75
5	22.	16.25
16	16.75	18.5
2	17.	18.5
3	23.75	17.5
6	19.75	18.75
1	19.	18.75
7	19.75	17.75
	268.5	284.

12. ST. LOUIS

Code no.	Off.	Def.
16	16.75	18.5
13	23.75	15.75
25	24.25	11.75
7	19.75	17.75
13	23.75	15.75
8	19.75	18.25
2	17.	18.5
10	10.	23.75
3	23.75	17.5
8	19.75	18.25
21	26.25	13.25
3	23.75	17.5
6	19.75	18.75
10	10.	23.75
	278.25	249.

13. WASHINGTON

Code no.	Off.	Def.
7	19.75	17.75
12	12.	22.5
22	14.75	31.5
10	10.	23.75
12	12.	22.5
3	23.75	17.5
8	19.75	18.25
23	25.5	23.75
8	19.75	18.25
1	19.	18.75
5	22.	16.25
10	10.	23.75
3	23.75	17.5
14	19.	26.5
	251.	298.5

14. BUFFALO

Code no.	Off.	Def.
23	25.5	23.75
11	24.5	19.25
16	18.75	18.5
22	14.75	31.5
24	24.5	17.25
21	26.25	13.25
25	24.25	11.75
21	26.25	13.25
23	25.5	23.75
22	14.75	31.5
15	21.5	17.
16	16.75	18.5
4	24.5	20.25
13	23.75	15.75
	309.5	275.25

15. CLEVELAND

Code no.	Off.	Def.
5	22.	16.25
10	10.	23.75
17	18.25	15.25
20	20.5	18.5
2	17.	18.5
19	11.75	25.25
21	21.75	24.
19	11.75	25.25
26	19.	24.75
25	24.25	11.75
25	24.25	11.75
17	18.25	15.25
23	25.5	23.75
	263.25	280.5

16. BALTIMORE

Code no.	Off.	Def.
12	12.	22.5
25	25.5	23.75
14	19.	26.5
26	19.	24.75
3	23.75	17.5
25	25.5	23.75
21	26.25	13.25
12	14.75	31.5
11	24.5	19.25
18	18.25	15.25
22	14.75	31.5
14	19.	26.5
20	20.5	18.5
21	26.25	13.25
	289.	307.75

17. CINCINNATI

Code no.	Off.	Def.
22	14.75	31.5
25	24.25	11.75
15	21.5	17.
18	21.75	24.
20	20.5	18.5
6	19.75	18.75
19	11.75	25.25
25	24.25	11.75
24	24.5	17.25
16	16.75	18.5
2	17	18.5
8	19.75	18.25
15	21.5	17.
19	11.75	25.25
	269.75	273.25

18. DENVER

Code no.	Off.	Def.
19	11.75	25.25
26	19.	24.75
20	20.5	18.5
17	18.25	15.25
7	19.75	17.75
24	24.5	17.25
15	21.5	17.
8	19.75	18.25
6	19.75	18.75
24	24.5	17.25
1	19.	18.75
20	20.5	18.5
26	19.	24.75
22	14.75	31.5
	272.5	283.5

19. HOUSTON

Code no.	Off.	Def.
18	21.75	24.
21	26.25	13.25
23	25.5	23.75
24	24.5	17.25
25	24.25	11.75
15	21.5	17.
17	18.25	15.25
15	21.5	17.
10	10.	23.75
5	22.	16.25
26	19.	24.75
1	19.	18.75
25	24.25	11.75
17	18.25	15.25
	296.	249.75

20. KANSAS CITY

Code no.	Off.	Def.
21	26.25	13.25
9	17.	25.5
18	21.75	24.
15	21.5	17.
17	18.25	15.25
10	10.	23.75
26	19.	24.75
24	24.5	17.25
25	24.25	11.75
26	19.	24.75
24	24.5	17.25
18	21.75	24.
16	16.75	18.5
1	19.	18.75
	283.5	275.75

21. MIAMI

Code no.	Off.	Def.
20	20.5	18.5
19	11.75	25.25
7	19.75	17.75
23	25.5	23.75
26	19.	24.75
14	19.	26.5
16	16.75	18.5
22	14.75	31.5
23	25.5	23.75
12	12.	22.5
22	14.75	31.5
8	19.75	18.25
16	16.75	18.5
	254.75	327.5

22. NEW ENGLAND

Code no.	Off.	Def.
17	18.25	15.25
1	19.	18.75
13	23.75	15.75
14	19.	26.5
23	25.5	23.75
25	24.25	11.75
23	25.5	23.75
16	16.75	18.5
21	26.25	13.25
16	16.75	18.5
14	19.	26.5
9	17.	25.5
18	21.75	24.
	299.	275.

23. NY JETS

Code no.	Off.	Def.
14	19.	26.5
16	16.75	18.5
19	11.75	25.25
21	26.25	13.25
22	14.75	31.5
16	16.75	18.5
22	14.75	31.5
13	23.75	15.75
14	19.	26.5
21	26.25	13.25
4	24.5	20.25
9	17.	25.5
24	24.5	17.25
15	21.5	17.
	276.5	300.5

24. OAKLAND

Code no.	Off.	Def.
25	24.25	11.75
5	22.	16.25
26	19.	24.75
19	11.75	25.25
14	19.	26.5
18	21.75	24.
6	19.75	18.75
20	20.5	18.5
17	18.25	15.25
18	21.75	24.
20	20.5	18.5
26	19.	24.75
23	25.5	23.75
2	17.	18.5
	280.	290.5

25. PITTSBURGH

Code no.	Off.	Def.
24	24.5	17.25
17	18.25	15.25
12	12.	22.5
3	23.75	17.5
19	11.75	25.25
22	14.75	31.5
14	19.	26.5
18	18.25	15.25
20	20.5	18.5
15	21.5	17.
7	19.75	17.75
15	21.5	17.
19	11.75	25.25
26	19.	24.75
	256.25	291.25

26. SAN DIEGO

Code no.	Off.	Def.
11	24.5	19.25
18	21.75	24.
24	24.5	17.25
16	16.75	18.5
21	26.25	13.25
4	24.5	20.25
20	20.5	18.5
3	23.75	17.5
15	21.5	17.
20	20.5	18.5
24	24.5	17.25
18	21.75	24.
25	24.25	11.75
	306.75	262.25

[a] Defense means points allowed, and offense means points made.

TABLE 13.4a

Trimeans for the Season (1971) by the Opponents of the Team Given at the Head After Second-Order Adjustments[a]

1. ATLANTA Opponents			2. CHICAGO Opponents			3. DALLAS Opponents			4. DETROIT Opponents			5. GREEN BAY Opponents			6. LOS ANGELES Opponents		
Code no.	Trimean Off.	Def.	Code no.	Trimean Off.	Def.	Code no.	Trimean Off.	Def.	Code no.	Trimean Off.	Def.	Code no.	Trimean Off.	Def.	Code no.	Trimean Off.	Def.
11	21.5	17.5	25	19.75	21.	14	8.75	24.25	7	17.25	8.62	8	13.5	23.25	9	18.25	22.62
6	20.38	18.25	7	17.	8.62	10	15.62	19.88	22	17.	21.5	18	15.5	17.	1	20.25	19.62
4	23.25	21.	6	21.5	19.25	13	20.88	13.12	1	18.25	19.5	17	22.	19.75	2	12.75	19.
12	16.75	20.	9	19.5	21.5	8	13.62	23.38	5	19.	20.75	4	24.75	20.5	11	23.5	15.88
6	20.38	18.25	11	23.	17.75	9	19.5	23.75	19	16.5	22.75	7	17.75	9.5	1	20.25	19.62
9	20.	22.88	4	24.	21.38	22	17.	21.5	2	11.38	17.88	6	20.	19.25	5	20.5	19.
15	20.75	18.25	3	28.5	14.25	2	10.	19.	5	19.	20.75	4	24.75	20.5	21	22.75	12.
17	22.	20.5	5	18.38	23.88	12	17.75	19.12	18	13.25	17.75	2	12.62	18.38	16	22.25	9.25
8	13.5	24.25	13	21.	12.5	10	15.62	19.88	6	20.25	19.25	7	17.75	9.5	4	26.25	21.
5	18.75	19.25	4	24.	21.38	13	20.88	13.12	2	11.38	17.88	1	18.25	19.5	11	23.5	15.88
7	17.5	9.	21	22.	13.	6	20.25	17.25	20	20.75	13.75	9	19.5	23.5	3	24.5	14.25
24	27.	19.25	18	15.5	21.25	23	15.5	16.5	10	13.	21.	12	16.75	20.	9	18.25	22.62
11	21.5	17.5	5	18.38	23.88	8	13.62	23.38	7	17.25	8.62	2	12.62	18.38	13	19.5	12.25
9	20.	22.88	7	17.	8.62	12	17.75	19.12	11	19.75	15.75	21	22.25	13.	25	19.75	18.5
	283.25	268.75		289.5	248.25		226.75	273.25		234.	245.75		258.	252.		292.25	241.5

7. MINNESOTA			8. NY GIANTS			9. NEW ORLEANS			10. PHILADELPHIA			11. SAN FRANCISCO			12. ST. LOUIS		
4	27.	20.12	5	17.	19.	6	20.38	16.25	17	20.5	19.75	1	21.12	19.62	13	19.38	13.75
2	11.75	18.5	13	19.25	15.38	11	20.12	14.38	3	26.75	17.12	9	18.62	22.62	23	15.5	18.5
14	13.5	27.5	12	16.	20.25	19	16.5	26.75	11	19.75	17.75	10	14.5	20.25	8	14.38	24.62
10	14.5	21.75	3	26.75	15.88	2	10.	19.	7	18.	10.	6	21.12	19.88	1	21.	19.5
5	21.38	21.88	16	20.5	11.5	3	29.25	14.25	24	22.5	20.	2	12.75	19.	13	19.38	13.75
16	22.75	11.5	10	12.	21.75	1	18.	20.38	8	13.5	22.62	12	16.75	19.75	11	20.	17.5
8	13.5	24.25	7	17.75	9.	13	19.5	12.5	18	14.	19.75	22	17.	23.	14	8.75	25.5
11	23.	17.75	26	22.25	22.5	24	25.5	20.	13	20.88	14.62	7	18.	9.	3	27.12	16.12
5	21.38	21.88	1	19.25	19.5	11	20.12	14.38	3	26.75	17.12	9	18.62	22.62	26	22.25	23.25
9	19.5	22.5	25	19.5	21.75	7	17.75	9.	12	17.38	19.12	6	21.12	19.88	10	12.5	21.75
1	21.	19.5	12	16.	20.25	5	18.75	19.	13	20.88	14.62	23	14.	16.5	8	14.38	24.62
26	22.25	23.25	13	19.25	15.38	6	20.38	16.25	4	24.75	21.	20	20.75	14.5	5	20.25	22.75
4	27.	20.12	3	26.75	15.88	15	20.25	22.	12	17.38	19.12	1	21.12	19.62	10	12.5	21.75
2	11.75	18.5	10	12.	21.75	1	18.	20.38	8	13.5	22.62	4	23.25	21.	3	27.12	16.12
	270.25	289.		264.25	249.75		274.5	244.5		276.5	255.25		258.75	267.25		254.5	279.5

13. WASHINGTON			14. BUFFALO			15. CLEVELAND			16. BALTIMORE			17. CINCINNATI			18. DENVER		
12	17.38	19.12	3	24.5	14.25	19	16.38	22.	23	15.12	18.5	10	14.	20.25	21	23.75	12.
8	15.	23.88	21	20.75	12.5	16	22.75	10.	15	20.75	22.	25	17.38	22.38	5	17.	22.75
3	30.38	15.	7	17.75	10.	24	22.5	20.	22	17.88	25.12	5	18.75	22.75	20	20.62	15.88
19	16.5	25.25	16	20.12	12.25	25	18.38	20.	14	14.5	25.38	21	22.75	12.	24	25.	21.12
12	17.38	19.12	23	13.38	20.	17	19.25	16.5	8	13.5	23.25	15	19.62	18.38	26	21.25	25.38
20	20.5	13.75	26	22.25	23.25	18	13.25	21.25	7	18.	10.	24	22.5	19.25	15	20.75	18.25
9	19.5	22.5	12	16.75	20.	1	18.25	20.75	25	17.5	17.75	19	17.88	25.	10	14.	21.
10	15.25	21.75	21	20.75	12.5	25	18.38	20.	6	21.5	17.25	1	21.	20.75	4	24.75	21.
2	10.75	19.	22	14.38	21.62	20	21.25	15.5	23	15.12	18.5	18	15.5	17.75	17	20.5	20.5
3	30.38	15.	23	13.38	20.	22	17.	23.	21	24.88	11.38	19	17.88	25.	20	20.62	15.88
10	15.25	21.75	22	14.38	21.62	19	16.38	22.	24	27.	19.25	26	22.5	23.25	25	19.75	18.5
8	15.	23.88	16	20.12	12.25	17	19.25	16.5	14	14.5	25.38	25	19.62	18.38	12	17.25	19.
6	20.	17.25	19	16.5	26.75	9	19.5	23.5	21	24.88	11.38	25	17.38	22.38	26	21.25	25.38
15	20.75	22.	20	20.75	14.5	13	21.	12.25	22	17.88	25.12	23	14.	17.	24	25.	21.12
	264.	279.25		255.75	242.5		263.5	263.25		263.	270.25		260.75	284.5		287.	277.75

19. HOUSTON			20. KANSAS CITY			21. MIAMI			22. NEW ENGLAND			23. NY JETS			24. OAKLAND		
15	19.62	20.25	26	22.38	23.25	18	15.5	21.25	24	27.	20.	16	23.38	11.	22	17.	26.
20	21.25	14.5	19	16.5	25.25	14	12.38	24.75	4	23.25	21.5	12	16.75	20.	26	22.	21.88
9	19.5	23.75	18	15.88	18.38	23	14.25	18.	16	23.12	10.	21	23.38	11.38	15	20.75	18.25
13	19.75	13.	26	22.38	23.25	17	22.	19.25	23	15.12	19.25	22	17.88	26.5	18	14.75	17.25
4	23.25	21.5	25	19.5	17.75	22	17.	23.75	21	22.5	12.5	14	12.	27.	10	14.5	20.25
25	18.62	19.38	24	27.38	20.25	23	14.25	18.	3	24.5	14.25	21	23.38	11.38	17	20.5	20.5
17	21.25	20.75	23	14.75	19.5	6	21.5	17.25	11	19.75	17.5	26	21.5	23.25	20	21.38	14.25
22	17.	25.	15	20.75	22.	14	12.38	24.75	19	16.5	22.75	20	21.25	15.5	9	19.5	23.5
24	22.5	20.	18	15.88	18.38	25	17.5	18.5	14	7.88	25.88	16	23.38	11.	19	16.25	22.75
17	21.25	20.75	4	23.25	21.	2	12.75	18.	15	20.25	22.	14	12.	27.	26	22.	21.88
15	19.62	20.25	11	22.	15.75	22	17.	23.75	14	7.88	25.88	11	20.	15.75	16	20.5	10.
25	18.62	19.38	24	27.38	20.25	16	23.75	10.	21	22.5	12.5	3	24.5	15.25	1	19.25	20.75
14	10.25	27.5	14	12.75	27.5	5	20.5	19.25	23	15.12	19.25	22	17.88	26.5	20	21.38	14.25
26	21.5	22.5							16	23.12	10.	17	22.	18.25	18	14.75	17.25
	274.	288.5		280.5	284.75		244.5	266.5		268.5	253.25		279.25	259.75		264.5	266.5

25. PITTSBURGH			26. SAN DIEGO		
2	10.75	19.	20	20.88	14.5
17	22.62	18.25	24	22.12	19.62
26	22.25	23.25	25	17.5	21.
15	21.	20.25	20	20.88	14.5
20	20.5	14.5	18	13.5	18.38
19	15.25	26.25	14	12.75	27.5
16	20.5	9.25	23	14.	16.5
15	21.	20.25	8	13.5	24.25
21	22.25	12.	12	16.75	20.
8	13.5	24.25	24	22.12	19.62
18	13.25	21.25	17	20.5	20.5
19	15.25	26.25	7	17.75	9.
17	22.62	18.25	18	13.5	18.38
6	20.25	19.25	19	16.25	22.75
	261.	272.25		242.	266.5

[a]Defense means points allowed, and offense means points made.

TABLE 13.4b

Trimeans for the Season (1972) by the Opponents of the Team Given at the Head After Second-Order Adjustments[a]

1. ATLANTA

Code no.	Off.	Def.
2	17.	15.75
22	14	32.75
6	20.25	18.38
4	24.	20.
9	16.5	25.
5	22.	16.25
11	23.75	20.5
6	20.25	18.38
9	16.5	25.
13	23.75	15.75
18	21.75	24.
19	12.5	25.5
11	23.75	20.5
20	20.5	19.25
	276.5	297.

2. CHICAGO

Code no.	Off.	Def.
1	19.	18.75
8	20.	18.75
4	24.88	20.88
5	22.25	16.25
15	24.75	17.
7	20.88	18.88
12	12.	22.25
4	24.88	20.88
5	22.25	16.25
11	22.75	19.
17	19.	15.5
7	20.88	18.88
10	9.25	24.
24	24.	17.
	286.75	264.25

3. DALLAS

Code no.	Off.	Def.
10	11.	22.38
8	20.	18.38
5	22.	16.25
25	26.	10.5
16	18.5	18.
13	23.62	14.12
4	25.	20.
26	17.5	22.
12	12.12	21.88
10	11.	22.38
11	23.5	20.5
12	12.12	21.88
13	23.62	14.12
8	20.	18.38
	266.	260.75

4. DETROIT

Code no.	Off.	Def.
8	21.5	17.25
7	18.75	18.75
2	17.	17.38
1	19.	18.75
5	20.62	16.12
26	18.5	22.
3	22.75	15.75
2	17.	17.38
7	18.75	18.75
9	17.	24.
23	26.5	23.
5	20.62	16.12
14	19.	27.25
6	19.75	17.
	276.75	269.5

5. GREEN BAY

Code no.	Off.	Def.
15	24.75	17.
24	25.25	17.75
3	25.5	19.25
2	17.62	17.25
4	26.12	19.88
1	19.25	19.5
7	20.38	17.
11	23.5	18.25
2	17.62	17.25
19	12.5	25.5
13	23.75	15.75
4	26.12	19.88
7	20.38	17.
9	17.	24.
	299.75	265.25

6. LOS ANGELES

Code no.	Off.	Def.
9	16.5	25.88
2	17.	20.
1	19.12	19.5
11	25.5	16.38
10	10.75	23.25
19	19.	15.5
24	24.	17.25
1	19.12	19.5
18	22.5	24.
7	17.75	16.25
9	16.5	25.88
11	25.5	16.38
12	11.5	23.5
4	23.	20.5
	267.75	283.75

7. MINNESOTA

Code no.	Off.	Def.
13	23.75	15.5
4	27.25	20.38
21	27.	13.25
12	12.	22.75
18	21.75	24.
2	18.5	19.38
22	22.5	16.12
9	17.	23.5
4	27.25	20.38
6	18.5	17.
25	24.25	13.
2	18.5	19.38
5	22.5	16.12
11	25.5	19.5
	306.25	260.25

8. NY GIANTS

Code no.	Off.	Def.
4	24.	20.75
3	26.	17.62
10	9.	22.5
9	17.	23.5
11	25.5	19.
12	12.38	23.38
13	23.5	16.
18	22.5	23.5
13	23.5	16.
12	12.38	23.38
10	9.	22.5
17	19.	15.5
21	27.	13.25
3	26.	17.62
	276.75	274.5

9. NEW ORLEANS

Code no.	Off.	Def.
6	19.	18.5
20	20.5	19.25
11	23.75	20.12
8	18.	17.25
1	17.12	19.
11	23.75	20.12
10	10.75	24.
7	17.75	18.5
1	17.12	19.
4	24.	20.75
6	19.	18.5
23	26.5	25.
22	14.	32.75
5	21.5	16.25
	272.75	289.

10. PHILADELPHIA

Code no.	Off.	Def.
3	22.38	21.12
15	20.75	17.
8	17.5	20.
13	24.12	17.12
6	18.5	19.
20	20.5	17.75
9	17.	27.5
12	12.12	24.12
19	11.	35.5
3	22.38	21.12
8	17.5	20.
13	24.12	17.12
2	17.	20.25
12	12.12	24.12
	257.	291.75

11. SAN FRANCISCO

Code no.	Off.	Def.
26	19.75	22.
14	19.	27.5
9	17.	25.12
6	18.38	20.
8	18.	19.25
9	17.	25.12
1	20.38	18.25
5	21.5	16.
16	16.75	17.75
2	17.	15.75
3	25.5	15.75
6	18.38	20.
1	20.38	18.25
7	20.75	17.
	269.75	277.75

12. ST. LOUIS

Code no.	Off.	Def.
16	18.5	20.5
13	23.25	17.12
25	24.25	10.
7	20.75	17.
13	23.25	17.12
8	20.12	18.38
2	17.	20.25
10	9.	24.62
3	21.75	18.25
8	20.12	18.38
21	25.25	13.25
3	21.75	18.25
6	20.	18.75
10	9.	24.62
	274.	256.5

13. WASHINGTON

Code no.	Off.	Def.
7	18.75	16.25
12	15.	22.12
22	14.	32.75
10	11.38	24.88
12	15.	22.12
3	23.25	15.12
8	21.88	16.75
23	26.75	23.
8	21.88	16.75
1	19.25	18.75
5	22.	16.
10	11.38	24.88
3	23.25	15.12
14	19.	27.5
	262.75	292.

14. BUFFALO

Code no.	Off.	Def.
23	21.5	25.38
11	25.5	18.25
16	16.	21.12
22	14.	31.62
4	24.	17.25
21	26.25	10.88
25	23.5	10.
21	26.25	10.88
23	21.5	25.38
22	14.	31.62
15	20.75	18.75
16	16.	21.12
13	23.75	15.5
	298.	277.75

15. CLEVELAND

Code no.	Off.	Def.
5	21.5	16.25
10	8.	23.5
17	19.	13.
20	20.	19.25
2	17.	20.25
19	11.75	27.
18	21.75	24.
19	11.75	27.
26	19.5	25.5
25	24.	12.
14	20.5	25.75
25	24.	12.
17	19.	13.
23	26.75	23.25
	264.5	281.75

16. BALTIMORE

Code no.	Off.	Def.
12	12.	23.5
23	23.62	23.12
14	21.38	26.38
26	18.5	25.5
3	24.75	20.75
23	23.62	23.12
21	27.75	14.
22	15.12	32.88
11	23.5	19.
22	15.12	32.88
14	21.38	26.38
20	20.5	19.25
21	27.75	14.
	292.75	315.75

17. CINCINNATI

Code no.	Off.	Def.
22	16.25	32.
25	24.75	10.
19	19.75	18.12
2	22.5	24.
20	20.75	17.25
6	19.75	19.
11	11.26	24.5
25	24.75	10.
24	25.25	17.75
16	16.75	19.
2	17.	20.
15	21.75	19.25
11	21.25	24.5
	271.5	273.5

18. DENVER

Code no.	Off.	Def.
19	11.	25.
26	18.25	23.75
20	18.75	17.25
17	17.75	15.5
7	10.75	17.
24	24.5	16.75
15	20.75	17.
8	18.	19.25
6	20.	18.75
24	24.5	16.75
1	19.	18.75
20	18.75	17.25
26	18.25	23.75
22	14.	30.75
	262.25	277.5

19. HOUSTON

Code no.	Off.	Def.
18	20.25	24.
21	25.25	13.25
23	26.5	23.25
24	24.	17.75
25	25.5	14.25
15	21.88	18.88
17	16.75	16.12
15	21.88	18.88
10	8.	24.25
5	22.	16.25
26	17.5	25.5
1	19.	19.5
25	25.5	14.25
17	16.75	16.12
	290.75	262.25

20. KANSAS CITY

Code no.	Off.	Def.
21	27.	13.25
9	17.	27.
18	21.62	23.25
15	24.75	17.
17	17.75	15.
26	18.25	24.75
25	25.88	17.38
26	18.25	24.75
25	26.	13.
26	18.25	24.75
24	25.88	17.38
18	21.62	23.25
16	16.75	17.75
1	19.	18.75
	287.75	276.75

21. MIAMI

Code no.	Off.	Def.
20	20.75	17.75
19	11.	24.
7	21.25	18.5
23	25.62	23.25
26	19.75	24.
14	19.	26.5
16	20.25	18.12
14	19.	26.5
22	15.12	30.38
23	25.62	23.25
12	12.	22.25
22	15.12	30.38
8	21.75	17.25
16	20.25	18.12
	266.5	320.25

22. NEW ENGLAND

Code no.	Off.	Def.
17	17.5	15.5
1	19.	18.75
13	23.75	15.5
14	17.25	28.
23	22.38	26.25
23	23.5	14.
23	22.38	26.25
16	14.75	20.25
21	24.62	13.12
14	17.25	28.
16	14.75	20.25
21	24.62	13.12
9	17.	27.5
18	20.25	24.
	279.	290.5

23. NY JETS

Code no.	Off.	Def.
14	20.12	23.88
16	15.25	16.88
19	11.	25.5
21	25.5	10.75
22	15.	30.75
16	15.25	16.88
22	15.	30.75
14	20.12	23.88
25	24.75	10.
24	25.25	17.75
4	23.	20.5
9	17.	27.5
24	25.	17.25
15	20.75	18.75
	272.25	289.75

24. OAKLAND

Code no.	Off.	Def.
25	23.5	10.
5	22.	16.25
26	19.	26.6
19	12.5	24.
14	19.	25.75
18	20.88	23.25
6	19.75	17.
18	20.88	23.25
17	18.75	15.
18	20.88	23.25
20	20.38	18.25
26	19.	25.5
23	26.75	24.25
2	17.	15.75
	279.75	282.

25. PITTSBURGH

Code no.	Off.	Def.
24	24.	17.
17	20.	14.88
12	12.	22.25
3	25.5	19.25
19	13.88	26.75
22	16.25	31.
14	19.	24.5
17	20.	14.88
20	20.75	19.25
15	22.75	16.5
7	21.25	16.25
15	22.75	16.5
19	13.88	26.75
26	19.75	24.
	271.75	289.75

26. SAN DIEGO

Code no.	Off.	Def.
11	22.75	20.5
18	21.38	23.75
24	26.62	17.75
16	16.75	18.
21	27.	13.25
4	23.	20.5
3	22.75	15.75
15	22.25	17.
20	19.52	18.25
19	11.	24.
24	26.62	17.75
18	21.38	23.75
25	24.25	14.
	305.	262.5

[a]Defense means points allowed, and offense means points made.

TABLE 13.5a
Defensive Scoring (1971)

	Offense			Defense		
	Expected Score	14 × Trimean	Net	Expected Score	14 × Trimean	Net
1. Atlanta	270.25	269.5	−.75	279.25	276.5	2.75
2. Chicago	237.75	164.5	−73.25	285.50	266.0	19.50
3. Dallas	283.00	371.0	88.00	223.25	203.0	20.25
4. Detroit	255.50	336.0	80.50	242.25	294.0	−51.75
5. Green Bay	252.75	273.0	20.25	255.00	294.0	−39.00
6. Los Angeles	249.75	287.0	37.25	284.50	255.5	29.00
7. Minnesota	286.50	248.5	−38.00	254.25	126.0	128.25
8. N.Y. Giants	240.00	189.0	−51.00	274.25	329.0	−54.75
9. New Orleans	250.00	273.0	23.00	277.75	322.0	−44.25
10. Philadelphia	246.50	199.5	−47.00	275.75	294.0	−18.25
11. San Francisco	268.75	294.0	25.25	255.50	234.5	21.00
12. St. Louis	268.50	234.5	−34.00	256.00	280.0	−24.00
13. Washington	277.50	276.5	−1.00	251.75	178.5	73.25
14. Buffalo	234.75	161.0	−73.75	273.75	371.0	−97.25
15. Cleveland	270.50	287.0	16.50	270.25	283.5	−13.25
16. Baltimore	271.25	315.0	43.75	245.75	150.5	95.25
17. Cincinnati	281.50	297.5	16.00	262.00	273.0	−11.00
18. Denver	270.00	206.5	−63.50	286.75	262.5	24.25
19. Houston	284.50	231.0	−53.50	279.50	336.0	−56.50
20. Kansas City	282.75	294.0	11.25	268.25	210.0	58.25
21. Miami	274.25	315.0	40.75	237.25	168.0	69.25
22. New England	250.50	238.0	−12.50	274.50	336.0	−61.50
23. N.Y. Jets	255.50	203.0	−52.50	275.75	248.5	27.25
24. Oakland	276.25	336.0	59.75	266.75	280.0	−13.25
25. Pittsburgh	268.00	259.0	−9.00	265.25	276.5	−11.25
26. San Diego	267.50	311.5	44.00	249.75	325.5	−75.75

(See Notes following Table 13.5b.)

points. The reader should note that it is this net figure that gives consideration to the strength of the opposition in the schedule.

DEFENSIVE SCORING (Tables 13.5 and 13.6)

If we compute the trimean for the season's offensive scoring by each team, we can get a measure of their attacking strength, and thus find out how many points a team with a given schedule can expect to have scored upon it if it is an average team. Then we can subtract from this 14 times the trimean of what the opponents actually scored. If this is positive, it is what the defense saved in points during the season, compared to an average team.

Again for Atlanta in 1971, the opponents were expected to make 279.25 points (Table 13.3) and 14 times the trimean for the opponents in their games against Atlanta was actually 276.5 (14 × 19.75). The difference of 2.75 (Table 13.5) means that over the season the Atlanta defense saved 2.75 points compared to average.

Other teams were not so close to average—Minnesota's defense saved 128.25 points, while Buffalo's lost 97.25 compared to average.

TABLE 13.5b
Defensive Scoring (1972)

	Offense			Defense		
	Expected Score	14 × Trimean	Net	Expected Score	14 × Trimean	Net
1. Atlanta	297.00	266.0	−31.00	278.50	262.5	16.00
2. Chicago	261.00	238.0	−23.00	282.00	259.0	23.00
3. Dallas	271.25	332.5	61.25	262.00	245.0	17.00
4. Detroit	278.75	343.0	64.25	280.25	283.5	3.25
5. Green Bay	269.25	308.0	38.75	288.25	227.5	60.75
6. Los Angeles	286.25	276.5	−9.75	268.75	262.5	6.25
7. Minnesota	260.75	276.5	15.75	296.25	248.5	47.75
8. N.Y. Giants	276.50	276.5	0.00	271.25	255.5	15.75
9. New Orleans	283.50	238.0	−45.50	283.25	357.0	−73.75
10. Philadelphia	271.50	140.0	−131.50	266.00	332.5	−66.50
11. San Francisco	284.00	343.0	59.00	268.50	269.5	−1.00
12. St. Louis	249.00	168.0	−81.00	278.25	315.0	−36.75
13. Washington	298.50	332.5	34.00	251.00	220.5	30.50
14. Buffalo	275.25	266.0	−9.25	309.50	371.0	−61.50
15. Cleveland	280.50	301.0	20.50	263.25	238.0	25.25
16. Baltimore	307.75	234.5	−73.25	289.00	259.0	30.00
17. Cincinnati	273.25	255.5	−17.75	269.75	213.5	56.25
18. Denver	283.50	304.5	21.00	272.50	336.0	−63.50
19. Houston	249.75	164.5	−85.25	296.00	353.5	−57.50
20. Kansas City	275.75	287.0	11.25	283.50	259.0	24.50
21. Miami	327.50	367.5	40.00	254.75	185.5	69.25
22. New England	275.00	206.5	−68.50	299.00	441.0	−142.00
23. N.Y. Jets	300.50	357.0	56.50	276.50	332.5	−56.00
24. Oakland	290.50	343.0	52.50	280.00	241.5	38.50
25. Pittsburgh	291.25	339.5	48.25	256.25	164.5	91.75
26. San Diego	262.25	266.0	3.75	306.75	346.5	−39.75

Notes: Expected score = sum of trimeans of opponent's defensive scoring.
14 × trimean = 14 × trimean of team's scores against opponents.
Defensive expected score = sum of trimeans of opponent's scores against their opponents.
Defensive 14 × trimean = 14 × trimean of team's opponent's scores against their opponents.

TABLE 13.6a
Defensive Scoring (1971) With Second-Order Adjustments

		Offense			Defense	
	Expected Score	14 × Trimean	Net	Expected Score	14 × Trimean	Net
1. Atlanta	268.75	269.5	.75	283.25	276.5	6.75
2. Chicago	248.25	164.5	-83.75	289.5	266.	23.5
3. Dallas	273.25	371.	97.75	226.75	203.	23.75
4. Detroit	245.75	336.	90.25	234.	294.	-60.
5. Green Bay	252.	273.	21.	258.	294.	-36.
6. Los Angeles	241.5	287.	45.5	292.25	255.5	36.75
7. Minnesota	289.	248.5	-40.5	270.25	126.	144.25
8. NY Giants	249.75	189.	-60.75	264.25	329.	-64.75
9. New Orleans	244.5	273.	28.5	274.5	322.	-47.5
10. Philadelphia	255.25	199.5	-55.75	276.5	294.	-17.5
11. San Francisco	267.25	294.	26.75	258.75	234.5	24.25
12. St. Louis	279.5	234.5	-45.	254.5	280.	-25.5
13. Washington	279.25	276.5	-2.75	264.	178.5	85.5
14. Buffalo	242.5	161.	-81.5	255.75	371.	-115.25
15. Cleveland	263.25	287.	23.75	263.5	283.5	-20.
16. Baltimore	270.25	315.	44.75	263.	150.5	112.5
17. Cincinnati	284.5	297.5	13.	260.75	273.	-12.25
18. Denver	277.75	206.5	-71.25	287.	262.5	24.5
19. Houston	288.5	231.	-57.5	274.	336.	-62.
20. Kansas City	284.75	294.	9.25	280.5	210.	70.5
21. Miami	266.5	315.	48.5	244.5	168.	76.5
22. New England	253.25	238.	-15.25	268.5	336.	-67.5
23. NY Jets	259.75	203.	-56.75	279.25	248.5	30.75
24. Oakland	266.5	336.	69.5	264.5	280.	-15.5
25. Pittsburgh	272.25	259.	-13.25	261.	276.5	-15.5
26. San Diego	266.5	311.5	45.	242.	325.5	-83.5

TABLE 13.6b
Defensive Scoring (1972) With Second-Order Adjustments

		Offense			Defense	
	Expected Score	14 × Trimean	Net	Expected Score	14 × Trimean	Net
1. Atlanta	297.	266.	-31.	276.5	262.5	14.
2. Chicago	264.25	238.	-26.25	286.75	259.	27.75
3. Dallas	260.75	332.5	71.75	266.	245.	21.
4. Detroit	269.5	343.	73.5	276.75	283.5	-6.75
5. Green Bay	265.25	308.	42.75	299.75	227.5	72.25
6. Los Angeles	283.75	276.5	-7.25	267.75	262.5	5.25
7. Minnesota	260.25	276.5	16.25	306.25	248.5	57.75
8. NY Giants	274.5	276.5	2.	276.75	255.5	21.25
9. New Orleans	289.	238.	-51.	272.75	357.	-84.25
10. Philadelphia	291.75	140.	-151.75	257.	332.5	-75.5
11. San Francisco	277.75	343.	65.25	269.75	269.5	.25
12. St. Louis	256.5	168.	-88.5	274.	315.	-41.
13. Washington	292.	332.5	40.5	262.75	220.5	42.25
14. Buffalo	277.75	266.	-11.75	298.	371.	-73.
15. Cleveland	281.75	301.	19.25	264.5	238.	26.5
16. Baltimore	315.75	234.5	-81.25	292.75	259.	33.75
17. Cincinnati	273.5	255.5	-18.	271.5	213.5	58.
18. Denver	277.5	304.5	27.	262.25	336.	-73.75
19. Houston	262.25	164.5	-97.75	290.75	353.5	-62.75
20. Kansas City	276.75	287.	10.25	287.75	259.	28.75
21. Miami	320.25	367.5	47.25	266.5	185.5	81.
22. New England	290.5	206.5	-84.	279.	441.	-162.
23. NY Jets	289.75	357.	67.25	272.25	332.5	-60.25
24. Oakland	282.	343.	61.	279.75	241.5	38.25
25. Pittsburgh	289.75	339.5	49.75	271.75	164.5	107.25
26. San Diego	262.5	266.	3.5	305.	346.5	-41.5

NET PERFORMANCE (Table 13.7)

By adding the excess of points gained by the offense and the excess of points saved by the defense (-0.75 + 2.75 = 2 for Atlanta), we have a measure of the performance of each team for the whole season adjusted for inequities in its schedule. Of course it is not surprising that the teams are ranked in an order similar to what would have been obtained from the actual won–lost records. But more detail is offered, since we get information on both offense and defense and we have a more sensitive spacing for the teams.

We can think of the points indicated as the number of extra points the team scored or prevented from scoring compared to the average. The range in 1971

TABLE 13.7a
Adjusted Ratings of Teams (1971)

Code No.	Team	Final Rating				Schedule Effect: Expected Score		
		Offense	Defense	Total	Rank	Opponent	Own	Net
		National Football Conference						
1.	Atlanta	-.75	2.75	2.00	13	279.25	270.25	9.00
2.	Chicago	-73.25	19.50	-53.75	20	285.50	237.75	47.75
3.	Dallas	88.00	20.25	108.25	3	223.25	283.00	-59.75
4.	Detroit	80.50	51.75	28.75	10	242.25	255.50	-13.25
5.	Green Bay	20.25	-39.00	-18.75	14	255.00	252.75	2.25
6.	Los Angeles	37.25	29.00	66.25	7	284.50	249.75	34.75
7.	Minnesota	-38.00	128.25	90.25	4	254.25	286.50	-32.25
8.	N.Y. Giants	-51.00	-54.75	-105.75	24	274.25	240.00	34.25
9.	New Orleans	23.00	-44.25	-21.25	16	277.75	250.00	27.75
10.	Philadelphia	-47.00	-18.25	-65.25	22	275.75	246.50	29.25
11.	San Francisco	25.25	21.00	46.25	9	255.50	268.75	-13.25
12.	St. Louis	-34.00	-24.00	-58.00	21	256.00	268.50	-12.50
13.	Washington	-1.00	73.25	72.25	5	251.75	277.50	-25.75
		American Football Conference						
14.	Buffalo	-73.75	-97.25	-171.00	26	273.75	234.75	39.00
15.	Cleveland	16.50	-13.25	3.25	12	270.25	270.50	-.25
16.	Baltimore	43.75	95.25	139.00	1	245.75	271.25	-25.50
17.	Cincinnati	16.00	-11.00	5.00	11	262.00	281.50	-19.50
18.	Denver	-63.50	24.25	-39.75	19	286.75	270.00	16.75
19.	Houston	-53.50	-56.50	-110.00	25	279.50	284.50	-5.00
20.	Kansas City	11.25	58.25	69.50	6	268.25	282.75	-14.50
21.	Miami	40.75	69.25	110.00	2	237.25	274.25	-37.00
22.	New England	-12.50	-61.50	-74.00	23	274.50	250.50	24.00
23.	N.Y. Jets	-52.50	27.25	-25.25	17	275.75	255.50	20.25
24.	Oakland	59.75	-13.25	46.50	8	266.75	276.25	-9.50
25.	Pittsburgh	-9.00	-11.25	-20.25	15	265.25	268.00	-2.75
26.	San Diego	44.00	-75.75	-31.75	18	249.75	267.50	-17.75

TABLE 13.7b
Adjusted Ratings of Teams (1972)

Code No.	Team	Final Rating				Schedule Effect: Expected Score		
		Offense	Defense	Total	Rank	Opponent	Own	Net
	National Football Conference							
1.	Atlanta	−31.00	16.00	−15.00	17	278.50	297.00	−18.50
2.	Chicago	−23.00	23.00	0.00	15	282.00	261.00	21.00
3.	Dallas	61.25	17.00	78.25	5	262.00	271.25	−9.25
4.	Detroit	64.25	−3.25	61.00	8	280.25	278.75	1.50
5.	Green Bay	38.75	60.75	99.50	3	288.25	269.25	19.00
6.	Los Angeles	−9.75	6.25	−3.50	16	268.75	286.25	−17.50
7.	Minnesota	15.75	47.75	63.50	7	296.25	260.75	35.50
8.	N.Y. Giants	0.00	15.75	15.75	13	271.25	276.50	−5.25
9.	New Orleans	−45.50	−73.75	−119.25	23	283.25	283.50	−.25
10.	Philadelphia	−131.50	−66.50	−198.00	25	266.00	271.50	−5.50
11.	San Francisco	59.00	−1.00	58.00	9	268.50	284.00	−15.50
12.	St. Louis	−81.00	−36.75	−117.75	22	278.25	249.00	29.25
13.	Washington	34.00	30.50	64.50	6	251.00	298.50	−47.50
	American Football Conference							
14.	Buffalo	−9.25	−61.50	−70.75	21	309.50	275.25	34.25
15.	Cleveland	20.50	25.25	45.75	10	263.25	280.50	−17.25
16.	Baltimore	−73.25	30.00	−43.25	20	289.00	307.75	−18.75
17.	Cincinnati	−17.75	56.25	38.50	11	269.75	273.25	−3.50
18.	Denver	21.00	−63.50	−42.50	19	272.50	283.50	−11.00
19.	Houston	−85.25	−57.50	−142.75	24	296.00	249.75	46.25
20.	Kansas City	11.25	24.50	35.75	12	283.50	275.75	7.75
21.	Miami	40.00	69.25	109.25	2	254.75	327.50	−72.75
22.	New England	−68.50	−142.00	−210.50	26	299.00	275.00	24.00
23.	N.Y. Jets	56.50	−56.00	0.50	14	276.50	300.50	−24.00
24.	Oakland	52.50	38.50	91.00	4	280.00	290.50	−10.50
25.	Pittsburgh	48.25	91.75	140.00	1	256.25	291.25	−35.00
26.	San Diego	3.75	−39.75	−36.00	18	306.75	262.25	44.50

is 310 from the Baltimore Colts to the Buffalo Bills. The Bills were much worse than the next lowest team, the Houston Oilers. Several top teams are close in total points.

We have given a ranking based on the points scored in the rating column. Teams within each conference probably have more reliable comparisons than the comparisons across conferences. In making point comparisons between teams on a per-game basis, one would take the difference in ratings and divide by 14. Thus, in 1971 Miami is favored by 3 points against Kansas City $[(110 - 69.5)/14 \approx 3]$ but, as we shall see, this is more than reversed if they play in Kansas City.

STIFFNESS OF SCHEDULE

One bonus of this analysis is that it gives a ready way to calculate the toughness of a team's schedule in retrospect. In the third column after the ranking we have given a net expected gain or loss compared to an average team. Positive numbers in the last column mean a tougher than average schedule. In 1971, Dallas had the easiest schedule, with a net gain of 59.75 points, while Chicago had the toughest with a net loss of 47.75 points. These differences, however, have already been taken into account in computing the rating.

The reader will readily think of other variables that we have not taken into account, such as "at home" and "away," the fact that the composition of the teams changes during the season due to injuries, changes in personnel, and training and experience.

A FURTHER REFINEMENT

In making the adjustments presented in Table 13.7, we have allowed each team to contribute to its own opponents' total offensive and defensive scoring distributions. If it were desired to remove this effect, it could readily be done, as shown in Table 13.8. All that is done is to recompute everything with one's

TABLE 13.8a
Second-Order Adjusted Ratings of Teams (1971)

Code No.	Team	Final Rating				Schedule Effect: Expected Score		
		Offense	*Defense*	*Total*	*Rank*	*Opponent*	*Own*	*Net*
		National Football Conference						
1.	Atlanta	.75	6.75	7.50	11	283.25	268.75	14.50
2.	Chicago	−83.75	23.50	−60.25	20	289.50	248.25	41.25
3.	Dallas	97.75	23.75	121.50	3	226.75	273.25	−46.50
4.	Detroit	90.25	−60.00	30.25	10	234.00	245.75	−11.75
5.	Green Bay	21.00	−36.00	−15.00	14	258.00	252.00	6.00
6.	Los Angeles	45.50	36.75	82.25	6	292.25	241.50	50.75
7.	Minnesota	−40.50	144.25	103.75	4	270.25	289.00	−18.75
8.	N.Y. Giants	−60.75	−64.75	−125.50	25	264.25	249.75	14.50
9.	New Orleans	28.50	−47.50	−19.00	15	274.50	244.50	30.00
10.	Philadelphia	−55.75	−17.50	−73.25	22	276.50	255.25	21.25
11.	San Francisco	26.75	24.25	51.00	9	258.75	267.25	−8.50
12.	St. Louis	−45.00	−25.50	−70.50	21	254.50	279.50	−25.00
13.	Washington	−2.75	85.50	82.75	5	264.00	279.25	−15.25

(continued)

TABLE 13.8a (*continued*)

American Football Conference

14.	Buffalo	–81.50	–115.25	–196.75	26	255.75	242.50	13.25
15.	Cleveland	23.75	–20.00	3.75	12	263.50	242.50	.25
16.	Baltimore	44.75	112.50	157.25	1	263.00	270.25	–7.25
17.	Cincinnati	13.00	–12.25	.75	13	260.75	284.50	–23.75
18.	Denver	–71.25	24.50	–46.75	19	287.00	277.75	9.25
19.	Houston	–57.50	–62.00	–119.50	24	274.00	288.50	–14.50
20.	Kansas City	9.25	70.50	79.75	7	280.50	284.75	–4.25
21.	Miami	48.50	76.50	125.00	2	244.50	266.50	–22.00
22.	New England	–15.25	–67.50	–82.75	23	268.50	253.25	15.25
23.	N.Y. Jets	–56.75	30.75	–26.00	16	279.25	259.75	19.50
24.	Oakland	69.50	–15.50	54.00	8	264.50	266.50	–2.00
25.	Pittsburgh	–13.25	–15.50	–28.75	17	261.00	272.25	–11.25
26.	San Diego	45.00	–83.50	–38.50	18	242.00	266.50	–24.50

own performance from the opponent's opponents. These are our final ratings. Table 13.7 shows the simply adjusted ratings and Table 13.8 the second-order adjusted ratings. (Table 13.4 shows the intermediate calculations.)

Figure 13.1 shows, for ready reference, the ranks for 1971 and 1972. Miami's beautiful 2-year performance is shown by the point nearest the origin. Baltimore's 1972 disaster after its great 1971 performance makes it the top left-hand point. The 45° lines are intended to guide the eye and show which three teams are most changed in rank, up and down. Points on the middle 45° line represent teams with unchanged ranks.

TABLE 13.8b
Second-Order Adjusted Ratings of Teams (1972)

Code No.	Team	Final Rating				Schedule Effect: Expected Score		
		Offense	Defense	Total	Rank	Opponent	Own	Net
		National Football Conference						
1.	Atlanta	–31.00	14.00	–17.00	17	276.50	297.00	–20.50
2.	Chicago	–26.25	27.75	1.50	15	286.75	264.25	22.50
3.	Dallas	71.75	21.00	92.75	5	266.00	260.75	5.25
4.	Detroit	73.50	–6.75	66.75	8	276.75	269.50	7.25
5.	Green Bay	42.75	72.25	115.00	3	299.75	265.25	34.50
6.	Los Angeles	–7.25	5.25	–2.00	16	267.75	283.75	–16.00
7.	Minnesota	16.25	57.75	74.00	7	306.25	260.25	46.00
8.	N.Y. Giants	2.00	21.25	23.25	13	276.75	274.50	2.25
9.	New Orleans	–51.00	–84.25	–135.25	23	272.75	289.00	–16.25
10.	Philadelphia	–151.75	–75.50	–227.25	25	257.00	291.75	–34.75
11.	San Francisco	65.25	.25	65.50	9	269.75	277.75	–8.00
12.	St. Louis	–88.50	–41.00	–129.50	22	274.00	256.50	17.50
13.	Washington	40.50	42.25	82.75	6	262.75	292.00	–29.25

(*continued*)

TABLE 13.b*(continued)*

American Football Conference								
14.	Buffalo	−11.75	−73.00	−84.75	21	298.00	277.75	20.25
15.	Cleveland	19.25	26.50	45.75	10	264.50	281.75	−17.25
16.	Baltimore	−81.25	33.75	−47.50	20	292.75	315.75	−23.00
17.	Cincinnati	−18.00	58.00	40.00	11	271.50	273.50	−2.00
18.	Denver	27.00	−73.75	−46.75	19	262.25	277.50	−15.25
19.	Houston	−97.75	−62.75	−160.50	24	290.75	262.25	28.50
20.	Kansas City	10.25	28.75	39.00	12	287.75	276.75	11.00
21.	Miami	47.25	81.00	128.25	2	266.50	320.25	−53.75
22.	New England	−84.00	−162.00	−246.00	26	279.00	290.50	−11.50
23.	N.Y. Jets	67.25	−60.25	7.00	14	272.25	289.75	−17.50
24.	Oakland	61.00	38.25	99.25	4	279.75	282.00	−2.25
25.	Pittsburgh	49.75	107.25	157.00	1	271.75	289.75	−18.00
26.	San Diego	3.50	−41.50	−38.00	18	305.00	262.50	42.50

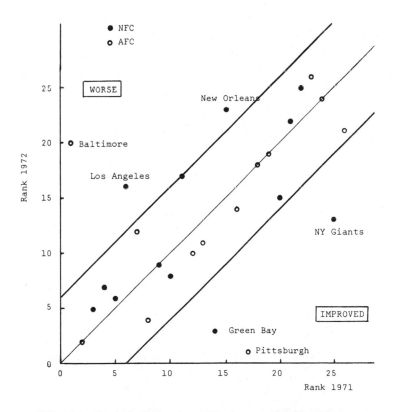

FIG. 13.1.   Ranks in 1971 versus 1972 after second-order adjustments.

TABLE 13.9a
Home Versus Away (1971)[a]

Opp.	Home			Away			
no.	Own	Opp	Net	Own	Opp	Net	Δ
1. ATLANTA							
6	16	24	-8	20	20	0	-8
9	28	6	22	24	20	4	18
11	20	17	3	3	24	-21	24
						Total	34
2. CHICAGO							
4	3	28	-25	28	23	5	-30
5	14	17	-3	10	31	-21	18
7	10	27	-17	20	17	3	-20
						Total	-32
3. DALLAS							
8	20	13	7	42	14	28	-21
10	20	7	13	42	7	35	-22
12	31	12	19	16	13	3	16
13	16	20	-4	13	0	13	-17
						Total	-44
4. DETROIT							
2	23	28	-5	28	3	25	-30
5	31	28	3	14	14	0	3
7	13	16	-3	10	29	-19	16
						Total	-11
5. GREEN BAY							
2	31	10	21	17	14	3	18
4	14	14	0	28	31	-3	3
7	13	24	-11	0	3	-3	-8
						Total	13
6. LOS ANGELES							
1	20	20	0	24	16	8	-8
9	45	28	17	20	24	-4	21
11	17	6	11	20	13	7	4
						Total	17
7. MINNESOTA							
2	17	20	-3	27	10	17	-20
4	29	10	19	16	13	3	16
5	3	0	3	24	13	11	-8
						Total	-12
8. NY GIANTS							
3	14	42	-28	13	20	-7	-21
10	28	41	-13	7	23	-16	3
12	7	24	-17	21	20	1	-18
13	3	30	-27	7	23	-16	-11
						Total	-47
9. NEW ORLEANS							
1	20	24	-4	6	28	-22	18
6	24	20	4	28	45	-17	21
11	20	38	-18	26	20	6	-24
						Total	15
10. PHILADELPHIA							
3	7	42	-35	7	20	-13	-22
8	23	7	16	41	28	13	3
12	19	7	12	37	20	17	-5
13	13	20	-7	7	7	0	-7
						Total	-31
11. SAN FRANCISCO							
1	24	3	21	17	20	-3	24
6	13	20	-7	6	17	-11	4
9	20	26	-6	38	20	18	-24
						Total	4
12. ST. LOUIS							
3	13	16	-3	12	31	-19	16
8	20	21	-1	24	7	17	-18
10	20	37	-17	7	19	-12	-5
13	17	24	-7	0	20	-20	13
						Total	6
13. WASHINGTON							
3	0	13	-13	20	16	4	-17
8	23	7	16	30	3	27	-11
10	7	7	0	20	13	7	-7
12	20	0	20	24	17	7	13
						Total	-22
14. BUFFALO							
16	0	43	-43	0	24	-24	-19
21	14	29	-15	0	34	-34	19
22	27	20	7	33	38	-5	12
23	7	20	-13	17	28	-11	-2
						Total	10
15. CLEVELAND							
17	31	27	4	27	24	3	1
19	31	0	31	37	24	13	18
25	27	17	10	9	26	-17	27
						Total	46
16. BALTIMORE							
14	24	0	24	43	0	43	-19
21	14	3	11	14	17	-3	14
22	17	21	-4	23	3	20	-24
23	22	0	22	14	13	1	21
						Total	-8
17. CINCINNATI							
15	24	27	-3	27	31	-4	1
19	28	13	15	6	10	-4	19
25	13	21	-8	10	21	-11	3
						Total	23
18. DENVER							
20	3	16	-13	10	28	-18	5
24	16	27	-11	13	21	-8	-3
26	20	16	4	17	45	-28	32
						Total	34
19. HOUSTON							
15	24	37	-13	0	31	-31	18
17	10	6	4	13	28	-15	19
25	29	3	26	16	23	-7	33
						Total	70
20. KANSAS CITY							
18	28	10	18	16	3	13	5
24	16	14	2	20	20	0	2
26	31	10	21	14	21	-7	28
						Total	35
21. MIAMI							
14	34	0	34	29	14	15	19
16	17	14	3	3	14	-11	14
22	41	3	38	13	34	-21	59
23	10	14	-4	30	14	16	-20
						Total	72
22. NEW ENGLAND							
14	38	33	5	20	27	-7	12
16	3	23	-20	21	17	4	-24
21	34	13	21	3	41	-38	59
23	20	0	20	6	13	-7	27
						Total	74
23. NY JETS							
14	28	17	11	20	7	13	-2
16	13	14	-1	0	22	-22	21
21	14	30	-16	14	10	4	-20
22	13	6	7	0	20	-20	27
						Total	26
24. OAKLAND							
18	21	13	8	27	16	11	-3
20	20	20	0	14	16	-2	2
26	34	33	1	34	0	34	-33
							-34
25. PITTSBURGH							
15	26	9	17	17	27	-10	27
17	21	10	11	21	13	8	3
19	23	16	7	3	29	-26	33
						Total	63
26. SAN DIEGO							
18	45	17	28	16	20	-4	32
20	21	14	7	10	31	-21	28
24	0	34	-34	33	34	-1	-33
							27

[a]Δ = net home score minus net away score.

TABLE 13.9b
Home Versus Away (1972)[a]

1. ATLANTA

Opp. no.	Home Own	Home Opp	Home Net	Away Own	Away Opp	Away Net	Δ
6	31	3	28	7	20	-13	41
9	36	20	16	21	14	7	9
11	14	49	-35	0	20	-20	-15
						Total	35

2. CHICAGO

Opp. no.	Home Own	Home Opp	Home Net	Away Own	Away Opp	Away Net	Δ
4	24	38	-14	0	14	-14	0
5	17	23	-6	17	20	-3	-3
7	13	10	3	10	23	-13	16
						Total	13

3. DALLAS

Opp. no.	Home Own	Home Opp	Home Net	Away Own	Away Opp	Away Net	Δ
8	3	23	-20	23	14	9	-29
10	28	6	22	28	7	21	1
12	33	24	9	27	6	21	-12
13	34	24	10	20	24	-4	14
						Total	-26

4. DETROIT

Opp. no.	Home Own	Home Opp	Home Net	Away Own	Away Opp	Away Net	Δ
2	14	0	14	38	24	14	0
5	23	24	-1	7	33	-26	25
7	10	34	-24	14	16	-2	-22
						Total	3

5. GREEN BAY

Opp. no.	Home Own	Home Opp	Home Net	Away Own	Away Opp	Away Net	Δ
2	20	17	3	23	17	6	-3
4	33	7	26	24	23	1	25
7	13	27	-14	23	7	16	-30
						Total	-8

6. LOS ANGELES

Opp. no.	Home Own	Home Opp	Home Net	Away Own	Away Opp	Away Net	Δ
1	20	7	13	3	31	-28	41
9	34	14	20	16	19	-3	23
11	31	7	24	26	16	10	14
						Total	78

7. MINNESOTA

Opp. no.	Home Own	Home Opp	Home Net	Away Own	Away Opp	Away Net	Δ
2	23	10	13	10	13	-3	16
4	16	14	2	34	10	24	-22
5	7	23	-16	27	13	14	-30
						Total	-36

8. NY GIANTS

Opp. no.	Home Own	Home Opp	Home Net	Away Own	Away Opp	Away Net	Δ
3	14	23	-9	23	3	20	-29
10	62	10	52	27	12	15	37
12	27	21	6	13	7	6	0
13	16	23	-7	13	27	-14	7
						Total	15

9. NEW ORLEANS

Opp. no.	Home Own	Home Opp	Home Net	Away Own	Away Opp	Away Net	Δ
1	14	21	-7	20	36	-16	9
6	19	16	3	14	34	-20	23
11	2	37	-35	20	20	0	-35
						Total	-3

10. PHILADELPHIA

Opp. no.	Home Own	Home Opp	Home Net	Away Own	Away Opp	Away Net	Δ
3	7	28	-21	6	28	-22	1
8	12	27	-15	10	62	-52	37
12	6	6	0	23	24	-1	1
13	7	23	-16	0	14	-14	-2
						Total	37

11. SAN FRANCISCO

Opp. no.	Home Own	Home Opp	Home Net	Away Own	Away Opp	Away Net	Δ
1	20	0	20	49	14	35	-15
6	16	26	-10	7	31	-24	14
9	20	20	0	37	2	35	-35
						Total	-36

12. ST. LOUIS

Opp. no.	Home Own	Home Opp	Home Net	Away Own	Away Opp	Away Net	Δ
3	6	27	-21	24	33	-9	-12
8	7	13	-6	21	27	-6	0
10	24	23	1	6	6	0	1
13	3	33	-30	10	24	-14	-16
						Total	-27

13. WASHINGTON

Opp. no.	Home Own	Home Opp	Home Net	Away Own	Away Opp	Away Net	Δ
3	24	20	4	24	34	-10	14
8	27	13	14	23	16	7	7
10	14	0	14	23	7	16	-2
12	24	10	14	33	3	30	-16
						Total	3

14. BUFFALO

Opp. no.	Home Own	Home Opp	Home Net	Away Own	Away Opp	Away Net	Δ
16	0	17	-17	7	35	-28	11
21	16	30	-14	23	24	-1	-13
22	38	14	24	27	24	3	21
23	24	41	-17	3	41	-38	21
						Total	40

15. CLEVELAND

Opp. no.	Home Own	Home Opp	Home Net	Away Own	Away Opp	Away Net	Δ
17	27	6	21	27	24	3	18
19	20	0	20	23	17	6	14
25	26	24	2	0	30	-30	32
						Total	64

16. BALTIMORE

Opp. no.	Home Own	Home Opp	Home Net	Away Own	Away Opp	Away Net	Δ
14	35	7	28	17	0	17	11
21	0	23	-23	0	16	-16	-7
22	31	0	31	24	17	7	24
23	34	44	-10	20	24	-4	-6
						Total	22

17. CINCINNATI

Opp. no.	Home Own	Home Opp	Home Net	Away Own	Away Opp	Away Net	Δ
15	24	27	-3	6	27	-21	18
19	30	7	23	61	17	44	-21
25	15	10	5	17	40	-23	28
						Total	25

18. DENVER

Opp. no.	Home Own	Home Opp	Home Net	Away Own	Away Opp	Away Net	Δ
20	24	45	-21	21	24	-3	-18
24	20	37	-17	30	23	7	-24
26	38	13	25	14	37	-23	48
						Total	6

19. HOUSTON

Opp. no.	Home Own	Home Opp	Home Net	Away Own	Away Opp	Away Net	Δ
15	17	23	-6	0	20	-20	14
17	17	61	-44	7	30	-23	-21
25	3	9	-6	7	24	-17	11
						Total	4

20. KANSAS CITY

Opp. no.	Home Own	Home Opp	Home Net	Away Own	Away Opp	Away Net	Δ
18	24	21	3	45	24	21	-18
24	27	14	13	3	26	-23	36
26	17	27	-10	26	14	12	-22
						Total	-4

21. MIAMI

Opp. no.	Home Own	Home Opp	Home Net	Away Own	Away Opp	Away Net	Δ
14	24	23	1	30	16	14	-13
16	16	0	16	23	0	23	-7
22	52	0	52	37	21	16	36
23	28	24	4	27	17	10	-6
						Total	10

22. NEW ENGLAND

Opp. no.	Home Own	Home Opp	Home Net	Away Own	Away Opp	Away Net	Δ
14	24	27	-3	14	38	-24	21
16	17	24	-7	0	31	-31	24
21	21	37	-16	0	52	-52	36
23	13	41	-28	10	34	-24	-4
						Total	77

23. NY JETS

Opp. no.	Home Own	Home Opp	Home Net	Away Own	Away Opp	Away Net	Δ
14	41	3	38	41	24	17	21
16	24	20	4	44	34	10	-6
21	17	27	-10	24	28	-4	-6
22	34	10	24	41	13	28	-4
						Total	5

24. OAKLAND

Opp. no.	Home Own	Home Opp	Home Net	Away Own	Away Opp	Away Net	Δ
18	23	30	-7	37	20	17	-24
20	26	3	23	14	27	-13	36
26	17	17	0	21	19	2	-2
						Total	10

25. PITTSBURGH

Opp. no.	Home Own	Home Opp	Home Net	Away Own	Away Opp	Away Net	Δ
15	30	0	30	24	26	-2	32
17	40	17	23	10	15	-5	28
19	24	7	17	9	3	6	11
						Total	71

26. SAN DIEGO

Opp. no.	Home Own	Home Opp	Home Net	Away Own	Away Opp	Away Net	Δ
18	37	14	23	13	38	-25	48
20	14	26	-12	27	17	10	-22
24	19	21	-2	17	17	0	-2
						Total	24

[a]Δ = net home score minus net away score.

HOME VERSUS AWAY (Tables 13.9 and 13.10)

We made an additional study of at home versus away scores. Since each team plays three or four teams both at home and away, we can look at balanced pairs of games. The leagues differ. Surprisingly, in these paired games in the National Football Conference in 1971, the "away" team had the advantage by about 2 points. Let a pair of teams be labeled C and D and for their scores against one another the same letters with subscripts H or A according to

TABLE 13.10a
Stem-and-Leaf Plots of Δ on Pairs of Games (1971)[a]

National					American	
			5	99		
			4			
			3	2233		
Hinge	16	2 1144	2	11777788	Hinge	27
Median	−6	1 3366668888	1	2244889999	Median	13
Hinge	−18	0 333344	0	11223355	Hinge	−2
Trimean	−3.5	−0 55668888	−0	2233	Trimean	12.75
Home effect					Home effect	
(trimean/2)	−1.75	−1 117788	−1	99	(trimean/2)	6.38
		−2 00112244	−2	0044		
		−3 00	−3	33		

[a] Δ = net home score minus net away score. Each Δ appears twice in this stem-and-leaf plot.

TABLE 13.10b
Stem-and-Leaf Plots of Δ on Pairs of Games (1972)[a]

National					American	
		4 11	4	88		
		3 77	3	226666		
		2 3355	2	1114488		
		1 44466	1	11114488		
		0 000011117799	0			
Hinge	14	−0 2233	−0	2244666677	Hinge	24
Median	0.5	−1 225566	−1	3388	Median	11
Hinge	−15	−2 2299	−2	112244	Hinge	−7
Trimean	0	−3 0055	−3		Trimean	9.75
Home effect	0				Home effect	
(trimean/2)					(trimean/2)	4.88

[a] Δ = net home score minus net away score. Each Δ appears twice in this stem-and-leaf plot.

whether the team plays at home or away, respectively. Then we have computed

$$\Delta = (C_H - D_A) - (C_A - D_H).$$

In 1971 the estimated standard deviation of this difference of differences was about 26 points. The advantage for the "at home" team is half the average of this difference of differences. In the American Football Conference the "at home" team had the edge by a trimean of about 6 points, and the pseudo standard deviation of the difference of the differences was about 22 points. (In both conferences the standard deviation was estimated as ¾ of the midspread, that is, ¾ of the distance between the hinges or quartiles.)

In 1972 in the National Conference, the trimean of Δ was zero, indicating no differences between home and away; in the American Conference the trimean was in favor of the home team by 5 points per game. The standard deviation is estimated as 22 for NFC and as 23 for AFC. We have not investigated home and away effects among teams playing one another only once.

In 44 paired games, the games were split 18 times in 1971 and 12 times in 1972. Perhaps we are observing increased consistency.

RELIABILITY OF DIFFERENCES

Our "totals" from Table 13.8 can be used to estimate the difference in score between two teams when they play during the season. For example, in 1971 Baltimore had a Table 13.8 total of 157.25, and the New York Giants had a total of -125.5. Thus their "fitted" difference per game would be [157.25 - (-125.5)]/14 $\approx$ 20. The observed difference was 31 - 7 = 24 favoring Baltimore, and so the the residual is:

residual = observed - fitted = 24 - 20 = 4

We have tabulated the stem-and-leafs of the residuals for a few sorts of teams (Table 13.11). For example, for the eight top-rated teams, we got the distributions of residuals when they played each other. We also did this when the eight top-rated teams play teams from the eight bottom-rated teams. We would expect these results to be distributed approximately symmetrically around zero. It is a little surprising that the variability is about the same when the top play the top as when the top play the bottom. It probably means that the better teams do not try to beat the poorer teams as badly as they can. And this may be one reason why Miami, in spite of its marvelous won–lost record in 1972, did not come out first in the adjusted scoring (see Table 13.8b).

TABLE 13.11
Stem-and-Leaf of Plots Residuals

Top 8 Teams Versus Top 8

1971				1972	
1	046			2	33
0	02349			1	3
-0	2577			0	1122279
-1	1			-1	7

Top team won 8,
lost 4, tied 1

Top team won 12,
lost 5, tied 0

Hinge	9		Hinge	7
Median	2		Median	1
Hinge	-5		Hinge	-5
Trimean	2		Trimean	1

Top 8 Teams Versus Bottom 8

1971			1972	
2	13		2	5
1	012588		1	01556
0	01134444558899		0	0013357
-0	112445789		-0	1111126667788
-1	011111257		-1	11447779
-2	14		-2	4
-3	6			

Top team won 35,
lost 6, tied 2

Top team won 30,
lost 4, tied 1

Hinge	8		Hinge	3
Median	0		Median	-1
Hinge	-11		Hinge	-11
Trimean	-0.75		Trimean	-2.5

FORECASTS OR HISTORY?

Several people have expressed surprise at the position that: (1) the purpose of the analysis above is merely to compare the performance of the teams for the season (adjusting for schedule); and (2) the method is not especially designed to forecast the results of future games.

Admittedly, the results can be used to forecast future games and indeed in our forecast got four right, two wrong, and one no prediction (ratings closer than one point) in both 1971 and 1972 playoffs. Were we to develop a forecasting system, there are additional, different steps we would want to

take, even if we were confined to using the outcomes of past games, and even if we planned to do an analysis in the spirit of the present one.

BUILDING A FORECASTER

What are examples of such steps?

1. *Use the past to predict the future.* We would use only past scores to predict future ones. As things stand now, we essentially use the scores for the whole season to fit (postdict) the scores of any game, including the first one of the season. Using all the data is a reasonable procedure if we want to give games a basically equal weight all through the season, which is our plan in adjusting for schedule.

2. *Use weights.* We would try to discover a good weighting scheme. Very likely for forecasting next week's game, this scheme would weight recent weeks' games much more highly than games early in the season. To do a good job here, one probably has to develop the method from data for several years.

3. *Use last year's data.* For early games one would weight up last year's last few games to help the prediction. This has no interest for adjusting for this year's schedule, which is our present purpose. As the season progressed, no doubt, last year's games would be weighted less and less.

4. *Estimate both strength and variability.* This chapter deals primarily with strength for single teams and treats variability as incidental intelligence for a whole league or conference, not for a team. In forecasting outcomes for games, one would like to know about both variability and strength. Estimating variability for each team would be a troublesome job and would probably require considerable sophistication both in model-building and data analysis. It is needed to provide good estimates of odds. It may be that this could be done roughly.

As a side study, I looked at the top eight teams in my 1971 ratings. For games where the teams played one another during the regular season, I subtracted the score of the team with a poorer rating from that of the team with the better rating. That distribution had a standard deviation of about 10. Very roughly, this means that if strong teams play each other and one is 1 point better than the other (in the long run), then its chance of winning is about 0.54 instead of the 0.50 it would have had if they had been even. Two points would give 0.58, but it is probably nonlinear after that. I merely emphasize here that variability matters.

5. *Adjust for "at home" and "away."* One needs to keep track of this. It seems to change a bit from year to year and from conference to conference.

6. *Adjust for trends.* Over and above differential weights for weeks, we could afford to try to pay attention to trends. This would be a way of detecting

that some team was losing important players because of serious injuries or was having its strengths "found out" and adjusted for by other teams.

If we later reanalyze the football data using an alternative method, we will probably look for the team trends for the season. We could do it now with our current analysis but there are some drawbacks, and because we would be computerized in the alternative analysis, it would be best to do it by machine. Otherwise it is a tiresome, long job and hard to keep accurate.

7. *Develop scores for injuries.*   From newspaper or inside accounts, we could discover the extent of a team's injuries and gradually develop adjustments for such information.

No doubt others will suggest items, H, I, J, and so on. But these items are enough to make clear that even without trying to assess soft variables like morale, a serious attack on game by game forecasting could profitably use more effort on outside variables than we have exerted here. An example of such an effort before the 1972 season is Stat-Key®, shown in *Game Plan Magazine Pro Football*, 1972, pp. 13–17.

One should not suppose that making such developments is an entirely frivolous venture. It would be hard to do a good job of such forecasting without developing techniques of significant value to the business community or ideas that would help solve the problems of timeliness and accuracy in government statistics, always a pressing problem. Of course, one is likely to do better sooner on such problems by direct attack, but work in the mathematical sciences often finds happy homes far from its origins.

CONCEPTS OF BETTER

A few people have asked whether the playoff game between Miami and Pittsburgh didn't prove that these ratings were mistaken. Not at all. The ratings deal with history and assess how well the teams performed during the season adjusting for their schedule. That is the task.

1. Games played some other time do not have much relevance to that task.
2. In the excitement of playoff games, fans who know well that much of the fun of sports lies in the uncertainty of the outcome, and who know that when teams play twice they often split or worse yet, the obviously superior team may lose both games, lose their cool, and begin thinking that the outcome of one game shows which team is superior. All that is going on here is a routine mixup of two concepts. What are they?

Concept A. Winning the cup (or pennant or World Series). The team that wins the Super Bowl wins the cup and by the rules of the league it becomes the champion. That is straightforward. No one can argue with this.

Concept B. Superiority. If these teams, with their present strength, age, composition, and skill, could somehow keep playing this game over day after day, year after year, recuperating every night to present strength, Team *A* would win most of those games. Team *A* would then be superior to Team *B*. This long-run concept, though hard to keep in mind in the excitement of a playoff game, is actually well understood by sports fans during the off-season when they say such things as "Well, if they played again, I'd bet on *X* (the team that lost)." In this concept, better is not observable directly; sometimes we say it is a latent attribute.

Consequently, although the higher ranking of Miami against Washington in 1972 could be used to predict the Super Bowl outcome, and indeed the prediction to be correct, one 14–7 score does not do a great deal to strengthen our belief in Miami's superiority, especially when we think of a standard deviation of 10 points, which is larger than the difference of 7 observed. We would get a difference bigger than 7 half the time if the teams were perfectly matched. In the same way, a 4-point difference between Miami and Pittsburgh adds little to our knowledge about the relative strengths of the teams, no matter which way it goes.

One can go a little way on this by thinking of the first half and second half as two "short games" and recalling how different they often are.

Concept C. How well a team performs on the average gives its rating. We think of a team as playing every team many times, and we credit it with its scoring advantage over each team. Then its average performance, with the extremes weighted lightly, gives the rating. This idea is the one we use. It correlates closely with Concept B, but not exactly. For example, if a team always beat every team it played by one point it will be rated below a team that wins by large scores ¾ of the time and loses ¼ of the time. It must be remembered that every index has features that violate some of our preferences. Just who wins this race depends on the average chosen.

RELIABILITY OF DIFFERENCES

To repeat, for the regular season, Miami was rated here as ahead of Washington. Accepting our rating process for the purpose of this discussion, we have a considerable amount of evidence that Miami is a little better. But we do not have infinitely many games. There is some uncertainty in the final ratings I have given, as there will be in any such rating scheme. Won–lost records have the same problem. They are the *results* of Concept B. When we think about them as *estimates* of the *long-run ordering* that Concept B would provide, we appreciate their variability. I have not estimated these uncertainties, but probably it could be done.

Let us remember that if a lot of people pair off, match coins to see who is "better," and then the winners pair off again, as in a tennis ladder, or the

football playoffs, and continue matching, and so on, then in the end there is one winner—Concept A. But recalling Concept B, if the coins *are all fair*, then actually these people *were all equally good* at matching. The outcome proved nothing about superiority.

HOW OFTEN DOES THE BEST TEAM WIN?

That raised the question, given the sorts of differences between the football teams that actually exist: What is the chance that the *best* of the eight teams (Concept B) entering the playoffs actually is the Super Bowl winner? Mind you, we will never know which team is best, but we might figure out the answer to this question all the same. I did once figure out that the probability that the better team won the World Series is .85. That was quite a while ago. It may be less now. It is remarkable that we don't need to know the name of the better team to make this estimate. You may be amused to know that Lewis Carroll, author of *Alice in Wonderland*, computed the probability that the second-best man in a tennis ladder arranged at random would be runner-up when the better man always won. We are asking a harder question because we admit the better team doesn't always win.

ASPECTS OF TRIMEANS

Some have asked why I "throw away" the extreme games and why three instead of one, two, or four.

1. I do not throw away anything! I order the data for the 14 games (see Table 13.2). Then after the ordering I take an average which weights some observations near the middle higher and weights the end ones zero. They counted, though, because they helped decide which measurements were in the middle.

2. Why three? It has nothing to do with football. A great many theoretical and empirical studies show that if one has data contaminated by outliers (like runaway games) and wants to measure where the center of the true distribution is, taking some advantage of the middle 50% (give or take a few percent) of the numbers usually is better than giving them all equal weight as we do when we take a mean. The idea is that a robust method will give almost the same answer if a few numbers are changed a lot. Means do not have this property. One wild observation has a big effect on the whole analysis when we use means. The three is approximately one-quarter of the number of measurements, here 14.

3. Accepting the three, why the trimean? Studies show that it is often more reliable than the median, which would be an important competitor (a competitor that does *not* "throw away" all but one observation). I could have averaged the middle eight numbers. One reason I didn't was that it was more work. I was working by hand. I was tempted to use the median, but I thought the trimean would be better. The grounds are not presented in this chapter but in the extensive research done by other scholars..

4. Why not use won–lost records? Wouldn't they provide a resistant analysis? Yes, I could develop such an analysis and adjust for schedule. There were three reasons I didn't. First, I already knew a good deal about that. Second, I thought the result wouldn't be as reliable as the analysis I did because I believed it would disregard some valuable information. Proving that I am right or wrong about that might require a serious effort. Third, the problems I am likely to use this method on in serious work will rarely be of the won–lost type with only one or two comparisons (games) between objects (teams).

5. Might an analysis using medians or the midmean (average of the middle eight scores) give a different ranking from the one given? Yes, a little. Well, then, which is right? Each is right on its own terms. I can express some preferences based on research, but slight rearrangements of the rankings will not upset me. For example, if the first and second teams are far apart, then both methods should tell that. If they are nearly equal, both methods should also tell that. Once they are nearly equal, I know the season isn't long enough to give me strong likelihood that the top rated one is really superior in the Concept B sense. And so, although I am as interested as others in outcomes (Concept A), I am not greatly impressed by small differences in ratings between teams. They might readily change with changed measures, but I would not be impressed with the sizes of the differences.

ACKNOWLEDGMENTS

I wish to express my appreciation to Mrs. Cleo Youtz, who carried out and checked the calculations that are presented here.

REFERENCES

The 1971 scores used in this analysis were printed in:
  The Football News, January 1, 1972, p.4.
The 1972 scores were taken either from the:
  Boston Herald American (formerly *Herald Traveler and Record American*), or from *The Boston Globe* the day after games were played.
Tukey, W. *Exploratory data analysis*. Reading, Mass.: Addison-Wesley, 1977.

14
Outcomes in Professional Team Sports: Chance, Skill, and Situational Factors

Jeffrey H. Goldstein
Temple University

ASSUMPTIONS ABOUT SPORTS

One of the most fundamental assumptions made about professional team sports—one, indeed, that is made in most of the chapters in this book—is that success (winning) is an indication of a team's superiority. It has been estimated that over $150 billion are wagered each year on professional sports in America (Michener, 1976, p.406; see also Merchant, 1973). Underlying most gambling is the assumption that some teams are better than others and are, therefore, likely to defeat their opponents in a particular game or series of games. It is this assumption of superiority that not only fosters gambling in sports, but keeps millions of people so highly involved in football, baseball, basketball, horse racing, soccer, and hockey.

How does one know whether Team *A* is better than Team *B*? Because *A* defeats *B*. Why does *A* defeat *B*? Because it is better. This kind of circular reasoning lies behind most devotees' attachment to a team. Because the notion of team superiority is so widely shared, it is generally unquestioned. The consequences of *not* making this assumption are great. The World Series, the Super Bowl, the Stanley Cup, the Olympic Games—all these become meaningless for many spectators, and indeed for many participants, unless it is assumed that such contests determine the best team. (Of course, even if

JEFFREY GOLDSTEIN is Professor of Psychology and former Director of Social Psychology at Temple University. He is author of *Aggression and Crimes of Violence* and editor, with Paul McGhee, of *The Psychology of Humor*. He turned to psychology when it became clear that he would play neither basketball in Madison Square Garden nor the guitar in Carnegie Hall.

superiority is not determined by such competitions the games may be meaningful on an altogether different level, and this will be discussed subsequently; see also Goldstein & Bredemeier, 1977).

Let us take a skeptical view of professional team sports. We begin with the assumption that winning and losing are chance or random events, unless they can otherwise be demonstrated to be caused by some specifiable set of factors. Taking this vewpoint immediately calls into question a host of beliefs and presuppositions:

1. Competitions to determine which team is most skilled (such as the World Series, Olympics, Super Bowl, etc.) are capable of doing so.

2. The quality of players on a team is an important determinant of team success.

3. Management is influential in team performance.

4. Betting on professional team sports is meaningful (i.e., nonrandom), because the outcome of a game or series of games is systematically determined.

Given a professional football game between,say, the Pittsburgh Steelers and the Oakland Raiders, a true skeptic will bet on whichever side comes up in the toss of a coin. To the person betting, the odds that the Steelers will win any given game is 50–50 (excluding ties). In fact, the odds in any two-team game will always be 50–50 regardless of where the game is to be played, what the weather is, who the coaches are, who the players are, and what each team's won–lost record is. To do otherwise would be to assume that some factor or factors systematically influence the outcome of the game. In order to evaluate the outcome of some future game at other than 50–50, the skeptic would need evidence either that one team is superior to another or that some other nonrandom factors influence game outcome.

Most people seem to assume that certain teams are better than others because they have particular players or coaches who are deemed especially proficient. A team with several superstars is assumed to win because of them. The skeptic's interpretation of team personnel is somewhat different. In a good many professional team sports, football and basketball among them, there is a draft lottery that acts to equalize the quality of a team's players. This is accomplished by taking the team with the worst won–lost record from the preceding year and allowing it the first draft choice for the following year. Assuming that there is a homogeneous population of able college talent, the pro draft works to the equalization of teams from one year to the next. That such equalization actually occurs can be seen in Table 14.1, which shows the average weight of each professional football team for 1972. That the deviations from the league average are so slight suggests that all the teams were drawn from same population. Naturally, if we were to be concerned

TABLE 14.1
Mean Player Weight: 1972 NFL[a]

Team	Mean Weight	Deviation from League Average
American Football Conference		
Baltimore	220.25	2.26
Buffalo	225.04	2.53
Cincinnati	221.75	0.76
Cleveland	225.50	2.99
Denver	224.58	2.07
Houston	225.76	3.25
Kansas City	224.61	2.10
Miami	220.33	2.18
New England	218.85	3.66
New York Jets	218.68	3.83
Oakland	226.15	3.64
Pittsburgh	224.22	1.71
San Diego	225.08	2.57
National Football Conference		
Atlanta	223.39	0.88
Chicago	226.31	3.80
Dallas	221.55	0.96
Detroit	221.24	1.27
Green Bay	223.80	1.29
Los Angeles	222.31	0.20
Minnesota	220.30	2.21
New Orleans	218.12	4.39
New York Giants	221.46	1.05
Philadelphia	222.46	0.05
St. Louis	222.27	0.24
San Francisco	219.59	2.92
Washington	220.26	2.25

[a]Data are from *The Complete Handbook of Pro Football* (New York: Lancer, 1973). Mean player weight for the entire league ($n = 1268$) = 222.51 pounds.

with individual players rather than with teams, there would be some players who were heavier, taller, younger, stronger or faster than others. On the average, however, all teams are probably equivalent in terms of physical characteristics of their players.

Given teams that are comparable in terms of player characteristics, our skeptic would place the odds on any game at 50–50. Experience, however, suggests that even-odds are not always the best assumption. In 1972, for example, the Miami Dolphins won 14 games and lost none. The Houston Oilers won one and lost 13. Clearly, one would have to argue that in 1972, the

Dolphins were significantly better than the Oilers. It is unlikely that these two won-lost records would occur by chance (the probability of such a chance occurrence is less than one in 3000). How does the skeptic account for such dramatic differences? There are two possible responses that he or she might have. The first is that over any relatively short series of "trials" (each game counting as a trial), there are apt to be occasional statistical flukes. If a fair coin is flipped only 14 times, on occasion it will come up 11 or 12 heads. However, if it were flipped some 10,000 trials, there would be a more equal number of heads to tails. Although it may appear at particular times that the coin is biased, in the long run it indeed proves to be a fair coin operating on random principles. Similarly with football games. In the relatively few trials in a football season (14 in 1972), there are bound to be occasional runs that appear to be nonrandom. If the season were extended to several hundred games, however, the won-lost record of each team would approximate 50% wins. In the considerably greater number of games in a professional baseball season, the percent of games won typically falls between 35 and 65 (see Cook, 1966).

NONSKILL FACTORS IN OUTCOMES

Another possible response from our skeptic is that nonrandom factors *other than skill* act to determine the outcome of a game or series of games. Although we are dealing here with nonrandom events they are not generally those that the sports fan or gambler thinks of as causing game outcomes. Such factors as team morale, attitudes of the home-team crowd, whether the team had a good flight on the way to the game, whether they are playing at home or away, and so on, may influence the outcome of a game. Just as there are "mudders" in horse racing, so, too, might extraneous factors influence the outcomes of other sports. These factors might be considered nonskill, extra–personal, or *situational* variables. We could, for example, operationally define morale as a function of two independent variables, and then examine the effects of morale on winning and losing. As a demonstration of how extra-personal factors may influence outcomes in professional football, let us define team morale as influenced by winning or losing the previous game and by the location of the present game. Morale would be considered highest if a team was about to play at home (Fisher, 1976, p. 3; see also Chapter 15, this volume) and if it had won its previous game. It would be lowest if it had lost the previous game and was about to play away against a team that had won its previous game. If we wanted to predict the outcome of a game from these variables alone, we could assign a team the highest probability of winning if it: (1) won its previous game; (2) was playing an opponent who had lost its previous game; and (3) was playing a home game. Table 14.2 shows the outcomes of the 1972

TABLE 14.2
Professional Football Games Won as a Function of
Extra-Personal Factors

Number of Favorable Conditions	N	% Won
0	29	27.6
1	122	45.1
2	121	52.9
3	32	75.0

Note: Ties excluded from this analysis. Favorable conditions = home game, won previous game, opponent lost previous game. Unfavorable = away game, lost previous game, opponent won previous game.

professional football games based only on these factors. We can see that this operational definition of morale is capable of predicting outcomes at better than a chance level ($\chi 2 = 23.2$, $p < .01$).

It is thus possible to predict the outcome of professional team sports by reference largely to extraneous, situational variables (see Chapter 15, this volume; and Schwartz & Barsky, 1977). This is not to say that they alone are the sole determinants of outcome. What determines previous wins and losses in the above analysis, for example, is left unspecified. The purpose of this brief exposition is simply to raise a number of questions about the assumptions underlying much of the analysis of sport. As Gaskell and Pearton (Chapter 10) note, there are a number of latent propositions about sports that might be raised for question. This analysis does raise a number of such questions. The assumption that there are systematic personality and sensori-motor skills associated with athletic team success can be questioned, at least insofar as professional team sports are concerned where players are drawn from a large and fairly homogeneous population. The emphasis placed on winning, both by athletes and fans, as well as by researchers in the social psychology of sport, may be questioned. The notion that winning is an indication of superiority is undermined by the finding that extraneous factors can, statistically speaking, account for considerable variance in outcome. There is some anecdotal evidence that supports this argument. One of the most often heard statements by coaches and players prior to a professinal football, basketball, or hockey game is that "on any given day, any team is capable of defeating any other team." If this is so, then it must be attributable to nonskill factors; otherwise, the "best" team would always win.

This analysis raises two questions that I would like to explore in somewhat more detail. Why is the belief so persistent that skill is related to winning? And, if game outcome is not as strongly associated with superiority as is commonly believed, what does this bode for professional team sports?

PERSISTENCE OF THE "SKILL = SUCCESS" BELIEF

Why do players, coaches and sports fans so firmly hold to the belief that players' and coaches' abilities influence the outcome of a game? One reason probably has to do with the almost endless details of most games that are available to the devotee. There is something nearly mystical, for example, about baseball statistics. As a youngster, I knew the batting average of every New York Yankee—and the averages changed from day to day; the starting lineups of every American League team; the earned run average of most of the league's pitchers; the number of home runs hit by every player. I knew, too, schoolmates who could recite these and other statistics not only for the current season but for every season over the past two or three decades. There are millions of Americans who commit these statistics to memory. Such statistics are real: these computations have a hard existence, they are in most newspapers every day, and books of sports records abound. With such hard data before them, how can people be expected to conclude that the final outcome of the season is a random occurrence? Because of the many statistical realities of sports, the millions of correlations that can be computed from them, the meaning that can be read into them, it is difficult to dismiss them as the mere side effects of fate.[1]

There is a good deal of psychological theory and research that bears directly on the belief that what may be essentially random events are often interpreted causally. Ellen Langer (1975) has proposed a number of hypotheses on the "illusion of control." To the extent that one perceives choices, one tends to think of outcomes as caused. For instance, if a football coach can put either Johnson or Smith in as quarterback, then he is apt to believe that the outcome of the game was influenced by that decision. If Johnson is put in and the team wins, then that verifies the correctness of the decision. Likewise, the quarterback must make hundreds of decisions during a game and so is also likely to believe that he influenced the outcome of the game. To the extent that options are available, outcomes seem nonrandom. This is probably as true for spectators. Knowing that coaches and players have options available to them increases the belief that players and coaches have an effect on outcome (see Ayeroff & Abelson, 1976; Gamson & Scotch, 1964).

It would not come as a surprise to most sports fans to learn that successful outcomes are apt to be seen as personally caused, while losses are likely to be interpreted as extra-personally caused. A fan, player or coach whose team has just won a game is likely to point to the marvelous defense of the tackle, the important interception in the fourth quarter, the fine passing of the

---

[1]The same is true of analyses of the stock market (see Malkiel, 1973).

quarterback. A fan, player or coach whose team has just lost a game is more likely to refer to the tough break in the third quarter, the bad refereeing, the slippery Astro-turf, or the plain bad luck that only just prevented a winning touchdown. There is considerable experimental evidence that supports such an interpretation in other, nonsports, contexts (e.g., Cohen, 1964; Hastorf & Cantril, 1954; Kelley, 1976; Langer & Roth, 1975; Weiner *et al.*, 1971).

If professional team sports have random or extra-personal outcomes, there are still enough decisions to be made within them, enough complexity and subtlety, to foster the illusion that they are contests of skill. This is one reason that post-season analyses of statistics are so appealing: they provide order and meaning where none was present.

I do not contend that all professional sports are randomly determined. Certainly individual contests—such as tennis and golf—are likely to be determined largely by skill factors, although extraneous factors may also play an important role. Team sports are more susceptible to nonskill factors, and professional team sports more than amateur sports. My primary purpose is to raise for discussion the point that outcome may be based on chance and situational variables.

IMPLICATIONS OF NONSKILL OUTCOMES

If it is true that the outcomes of professional team sports are less than perfectly correlated with superiority, what are the implications for sports? There are several perhaps, both for the participant and the fan. The most obvious is that the emphasis on winning is misplaced and should probably be shifted away from outcome to other aspects of sports, to what has been referred to elsewhere as process characteristics of sports (Goldstein & Bredemeier, 1977). To the extent that nonskill factors rather than superiority determine outcome, then winning is not only *not* the only thing, it is hardly anything at all. But it still matters how the game is played: It can be played with finesse, with grace, daring and beauty. One can still attempt to engage in strategic battles with limited ends in mind (see Chapter 8), for even if outcomes are random, there is still sufficient variability to allow for strategic maneuvering within a game. If the emphasis on winning is diminished, there should be a corresponding increase in the intrinsic motivations and satisfactions inherent in sports.

ACKNOWLEDGMENTS

I gratefully acknowledge the assistance of David D. S. Poor and Carole Oglesby, who provided helpful comments on a preliminary draft of this chapter.

REFERENCES

Ayeroff, F., & Abelson, R. P. ESP and ESB: Belief in personal success at mental telepathy. *Journal of Personality and Social Psychology*, 1976, *34*, 240–247.

Cialdini, R. B., Borden, R. J., Thorne, A., Walker, M. R., Freeman, S., & Sloan, L. R. Basking in reflected glory: Three (football) field studies. *Journal of Personality and Social Psychology*, 1976, *34*, 366–375.

Cohen, J. *Behavior in uncertainty.* London: Unwin, 1964.

Cook, E. (with W. R. Garner). *Percentage baseball.* Cambridge, Mass.: MIT Press, 1966.

Fisher, A. C. *The psychology of sport.* Palo Alto, Calif.: Mayfield, 1976.

Gamson, W. A., & Scotch, N. Scapegoating in baseball. *American Journal of Sociology*, 1964, *70*, 69–72.

Goldstein, J. H., & Bredemeier, B. J. Sports and socialization: Some basic issues. *Journal of Communication*, 1977, *27*, 154–159.

Hastorf, A. H., & Cantril, H. They saw a game: A case study. *Journal of Abnormal and Social Psychology*, 1954, *49*, 129–134.

Kelley, H. H. Attribution theory in social psychology. In D. Levine (Ed.), *Nebraska Symposium of Motivation* (Vol. 15). Lincoln: University of Nebraska Press, 1967.

Langer, E. J. The illusion of control. *Journal of Personality and Social Psychology*, 1975, *32*, 311–328.

Langer, E. J., & Roth, J. Heads I win, tails it's chance: Illusion of control as a function of sequence of outcomes in a purely chance task. *Journal of Personality and Social Psychology*, 1975, *32*, 951–955.

Malkiel, B. G. *A random walk down Wall Street.* New York: Norton, 1973.

Merchant, L. *The national football lottery.* New York: Rinehart & Winston, 1973.

Michener, J. A. *Sports in America.* New York: Random House, 1976.

Schwartz, B., & Barsky, S. F. The home advantage. *Social Forces*, 1977, *55*, 641–661.

Weiner, B., Frieze, I., Kukla, A., Reed, L., Rest, S., & Rosenbaum, R. M. Perceiving the causes of success and failure. In E. E. Jones, D. E. Kanouse, H. H. Kelley, R. E. Nisbett, S. Valins, & B. Weiner (Eds.), *Attribution.* Morristown, N.J.: General Learning Press, 1971.

15 The Home-Field Advantage

John Edwards
Loyola University of Chicago

INTRODUCTION

Sports lore has long held that a team playing on its home ground has an advantage over its opponent. Many experts such as coaches, players and sportswriters give as much attention to the home-field advantage as to almost any other factor that might determine the outcome of a contest—at least in some sports. For example, in an informal content analysis of the sports pages of Chicago newspapers during a 2-week period in late 1975, more references were found to the difficulty of defeating a team on its home ground than to any other single factor such as the talent of, or injuries to, key players, momentum, and so on. On the other hand, since in most sports each team plays only about one-half of its games on its home field, there must be other important factors that determine a team's success. Otherwise, each team would have about the same record.

Despite the pervasive concern about and belief in the home-field advantage, there has been little systematic research by social scientists on this phenomenon, nor has there been a theoretical analysis of its possible causes. We first examine some statistics from several sports with the aim of documenting the home-field advantage and some of its possible limitations.

JOHN EDWARDS, Associate Professor of Social Psychology at Loyola University, received his B.S., M.A., and Ph.D. degrees from The Ohio State University. As a graduate student, his office was under the football stadium which probably stimulated his interest in the home field advantage. In addition to being a sports fan and competent athlete (at least in his own back yard), Dr. Edwards has published numerous articles on values, person perception and attitude change.

Second, we review some of the theories about social behavior that seem relevant to explaining this phenomenon. Particular attention is given to the notion of territoriality based on the writings of ethologists and environmental psychologists, and to the idea of social facilitation/inhibition originating in the work of social psychologists. Finally, we briefly explore the possible relevance of the home field advantage in other arenas of competition such as politics and warfare.

LOOKING FOR THE HOME-FIELD ADVANTAGE IN VARIOUS SPORTS

Football

Perhaps the most important sport in America today in terms of the size and recent growth of attendance, degree of live media coverage, and annual expenditure is football. This popular sport was selected for a somewhat detailed analysis in order to determine the extent of the home-field advantage. Football, as with many other sports, is played at many levels from informal sandlot games among children to professional contests in mammoth stadiums among some of the most highly paid individuals in our society. It is possible that the home-field advantage would be different among the different types of players. Professional teams might show less of an effect if for no other reason than that they are professionals and have more experience in playing under a variety of conditions. For this reason, some comparisons were made between professional and college teams.

Using various sources such as the newspaper, *Sporting News*, and the press guides provided by the professional leagues, the results of 349 professional and 577 college football games played during the 1974, 1975, and 1976 seasons, spread about evenly across the season, were selected. Considering the professional games, 190 or 54.4% were won by the home team. According to the binomial test (Siegal, 1956), this percentage is not statistically significantly different from the theoretical percentage (50.0%), assuming that each team has an equal chance of winning ($z = 1.61$, $p < .107$, two-tailed). Such a winning percentage would, of course, be different from chance if it were to hold up using a larger sample of games. An examination of the points scored in these 349 games reveals that the home-field advantage, while statistically marginal, would be sufficient for making a difference between winning and losing. The average number of points scored by home teams was 21.08, while the average number of points scored by visitors was 18.29. As a further check, games were divided into those won by the home team versus those won by the visitors. Table 15.1 shows the mean number of points scored and points given up for both sets of winners. These figures indicate an average

TABLE 15.1
Mean Number of Points Scored and Given Up in 349
Professional Football Games by Home and
Visiting Winning Teams

	Home Winners	Visiting Winners
Points scored	27.03	25.45
Points given up	12.29	13.97

point spread margin of victory by home team winners of 14.74 points while visiting team winners had an average margin of 11.48 points. Examination of "points for" versus "points against" indicates that these differences in victory margins were about equally due to offense and to defense proficiency. That is, home winners scored 1.58 points more per game than did visiting winners, and home winners gave up 1.68 fewer points than visiting winners. Thus, in terms of mean points scored and margin of victory, home teams in the professional ranks had about a 3-point advantage.

Considering the college games, 338 or 58.6% were won by the home team. This margin over the theoretical 50.0% figure is highly significant statistically according to the binomial test ($z = 4.14$, $p < .00006$, two-tailed). The average number of points scored by home and visiting teams were 23.08 and 17.63, respectively. Table 15.2 shows the points for and against the home winners versus the visiting winners. The average point spread for home winners is 19.12 while for visiting winners the average margin is 13.89. Examining the "points for" and the "points against" reveals that this difference in point spreads is somewhat due more to offense than defense. That is, home winners scored 3.41 more points per victory than did visiting winners, while giving up 1.82 fewer points. Thus, in terms of mean points scored and the margin of victory, college home teams had slightly more than a 5-point average.

In general, both professional and college football game outcomes show that being the home team is a factor in winning—although the effect was higher for the college teams in this sample of games. As a further test of this

TABLE 15.2
Mean Number of Points Scored and Given Up in 577
College Football Games by Home and
Visiting Winning Teams

	Home Winners	Visiting Winners
Points scored	30.25	26.84
Points given up	11.13	12.95

difference, the point spreads for home winners versus visiting winners were compared for college and professional teams using a 2 × 2 analysis of variance. This analysis confirmed that the point spread was greater for college than professional victors [$F(1,922) = 8.76$, $p < .005$], that the point spreads were larger for home winners than visiting winners [$F(1,922) = 5.43, p < .025$], and that there was no interaction between these two factors [$F(1,922) = .19$]. These statistics correspond with common assumptions and previous findings. For example, Schwartz and Barsky (cited in Lane, 1976) found that in a sample of 410 college games played during 1971, 60% were won by home teams; and in 182 professional football games played in 1971, 58% were won by the local team. Altman (1975) reported that over a 3-year period the University of Utah football team won two-thirds of its home games and less than one-half of its away games.

The finding of a home-field advantage in football, while seemingly reliable in general, may not always be a helpful guide for the sports gambler. We found that on any given weekend, the percentage of home winners among the pro teams ranged from over 70% to less than 30% while among college teams the range was from slightly less than 70% to slightly more than 40%. These figures also indicate that the home effect is more reliable for the college teams in this sample. A week-by-week analysis of the professional games showed a nonsignificant tendency for the home effect to increase over the season. That is, in the first half of the season, home teams won only 52% of the time while they won 58% in the latter half ($X^2 = 1.53, p > .20$). Among college teams, this trend was reversed with the home teams winning 64% early in the season and 52% at the second half ($X^2 = 8.94$, $p < .005$). The general impression that arises from inspecting the weekly fluctuations is that they may be due to scheduling. That is, a very high percentage of home team victories in any given week may be the result of the coincidence of many of the better teams playing on their home turf against less effective opponents. In order to further investigate this possibility as well as to explore some of the potential origins of the home team advantage in terms of specific skills, a more in-depth analysis was performed on the results of a sample of professional football games played in 1976.

For this analysis, over 100 games were selected from the 1976 professional football season. For each game, both home and visiting teams were categorized according to whether they had winning or losing records at the time each game was played. (Categorization for games selected from the first week of the season was based on the team's 1975 record.) Teams that had .500 records were deleted. This resulted in a final sample of 97 games with each team assigned to one of four "conditions" (i.e., being either a home or visiting team, and having either a winning or losing record).

The resulting four types of teams were then compared in terms of 17 variables reflecting performance such as total points scored, number of first

downs, fumbles lost, and others to be described below. These variables were tested in a 2 × 2 multivariate analysis of variance with univariate tests on each of the 17 variables. The mean values on each variable for the two main effects are shown in Table 15.3.

Examination of this table reveals that home teams and teams with winning records were generally more effective than visitors or teams with losing records along the same dimensions. Specifically, home teams and teams with winning records score more points, make more first downs, run more rushing plays, gain more yards rushing, gain more yards passing, have higher completion records, and punt less often than visitors or teams with losing records. There are no differences in other factors such as yardage in returning punts and kickoffs, pass attempts, having passes intercepted, punting average, number of fumbles or fumbles lost, or number of penalties or yards penalized.

It should be noted that the interaction between the home/visitor and winning/losing record factors was not significant for any of the 17 variables. The implication of this important finding is that the home field does not

TABLE 15.3
Comparison of Home Versus Visitors and Teams with Winning Versus Losing
Records on 17 Performance Variables

Variables	Home	Visitors	Winning Record	Losing Record
1. Total points	21.6	15.5 (.001)	21.9	15.2 (.001)
2. Number of first downs	19.1	16.3 (.001)	19.6	15.8 (.001)
3. Total rushing plays	39.4	34.3 (.001)	38.9	34.8 (.003)
4. Net yards rushing	162.4	136.6 (.004)	160.0	139.0 (.020)
5. Total yards passing	174.3	139.9 (.009)	187.3	126.9 (.001)
6. Total yards gained	325.8	276.9 (.001)	336.6	266.1 (.001)
7. Return yards	70.3	66.2 (.605)	60.7	75.7 (.071)
8. Passes attempted	25.7	26.7 (.298)	26.6	25.7 (.367)
9. Passes completed	14.1	13.4 (.385)	14.7	12.8 (.009)
10. Percent pass completions	54.8	50.3 (.051)	55.2	49.9 (.050)
11. Passes had intercepted	1.0	1.3 (.076)	1.1	1.2 (.233)
12. Attempted punts	5.7	6.6 (.067)	5.5	6.8 (.017)
13. Average punt yards	38.2	39.2 (.144)	38.2	39.2 (.099)
14. Number of fumbles	2.1	2.3 (.439)	2.1	2.3 (.617)
15. Fumbles lost	1.1	1.2 (.662)	1.2	1.1 (.791)
16. Number of penalties	6.9	6.7 (.531)	6.7	6.9 (.724)
17. Yards penalized	58.7	55.8 (.467)	56.1	58.4 (.562)

Note: The numbers in parentheses are the probability levels for the home/visitor and winning/losing record main effects from the univariate F tests. For example, the difference between home and visitors and between winning and losing teams on the total points variable was significant at beyond the .001 level ($df = 1,190$ in all cases).

combine in any synergistic fashion with a team's overall effectiveness due to other factors such as player talent. Rather, the home-field advantage and having a winning record combine in a more or less additive fashion in such a way that home teams with winning records are the most effective and visiting teams with losing records are the least.

No unambiguous conclusions can be drawn from such results as to whether the home field advantage or the superiority of winning teams resides in offensive rather than defensive proficiency. Any statistic could reflect either an offensive strength of a home/winner or a defensive weakness of a visitor/loser, or some combination of both. However, some indication regarding the relative role of each of the variables can be obtained by examining the correlations among the variables and their relationship to the criterion of total points scored. For home teams, the variables that were most highly correlated with total score were: number of first downs ($r = .74$), total yards ($r = .71$), number of attempted punts ($r = -.68$), yards rushing ($r = .56$) and number of rushing plays ($r = .53$). All other correlations were smaller than $\pm.50$. For visiting teams, the variables most associated with total points were: total yards ($r = .75$), number of first downs ($r = .72$), yards passing ($r = .59$), and yards rushing ($r = .50$). Thus, home teams and visitors differ somewhat in the variables associated with scoring points with home teams apparently superior in factors relating to ball control.

A factor analysis of these correlations (varimax rotation) yielded four interpretable factors that accounted for over 93% of the variance. Factor I, "Ground Control," (accounting for 40% of the variance) had loadings of .70 or greater on the following variables: number of first downs, number of rushing plays, yards rushing, total yards, and (for home teams only) low number of attempted punts. Factor II, "Passing," (accounting for 21% of the variance) had loadings of .70 or greater for: number of passing attempts, number of pass completions, and percent completion, with total yards passing loading somewhat lower. Factor III, "Penalties," (accounting for 17% of the variance) included number of penalties and yards penalized with loadings of .70 or greater. Factor IV, "Fumbles" (accounting for 15% of the variance), included number of fumbles and number of fumbles lost with loadings greater than .70.

Based upon this particular set of variables, therefore, the most important factors involved in scoring points—whether by home or visiting teams—are controlling the ball on the ground, an effective passing attack, and minimizing penalties and fumbles. It is conceivable that other factors not included here such as percentage of third down conversions, "sacking" the quarterback, and so on, would also be good predictors of scoring. It is also possible that other factors or combinations of factors would emerge as important with other samples of games (Marshall, 1974). Nevertheless, these data are consistent with a fundamentalist approach to football that

emphasizes the running game supplemented by passing and reducing mistakes.

In summary, our findings, along with those of other investigators, support the expectation of a home-field advantage in football. Home teams win about 55% to 60% of their games by margins of up to about the equivalent of one touchdown. The effect appears somewhat stronger in college than in the professional ranks. This advantage is reflected in various offensive statistics. In our professional sample, the home team on the average chalked up about three more first downs, ran about five more rushing plays, gained 25 more yards rushing and nearly 35 more yards passing, completed a greater proportion of passes, and (as a result) had to punt about one less time per game than their visiting opponents. The avoidance of mistakes such as penalties and fumbles were less discriminating factors. In addition, the figures shown in Table 15.3 indicate that other factors that contribute to a team's overall record are at least as important as the home field in determining game outcome. For example, in the 1976 professional season in the games sampled, teams with winning records going into a game won 65.7% of their games, teams with losing records won only 35.4% of their games, and teams with .500 records at the time of a game won 43.8% of their games. It was very rare for a team with a winning record to lose on its home field—especially to a visitor with a losing record. In those cases when "losers" upset "winners," it occurred almost invariably on the "losers" home field. The following sections are concerned with the generalizability of the home field effect to other sports.

Baseball

The consensus of newspaper sportswriters and radio and TV newscasters we contacted was that a home-field advantage would be least likely to occur among the major sports in baseball. To see whether the game traditionally called the national pastime is indeed immune from home-field effects, we examined the 1975 records of four professional teams. Two teams from both the National and American leagues were selected at random with the restriction that one had an overall winning record for the year and the other an overall losing record. The results of 288 home games played by these four teams showed that 160 or 55.6% were won by the home team. According to the binomial test, this result is only marginally significant ($z = 1.83, p < .067$, two-tailed). Of course, if this percentage were to hold up for a larger sample, it would be significant statistically. However, in terms of runs scored, home teams averaged 4.40 per game while visiting teams averaged 4.25, yielding a nonsignificant average point spread.

As with the football scores, the total runs were compared for home winners versus visiting winners. Home winners outscored their opponents by 5.7 to 2.4, or an average spread of 3.3 runs. Visiting winners outscored their hosts by

an average of 6.5 to 2.8, or an average spread of 3.7 runs. In other words, while home team winners gave up about 0.4 fewer runs per game than visiting winners, they also scored about 0.8 fewer runs themselves. Thus, in terms of proportion of games won, there was a slight home-field advantage, but this was not reflected in terms of average runs or margins of victory. This suggests that home teams were more effective in winning close games.

In the football results, it was found that having a winning record was comparable to the home-field advantage in terms of determining game outcomes. A similar analysis was done with baseball scores by comparing games in which the home team had a winning record at the time of the game versus home teams who were below .500 at the time of the game. Of the 160 games won by home teams, 118 or 73.8% were won by the teams that had winning records at the time of the game ($z = 5.93$, $p < .0001$); and they won by an average margin of 5.6 to 2.2. Home winners who had losing records at the time of the game outscored their opponents by 5.9 to 3.1; that is, home teams with losing records both scored and gave up more runs than home teams with winning records. In the 128 games won by visitors, only 60 or 46.9% were against those home teams having a winning record at the time of the game; their spread was 5.8 to 2.6. When visitors prevailed over home teams with losing records, they won by an average of 7.2 to 2.9. Taken together, these findings suggest that a team's record is more important than whether or not they are playing at home or away, and that the home field does not produce consistent or significant advantages in terms of runs scored or given up. Home teams who win tend to do so in close, low scoring games. Perhaps this stems from the technical advantage in baseball that allows home teams to bat last when behind or tied.

In their sample of over 1800 major league baseball games, Schwartz and Barsky (cited in Lane, 1976) also found a slight advantage for home teams (i.e., home teams won 53% of their games). They concluded that this effect is due more to offensive than defensive action. Both home and visitors made 2.3 defensive errors for each 100 times their opponents were at bat, but they found home teams averaged nearly 4 more runs per 100 times at bat, and collected slightly more total hits and extra base hits than visitors. These differences, while modest, could be sufficient in a "game of inches" to tip the outcome in the home team's favor.

Other Sports

Of all the major sports, the one nominated most frequently by various experts as most likely to show a home-field advantage is basketball. No less of an authority than Jimmy "The Greek" Snider stated ("Jimmy 'The Greek,' " 1976), "In evaluating pro basketball, the home court is the big factor. Home teams have a 71% rate for success, with increased travel due to expansion and

greater balance the main reasons. Figure the home court to be worth 3 to 7 points depending on the team and the floor [p. 17]." During the 1976 season, none of the NBA teams had a winning road record, while the teams that made the playoffs won over 85% of their home games. The superiority of some teams on their home floor may arise mainly from offensive effectiveness. For example, the Chicago Bulls shooting percentage for both field goals and free throws was nearly 10% higher on the home floor while points given up showed a much less dramatic difference. The same effect appears to hold for some college teams. Schwartz and Barsky (cited in Lane, 1976) reported that the Philadelphia area Big Five college teams won 82% of their home games versus 58% of their away games. Altman (1975) reported that while the University of Utah basketball team won two-thirds of its home games, it won only one-fourth of its away games over a three year period.

As Jimmy "The Greek" implied, some teams are almost never defeated on their home courts. Since all basketball courts have to be the same in many respects (i.e., the playing area is certainly more uniform in size than are baseball parks), the invincibility of certain teams in certain arenas cannot be totally attributed to aspects of the physical environment. It seems to be usually the case that teams with this sort of special advantage are those with great winning traditions (not only at home but also on the road). For example, UCLA, a team that dominated college basketball for a decade, lost less than five home games during that period. Their visiting opponents ran into a self-fulfilling prophecy. No one expected them to win in Pauley Pavillion, and there was little disgrace in losing there.

The idea that success breeds success is reflected in another fashion involving the home-field advantage as well. In some sports such as professional basketball and hockey (which, incidentally, also shows a dramatic home rink effect), the home arena is deemed so valuable that earning the right to play there becomes one of the objectives of an entire season. That is, in a playoff series, usually featuring up to seven games if necessary, the team with the better record is assigned the home field as a reward. That is, four of the seven games are scheduled to be played on the home floor of the team with the better season record. During this short "second season," this system supposedly enhances the chances of the better team winning. It is also a reward for owners, fans, concessionaires and other allies of the winningest team for their support throughout the year.

Individual Sports

Sports are sometimes categorized into two kinds: those involving competition between teams and those involving individual competition. In some sports such as track and field, the individuality of competition is very clear-cut such as when a number of runners are all lunging at the tape at about the same time.

But, of course, in most sports (even between teams) there is also head-to-head competition between individuals. Sports such as baseball and football can be seen as a collection of miniature battles between pitcher and base stealer, wide receiver and defensive halfback.

Individual versus team competition, therefore, does not lie in the type of game itself, but in the reward structure of the situation. Almost any kind of sporting event from boxing to chess can be played by a single individual competing for his or her own sake, or as a member of a team. The Olympic Games is a good case in point. While it is true that some events such as the Decathalon focus on the single athlete, that person is still part of a national team. The effort and performance of a person who is part of a team, whether it means actually interacting with other players to determine the game outcome, or whether it means just wearing the same colors, has an impact not only on the other team members, but also on the spectators who identify with the team. The team member represents not only himself or herself, but also a school, town or nation. In contrast, when a person is competing as an individual, which is the case, for example, in many sports such as boxing, auto racing, bowling, tennis and golf, the athlete's effort and performance has an impact primarily on his or her own rewards and gratifications.

Except for hero worship, there is little that the spectator can identify with in the case of individual competition. Perhaps for this reason individual sports appear to hold somewhat less fascination for sportswriters and statisticians than do team sports in which home town pride may be at stake. With the exception of a few major tournaments, the sports pages and TV-radio newscasts devote less attention to individual sports such as golf and tennis than they do major team sports such as baseball and hockey. Although such comparisons are probably unfair, given the greater number of team as opposed to individual contests, this latter fact may speak for itself. The popularity of a sport among spectators may hinge upon the idea that it is easier to identify with a team that carries the name of a place than to identify with an individual whose glory is hard for others to share.

More important for our purposes is the fact that individual sports, at least at the professional level, are not tied to a home field. Rather, an athlete travels from place to place competing against the same group of other traveling athletes. Only occasionally is any one of the pros in tennis, bowling, golf, and so on in or near his or her home town. Even then there is no guarantee that the player will feel that much at home, compared with other players.

In some cases, though, there could be an advantage for the peripatetic individual due to the moral support of local fans. A number of prize fighters have reported being stimulated to new heights of endurance because of the chants of the home town fans. The same may apply in other sports such as tennis. In commenting on a loss to Jimmy Connors, Vijay Amritrah ("St.

Louis likes Connors," 1977) said, "He was playing in his home town and he is the best. If it had been in my home town, it'd be different—not the result, perhaps, but at least the reception." Connors agreed, "When you get something like that (the home town accolade), you know people appreciate you." In sum, the question of whether a home-field advantage also applies to individual sports is difficult to answer. For one thing, people who compete as individuals as defined here are not strongly identified with a home field since they travel around rather than standing their ground in one place. Moreover, the various factors that are thought to contribute to the home-field advantage to be discussed below, especially the support of local fans who might identify with the winner, are missing. Finally, very little information about the details of performance or the distance of a player from his or her home town is provided or even collected by sports statisticians. However, as the above quotations from the sport of tennis suggest, a player—perhaps especially a good player—may benefit from being on home ground.

Review

The foregoing analysis of the home-field advantage, while selective and far from thorough, contains some common themes. First, there does appear to be a significant advantage to the home field, thus confirming sports lore. Second, this advantage is stronger in some sports such as football and basketball than it is in others such as baseball. Third, on the basis of certain statistics, it appears that the advantage may be somewhat more due to offensive factors leading to scoring points as opposed to defensive factors such as preventing the other side from scoring. This conclusion is tenuous, though, since, as noted earlier, offense and defense are difficult to separate. The ability to get more extra base hits or complete more passes could be due to the enhancement of the home team offense, inhibition of the visitor's defense, or a combination of the two. Fourth, the home field is only one factor in determining the outcome of a contest. The other major factor found here is overall team performance that is probably a reflection of athletic talent. Some teams and individuals are simply better than others regardless of where they play. However, whether a team finishes the season with a winning or losing record is often a consequence of a team's home performance. Most coaches and players count themselves fortunate if they can break even on their road games. What separates winners from losers is the ability to win at home. Those teams with the best records in sports are those who prevail much more than half the time on their own field. Those with losing records are those who do not take advantage of their home field. The following sections present some theoretical notions and supporting research that help to shed some light on the reasons underlying these findings and conclusions.

TERRITORIALITY

The notion that people, as well as other organisms, possess specific places or territories with which they identify and which they protect against intrusion is gaining increasing popular acceptance. Evidence for this idea is readily apparent in everyday life in many forms, ranging from "no trespassing" signs and barking watch dogs that people use to keep intruders off their lawns to the tireless resistance of one nation to the attempted take-over by an enemy. Territoriality has several implications for the psychology of sports including such issues as identification with a home field, familiarity with a place, the relationship between territoriality and dominance, and the role of sports as an outlet for territory-related aggression.

The concept of territory stems from two lines of work in the social sciences. First, for about 50 years sociologists have been studying the dynamics of neighborhood groups, particularly juvenile gangs and their "turf" (e.g., Whyte, 1943; Suttles, 1968). Second, naturalists and ethologists have observed the territorial behavior of animals in their natural habitats (e.g., Ardrey, 1966; Eibl-Eibesfeldt, 1970). Although there are some important differences between human and animal territory (cf. Edney, 1974), there are several common themes that run through the various definitions of this concept. In discussing animal behavior, Hediger (1950) wrote: "Territories are geographical areas where an animal lives and from which it prevents others of the same species from entering. They are often demarcated by optical, acoustical and olfactory means. Thus, they are areas that are rendered personally distinctive and that are defended against encroachment [p. 111]." Similarly, Pastalan (1970), in discussing people, stated: "A territory is a delimited space that a person or group uses and defends as an exclusive preserve. It involves psychological identification with a place, symbolized by attitudes of possessiveness and arrangement of objects in the area [p. 94]."

These and other definitions of territoriality share several themes. First, all involve the idea of a single place where the organism carries out certain functions. In the case of sports, this place, of course, is the home field on which a game is played. In contrast to animals that conduct all of their basic functions such as eating, sleeping, mating and child rearing in one place, humans often have different places for where they eat, sleep, and play games. Nevertheless, with the exception of some individual sports and championship games, most sports contests are carried out in a place that more clearly "belongs" to one of the teams.

A second aspect of territoriality is personalization of the place by some kind of marking device. Although in animals this usually takes a different form (e.g., urination, defecation, glandular secretions) than it does in humans, the human forms are just as potent. A sports arena is usually decorated with signs and banners that make it very clear to all observers

whose arena they are visiting. There are also reminders of past accomplishments such as championships won and plaques commemorating athletic stars. The uniforms of the players, the band, the cheerleaders and the fans, the paint on the walls, seats and sometimes the playing surface are often in the colors of the home team. These and other symbols all serve to personalize an area in the sense of making the home team feel more at home and the visitors feel more like strangers or intruders.

A third aspect of territoriality is defense against intrusion. In the case of animals, defense can take many forms ranging from vocalization to physical combat. For example, the chirping of birds, once thought (by poets at least) to be songs of joy, are now regarded by ethologists as warnings to possible intruders to stay away. Although it is tempting to draw an analogy between the singing of birds and the howling of wolves on the one hand, and the playing of fight songs and the chants of home town fans on the other, this temptation will be avoided.

One problem in drawing analogies between animals and humans in terms of territoriality is that while animals usually have only one place, humans have many. In discussing this point, Altman (1975) argues that there are three types of territories in which people are found. A primary territory is one that is exclusively owned and used by particular people or groups. Some examples might be a private home (or a room within a house) or a private club with a limited membership. A secondary territory is a place that is open to the public in a sense, but that is normally occupied by a restricted clientele. A neighborhood bar or restaurant that is usually visited only by "regulars" would be an example of this type. A third type is the public territory such as a library or playground that features very temporary and occasional use by a wide variety of persons. These types of territories differ in many respects such as the extent to which a person feels personally identified with them and the legitimacy of defending them against intrusion by others. Of these three types, a sports arena is probably most like a secondary territory. As a number of authors (e.g., Edney, 1974; Lyman & Scott, 1967) have noted, humans, unlike animals, invite other members of their species into certain territories (e.g., living rooms but not bathrooms) for some kinds of social interaction. The host, in making the invitation, still retains certain rights not shared by the visitor (e.g. rearranging the furniture), but allows the guest certain opportunities for making use of the territory. A sports arena fits this description with the implication being that the home team will feel more free to take liberties that make the situation more suitable for them. Thus, a home team can make itself feel more at home not only through pennants and martial music, but also through subtle arrangements of the home field. For example, in hockey, a home team can slow down the attack of a swifter visiting club by allowing the ice to soften somewhat before game time. In baseball, changes in the pitching mound and base paths can be managed that

are designed to hinder certain visiting players. Although such personaliza-
tions of the home field can only be carried so far, and although they may be
regarded as unsportsmanlike, rumor in sports circles suggest that they are
fairly common.

In sum, as a secondary territory, a sports arena is unlike the home ground
of an animal, but it may share some of the characteristics of animal
territoriality such as being a focus for identification, possessing greater
familiarity of its idiosyncratic features, being a place in which defensive
abilities are enhanced and in which one plays a dominant role in determining
who can enter and what intruders can do. Each of these points is discussed in
somewhat more detail in the following sections.

Identification

When a player joins a team, part of his or her identity becomes associted with
the home base of that team. Thus, an athlete becomes a Chicago Bear, an
Ohio State Buckeye, or an Arizona Sun Devil. While it is true that members
of both home and visiting teams usually wear the name of the place they are
representing on their uniforms, the home team is surrounded by more
supportive reminders of this identification. However, in the collegiate ranks,
and even more so among professionals, the team an athlete plays for is often
not the player's original home town. With the frequency of trades, drafts and
so on, athletes in general are probably not extremely wedded to any particular
place. However, there is another type of person involved in the sporting
enterprise who is more strongly and permanently identified with the home
team and its performance. This other person, of course, is the home town fan.
That is, even though players may have a loose allegiance to the town they
represent on the playing field, it is not unusual for entire cities to invest a
considerable proportion of their identity with local sports teams. This is
especially true when the team is having a winning season. Thus, whether it is
"Packer Power" in Green Bay, or "Blazer Mania" in Portland, the home town
fans convey their identity with a team by going through the turnstyles at the
arena and shouting their encouragement to the local heroes.

Cialdini, Borden, Thorne, Walker, Freeman and Sloan (1976) reported
some interesting indicators of the strength as well as the fickleness of the home
town fan. For example, they observed that on the Monday following a victory
by the home team, college students were more likely to wear clothing such as
sweatshirts that identified them with the home school than following a home
team loss. Second, they found that in a survey of knowledge about recent
campus events, students were more likely to use the pronoun "we" in
describing the outcome of a game (i.e., "we won"), but used the third person
pronoun in describing the home team's losses (i.e., "they lost"). Referring to
this phenomenon as "basking in reflected glory," these authors argue that

claiming identity with a winner is a way of enhancing one's image even though the claimant is in no way responsible for the team's success. In many cases when the pride of the home town is jeopardized by an unfavorable call by an official, or even worse, when the home team loses a game, fans have been known to express their hurt in violent ways (Bryan & Horton, Note 1). This type of aggressiveness takes many forms from minor "rowdiness" during a game to brutal killings in the parking lots and streets afterwards. Common observation of sporting events tells us that the fans' passion to win and to be identified with a winner is clearly communicated to the players. And regardless of their devotion to a particular team or particular group of fans, athletes share this desire to be identified with a winner (see Chapter 9.)

Familiarity With the Territory

Although the playing fields in most sports must conform to certain standards, it is also true that no two fields are exactly alike. This is especially obvious in baseball where the distance and height of the fence, distance from the base paths to the dugouts and seats and other dimensions vary from park to park. But the same holds for other playing surfaces as well. For example, football fields have either natural grass or various kinds of artificial turf, some stadiums are enclosed and have fairly constant climatic conditions while others are open to the vagaries of weather, basketball floors and tennis courts differ in the liveliness of the bounce they give to the ball, and so on. In discussing this point, Sommer (1969) states:

> It is not only the presence of the hometown fans that makes the difference, but also a player's intimate knowledge of the special characteristics of the environment—every little mound on the diamond, the height and location of fences and guardrails, and so on. Minnesota Fats, the pool hall genius, emphasized how a man had to be a real expert to travel from town to town and still win: 'You really have to be a good player to beat a man in his hometown. Every table is different. The rubber is just like a person, it dies a little each year [p. 14].'

Thus, even though players—especially in the professional ranks—may have some familiarity with every field, in general, familiarity is greater among the home team players. In the heat of action, when movements must be made reflexively, familiarity may operate in the home team's favor at the unconscious level. Often without awareness a quarterback knows from various cues in his surroundings how hard to throw the ball, the basketball player knows when to pull up and take a shot when he has reached his best spot, an outfielder chasing a fly ball feels when he is getting close to a fence, a running back can tell without looking how much room he has before going

out of bounds. The lack of this kind of intimate knowledge among the visitors can work against them in many ways. For example, in a study of sports injuries (Gomolak & Gomolak, 1975), it was found that injuries due to field obstructions such as TV cameras and yard markers happened mainly to visiting team players. However, if familiarity with the idiosyncracies of the home field were an all-important factor, we might expect a more dramatic influence in some sports than others. For example, since pro football teams play more games per season on their home field and since pro players on the average spend more years on the same team than is the case with college teams, the home-field effect should be stronger in the professional ranks. The data reported earlier suggest that this is not the case. As will be argued below, there are other aspects of being on the home field that may carry more weight than mere familiarity.

Territorial Dominance and Resistance to Encroachment

Most definitions of territoriality include the notion of defending a place against intrusion by outsiders. This idea has several implications for the psychology of sports. First, it is apparent that many kinds of sports from chess to ice hockey can be regarded as territorial, i.e., a major part of the game is to prevent the opponent from entering some region. In fact, sports can be categorized according to the extent to which they involve defense of some piece of turf, ranging from the highly territorial, such as football, to nonterritorial races such as swimming and track.

In his analysis of the consequences of territoriality in animals and men, Ardrey (1966) argues that being on one's home ground energizes the defender against attack by outsiders. He uses this notion to explain both the victories of small animals in defending their nests against larger invaders, as well as the failure of human invaders to conquer on foreign soil. This was the lesson that Napoleon learned in Russia and which the United States learned in Viet Nam. All of this might lead to the conclusion that not only should there be a home field advantage, but that it should be stronger in territorial sports than in nonterritorial ones. This deceptively simple hypothesis reveals another problem in drawing analogies between animal and human behavior. That is, the goal regions in territorial sports such as the end zone in football, are not comparable to animal territories. Rather, goal regions are actually subterritories within larger, secondary territories. In fact, the area that a team has to defend regularly changes from one end to the other as a game proceeds. Except for certain advantages such as lighting or wind direction, there is little reason to prefer one goal over another. This is in contrast to the territories of animals upon which their survival as individuals and as species depend.

Nevertheless, the connection observed in animals between being on one's home ground and domination over intruders may have some merit when

applied to people. One line of research has investigated the relationship between a person's dominance in a group and the size of that person's territory. Although the results have not been entirely consistent (DeLong, 1973; Esser, Chamberlain, Chapple, & Kline, 1965; Esser, 1968; Esser, 1973), the general conclusion that follows from this work so far is that, at least within stable groups, the more influential members have larger territories. This conclusion, if stretched considerably, is consistent with the observation that successful teams draw larger crowds and sometimes build larger stadiums to accommodate them.

Several other studies have looked at the amount of influence people have as a function of being in their own territory. Esser (1970) found that psychotic patients were more successful in influencing others when in the area of the hospital that they had staked out as their own than when in other areas. Martindale (1971) found that college students won more negotiations in a bargaining game when playing in their own room than visitors did. Thus, although the evidence is scanty and often based upon some unusual types of subjects (usually people living in some kind of institution), it is consistent with Ardrey's notion about the advantage for home defenders in giving them more energy to fight and encouraging the intruder to submit. It would not necessarily follow, therefore, that sports statistics should show that the home-field advantage stems mainly from defensive proficiency. The statistics reported earlier which suggested that the advantage was primarily in terms of offense may reflect both enhanced energy on the part of the offense of the home team and submissiveness of the visitor.

One other aspect of the possible energizing effect of being on one's home ground warrants some attention. Most sports involve physical exertion and contact that can result in injuries and pain. It is possible that the high arousal stemming from being on home ground as well as fan support help the home town player to withstand more pain. A number of studies have shown that when one's reference group is made salient and when its courage in withstanding pain is impuned, tolerance for pain increases (e.g., Buss & Portnoy, 1967).

In sum, although the connection between territoriality and dominance is tenuous at best when applied to humans, there is some evidence to suggest that part of the home-field advantage stems from the relatively greater confidence and tolerance for injury of the home team. Whether this represents a residue of our animal ancestry or whether it results from training remains to be seen (Scott, 1958). In fact, when one observes the grunts and groans in contact sports and the occasional vicious attack of one player on another, it may be a disservice to animals to say that we acquired this aggressiveness from them. As we'll see in the following section, some ethologists have argued that the type and level of aggression among people is unprecedented in the animal world, but that sports may provide one safety valve.

Sports as Ritualized Violence

A number of ethologists, particularly Nobel prize winner Konrad Lorenz (1966), have argued that all animals, including humans, are instinctively aggressive. This instinct for aggression, at least of a nonlethal variety, came about, he argues, because it serves certain functions for a species such as ensuring that the strongest members will propagate, that children will be protected, and that the food supply will not be burdened. The aggression that occurs, however, is ritualized—a kind of dance rather than a fight to the death. The purpose of the ritualized fight is to determine which animal is the more dominant without hurting the weaker. Sometimes this can be achieved by noisy displays without any combat at all. Once a dominance hierarchy is determined, though, the challenger accepts his position in the group or may move on to another area.

Lorenz further contends that all human sports have a similar aim, i.e., they are ritualized fights to determine which person or team is the better. Lorenz further argues that, "the value of sport, however, is much greater than that of a simple outlet of aggression in its coarser and more individualistic behavior patterns. It educates a man to a conscious and responsible control of his own fighting behavior. More educational still is the restrictions imposed by the demands for fairness and chivalry which must be respected even in the face of the strongest aggression-eliciting stimuli." Thus, Lorenz endorses sports as a way not only of releasing aggressive impulses, but as a way of bringing people together under a set of rules that encourage fair play. That is, contests such as the Olympic Games are thought to provide a way for potential enemies to become acquainted and to learn what they have in common. In practice, however, recent Olympic Games as well as contests of less global significance have not proven to be entirely peaceful to say the least. Recent research testing the notion that participating in or witnessing the aggression of sports is cathartic has not supported Lorenz' position. In fact, although some laboratory studies (e.g., Feshbach, 1961) support the idea of catharsis, the bulk of empirical studies supports the opposite conclusion that participating in or witnessing competition actually increases aggressive tendencies (e.g., Christy, Gelfand, & Hartmann, 1971; Goldstein & Arms, 1971).

One of the important features of the ethological approach to social behavior is that aggressiveness is a latent possibiity that will become manifest in the presence of proper environmental cues or "releasers." The favorite illustration of this phenomenon in the animal world is the fighting behavior of male stickleback fish when presented with another stickleback or similar object that has a red dot (Tinbergen, 1953). Another, perhaps more familiar example, is the apparent anger produced in fighting bulls when they see the flapping cape of a bullfighter. Anyone who doubts that the same type of aggression-eliciting cues operate in humans should go to Columbus, Ohio in

November, wearing the colors of the University of Michigan. The point of this illustration is that even though hostility-producing cues among humans are acquired through experience, they produce the same result and occasionally a more extreme result as they do in lower organisms. When rivalries are built up between certain teams, the sight of the opponent is enough to make the players and the home town spectators "fighting mad."

Further analogies between ritualized fighting in animals and human sport have been noted by other ethologists. Etkin (1964) writes, "As for team sports... the major affective experience of both audience and players seem to be the stimulation and ascendancy experienced in the defeat of opponents... Only in sports do men come so close to mayhem and yet usually avoid it, and it seems that basic hominid motivations are involved [p. 183]." Even more intriguing is Etkin's (1964) observation that:

> The forms which team sports take seem closely related to their probable inception as ritualized competitions among hunters and warriors. Most team sports emphasize running and accurate propulsion of missiles.... It is pertinent that accurate throwing is also found in nature among primate species and it is probable that hominid youngsters, like chimpanzees, take readily to stick and stone weaponry as a result of hominid evolution [p. 184].

In a related vein, Washburn (1965) argues that "the basis for the majority of contemporary sports was the preparation for war, and the purpose of sports was to render the individuals taking part in them physically and psychologically tough, so they would be capable of, and would enjoy, the physical destruction of other human beings [p. 11]."

In what may seem to be a blatantly sexist approach, Lionel Tiger (1970) argues that sport is a manifestation of what he calls a male bond. That is, in his view, the relationship between men (e.g., in the form of hunting parties) is the cornerstone of civilization as it has evolved, and this type of bond among men in common cause is a central organizational feature of sport. On this basis, he justifies his conclusion that public interest is greater in male than female sport. Moreover, he argues, admittedly without systematic supporting data, that males are superior to females in all sports with the possible exception of long-distance swimming, which he dubs "a precisely inappropriate skill for terrestrial animal." Even though the phylogenetic validity of his argument is debatable, some of his conclusions are true at the present time. Indeed, women are less frequently found in contact sports, and fewer people attend women's than men's events. It is also apparent that a certain degree of *esprit de corps* characterizes winning teams (although this is not limited to males), and there is also evidence that males may be biologically (rather than merely sociologically) more aggression-prone than women (Maccoby & Jacklin, 1974). All of these points are consistent with the view that aggressiveness in

defending a home ground is somehow "natural," particularly among males, and that modern sports are a means of reliving our primitive past.

In sum, ethologists have argued that there are direct parallels between animals and people in terms of such notions as identification with a territory, the dominance of organisms over intruders on their home ground, and the prevention of lethal aggressiveness through ritualized competition. On the other hand, we have argued that these analogies should not be lightly taken at face value. Although it is true (as Tiger and other ethologists are fond of noting) that many sports teams are named for "ferocious" animals such as Lions, Tigers and Bears, it is also true that they are named for Dolphins, Orioles, and Gophers. Despite the potential oversimplification in embracing the ethological argument, this approach has provided several useful insights. Perhaps violent sports do provide an outlet for those individuals who, because of their size, physiological makeup or social experience, are prone toward assertive action which, in the absence of sports, would find expression in less socially approved ways.

In contrast to the ethological argument, though, human aggression is often expressed in athletic forms that seemingly have little to do with defending one's home territory. That is, although many sports such as football have certain territorial meanings, other violent sports such as boxing and the roller derby do not. In addition, the advantage of familiarity with a home field as well as the enhancement of energy of the home defender probably does not apply in the same degree in the case of human sports as it does among animals defending their homes. And there is little evidence of appeasement gestures on the part of visiting teams which naturalists have observed in other species. Of all the factors suggested by ethologists, the one that seems most promising in accounting for the home-field advantage is identification with the team. By this we mean not only the spirit of cohesiveness among the players and coaches, but also the feelings of the sports fans towards their team and the place it represents. These socio-emotional relationships among players and between players and their fans are discussed in the following section.

EFFECTS OF OTHER PEOPLE ON PERFORMANCE

A fundamental fact about athletic performance is that it is typically carried out in the presence of others. Although an athlete may often work on individual skills alone, the contest situation involves several kinds of social relations and interpersonal dynamics. From the perspective of the individual player, there are two kinds of persons who can influence his or her activities: the other players, coaches and officials who are part of the game; and the fans who are watching. These people exert two types of social influence, called coaction and audience effects, which have been studied by social psychologists for 80 years.

Coaction Effects

Interest in the question of the effects of the presence of others on performance, termed "social facilitation" (Allport, 1920), originated in the work of Triplett (1897) who was apparently inspired by his observation that the speed of bicycle races varied with the type of competition. He noted that times were faster when several racers competed against each other than when solitary riders raced against the clock. Triplett conducted some laboratory experiments to test his theory that the presence of competing coactors enhanced energy level. He found that children working on various simple motor tasks such as winding fishing reels generally went faster when competing with others than when alone.

Subsequent studies with various kinds of animals as well as people produced mixed results in testing for audience effects. For example, birds were found to eat more food in the presence of others than when alone (e.g., Harlow, 1932), whereas other activities such as learning a maze were found to be inhibited in a coaction situation (e.g., Gates & Allee, 1933). In another early study, Allport (1920) compared the performance of solitary and coacting persons on a variety of tasks. His findings indicated that the presence of coactors facilitated some tasks such as word association, multiplication problems and canceling out all the vowels on sheets of prose, while performance was inhibited on other tasks such as complex problem solving. Thus, the early literature contained some apparent contradiction. Zajonc (1965) offered an elegant resolution of this line of research by suggesting that the presence of coactors would facilitate the performance of simple, well-learned tasks (such as eating or letter canceling) while it would interfere with more complex, unfamiliar tasks (such as learning a maze or resolving philosophical problems).

The basis of Zajonc's reasoning was the assumption that the mere presence of others produces arousal, and that heightened arousal would energize and increase the probability of the dominant response in a situation. Since a simple, unfamiliar task is one that, by definition, does not have a single dominant response associated with it, heightened arousal increases the competition among alternative responses and inhibits performance. In contrast, for simple tasks there is a dominant response and if it happens to be the correct one (as would usually be the case), then increased arousal due to the presence of others should facilitate performance.

Although Zajonc's theory was consistent with the early studies and has been supported by later work, some debate has centered on his assumption that the mere presence of others produces arousal. In his 1965 paper, Zaonc noted that there was some evidence supporting his assumption that other people are arousing. He also noted that there was evidence that other people can reduce arousal. In fact, the latter point is a basic assumption in the work of Schachter (1959) and others on the psychology of affiliation. That is, when

people are highly aroused by fear they often choose to join other people rather than remain alone, presumably because other people have a calming effect. These conflicting assumptions have yet to be fully resolved, although it is probably safe to say that whether other people are arousal producing or reducing depends upon what these other people are doing. That is, other people can reduce arousal if they are similar to the aroused person and sympathetic, but may increase arousal if they are making judgments about the person.

In a revision of Zajonc's theory, Cottrell (1972) maintained that the coaction effect would occur, among humans at least, only when the presence of others arouses anticipation of positive or negative outcomes. That is, in contrast to Zajonc's position, Cottrell argued that arousal is not an innate response to the mere presence of others, but a learned reaction based on previous experience in which coactors can make rivalrous comparisons in performance. Several studies (e.g., Klinger, 1969) have supported Cottrell's position.

In a competitive situation, not only can the players from the opposing side determine one's outcome (i.e., they could win the game), it is also true that they can provide evaluative information about one's performance. The euphemism, "rivalrous comparison," is hardly adequate to describe the usually profane badgering that goes on during a game. A number of studies (e.g., Van Turien & McNeel, 1975) have shown that the coaction effect occurs under competitive but not under noncompetitive, mere presence conditions.

It is reasonable to assume that the tasks carried out by athletes are well-learned and familiar based on years of practice. Therefore, performance should be better under actual game conditions than during practice. Obviously, this effect should apply to visitors as well as home teams and, therefore, cannot by itself account for a home-field advantage. However, since coacting with competitors enhances dominant responses, it should have more influence on players who have more clearly defined response dominance hierarchies (i.e., the better players). In his pioneering studies, Triplett observed that while the majority of children improved on their solitary performance when competing, others showed no change and some actually became less proficient. Thus, the actions of other players can either help or hinder performance, depnding on the athlete's level of skill.

Another way in which individual differences in a coaction situation might arise is through the level of arousal that is produced in each participant. One of the oldest principles in psychology postulates an inverted U-shaped relationship between arousal and performance (Yerkes & Dodson, 1908). That is, if arousal is either very high or very low, performance is inhibited, but for different reasons. In preparing for a game, players have to get "psyched-up" enough to put forth their best effort, but not get so high that they lose control. The "coldness" of teams, e.g., in shooting baskets or catching passes,

frequently occurs in the early stages of a game and especially in important games. Since a moderate level of arousal produces optimum performance, players who are able to reach and maintain this level during a game will have an advantage. This is more likely to apply to more experienced athletes. Therefore, it is reasonable to conclude that the more talented and experienced players would be less susceptible to the coaction effect. This conclusion is consistent with the findings reported earlier that a team's overall record is as important as the home-field advantage in determining game outcome, and may help to explain the difference in point spreads between college and professional football teams reported earlier.

In sum, studies on coaction effects reveal that winners will be winners. Moreover, as the football statistics showed, teams with winning records are more effective at home than on the road. However, this was also true for teams with overall losing records. Thus, there is little evidence, contrary to what the ethologists might predict, that the arousal produced by competition is more optimal (although it might be higher) on one's home ground. The emotional factor that promises to favor more clearly the home team would be, naturally, the presence and behavior of the home team supporters including bands, cheerleaders and, of course, the fans.

Audience Effects

Interest in the effects of an audience on performance has almost as long a tradition and has been subjected to the same theoretical analysis as the coaction effect. The early studies on this topic produced mixed results. For instance, Travis (1925) found that subjects performed more effectively on a simple motor task when in front of a small audience than when alone. But Pessin (1933) found that performance on a learning task was inhibited by the presence of an audience. Again, Zajonc (1965) interpreted these and similar conflicting results by suggesting that while emission of easy, well-learned responses is facilitated by the arousal produced by the mere presence of an audience, the acqustion of new responses is inhibited by this arousal.

Cottrell's (1972) alternative interpretation maintains that the presence of others will enhance the emission of dominant responses only when the spectators can *evaluate* performance. A number of studies have supported this interpretation. Henchy and Glass (1968) showed that dominant responses were enhanced only when performance was being evaluated (or going to be evaluated later) by experts but not when performance was carried out alone or in view of nonexperts. Paulus and Murdock (1971) manipulated presence of an audience and anticipated evaluation separately. The presence of an audience did not enhance dominant responses, but anticipated evaluation did—regardless of whether the audience was physically present during the performance or not.

The general conclusion that follows from this line of work is that it is not the mere presence of spectators that affects performance, but what kind of feedback, if any, they are providing, or are expected to provide. It should be noted that in these studies the audiences were generally passive observers. This is in contrast to the behavior of sports fans who voice their approval or disapproval during a game. It could be argued, then, that a passive, listless group of spectators would have little influence on a game while a noisy crowd should enhance the performance of players on both sides. A number of athletes and sportswriters we consulted agreed with this conclusion. That is, even the members of a visiting team can be sometimes aroused by the home crowd. In order to account for the home-field advantage, therefore, we must examine the characteristics of this crowd and the selectivity of its feedback.

Audience Composition. The basic fact about sports crowds is their partisanship. Although it is conceivable that the crowd could be evenly divided between home and visiting team supporters, in practice the home supporters turn out in greater numbers. This stems from very practical considerations such as travel distances, as well as from actual limitations imposed in some cases on the number of tickets made available to visiting fans. Although there are a few loyal fans who follow their favorite teams from place to place, such devotion is not possible for most people. In fact, the travel distance is probably a major factor in establishing traditional rivalries. Teams whose home fields are within reasonable travel distance are probably more likely to be rivals (for fan dedication and dollars) than are teams who are farther apart. The rivalry is intensified by a potentially more even distribution of fans in the stands.

Given that the sports audience is composed primarily of home team fans, the relevant question is to find out what they are doing. As Fisher (1976) wisely points out, the home crowd does not cheer the visiting team. Rather, the home crowd acts as a reinforcing agent for the home players—cheering their successes and booing their failures. Thus far there has been no systematic analysis of the type and magnitude of spectator feedback on performance. However, informal observation and comments from those directly involved in sports indicates a mutual feedback system between players and fans. Sometimes a game can be turned around after a spectacular play by a team or individual. This feeds the crowd which in turn feeds the players with approval. A cycle is created that can demoralize the visiting team, thus perpetuating the cycle.

To be realistic, though, the glorious situation described above does not always occur. On those occasions when things are not going well for the home team, fans can be cruelly critical. Again, there is little research on the effects of negative audience feedback, although one early study (Laird, 1923) showed that "razzing" inhibited performance on a simple motor coordination task. It

is conceivable that crowd noise, perhaps especially of a negative type, can be distracting. In fact, home crowds sometimes attempt to interfere with visiting team performance in critical situations such as shooting free throws or on a fourth-down-and-goal-to-go situation.

In postgame interviews, victorious players often give some credit to the home town fans for the vocal support. Research on social facilitation suggests that this credit is due not only for energizing the home squad but for actively discouraging and distracting the visitors. This conclusion, while consistent with findings about the home-field advantage in general, does not account for the variation in the advantage across different sports. To explain this phenomenon, we must examine other aspects of the crowd besides its partisanship.

Audience Size, Density, and Intimacy. The statistics reported earlier suggest that the home-field advantage is greater in basketball than in football and even less important in baseball. Examining the size of the arenas and stadia in which these sports are played as well as attendance figures reveals that crowd size cannot account for the home-field effect. That is, basketball arenas typically hold less than 15,000 people, while baseball and football stadia can accommodate three to six times more people. Unfortunately, past research on audience effects has varied only presence versus absence of an audience and not audience size. Thus, there is little basis for arguing that size is an important factor. Intuition and some data (Paulus, Note 2) suggest that the density of a crowd (i.e., ratio of fans to available seats) is a more important factor. Density, though, is usually not an unconfounded factor. Crowds are more dense when the home team is having a winning season, so it is difficult to separate the effects of fan support from team talent.

A more clear-cut variable that differentiates among sports is the intimacy of the relationship between fans and players. In football and baseball the fans are much more physically remote from the action than in basketball where, in some cases, many fans can reach out and touch the players. It is also true that basketball is played in an enclosed arena which intensifies whatever noise the crowd is making, while in other sports played primarily in open-air stadia, the crowd reaction is dispersed. Basketball is more intimate than many other sports in another respect as well. The players are performing in very scanty attire while in other sports they are more fully clothed. The padding and helmets worn in football not only cut down on the amount of "feedback" that a player can receive, they also serve as a psychological barrier shutting out the fans. While the density and closeness of a crowd provides a reasonable account of the greater home-field advantage in basketball than in some other sports, it does not explain the difference between football and baseball. Some further insight into the home field advantage can be gained by exploring the effects of arousal on the type of activity required in different sports.

Audience Arousal.   Given the assumption of social facilitation theory that audiences can produce arousal, the question arises as to how helpful the arousal is in enhancing performance. Different sports require different degrees of stamina and intensity. Baseball, as its critics point out, is a relatively slow-paced game. Most players experience fairly long periods of waiting interrupted by occasional bursts of very quick action. Football requires somewhat longer periods of sustained action but is interrupted by rest periods between each play, and with the advent of "two-platoon" systems and specialty teams, most players spend about half the time on the sidelines. Basketball and other sports such as soccer and hockey involve more continuous activity. In fact, many athletes—especially basketball players—regard basketball as the most grueling sport. The arousal produced by home fans, therefore, would seem to be more of an advantage in this sport in sustaining players not only during a game but throughout an exhausting season.

Besides providing the extra energy needed to keep up the pace in certain sports, the arousal produced by a home crowd has other implications. For example, there is considerable evidence (Rule & Nesdale, 1976) that generalized arousal increases aggressive tendencies when appropriate targets are available. This finding has obvious implications for sports such as football, where aggressive action is part of the game, but it also applies to basketball which is a "no-contact" sport in name only. Baseball allows few opportunities for physical aggression within the context of the game itself. That is, aggressiveness produced by arousal can be functionally advantageous in some sports but not others. In addition, as was noted in the case of coaction effects, the presence of an audience may have more effect on some athletes than others. For example, Kohfeld and Weitzel (1969) found that people who were more achievement-oriented, conscientious, dependable and eager to make a good impression were less affected by the presence of an audience than were other personality types. Furthermore, they found that people who were generally more proficient at the task showed a greater benefit from an audience than less proficient performers. These results bring us to a definition of a "star" as an athlete who "shines" in front of a crowd—especially a home town crowd.

In sum, there are several ways in which the home audience can provide an advantage for the local favorites. They reward good performance, intimidate the opposition, stimulate energy and aggressiveness, and bring out the best in the best players. They do so not only for reasons of home town and personal pride as discussed earlier, but also because they have paid to do so. It should be kept in mind that sports is not only a means of expression, it is a form of entertainment. By buying a ticket the fan has purchased the right to observe and to take some part in the performance. It is doubtful that sports as we know it today would continue to exist if fans were totally replaced by TV

cameras. At least it is unlikely that the home-field advantage would remain at its present level.

Other Factors.   In focusing on the various aspects of territoriality and social facilitation, I have not directly addressed the many other possible determinants of the home-field advantage. A thorough account of this phenomenon requires at least some consideration of other factors. One possibility suggested by various sources was rulings by officials that favored the home team. This suggestion does not seem to be borne out by informal observation or game statistics such as those reported in Table 15.3. The one other factor that appears most promising in furthering our understanding of the home team advantage is the fact that the visiting team is away from "all the comforts of home." That is, being away from the support of family and friends as well as the freedom of choice about such matters as eating and sleeping can lower the morale of the visiting team. In addition, the fatigue and boredom entailed in traveling can reduce physical preparedness. The problems of travel may be somewhat reduced by the use of jet planes, but even this can be disorienting, especially when long distances are involved. Moreover, if travel is a factor, it should have a greater effect in sports such as basketball and baseball where it occurs more often and for longer periods than in football. Since there seems to be little correspondence between extent of travel and size of the home team advantage across these sports, perhaps travel is only a minor factor.

In general, it seems likely that the disadvantages of being away from home operate in conjunction with the advantages discussed above that accrue to the home team. In other words, the home team advantage represents not the operation of a single variable, but a combination of variables. Finally, although the relative importance of each of the variables discussed here may vary as a function of type of sport, particular teams, and particular home field, the general impression that arises from the present analysis is that familiarity with the "territory" and fan support are the most important and generalized factors contributing to the home team advantage.

APPLICATIONS TO OTHER "GAMES"

While the present analysis has centered on sports, it seems fitting to close by briefly exploring the ramifications of the issues raised here for other, perhaps more serious forms of competition. There are many arenas outside the realm of sports where familiarity with the territory and the support of local "fans" might give an advantage to the home side. For instance, in discussing his successful prosecution of Patricia Hearst, U.S. Attorney J. L. Browning (1976) admitted that his chief opponent, the flamboyant F. Lee Bailey, was

more articulate but that he had the advantage, as prosecutor, of knowing the territory. Browning said that Bailey's scathing cross examinations "may work on the East Coast, but not on the West."

An even more significant example of the home-field effect is provided by a report on the way in which Abraham Lincoln came to receive the Republican presidential nomination in 1860. Illinois Republicans had Lincoln's candidacy in mind when they persuaded the party to come to Chicago (in Lincoln's home state) for the convention; they even built a special structure for the occasion. According to one account ("Whooping it up at the Wigwam," 1976), when Lincoln's name was placed in nomination, "A thousand steam whistles, 10 acres of hotel gongs, a tribe of Comanches, headed by a choice vanguard from pandemonium, might have mingled in the scene unnoticed." When Lincoln finally pulled ahead on the third ballot, "The cannon boomed the news to the multitude below and 20,000 throats took up the cry. The city heard it, and 100 guns on the Tremont Hotel, innumerable whistles on the river and lake front, on locomotives and factories, and the bells in all the steeples broke forth. For 24 hours the clamour never ceased." This boisterous support sent Lincoln on to become one of our greatest Presidents, and perhaps thereby changed the course of history.

Of all the forms of human competition, the most severe is war. As Ardrey (1966) noted, territorial encroachments and occupations that are part of warfare are rarely if ever permanently successful. There are many historical incidents to support this view. The Crusaders had to withdraw, the Romans failed to conquer the hearts of the subjects in their many lands, the Americans pulled together after Pearl Harbor, and Hitler's Third Reich fell far short of its promised 1000-year reign. There are contrary examples as well. Russia still controls much of Europe, but perhaps it is too soon to tell how permanent that situation will be. An apparently more successful invasion is the take-over in America of Indian territory by white settlers. But this, as we know, entailed an unprecedented degree of disorganized defense, deception and annihilation. And, again, it may be too early to tell the final outcome of this invasion.

The lessons to be learned from studying the home-field advantage in sports are clear and widely applicable. The value and meaning of home is conveyed in history, song, and rhyme as well as sports statistics. If the goal is to win, then, indeed, there is no place like home.

REFERENCE NOTES

1. Bryan, C., & Horton, R. *Athletic events and spectacular spectators.* Paper presented at the meeting of the American Educational Research Association, San Francisco, April 1976.
2. Paulus, P. B. *Social facilitation and sports.* Paper presented at the meeting of the North American Society for the Psychology of Sport and Physical Activity, Arlington, Texas, April 1976.

REFERENCES

Allport, F. H. The influence of the group upon association and thought. *Journal of Experimental Psychology*, 1920, *3*, 159–182.

Altman, I. *The environment and social behavior.* Monterey, Calif.: Brooks/Cole, 1975.

Ardrey, R. *The territorial imperative.* New York: Atheneum, 1966.

Browning—How to blunt a scalpel. *Time*, March 29, 1976, p. 24.

Buss, A. H.. & Portnoy, N. W. Pain tolerance and group identification. *Journal of Personality and Social Psychology*, 1967, *6*, 106–108.

Christy, P. R., Gelfand, D. M., & Hartmann, D. P. Effects of competition-induced frustration on two classes of modeled behavior. *Developmental Psychology*, 1971, *5*, 104–111.

Cialdini, R. B., Borden, R. J., Thorne, A., Walker, M. R., Freeman, S., & Sloan, L. R. Basking in reflected glory: Three (football) field studies. *Journal of Personality and Social Psychology*, 1976, *34*, 366–375.

Cottrell, N. B. Social facilitation. In C. G. McClintock (Ed.), *Experimental social psychology.* New York: Holt, Rinehart & Winston, 1972.

DeLong, A. J. Territorial stability and hierarchical formation. *Small Group Behavior*, 1973, *4*, 56–63.

Edney, J. J. Human territoriality. *Psychological Bulletin*, 1974, *81*, 959–975.

Eibl-Eibesfeldt, I. *Ethology: The biology of behavior.* New York: Holt, Rinehart & Winston, 1970.

Esser, A. H. Dominance hierarchy and clinical course of psychiatrically hospitalized boys. *Child Development*, 1968, *39*, 147–157.

Esser, A. H. Interactional hierarchy and power structure on a psychiatric ward. In S. J. Hutt & C. Hutt (Eds.), *Behavior studies in psychiatry.* New York: Oxford University Press, 1970.

Esser, A. H. Cottage fourteen: Dominance and territoriality in a group of institutionalized boys. *Small Group Behavior*, 1973, *4*, 131–146.

Esser, A. H., Chamberlain, A. S., Chapple, E. D., & Kline, N. S.. Territoriality of patients on a research ward. In J. Wortis (Ed.), *Recent advances in biological psychiatry.* New York: Plenum, 1965.

Etkin, W. *Social behavior from fish to man.* Chicago: University of Chicago Press, 1964.

Feshbach, S. The stimulating versus cathartic effects of a vicarious aggressive activity. *Journal of Abnormal and Social Psychology*, 1961, *63*, 381–385.

Fisher, A. C. *Psychology of sport.* Palo Alto, Calif.: Mayfield, 1976.

Gates, M. F., & Allee, W. C. Conditioned behavior of isolated and grouped cockroaches on a simple maze. *Journal of Comparative Psychology*, 1933, *15*, 331–358.

Goldstein, J. H., Arms, R. L. Effects of observing athletic contests on hostility. *Sociometry*, 1971, *34*, 83–90.

Gomolak, L., & Gomolak, C. Pro football—world's most dangerous sport. *Chicago Tribune*, November 30, 1975, p. 1.

Harlow, H. F. Social facilitation of feeding in the albino rat. *Journal of Genetic Psychology*, 1932, *41*, 211–221.

Hediger, H. *Wild animals in captivity.* London: Butterworth, 1950.

Henchy, T., & Glass, D. C. Evaluation apprehension and the social facilitation of dominant and subordinate responses. *Journal of Personality and Social Psychology*, 1968, *10*, 446–454.

Jimmy "The Greek." *Chicago Daily News*, February 23, 1976, p. 17.

Klinger, E. Feedback effects and social facilitation of vigilance performance: Mere coaction versus potential evaluation. *Psychonomic Science*, 1969, *14*, 161–162.

Kohfeld, D. L., & Weitzel, W. Some relations between personality factors and social facilitation. *Journal of Experimental Research in Personality*, 1969, *3*, 287–292.

Laird, D. A. Changes in motor control and individual variations under the influence of razzing. *Journal of Experimental Psychology*, 1923, *6*, 236–246.

Lane, E. Home, sweet home, for athletes. *Chicago Sun Times,* August 20, 1976, p. 54.

Lorenz, K. *On aggression.* New York: Harcourt, Brace & World, 1966.

Lyman, S. M., & Scott, M. B. Territoriality: A neglected sociological dimension. *Social Problems,* 1967, *15,* 235–249.

Maccoby, E. E., & Jacklin, C. N. *The psychology of sex differences.* Stanford, Calif.: Stanford University Press, 1974.

Marshall, J. Doing it by the numbers. *Sports Illustrated,* January 14, 1974, 42–49.

Martens, R., & Landers, D. M. Motor performance under stress: A test of the inverted-U hypothesis. *Journal of Personality and Social Psychology,* 1970, *16,* 29–37.

Martindale, D. A. Territorial dominance behavior in dyadic verbal interactions. *Proceedings of the American Psychological Association Convention,* 1971, *6,* 305–306.

Pastalan, L. A. Privacy as a behavioral concept. *Social Forces,* 1970, *45,* 93–97.

Paulus, P. B., & Murdoch, P. Anticipated evaluation and audience presence in the enhancement of dominant responses. *Journal of Experimental Social Psychology,* 1971, *7,* 280–291.

Pessin, J. The comparative effects of social and mechanical stimulation on memorizing. *American Journal of Psychology,* 1933, *45,* 263–270.

Rule, B. G., & Nesdale, A. R. Emotional arousal and aggressive behavior. *Psychological Bulletin,* 1976, *83,* 851–863.

St. Louis likes Connors. *Chicago Daily News,* February 7, 1977, p. 15.

Schachter, S. *The psychology of affiliation.* Stanford, Calif.: Stanford University Press, 1959.

Scott, J. P. *Aggression.* Chicago: University of Chicago Press, 1958.

Siegal, S. *Nonparametric statistics for the behavioral sciences.* New York: McGraw-Hill, 1956.

Sommer, R. *Personal space.* Englewood Cliffs, N.J.: Prentice-Hall, 1969.

Suttles, G. D. *The social order of the slum.* Chicago: University of Chicago Press, 1968.

Tiger, L. *Men in groups.* New York: Random House, 1970.

Tinbergen, N. *Social behaviour in animals.* New York; Wiley, 1953.

Travis, L. E. The effect of a small audience upon eye–hand coordination. *Journal of Abnormal and Social Psychology,* 1925, *20,* 142–146.

Triplett, N. The dynamogenic factors in pacemaking and competition. *American Journal of Psychology,* 1897, *9,* 507–533.

Van Turien, M., & McNeel, S. P. A test of the social facilitation theories of Cottrell and Zajonc. *Personality and social Psychology Bulletin,* 1975, *1,* 604–607.

Washburn, S. L. Conflict in primate society. In I. DeVore (Ed.), *Primate behavior: Field studies of monkeys and apes.* New York: Holt, Rinehard & Winston, 1965.

Whooping it up at the wigwam. *Panorama-Chicago Daily News,* July 10, 1976, p. 2.

Whyte, W. F. *Street corner society.* Chicago: University of Chicago Press, 1943.

Yerkes, R. M., & Dodson, J. D. The relation of strength of stimulus to rapidity of habit-formation. *Journal of Comparative Neurology and Psychology,* 1908, *18,* 459–482.

Zajonc, R. B. Social facilitation. *Science,* 1965, *149,* 269–274.

INDEXES

Author Index

442   AUTHOR INDEX

Blumer, H., 337, 340, 366
Bock, H. E., 298, 334
Borden, R. J., 235, 259, 307, 309, 332, 338, 366, 422, 437
Boslooper, T., 122, 146
Bouet, M., 228, 231, 259
Boyle, A., 185, 187
Bramel, D., 230, 259
Brazelton, T. B., 14, 26
Bredemeier, B. J., 402, 407, 408
Bronfenbrenner, U., 281, 293
Brown, R., 354, 366
Browning, J. L., 435, 437
Bruner, J. S., 8, 24, 26
Bruns, W., 106, 113, 256, 262
Bryan, C., 423, 436
Bryant, J., 299, 307, 320, 324, 325, 328, 332, 334, 335
Bryson, F. R., 302, 332
Burmeister, E., 66, 71, 98
Bush, R. R., 66, 98, 235, 261
Buskirk, E. R., 298, 333
Buss, A. H., 231, 259, 275, 283, 293, 425, 437
Buttenwieser, P., 50, 62
Byrne, D., 232, 259
Byrne, R., 37

C

Caillois, R., 223, 224, 228, 259
Campbell, D. T., 267, 295
Candell, P., 120, 146
Cantor, J. R., 298, 312, 320, 325, 332, 335
Cantril, H., 282–283, 294, 338, 359, 367, 407, 408
Caplow, T., 279, 293
Carew, J., 1, 25
Carlson, F. R., 45, 63
Carroll, C. M., 43, 62
Cattell, R. B., 125, 126, 146, 278, 293
Chafetz, J. S., 120, 146
Chakotin, S., 350, 366
Chamberlain, A. S., 425, 437
Chan, I., 1, 25
Chandler, M., 14, 27
Chapple, E. D., 425, 437
Charness, N., 36, 38, 41, 62
Chase, W. G., 36, 39, 41, 42, 53, 62, 63

Chess, S., 13, 14, 28
Chi, P. S. K., 117, 118, 139, 144, 147
Christenson, A., 234, 259
Christy, P. R., 426, 437
Cialdini, R. B., 235, 240, 241, 242, 259, 307, 309, 332, 338, 366, 422, 437
Clark, R. A., 160, 187, 235, 261
Cleveland, A. A., 39, 40, 62
Clinchy, N. G., 233, 259
Cockburn, A., 54, 62
Cohen, J., 407, 408
Coleman, J. C., 178, 187
Collins, J. W., 37, 43, 62
Collins, M., 31, 62
Cominsky, P., 324, 332
Conlee, M., 242, 260
Cook, E., 404, 408
Cooper, L., 115, 146
Corbin, C. B., 222, 259
Corrigan, P., 289, 290, 291, 292, 293
Coser, L. A., 238, 259
Cottrell, N. B., 430, 431, 437
Couch, C. J., 340, 366
Cozens, F. W., 300, 307, 333
Cratty, B. J., 227, 259
Cullen, F. T., 233, 259

D

D'Andrade, R. G., 66, 76, 86, 98
Dansky, J. L., 17, 26
Darrach, B., 58, 62
Davies, J. C., 355, 366
Davis, S., 116, 148
Davis, W. N., 160, 187
Day, K. D., 298, 299, 301, 332, 335
de Groot, A. D., 38, 39, 40, 46, 47, 53, 56, 62
De Long, A. J., 425, 437
Dennis, L. B., 13, 20, 21, 22, 25
Deutsch, M., 357, 366
Deutscher, I., 280, 293
Dixon, D., 9, 10, 12, 17, 20, 25
Dodson, J. D., 430, 438
Dollard, J., 230, 259, 272, 273, 294, 304, 333, 354, 366
Doob, L. W., 230, 259, 272, 273, 294, 304, 333, 354, 366
Doshi, R., 18, 20, 27
Draper, N., 50, 51, 62

Michener, J. A., 219, 221, 229, 232, 233, 234, 261, 401, 408
Milavsky, B., 299, 335
Milgram, S., 229, 261, 342, 367
Miller, D., 363–364, 367
Miller, D. L., 233, 261
Miller, J. L., 365, 366
Miller, N. E., 230, 259, 272, 294, 304, 333, 354, 366
Mills, C. W., 273, 294
Minner, D. G., 14, 26
Mischel, W., 117, 147
Montagu, M. F. A., 271, 294
Moore, B., 10, 27
Morgan, W. P., 121, 124, 147, 298, 334
Morris, D., 227, 228, 230, 235, 261
Morris, W. E., 298, 333
Mowrer, O. H., 230, 259, 272, 294, 304, 333, 354, 366
Murdock, P., 431, 438
Murphy, L. B., 15, 27
Murray, H. A., 235, 261
Musselman, B., 234, 261

N

Nabokov, V., 31, 62
Nahme-Huang, L., 18, 27
Nerlove, S. B., 66, 99
Nesdale, A. R., 434, 438
Newborn, M., 43, 62
Nie, N., 130, 147
Noel-Baker, P., 264, 294
Novak, M., 220, 232, 234, 261

O

Ogilvie, B. C., 115, 116, 131, 147, 162, 172, 188, 225, 233, 235, 261, 278, 279, 294
Olsen, J., 175, 187
O'Neil, E. C., 344, 366
Orne, M. T., 244, 251, 261

P

Parker, S., 300, 333
Pastalan, L. A., 420, 438

Patterson, A. H., 299, 332
Paulus, P. B., 431, 433, 436, 438
Pavenstedt, E., 23, 27
Pearton, R. B., 268, 293, 405
Perls, F. S., 230, 261
Pessin, J., 431, 438
Peterson, J. A., 239, 261
Peterson, K., 116, 147
Peterson, S., 116, 147
Petrie, A., 228, 261
Piaget, J., 2, 3, 5, 6, 7, 13, 23, 27, 232, 261
Pleck, J. H., 120, 130, 131, 147
Plessner, H., 298, 334
Portney, N. W., 425, 437
Potepan, P. A., 161, 188
Prentice, N. M., 22, 27
Pulaski, M. A., 5, 15, 18, 27

Q

Quanty, M. B., 299, 334

R

Reed, L., 161, 188, 408
Reider, N., 29, 31, 53, 54, 55, 62
Reiss, A., 10, 25
Rest, S., 161, 188, 408
Richards, J. W., 237, 262
Richards, M. P. M., 14, 27
Richardson, A., 3, 27
Roberts, J. M., 11, 28, 66, 74, 98, 99, 121, 124, 148, 235, 261, 301, 334
Roberts, M., 102, 113, 219, 221, 236, 237, 261
Robertson, A., 5, 25
Romney, A. K., 66, 99
Rosenbaum, D. A., 7, 8, 27
Rosenbaum, R. M., 161, 188, 408
Rosenberg, D., 298, 333
Rosenblum, L. A., 14, 27
Rosenhan, D., 10, 27
Rosenthal, S. R., 228, 261
Ross, G. S., 16–17, 26
Roth, J., 407, 408
Rubin, E., 33, 50, 51, 63
Rubin, K. H., 15, 27

Subject Index